W9-CAN-301

The LPGA:

The Unauthorized Version

the History of the Ladies Professional Golf Association

Liz Kahn

Group Fore Productions, Inc.

Menlo Park, California

1996

The LPGA:
The Unauthorized Version

Printed in Korea

ISBN 0-88197-126-X

Group Fore Productions, Inc.
1259 El Camino Real, Suite 153
Menlo Park, California 94025
(415) 327-5207
FAX (415) 327-5208

This book is dedicated to all the women of the LPGA—past, present, and future.

Contents

CONTENTS (continued)

Foreword

You are holding in your hand the only comprehensive and accurate book ever published on the history of women's professional golf. The author is Liz Kahn, an insightful, empathetic reporter and tireless researcher—and a British citizen.

In the late 1970s, Mrs. Kahn had the audacity to touch down on United States soil, hustle to the nearest LPGA tournament site, don her press badge, and announce, "I'm here to write a book about the LPGA." Some LPGA players viewed her as though she were a London tabloid muckraker. One Hall-of-Famer refused to be interviewed; younger players could be equally uncooperative, doubting that a Brit could truly write the mother language.

But Liz's obvious sincerity, her literary credits, her instant warmth, her British-style feminism, and her inexhaustible sense of humor won over even the most obdurate ones. Most of us, pleased that finally someone was writing a real history of the LPGA, hit our cooperative mode button faster than Babe Zaharias could take a free drop from ground under repair. We scoured our memories for heretofore unrevealed anecdotes of tour experiences. We pawed through our archives for unpublished pictures. We provided Liz with lists of phone numbers of rich information sources—former tour players who had scattered to the vast hinterlands.

Betty Hicks, a founder of the Women's Professional Golf Association, embarks from her Beechcraft multi-engine airplane in San Jose, California, after a series of clinics promoting LPGA tournaments. The year was 1960.

Except for her on-again-off-again exclusion from the locker room, from which all media are now barred, Liz became a fixture on the tour. (After all, of what significance are out of bounds stakes around LPGA locker rooms after one has been bodily removed from the locker room at St. Andrews, which Liz has been?) When she is home in the London suburb of Herts, our phone calls from Liz, punctuated abundantly with shared laughter, are frequent and welcome, particularly since Liz is meticulously attentive to time differences.

Liz Kahn's nearly 20-year effort to gather the material essential to an unmitigated LPGA history was Herculean. She filled hundreds of tapes with interviews—thousands of hours of intense, often intimate conversations with the heroines and the near heroines of women's professional golf. She transcribed all of those tapes in tedious longhand. I chided her often on her medieval methods. "Longhand, Liz? You write in longhand!" Liz Kahn writes in longhand.

Liz dined with headliners in their homes. She lunched with the stars at tournament clubhouses.

She compiled what began as a modest account of the WPGA/LPGA and emerged as a remarkable oral history. Liz Kahn knows more about LPGA professionals than they know about one another.

Several elements of *The LPGA, The Unauthorized Version*, particularly impress me. Kahn achieved an uncommon balance. Nancy Lopez and Joan Joyce were rationed almost equal verbiage. Patty Berg and Sandra Post were allowed to speak with commensurate import. The stars and the cast were awarded equal billing. This is not merely a book about JoAnne Carner, Patty Sheehan, Carol Mann, Louise Suggs, and Betsy Rawls. The book is about the Women's Professional Golf Association and the Ladies Professional Golf Association, both of which featured star systems, but both of which would have been simply exhibition tours without their chorus lines.

The WPGA has been placed in proper perspective to the LPGA; the WPGA was a predecessor and the LPGA a successor to the grandmother organization. The claim that the term "Ladies" was chosen by Fred Corcoran for his new association of women professionals because the definitive "Women's" was already usurped by the WPGA is untrue. The WPGA was legally disbanded months before the LPGA was formed.

Liz Kahn's research revealed, thoroughly and understandably, the non-competitive era in women's sports from which highly competitive golf for women emerged. Those LPGA members, who shriek in horror as they sniff the attar of burning bras, need to understand the near-complete suppression of women's athletics in the 1920s, 1930s, and even into the 1940s. The only "nice" sports for girls and women were croquet, swimming, tennis, and golf, as long as the competition did not reach any level of ferocity, accompanied by the stricture that the women played only for the joy of the sport and never for money. When I attended a small liberal arts college in California in 1944, we were not permitted to keep score in any physical education class, in deference to playing only for the joy of the activity. Liz Kahn knows that era well, not because she lived it, but because of her meticulous sociological research of it.

The LPGA tour, as other women's sports, lives in horror of mention of the "L" word. We exist in a homophobic society. The etiology of the unreasonable phobia is varied, but it is usually rooted in ignorance, fear, and the irrational aspects of religious beliefs. Liz Kahn handles the potentially explosive issue of lesbianism on the

LPGA professionals Helen Dettweiler, Beverly Hanson, Babe Zaharias, and Betty Hicks starred with Katharine Hepburn and Spencer Tracy (pictured here) in MGM's "Pat and Mike", a hit film about a star woman athlete. Photo courtesy: Betty Hicks.

Betty Hicks interviews one of the LPGA's all-time greats, Patty Berg, at Chicago's famous Tam O'Shanter tournament in 1947. Because Betty did publicity for the WPGA and LPGA, she has one of the most extensive collections of photos in women's professional golf. Many of her photo, like this one, are included in this book.

LPGA tour with delicacy and tolerance. There are, Mrs. Kahn agrees, lesbians on the tour, just as there are lesbian schoolteachers, doctors, lawyers, tennis professionals, politicians, gardeners, corporate executives, and carpenters. She has never been attacked by anyone on the tour, she laughs. She has never observed untoward behavior by any of the tour's thusly oriented women. Although she knows who the women-identified women are on the tour's membership rolls, she has no inclination to reveal them. They include some of the LPGA's most attractive, talented, and feminine women, who are waging a battle over two fronts—the confrontations of tournament golf itself and the necessity to hide an important aspect of their existence. They are courageous women. Kahn is courageous to address the subject.

Liz Kahn also deals objectively with the issues produced by the tour's "God Squad"—the Bible study group. The author allowed the born-agains to speak for themselves, and she listened even when they spoke in tongues. Liz hopes that one of the tour's major stars will share with her the humor of the event: the star demonstrating—speaking in tongues—when a potent electrical storm drove the clubhouse into darkness!

Her oral histories of 50 professionals and conversations with others portray the WPGA/LPGA from the former's inception in 1943 to the LPGA's meteoric ascent to what the organization has become today. The individual portraits are the heart of *"The LPGA, The Unauthorized Version."* I was fascinated by being reintroduced to professionals I thought I had known well, but actually had only a superficial acquaintance with. Through the depths of Kahn's interviewing, we learn the commonalities of these touring professionals, and we also learn the incredibly diverse backgrounds from which they emerged to earn their LPGA tour cards.

This is a few-holds-barred sociological treatment of the phenomenon of women's professional golf as it relates to the massive jigsaw which is women's sport in America today. Kahn's work is an intimate perspective of the stars and the cast. She is a dedicated interviewer, omitting no contacts which would contribute to her own stated purpose for undertaking a gargantuan task.

How well she delivered!

Betty Hicks
WPGA, LPGA

Introduction

You can't help loving them; they're an amazing bunch of brave women, a different breed: women professional golfers.

You can knock them, you can criticize their way of life, their mores, their success, their failure, but when all is said and done, they've got guts. They stick by each other in mutual respect, in suffering, achieving, doing a job, and recognizing their common bond.

Being a touring woman professional is a tough existence. Inevitably, the way of life, traveling week in week out, living on a high and in a state of tension, breeds a tight, closed society, friendly to its members and wary of those outside. Their perception is heightened; they are more aware as a group, more constantly tense, emotionally involved. They luxuriate in it, and they are hurt by it.

A woman professional golfer has chosen to make sport her career. For a woman always on the move, it is a hard lifestyle to combine with domesticity and the raising of a family. Increasingly, women golfers are traveling with families, but to reach the top in the manner of Nancy Lopez is the exception rather than the rule.

The sportswoman has traits more akin to those regarded by society as male: aggression, assertion, and achieving job satisfaction. She is less likely to identify with the role of wife and mother, since her existence is far removed from the majority of women who marry, raise children, and possibly take a job to help achieve a higher standard of living.

When you play and practice golf all day, that is your life, and you are remote from much of the outside world, from the daily grind of family living. Instead, a pattern emerges of life on tour. Monday is moving day, you get to the next town, near or far. Tuesday is practice day, and Wednesday you play the Pro-Am. Thursday to Sunday you are involved in the tournament if you are successful, and then the pattern repeats itself. You may live in a trailer, stay in hotels, or take advantage of private housing. You may travel by car, by plane, or hitch a ride with someone else.

At some point in the week, the women have to do their washing and ironing and necessary shopping. Every day they wash their hair, shave their legs, cream their faces and bodies so that the long hours of exposure to all types of weather takes the least possible toll. Great care is given to the choice of clothes, and packing becomes an art.

You see the outward confidence and the inward uncertainties of the youngsters joining the tour. The problems of settling into the rhythm of life are enormous, and the women are on a constant tightrope between depression and joy. They arrive with a sense of hope and expectation, knowing they have ability but wondering just how much. Some do not last the pace and go out with a shattered sense of self and without any pride in themselves or their performance, which may be high, but it appears to have no worth.

There are women professionals who travel together and who travel alone. Some are married with a family, which sometimes travels with them; some are divorced; some are separated. There's a fair mix, but generally among themselves they are companionable, effervescent, emotional, aggressive, and competitive. They're high flyers, and they know it.

The reason for writing this book about the LPGA and its members is part identification, part admiration, and an innate curiosity for the mind and make-up of the career sportswoman. Is there a common denominator in their background? Are they interested in money or motivated by glory, winning, the pure enjoyment of competition?

How do they cope with their emotions, the strains, the tensions of such an uncertain life? How do they see their role as women? What is their criteria for success and failure? Where do old pros go? These and many other questions formed the springboard and motivation for the book. The answers are to be found inside.

The tour and the association unfolds through the eyes of the women from the 1930s onward. Women's competitive professional golf began to take shape in the 1940s, and I have talked to the older founder members, to those who continued to carry it through, and to the present generation. I have talked to those who have found success and failure, and I have endeavored to take a representative cross-section of the women who are a phenomena in sport. I have placed the women in decades—each woman in the decade she joined the tour.

In my years of research I made friends on the tour, but it is not necessarily those people who were interviewed or who made the best interviewees. I have tried to be objective. I have let the women speak for themselves, but interaction must vary, and obviously some people are more able and willing to draw on their emotional depths than others.

At first I was intimidated by the women, to whom I was unacceptable because I represented the media, of whom they were very wary. I had a tremendous shock finding myself excluded from locker rooms. I had covered men's golf and been barred from entering their locker rooms in Britain on the grounds of my sex. Now, I found myself on a women's tour, and I was still on the outside. If I got permission to go and find a player, I was frozen out by the atmosphere. There were various explosions and incidents when I said that I felt regular golf writers should be allowed to enter the locker room. The security people at the doors, wearing guns, terrified me, and the women inside the locker rooms were intimidating. Although, after about a year I was given an LPGA card to allow my entry into locker rooms, the issue was not permanently resolved, and I was again excluded.

Gradually, I was more accepted as the players became interested in the project of my book, and wariness turned to enthusiasm for reading the finished product. About two years through my research, I arrived from England at a tournament and saw one of the professionals who said "hello" and then spontaneously added, "You know you're a very nice addition to our tour." I was more than touched.

It has been a mammoth undertaking, but I enjoyed becoming part of the LPGA tour, and I am indebted for the co-operation given to me by all the women professionals who helped make this book a reality. When the LPGA was in New York, staff members gave me free run of their files and their offices, and they answered endless questions for which I am most grateful.

The story that has emerged is enlightening for those who love golf and for anyone who wants to better understand women.

Liz Kahn

The Early Years

Women in America took to golf as a sport shortly after their counterparts in Britain entered into it competitively in 1893, when Lady Margaret Scott won the first British Women's Amateur Championship.

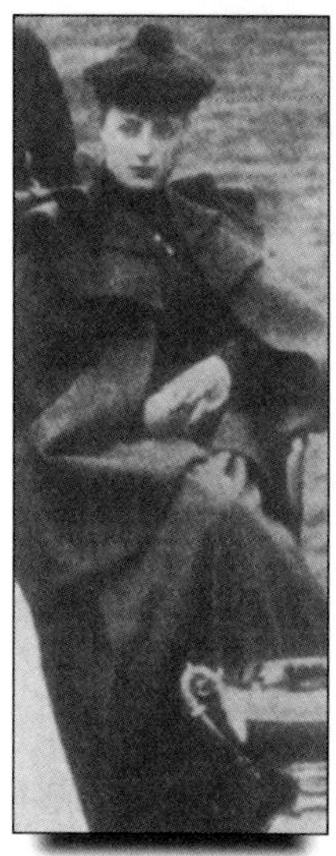

Lady Margaret Scott, the first great woman golfer, won the first three British Ladies Golf Championships in 1893, 1894, and 1895.

In spite of some early all-male American golf clubs that were called "Eveless Edens," the women identified more with the feelings of the 1899 and 1902 British amateur champion May Hezlet, who wrote in a book published in England in 1907: "It is now generally acknowledged that golf is a game—par excellence—for women. It is essentially a game for women: the exercise is splendid without being unduly violent as is sometimes the case in hockey or tennis. "The life that a girl led in olden times must have been a very narrow one. Now all is changed and women have become a power in the world with a right to their own opinions on matters of importance. This change has partly been brought about by the natural progress of events and partly by the increase of athletic sports among girls."

The first American Women's Amateur Championship was held under the auspices of the USGA in November 1895, at the Meadow Brook Club, Hempstead, Long Island. There were thirteen entries. Play consisted of an 18-hole medal round, and the winner was a Mrs. C. S. Brown of Shinnecock Hills, who came in with a score of 132. In the following years the championship became a matchplay event, which for three successive years from 1896 was dominated by the victorious Beatrix Hoyt.

In 1900, the Women's Championship, held at Shinnecock Hills, was won by Frances C. Grimscom of the Merion Cricket Club, one of the first women to take up golf in America. She defeated Margaret Curtis of the Essex Country Club by six and five in the final.

In 1904, golf was an official Olympic sport. At the 1900 games in Paris, which by all accounts were a shambles, only men participated in the golf, which, with cricket and croquet, comprised the three official events. In the more orderly events of the 1904 Olympic games held in St. Louis, Missouri,

Miss Beatrix Hoyt won the U.S. Women's Amateur crown in 1896, 1897, and 1898. The tourney in 1896 was the USGA's second, and it was the first match play event for women.

there were both men's and women's golfing competitions. The women's singles events were dominated by three Americans—Margaret Abbott from Chicago took the gold, Polly Whittier the silver, and Daria Pratt the bronze. Thereafter, golf was discontinued as an Olympic sport.

The early American women's golf associations were founded around the same time: The Women's Golf Association of Philadelphia in 1897, followed by the Women's Metropolitan Golf Association (New York) and the Women's Golf Association of Boston in 1900, and finally the Women's Western Golf Association in 1903 completed the quadruplet that covered the country.

By 1905, American women were going to Britain to compete in the Amateur Championship, including the Curtis sisters (Harriet and Margaret) from Boston, who took part in an unofficial match of England versus the United States, in spite of the home team having members from Ireland and Scotland.

In 1930, the last of these unofficial matches took place at Sunningdale in England, of which British golf writer, Enid Wilson, wrote: "What had begun as an informal occasion was written up so much by the press and attracted such crowds that the general impression became that it was a full-scale International." The Curtis sisters, who were both U.S. Amateur champions, donated a trophy, and the Curtis Cup began its history in 1932.

Cigarette cards have become collectibles, and these feature England's greatest women golfers. Joyce Wethered won the English Ladies Championship five years in a row beginning in 1920, and she played for England in many international matches. Pam Barton was Britain's winningest golfer and successor to Wethered. At nineteen she won the British and American Championships as well as matches around the world.

In America, Glenna Collett and Alexa Stirling led a new wave of American women golfers that would rival Britain's golfers for years to come.

In 1906, Rhona Adair, an exceptionally talented Irish scratch golfer, toured the United States playing competitive golf. During her adventurous trip, she won 16 golfing trophies, being defeated only once by an American golfer. Rhona was the British Women's Open Amateur champion of 1900 and 1903, won the Irish Championship four times, and was ranked consistently as the finest player in the world. The American woman golfer who impressed her the most was Mrs. Charles C. Stout, who as Genevieve Hecker was the Women's Amateur champion in 1901 and 1902.

May Hezlet, in her book *Ladies Golf* published in 1907, quoted Rhona Adair, saying of the American golfer: "Mrs. Stout is an example of the perfect orthodox form of the royal and ancient game. She learned her game from different professionals, and being very agile and apparently optimistic, with a repose and ease of play, she stands today as the best exponent of the game in America. I consider her, all things taken into consideration, a wonder. Never have I seen a player display more ideal form than does she in every particular, and in my opinion she is quite the equal of any woman golfer in the world."

Glenna Collett shakes hands with Alexa Stirling after winning the National Women's Amateur Golf Championship in 1925.

Her photograph shows Mrs. Stout as a lissome young woman, with a full, free-flowing swing. Attractive, with hair piled up on her head, she wears a long sleeved blouse and a full length skirt stopping just short of some sturdy lace-up shoes.

Accounting for the professional and highly competitive attitude associated with the American woman golfer, Rhona Adair said of her female counterparts in the U.S. at the beginning of the century: "Never in all my experience have I seen such universal grit and nerve as is displayed by every woman golfer. It is really astonishing. In England it is uncommon to find a woman playing out a hole if she has been bunkered, driven out of bounds, or is playing several strokes more than her opponent.

"I find in America that with the never-say-die spirit, which I had always heard was typical of all Americans, they keep right on playing until their opponent's ball is actually in the hole. Nor does this apply to one hole only of a match. I have seen women with a score of four down and five to go staring them in the face, tee up with quite as much pluck and cheerfulness as they showed on the first tee, and in a good many instances with much more. That is the spirit which wins golf matches, and while I am loyal to the last to my home and friends, I must, in fairness, admit that American women seem better able to rise to a bad situation and play better than they know how, when such a feat is demanded by the exigencies of the score, than either English, Irish or Scotch women.

"I cannot express myself too strongly in praise of the American women. They are such a jolly lot. I was surprised to see what splendid sportswomen they all are. They go into athletics even more strenuously than we do. Everyone I have met has

Helen Hicks was the first women pro to promote golf equipment and clinics. She represented the Wilson Sporting Goods Company for many years, beginning in 1934.

impressed me by reason of her splendid physical development. Golf has done wonders for them. Splendid achievements in athletics to them seem just as desirable as they do to American men."

After those early American golfing pioneers, came two dominant women: Alexa Sterling, three times consecutively an Amateur champion on either side of World War I, and following her Glenna Collett Vare, who won six Amateur championships from 1922 to 1935. Glenna, a greatly revered golfer who died in 1989, hit the golf ball harder than any of her contemporaries.

Women started to appear at golf clubs in the professional ranks in the 1920s and the 1930s, including Bessie Fenn, Virginia Hayes, May Dunn, Helen MacDonald, and Virginia Pepp. Helen MacDonald, who turned professional in 1924 and taught at the Golf Studio in Chicago, was the first woman to join a major sporting goods manufacturer, Hillerich & Bradsby of Louisville, Kentucky.

The first woman to go on the road promoting a manufacturer's products and giving golf clinics was Helen Hicks, who joined the Wilson Sporting Goods Company in 1934. Her work was furthered by Opal Hill in 1938, Helen Dettweiler in 1939, and Patty Berg in 1940—all joining the same company.

For women professionals in the 1930s, there was little competition. They could play only in the Hardscrabble Open in Arkansas, the Texas Open, the Western Open which began in 1930, and the Titleholders, started in 1937 at the Augusta Country Club. The latter two were regarded as the premier events in women's golf, but initially they offered no prize money. Helen Dettweiler won the Western Open as a professional in 1939 and carried off a silver bowl, while in 1941 Patty Berg was victorious and received the first-ever prize money from the Women's Western Golf Association, which was worth $100.00 in war bonds.

Glenna Collett Vare and Patty Berg contended in the 1930 Women's National Amateur. USGA President Prescott Bush presented the winners trophy to Mrs. Collett Vare.

With the advent of World War II, golf competition nearly ceased except for the combined All American and World Championships presented by George S. May of the Tam O'Shanter Country Club. Helen Dettweiler (left) was a member of the Women's Airforce Service Pilots (WASP). Patty Berg (right) enlisted in the Marines. Betty Hicks served in the Coast Guard Women's Auxiliary.

The woman who won the Western Women's Open in 1940 was Babe Didrikson Zaharias, who had married wrestler George Zaharias in 1938. At the time of winning, Babe was a professional golfer who had applied for reinstatement as an amateur, but she was able to compete in Open events without taking money. Her change in status in 1935 had come about in a dubious manner, when she competed in the Texas Amateur championship, only the second golf tournament she ever entered, and won it. Afterwards, a complaint was lodged, referring to her endorsement of a car. Her connection with professional basketball following her phenomenal achievements in the 1932 Olympics also contributed to her disputed status. It was said that if she had been a professional in one sport, she must be in another, and the unfair assumption was upheld by the USGA.

Babe made the best of this by joining the Goldsmith Company, which later merged with the MacGregor Golf Company, and they started a line of clubs for her. As a publicly idolized figure, she promoted their goods with great panache at clinics and exhibitions, but she was hungry for more competitive golf. After winning the Western Open, she applied for amateur reinstatement, which took a statutory three years.

Those early years of the Second World War saw little in the way of golf competition other than the combined All American and World Championships presented in show business style by the flamboyant George S. May of Tam O'Shanter Country Club, Chicago. His event in its early days offered a large purse in the ratio of $1.00 for the women professionals to each $28.00 for the men, which meant that Byron Nelson received $14,000 for his victory, and Betty Hicks, winner of the 1941 National Amateur, received a mere $500 for hers. It was an insult, which helped to prompt a young club professional in Greensboro, South Carolina, by the name of Hope Seignious, to become instrumental in forming the Women's Professional Golf Association. It was an idealistic but not altogether practical undertaking. The WPGA was incorporated in 1944 and had a life span of some five years.

Its first president, Betty Hicks, later colorfully wrote: "The first organization of women's professional golf was conceived in wrath, born into poverty, and perished in a family squabble. Thus was the Women's Professional Golf Association born: a bawling scrawny child of early day feminists, a beggar of a child pleading for tournaments and for amateurs to become professionals to play in those tournaments."

The three pathfinders of the WPGA—Hope Seignious (treasurer and secretary), Betty Hicks (president), and Ellen Griffin (vice president)—were responsible for innovations that were to carry on right through the burgeoning life of women's professional golf. Hope's energy initiated the Women's U.S. Open in 1946, and the inaugural event took place at the Spokane Country Club of

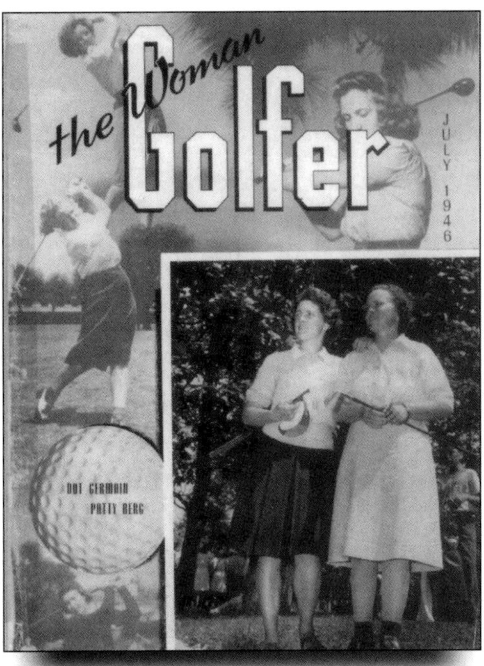

Thirteen issues of "The Woman Golfer", the official monthly publication of the WPGA, were published beginning in July 1946. It covered women's amateur and professional golf and sold for 25 cents. Magazine courtesy: Betty Hicks.

Washington State, sponsored by the Spokane Athletic Round Table, an organization which made a considerable income from slot machines. This enabled them to put up a prize fund of $19,700 in war bonds. Patty Berg was the winner, defeating Betty Jameson in the final. She received $5,600, in the only matchplay format in the history of the championship. The following year Betty Jameson achieved victory and became the first woman to break 300 in a 72-hole strokeplay tournament, taking the honors with a total of 295. In 1948 Babe Zaharias put her name on the trophy, for the first of three occasions.

The WPGA, in its short lifetime, instigated a women's winter tour in Florida in 1945. The foundations of the teaching division were firmly established by Ellen Griffin and Betty Hicks, who together wrote a book that became the bible for teaching golf in colleges. A monthly magazine called *The Woman Golfer* produced 13 issues at 25¢ a copy in 1946 and 1947, with the help of Greensboro journalist Smith Barrier (who died in 1989). He was the anonymous editor and wrote a column under the pen name of Margaret Allen, the name of his wife, who still lives in Greensboro.

Smith Barrier, former executive sports editor of the Greensboro Daily News, told me: "I became friendly with Hope Seignious, the daughter of a cotton broker, whose father, George, had some money. She was an only child, and he had wanted a boy, so she was his boy. He got her interested in golf, and she was not a competitor, but she became a good teacher, first as an assistant club professional, then as a head professional. Her father was prepared to indulge her interest in starting the WPGA and the magazine—he just wrote the checks for her—and I became very interested in the project of the WPGA and thought that women's athletics should be run by women."

The magazine's circulation was under 2,000 and thus couldn't get any advertising, so it eventually went out of business. The name was turned over to Bob Harlow, who was doing well with the weekly Golf World magazine. Harlow, who was the first tournament bureau manager of the men's PGA in the mid-1930s and was responsible with Fred Corcoran for creating their tour, thought highly of

WPGA founder Hope Seignious and bandleader Jimmy Dorsey are shown during WPGA Pro-Am. Hope and her family's money funded the tour as well as the National Opens in 1947 and 1948.

professional golf as a career for women. He considered it likely that important women's golf events, barring the National, might develop into open events. A man of vision, he wrote in 1940: "I know that a good winter circuit can be built up with open events to replace the amateur events. The basis should be free accommodation for the pros—two-day, 36-hole medal play for purses of $1,000, and 3-day, 54-hole events for purses of $1,500. The purses would increase as the girls made the events attractive and the fields got stronger."

The idea was sound but ahead of its time, as were the hopes for success of the WPGA, which foundered over the years with lack of cohesion, opposition, and funding that was dependent on Hope Seignious. Hope injected her father's money into the WPGA, spurred on by a genuine concern to do something to launch women's professional golf. She also harbored a desire to become its first tournament director.

The problem of the vast size of the country, and the slowness of communicating by letters and the occasional telegram was highlighted when Helen Dettweiler in California took it upon herself to appoint a WPGA tournament director in 1947. It was an issue that had been discussed but never confirmed with Hope, who held the purse strings.

In a long, disillusioned letter, Hope wrote to Helen: "When I told you the financial outlay for 1946 was $28,000 in round figures, which includes the magazine, the WPGA office expense, publicity for the National Open, and telephone and telegraph amount to $6,649.69, you immediately skipped over it." After berating Dettweiler and Hicks for their lack of financial acumen, she continued: "With the exception of you and Hicks, the rest of the contribution has amounted to nothing but hot air and good intentions, which die as they walk out the door. I honestly don't see why it isn't possible for all of us to work together instead of hiring someone to work for us."

The problems of making the WPGA a viable organization eventually became overwhelming, and when its demise came about in 1949, Hope Seignious went into organizing a trucking business in Greensboro.

Golf legend Bobby Jones, like most of the world, knew that Babe Zaharias would be a star of women's golf. Here, they are at Augusta National in 1947, the year she again became a pro, rejoining the WPGA.

On August 16, 1947, Babe Zaharias once again became a professional golfer, having completed her amateur career with an outstanding run of tournament victories, including the 1946 American and 1947 British Amateur championships. Although legend claims that she won 17 consecutive events, she actually won 13 and then forgot to record her loss in the opening round of the first National Women's Open—the one that Hope Seignious got off the ground in August 1946 at Spokane.

Babe joined the Wilson Sporting Goods Company and employed Fred Corcoran as her manager, whom Smith Barrier had approached unsuccessfully to take over the WPGA affairs. By 1949 the combination of L. B. Icely, the dynamic president of Wilson, and Fred Corcoran, who had been employed by the men's PGA from 1937, created a more organized format of women's professional golf. Babe Zaharias was its drawing card, spearheading a handful of illustrious women professionals.

Louise Suggs and Patty Berg, two founders of the LPGA, exchange scorecards at the 1946 Women's Western Open.

In May 1949, The Ladies' Professional Golf Players' Association was formed during the Eastern Open at Essex Falls, New Jersey, and Fred Corcoran was formally appointed tournament manager. Corcoran was able to take this position for a nominal $1.00 a year, since L. B. Icely added Corcoran's name to the staff of Wilson, which with the Golf Manufacturers' Association, provided the essential financial backing for the women. It was thought that Corcoran would benefit further when the established tournament circuit produced an income. Meanwhile his salary from Wilson was in addition to handling Babe Zaharias and baseball player Ted Williams, and he had an interest in a Massachusetts Ford Agency.

According to a later article in *Golf World* in 1950, the word "Ladies" instead of the former "Women" was used because Fred Corcoran advised it: "He did not feel the new association had a right to the old name and wanted no headaches about that item. He had plenty as it was." However, as Betty Hicks states in the *Foreword*, the WPGA had, in fact, been legally disbanded months before the LPGA was founded.

At the Eastern Open—the first to be organized by Corcoran—Babe demonstrated the considerable possibilities of a women's tour. She put on a fine show and took the title by a triumphant 13 shots, earning the $1,000 top prize in the $3,500 event, and the tournament was immediately booked for the following year.

The decade came to a close with expectations raised for a handful of women professionals nicknamed "The Dough Girls," who signed up with the newly formed association. Patty Berg was appointed president, and the rest of the members, Babe Zaharias, Betty Jameson, Helen Dettweiler, Bettye Mims White, and Helen Hicks, were all on the tournament committee. As new members had to be elected, the first invitation went to Louise Suggs, who had been unable to compete at Essex Falls due to a prior engagement to play an exhibition for her sponsors.

These few women professionals of the 1930s and 1940s extended the boundaries of their predecessors, and they provided an important role model to inspire their successors. They had determination, a sense of adventure, courage, talent, and above all, a great love for the game of golf.

George S. May smiles over Babe Zaharias' record 70 on the Tam O'Shanter course in 1946. She won the event that year, and his tournaments sustained women's professional golf during and after the war years.

Patty Berg

Patty Berg has been an outstanding competitor and contributor to the world of golf. Fellow professional Betsy Rawls rates her as being in the top five players of her era, and in the top ten of all-time great golfers. "Patty was the best fairway wood player and greatest sand player we ever had," says Betsy. While Mickey Wright says, "Babe Zaharias couldn't carry Patty Berg's golf clubs."

Patty has received almost every known accolade for a tremendous career, which competitively spanned five decades (she won in four of them). As an amateur she won 29 titles; 1938 was her finest year, when she won 10 of the 13 tournaments she entered, including the U.S. Amateur Championship. She played for her country in the 1936 and 1938 Curtis Cup teams.

In professional golf her involvement started in 1940, when she was 22, and continued as a founding member of the LPGA in 1950. Patty achieved 55 professional victories, 42 of them LPGA events; her tournament-playing spanned over 30 years, until she had a hip replacement and was forced to retire in 1980.

Her association with the Wilson Sporting Goods company has continued throughout her professional career, and she developed a famous showpiece clinic, which she gave all over the world. I was lucky enough to see, admire, and enjoy one in Florida, when I and the entire audience were rocking with laughter at her polished patter, and marveling at the quality of her shotmaking.

In 1995, at the 50th US Women's Open held at the Broadmoor, where there was an historic gathering of past Open champions, Patty gave a clinic, including some of the women professionals she had trained through the years. The likes of Betsy Rawls, Sandra Palmer, Donna Caponi, Mary Mills, Carol Mann, Murle Breer and Jerilyn Britz (US Open champions, all) demonstrated their shots to the crowds, as did Patty, who called the tune.

Patty won the first U.S. Women's Open Championship (played at Spokane, Washington), a matchplay format in which she defeated Betty Jameson by five and four. She was the first president of the LPGA and one of the original four women in the Hall of Fame (she is in eleven halls of fame). She had her own Patty Berg Classic

Patty, shown here as a youthful ice skater, became one of the foremost competitors and contributors to women's golf.

LPGA tour event, and in 1979 she established the annual Patty Berg award for sportsmanship and contribution to the game of golf, of which Marilynn Smith was the first recipient.

In modern financial terms, Patty never won much money. Her career earnings totaled $190,760, which indicates the level of prize money in the decades she was winning. Her top money-winning year, 1957, which included five victories, gave her $16,272.

Mickey Wright said of her: "Patty is the consummate perfect golfer for a woman, which shows in the fact that she could still swing the club as beautifully, and with all the class, in her sixties, as she had when I was coming along."

Betty Hicks has written: "When Patty Berg grasps a golf club, the butterfly emerges from the cocoon. Some of the greatest shots in women's golf have come off the faces of her clubs. No woman has abstracted more from golf, and none has returned more. There are many dedicated professionals of whom it is said that golf is their life. For Patty, golf is life."

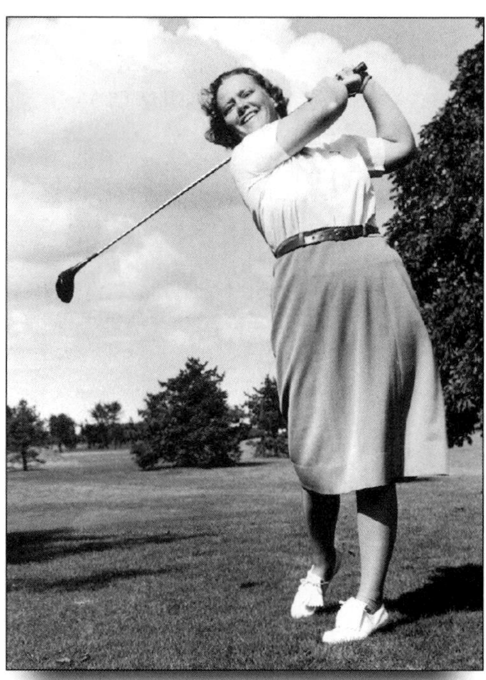

With a smile as famous as the swing, Patty is still one of the best ambassadors of the game of golf.

Betsy Rawls sees Patty thus: "Patty is a supreme diplomat and hides her feelings. Her public image is most important—she would never damage it—and the public adores her. She is at her most comfortable in front of a large audience. When I turned professional and Wilson hired me, they sent me to Patty as a training program for giving clinics and exhibitions. She was absolutely great, everyone loved her, and she put on a great show. She did not relate as well on a one-to-one basis, but she worked all her life to be a good "showperson" and to get feedback from the audience. She took lessons in dancing, diction, and everything a Broadway star would do. It is nice because she has entertained a lot of people, who just love her, and she has given a lot.

"Her father would make her work and practice, and he was the driving force behind her. In the process he could make her feel that if she wasn't a successful golfer, she was nothing. She's a very bright, intelligent woman, with a high IQ, and she thinks well."

Patty, 5 feet, 2 inches, in her spikes, as a young woman had bright, curly red hair, a freckled face, and a chunky figure. She was a great favorite with the galleries.

I went to see Patty at her home in Fort Myers, where she was very welcoming, taking me out for dinner and making me feel that she was more than happy to be contributing. She had her secretary send me details of her achievements, she wrote to me herself, and since that day I have received a Christmas card from her every year.

Patty is very keen on lists, on detail, on charting progress. She shared with me the list she made of what she believes it takes to win, and told me it is compiled from a variety of sources:

1. Believe you have to have a will to win, not a wish to win.
2. Inspiration.
3. Don't think you really win until you live up to that high thing within you, that makes you do your best, no matter what.
4. Never give up.
5. Desire, dedication, and determination.
6. Fighting heart.

7. Strive for perfection.
8. Faith, confidence, courage, spirit, and enthusiasm.
9. Self-control and patience.
10. Use your mind, concentration, visualization.
11. Take defeat and bounce back to victory.
12. Take God with you.

Patty was born and grew up in Minneapolis, in a religious Catholic family, with two sisters, Helen and Mary, three and four years older, and a brother, Herman Jr., four years younger. As the third child and a girl, she wanted to be noticed, and claimed her father's attention with her golf. Her father worked for a grain company, and the family was in the upper income group.

"I played all sports and loved them, I did speed skating, I won medals for track, and I was the quarterback for our local football team, called the 50th Street Tigers. I was the only girl and the only one who could remember signals. Charles `Bud' Wilkinson [the famous football coach] was guard, coach, and captain of the Tigers. I tore so many dresses and got so many bruises that my mother decided I should get into another sport.

"My dad played football and loved baseball, but golf became his first love, and he was a ten-handicap player. He was the biggest influence in my life because he started out with me in 1932 when I began to play golf, and he was a great inspiration.

"In 1933 I played the Minneapolis City Championship, which completely changed my life. I qualified in the last flight with the highest score of 122. I was in almost every trap, and the woman who was my opponent beat me on almost every hole. After the match was over, and it was over soon, I congratulated her and started walking back to the clubhouse. As I walked, I said to myself that I would dedicate the next 365 days to shooting better than 122 in the next championship, by taking golf lessons and working at it. It was going to be dedication, desire, and determination, and a real challenge.

"The following day I started practicing and playing, and I took lessons from Lester Volstad, who was to become my teacher for the next 40 years. I learned the short game, the irons, fairway woods, and the driver, and was determined I would jump from that last flight in the championship to at least the second or third flight. All I did was think and talk about golf the whole year.

"In 1934, I played in the same event and qualified as medalist. Then I won the tournament, and not only did it change my whole outlook on life, it was also the most satisfying victory of my entire life. I never thought I would win, and when I realized what I'd done in 365 days, I thought I could go on to play the big amateur tournaments and maybe some day I could have a future in golf. That began my eight years in amateur golf, and I loved it because I enjoy anything pertaining to golf. I love golf, and I love people.

"My daddy said it was fine for me to play a lot of golf, but on Saturdays and Sundays he wanted me to do something for charity. So every weekend I was home, I played exhibitions locally and in towns all over Minnesota, and some in Iowa and Wisconsin. My dad paid all the expenses; he was the MC for the clinics; and sometimes we took a popular football player, other locally known celebrities, or my brother Herman, Jr.

"We would drive somewhere on a Saturday, give a half-hour clinic, and then play 18 exhibition holes, after which we would drive on, stop overnight, go to church in the morning, drive to the next club, and do the same thing again. We would involve the club professional, and all donations went to charity.

"In 1937 I became a student at the University of Minnesota, where I majored in history and studied English, but I stayed only for two and a half years and didn't graduate. My amateur golf was halted during 1939, when I had appendicitis and could not play. On Christmas day that year, my first mother, who was badly crippled with a dislocated hip, had a stroke at 11 in the morning and died a half an hour later. It was a deep loss, but my college friends, my family, and my golf helped me in getting over it.

Patty's "first" mother, as she calls her, died when Patty was 21. Three years later her father remarried, and Patty called Vera, his new wife, "mother," though she was only 11 years older

Patty and Babe squared off in the final of the 1941 Western Open, a match play event. Patty won it, and later, in 1948, she put a dent in Babe's supremacy, edging her 1-up in a 36-hole cliff hanger to win the Western Open again. Photo Courtesy: Betty Hicks.

than her new daughter. There was a remarkable resemblance in their looks, and they had a close and continuing relationship until Vera died in 1993.

"My father married again, as the result of my having played an exhibition in 1941 in Charlotte, North Carolina, where a widow named Vera Parks had us to lunch. A year and a half later they were married. Vera became my mother, and she was a fine golfer, who won the Minnesota State Championship four times and the Florida Seniors on three occasions. She was my biggest booster; she saw me through illness and my golf, and she was the reason I'm where I am today. She was a great inspiration.

"In June 1940 I decided to turn professional. There were only around three tournaments with prize money of perhaps $500, and about five professionals. I had spent eight years in amateur golf and had to think about the prospect of being away for ten months, with different people, on different golf courses, packing, unpacking, ironing out all the wrinkles from my clothes, and promoting Wilson merchandise. I knew that I would have my name on a golf club and get royalties, that Wilson would pay me a salary and my traveling expenses. I loved clinics and exhibitions so much, I made the decision to become a professional, and I thought one day we would get a women's tour started.

"Helen Hicks, who had a marvelous personality, had paved the way with Wilson, starting in 1934 doing clinics and exhibitions right round the country. Then she got married and stopped most of the traveling, and I took it up. Opal Hill and Helen Dettweiler were also Wilson pioneer professionals. It was L. B. Icely, the president of Wilson, who started an advisory staff in sports. When I arrived, everyone was wonderful to me and so welcoming, and in nearly 50 super and wonderful years, I have done more than 10,000 clinics for Wilson and trained 20 girls. When I started, I would do three clinics a day, and I could have done them all day and all night.

"In 1941 I won the Western Open, North Carolina Open, and New York Invitational. Then in December that year, I was a passenger in a car traveling to a exhibition with Helen Dettweiler, and another car hit us. My left knee went into the dashboard, and I had a compound fracture and couldn't play golf for 18 months. The knee took so long to heal it looked like it might go stiff and not get right. Finally it got better, and I went to train with a boxer I knew in Mobile, Alabama, to build up the strength in my leg.

"In 1943 I won the Western Open and All-American Open, and then in September I joined the Marine Corps to do my part for my country in the Second World War. I went to officer cadet school and graduated as a second lieutenant. I became a recruiting officer in Philadelphia and was in charge of women in five departments, and I did a lot of public speaking about the Marines.

"I got out of the Marines in October 1945 and resumed my golfing life. In 1946 I won four tournaments, including the first U.S. Women's Open, which was started by Hope Seignious, a founder of the WPGA in 1945. The WPGA survived for several years. In January 1948, Babe Zaharias, who was then a professional with Wilson, her husband George, and I, went to see L. B. Icely about setting up a tour. He agreed to hire Fred Corcoran, who had been running the PGA, to set up a tour for us, and I became the first president in 1948, remaining until 1952.

"It was a group effort in the early days. Babe was a household name, and people came to see her. Corcoran created a 'Big Four' of women professionals doing exhibitions, using Babe and Betty Jameson to play against Louise Suggs and me, and it was very successful.

"Babe was the greatest woman athlete I've ever known and a great friend. She brought a power to the game that I had not seen before. When she died at 42, before she could see the result of all the doors she had opened, it was very sad and a tremendous loss. On the day after she died, President Eisenhower opened his news conference by talking about her death.

"When the LPGA tour got going, I never played full time because I was doing clinics and exhibitions. I was money leader three times, but the most I ever won in a season in my entire career was $16,272 in 1957. I never worried that much about money or really thought about it. I just liked to play golf, which has been my whole life. I loved the competition and the people.

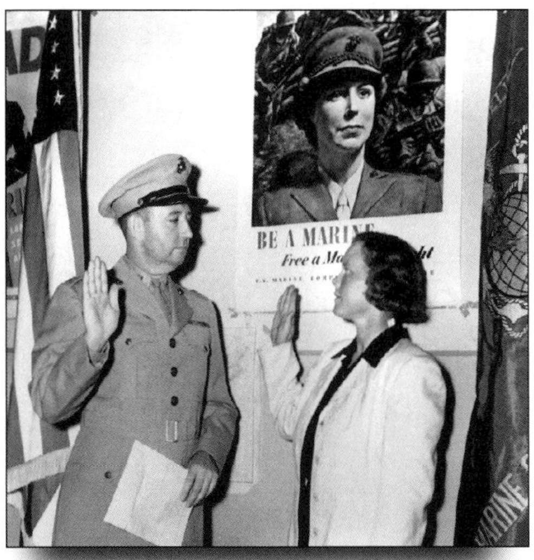

Patty joined the Marines in 1943, to do her part for her country. She served as recruiting officer for the Marines. Later, she recruited thousands of fans for the LPGA and still does so today.

Patty won the Titleholders championship in 1953 just one of her 57 LPGA victories.

"I always worked on my game and practiced hard, trying to improve, to do better or hold on to what I had. I feel muscle memory and the same swing are very important, to be prepared is important, and pace is too. You should start to pace yourself the minute you get out of bed. Don't run into the bathroom and start brushing your teeth, just move at a steady playing pace to avoid everything becoming fast and jerky. On the course breathe out slowly, let your arms hang loose, and walk at a steady pace all the way. No one will ever master golf because it is too much to do with the nervous system and so much can transpire in the mind."

Patty won tournaments, played exhibitions, gave clinics, and made friends around the world. Her father died at 77 in 1962, her two sisters died of cancer, and Herman, Jr., had two open-heart operations. In 1971 Patty was operated on for a malignant cancerous tumor and recovered well. In 1967, she was unlucky enough to be burglarized, and all her precious and sentimental trophies were stolen from her.

For her 60th birthday, Wilson gave her a surprise party: "It was the most thrilling thing I ever had happen to me. They were screaming and hollering `Happy Birthday.' My mother Vera was there and my niece, and the band played. Ray Volpe spoke, so did Kathy Whitworth, Carol Mann, Donna Caponi, and Beth Stone. Betsy Rawls and Betsy Cullen were there. There was a huge cake, and my hands were shaking so much I thought I would cut Donna Caponi's hand.

"There were flowers and lovely things, but most of all I appreciated the wonderful thoughtfulness and kindness. It was the greatest honor. Imagine your fellow golfers giving this big party for you. I didn't sleep for two or three nights just thinking about it.

"Some years ago, Mickey Wright asked me what I would change if I had to do it again. I said I wouldn't change a thing; I couldn't be this lucky twice. I did it myself. It's the life I chose, and it has brought me a lot of happiness."

Patty talks with Helen Dettweiler at the 1987 Marilynn Smith Founders' Classic in Dallas. Today, Patty still represents Wilson Sporting Goods promoting golf to her fans, young and old.

Member LPGA Hall of Fame 1951

LPGA Victories: 1941 Western Open, North Carolina Open, New York Invitational. **1943** Western Open, All-American Open. **1945** All-American Open. **1946** Northern California Open, Northern California Medal Tournament, Pebble Beach Open. U.S. Women's Open. **1947** Northern California Open, Pebble Beach Open, Northern California Medal Tournament. **1948** Titleholders Championship, Western Open, Hardscrabble Open. **1949** Tampa Open, Texas PGA Championship, Hardscrabble Open. **1950** Eastern Open, Sunset Hills Open, Hardscrabble Open. **1951** Western Open, Sandhills Open, Weathervane Women's Open Pebble Beach, Weathervane Women's Open Westchester, Weathervane Women's Open Playoff. **1952** New Orleans Open, Richmond Open, New York Weathervane Open. **1953** Titleholders Championship, All-American Open, World Championship, Jacksonville Open, New Orleans Open, Reno Open, Phoenix Weathervane Open (T1). **1954** World Championship, Triangle Round Robin, Ardmore Open. **1955** Titleholders Championship, Western Open, All-American Open, World Championship, St. Petersburg Open, Clock Open. **1956** Dallas Open, Arkansas Open. **1957** Titleholders Championship, Western Open, All-American Open, World Championship, Havana Open. **1958** Western Open, American Women's Open. **1960** American Open. **1962** Muskogee Civitan Open. Unofficial Victories: **1944** Pro-Lady Victory National (with Johnny Revolta). **1950** Orlando Two-Ball (with Earl Stewart). **1954** Orlando Two-Ball (with Pete Cooper).

Patty Berg's LPGA Record

Year	No. of Events	Best Finish	Money	Rank	Scoring Average
1950	10	1	$1,500	NA	77.64
1951	14	1	4,537	NA	75.76
1952	11	1	4,794	NA	75.39
1953	19	1	14,500	NA	74.94
1954	16	1	13,947	NA	77.29
1955	17	1	9,873	NA	77.29
1956	21	1	12,055	NA	75.54
1957	19	1	16,272	7	74.83
1958	16	1	8,014	4	75.13
1959	22	2	11,495	7	74.95
1960	17	1	9,019	7	75.27
1961	8	4	4,574	15	76.63
1962	19	1	11,552	7	74.47
1963	5	6	998	33	78.05
1964	16	T4	4,791	17	75.54
1965	14	2	6,065	24	75.76
1966	13	T6	3,177	28	75.78
1967	10	T9	4,562	34	75.68
1968	10	T9	3,909	37	75.45
1969	14	3	6,460	32	75.54
1970	7	T11	3,213	39	75.13
1971	DNP				
1972	8	T32	1,975	71	78.05
1973	9	T28	1,512	79	79.11
1974	8	T39	1,077	86	77.82
1975	8	T49	522	100	78.05
1976	7	T49	738	105	78.78
1977	3	NA	NA	NA	81.00
1978	5	T66	190	119	81.71
1979	4	68	200	130	83.75
1980	1	71	220	153	83.00

Helen Dettweiler

Helen Dettweiler, born in 1914 at the beginning of World War I, was a woman of remarkable achievement, combined with great charm, considerable self-effacement, and an apparent lack of aggression.

When she was only 14 years old, an essay that she wrote on the subject of the typical all-American girl—which is how she was later described in print—won her a six-week trip to France and England.

"I remember one highlight in England was having lunch on the yacht of Nancy, Lady Astor, who was the first woman member of Parliament. The other was having tea with the Prince of Wales—who became Edward VIII—at his home in London. He gave us each a cigarette with `HRH' on it, which I kept for many years."

A highly academic student, by the age of 21, Helen had a degree in English and History from Trinity College in Washington, D.C., which she achieved at the same time as completing, at night, two years of law at Columbus Law school.

Betty Hicks says of Helen: "She came from a devout Catholic family, and I remember her telling me that she had made a vow to go into a convent if she didn't win the Washington District Championship. Luckily she did. Maybe Helen wasn't aggressive enough to be a winner, but she was so diversified that I found her one of the most remarkable women in golf."

When Helen died of cancer in 1990, I felt I lost a friend of great warmth, even after our relatively short acquaintance. I saw Helen at her home during her final illness, visiting her with Marilynn Smith. We were made most welcome and enjoyed the time we spent chatting and gossiping with her.

Helen's list of accomplishments includes becoming the first woman baseball radio commentator; the third woman professional to work for a golf club manufacturer, doing exhibitions and clinics all over the country; the first woman to design and build a golf course; the second president of the WPGA in 1946, the second president of the LPGA, of which she was a founding member in 1950; and the first woman to receive the LPGA teaching award of the year in 1958. When she attended the inaugural 1987 Marilynn Smith Founders' Classic, she received her jacket from Ben Hogan, with whom she played an exhibition match in the 1940s.

Helen shows her fine form on the driving range, and it was good enough to win the 1939 Western Open.

In World War II Helen became a pilot, flying B-17s after she joined the WASPs, a group of women who flew over 60 million miles during the war, and about whom a book was written, entitled *Those Wonderful Women in Their Flying Machines.*

My first meeting with Helen was during the 1986 Dinah Shore Tournament in Palm Springs, after which we corresponded. Helen was an excellent letter writer, and we met again at Marilynn Smith's tournament. Helen was warm, helpful, and supportive. She had a shy, self-effacing quality, and always made light of her achievements, such as flying a B-17: "It flew itself, it really did. It was such a beautiful, sensational plane, which responded so well that it was easier than flying the training planes. It was not a matter of strength, more coordination, timing, and good depth perception for landing. It was exhilarating to be up there with God and four engines, in a plane that would fly on one engine."

Helen was born and brought up in an upper middle class family in Washington, D.C. Her father was a dentist, and she had two brothers, three and six years younger. Her brother, Bill, three years younger, was a very fine golfer, who at 14 was the youngest player ever to qualify for the National Amateur.

"I always liked outdoor sports, particularly baseball. When I was 17, I saw Joyce Wethered play a local exhibition golf match, which inspired me, and she was my ideal in every phase of the game.

Helen, a golfing pioneer, was a pilot. She flew B-17s and B-29s, logging 750 hours. She was also the first woman baseball commentator, and the first woman to design and build a golf course.

Helen gives Secretary of State Cordell Hull an impromptu putting lesson.

From about 16, I won the District of Columbia title, the Maryland State Championship, and the Mid-Atlantic several times."

Later, a newspaper columnist, Vincent X. Flaherty, wrote: "Helen became the princess of the Washington sports pages when she was no older than 14 or 15. She regularly defeated top female stars who were old enough to be her mother. She presented a curious spectacle as she strode down the fairways among these golfing matrons, appearing to be more of a rollicking schoolgirl than a contender." At the end of his column, Flaherty said: "Helen Dettweiler comes nearer to personifying the conception of the American girl, than any girl I have ever seen."

Because of Helen's friendship with Washington Senators' owner Clark Griffith, with whom she played golf, in the mid-1930s she became involved as a national radio commentator in major league baseball. "I used to sneak out of school and sit in Clark's box, whenever there was a home game. Wheaties sponsored the radio reports, and after I did a dummy run, I was offered quite a lot of money to be a commentator. I knew the game backwards and forwards and loved it. I traveled all over the country and had a wonderful time, sometimes being given grand accommodation in bridal suites.

"I had been playing amateur golf and doing pretty well, when in 1939 the Wilson Sporting Goods Company approached me and asked me to become a professional for them—doing clinics and promoting women's golf and their product. They offered me a lot of money—$2,500 a year, 8 cents a mile, and my expenses. I thought it was a great opportunity. So did my parents, who were always behind me in everything I did.

"I bought my own car, a Chrysler convertible. I had it done inside with Scottish plaid upholstery. I had a horn fitted which played 'The Campbells Are Coming,' and I was over the moon. My most embarrassing moment came when I went to do a clinic at a club in the Adirondacks, and my horn got stuck right outside the front door."

"After I turned professional, I immediately won the Western Open, for which I received a silver bowl (there was not any prize money), and it was my biggest moment in golf. I'm not a great competitor; I never have been. I didn't feel that competitive; winning was not that important to me. I enjoyed people more than competition.

"Helen Hicks had turned professional in 1934 and gone with Wilson, as did Opal Hill in 1938.

Helen, on the set of "Pat & Mike" with Katharine Hepburn and Spencer Tracy, was one of several LPGA pros used in the movie. Betty Hicks, Babe Zaharias, Bev Hanson, and Virginia Nance also appeared in the movie.

Helen took me under her wing until, three months later, Patty Berg followed me into the professional ranks, and I took her with me on the road. Patty was a great golfer and the greatest competitor. She was also very naive, and I almost had to tell her the facts of life. Her hypochondria was legendary: If Patty cut a toe nail, it would be like cutting her leg off. There was never a day when there wasn't something wrong.

"I came near to getting married a couple of times, but I never found anyone with whom I wanted to share my life, and as I became more independent from traveling I was less interested in marriage.

"When America entered the Second World War, I got a job in Washington in the Air Force's cryptographic section, of which I became manager, training people to encode and decode, and they sent me all over the country to organize other sections.

"I was interested in flying and had been taking lessons, when I applied to join the WASPs, the Women's Air Force Service Pilots. We went through the same training process as the men, but we were civilians flying for the Air Force and were never allowed to be part of the military. For that reason they kept us in the United States because had we gone to foreign war territory, we could have been shot as spies. We were ferrying planes, test hopping, tow targeting, doing domestic flying, all the duties which would release the men for flying overseas. From 1943 to 1944 I flew the B-17s, logging 750 hours.

"Following that I was in the Pentagon with Jacqueline Cochran, the pioneer woman pilot who was the inspiration behind the WASPs. She was their director, and I acted as her aide, inspecting bases and handling the press. When the war was over, Jackie asked me to go to Indio in Palm Springs to help her write the history of women pilots for the U.S. Air Force archives. The point had been proved that women could do the same flying duties as men, with almost identical results.

"When I went to Palm Springs, there was only one golf course, O'Donnell, which was nine holes. Jackie's husband, Floyd Odlum, was a financier. I asked him why he didn't build nine holes at the Cochran Ranch and open it to the public. He said if I would design and build a course and stay as professional for at least a couple of years, he would back the idea.

"I carried out the design and construction of the course, and I stayed for six years. I joined MacGregor, for whom I did clinics and exhibitions, and I did a lot of teaching at the club.

"The next course to open in Palm Springs was Thunderbird, where Jimmy Hines was the professional, followed by Tamarisk in 1952. Tamarisk obtained Ben Hogan for its course, and at the opening, Ben, Jimmy, and I—along with George Howard—played an exhibition match. Ben and I were against the other two; there were a lot of bets, which Hogan didn't like, and on the 18th, where he had a six-foot putt, I'm sure he missed it on purpose."

"At that time, Jimmy Hines offered me a teaching job at Thunderbird, and as Floyd [Odlum] didn't want to build another nine holes at Cochran

Ben Hogan presents Helen her jacket as an LPGA charter member at the Marilynn Smith Founders' Classic, Dallas, 1987.

Ranch, I took it. While I was there, I taught President Eisenhower, whom I had met previously, during his term of office. Later, when he had a house at Eldorado, he came and took lessons every morning at 8:30, except on Sundays. When he was returning back East, he asked me how much he owed me for the lessons, and I said I should be paying him. When he insisted, I said I would love one of his own paintings, as that was his hobby. Two weeks later, I received a signed oil painting of a winter farm scene in Gettysburg, which I have treasured.

"Because I met and taught many show-business people in Palm Springs, I became involved in the film Pat and Mike, made in the late 1940s with Spencer Tracy and Katharine Hepburn. Betty Hicks, Bev Hanson, and Babe Zaharias were also involved, and we had a great time filming at the Riviera Country Club in Los Angeles. Katharine Hepburn did all her own golf shots—she was very athletic and loved to play—and I gave Spencer Tracy a golf lesson."

Helen played in some tournaments, but mainly she continued teaching golf, for which she became renowned. In the late 1960s, she opened a sportswear shop in Palm Springs, which she owned for ten years, before selling it. "I enjoyed pioneering; there was always a new challenge. I would like to have continued flying after the war, but it was too expensive, and I didn't really miss it, since I went on to do other things."

Helen's adventures included going on safari in Africa, where she was a regular visitor in the 1980s, and she asked me to join one of her trips, but sadly I was unable to make it. Asked to attend the second Marilynn Smith Founders' Classic in 1988, Helen declined because she was off on safari: "Africa comes before almost everything," she explained.

Professional Victories: 1939 Western Open.

Ellen Griffin

Ellen Griffin was a pioneer. She had the look of the pioneer woman. She was small and athletic, with a wonderfully lined face when I met her. Her voice was warm, low, and strong; her humor always apparent; and we had long discussions on life, death, religion, and sport.

After years of courageously fighting cancer and heart problems, Ellen died at 67 in 1985. Some years previously, when Ellen and I talked about growing older and dying, she told me: "Growing older and playing golf, I accepted a lower standard. For a long time you use an extra club, then you run out of clubs. Physically I know I can't do what I used to, although I feel just the same. I don't resent being old, but I find there are limits. I chop wood, haul bales of hay, cripple myself, but my limit is now 50 pound bags.

"Only the good die young, and I forgot to tell anyone the good I'd done. I don't believe I'm going to be blotted out when I die. But it's a new experience, and no one knows about it, so why worry? I'm not in a hurry. I'm curious, and I'm going to know about it one day, but it's last on my list of priorities."

Ellen was a legend in the world of teaching golf. As someone said humorously at a dinner given in her honor in 1983: "Ellen is a legend in her own mind." That legend lives on, through the many people whose lives she touched and whose golf games she influenced with her highly individual style, enthusiasm, and enjoyment.

In 1989 the Ellen Griffin Rolex Award was instituted by the LPGA Teaching Division to honor the woman who dedicated so much of her life to teaching and who was LPGA Teacher of the Year in 1962. The award is given to a male or female who has made a major contribution to the teaching of golf and who has demonstrated the spirit, love, and dedication that Ellen Griffin imparted to her golf students in teaching the skills and game of golf. The first three awards were received by Peggy Kirk Bell, Linda Craft, and Shirley Englehorn.

Together with Betty Hicks, Ellen wrote *The Golf Manual for Teachers*, which became a teaching bible. Ellen achieved master professional status, and in 1976, she was cited as one of the six outstanding teachers in the United States.

In 1944, Ellen Griffin and Hope Seignious, based in Greensboro, together with Betty Hicks in California, formed the WPGA, the first organization of any kind for women professional golfers. With journalist Smith Barrier, they put out a magazine called The Woman Golfer, which was both entertaining and informative, appearing in 1946 and 1947.

Ellen Griffin, shown here in 1947, was a founder of the WPGA. Together with Betty Hicks, she wrote the "Golf Manual for Teachers", which became a teaching bible.

Ellen was an exciting piece in my jigsaw puzzle of tracing women professionals. I met her in 1979 while staying with Dot Germain, professional golfer, protégée, and student of the Ellen Griffin school. Dot lived next door to where Ellen ran her teaching "Farm," to which so many grateful students came over the years and continue to come.

Ellen gave me a book of her sayings and poetry, from which I quote: "A child asks questions, an adult questions answers; a little of both in both is the balance of human nature."

She battled the repression of her era directed against the athletic woman, and she strove to establish that competition in golf was healthy for women, that intercollegiate athletics and intermural activities were acceptable. She remained dedicated to teaching as she struggled for her ideals.

Ellen was born in 1918, the only daughter and the oldest of the three children in an army family. Her father died in 1948, but her mother outlived her. The family was constantly on the move, and Ellen attended eight different grade schools.

"I loved moving and traveling, and I loved school. From the time I was seven I wanted to go to West Point. I was told they didn't take girls at the Military Academy, so I said, `Well, how do you get to be a boy? `Kiss your elbow,' they told me teasingly. I tried it, fell over, and nearly broke my ankle.

"My father was a great sportsman, and he played golf. When I was eight and we were living in Georgia, he took me to the local professional and told him to give me a golf club and one lesson. The professional gave me a cut-down hickory-shafted two iron, and I imitated what he did. It was a great way to start.

"I was a tomboy who loved sport, and I loved my two iron, which I used for every shot. It was lucky my father was in the Army because we could open the golf course every Sunday at 6 a.m. He played 18 holes with me, then took me for a chocolate milk, after which I went to church, and Dad played golf with his men friends.

"In my junior year of high school I found you could do physical education at college, and I went to the Woman's College of the University of North Carolina in Greensboro. It wasn't until I got to college that I realized you were regarded as a dumb-head if you were in physical education. You couldn't make Phi Beta Kappa, since every class was taken without credit. Although I had the same liberal-arts degree as my brother, who was a pre-med, there was a stigma attached to 'phys. ed.' People called it 'PE' in a derogatory way and thought it was the lowest thing on the academic totem pole, although the course included anatomy, physiology, chemistry, biology, and English. Physical education was regarded as a male pursuit, and women involved were thought of as dumb, lesbian jocks, although no one voiced it in those terms. No part of it was seen as healthy and wholesome.

"When others condemned us for our subject, they would say in a derisory tone: 'You walk like a PE major.' Our teacher said that any time anyone told us we walked, talked, or looked like a phys ed major, we should turn round and say only one thing: 'Thank you.' She said, 'You should be happy with the way you walk, the way you talk, at the exuberance and vitality you have. Don't let others tell you what you are.' I always remembered that.

"Although swimming, golf, and tennis were respected as individual sports for women, varsity or interscholastic athletics were dirty words. There was a constant fight in the 1940s to establish competitive athletics for women, with section committees being set up to establish standards and guidelines for women participating in sport. Research was done on menstrual problems and athletics, and they said you could not menstruate and swim or participate in any heavy exercise. Later, research showed this to be untrue, but prior to the invention of the tampon, it was a sanitary protection not to swim, and when you were menstruating, you were told not to shower, since you were regarded as sick and not in a normal state.

"It was thought masculine to compete, and no one would dare mention lesbian or indeed homosexual, which were very guarded words. I had to teach sex education in my first job, and it was very difficult just talking about menstruation and the birth of a baby. There were so many words you couldn't say that you had to struggle to express yourself, but it was safe to stick to the description in the anatomy book.

"The first talk I ever gave on boy-girl relations was at a junior high school, and I was told they wanted 15 minutes at the end for a question and answer session. I thought, `Boy, I'm not going to get involved in that,' and I went on talking almost to the bitter end of my allotted time.

"With a couple of minutes remaining, all the hands shot up with questions, and I picked out a little girl who was the homeliest I've ever seen, with black horn-rimmed glasses, and I asked for her question. `If a boy takes you to a movie and all he wants to do is sit and smooch, what do you do?' asked this homespun creature. I can't remember what I replied, but I know that I took enough time with my answer to avoid all further questions."

It was in 1940, just after the war began in Europe, that Ellen obtained her physical education degree. She wanted to join the armed services, but her father refused to allow it, so she worked for the Victory Corps and stayed on at college to obtain her master's degree. Her teaching association with the University of North Carolina continued for the next 28 years, and she became a professor of physical education.

"The Second World War, like the First, gave women an opportunity to enter a field of close competition with men because during those years women were needed in men's jobs and were earning men's wages. For some women, the effect carried over into other areas.

"The emergence of athletics for women began in the 1940s when a woman called Gladys Palmer initiated at Ohio University the first collegiate golf tournament for women. I was teaching in Greensboro, and I took the invitation to the head of my department and nearly fell on my face when she told me to get some girls and go. Only two years earlier, she had preached against competition for women... and certainly not intercollegiate competition.

"We didn't have a team, but I got together some girls. We went, and it was beautiful. The tournament continued in Ohio for ten years, then looked like it would die. So I said, `We've got to keep it alive,' and I brought it to Greensboro. After that, others kept it alive, and it became the model for collegiate tournament golf and a spearhead for greater developments.

"In the 1950s, prior to a huge national convention for the physical education of college women, a tripartite committee was formed at Purdue University, in West Lafayette, Indiana, which proved one of the most significant events I ever attended. All the people who formerly pushed out women's athletics, now voted them in unanimously. Collegiate golf had proved the forerunner that kept alive athletics for women in colleges, leading to competition at a high level in all women's sports."

When the WPGA was formed, Ellen was in charge of the physical education program, which offered its services to teachers in universities and high schools. The first National Golf Clinic of Physical Education Teachers, under the auspices of

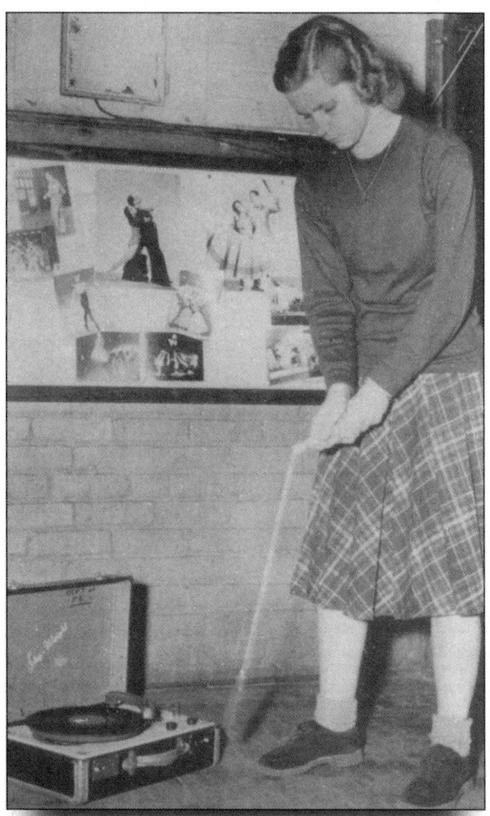

Ellen demonstrates the "Swing Wonder" with the aid of a phonograph. It developed the feel of the swing in close environs. The photo accompanied one of her articles for "The Woman Golfer". Magazine photo courtesy: Betty Hicks.

the WPGA, was held in 1946 at Purdue University, where golf had been taught to women students as far back as 1933. Ellen, Betty Hicks, Patty Berg, Betty Jameson, Shirley Spork, and Hope Seignious were all involved in this innovative national clinic.

The Woman Golfer magazine campaigned for more participation in women's athletics, saying in the first issue of July 1946: "Women of today are anxious to build leadership among and within themselves. They have learned to organize and assume responsibility. The field of sports gives them a chance to do all of these things."

In 1949, as a culmination of their work in teaching and playing, The Golf Manual for Teachers was published, written by Ellen Griffin and Betty Hicks. Ellen said: "Betty was the name player, while I had the teaching experience. She wrote it and we agreed on everything. About 10,000 copies were sold, and it became the accepted teaching manual.

"I remember Betty showed it to Babe [Zaharias], who said: `How long did it take you to write that?' Betty told her three or four years. `Good Lord,' said Babe. `I'm going to New York, and I'm going to get out mine this weekend.'

"I remember being influenced by Babe when I was in high school. She was my idol and was always on the sports pages. I didn't realize until much later that on the other pages of the newspapers it said, `There is a woman doing masculine things in a masculine way and looking masculine.' Even when she painted her nails, changed her image, and married, it didn't make much difference in the way they wrote about her. It was predetermined that as a woman athlete you'd be masculine or a lesbian. There always have been and probably always will be innuendoes of masculinity and lesbianism on the golf tour, but it hasn't caused and won't cause the end of it.

LPGA golfer, protegeé, and student of the Ellen Griffin School, Dot Germain pays Ellen a neighborly visit to "The Farm" near Greensboro.

"As a teacher, I spent a lot of time talking to parents, trying to convince them that what their daughters were doing in phys ed was a beautiful art and a science. All the things they imagined were not the ones I knew. Their daughters would turn out the same way, I told them, whether they were in music, art, or biology. It was nothing to do with phys. ed.

"I used to take my students to see women wrestlers because I said, `How can you form opinions when you haven't seen them?' My students were against going, but I said, `I want you to watch and tell me how you feel. If you had a daughter, would you let her wrestle professionally?' They were horrified and said absolutely not, because they considered it a put-up job. I told them it was the best tumbling act I'd ever seen, and they ought to look for the beauty, skill, and gymnastics needed to do it. There were prejudices against women wrestling and playing football, as there were about running and swimming during menstruation.

"I guess I was a pioneer, though I've never thought of it like that, but I suppose I was excited about things because they had never been done before. I love teaching because it's a challenge, and although I personally don't feel particularly motivated, the sport is self-motivating. I've always believed in the worth of women in golf, and I enjoy any way that I can be part of it. Teaching is common sense; it is the mental aspect that is important. I don't charge a whole lot for my golf lessons, but my couch time is terribly expensive."

Betty Hicks

Betty Hicks is a remarkable woman, short in stature at 5 feet, 1 inch, but long on achievement. You get the feeling that she has always made waves, that she has never been swimming with the tide, although she made a few token gestures.

Born in 1920, she has all the instincts of the competitive pioneer woman, and although she is a naturally shy person, she is highly intelligent, with a quick, razor-sharp wit. A wonderful observer, she penned in the Saturday Evening Post what is probably the best article ever written about the LPGA, entitled, "Next to Marriage We'll Take Golf," in which she did not mince words and gave an excellent, pithy insight into the women's golf tour of that era.

Patty Berg, whom Betty referred to as "our troupe's healthiest hypochondriac," did not speak to her for some time afterwards, and Babe Zaharias, of whom Betty wrote: "Babe's supremacy would be much easier for us to swallow if she didn't cram it down our throats," threatened to resign from the tour unless she was in control, ousting Betty Hicks from her post of publicity director, and using the article against her.

Betty Hicks, comes up with a win at the 1940 Palm Beach Championship. The next year, she captured the National Women's Amateur at the Country Club of Brookline in Massachusetts. Photo courtesy: Betty Hicks.

"The article wasn't malicious," says Betty. "It was somewhat humorous, as the women have humorous frailties. It was resented to some extent, a little jealousy was involved, and although the criticism was largely unwarranted, there may have been a basis for being upset about it."

The impact of Betty's article was described by newspaperman, Dave Lewis of Long Beach, California: "Veteran golf observers are in unanimous agreement that the article by Betty Hicks in the Saturday Evening Post recently, was the best publicity the Ladies' Professional Golf Association has ever had. Gate receipts of the Tampa Open, played right after the article hit the newsstands, bear this out. All attendance records were broken."

Betty is a pilot, a journalist (she has taught both subjects), and a gourmet cook who has written excellent books on the subject. She is musical and artistic, at one time playing the cello and painting. She was also a winner in golf before she began to diversify. Betty, with Ellen Griffin, compiled and wrote *The Golf Manual for Teachers*, a first of its kind and highly successful. A founder and the first president of the WPGA, Betty was not involved in the beginnings of the LPGA because she was studying for a teaching degree at Wayne State University in Detroit. By rights Betty should have been acknowledged as a founder, since she founded the forerunner WPGA and played the LPGA tour in the 1950s, contributing much to the organization and promotion of the association.

Betty says of those years: "My role was that of an enthusiastic pioneer, somewhat naive in the ways of the business world. We were all sportswomen, who thought our game would sell itself, and we had no concept of how to sell. We all had to work together, and I started to provide the communication, but in those days women didn't trust each other to have expertise in any area."

Through my years of research, Betty has been a good friend, who has given unfailing support and encouragement for a project that she could well have undertaken herself, and she has supplied me with invaluable documentation and photographs of the early era. I have always been made a welcome guest at her home in California.

Although she struck out for herself, Betty was influenced by fellow pioneer and professional golfer, Helen Dettweiler: "Helen thought I could be a good professional and I greatly admired her."

Betty was born and brought up in Long Beach, California, to an upper middle income family. Her father was a high school principal, she had a sister four years her junior, and the entire family loved athletic pursuits.

"I played softball, basketball, and touch football, until I was 16. My father thought I should take up a game with a longer life span; so in 1937 I started lessons in golf classes at Long Beach City College. I progressed very rapidly and won the Long Beach City tournament only a year later.

"Golf was considered a dignified game, reasonably acceptable for a woman, but it was frowned upon to be very competitive. I hit the ball too hard and practiced too much for the local women. I established a daily practice routine, which was a self-imposed discipline, where I would hit 500 full shots a day, spend an hour playing trap shots, an hour putting and approaching, and I played 18 holes a day.

"After I spent one and one-half years at college, majoring in journalism, my father saw that it was a lost cause, and he let me quit to concentrate on golf. It took me 37 years to graduate, having started in 1937 and taking a few courses a year from San Jose State University, but I finally graduated with a double major in journalism and aviation in 1974.

"After playing golf for four years, I won the National Amateur at Brookline in 1941, when I was the youngest winner at the time. The trophy was presented on the clubhouse porch, because women were not allowed inside. I won 15 championships and probably thought that by becoming a good golfer, people would love me. I had to achieve something, and that was the way I could enjoy it.

"Being so small didn't bother me, because it was a publicity advantage. At 17, they wrote about me as "an infant prodigy." I was a strong, aggressive little kid, who hit the ball hard in other sports and translated it into golf. I was a follower of women like Amelia Earhart. I would bike out to the airport and watch the women pilots, but I wouldn't like to have been a pioneer pilot, since their engines quit too often.

"I saw Babe run in the 1932 Olympics in Los Angeles, and I was motivated by that and by reading about her. She was very boyish, and being a woman athlete made her unacceptable. She got lots of publicity and criticism, and they suspected she was not female. I remember reading Paul Gallico, who said she was very 'hirsute,' and I looked that up in the dictionary to find that it meant hairy, which probably indicated Babe didn't shave her legs, but at 11, I visualized her having hair all over. Anatomically Babe was a complete female; also, a

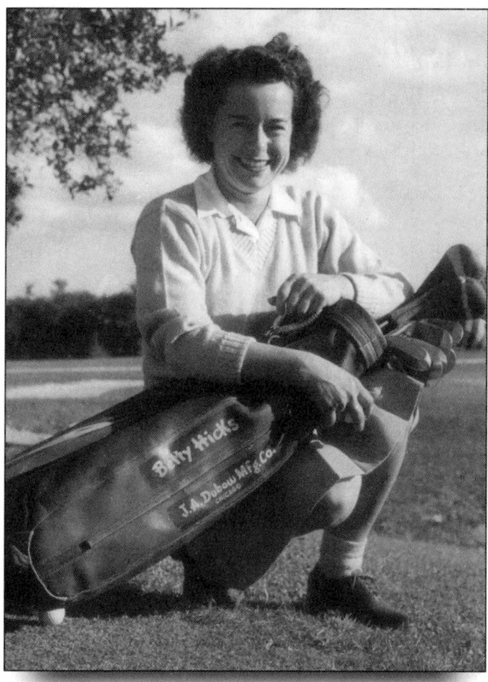

Betty turned pro in 1941 and signed with J.A. Dubow Manufacturing. Later, she signed with Wilson and continued to teach and give clinics for Wilson until the early 1990s. Photo courtesy: Betty Hicks.

woman driven by poverty to achieve.

"I saw her at her greatest moment of glory in the Olympics and also at the end of her life when she died at 45 in September 1956. Her influence was profound. In golf, she gave them the show they wanted, yet her histrionics and behavior would sometimes perpetuate the myth that professional athletes are not all woman. Babe metamorphosed women golfers into becoming attacking hitters, and professional women golfers owe her so much.

"As a youngster I didn't gain approval because I was too competitive, so I withdrew socially to show my resentment. Later my mother, who didn't say much, was demonstrably unhappy about `that awful golf tour'; she wanted me to marry and settle down, but my father was happy, since he wanted me to be an athlete.

"Both my parents were strong personalities, and my father, who was an innovative educator, encouraged me in golf. My mother would sit around clubhouse porches and listen to all the rumors about the women professionals, implying that one of those horrible women would seduce me, but I didn't know what she was afraid of because no one made passes at me. When I went on the tour, the general criticism was that either you slept with far too many men, or you didn't sleep with enough.

"When I married at 20, I felt totally stultified after two years, and I got divorced. I married a man who later became a professional golfer, but at the time he was working as an engineer for Douglas Aircraft. When L. B. Icely from Wilson came to the house shortly after I won the National Amateur and offered to pay all my expenses if I would play eight tournaments a year as an amateur, my husband refused to let me go and compete.

"I thought I should bring some money into the household, so I turned professional in October 1941, taking a job for $83 a month at Recreation Park Golf Club in Long Beach. My duties were club repair, working in the shop, and giving lessons. My own club greeted the news with horror. A few months later I signed a contract with the Dubow Company in Chicago, which was a sporting goods manufacturer. They designed my own line of golf equipment, and the contract turned out to be

Betty gives actor William Bendix a few tips while filming a sequence of "The Life of Riley".

worth $8,000 to $10,000 a year from royalties.

"I joined the women's Coast Guards Reserve (SPARs) in World War II, and I was a recruiting officer for three years. By 1943, there were a few tournaments, including the Tam O'Shanter in Chicago, sponsored by the innovative George S. May, who was the first to build grandstands for the galleries, to put numbers on the players, and to have leader boards and greenside bars.

"It was a big tournament for men and women. Byron Nelson won $14,000 for his victory, while I won $500 for mine. There I met Hope Seignious from Greensboro, North Carolina, and we decided that the women professionals needed their own professional division, and we sowed the seeds of the beginning of the WPGA.

"The Charter of the WPGA was incorporated in November 1944, with Hope Seignious becoming Secretary and Treasurer, Ellen Griffin Vice President, I President, and we were all unanimously elected by our own vote of three. The WPGA was the first sports organization whose constitution did not include a Caucasian-only clause. Our objectives were to promote money tournaments for women, which Hope would do, and for Ellen and myself to promote golf for women in schools and colleges.

"Hope's finest bequest to women's golf was the 1946 Women's National Open, sponsored by the Spokane Athletic Round Table (a group that made money at gaming tables) for $19,000 in war bonds, and in 1947 she personally financed the next Open at Greensboro. Hope was the real founder of professional tournament golf for women.

"Ellen and I started the first National teaching clinics; together we wrote the teaching manual, *Golf Manual for Teachers*, and I toured colleges, promoting golf and the improvement of golf instruction. By 1947 the WPGA was disintegrating, and Hope had lost a lot of her family money in supporting it. Babe became a professional again, and Fred Corcoran became involved, later being hired by the Manufacturers' Association as the LPGA tournament manager.

"I returned to college, which I did every few years, and then I joined the LPGA tour in 1953, at a time when we didn't have any grandiose ideas. We just enjoyed golf and were trying to make a living. Most of us were upper middle class Caucasians, and someone with the name of Lopez would not have been very acceptable. We had to strive hard for Jackie Pung from Hawaii to be accepted.

"We were raised in an era when young women were supposed to be modest, and that modesty excluded trying to seek publicity, which meant you were happy to see an article about yourself in the paper, but you really didn't have anything to do with the press. I had to force the women to co-operate on publicity; they were so reticent.

Betty Hicks, played competitive golf until 1965, when she became a flight instructor. Photo courtesy: Betty Hicks.

"The milestone came in 1953 with the USGA assuming sponsorship for the first time of the Women's National Open, which was at Rochester, New York, and was won by Betsy Rawls. In 1954, when I was LPGA publicity director and Fred Corcoran had gone, my *Saturday Evening Post* article was published, which Babe said was a pack of lies. She threatened to resign from the association and said we had fired Fred Corcoran, which was not true. We had never even hired him. It was the Golf Manufacturers' Association that withdrew from paying him. Babe had her husband George tell me that she would stay only if I resigned as publicity director. So I resigned. It was emotional blackmail and ridiculous.

"Babe would say, 'I'll quit the tour and then see how Suggs will make her money.' The LPGA asked me to write the by-laws and George told me: 'I don't give a shit about those by-laws. Don't lawyer me; we don't want none of this Parliamentary stuff.' George was a monstrous man, who could crunch you in two in a hurry, so facing up to him gave you a life-threatening feeling.

"There was a big commotion at a meeting with half the people walking out, and Peggy Kirk being sent to retrieve them, and finally the tournament committee was decided with Babe as director. I think it was all a publicity-seeking gimmick; George told me that women's golf was a racket like wrestling and should be run the same way. Babe told me in 1946 that the two of us should start a feud, get some publicity, and go on an exhibition tour. Babe kept the job as tournament director for two months and then walked up to me on the practice putting green at the New Orleans Open and said, 'I resign.' She just couldn't cope with it.

"I took over the job for two years. I carried round my typewriter, files, promotion material, cameras, tape recorder, and the scoreboards on top of the car. I did advance publicity, increased the purse for 72-hole events to a minimum $5,000, and gained a few new sponsors. Golf Digest gave us a scoreboard and office space in Evanston, Illinois, and by 1955 we had prize money of $150,000.

"The last year I played the tour full time was in 1955, when I was sixth on the money list and earned $7,600. I made my expenses and realized I needed a second career. In 1956 I had surgery for a cyst and intestinal problems, brought on as the result of reacting to the pressure of playing in tournaments and the internal havoc caused from being in contention.

"I played the tour part time in 1957 and took a club job as head professional at Los Coyotes Country Club, Buena Park, California, during which time a pilot friend of mine convinced me that I should take flying lessons, which I had been wanting to do for some time. I got my license and shared the ownership of a Cessna 172 with a friend, and I would fly to tournaments or to give exhibitions. One time when I took Kathy Whitworth to a clinic at Whittier, I landed my plane on the fairway.

"I had a cockpit pass whenever I flew on an airline jet, and I acquired about ten hours of jet flying time on a 747. I would like to have been a 747 pilot; it's like balancing a bathtub on a steel rod."

Betty played tour golf until 1965, when she became a flight instructor. She acquired more flight training time to become an airline transport certified pilot, and she has logged over 3,000 hours of instruction time. Over the years she obtained her college degree, taught golf and coached the women's golf team at San Jose State, taught flying and co-ordinated the aviation program at Foothill Community College, wrote articles for a wide variety of publications, and taught journalism.

Predictably, Betty identified with women's liberation. "I thought the women's liberation movement was long overdue, and the women in it had to be militant in the early days to achieve something. Indirectly, I was involved in the feminist movement by trying to give women the opportunity to play golf for a living. An unfortunate connotation has been created of women's lib, and I get very angry when an athlete says, `I'm not a women's libber,' because she is taking advantage of the fact that someone else is or was. What she is saying is, `I don't want you to think of me as one of those people who burns her bra or loves other women, but I'll take advantage of the fact that other women stuck out their necks.'

Betty, the pilot and player, then and still today, was able to do advance publicity for the tour thanks to her ability to fly. Photo: Wayne Glusker.

"I was involved in a college study of athletes based on social concepts of what is masculine and feminine, and I scored very highly on the masculine side, although I don't consider myself masculine. One of the questions was: `Do you stick up for your friends?' I answered, `Yes.' Apparently, sticking up for your friends is considered a masculine trait.

"My mother told me that with above average competitive drive and above average intelligence, you can do practically anything you want. You need ability and enjoyment of doing what that ability makes possible, and you have to create your own opportunities. Although it was frustrating that we never had access to the top reward and that top posts were unattainable in our era, it was exciting, if difficult, to be a pioneer."

Championships: 1939 Southern California Championship, Palm Springs Invitational, Western Medal Play. **1940** Palm Springs Invitational, Southern California Championship, South Atlantic Championship, Palm Beach Invitational, Western Medal Play. **1941** United States National Championship, California State, Miami-Biltmore Invitational. **1943** Chicago Victory Open, All-American Open. **1944** Chicago Victory Open, Portland Open.

Betty Jameson

Sandra Haynie says of Betty Jameson: "Betty is a fascinating and interesting lady, a very free spirit. She has large hands, and I always have a mental picture of how pretty her hands look sitting on a golf club."

While Betty Hicks wrote of her in 1957: "Soft spoken Betty Jameson feels very little need for applause and probably feels as deep a love for the game of golf as anyone has ever felt. Devoted to practice, Betty came one rainy night, with putter and chipping iron in hand, into a resort hotel where a tournament was in progress.

"Where have you been?" inquired several incredulous competitors.

"Out putting and chipping," was Betty's matter of fact reply. "But it's dark and it's raining." Betty, starry-eyed as a teenager deep in her first love affair, answered: "It's light enough for me."

Betty Jameson's initial impact is a physical one. She is a tall, strong, graceful woman, with curly hair, that has been white since the age of 33. She appears to have changed very little, is arty and attractive, and says: "Before I became a professional, I toyed with the idea of giving up golf and becoming a painter. That's what I would really like to have done."

Yet Betty was obviously a natural golfer, who was a prodigy from the age of 13, when she won the Texas Public Links Championship, followed by the Texas State Championship, and at 15 she was the youngest player ever to win the Southern Championship, which she won four years in a row. In 1939 and 1940, Betty achieved consecutive victories in the U.S. Amateur Championship, while her victory in the 1947 U.S. Women's Open set a record, with her total of 295 being the first recorded under 300 for a 72-hole women's tournament.

By 1951, Betty was inducted into the Hall of Fame, at the age of 32, when the LPGA tour was in its infancy, and Betty, together with Babe Zaharias, Patty Berg, and Louise Suggs, formed "The Big Four" in women's golf. Betty recalled, "The Hall of Fame was at the Augusta Country Club, Georgia, and we four were selected previously by journalists, on the strength of our amateur records, when the list included Joyce Wethered and Glenna Collett Vare."

Betty was a proud charter member of the WPGA in 1945 and similarly, in 1950, of the LPGA. In 1952 she donated a trophy to the LPGA to be awarded to the player with the lowest scoring average for the year, named the Vare trophy, in honor of her idol, Glenna Collett Vare.

Hall of Fame member Betty Jameson, shown here at the 1946 Women's Western Open, won this event in 1942 and 1954.

Betty is remembered for her superb golf swing, as well as for her wonderful hands. Golf professional Lawson Little said of her: "Betty Jameson has the soundest swing, the best pivot and the greatest follow through of the hips, of any woman player except Joyce Wethered." As a professional she achieved ten victories, which reflects, perhaps, the fact that she never relished strokeplay golf.

I met Betty when I was staying with Hollis Stacy in Florida. She came to see me with all the treasures of her golfing life, the recorded items and photographs, which were obviously important to her. She is not an easy woman to interview, as her mind jumps around, and she has the reputation for blowing hot and cold, but she has always been most helpful and warm to me. She is a liberated woman, who has identified with feminism and lauds it.

Betty was born in Norman, Oklahoma, and brought up, with a brother one year older, in San Antonio, Texas, where her father was in the advertising side of newspapers. Her mother was a fine horsewoman and a good shot.

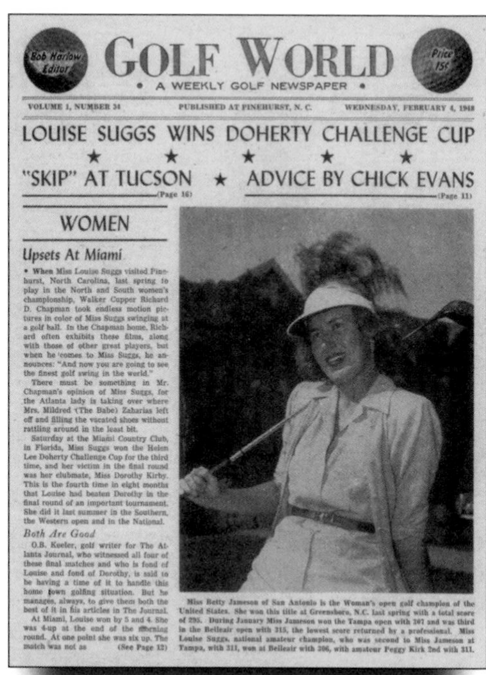
Bob Harlow Editor

GOLF WORLD

• A WEEKLY GOLF NEWSPAPER •

Price 15¢

VOLUME 1, NUMBER 34 PUBLISHED AT PINEHURST, N. C. WEDNESDAY, FEBRUARY 4, 1948

LOUISE SUGGS WINS DOHERTY CHALLENGE CUP

★ ★ ★ ★ ★

"SKIP" AT TUCSON (Page 16) ★ ADVICE BY CHICK EVANS (Page 11)

WOMEN

Upsets At Miami

• When Miss Louise Suggs visited Pinehurst, North Carolina, last spring to play in the North and South women's championship, Walker Cupper Richard D. Chapman took endless motion pictures in color of Miss Suggs swinging at a golf ball. In the Chapman home, Richard often exhibits these films, along with those of other great players, but when he comes to Miss Suggs, he announces: "And now you are going to see the finest golf swing in the world."

There must be something in Mr. Chapman's opinion of Miss Suggs, for the Atlanta lady is taking over where Mrs. Mildred (The Babe) Zaharias left off and filling the vacated shoes without rattling around in the least bit.

Saturday at the Miami Country Club, in Florida, Miss Suggs won the Helen Lee Doherty Challenge Cup for the third time, and her victim in the final round was her clubmate, Miss Dorothy Kirby. This is the fourth time in eight months that Louise had beaten Dorothy in the final round of an important tournament. She did it last summer in the Southern, the Western open and in the National.

Both Are Good

O.B. Keeler, golf writer for The Atlanta Journal, who witnessed all four of these final matches and who is fond of Louise and fond of Dorothy, is said to be having a time of it to handle this home town golfing situation. But he manages, always, to give them both the best of it in his articles in The Journal.

At Miami, Louise won by 5 and 4. She was 4-up at the end of the morning round. At one point she was six up. The match was not as (See Page 12)

Miss Betty Jameson of San Antonio is the Woman's open golf champion of the United States. She won this title at Greensboro, N.C. last spring with a total score of 295. During January Miss Jameson won the Tampa open with 207 and was third in the Belleair open with 315, the lowest score returned by a professional. Miss Louise Suggs, national amateur champion, who was second to Miss Jameson at Tampa, with 311, won at Belleair with 306, with amateur Peggy Kirk 2nd with 311.

Betty Jameson, featured in "Golf World", won the U.S. Open in 1947 with a 245 total. This marked the first time a female golfer scored better than 300 in a 72-hole tournament.

"My father was a left handed golfer, who played on a public course. I would turn his clubs upside down and around, and try to play. One day a little lady on a putting green asked me if I would like to try, which I did and I enjoyed it, so my brother and I played miniature golf.

"I had my first round of golf at 11, when I persuaded my mother to let me go to Oak Grove in Dallas to rent a set of clubs for 50¢ and pay the 50¢ green fee. I played alone until the back nine, when I picked up a man who kept my score. I don't know how I connected with the ball, but not counting whiffs my score was about 118, and I treasured the card for a long time.

"My father got me some cut-down hickory shafted clubs for Christmas and when spring came, I started to play at Oak Grove. I played every day, 45 to 50 holes sometimes, and often I teamed up with a boy and played for a bottle of pop. I had a 39 for nine holes that summer and got my picture in the paper.

"When I was 13, I went to a driving range to compete in a long driving contest, and I met Francis Sheider, who was a great teacher and offered to help me. I was blessed by making his acquaintance. He was the professional at Brook Hollow, the best golf club in Dallas, and I would go and work with him there every Saturday, even though I lived miles away on the other side of town.

"I was young enough to be able to copy his golf swing, which was the best I've ever seen, and I developed one of the best golf swings that ever was. I was pretty strong, and I had good hands. The hands are the only connection with the club, and the reason I could hold it softly was because I had a very good grip, which I devised through my golf swing.

"My mother and grandmother were great figures in my life. My mother knew I could be a world beater—that was the old fashioned term—and my grandmother, on the other hand, would say, 'Are you still playing golf?'

"My mother never knew I turned professional because she died in 1942. I cried a lot at her death, for everyone needs someone to sit in her corner, and my mother was a great motivator. Maybe I didn't have the same stimulus after that.

I continued to visit my grandmother, who was an Englishwoman, one of 13 children, and she lived until 95. She had red hair, an arranged marriage, and her father was a shoemaker in Cardiff (South Wales).

"I started winning amateur tournaments in 1932 at 13, and I remember when I won my first Southern Championship in 1934. Playing the semi-finals, I won at the 19th with a stymie. I used a nine iron, and I made the ball jump quite high, right over my opponent's ball, to about six inches from the hole. I won the finals 10 and 8.

"In 1934, I went to my first National Amateur Championship, where I met Glenna Collett Vare. In 1935, I saw her defeat Patty Berg. Glenna had won five times, and she was my idol. In 1937, I attended the University of Texas for one semester, but I was more interested in golf. I wasn't much of a scholar, so they let me play golf and not bother with grades. There was a French teacher who told me: `If you drop the course, I'll give you a C.' I left college and continued to play amateur golf. I loved matchplay, the dramatic one-to-one rivalry, and I always had an exciting time playing matches.

"Because of the war, tournaments stopped after 1942. I was on the city desk of the Dallas Times Herald, for which I had written a golf column when I was 12. I liked the idea of writing, but I wasn't a good typist, and I couldn't meet the deadlines; so I went to an Army depot and drove generals around in trucks in San Antonio. I had to earn a living.

"When the war finished, someone came to me in 1945 from the Spalding Company and convinced me to turn professional. They offered me $5,000 a year and my expenses for doing clinics, which was a lot of money. I also received royalties on my own clubs. It was a very charismatic company, but it didn't really know what to do with a woman golfer. They just wanted me to do what Patty Berg did for Wilson, without training me.

"I thought if I wanted to be the best in the world, I should turn professional, where at least I would be making money. I couldn't afford the amateur game, but a few of the tournaments were open to professionals, and a few others were starting just for them. I didn't dream that without matchplay the whole essence and drama of golf would disappear. I didn't realize how humdrum it is, playing hole after hole and not daring to take chances."

Betty gives putting pointers to a young Betty Dodd.

In 1945, the WPGA was started by Betty Hicks in California, and Hope Seignious and Ellen Griffin in North Carolina. Betty Jameson became a charter member with a document which read:

> ***No. 2. Membership of the Women's Professional Golf Association Inc.***
>
> *This certifies that Betty Jameson is the owner of one Charter Membership of the WPGA Inc. Each Charter Membership shall be entitled to one vote.*
>
> *These certificates shall be transferable, but shall be offered to other charter members of this corporation through the Secretary, pro rata to their holdings of charter memberships, and for a sum not less than their original cost and not more than the book value of this unit of ownership of the corporation assets. The book value is to be determined by the Directors of the*

corporation and the determination of the Directors is final. Upon the death of a member holding a charter membership, her personal representative shall offer the holdings of the deceased to the other holders of charter memberships in the same manner as the living member is required to do and for the same amount.

Charter memberships are without par value and the cost shall be fixed by the Directors of this corporation, which may be changed from time to time. There shall only be one cost of a charter membership except for special assessments as provided by the by-lays of this corporation.

In Witness whereof, the said corporation has caused this certificate to be signed by its duly authorized officers and its corporate seal to be hereunto affixed this the 6th day of August, 1945.

Attested:

Hope Seignious, Secretary
Betty Hicks, President

Says Betty Jameson: "Hope's father put up the money for starting the WPGA. She was a fair golfer, who wanted to be the Diaghilev of women's golf. The history of the WPGA and the LPGA mean a lot to me, and I was the one, who when the WPGA fizzled out and the next organization began, suggested the name LPGA, keeping tradition with the Ladies' Golf Union in Britain.

"I loved my career, although I think it was a little time wasting. I stayed too long in competitive professional golf, from 1945 to 1963, since I wasn't shooting that well and I let my game slip. My best year was 1955 when I won five tournaments, but I was never leading money winner.

"As a woman I always thought I was swimming with the tide. I thought women could do anything and I still do. Women's place in the world meant something to me, as did Gloria Steinem and the women's movement. I was not active in the women's movement because I didn't mix with many of those people, but I supported it. The whole world is coming around to sensing a little more equality, and I agree with Orson Welles, whose mother was a Suffragette. He said, 'Vive La Difference.'

"When I came off tour I thought of being a painter in a loft in New York, but that did not work out, and then I lost some money going into business. I started teaching in Florida, and it was kind of nice, but I was a better learner than teacher, and I feel I missed out doing anything great with my painting and drawing.

"Now, I have returned to art. I love doing still life, the human figure, painting in oils and drawing. Art and painting make you feel so alive, there's never a dull moment. I'm very devoted to it and I may have to paint for the rest of my life."

Member LPGA Hall of Fame 1951

LPGA Victories: 1947 U.S. Women's Open. **1948** Tampa Open. **1949** Texas Open. **1952** World Championship. **1953** Serbin Open. **1954** Women's Western Open. **1955** Sarasota Open, Babe Zaharias Open, White Mountains Open, Richmond Open.

Betty Jameson's LPGA Record

Year	No. of Events	Best Finish	Money	Rank	Scoring Average
1950	10	3	$1,425	NA	79.19
1951	12	3	3,312	NA	77.18
1952	12	1	10,684	NA	75.54
1953	18	1	5,785	NA	77.03
1954	18	2	8,038	NA	77.56
1955	22	1	7,720	NA	80.98
1956	22	2	8,997	NA	76.72

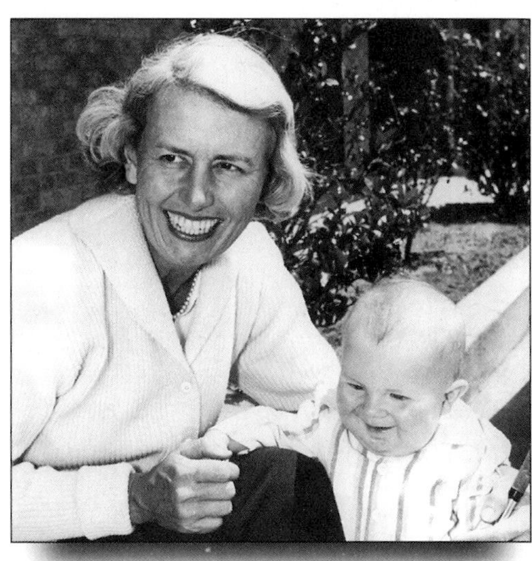

Betty is shown here with Heidi Hagge, daughter of Alice and Bob Hagge.

Marilynn Smith

At the inaugural 1988 Marilynn Smith Founders' Classic, held in Dallas, Texas, the evening guest of honor, Ben Hogan, got up and said: "Here you have the best sponsor in the world—Marilynn Smith. She has done many things in her time. She's never made a mistake; she's always been successful. They tell me Jesus Christ was a man, but I don't believe it. We have Jesus Christ right here."

It was an unusually emotional declaration from Ben Hogan, who hugged Marilynn Smith and then put the special maroon jackets on each of nine women founder members of the LPGA, kissing every one of them.

Marilynn Smith and her golf won many friends for the LPGA. To this day, she recalls many fans whenever she meets them.

At the dinner the previous night, for the 48 women who were attending this joyous reunion (many of whom had not seen each other in the previous 20 years), Patty Berg said: "The reason this tournament is such a huge success is because of Marilynn Smith. Marilynn has as many friends as I have freckles. It is a most wonderful gathering, a dream come true. In a few months I will be seventy years old. I want you to know that it is wonderful to be with each and every one of you."

In her own speech, Marilynn said: "That the LPGA has survived is a credit to perseverance, to the love of the game and the love of life. We may have come from different walks of life, but we had one thing in common—we all wanted the tour to succeed. We persevered, did a lot of hard work, had plenty of heartache and a lot of happiness. What was really meaningful was that we were a family, all out there to help each other. There were just twelve of us in 1950. I was around, I was 20, and we were a team that worked together. Some scored better than others, but we all had our own charisma; we were all stars and we earned it. I dedicate this tournament to the founders of the LPGA."

Marilynn worked long and hard to get that first Founders' Classic off the ground. Nicknamed by Wiffi Smith "The Open Arms Open," Marilynn's Founders' Classic continued for three years, but the week in 1987 was very special, a memory that everyone there will carry in their hearts because the love and the warmth, so obviously alive, had lasted through the years.

The only sadness was the lack of recognition from the LPGA, which decided not to support those women to whom they owe their existence. They refused to take any space in the program and took no part in the event, other than the attendance of some individual members.

Carol Mann said at the players' dinner: "I am a product of the early 1960s. The women of the 1930s, 1940s, and 1950s are basically my mothers. They instilled in me values, ethics, and standards of performance. My hope is that those of the 1960s and 1970s will pass some of those ethics on to the next generation: it is very important that the baton continues to be passed."

Of the LPGA's failure to recognize the tournament in which Carol played, she said: "In John Laupheimer's eyes it is in competition with the LPGA. I don't see it that way at all. This tournament was conceived and born out of love. Love for Marilynn Smith and for an era in women's

Marilynn clutches the trophy she won at the 1964 Titleholders Championship in Augusta, Georgia.

golf. I cried so much just thinking about it. I understand the LPGA's point of view from Laupheimer's perspective, but I don't like it. The young players should know about these feelings of regard for one another."

For Marilynn Smith, the week at Dallas was one of great fulfillment, a highlight in her golfing career, which included considerable achievements. She won 22 tournaments from 1954 to 1972 and continued to play full time until 1976. Like others, she suffered when it was time to leave the tour, which she did in the 1980s to teach in Dallas and to take groups abroad on golf travel trips.

Dubbed from the outset the "Personality Girl" (some thought to the detriment of her golf game), Marilynn has an engaging personality, all the social graces, and she has always been aware of her image as a woman golfer.

We met and talked in the late 1970s. On tour, Marilynn always greeted me with great friendliness and would include me in whatever she was doing. Over the years we struck up a warm friendship, keeping in touch by letter and telephone, and I was thrilled to be at her first Founders' Classic in 1987, won by Kathy Whitworth. Among other things she has given me are some of her personal tees, on which is engraved: "Marilynn Smith, Live, Love and Laugh."

Marilynn was born in Topeka, Kansas, and grew up in Wichita. She comes from a comfortable middle-class background, having one sister twelve years younger. Her father worked in life insurance, and both of her parents played golf.

"I thought golf was a sissy sport, since I ran a boys' baseball team, where I was the pitcher, coach, and manager. One day I came home from playing baseball, and my mother asked how I'd done. I used a four-letter word, and my mother marched me into the bathroom and washed out my mouth with Lifebuoy soap. To this day I can still taste it.

"My mom told my dad, who suggested taking me to Wichita Country Club for the more ladylike sport of golf. I began at 11½, and Dad said he would give me a bike when I broke 40 for nine holes, which I did when I was fourteen. I won the Kansas State Amateur for three years from 1947, and they called me the blonde bomber, since I hit the ball twenty-five yards farther than anyone else.

"When I went to the University of Kansas as a physical education major, I won the Intercollegiate in my sophomore year. After that I had an offer from Spalding to turn professional, which I did on July 1, 1949. Spalding offered me a salary of $5,000, which was a lot of money then. I was to give 50 to 100 clinics a year, promote Spalding equipment, and get youngsters and women interested in the game. They said I never had to win a tournament, just play as well as I could and do PR for them.

"I love traveling and meeting people, so I thought it was fantastic. I went to the Spalding factory, and they gave me a blue Dodge car and a set of golf clubs. I told them I had to have a couple of baseball gloves, since baseball was my favorite sport, so they gave me two mitts and a baseball, and off I went. I did an awful lot of clinics, because we only had six or seven tournaments to play in until the LPGA was founded in 1950 in Wichita. Then, we had 11 tournaments.

"I never had a lot of confidence in myself, and winning wasn't an all-consuming passion, but if someone said they thought I couldn't play, it would spur me on to win. I was scared to death to win; I lacked that dog-eat-dog attitude, and I was always happy if someone else won. I enjoyed team things and rally 'round the flag occasions. I was always trying to find the perfect swing, listening to everybody with my big rabbit ears, and for many years I wore a rabbit's foot on my waist band.

"In the early years it was important to have a good image, since it was frowned upon to play a lot of golf. We had an Amazon image, and I always tried to erase that stigma by wearing earrings and pearls, by being well groomed, and by behaving like a lady. Showing an aggressive attitude on the golf course was taken for masculinity, and I didn't want to be considered masculine. A lot of people thought we pros should be married, raising a family and staying at home, and I was always very conscious of trying to set a good example for womanhood.

"My role in public relations has been my main forté, and when I was president of the LPGA for three years beginning in 1958, I arranged parties for the press and sponsors, so they got to know us better. We always felt we had a great show but that no one knew about it. It's hard when no one is tooting your horn. *Golf World* magazine did a good job, but that was all. Betsy Rawls said that communicating with the public takes a lot of energy, but I didn't realize it, and although I was a natural at PR, it did sometimes drain me.

"I was always involved in a lot of things. I used to love South American dancing, and I enjoyed history, music, and sightseeing. I was always interested in politics, and my uncle was the governor of Kansas. I was a member of President Nixon's Physical Fitness Conference for promotion of all sports, and during his second campaign, I had 2,000 golf tees made up, which said: 'Re-Elect Richard Nixon.' I gave them out at clinics and to members of the gallery. I was always promoting some cause.

"My biggest golfing thrill was beating Mickey Wright in the Titleholders at Augusta Country Club in 1963, in an 18-hole playoff, when I had 72 and she had 73. When Babe won her last tournament, the Serbin Open, I was runner-up. I was really glad she won. I was leading by four shots with nine holes to go, and it was like God was on my shoulder and put my ball into the trap. I lost five shots in the last nine holes, and it was as though Babe was destined to win. I got a great kick out of Babe, who was our main drawing card. I wasn't any threat to her. I felt like a little kid around her, and it was a great loss to our tour when she died.

"I loved the exciting life, and I guess that deep down I'm more competitive than I make out. When I had pancreas trouble in the late 1970s, I thought there was something terribly wrong with me, and I became very nervous. Your pancreas is your stress organ, and I think it rebelled from all that I had done over the years.

Marilynn, always fashionable, participated in the style show at the 1958 Civitan tournament.

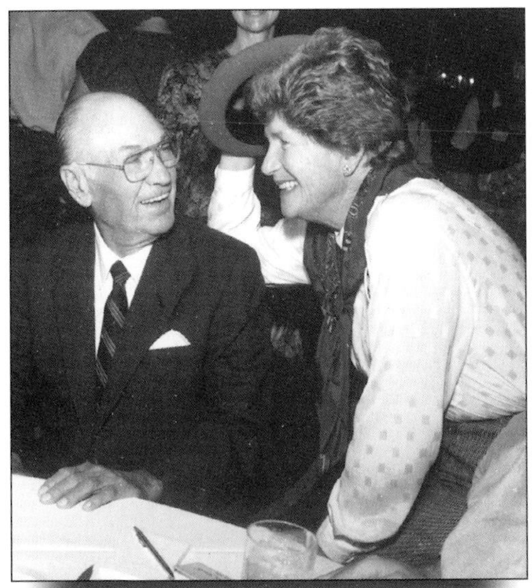

Marilynn and Ben Hogan share mutual admiration at the 1987 Founders' Classic which she worked hard to get off the ground.

"I don't rest too well. I'm not a very calm person. I'm energetic, gregarious, and hyperactive. If I don't have something to think about, I'll manufacture it. Even my golf swing is very fast, and there was never a moment on tour when I completely relaxed.

"I adjusted to my changing environment every week by carrying pictures of family and friends. I would make my motel room look like my bedroom, like home. I'm sentimental, and I carried a candle that I would light at night when I was reading or watching television. It was something homey, which gave me roots and stability.

"I always thought I'd be married at 30, and it would be nice to have kids. Although there was pressure from my mom, it didn't worry me. My dad was happy for me to have a career. My sister married and had two children.

"Years ago, I thought I'd marry a rancher, live on a ranch, and have animals. It was my ideal dream as a teenager. One goal has been reached: I do now live in the country, on a mini-ranch with horses, dogs, and cats.

"Someone had to be a pioneer; Betty Hicks, Hope Seignious, and Ellen Griffin, who actually founded the whole thing, were the original pioneers, but I'm proud I was a charter member of the LPGA and helped to get it going. That was exciting. It's great to see it having come a lot further than we ever imagined."

LPGA Victories: 1954 Fort Wayne Open. **1955** Heart of America Open, Mile High Open. **1957** Homestead Four-Ball. **1958** Jacksonville Open. **1959** Memphis Open. **1962** Sunshine Open, Waterloo Open. **1963** Titleholders Championship, Peach Blossom Open, Eugene Open, Cavern City Open. **1964** Titleholders Championship, Albuquerque Pro-Am. **1965** Peach Blossom Invitational. **1966** St. Petersburg Open, Delray Beach Invitational. **1967** St. Petersburg Open, Babe Zaharias Open. **1968** O'Sullivan Open. **1970** Golf Charities Open. **1972** Pabst Open.

Marilynn Smith's LPGA Record

Year	No. of Events	Best Finish	Money	Rank	Scoring Average
1957	23	1	$5,210	17	76.51
1958	24	1	6,672	15	76.71
1959	28	1	7,739	15	76.35
1960	24	3	6,430	19	75.65
1961	15	2	10,687	10	75.20
1962	29	1	12,075	8	75.09
1963	32	1	21,691	4	74.14
1964	30	1	12,738	10	74.18
1965	28	1	16,692	6	73.69
1966	29	1	16,412	6	74.38
1967	25	1	13,045	8	73.96
1968	30	1	20,945	4	73.89
1969	16	T2	12,139	18	74.72
1970	21	1	22,391	4	73.57
1971	20	4	13,721	13	74.48
1972	27	1	29,910	8	73.81
1973	27	T2	12,292	37	76.51
1974	18	T2	9,733	43	75.66
1975	20	T2	6,815	54	76.07
1976	22	T12	4,815	54	77.16
1977	11	T23	3,513	87	76.47
1978	6	T55	482	115	78.71
1979	6	T47	690	127	76.74
1980	9	T40	714	142	78.48
1981	6	T63	262	150	77.39
1982	6	T12	640	148	77.00
1983	8	T65	NA	NA	78.26
1984	7	T59	368	180	78.60
1985	5	NA	NA	NA	NA
1986	DNP				
1987	1	NA	NA	NA	NA

Babe Zaharias

So many words have been written about the legendary Babe Zaharias, but perhaps none more picturesque than those of the British golf writer, Enid Wilson, who saw Babe win the 1947 British Women's Amateur Championship at Gullane, Scotland. She wrote in Golf Illustrated:

"She is above average height, slender in build and moves with a lithe grace as though she had not got a bone in her body. She has fair hair, blue eyes and a large mouth. Her eyes and mouth are perpetually mobile with the sparkling alertness and puckish grin of a good-humored child. She is so fit that sheer joie de vivre prevents her from being motionless. She has a ready and nimble wit and brims over with what the Americans call `wisecracks,' and we term repartee. She wears her fingernails long and paints them bright red, and she likes brightly colored clothing. She does not drink alcohol, and smokes in moderation.

"There are moments on the golf course when her mouth sets in a straight line like a steel trap, but that is when she is displeased with herself, and is the only indication that she might own a temper. Her golf is without frills. She has one mannerism; before finally taking up her stance for a drive or an iron shot she raises her left hand and touches the glove on it with the tip of her tongue, then gravely wriggles her fingers and brushes this hand against her left thigh, before she carefully grasps the club with it. She takes up her stance with deliberation, and hits the ball with great power.

"Unless I had been at Gullane and seen Mrs. Zaharias play, I would not have believed it humanly possible for a woman to hit a golf ball so far as she did. The ground was thoroughly sodden and there was none of the run on the ball that we normally expect on a seaside course in June. The 16th hole at Gullane is 550 yards, the last 160 yards being uphill. I saw Mrs. Zaharias reach that with a drive

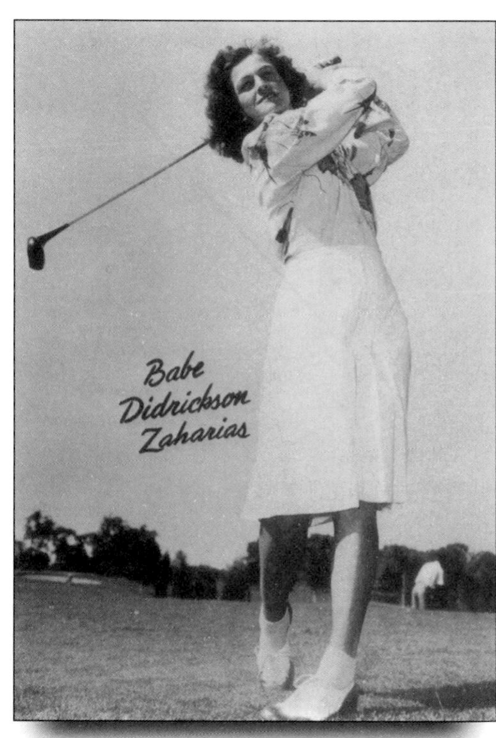

Babe Zaharias had the name and the golf game to propel the LPGA to its initial success against all odds.

and an iron—the ball pitched on the back edge of the green and finished in the rough beyond.

"When Mrs. Zaharias was in need of it, 'she trod on the gas.' Mrs. Zaharias was undoubtedly the best golfer at Gullane, and no one can begrudge her most worthy victory."

After Babe won the prestigious British title, she arrived home by ship, doing a highland fling in her kilt down the gang plank of the Queen Elizabeth into the arms of her wrestler husband, George Zaharias. Back in Denver, where she and George were living, she was given one of the greatest public demonstrations ever accorded an individual in the Mile High City. Thousands lined the streets and cheered her all the way to the city hall as an airplane above scrawled "Hi Babe" in skywriting. Accompanied by her husband, Babe was presented with the 14 foot high, 250 pound key to the city, which was hauled into position by six policemen. "Don't worry about it any more," Babe told them, "George will carry it home."

That Babe was a superb athlete, a tremendous competitor, and a terrific showperson was undisputed. She brought all of those qualities to golf, from her early years as an athlete, where her crowning performance was at the 1932 Olympic games. For golf and the LPGA, Babe was a tremendous boost, even if some of her actions might cause fellow competitors to shudder.

Professional golfer, Beverly Sfengi Hanson, recalls: "Babe was a hero, a super person and very helpful. She was so good that other people were jealous. She was so competitive, that although she played within the rules, she would try to get you to see them from her standpoint. If she could convince you that the Mississippi River was a mere creek, she would.

"Babe put a lot of her own money and effort into the LPGA. She would use her personal position to badger sponsors into putting up money for tournaments. If we hadn't had Babe, the tour would have taken 10 years longer to get off the ground."

Nelson Cullenward, who wrote about golf for 45 years and was editor of the National Golfer magazine in the days of Babe Zaharias, said: "I never thought of her as a man, woman or athlete, I just thought of her as a good friend. She was the greatest hustler I've ever seen. She would give you her house to stay in, but on the golf course playing you for 50¢, she would try to kill you every way she could to win four bits, and then she would spend $20.00 on you."

Everyone has his own anecdote about this greatest ever American woman athlete, whose year of birth is obscured by her various and differing pronouncements of her age. Only from a baptismal certificate (there is no record of a birth certificate from her hometown), found by her sister Lillie, would it appear that she was born on June 26 in the year of 1911, the sixth of seven children.

Her parents were immigrants from Norway, Ole and Hannah Didriksen, and her birthplace was in a house in Port Arthur, Texas, built by her father, a furniture restorer and cabinet maker. She was born Mildred Ella Didriksen. Her parents spelled their name with an "sen" at the end; Babe changed hers to "son," claiming erroneously that it was more Norwegian.

After a terrifying hurricane in 1915, which filled their Port Arthur home with water, the Didriksens uprooted and moved seventeen miles away to Beaumont, where they lived not far from the town's largest industrial complex, an oil refinery. In the back garden, Ole Didriksen built his children a gymnasium, which included a weight-lifting device and a trapeze; it was here where Babe got her first taste for athletics and jumping. She would set up a row of hurdles by getting the neighbors to cut down all their hedges to the appropriate height, and she would race her sister Lillie, who ran along the road, while Babe leaped over the greenery.

George Zaharias, always the promoter, viewed the WPGA and LPGA tours as entertainment with Babe as the big drawing card.

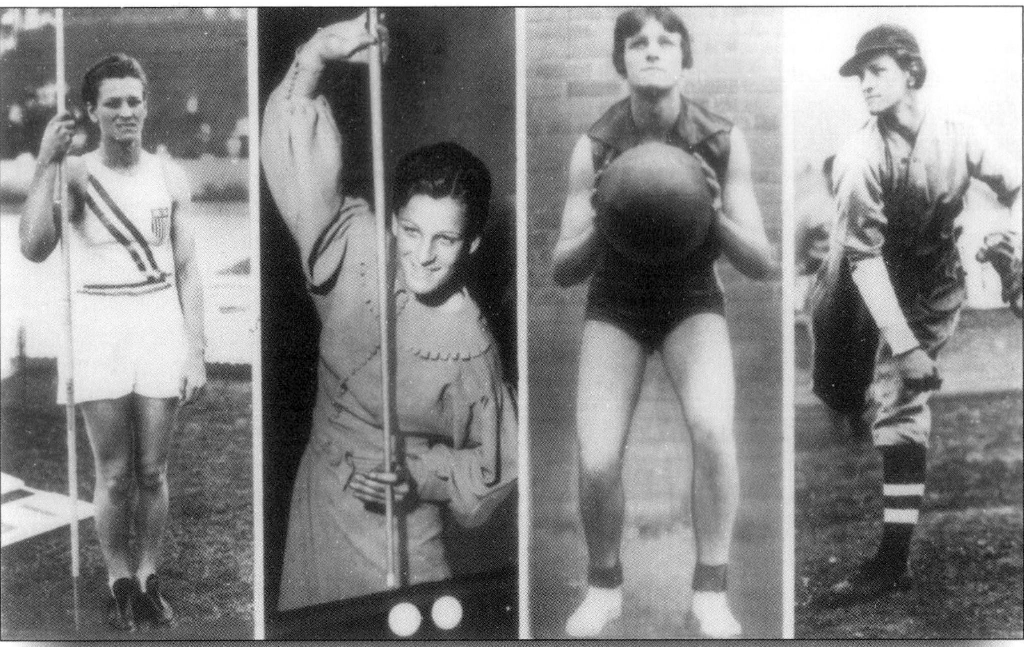

Babe, an Olympic athlete, excelled at most sports. Here, she poses with a javelin as a member of the U.S. Olympic team in 1932, she demonstrates her billiard technique in Chicago in 1932, she practices basketball, and she warms up to pitch for a New Orleans team against the Cleveland Indians in an exhibition game.

A wonderfully natural athlete, who excelled at and reveled in each sport she tried, Babe was on every team at Beaumont High school: volleyball, tennis, basketball, swimming, and baseball. She began golf in the 1920s with a woman called Beatrice Lyte, her physical education teacher, who played at the municipal club, but it was basketball that was Babe's dominant sport and through which she became an Olympic athlete. When she started hitting home runs in ball games, she was nicknamed after the baseball hero of the day, Babe Ruth.

Because of the discrepancy in her estimated age, it is impossible to know which year she was discovered on the girls high school basketball team by a Colonel McCombs (quoted in one book as 1930, which would have meant Babe was 19 and still in high school). A scout for a Dallas insurance company, called Employers' Casualty, he saw Babe and asked her to come to work for the company in Dallas as a $75-a-month stenographer, in order to play on their Golden Cyclones women's basketball team.

After Babe joined the company and became the outstanding member of the basketball team, the colonel introduced her to track and field sports—to the javelin, the shot put, baseball throw, long jump, and high jump. She speedily started creating world records, acquiring a cupboard full of gold medals, and she decided to train for the 1932 Olympics.

In August 1931, the Dallas Morning News declared that Babe was "probably the world's outstanding all-round feminine athlete." Female, she certainly was, but feminine she was not. Judging from photos, she was decidedly boyish and her attacking, competitive attitude added to the masculine image. To Babe, it was the natural behavior of a youngster immersed in the world of sport and athletics.

Another Dallas newspaper wrote of Babe: "Her lines and features are almost wholly masculine, a husky voice, a direct manner of speech that often drops into the sporting argot and an almost complete absence of feminine frills heighten the impression of masculinity. She follows no particular plan with her clothes."

In 1989, the president of the Women's Amateur Athletic Association, British octogenarian Vera Searle, and the 250 world champion runner after the First World War, spoke of the significance of women partaking in sport in her era, and in particular of their clothing. She said in an article in the Sunday Times in London: "Sport was a sign of freedom. Changing into freer clothes and running was the symbol. Athletics for women was very, very new and the medical profession was telling us we would leave our womanhood on the track. They said none of us would ever have children. We were determined to prove the bloody men wrong."

Sport was a complete freedom of spirit and expression for Babe, who never experienced the restrictions of Vera Searle, but she was out of tune with most of the young women of her day, and she became a symbol when she competed in the 1932 Olympics for many of those women who wanted to express themselves in sport and needed a role model. She was the first woman athlete to became a national hero.

It was in 1932 at the AAU meeting and Olympic tryouts at Evanston that Babe really made her mark. She entered eight events, won six gold medals, and broke four world records, two of them her own. Her cocky attitude may not have made her the most popular member chosen for the Olympics among her teammates, but certainly she was the most flamboyant and outstanding, and attracted the greatest publicity.

The 1932 Olympic Games at Los Angeles were the first of the modern lavish spectacles. The largest ever crowd of 105,000 attended the opening ceremony, and Olympic hysteria gripped a nation, otherwise enshrouded in the Depression.

Babe's first event was throwing the javelin, in which she unleashed an almighty throw of 143 feet, 4 inches, which staggered the audience, since it broke the world record by more than 11 feet. She followed this with the 80 meter hurdles and won her second gold medal when she breasted the tape in a world record time of 11.7 seconds. In her high jump event, she and fellow competitor Jean Shiley both cleared 5 feet, 5$^{1}/_{2}$ inches, but Shiley was awarded the gold due to a technicality of that era: Babe's last jump was deemed illegal because her head rolled over the bar before the rest of her, and although she was awarded the silver medal, she was announced as co-holder of the world record.

Babe was given an extravagant reception back in Dallas, which lasted for two days, and a heart-warming welcome of thousands in her hometown of Beaumont. In the press, sportswriter Grantland Rice put her on a pedestal as "the Ultimate Amazon and the greatest athlete of all mankind for all time. An incredible human being. She is beyond all belief until you see her perform. Then you finally understand that you are looking at the most flawless section of muscle harmony, of complete mental and physical co-ordination the world of sport has ever known. This may seem to be a wild statement, yet it happens to be 100 per cent true. There is only one Babe Didrikson and there has never been another in her class—even close to her class."

With rave reviews like that, it is understandable that Babe should have begun to believe her press clippings and to enjoy her status as one of the most famous people in the United States. She then fell from grace when she acquired a Dodge car, and her name and photograph accompanied an advertisement for it. A question of her amateur status arose, and she was suspended from the AAU

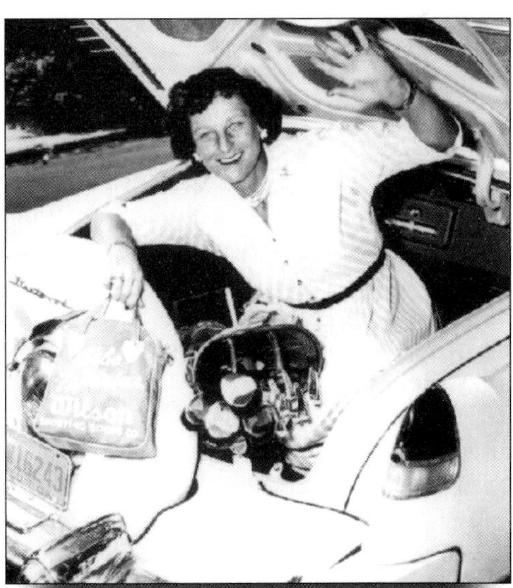

This is one of many publicity shots Babe was famous for. It is not unlike the advertisement for Dodge that cost Babe her amateur status.

Babe, always the showperson, demonstrates the vigor for which she was so well known, and she did it in high heels in between rounds at the Tam O'Shanter in Chicago.

and then reinstated when she said she had no knowledge of the advertisement or of endorsing the car.

Following this she went into vaudeville in Chicago. She was billed as the star; she sang and played the harmonica (a talent she had acquired as a child of seven), ran on a treadmill, and hit plastic golf balls from the stage into the audience. From being a theatrical success, she moved into professional basketball, pocket billiards, and then went on the road with "Babe Didrikson's All Americans," a mixed basketball sideshow, for which she earned a high reward of $1,000 per month. This was followed by touring with the House of David baseball team.

In 1933, having been encouraged by an earlier game of golf with Grantland Rice, Babe decided to put her earnings to good use in a bid to become a championship golfer and enter a socially acceptable world of sport. With her mother and sister Lillie, she went for six months to Los Angeles, where she worked incessantly and obsessively with a club professional, Stan Kertes. She practiced by hitting up to 1,500 balls a day in her efforts to become proficient. Not only did she have the ability to hit the ball huge distances, but she acquired a most delicate touch in her short game.

In her first tournament in 1934, the Fort Worth Women's Invitational, she achieved a tremendous 77 in the qualifying and then lost in the opening round of matchplay. The following year at the Texas Women's Amateur championship, Babe made an indelible impression on her newly acquired golfing set, although there was no shortage of snide remarks about her lowly social status, made before the event began.

Babe progressed to the matchplay stage, where she won her opening round by six and five, the second round by eight and six, and the third by three and two; in her semifinal, interrupted by rain, she sank a 20 foot putt to gain a place in the final against Peggy Chandler. Chandler, a classy golfer and a member of the country club set, had been prompted earlier to refer to Babe as "a truck driver's daughter."

In the 36 hole final, Babe eagled the 34th by chipping into the hole, before taking the title two holes later. All of this excited the press and her many hometown fans, who had arrived as spectators. But it did nothing to further the golf career of Babe, whose amateur status was questioned by someone in the Texas Women's Golf Association on the grounds of her being a professional athlete in other sports, and shamefully she was denied the right to play amateur golf by the USGA.

Following this, Babe signed up with the Goldsmith Golf Company, doing clinics and exhibitions for them and touring with the great professional, Gene Sarazen, the two of them being a tremendous draw.

Babe was an awesome force on the course, and in everything she did, including her efforts to promote the LPGA.

She also established her friendship with Al and Bertha Bowen, whom she had met during the Fort Worth Invitational. A wealthy golfing pair, who lived in the city, they took her under their wing, managing to make the local Invitational event an open one so that Babe could compete in it. Bertha was responsible for a considerable change in Babe's appearance to a much more feminine young woman, since she generously outfitted her in clothes from Neiman Marcus.

In this period of golf professionalism, Babe met her future husband, a showman and professional wrestler, George Zaharias. Babe was later to utter these words about her husband of Greek origin, possibly in jest: "When I married him, he looked like a Greek god, and now he looks like a gawddamned Greek." Because of the acted out part he played as a wrestler, sobbing for mercy as he was beaten, George was known as the Crying Greek from Cripple Creek, a town forty miles from his home in Pueblo.

When Babe met George, they were both competing in the 1938 Los Angeles Open. He was a well known figure, making more than $100,000 a year (his successful show could earn him $15,000 a night). She was living in Los Angeles, where she achieved the distinction of becoming the first and perhaps only woman ever to enter the Los Angeles Open, a men's PGA tournament. Just what George was doing competing is not clear, but he was a good amateur golfer. For Babe, it was an opportunity to play some competitive golf, even if she did not stand a chance of making any money.

As it turned out, both she and George missed the halfway cut, but their chemistry blended, and they were married on December 23 in St. Louis, in the home of a wrestling promoter Tom Packs.

The relationship of this unusual couple is described in other parts of this book in the chapters on Babe's two best friends, Betty Dodd and Peggy Kirk Bell, both of whom see it from different perspectives. George and Babe, who obviously had their times of happiness in a relationship which ultimately deteriorated, did not have children, much to Babe's sorrow. After she had miscarried, they did try to adopt a child but were considered an unsuitable couple since so much of their life was spent on the road.

Babe, who earned many trophies in many sports, is shown with U.S. and British amateur championship trophies in 1947.

In this period Babe, whose home with George was in West Los Angeles, entered into the role of homemaker, which she enjoyed. She was a good cook and seamstress, and she liked gardening. For a time she also devoted herself to her newly discovered passion, tennis, taking lessons from Eleanor "Teach" Tennant, a famous coach. Babe practiced with all the fervor she had previously put into her golf, and finally she entered a tournament in 1941. When her entry was refused, and she was told by the USLTA (in a decision equally absurd to that in golf) that because she had been a professional in another sport she was unacceptable, she never touched a racquet again. She followed tennis with bowling, where she became successful enough to set records in yet another area of endeavor.

In January 1940, Babe decided to retrieve her amateur golf status since there were more tournaments in those ranks. She applied to the USGA and had to wait the statutory three years. She was able to compete in the 1940 Western and Texas Opens, since she could play in open events without taking the prize money, so long as the organizers agreed, and she won them both. On behalf of the war effort, she played benefit matches and exhibitions, often with Bing Crosby, Bob Hope, and Patty Berg.

In 1943, the year her father died of a heart attack, Babe was once again accorded amateur status, and she relished the extra competition that became available to her after the war ended in 1945. While Babe was playing the Western Women's Open that year, her mother died. Babe was unable to get any transport out of the city, so she stayed at the tournament and won it, then went home for the funeral.

In 1946, with the amateur tournaments in full swing, Babe began a domination of the game that lasted for almost a year. Although the records show 17 consecutive victories, they are not accurate. After 13 consecutive victories, Babe lost in the first round of the inaugural Women's U.S. Open at Spokane, and from there she won the National Women's Amateur championship at the beginning of a run of 14 consecutive wins, which included the 1947 British Women's Amateur Championship, her penultimate title as an amateur.

Wanting to cash in on some lucrative offers if she turned professional, Babe did just that on August 14, 1947, before she had a chance to defend her U.S. Amateur title. She signed with Wilson Sporting Goods and appointed Fred Corcoran as her business representative, capitalizing on her fame with a punishing schedule of commitments.

In 1948, Babe announced she was going to enter the men's U.S. Open in Los Angeles (won by Ben Hogan), but her plan was thwarted by the USGA, which contended: "As the championship has

Patty Berg and Babe Zaharias display the National Open trophy. Babe won it in 1948, 1950, and 1954, Patty won in 1946.

always been intended to be for men, the eligibility rules have been rephrased to confirm that condition." Babe did win the women's U.S. Open that year by the considerable margin of eight shots, taking the $1,200 top prize on her way to being leading money winner with her total of $3,400.

When Fred Corcoran was retained by Wilson in 1949 to start a women's professional tour, Babe, who always craved competition, was a willing participant helping to get it off the ground. Babe needed a vehicle and a place to demonstrate her talent, and the tour needed her drawing power. Babe's showmanship—her harmonica, which she played in tandem with guitarist Betty Dodd, 19 years her junior; her ability to enchant the crowds and the press with her quick wit; and even her marriage—all added to the aura that followed her. Golfing talent, innate athleticism, her desire to compete and to win were the icing on the cake. Any lack of the social graces, any surfeit of extravagant claims and egocentricity, and her sometimes rocketing weight were only parts of a fascinating woman, who pushed herself to the limit for the whole of her short life.

In 1950, the year of the real beginnings of the LPGA tour and Babe's second U.S. Open victory, she was retained by the Sky Crest Country Club near Chicago on a $20,000 contract as their teaching professional, with time off for tournaments and exhibitions. She and George moved there, until 1951, when she left after it was alleged that she hustled the members. She and George bought their own golf course in Florida, which became the Tampa Golf and Country Club.

Babe's first experience of something troubling her physical well being occurred in 1948, when she experienced a swelling and an extremely sharp pain in her left side. Never a woman to admit to physical weakness, she did not consult a doctor as the pain and swelling subsided and re-occurred over the next four years, until finally she collapsed and went to a hospital in Beaumont in May 1952. There doctors performed an operation for a strangulated hernia. She recovered well, but then her health deteriorated, and by the following April, after a superhuman effort of winning her hometown tournament in Beaumont, she collapsed

Babe's career was cut short after cancer was discovered in 1952. Until her death in 1956, she rallied several times to play in tournaments — winning several. She also made many personal appearances to raise money for the Damon Runyan Society to fight cancer.

again and was forced to consult a doctor. Cancer of the rectum was diagnosed, which required a colostomy, a shattering blow to anyone, let alone a Babe Zaharias. She had pushed her extraordinarily well co-ordinated body to the limit for too long.

Her mental toughness did not desert her, and her fighting spirit enabled her to make her last and most indelible imprint in the record books. She was determined to play golf again and returned to the tour in July 1953, only three months after her operation. She was not back to her normal strength, but she played three tournaments that season and finished in sixth place on the money list.

The following year she performed astonishingly well, achieving five victories including her third U.S. Women's Open, which she won by the huge margin of 12 strokes from Betty Hicks. She crowned her season by winning the Vare trophy for the lowest scoring average, coming second on the money list, and being voted by the Associated Press the outstanding Woman Athlete of the Year for a record sixth time.

Babe was not only competing at golf tournaments, she made constant personal appearances across the country, on television and radio, to raise money for the American Cancer Society. Also, while on tour she visited cancer patients to encourage them. It is said that Babe was mercenary in her demands for appearance money on some of these public occasions, but the end result was a boost for the cancer charity.

Partly needing to compete for her own self-esteem and partly to encourage others, Babe doggedly endeavored to keep playing in 1955, and she was successful in winning two tournaments. She won the Tampa Open in January, and her last victory, a two stroke margin over Marilynn Smith in the Peach Blossom Betsy Rawls Open in Spartanburg, was achieved in considerable pain.

Finally, her tortured body could not respond, and following an operation in June 1955, she never regained any physical well being. Her indomitable spirit carried her through, but perhaps she would have had a gentler decline had she not been such a fighter. George was unable to cope with her illness, so it was Betty Dodd who took over the supportive and caring role that sustained Babe until she died on September 27, 1956.

Patty Berg called Babe a great friend and the greatest woman athlete she'd ever known. "It was a very sad and tremendous loss when she died at 42, before she could see the results of all the doors she opened."

There were many memorials to Babe, but the most touching has to be in San Antonio's Sea World, where a statue of her is to be found among the tributes to famous Texans. It is touching, because the woman who unveiled it in 1988, then much older than Babe when she died, was San Antonio resident Betty Dodd, who died in 1993. The former protégée of Babe's, who treasured their special friendship, was still able to be excited by the statue and by her memory of a woman who touched the hearts of so many.

Member LPGA Hall of Fame 1951

Professional Victories: 1948 All-American Open, World Championship, U.S. Women's Open. **1949** World Championship, Eastern Open. **1950** All-American Open, World Championship, U.S. Women's Open, Titleholders Championship, Weathervane, Western Open. **1951** All-American Open, World Championship, Ponte Verde Open, Tampa Open, Fresno Open, Richmond Open, Texas Open. **1952** Titleholders Championship, Fresno Open, Texas Open, Miami Weathervane. **1953** Sarasota Open, Babe Zaharias Open. **1954** All-American Open, U.S. Women's Open, Sarasota Open, Serbin Open, National Capital Open. **1955** Tampa Open, Peach Blossom Classic.

Babe Zaharias' LPGA Record

Year	No. of Events	Best Finish	Money	Rank	Scoring Average
1950	10	1	$2,875	NA	75.88
1951	14	1	6,812	NA	74.92
1952	8	1	4,730	NA	75.76
1953	10	1	5,132	NA	75.70
1954	17	1	11,437	NA	75.61
1955	8	1	3,398	NA	75.60

The 1950s

At the beginning of the 1950s a fascinating era of women's golf began to fight for its existence. As Fred Corcoran was later to write in his memoirs: "The announcement that we had formed the Ladies' Professional Golf Association touched off a national storm of indifference." The decade in its earlier years was dominated by the presence of Babe Zaharias, the catalyst for sponsors and the tour, but after her premature death in 1956, a handful of women professionals struggled for credibility and survival.

Dropping the previously included "Players" from their title, the Ladies' Professional Golf Association of America had its certificate of incorporation "witnessed, made, subscribed and acknowledged," on two days in 1950: first, at the Women's Open at the Rolling Hills Country Club in Wichita, Kansas, on September 30; then more formally on October 9 in New York County. The certificate, which was signed by Patty Berg, Helen Dettweiler, Sally Sessions, Betty Jameson, and Helen Hicks, was stamped by New York notary Lawrence B. Simons and sworn in front of New York lawyer Lee V. Eastman, who also signed the document. The above names and those who were at Wichita came to be regarded as the charter members. At Wichita were Alice and Marlene Bauer, Bettye Mims Danoff, Opal Hill, Marilynn Smith, Shirley Spork, Louise

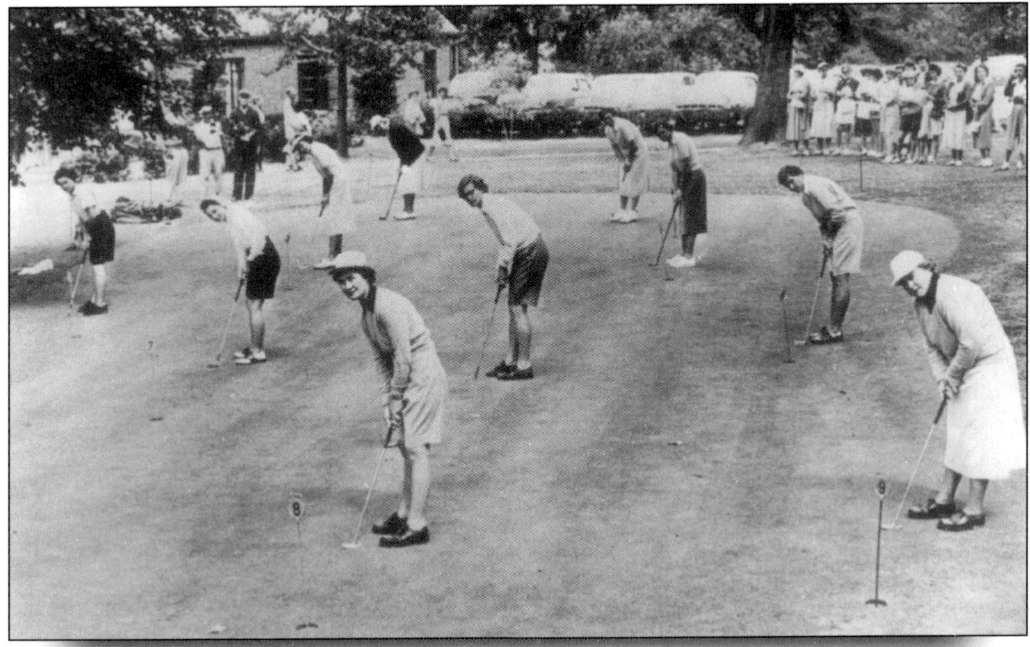

This innovative photo of the LPGA at work during the 1954 LPGA Championship was used to publicize the tour. Reading clockwise from front center are Louise Suggs, Marlene Bauer, Betty Hicks, Betty MacKinnon, Betty Jameson (dark sweater, at back), Fay Crocker, Betsy Rawls, Pat O'Sullivan, and Patty Berg. Beverly Hanson, wearing glasses, is in the center.

Bettye Mims Danoff, housewife and mother, was one of the 13 founders of the LPGA. When she won the Texas Open in 1947, she put an end to Babe Zaharias' phenomenal run of 17 straight victories.

Suggs, and Babe Zaharias, who won her second Open title that week.

Officially, there were 13 LPGA charter members, yet Helen Hicks who signed the certificate of incorporation, has never been listed as one of them. Helen died of throat cancer in 1974. Neither has Betty Hicks (no relation to Helen) ever been recognized as a charter member, in spite of her being responsible with Hope Seignious and Ellen Griffin for the formation of the WPGA in the 1940s and who, in the words of Betsy Rawls, "did as much as anyone to further the progress of the LPGA." When the charter was signed, Betty Hicks was at college studying for a degree in teaching but soon after was on the LPGA tour and instrumental in its organization and promotion. Recognition was accorded to Hope Seignious in 1954, when she was named the first honorary member of the LPGA.

The first tournament in 1950 was the $3,500 Tampa Open. Louise Suggs, five shots behind in second place, took the top $1,000 prize, because the event was won with a 5-under par 295 by amateur Polly Riley who, from 1948 to 1958, was a member of six Curtis Cup teams and was a formidable competitor. According to journalist Robin McMillan, the same Polly Riley, who became head of the marketing department for a chain called Pancho's Salad Bars, was many years later contacted by a representative of the LPGA, trying to sell her sponsorship of a tournament. A sum of $500,000 was suggested, which Polly politely declined. The caller tried to impress her with numerous details about the LPGA and its fine heritage, after which Polly Riley said: "Honey, I don't need to know about the LPGA. Why don't you look up your record books and see who won their very first tournament. It was me."

In the spring of 1950, during the 12th Titleholders' Championship at the Augusta Country Club, Fred Corcoran thought of an idea for attaining publicity by establishing a Women's Golf Hall of Fame to honor the great women golfers of the past. He felt that Augusta Country Club, the permanent home of the Titleholders, would be a good choice of venue. With the help of the Associated Press golf writer, who rejoiced in the name of Sterling Slappey, and Bert Prather, golf writer for the Atlanta Journal, he set the idea in motion.

Louise Suggs won the first LPGA tournament, the Tampa Open.

This is one of the Weathervane teams Alvin Handmacher took to Europe to play against men and women amateurs in the early 1950s. The American women won convincingly. Team members included Babe Zaharias, Peggy Kirk Bell, Betty Jameson, Betsy Rawls, Bonnie Randolph, and Patty Berg.

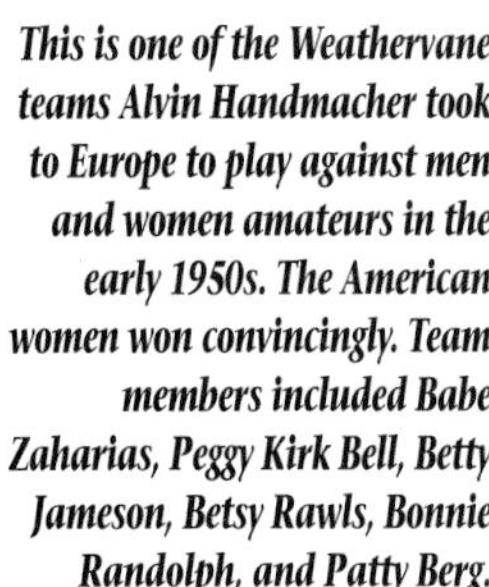

The original selection committee consisted of Kerr Petrie, retired writer for the New York Herald Tribune; O. B. Keeler of the Atlanta Journal; Bob Harlow, editor of *Golf World*; Herb Graffis, editor of a magazine called Golfdom; Grantland Rice of the North American Newspaper Alliance; and Lindy Fowler, former writer for the Boston Transcript.

A space was found in the clubhouse of Augusta Country Club, and a month after the Titleholders, during the Masters, the committee met and elected Beatrix Hoyt, Alexa Stirling Fraser, Dorothy Campbell Hurd, Virginia Van Wie, Margaret Curtis, Glenna Collett Vare, and British woman golfer, Joyce Wethered (Lady Heathcott Amory) as charter honorees. The committee met again in 1951, this time electing Babe Zaharias, Patty Berg, Betty Jameson, and Louise Suggs. The Vare Trophy for the player with the year's lowest scoring average was also housed at Augusta Country Club. It was presented to the LPGA by Betty Jameson in 1952, in honor of the great amateur golfer Glenna Collett Vare, already in the Hall of Fame. Patty Berg was the first recipient in 1953, and won again in 1955 and 1956, and Babe Zaharias won the prized trophy in 1954.

One man who played a big part in financial and competitive terms, to establish a tournament circuit for the LPGA in those early years, was Alvin Handmacher, a New York manufacturer of women's clothing. In 1950, Handmacher put up $17,000, ($3,000 per tournament and $5,000 for the overall low scorer) for a series of four Weathervane Opens to be played across the country—in California, Chicago, Cleveland, and New York. Babe Zaharias and Louise Suggs won alternate tournaments, and Handmacher was a delighted sponsor, who decided that in 1951 he would take the top six women professionals to play competitively in England.

At the Chicago Weathervane tournament in 1950, Shirley Spork, who became a leading light in the LPGA teaching division and who received the Teacher of the Year award in 1959 and 1985, had an unusual dubbing as a professional golfer. In a piece written for the LPGA records, she said: "While eating breakfast with Marilynn Smith, and Babe and George Zaharias, prior to the first round of play, Babe said: `Hey kid, why don't you turn pro? You are a top amateur from Michigan, we need more players on our ladies' tour.' I said: 'Babe, how do you turn pro?' She got up from the table, plunked her right hand down firmly on top of my head, and said, 'Kid, you're a pro. Go tell them on the first tee you're playing as a pro.' I did and was one of eleven women pros playing in that tournament." Shirley, a charter member of the LPGA, played the tour in its early years, when she was the trick shot artist at the Swing Parade Clinics, which were then a feature at LPGA tournaments.

Handmacher's 1951 Weathervane jamboree to Europe began in July, with a large party given by the sponsor at New York's Savoy-Plaza Hotel. An article in *Golf World* by Ruth Woodward, noted: "The Savoy-Plaza menu included vichyssoise, noisette of lamb, and ice cream in five technicolors. It all started with cocktails and finished with brandy."

The six women, each of whom was decked out in a Weathervane suit and presented with a gold brooch in the form of the Weathervane trademark of a rooster, were Babe Zaharias, Patty Berg, Betty Jameson, Betsy Rawls, Peggy Kirk, and Betty Bush, all of whom were scheduled to go to England to play top teams of British women and men amateurs and to contest for the European Weathervane trophy. To this day, the match against the men is a much talked of event by British golfers, and the meeting of Babe Zaharias and Leonard Crawley has passed into golfing folklore.

Golf World magazine of July 27, 1951, recorded the trip under the title of "The Amazing Amazons": "Britain has experienced some interesting invasions, all of which have left their mark of culture. The imprint of the Roman legionnaires and William's Norman knights is writ large on the pages of British history, but never has an invasion produced such a convulsion (in miniature to be sure) as the recent visitation by Alvin Handmacher, choreographer Fred Corcoran, and their line of six gals. The sextet of American women professionals gave British golf its most emphatic jolt of the decade. If nothing else, the transatlantic hop proved conclusively that between the pro and the amateur there lies a yawning psychological chasm."

Bob Renner was tournament director during 1950s. Photo credit: LPGA.

Starting at Sunningdale, the six Americans played a two day engagement with Diana Critchley's star international women's amateur team, for which Handmacher donated a beautiful Weathervane Cup. The American pros swept the three foursome matches on the first day and then polished off the six amateurs in head to head competition for a final score of nine to nothing. The Weathervane troop then progressed down the road to Wentworth, where they tackled a team of the finest British male amateurs, assembled by General Critchley—husband of Diana. The British men included four Walker Cup team members.

Said *Golf World*: "This Sunday show produced the sensation of post war golf in England. Meeting the men on level terms over a course they had never seen, the Floradora girls walloped the boys by 6½ to 2½, sweeping all six singles. It was an incredible showing. They matched the men drive for drive and iron for iron, and showed a clear-cut supremacy on the putting green.

"Babe Zaharias drew the crowd in her feature match against Leonard Crawley, ex-Walker Cupper and golf pundit for the *Daily Telegraph*. Time after time she outdistanced the nettled Crawley from the tee and when she negotiated a half-stymie at the 16th green to win by 3 and 2, Crawley was dazed. As Desmond Hackett put it: 'Crawley was shaken to the bristling tips of his ginger moustache'."

It was that moustache, according to legend, for which the match was wagered, as Babe had told Leonard that if she won the match he would have to shave off his moustache. The wager was said to be agreed, but at the end of the day Leonard did not remove his famous trademark. Babe also insisted that they played off the same tees as the male amateurs.

It was sensational golf and headline news, which was not repeated, as the Weathervane sponsorship was restricted to just two more LPGA tournaments

This was the LPGA in July 1957, at the Homestead Two-Ball tournament. Front row, left to right: Barbara Jon Snyder, Bonnie Randolph, Diane Garrett Penera, Alice Bauer, Louise Suggs; second row: Jackie Pung, Fay Ingalls (owner of the Homestead, famed Hot Springs resort, and tournament sponsor), Mrs. Ingalls, Pat Derany, Marlene Hagge, Kathy Cornelius, Bev Hanson; third row: Murle MacKenzie, Esther Foley, JoAnne Prentice, Peggy Kirk Bell, Betty Dodd, Ruth Jessen, Gloria Fecht, Gloria Armstrong, Fay Crocker; back row: the Homestead's assistant pro, Marilynn Smith, Barbara Rotvig, Vonnie Colby, Joyce Ziske, Mary Lena Faulk, Betty Jameson, Wiffi Smith, the Homestead's head pro. Photo: Stephen Blake.

in America, one in 1952 and another the following year.

The lucrative Handmacher sponsorship gauntlet was taken up by George S. May, who owned a business engineering company, and whose original Chicago tournament had sparked off the formation of the WPGA in the 1940s. Right through the decade, May put up huge purses for his two week Tam O'Shanter sponsored events for men and women, which amazingly in 1952 were said to be worth $250,000. May had bought time on radio and television and took full page advertisements in the *Chicago Tribune* and the golfing press. The Tam O'Shanter was easily the largest operation in golf.

As the number of women's tournaments and their purses started to increase, a tragic blow came in 1953, with the revelation that Babe Zaharias had cancer of the colon, requiring a colostomy. It was a personal tragedy with far reaching consequences, for Babe was the famous personality and the magnet for every sponsor. It was on Babe and her broad shoulders that the LPGA tour was being carried. She may, at times, have irritated some of her fellow professionals, bent the rules, or been a bit loud, but she personally demanded tournaments from sponsors. It was her star quality that brought in the money and her excitingly flamboyant style of winning golf that attracted the galleries.

Babe had won two tournaments by the beginning of April 1953, but she ignored physical signs that warned her of some serious complaint, which she sensed might be cancer. She was forced to face reality after her second victory, when somehow after summoning the strength to win the

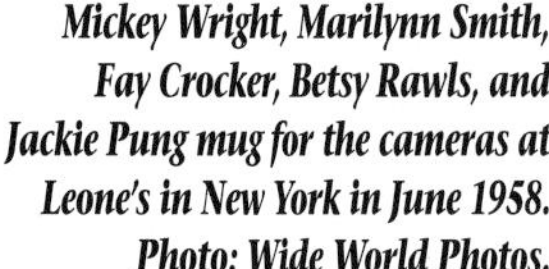

Mickey Wright, Marilynn Smith, Fay Crocker, Betsy Rawls, and Jackie Pung mug for the cameras at Leone's in New York in June 1958. Photo: Wide World Photos.

Babe Zaharias Open in her home town of Beaumont, she collapsed in a state of total exhaustion. By April 17 she was on the operating table, and in spite of the tremendous shock both physically and psychologically, she was back in tournament golf by the end of July. Her physical condition allowed her to control only her opening drive of 250 yards; she finished in 15th place. She played only two more tournaments that year, but was sixth on the money list. With courage and a superhuman will, Babe won two successive tournaments the following season, and then took her third U.S. Women's Open title in Salem, Massachusetts, the championship having come under the banner of the USGA for the first time the previous year.

Shown at a 1958 tournament in Alliance, Ohio, are (left to right) Marilynn Smith (LPGA president), Fred Corcoran (tournament director), Frank Hoiles (tournament chairman), and Eileen Stulb (marketing and advertising). Photo: Al Levine.

When the financial backing of the golf equipment manufacturers dissolved at the end of 1953, Fred Corcoran left to go back to the PGA. Babe, who had sufficient energy to become the focus of dissension, wanted, with husband George, to take control of the LPGA. She was prepared to engage in a mini-power struggle, which had her acting as tournament director for all of three months. After that period, she handed the reins over to Betty Hicks, who had been absent from the beginnings of the LPGA tour because she was in college. Returning in 1952, Betty was its most prolific publicist and a fine and entertaining writer.

At the 1954 New Orleans Open, Babe walked onto the practice green with the two small metal files containing the LPGA's business transaction records, set them in front of Betty Hicks, and said: "Ah've got my belly full. Here, Betty, you be tournament director." At a meeting in August 1954, Babe was elected president of the LPGA, while Betty Hicks formally became tournament chairman.

The first LPGA Championship, worth $6,000, was played at Fort Wayne, Indiana, in 1955. It began with strokeplay qualifying rounds and culminated in a 36-hole matchplay final between Louise Suggs and Beverly Hanson, with victory and $1,200 to Hanson, 4 and 3.

Following Babe's comeback in 1954, her powers declined. She put up a valiant fight until her tragic death in September 1956 at the age of 45. There was a huge void, which affected the fortunes of the struggling LPGA, and as Betty Hicks' health forced her off the tour for six months, Marilynn Smith and Fay Crocker jointly took over the post of tournament director.

With the organization still in some disarray in 1956, Marilynn Smith and Louise Suggs, the current LPGA president, consulted a group of businessmen, headed by Blaine Eynon at the Forest Lake Country Club. After setting up interviews, the committee recommended sportswriter Bob Renner of Fort Wayne, Indiana, for the post of LPGA tournament director. He was appointed at a considerable salary of $15,000, for the year. He worked for the association, but he struggled with fields of 25 women professionals, who drew only the faithful few. "Many newsmen do not regard women's sports as important," said Renner.

In 1956, Mickey Wright achieved her first victory after two years as a professional. She continued to win, taking her first U.S. Open in 1958, but it was not until the following decade that she acquired exceptional status. In the 1950s, Betsy Rawls, Louise Suggs, and Patty Berg were the names on tour, all claiming a considerable share of the prizes.

Continuity was lacking, since LPGA officials continued to change frequently. Ed Carter, from the men's PGA, succeeded Bob Renner in 1957, until Fred Corcoran returned to the fold in July 1958. Eileen Stulb and her advertising and public relations company in Augusta, were hired to promote the LPGA tour.

In 1958, Helen Dettweiler received the first Teacher of the Year award: "To honor the teaching professional who had most exemplified her profession during the year." Bev Hanson, who created the award to generate some off-season publicity, said: "I got this wild idea that we should have a teacher of the year award, and said, 'Let's name Helen Dettweiler.' That was it; there was no vote, but that's what you do when your base of operations is someone's motel room. Everyone's voice could be heard because there were so few, and we flew by the seat of our pants, which was great."

As the decade neared its close, the playing professionals numbered about 25 for a season of some 27 events, worth just over $200,000. LPGA President Marilynn Smith, desirous of further publicity, introduced sponsor and press cocktail parties at various tour stops, and by 1959 a further innovation was the one day Pro-Am preceding tournament play, which became an established event.

The 1959 LPGA International Challenge Team included: Patty Berg, Bonnie Randolph, Betsy Rawls, Louise Suggs, Marlene Hagge, Wiffi Smith in the front row; Kathy Cornelius, Mickey Wright, Betty Jameson, Marilynn Smith, Bev Hanson, and Fay Crocker in the back row. Photo by: Morgan Fitz. Photo courtesy: Eileen Stulb.

At the beginning of the 1950s, when women's golf had to fight for its existence, Patty Berg and Babe Zaharias shouldered the responsibility for its success as they became catalysts for sponsors and galleries.

Of those early years, when a sense of adventure and a love of golf were the prime requirements, Marilynn Smith said: "We often had to drive as far as 1,600 miles from one tournament to another, and we traveled caravan style, following each other in cars and doubling up to share expenses. When one considers all the facts, our scores were really rather remarkable. We played on some finely groomed courses as well as some rather poorly maintained layouts. The courses measured from 6,250 to over 6,900 yards, and we always played from the regular men's tees. Babe promoted the use of longer tee placements because she was the longest hitter of the ball at that time."

Just surviving was a remarkable achievement for the women professionals whose spirits remained high, in spite of their fluctuating fortunes. Marilynn Smith said at the end of 1959, in her president's role: "Let us endeavor to put our best foot forward and pull together for a stronger organization. Our tournament purses are higher, adding to the prestige of each event. Let us live up to this prestige that we have worked so hard to attain. This has not come easily, but by perseverance and hard work."

The Babe Zaharias Memorial Trophy, in honor of the famed woman athlete who passed away in September 1956, is held by golfer's Patty Berg and Betty Dodd before it was placed permanently in the Women's Golf Hall of Fame in Augusta, GA.

The Bauer Sisters

Alice Bauer & Marlene Hagge

Alice and Marlene Bauer were charter members of the LPGA. Alice played the tour only occasionally between three marriages and two children. The sisters attracted enormous publicity. When Alice's marriage to her first husband, Robert Hagge, was on the wane, the gossip was hot and fast around them. After Alice and Robert were divorced, Marlene and Robert married, confirming all the rumors. Two sisters marrying the same man was an unusual event in any walk of life.

In spite of her denial of any overt rivalry, Alice admits that initially she had to take up golf to be noticed. Marlene's admission of wanting to be like Alice in everything she did was carried to an extreme when she took as her husband the man formerly married to her older sister. The family and the sisters were close, and although they may have gone through a difficult patch, they have remained close friends.

They joined the tour at its inception in 1950, when Marlene was only 16 years old, and Alice six years her senior. They were, in Betty Jameson's words, "a real traveling circus," going everywhere as a family with their professional golfer father Dave and mother Madeline. Alice says, "I never found it a tough life because basically I'm a clown."

The two young girls created a sensation. Extremely glamorous show-business people, they were much in demand for golf exhibitions all over the country. They were managed by Fred Corcoran, the original LPGA tour director and manager of Babe Zaharias.

For me, meeting the "Bauer Sisters" was a real treat. I had heard of them and had seen Marlene, the younger sister playing the tour, but I had never spoken to her. The first sister I talked to was Marlene when she was competing in the mixed-team event in Florida. She is the more reserved, a private person. After a while, she suggested that I talk to Alice, who was at the tournament as a spectator and had been flinging remarks at us across the crowded room while I was interviewing Marlene. She seemed happier than Marlene to have questions fired at her. More than a year later I talked again with Marlene.

I so enjoyed my initial meeting with Alice that I called on her when I was in Sarasota, at her club,

Marlene and Alice Bauer, ages 12 and 18, in 1946, were hailed as the two greatest prospects in women's golf. Their father Dave, a golf pro, started them early—Alice at 11 and Marlene when she was only three. Photo from "Woman Golfer" magazine. Courtesy: Betty Hicks.

Marlene and Alice Bauer are shown with husband Bob Hagge. Photo courtesy: Betty Hicks.

Rolling Green, where she was greatly in demand as a teaching professional.

Before our meeting, she told me on the telephone that someone kept smashing the back windscreen of her car, and she was going to find her son's 34 shotgun and "let them have it."

Alice Bauer

Alice is an earthy, warm, and humorous woman, who talks in a forthright manner. She always puts on a good show, and you get the feeling that she has done plenty of living and had her share of joy and sorrow.

She dresses with flamboyant style—she was in marvelous canary yellow from top to toe when I met her in Sarasota—and she likes to identify with young people and the influence of the hippie generation. She is a strong character, very much her own person: She says she takes 24 hours to lose her temper, "and then I don't need a microphone; the whole world knows about it."

In the 1957 LPGA publicity brochure, her consistency as a golfer is often mentioned (she was the 14th money winner in 1956) as well as her popularity as a player: "While Alice's game was consistent, so was her following over the country as she parlayed beauty and ability into one of the top attractions in the sports world. The natural highlight when the galleries speak of Alice, is the amazing backswing of the 5 feet, 1 inch, 105-pound package of golfing dynamite. Galleries are always talking about her swing, which carries the clubhead back past her left leg on the backswing.

"Although Alice knows that this has become a trademark of her game, she stresses that this is necessary because of her small stature. 'I have to swing the club back that far to get the distance to keep at least in sight of the sluggers in this group.'"

Alice was a good player but never hit the heights like her sister Marlene. She admits that, in the words of Walter Hagen, "I like to stop and smell the flowers." Certainly, she has had a very busy life outside golf and gave up playing the tour for some long periods when she raised two children.

Alice was born in 1928, Marlene six years later, in Eureka, South Dakota, where their father, who was a teaching professional leased a golf course and had a driving range. He would like to have been a touring professional but settled down to marriage and a family. He wanted to make his children golfers. He tried to start Alice at the game when she was eight, but she was interested in other things; so when his second daughter came along, he taught her at the age of three and a half years.

"We had a range on the main highway in Long Beach, California," says Alice, "and when Marlene started playing golf and hitting balls, everyone stopped along the road and said 'Isn't she cute?'. She got all the attention, and I figured that if I wanted anyone to know that I was alive in any way, I'd better learn to play golf.

"I started in self defense and in some ways I liked it better than Marlene. She had natural talent and hated to practice, and I loved to practice—I preferred it to playing.

"I was 10 when I started, and most of my friends were boys in the high school golf team. I grew up in a world of boys, which wasn't all bad. I won quite a few amateur events, and then in 1950, when I was 22, I turned professional. I was always like a bridesmaid—I came in second six or seven times. I tied for the Heart of America Tournament in 1955 but lost in a playoff to Marilynn Smith.

"We traveled the tour as a family. My father was the only teacher we ever had. We always gave exhibitions, which were arranged for us by Fred Corcoran. Although it was hard work, I enjoyed the life and I don't think it was strange for my family to be together, so I could follow my profession. It's worse when society deems that at a certain age you go off and leave the ones you love, find your own way and lose your closeness—that to me is strange.

"Being a professional golfer was no different from going to New York or Hollywood to become an actress. A group of people live together to see if they can get their break in life. We began with 12, and then each year more joined us, and some played well and made it, and some didn't.

"There was money according to the expenses of the day, and Marlene and I had a great many exhibitions for which we were very well paid. We got $600 on weekdays, $700 on weekends, and we were booked solid. We made money out there; we didn't do it for laughs or love.

"I think it will take another 2,000 years for women to gain the same foothold in playing for the money that the men do, but in the course of history, it has taken 2,000 years for women to get where they are now.

"Women have made great strides. I'm not Women's Lib; I'm People's Lib, and there's a difference. I feel you should be able to do what you're talented to do. They freed the slaves 150 years ago, but I well remember some fantastic black baseball players who were banned from playing. Now they're finding out that women have some talent, and it just takes a while to progress."

When she was 25, Alice married a blonde adonis of a man, Robert Hagge. The marriage lasted about two to three years, and Alice said that he did not have a job the whole time they were married.

Later, after he had been married to her sister, Alice said, "He became a golf course architect and changed his name to 'Von Hagge' so that he could join the select group of 'Vons.' I really think I was well out of that one."

Alice's only positive memories of this marriage concern her daughter, Heidi, who was born in 1956. "I played golf for eight months while I was carrying Heidi. She was an 8 lb., 9 oz., baby, and that last month I was so heavy, it looked like I needed a wheel under me.

"I played Tam O'Shanter seven months pregnant. I was coming up the 18th; they had the bleacher seats all around, and my mother was watching me as I played in my maternity shirt. I was playing really well since I was swinging slower so that I wouldn't hurt the baby. My mother heard some lady say, 'My heavens, she must be wearing her husband's shirt' because they couldn't believe that I was dressed like that. Then the announcer at the 18th said 'Approaching the green is Alice' ('We won't discuss the last name right now', Alice told me) 'who is playing her own best ball.' He meant that because I was pregnant, Heidi and I were playing the field.

"When Heidi was born, my parents took care of her when I played in tournaments. Not too long after that, my marriage broke up. Having Marlene marry the same man was a strain, only because I was trying for her not to make a mistake, but,"

Marlene and Alice joined the tour at its inception in 1950. Both were popular with the galleries, but there was never any rivalry between them.

Alice claims now, "there was not a strain on our relationship.

"She was a young girl, and he talked a lot. I was dumb enough to marry him, but I got something very nice out of it—I got my little Heidi. The only strain was the fact that Marlene didn't believe me. But in later years I was proved right.

"As sisters, we were always friends. If you want to help someone, and they do something that will hurt them, you can only help if you're not aggravated with them. Marlene did me a favor. In essence, Bob was a terrible husband and a terrible father, and it was much easier getting rid of him that way. But Marlene hurt her life, and if you love someone you don't want them hurting themselves by making a mistake.

"I married again and had another child, Peter. To put it very simply, I'm a sucker for kids—I collect kids and get rid of husbands. My second husband, Harry Hovey, who was in the grocery business, was a good sport.

"He loved spectator sports and he used to laugh when I told people that we had a problem. 'We're incompatible,' I'd say. 'We do both like spectator sports—the problem is, he's a spectator and I'm a sport.'

"I gave up golf for a long time after my second marriage and only played occasionally. When the kids started going to school, there was no way I could take them with me. My kids may not have missed me, but I missed them so badly, there was no way on earth that golf could have been more important.

"I remember when Heidi was a baby, I left her for a couple of weeks with my parents and went to play a tournament. Coming back, when I was a mile from home, the anxiety of seeing that little girl gave me the worst headache in the world, and I said, 'Hey, it isn't worth it.'

"My priorities were my kids—and they are still. They're grown up now; Heidi plays guitar—Country and Western—and Peter plays lead guitar. They are both very good musicians. If there's something they need or if they want me, then I'll be there, not out shanking a couple of shots.

"My second marriage came to an end, and I married again. I kept trying because I was an optimist. But then finally I decided I had better give up. I don't even care to talk about my third husband. Boy, you can really make some stupid errors of judgment, and I did. It lasted a year and three months; I misjudged the person, that's all. Some people hide things rather well, and he was such a chauvinist, I couldn't believe it.

Marlene, Patty Berg, and Alice in 1951 were instrumental in helping the fledgling tour grow to its potential.

"Every time I got a divorce, I went out to the golf course—that was my escape. Everyone needs an escape, and that was where I went instead of to bars or out looking for trouble. I'd go off and play in tournaments and get into trouble all over again.

"My father always said one thing when we were young, and I love this statement—he said that he had two daughters, and if he taught them how to play poker, how to play chess, and how to play golf, then they could hold their own against anybody.

"In golf you try to beat the golf course. It's like chess, where you can only beat the other person if you don't make any first move mistakes. It's not a matter of personalities; it's a matter of how you perfect the game.

"I remember that one time my sister and I were going head to head in a tournament, and Marlene won because I couldn't decide whether I wanted to beat her or not. You have mixed emotions. It's not really rivalry, since you still play your own game.

"She's six and a half years younger and is like one of my kids. If something goes wrong or she needs help, I'm the first one she calls. I'm also the first one at whom she yells.

"Marlene was a great golfer at a very early age, but I was used to her and didn't think anything of it. Sometimes, though, when I got on the first tee and was paired with Louise Suggs, the Babe, or Patty Berg, I would stand there and look at them, look around, and think, 'What in the world am I doing out here?' I just couldn't believe that I was there playing with one of the three greats. Of course, I always played my brains out trying to beat them, but I felt I'd walked into another world.

"The Babe was fantastic for the tour. She was slapstick, and I loved it. She had charisma and knew how to make everyone have a good time. She was a showperson and a good golfer like Arnold Palmer. When she disappeared, it left a hole. Mickey Wright came out on tour and was a vastly superior golfer to Babe. Mickey is a quiet person, who had a much better golf swing. Whereas the Babe could always think of something funny in the blink of an eye.

"I was paired with Babe once at Beaumont, which is a very narrow course. When she teed off at the fifth hole and hit a tree, the ball bounced in front of her and went back under the bench behind her. She turned to the gallery and said, 'That's the one thing my pro told me when I first started to play golf—never let the ball get behind you.' It was beautiful and the crowd loved it.

"I guess that Marlene and I were the glamour girls of the tour in those early years because we were small and young and so different. There were some bothersome times with our clothing, in particular with shorts. Anything was short if it wasn't Bermudas, and they had to be no more than four inches above the knee. Well, I don't have an average leg, being so very short, and four inches above my knee is a long way up, though nothing like the short shorts worn today. Anyway, certain clubs didn't like it, and in a few places we were warned that we would have to wear skirts. It all came out in the papers, and there was a big fuss.

"Maybe there was some tension on tour from all the publicity we attracted, but basically I'm a happy person and was so busy trying to do my own thing that I wouldn't have known any tension existed.

"I thought it was a marvelous life. Maybe I wasted time sometimes, but my only regret would have been not to have had time with my children. My heart, once I'm gone, will have been with my kids and the people I've loved. No trophy on the shelf can ever replace that."

Marlene Hagge

Marlene Hagge is a phenomenon in women's professional golf. She was a child prodigy, starting golf at the age of three; she won 25 tournaments through 20 years of her golfing life, joining the LPGA tour in 1950. She still retained her looks, and

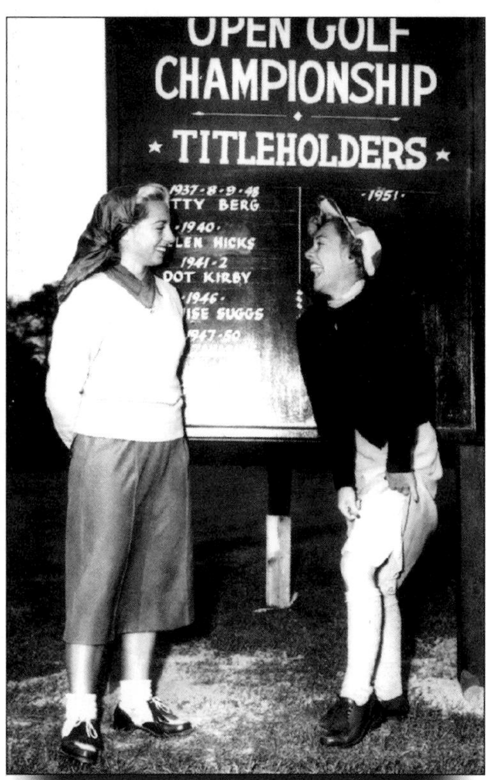

Alice (right) shows off her thermal underwear to sister Marlene after braving near-freezing temperatures during a practice round for the Titleholders Tournament, March 15, 1951. Photo: AP Wirephoto.

competed into the 1990s; 1979 was her best financial year when she won $26,812.

When you meet her, she seems small at 5 feet, 3 inches, but she is very athletic and has kept in marvelous trim. With a sweater girl figure, she is beautifully turned out, has long flowing hair, and is an attractive woman who is obviously aware of her body.

The year 1956 was her most spectacularly successful. The 1957 LPGA Publicity Brochure gives its leading money winner, whose picture graces the front cover, a rave review: "The usually close race for Golf Digest's most improved golfer award was a complete runaway in 1956, as petite Marlene Bauer Hagge outdistanced the field with her tremendous record-breaking performance during the year.

"Just take a look at these accomplishments: a world record of 284 for a 72-hole tournament; an all-time Ladies' PGA money record of $20,235; eight tournament championships; runner-up honors in both the scoring average race and the Babe Zaharias Trophy award, along with the most improved player trophy.

"Marlene has been in the golfing headlines for many years and actually gained recognition when she qualified in the championship flight of the South Dakota Championship at the age of eight. This brilliant golf prodigy set officials back on their heels, when at the age of 13 she won the Los Angeles Women's Golf Championship on a course where a sign stated 'Children Under 14 Are Not Allowed.'

"Now at 22, Marlene Bauer Hagge stands at the head of the top women professionals in the world. It's certain that a truly great future is in store for her, possibly the greatest career ever in women's professional golf history."

Marlene did not quite achieve that heady forecast, but her continued success has been remarkable. The recipient of accolades through the years, she has awards ranging from Teenager, to Athlete, to Golfer, to Woman for whichever year it may have been.

She is an opinionated woman, whose statements sometimes seem purposefully made to shock or to be funny, which often they are. She almost glosses over her success, and she appears to have the world in very reasonable perspective. Her claim that the tour has not been her number one priority in life is hard to take seriously. Undoubtedly it provided a good living, and she put her continued appearance down to wanting the money and having faith in her continued ability to win.

The golfing Bauer sisters, Alice and Marlene, arrive in style at Forest Lake Country Club in Bloomfield Hills, Michigan, an early stop on the tour.

Alice and Marlene were very stylish at the fashion show connected with the 1958 Dallas Civitan Open, held at the Glen Lakes Country Club.

She was said to have been dominated by her father's goals throughout his lifetime (he died in 1958), with her golfing achievements never quite reaching the dizzy heights he set for her. "My father tried to start Alice playing golf at an early age and, finding her interested in other things, thought that he would get hold of me before I had time to become interested in anything else. I'm told I played a lot of golf. I won the Western and National Junior Tournaments at 15.

"There were not any junior golf programs when I was growing up, and girls generally were not very athletic at that time, so I played my golf with men or with older boys on golf teams. When I was ten, I won the Long Beach junior event.

"I don't think it's fair to say my father pushed me. When you're a teenager, you want to be out doing what the other kids are doing, and you feel left out if you are not. Golf was important in our lives, and my father was trying to do what he thought was best for me and for Alice, and I'm certain he was right. It was similar to a kid not wanting to stay home and practice the piano while the other kids are out having fun. I don't feel I missed anything important, and my father wanted us to be able to function independently and to be able to make a living.

"There was not any rivalry between Alice and me. Alice treated me more like a little daughter rather than being in competition with me, and I always looked up to her and wanted to be like her in everything. It was a good relationship.

"When we both turned professional in 1950, I was a month short of 17 and the youngest by far on tour. It didn't seem very difficult. My dad had always taught us to take things in our stride and not to get things out of the proper perspective. He gave us a pretty good set of values, and we were never carried away with all the publicity. We knew it was not real life, and it really wasn't.

"Alice and I were not rivals out on tour. I know it sounds strange, but we've always been very close." [Here, Marlene and Alice called to each other across the room.]

Marlene: "Alice, she keeps asking me what was the rivalry like, and I say there wasn't any."

Alice: "I was trying to beat everyone else, and if she beat me, fine. There wasn't any rivalry. I always say that in my family I have four children—my daughter, my son, my mother, and my sister."

Marlene: "That's what I told her, that you treated me more like your daughter.

"I don't think there was any particular reason for our marrying the same man—it just happened. It wasn't necessarily difficult, though it was strange for a while. It was just one of those things. Alice and Bob didn't get along, and he and I got together. I married at 21 and got divorced eight years later.

"You can work out anything if you want to, but the problem was that I got married too young and had no idea what it was all about, none whatsoever. Who knows why I did it, except that I thought I was madly in love. Why does anyone get married?

"I don't know whether I regret not having a family. That's a hard question. I suppose the answer is, not really. I do not have one; so I'm not going to sit around worrying about it or regretting it. I have been pleased with my life, and one cannot always have everything.

"Although I think I would have been a good

parent, I'm not one of those people who has said, 'Oh I'd just love to have children.' It probably sounds bad, but it isn't something that has left a great big void in my life.

"I've always enjoyed competition and had a pretty keen sense of pride, which made me carry on with my golf. I liked winning and enjoyed the self-satisfaction of doing something well. The reasons for playing varied at different times; sometimes I needed to make a living, sometimes it was fun, especially if you do well.

"My progress on tour was slower at first than everyone expected, but from 1956 my career went really well. I was only interested in playing golf and getting out of practicing, which I have always disliked.

"From the initial 13 players, the tour grew in spite of ourselves, and we seemed to make progress. Over the years I have been involved in the administration as vice-president, as secretary, and on the tournament and pairings committees. Now that the tour has grown and is really big, it was inevitable that it would be taken over like any growing corporation, and there are more pluses than minuses in the way that it is run. Sometimes it can be frustrating to be involved in something and not be able to have a say in the decision-making, but it does mean that you have all your time to pursue your golf, while the more intelligent business heads are running the organization.

"If there's one thing that has been difficult on tour, it is the forming of close relationships or friendships because there is so much competitiveness and you always think of yourself. As a group, the girls on tour are super, and there is less pettiness than in any group of women you could meet. We get along really well, but past a certain point, it is hard to be really close.

"The life on tour is a cop-out. It's easy to be out there. You have freedom of choice which appeals to a lot of people who join the tour, and you have control over your destiny, in that your life, your weeks, your hours are your own and you don't have to punch a time clock. You can choose what you do without the responsibility of living in a set little society, in a little corner of a little town. I was taught to believe in myself, to be smart enough not to rely on other people, and I consider myself fairly intelligent. I don't feel the need to follow the dictates of society.

Marlene Hagge started golf at the age of three and has been playing tournament golf for more than 45 years, winning 25 tournaments in a 20-year time span. Here, she is shown after winning the USGA Junior Golf Championship in 1949.

"The fanfare and apparent glamour of our form of show business are very false. If you start to believe your press clippings, you're in serious trouble because you can be up one day, down the next. The main thing is to stay on an even keel emotionally and mentally.

"You do that by not placing golf first. Even though I was on tour for many years, golf was never the number one priority in my life. Being a woman and a good and well-adjusted person, who has concern for other people, comes first. I think any man or woman who makes work his or her life is making a terrible mistake. I like to cook, sew, and do all the things normal people do. For me, trying to do the best I can in each given instance is what matters.

"The only reason I was able to be out on tour and remain sane for more than 40 years, is because golf has never been number one. If I'd eaten, drank, and slept golf, I'd be a burnt out shell. Golf was the best way I knew how to make my living, with an income from endorsements, representing a club, and from prize money.

"When you start out, you have confidence because you don't know the pitfalls, so it can be blind confidence from not having failed. Then you go through a phase when you know what it's all about, and after that it can be a vicious cycle to get back up again. You get locked in and have to tell yourself to trust your capabilities and not get scared, but it can be frustrating when you don't play up to your expectations and capabilities.

"I'm very fond of the LPGA, and it's been a big part of my life, but I don't feel a need for it. You can be mentally effective to the world and yourself without bringing in a paycheck or having a career—it depends on your inner resources whether you vegetate or not. If you feel you can't do without it, you have become a slave to it.

"Leaving the tour, you miss the very few friendships and the competition. Looking back over my career, I will always wish that I had won the Open, but I very rarely look back."

LPGA Victories: 1952 Sarasota Open. **1954** New Orleans Open. **1956** Sea Island Open, Clock Open, Babe Zaharias Open, Denver Open, Pittsburgh Open, LPGA Championship, World Championship, Triangle Round Robin. **1957** Babe Zaharias Open, Lawton Open. **1958** Lake Worth Open, Land of Sky Open. **1959** Mayfair Open, Hoosier Open. **1963** Sight Open. **1964** Mickey Wright Invitational. **1965** Babe Zaharias Open, Milwaukee Open, Phoenix Thunderbirds Open, Tall City Open, Alamo Open. 1969 Strohs-WBLY Open. **1972** Burdine's Invitational.

Marlene Hagge's LPGA Record

Year	No.of Events	Best Finish	Money	Rank	Scoring Average
1956	23	1	$20,235	1	74.87
1957	25	1	10,260	6	75.48
1958	24	1	11,890	6	75.01
1959	26	1	12,056	4	75.40
1960	25	T3	7,208	16	75.83
1961	16	3	8,245	13	75.94
1962	24	3	6,777	17	76.31
1963	32	1	13,570	8	75.48
1964	32	1	18,843	5	73.78
1965	33	1	21,532	2	73.39
1966	31	2	10,117	15	75.57
1967	27	T8	6,189	22	75.44
1968	26	20	9,449	22	75.45
1969	23	1	15,469	15	75.38
1970	19	T4	7,474	24	74.76
1971	21	2	16,514	10	74.40
1972	30	1	26,318	11	74.24
1973	32	2	24,777	16	74.82
1974	28	T6	16,053	29	75.02
1975	24	T6	11,020	40	74.98
1976	28	3	24,154	24	75.01
1977	23	T25	4,831	76	76.30
1978	28	T4	15,837	48	75.35
1979	31	T4	26,812	40	74.90
1980	31	T15	15,151	66	75.29
1981	27	T10	24,770	56	74.41
1982	26	10	10,826	93	75.40
1983	28	T29	7,527	115	75.74
1984	26	7	14,865	102	75.21
1985	29	T21	8,377	128	75.97
1986	20	T34	7,125	134	75.82
1987	23	T26	7,153	135	75.88
1988	25	T35	7,590	145	75.62
1989	18	T28	2,236	168	76.64
1990	21	T57	1,805	179	76.82
1991	NA	NA	NA	NA	NA
1992	9	T63	630	199	77.32
1993	7	NA	722	187	76.25

Peggy Kirk Bell

Peggy Kirk Bell is a wonderful raconteur, a pioneer woman, a early member of the LPGA tour in the 1950s who flew her own airplane: "When I went to buy it, I chose the best looking plane, but when I found it was too slick for a learner, I chose one which was the color I liked best."

Tall and striking, with the cheekbones of a Katharine Hepburn, Peggy is a religious woman who was a close friend of Babe Zaharias. Although Peggy won tournaments as an amateur, she never had a professional victory, overawed by her admiration for Babe.

She married Warren (Bullet) Bell in 1953, and had three children, at first combining tour golf with raising a family. With pioneer teaching professional Ellen Griffin, she started "Golfaris" at Pine Needles golf course in North Carolina in the 1960s. Her husband died in 1984 of stomach cancer, having had heart bypass surgery previously, but Peggy remains at Pine Needles, host of the 1996 U.S. Women's Open. There she and her family carry on their flourishing business.

I first met Peggy in Florida in the early 1980s and interviewed her at someone's home where she was staying. It was an hilarious session, full of humorous, fascinating stories, and after we talked, Peggy donned a wig, which she said she needed to wear in order to go to some function. I told her, with cheekbones like hers the wig was superfluous, and she put it aside.

She invited me to Pine Needles, where I went to stay in 1983, enjoying her hospitality and company. The description of the round of golf I played with her and Wiffi Smith can be found in the chapter on Wiffi. It was one of the memorable days of my life.

"I was born and grew up in Findlay, Ohio, with a twin brother and a sister, two years older. My father owned oil wells and a wholesale grocery business, so we were an upper income family.

"I was a tomboy, the best high school athlete in basketball and other sports. I didn't play golf until after I graduated at 17, when I stopped going to summer camp in New Hampshire. I went to Findlay Golf and Country Club, two miles from home, tried playing golf, and lost all three of my golf balls before I reached the first green.

"I walked back in, asked for a teacher, and, pointing to my golf club, asked, 'How do you hold this thing?' Leonard Schmulte, the professional, said, 'Do you want a lesson tomorrow?' 'No,' I said, 'I am going to learn it all today.' After the lesson I told him I would play golf all summer, and he helped me without ever charging me a penny. It was the toughest challenge I'd ever faced, but I practiced every day till dark, I came along fast and won the club championship the following year.

"When I went to Sargent Physical Education College in Boston, I played in the first National Intercollegiate tournament, in Columbus, Ohio. There were about 30 girls; I had a 92, the worst score; and I met Patty Berg, who gave a clinic.

"I was in awe of Patty, who gave me a golf ball and asked me to give her a ride back to the hotel. My dad had bought me a Packard convertible, which was a really sharp car, and after Patty Berg sat on the front seat, I wouldn't let anyone sit there for a week.

"I transferred colleges, to Rollins in Florida, which was lovely, small, and had its own golf course. By 1942 I had a two handicap; I graduated in 1943 and worked for my father because it was the middle of the war and there were not any golf tournaments. It was also the time that women became more independent and started to get into business.

"Golf started again in 1946 and at the Western Open in Chicago, I met Babe [Zaharias]. I had heard about her, and I couldn't wait to see her. I watched her on the practice tee and couldn't believe how far she hit the ball.

"I was in the locker room when she came in, saw me, and said, 'Come on, kid, I'll play you at gin.' I said I didn't know how to play, and she said she would teach me. She dealt out, told me what to do, and after four hands said I owed her $12.50. I said I didn't know I was playing for money, and I never let her forget how she took advantage of an innocent young admirer.

"We became friendly, and she visited our home. Babe, who loved older people, called my dad 'Pop,' and she would stay up playing rummy with him until two in the morning. If she lost, she would stay until she won.

"She called me up one day and said, 'I need a partner for that Hollywood Fourball in Florida, and you might as well win a tournament.' We played three other tournaments in Florida, all of which Babe won, beating me in the final in the first one. I became a nervous wreck at the thought of the Hollywood tournament and told her, 'You've won the first three. Now, if you lose this one, it will be my fault.' She said, 'I can beat any two of them. I'll let you know if I need you.' So I relaxed.

"Babe and I got to the final, which was played over 36 holes, against Louise Suggs and Jean Hopkins, who were three up after 18 holes. We had it back to all square after the 33rd, and at the 35th it was getting really dark so that by the last hole the car headlights were on. There was a huge gallery, thousands of people, who were getting really excited, and when I knocked the ball on the final green in two, someone ran up and took it. Babe was on in two, Louise Suggs was in a bunker, and Jean Hopkins out of bounds. Babe called the match, saying it was too dark, which meant we had to play another 18 holes the next day.

"We played pretty well. I chipped and putted well, and we beat them by three and two. Louise Suggs, who was very proper and knew the rules better than anyone, hated Babe. Louise was a great golfer who was overshadowed by Babe's personality. I guess there are people in sports who don't like each other, and Babe's loudness and bluff scared some people. I always felt I didn't deserve to beat her.

Peggy Kirk Bell, a wonderful raconteur and early member of the LPGA, today lives and works at Pine Needles, in North Carolina, where she and her family carry on their flourishing business.

"Babe would play up to the press by coming in after a practice round and telling them she'd shot 70. When I would say later, you didn't have 70, she'd reply, 'Well, that's what they want to hear.' She was a real live wire, always on stage. Even when she was eating, she would be doing tricks with the silver. She was also a social climber, who liked to be seen in the company of doctors and lawyers at country clubs.

"She thrived on competition, was used to winning, and competed all the time. Physically she did everything well. She was always very confident, and when we arrived somewhere and unpacked, she would hang up an outfit and say, 'This is what I'm going to wear in the finals.' She made that kind of statement because she felt that way. If you have enough success you become confident. She was so strong, hit the ball farther than any woman I've seen, and sometimes would lose her balance because she hit it so hard. It could be tough on the other girls and not everyone loved her.

"After I won with her in Florida, she said, 'Once you win one, it's easy.' I went on to win the 1947 Ohio State Championship, later completing a hat trick. In 1948, I won three tournaments in Florida, in 1950 I was on the Curtis Cup team, and I played in the 1949 British Amateur, where I reached the quarter-finals.

"In June 1947, Babe turned professional for the second time, after winning 17 U.S. tournaments in a row and the British Amateur Championship. In 1948, Fred Corcoran, with the backing of the Wilson Sporting Goods Company, started organizing professional tournaments for the women. You felt like women's pro golf was going somewhere, and Babe encouraged me to turn professional. Spalding offered to pay me to do something that I would have paid to do, and when I became a professional in 1950, I signed a good contract with Spalding, doing clinics, sometimes 30 a month, and visiting stores where the clubs were sold. I have been with them ever since.

"I turned professional to play with the best. I didn't need the money, since my dad had set me up with a good income of more than $10,000 from stocks and property, which made me feel guilty. I handled it badly in my first season playing amateur tournaments, when I bought a new Cadillac 3500. By the end of the year, I couldn't pay my taxes and my dad had to bail me out. I grew up a bit after that.

"Right after I turned professional, I was playing a tournament in New Orleans, paired with Gloria Armstrong, then an amateur, and I told her I was dreading the drive to the West Coast in the car, even though it was a great big Cadillac convertible. In those days no one flew on airlines, and Gloria, who had her own plane in California, told me: 'You buy a plane. I'll fly it to California and teach you on the way. If you can drive a car, you can fly a plane.' I said, 'How neat.'

"I was playing in Dallas the following week, and she told me I could buy a plane at the airport. Gloria went with me, and I saw this Beech Bonanza, the best looking plane, and I said to the guy, 'I'll have that one.' Gloria said, 'You can't because it's too fast and slick to learn on, and I can't fly it either.' So I chose another, a top wing Cessna 170, because I liked the color.

"Gloria, trying to save me some money, told me I didn't need the radio and extra equipment, and she had it all taken out. I thought the radio was for music, and I didn't care whether I listened to music or not. I got the plane for $6,000, wrote the check, and off we went.

"We got up in the air, and I got so sick I told her to land the thing. I guess it was nerves; it was a little scary. Gloria told me to learn to do the charts and said, 'That's a river' and so on. When we got to California and came in to land, she said, 'You circle the tower—can you believe all this?—and they flash a light because they know you don't have a radio. They flash it green for landing or red to keep circling.'

"I am red/green color blind, so I said, 'I see the light but I'm darned if I know what color it is. Is that what the radio is for?' She said, 'Yes.' When we had landed, I had to pay $1,500 to get a radio put back. It was far more expensive than if I had left the original one in.

"I took about ten flying lessons and got a student license, which did not allow me to take a passenger—I could kill only myself until I passed the full test. I did some three point cross country flying, learned to navigate, land, take off, and fill up with gas.

"After my lessons, I had to get to New York to play in a Weathervane team tournament, so I told myself, 'Now you've got to fly it or sell it,' and I decided to fly home to Findlay. I took off, and because I wasn't very slick at landing and I bounced the plane, which made me feel sick, I stayed up until I got near Ohio. On the way, I climbed over a big mountain near Denver, going up and up until I got sleepy, my nose began bleeding, and I realized I was almost ready to pass out because I wasn't getting enough oxygen.

"A little while later, I was flying along, listening to my radio, and a guy was talking about a jet stream at such and such a height, which I didn't realize was an air current that takes you along faster. I thought it was a jet airplane streaming across the country. Eventually, I came down near Ohio because I needed gas, and finally I got home and went on to New York.

"It was amazing. You could do what you liked in those days. Some years later, I was flying, and I got in a snowstorm—you didn't have the same forecasting then—and I prayed to God. I said, 'You get me down, and I'll sell the plane.' I was flying along a railroad track, and I couldn't see anything except a field to the left. So I dumped the plane and walked to find a house.

"I called Bullet (I was married by then with kids) and said, 'I'm going to sell my plane.' He said, 'You can't leave it there. Wait a few days and fly home.' I said, 'You're trying to kill me. The Lord got me down, and I'm going to sell it. But I waited, flew home in a rainstorm, and enjoyed the experience."

In 1953, Peggy married Warren Bell, a former professional basketball player, with whom she had grown up, and who, following an injury, had gone to work for Spalding as a salesman. When they married, they bought a share in the Pine Needles development. Professional Julius Boros and his family bought them out two years later. Their first child, a daughter, was born in October 1954.

"Babe was a good friend, and she wanted to be there when our first baby was born. She was in Washington, when all of a sudden I had the baby. Babe got on a train, and Bullet picked her up and brought her to the hospital. The White House called, trying to locate Babe, who was supposed to be at a Republican dinner. She told them she had left Washington because her friend was having a baby. Babe organized photos at the hospital for the press; she set it all up, and said to the doctor, 'Come on, have your photo taken with the baby. You did a good job.' I was so embarrassed.

"Then Babe said, 'What are you going to name her? You're going to call her after me, aren't you?' I said, 'I can't stand the name Mildred, and neither can you, Babe.' 'Call her Babe,' she said. 'She's got to have a name,' I replied. 'Well, we've got to find something that looks good in print,' said Babe. We thought and thought. I had imagined it was going to be a boy, and we'd call him Kirk Bell. My family came from Scotland, so I said, 'How about Heather?' 'No,' said Babe, 'Bonnie Bell! That will look great in print.' Everything Babe did, she thought of the press."

Peggy had three children after Bonnie, her second daughter. Peggy, was born in 1958 and son Kirk in 1962. She played tournaments whenever she could, combining it with home and family until the early 1960s: "Bullet said he saved me from the tour, but I loved it out there. You get a lot of attention, you're spoiled, and I considered myself lucky because everyone wanted me to come and stay with them—the attitude to women professionals was awfully nice.

"There was only one woman professional in my day who said anything about being 'queer.' I'd never heard of it and didn't understand it, but she made some strong statements, and I didn't go near her. It isn't all right. I've got it in my Bible where God says that it is wrong." [Here, Peggy fetched a Bible.] "I go to Bible Study Fellowship every Wednesday, and I study the Bible every day. I guess I've always been religious. I was brought up Presbyterian, and my grandfather was a Presbyterian minister. In Romans, chapter 1, under 'The Downward Course of Man,' in verses 26 and 27 it says: 'For even their women did change the natural use into that which is against nature. And likewise also the men, leaving the natural use of the woman, burned in their lust one toward another.'

"I'm not being a judge because I'm not supposed to judge, but I think it is against God's word, that God didn't make woman to be with woman or man to be with man. They're not Christians because you can't love anything more than God; He's number one, then your husband and family. You can get over those things and the women on tour are lazy.

"I'm so dumb about all that stuff, I can't understand what goes on. A lot of girls travel together and are not queer. They are good friends who get along and don't want to live alone—friends in a rut. If some guy came along, they'd probably go with him. They would love to have a guy, but they're into golf. They're not 'that way.' It's just lonely out there. In my day over half the tour members were married. Many of the girls were dating, there were plenty of men to go out with, and you didn't have to sleep with them. We had fun. Babe played the harmonica in the bar every night, Betty [Dodd] played the guitar, and the Bauer sisters sang.

"I played with Babe in her last round of golf at Tampa. She got out of bed and wore loafers because she couldn't get her shoes on. We played the first hole, and she said: 'You've got to be the greatest golfer I've ever seen.' 'Why?' I asked. 'To hit it only this far and break 100. I don't know how you girls do it.' Of course, Babe was way past me when she was well, and she was still a long hitter, but her illness had weakened her.

"I went to see her once in Texas when she was sick and really thin. She was fighting. She never said to me she was going to die, but she did tell Bullet she wasn't going to make it.

"I was a good friend of Babe's and of her husband George, and they knew that. I tried to keep them happy together, but if you are married, you understand that couples argue a little bit and then patch it up. George's whole life was Babe, and although their relationship deteriorated because she was sick, if Babe had been healthy they would still have been together.

"Babe really loved George. He could get out of control because of his drinking—he was a big man, and I remember one time when he twisted my arm in fun, I thought he had broken it. He didn't realize his own strength. George was good to Babe, taking her out of baseball where she was pretty rough, into golf, where some of those rough edges were smoothed down. He had some money when they married, and then she made a lot of money later.

"My own career as a professional never really took off. I never won a tournament, which was tough. I felt I could play everyone except Babe. I wanted to be good at the game. I've always loved it and been sincere about it.

"When we went to Pine Needles, I had to teach golf. The first lesson I gave I told this woman, 'You've got to grip it right', and then I kept her there at least two and a half hours until finally she asked if she could leave. I told her everything I knew, and I didn't know a whole lot. Every time she swung the club, I would change something and give her a new thought. I reckoned I had to teach her in one day, get her ready for the tour in one lesson. I often wondered what happened to that woman; I think probably she quit.

"Later, I became a more experienced teacher, and with Ellen Griffin, who was the educated and dedicated authority on teaching, I began the first three-day golf schools for women. We then developed summer camp golf for young people. Ellen helped me set up Golfaris at Pine Needles where 60 women would come at a time. It was exciting, and it was also easy for me to be with my family."

Peggy has packed a lot into her productive life in a kind of organized chaos. "It's been a little more versatile than some," she says. Playing in the inaugural 1987 Marilynn Smith Founders' Classic in Dallas was a memorable highlight about which Peggy says: "There will never be another week like that. We spent so much time talking, laughing and saying to each other, 'You can't play either.' It was just great for all of us."

Highlight Victories: 1944 Florida Mixed Two-Ball (with Herb Smith). **1946** Florida Mixed Two-Ball (with Joe Kirkwood, Sr.). **1947** Ohio State Championship, Hollywood Four-Ball (T1). **1948** Ohio State Championship, Toledo District Championship, Everglades Championship (with Ted Berghaus), Florida Mixed Two-Ball (with Carl Dann). **1949** Ohio State Championship, North and South Championship, Titleholders Championship. **1950** Eastern Amateur.

Betty Dodd

Betty Dodd was the daughter of a general and the grand-daughter of a major general. She was a tall, impressive woman, with something of a military bearing: "My father, who was born in 1899, was a West Point graduate headed for a military career. Everything he did, I wanted to do, although I never wanted to go into the Army. He was a five handicap golfer, a big influence on me, and if he hadn't wanted me to play golf, I wouldn't have done it. He was the dominant member of the family.

"Father became a general and went to Korea in 1952 to get a command. While he was waiting for it, he was sent to Ko jima Island where there were 175,000 prisoners of war, a mixture of Korean Communists and anti-Communists, and he was supposed to sort out their politics.

"He was concerned about the killings in the camps, and it was a very touchy situation. He was there a long time, and one day the prisoners captured him and held him hostage for four days, negotiating concessions, which were granted, and he was freed. Afterwards, no one would admit giving the order to grant the concessions.

"My father was vindicated by a board from Washington who said he'd done a marvelous job; then General Mark Clark went to Korea to take General Ridgeway's job, who in turn took Eisenhower's job in Europe.

"Clark was furious at the rumpus and busted my father. They took away his star, and we returned to San Antonio where they put him in a menial job. It was horrible, and he retired soon after, totally destroyed.

"Major General Watlington tried to get my father's star back, and the year after my father died in 1973, they posthumously gave him back his star. My mother, who died in 1961 at age 53 of cancer, was the daughter of a major general in San Antonio.

Betty Dodd's golf game often took a backseat to the care and attention she gave Babe Zaharias during her battle against cancer. After leaving the tour in 1967, Betty remained in San Antonio, Texas, teaching golf everyday until she died in 1993.

My father's dishonor was very hard for her since she was deep-seated military."

Betty Dodd had not only a dominant father figure in her life, she also had a close and happy relationship with the most dominant of all LPGA women golfers, Babe Zaharias. The two of them became a musical duo. Betty sang and played the guitar, and Babe played the harmonica. On one occasion, Louise Suggs was less than pleased when they burst forth musically just as she was putting on the 18th green. When Babe was dying of cancer, she and Betty made a record, which was sold to raise money for cancer research. Betty's voice was considered so deep that she was asked to sing an octave higher.

"It was during the time that I was playing my very best golf," Betty said, "that I dropped off tour to take care of Babe. She got sick in 1953, died in 1956, and most of the time I was with her. She was such a strong, fantastic individual, who didn't trust anyone but me. I knew she wasn't going to live. They told me that at the beginning. I was always concerned about her and only went to a few tournaments.

"I didn't win anything until after she died. She wasn't going to be mad if I won, but I didn't realize that being involved with Babe hurt my golf game a great deal. It's a terrible thing to say about yourself, but later I realized I could have been an outstanding golfer.

"When we were playing a tournament, I would get off the 18th and run and see what Babe was doing; it can be very bad to be emotionally involved with someone. Babe would never have been that concerned about my golf. If I did well, okay, but it was a disaster if she didn't do well.

"If I'd been tougher or more selfish, I could have done a hell of a lot better. I don't regret it one bit. People have said I could have been one of the top players and asked me whether I was sorry. Yes, I'm sorry, but I don't regret my relationship at all. I'm sorry I wasn't a better player."

Betty Dodd was a fascinating woman with great stories to tell, and gives a completely different perspective on Babe Zaharias from Babe's other great friend, Peggy Kirk Bell.

I telephoned Betty in San Antonio, asking to see her on my researching travels. She warmly agreed and was wonderfully hospitable. I spent many hours at her home, riveted by her personality as she entertained me with her anecdotes, as well as dinner.

Betty was born in Portland, Oregon, the second of two children, having a sister fifteen months older. Her mother was an excellent horsewoman. "My sister and I were at high school in San Antonio, where I have lived all my life except for 18 months we spent in Germany. I was 15, and I had a ball since there was no school to go to. All I did was ski in the Bavarian Alps, or I played tennis and

Betty's father, General Dodd, was a five-handicap golfer and a big influence on her life.

dreamed of being a tennis professional. There was a nine hole golf course, and I had played a bit on an Army course, but tennis was my first love.

"When I returned to San Antonio, tennis was not a big deal; golf was. My handicap came down. I won some local tournaments and went alone by train to a few bigger ones.

"My father, who played a bit of golf, never quit telling me what to do and how to do it. He never let me alone, and I think it hurt me. He would object if I didn't practice, and we got into some terribly heated arguments since we were both very opinionated. Everything I wanted to do he knocked, so eventually I didn't do any of the things he criticized, and I always asked him what to do.

"I had a fear of failure because of his attitude and would have done a lot better without thinking about his reaction to everything. He kept interfering because I was his daughter. He loved me and wanted to be sure everything was all right. Until the day he died, I continued to ask him what to do and let him know everything I was thinking of doing. It was pretty silly.

"I met Babe in 1950 in Miami, where I was playing amateur tournaments. I was pretty much in awe of Babe, who was the outstanding paragon of golf. When I first saw her, her hair was dyed red, she was wearing a robin's egg blue suit with eyes that matched, and she was outstanding. She was not good looking, but she was strong and striking. The minute I saw her, I knew that had to be the Babe. We were introduced, and we struck it off right away, becoming friends from that moment.

"Babe talked me into turning professional, which I did in 1952 at 21. Betsy Rawls and I won the Hollywood Fourball, and after the National Open, Babe called my father and told him I should be a professional, and he agreed.

"I thought it was great since I wanted to be out there playing golf. I never thought about being famous because I was running around with the most famous person in the whole game, which in a lot of ways built up my confidence.

"Babe was a bit crude and rough at times, which went against my upbringing, but I would sit back and think, 'That's just Babe who hasn't had the advantages of other people.'

"There will never be another person like her. She could be a bit extreme. I remember one time she threw a guy to the ground. I'd never seen a woman do that. We were sitting in a clubhouse bar in Miami, where we were playing a tournament, and a short but well-built man with big shoulders slapped Babe on the back. She hadn't played well, and she cut him off curtly. He didn't like it, carried on, and she tried to ignore him, but he would not let her.

"Babe turned round and said: 'I'll have to do something about you if you don't go away.' He replied: 'You'll have to get George, that big, fat husband of yours,' and she told him she didn't need anyone to help her. She had her knee in his neck so fast, flipped the fellow onto his back, and left him there in a state of shock. She walked off to the locker room with her beer. No one else could do that and get away with it.

"Babe tried not to appear a strong woman, since women were not supposed to be like that. A lot of bad things were said about her, but physically she was a mighty person. She had phenomenal forearms like a man and unusually developed upper arms. She didn't watch her diet, and sometimes she was a bit heavy. Generally she was socially accepted and well liked, and she learned how to be more feminine. We were all in skirts then, but Babe on an impulse would leap hedges like a horse. She could run like a rocket or heave a baseball so hard that catching it was very painful.

"Her incredible co-ordination and physical strength gave her an adequate golf swing which was not good looking, but she made square contact, and she had finesse out of this world for any soft chipping or putting. She didn't win by hitting drives 300 yards, since she was in trouble more often than anyone else, but she was so sure of her ability that out of a trap it was like someone throwing the ball in the hole. She could hit a wedge off a concrete slab, and she was deadly from six feet.

"I'm sorry I didn't know about her Olympic achievements. I saw the medals in a cigar box. I never asked her, and she never talked about them. She never said anything unkind about anyone, nor did she gossip about people who put her down.

"She was full of ability and knew she could beat other people, many of whom would say: 'I don't want to be another Babe Didrikson. She's a freak.' Babe did so much for golf and became such a big

Betty and Babe Zaharias were a musical duo, with Betty on guitar and Babe on the harmonica. They even appeared on the "Ed Sullivan Show".

personality that the Queen of England would have said, 'Come in for tea.'

"On tour Louise Suggs hated her and made it very obvious, while Betsy Rawls liked her. Betty Jameson couldn't stand her and went into rigor mortis when her name was mentioned. Then Babe had a colostomy in 1953, and Betty did a complete turnaround and adored her. She wrote a letter of admiration and asked for help with her golf game. With Betty it's all black or white.

"When I turned professional in 1952, Babe was 37 and old enough to be my mother. I didn't look on her as an idol, but I admired her ability and athleticism. She figured I was more fun than some other people, and she didn't spend much time with anyone else except George, who interfered all the time. He was always there, and mostly they didn't get along too well. George got livid if she tried to do anything on her own, for fear of losing control over her.

"Babe was not socially sure of herself, but George was an unacceptable thug, who would barge in anywhere and not care what people said or thought. Babe was sensitive enough to care about how he behaved, even if she acted as though she didn't.

"When they first got involved, she felt confident around him because he said, 'You're the greatest, the best.' At the time she admired this quality in him, but later she came to hate it. I think she loved him, or thought that she did, when she married him. I couldn't say that for absolute fact, but I truly feel she loved him, maybe because she thought he could take care of her or she felt safe with him.

"Babe was afraid of George because he was liable to kill her—not that she would have made such a strong statement. But he was a really mean guy. She was physically afraid of him, and while 'kill' may be a little strong, he was liable to beat her up.

"When they were on their honeymoon in Australia, he had booked her at a bunch of golf exhibitions every day for three to four weeks, and she didn't even know about them. He told her when they arrived at the hotel. She got mad and said she was on her honeymoon and didn't want to be on the golf course every single damned day.

"They got into an argument, and he stopped the elevator between floors and beat the hell out of her, bruising her so badly that they had to go and have her made up to play golf and appear in public. If he did that once, I'm sure he was capable of doing it again, but she didn't say a lot about anything or anybody.

"As time went by, it got worse between George and Babe. The movie called *The Babe Zaharias Story* was enough to make you sick with all the lovey dovey stuff it included. If you were involved with them, you realized what a bunch of garbage it was. People were constantly phoning me to know if this or that scene were true. When I saw it a second time I got even more angry, but then it occurred to me that they do it with all films of 'true stories.'

"George saw Babe as his bread and butter, but to hear him talk, he had made all the money with his wrestling. If he made any money, he would throw it away. He was the kind of guy who would get drunk in a bar and someone would say; 'you've got $20,000, I'm going to let you invest in this professional ball team,' and he would. He lost his shirt on the Los Angeles Rams, also on a couple of hotels in Los Angeles that were fire traps, and a flea bag operation in Denver. Then he found Babe, who was a commodity.

"In 1953 when Babe had her cancer operation, she became more famous than you can imagine, since it was so highly publicized. She and I went to New York, and all of the talk shows wanted her to appear. She wouldn't appear for less than $1,000, and she made $10,000 for cancer societies in four days. She even appeared on the Ed Sullivan show. I played the guitar, she played the harmonica, and it was a lot of fun.

"Then we went to Canada where she played an exhibition, and I've never seen so many people in my life. You would have thought it was the National Open and the Masters combined. The crowds were unreal, and they were all there for her.

"All of a sudden a bell rang, and she realized she had the ability to make money and didn't need George. He would have sold her cheap, but she wanted to see how much she could get. He was always phoning, and they had traumatic conversations, which made her mad. When he realized what was happening, he didn't like it a bit.

"When Babe was dying, a wealthy stockbroker

friend, Janet Olson, who had invested some money for her, called me and said she had a check for $12,000 from investments for Babe, and she wanted to send it to someone so George didn't get it. I told Babe, who said she wanted her sister Lily to have it, but George found the check and that was it.

"One day in the hospital, he hit her intravenous tube, and she yelled at him to get out. She said, 'The goddamned son of a bitch is trying to kill me.' He went out like a scolded dog, with his tail between his legs. For a long time she didn't think she would die; she thought she would get out of hospital and get divorced. 'I'm not going to live with that man for the rest of my life,' she said.

Betty Dodd grew up playing golf on a military course, but tennis was her first love until she won some local tournaments in San Antonio a few years later.

"Others will tell you it would never have happened. Bertha and Aureol Bowen, from Fort Worth, who were wealthy, social, and influential people, and who helped her at 18 and became like her adopted parents, said there was no way they would have been divorced, there was too strong a tie between them. And who knows? It could well have been true.

"At first George didn't like me and was extremely jealous of me, but when Babe got sick, he loved me. He didn't want to be bothered with nurses and hospitals, and she had to have someone to take care of her. It was beyond him to do that. He was never by her side in the hospital. He was gone because he couldn't take the fact she had cancer. The colostomy was distasteful to him, and he took off like a big bird.

"The day she had her colostomy operation they brought her back to the recovery room, and the doctor told George and me that she had come through well, but they had found cancer elsewhere and she probably wouldn't live long. George cried and blubbered, hung around for four days, and then went to Denver. He never told Babe where he went. He would just reappear, and she resented his behavior.

"The first time Babe was ill in 1952, she had a hernia operation, which was nothing to do with cancer. Then in January 1953 she told me about her rectal bleeding, which I said was a danger signal of cancer, and she turned snow white. Her doctor in Beaumont said it didn't sound too bad and that she should see him when she got into town. She was completely relieved, since she wasn't going to Beaumont for five months. When we got there, she won the tournament and looked like death warmed over. If she had gone to a doctor right away, she might have been here today.

"I went back to San Antonio, where Babe called me and told me in a quivering voice that she had cancer and asked me to come to Fort Worth. I told her that I'd be there the next day. On the way, a truck hit my brand new car from behind, and it had to be towed in. Babe was transferred to a hospital in Beaumont, and I got on a plane and was with her from then on.

"She was terrified of the colostomy because she didn't know what it was. I knew someone who had had one; so I explained it to her. She got over the surgery quickly and started to play golf two months later. By special concession I played every round with her in the All American Open, since she wasn't sure what was going to happen and wanted me there. She coped very well but did not play well. Her putting was so bad that eventually she broke down, started to cry, and walked away. I said, 'You can quit. You don't have to go on. Everyone will understand.' But she finished way down the field. The following week she finished third, after taking nine on the 18th hole of the final round, where three times she bladed the ball into the Des Plains River in front of the green.

"I coped with the colostomy. I irrigated it every other day, and it was like nothing, like washing someone's face. At first it made her feel sick, but we made a big game out of it. It didn't bother me. Millions of nurses do it every day. If it hadn't been for me, I don't know what she would have done because George was gone.

"After the operation she returned to normal health and strength for a time because she was so strong. She lost weight, gained it back, looked marvelous, as though she could beat the world. She won two tournaments in 1953, five in 1954, including the National Open by twelve shots, and two more in 1955.

"In March 1955 we got the car stuck in sand one evening. We dug it out, but it got stuck again. We were digging again, when a guy who saw Babe, said to his friend, 'I ain't never seen a woman dig like that before.' Two days later Babe's back was so bad, she couldn't think straight. It was the beginning of the end.

"I got acute appendicitis and needed an operation; so I left Babe with her sister Lily in Beaumont. Peggy Kirk Bell, with whom I was friendly through Babe, took me to the hospital. Four days later she flew me out to Buffalo and I felt as though I'd been run over by a truck. When I was recovering, Babe, who was in hospital in Galveston, wanted me to come there. She was in bad shape. I flew into Houston at midnight, took a cab 40 miles, and found her in terrible pain. She was never all right after that.

"The doctor went on vacation, after telling her she was hooked on drugs. She wouldn't take any more, but the pain was tremendous, and she went nuts. She was screaming, shaking, and ringing bells, and a psychiatrist came and said she needed the drugs for her cancer pain. Ten days later, the lesions in the sacrum started to show.

"Babe went from the hospital to play tournaments a couple of times, and I gave her pain killing injections. I was a strong, healthy girl, and I took the emotional knocks, knowing she was going to die. She had tremendous courage and would never admit she was dying. I don't know whether she knew, since the doctors didn't tell her she was terminal. For her that was probably the right thing to do. They let her hope, but she must have known toward the end and wished she didn't have to go through any more. It seemed to me there were a lot of unnecessary things. She had a bowel obstruction, and they operated, but it never healed, and she lived another six weeks, which were pretty gross.

"Babe made me leave and go back on tour when she realized she didn't have much chance to live. She said, 'I think you should play some tournaments. I'll be all right.' I knew what was going to happen. I hated to leave, but I knew she was right. I had to go.

"I flew back to see her ten days before she died, and she only just knew me. It was fleeting. I stayed two or three days and left. When she died, my reaction was one of total relief. I was completely exhausted.

"I didn't go to the funeral—we had pre-arranged that—she didn't want me to go. I don't know why, but she made me promise not to and said she wouldn't go to mine. I'd done all I could when she was alive and felt it wasn't necessary for me to go. I was physically exhausted and slept for three days.

"They say her funeral in Beaumont was really something. The church was packed to the gills, and there was a procession the whole length of the city. They cremated and buried her, and George

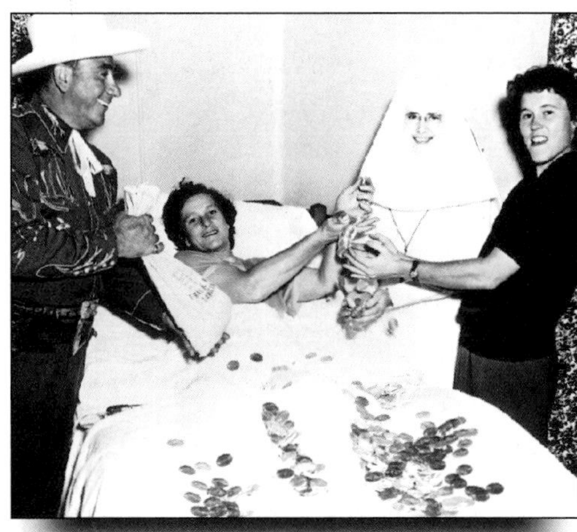

A hospitalized Babe Zaharias, her husband George, and Betty display money raised for the Damon Runyan cancer fund. Betty took care of Babe until her death in 1956.

had her mother and father exhumed from California and buried next to her, which I guess was the nicest thing he had ever done. I'm sure it would have pleased her, since she was crazy about both her parents. They were as close as you can get, that Didrikson family."

In 1956 and 1957 Betty had her first victories on the LPGA tour: "It was very exciting. I might have had some notion that I shouldn't win while Babe was alive, but I didn't win for her or so that she would have been proud of me. I didn't do it for Babe; I did it for me. And, I didn't think winning was sensational, or I might have won more. I played too well to think I was lucky in my first win in the Lawton Open in Oklahoma.

It had been raining for a week, and I shot 67 in the last round, over 6,800 yards, breaking the course record. Winning should have meant more. I thought it was great, but it didn't tear my insides out when I didn't win. There was a time when I had more course records, including a 64, than anyone. But, I was so inconsistent that under pressure I could easily blow it.

"In 1959 I was playing golf and walking down a hill when I twisted my ankle, cracked it, and spent six weeks in a cast. I injured it again in 1960 playing basketball, and if I did anything, it would turn black. My ligaments were gone. I had an operation, but I was through with golf. It was four years before I could hit a ball without it killing me.

"I had some money from my touring days, some money I inherited, and I returned to San Antonio to teach golf. At first I didn't enjoy it because I didn't know enough, and it scared me. I was so unsure that I didn't know if I was helping or hurting my pupils. When I got more involved and learned about the swing, I enjoyed it. I have a very fast eye, and I got into the mechanics of the golf swing.

"In 1967 I played a tournament, and they were going to give me my tour card if I finished in the top three. I shot a 67 and a 71 for the first two rounds. I couldn't believe it. In round three I went out of bounds twice and shot 75, but in the final round, it was as though I had never seen a golf course in my life. I blew it with an 83. I was more disappointed than ever before. It was a nightmare, a total shock, and a bad disappointment.

"When I came off tour I missed the girls I had been close to for so many years. I knew all the girls on tour. I knew their mothers, fathers, sisters, brothers, and cousins. I knew everything about them like a big happy family. If anyone on the outside said anything about anyone on the inside, I would go to bat for them.

"I enjoyed the fun of tour life. I loved playing cards and playing the guitar, although I don't play well—I was self taught. I got a beautiful guitar from Peggy and Bullet Bell. Peggy and I were walking down a street in Syracuse, New York, in 1955, when I saw a guitar in a music store window and said to Peggy, 'Isn't it gorgeous? You can buy it for me. Put your club name, Pine Needles, on it, and I'll advertise it for you.' I was kidding, and Peggy told me it cost $750 and the case another $150, and I could forget it. A week later, in comes Peggy with the guitar, with my name and Pine Needles on it. I've still got it. I've had it re-finished. It's the same one Elvis Presley played in old movies, and I've taken really good care of it."

Betty Dodd remained in San Antonio until her death in 1993, "teaching golf every damned day." Her devotion to Babe and her depth of feeling remained after all the years. She told me excitedly on the telephone in June 1988: "The largest ever Sea World was brought to San Antonio recently. In the acres of ground there is a Texas Walk, where there are 18 statues of famous Texans, and Babe is one of them. She is the only sports figure, and they invited me to the unveiling. When I arrived, the man who did the sculptures came up to me, introduced himself, and asked me to unveil Babe's statue. I did, and when I saw the statue I was amazed because it is so realistic. It looks exactly like her. It is wonderful."

LPGA Victories: 1956 Lawton Open. **1957** Colonial Open.

Betsy Rawls

In the 1950s, professionals Betsy Rawls and Betty Hicks sometimes traveled together on the LPGA tour. Betty Hicks recalls: "I'll never forget running out of gas in a swamp in New Orleans, and I was elected to go to a gas station. I had to hitch a ride with a truck driver, while Betsy sat in the car reading Will Durant's *The Story of Civilization.*"

Betsy is probably the only professional golfer, woman or man, to have combined an outstanding academic ability with a phenomenal golf career, which included 55 victories and entry into the Hall of Fame: "I thought I was going to be a winner, and as I went along, winning became easier and easier. It was something I expected to do. I always played well under pressure because it didn't bother me, which was why I won so many tournaments. I don't take much credit for it, but I could perform under tense situations. It was in my physical make-up to allow that to happen."

In 1959, Betsy Rawls won the Mt. Prospect Open, her sixth victory that year.

Due to her exceptional gift for applying her mind, Betsy was able to achieve her victories with more apparent ease and less trauma than some of the other great players: "I like to think I was less neurotic than some about winning." She gave up a future as a physicist to become one of the all time greats in golf, and she enjoyed every minute of it. She was renowned for her short game and in particular her magical touch with "slithering wedge shots," as they were called.

Her victories spanned a career lasting from 1951 through 1975, and included four U.S. Women's Open titles, the first in her rookie year. The second she won in 1953 in an 18-hole playoff against Jackie Pung: "I remember how well I played. It was one of my best rounds ever." Her third Open victory did not give Betsy much satisfaction since she won by default: Jackie Pung had an error on her score card for which she was disqualified. Betsy's fourth U.S. Open victory came in 1960. She won two LPGA Championships and had 10 tournament victories in 1959, the year she won $26,774, a considerable amount of money in those days. In her second season, 1952, she was leading money winner with $14,505: "Golf is a way of making a living and avoiding other work," Betsy claims.

When she retired from the competitive golfing arena, she became a much respected tournament director for the LPGA for six years, after which she took over the responsibilities of executive director for the McDonald's Championship, an LPGA tournament in Pennsylvania, and a leading contributor to charity. In 1993, McDonald's took over sponsorship of the LPGA Championship.

Another milestone was passed when in 1980 Betsy became the first woman to serve on the rules committee for the Men's U.S. Open and has continued regularly ever since. She has also chaired the LPGA sponsors' committee.

The 1957 Player Guide says of Betsy: "A total of 22 tournament championships and nearly $55,000 in earnings in just six short years. That's the amazing professional history of sharp, smart, and sedate Betsy Rawls. It truly has been a steady stream of championships, golf and glory for the Phi Beta Kappa graduate from the University of Texas.

"Her success has been continuous, and she had one of the most sizzling starts in professional golf history as she won four tournaments, finished as fourth leading money winner, and shocked everyone by knocking off the coveted National Open in her freshman year.

"Betsy entered the professional ranks with a great amateur background, winning in 1948 the Texas State Public Links Championship and the Austin City Championship. Her big win of 1949 was the Trans-Mississippi Championship, and in 1950 she was runner-up in the National Open to Babe Zaharias, winning the low amateur prize, leaving Louise Suggs two strokes behind and Patty Berg seven behind."

I first met Betsy during the 1970s at the Colgate tournament at Sunningdale, when she was riding the course in a golf cart in her capacity as tournament director. I said a few words to her and felt intimidated. I got to know Betsy when I was covering tournaments on the LPGA tour, and when I had problems entering the locker room, which was barred to the press, she would try to sort them out in a tactful manner. Eventually we became friendly; so when she left the tour I would telephone her in Pennsylvania, and on one occasion we met in Philadelphia, where we sat in a restaurant talking non-stop for four or five hours.

She is a shy woman for whom I feel much warmth and affection. I enjoy her mind and her company; I tend to idolize her, and she has been most helpful to me at all times, before and during the writing of this book.

Betsy was born in Spartanburg, South Carolina, and her family moved near Austin, Texas, when she was one year old. She was the youngest of two children, her brother being two years older, and hers was a middle income family, with her father working first as a wheat farmer and then a construction engineer.

Betsy won 55 LPGA events, ranked fourth behind Kathy Whitworth, Mickey Wright, and Patty Berg as having won the most titles in their careers.

"My father was once Indianapolis city golf champion, but then he didn't play much until I was 17 and became interested in the game. I had a lesson from Harvey Penick in Austin for $1.50, and then he never charged me again.

"I became good pretty quickly, got hooked on golf, and won some amateur tournaments, but having majored in physics at the University of Texas, I had every intention of being a physicist. I grew up isolated from the world of women's professional golf; there was no publicity about them. I didn't identify with them, and I hardly knew a tour existed. I played golf for fun and never considered turning professional, where there was no money and no glamour.

"I graduated in 1950, and in the spring of 1951 the Wilson Sporting Goods Company approached me about becoming a member of its staff. I decided it would be more fun to be in golf than physics, and Wilson paid me a salary and all my expenses and travel for the exhibitions I did for them.

"I was with Wilson until I retired; they paid my expenses for 20 years. One year I gave 120 clinics. Sometimes I skipped a tournament to do one. On occasions I did them alone, and at other times with Patty Berg. Patty trained me, which was tough because I couldn't put on a performance like hers, but I went along with it.

"I had to wear a hat, suit, and gloves to go on an airplane and to check into a hotel. I had to dress every night for dinner, and Patty ruled my life for a year. Eventually I could give a clinic on my own and was pretty good at it, but it was never easy. I never got much satisfaction from it, since I really wasn't a great showperson.

"There were enough tournaments to play, and I liked golf so much that the motivation was the tournaments and the competition. No one who turned professional at that time did it to make money, to get endorsements, or to be on television. It was purely for the sake of playing competitive golf and wanting to prove yourself.

"I joined the tour in 1951; I thoroughly enjoyed it then and all of the 25 years that I played. I never got tired of it, never woke up and said, 'I hate having to go to the golf course this morning.' I always looked forward to playing.

"There were about 20 players when I joined, and 20 tournaments, most of which averaged a purse of $5,000. Through the years, I held all the various LPGA offices; I was president in 1961 and 1962, member at large, secretary, and I headed the tournament committee of three, which set up the courses and gave rulings. The players made the pairings, kept statistics, had a staff including a treasurer and secretary. Altogether, we did a lot of hard work. The players today don't know how easy they have it.

"We made all the policy and procedure decisions as a group. We would get in a room and sometimes with great trauma we would thrash it out. I've written many a constitution for the LPGA. The players were involved, and due to all of them we have had continual growth, but at first our expectations were not very high.

"The crowds were all avid golfers and never bothered by roped fairways, since they walked with the players and talked to them. Babe [Zaharias] was a flamboyant, colorful, uninhibited woman, loved by the press. She was the mainstay of the tour and basically carried it for the first four to five years. I liked playing with her. She was funny and natural, not a phony. The Bauer sisters were the glamour girls. People always loved Patty Berg. Louise Suggs was renowned as the British and U.S. Amateur Champion. Betty Jameson was well known for having won the U.S. Amateur championship twice, and Marilynn Smith was immensely popular. Golf was an acceptable sport for women, since it was played by upper income people in country clubs.

"I wasn't surprised that I won the U.S. Open in my rookie year. I had quite a bit of confidence. When you start out, you think you are supposed to win. Only later are you surprised at important victories. I thought I was going to be a winner; it was something I expected to do. Later, when you start not winning so much, it is harder, and then you think you'll never win again. If you do, it's more surprising than your first victory.

"Winning is a combination that some have and some don't. Although it's an advantage to be physically strong, it is not a necessity. I never was. Temperament is important. Some people get so nervous they can't play under pressure. You need confidence in your ability to perform, which is not

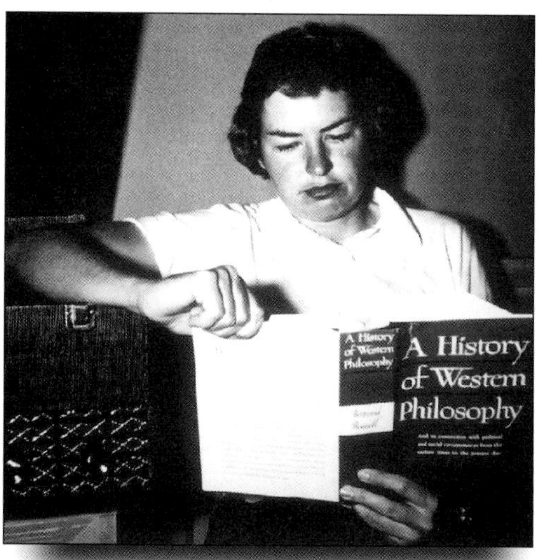

Betsy had planned to be a physicist until she took up golf at age 17. Here, she's shown with a little light reading. Photo courtesy: Betty Hicks.

the same as being a self-confident person.

"People who win a lot have a tremendous drive to win and a need to prove themselves to the world. There is a great confidence in one area and a great need in the other to prove you're a worthwhile person. You have the feeling inside that you're very worthwhile, but you need everyone else to know it. Winners take that avenue to prove to the world they are worthwhile, and they can do it through golf. I had a lot of drive, and any great player must have an obsession with winning and a need to win.

"Mickey Wright, a highly intelligent, articulate woman, who was the greatest player we ever had, put so much pressure on herself to win that she was really miserable when she was playing golf because she couldn't tolerate losing. She didn't have fun because there was always the fear she was going to lose. She was an amazing golfer, who won one in every three tournaments when she played regularly.

"It's a matter of style: Patty Berg was a complete extrovert who put on a show, Louise Suggs was withdrawn, and I was an introvert. What the good players have in common is that they are not interested in what the gallery thinks of them. There are players who are concerned with how they look and what impression they make on the gallery, which detracts from the golf game. You have to concentrate totally on what you're doing; any concern with other people is a distraction. You must be totally yourself, do it naturally, like Nancy Lopez, who is a naturally appealing person.

"I didn't set myself targets. I set out to win every tournament I could, which was the only goal I had. I was lucky to win early and win a lot. When you play golf, you know you're not completely in control of what happens. It takes a lot to win, and there is a certain amount of luck involved.

"It's such an emotional game, and golfers react so violently to things that happen on the golf course. Every good player works and works at controlling emotions because you put yourself on the line every time you go out. To great players, your whole world depends on what you shoot, and it's hard to control your reactions unless you don't care.

"Every golfer tries to blame a bad shot on a bad break. Mickey [Wright] did that, until she finally realized she was responsible for everything that happened on the course. She learned to play one shot at a time and zero in on it, without relating it to the score. When she could do that, she started winning a lot. Louise [Suggs] was so proud she wouldn't let anyone see she was upset. Patty [Berg] couldn't lose her temper and appear to have a poor image with the public.

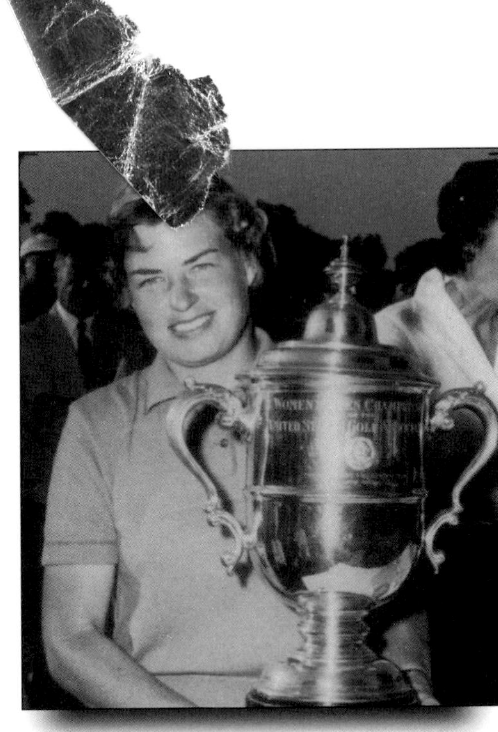

Betsy won the 1957 U.S. Open at Wingfoot. It was the third of four Open titles she captured during her 25 years on the tour.

"I learned that one bad shot does not mean the whole tournament, and then I learned the knack of not letting disappointment or frustration show, of not expressing anger. I turned negative feelings into determination. I didn't give up or feel sorry for myself.

"When people over-react, it's a reflection of not being able to accept a mistake in themselves. People who don't think highly of themselves or their ability can never really succeed. They give a great display of temper, and the bad shots reinforce their poor image to show the world what they think of themselves. For a lot of people, it is not in their script to win, it doesn't fit their self-image. I saw myself as a winner, but why that comes about I don't know.

"Mickey [Wright] had to prove herself to her father. Whether her father ever said, 'You're the

When Betsy Rawls retired from competitive golf in 1975, she became tournament director for the LPGA. In 1980, she became the first woman to serve on the rules committee for the USGA Men's Open. Photo courtesy: LPGA.

greatest golfer that ever lived,' I don't know, but that's what she wanted. She would have sacrificed anything to win. I guess great golfers have to prove themselves to somebody. I wanted to win for the recognition of my peer group.

"Winning my first U.S. Open didn't seem so important at the time. I thought that if I didn't win that one I could always win the next. My biggest thrill was the last LPGA championship I won, which was in 1969, because I had reached a point where I wasn't sure I could win again. It was on the toughest course on our schedule, which was Concord Country Club, New York. I played really well. I didn't have one bogey in the final round. I got a great kick out of that. I probably enjoyed that win the most.

"When you feel your ability slipping, there is a gradual change, a desperation at first that you're not winning. I've seen other golfers whose games don't change much, who don't hit it shorter or do anything different, but they stop winning on a regular basis. It happens to everyone. I was able to tolerate not winning, but I didn't like it, and I knew it was happening. I didn't suffer, but I don't think any athlete wants to quit. I didn't come to terms with it until the LPGA offered me a job as tournament director, and then I had to face it squarely. I wasn't ready to quit, but my better judgment prevailed. I knew it would be only a short time before I'd have to quit.

"It was a traumatic season in 1974, and I suffered a lot over making the decision. Once I got into the job the following year, I didn't suffer at all. I was so involved that I didn't miss golf, although I had thought I could hardly bear it if I didn't play a tournament every week. I was lucky not to have a total change in lifestyle.

"Golf changed me a lot as a person. When I started out, I was reluctant to talk, but as time went on it became easier to relate to people. The social aspect was difficult, since I was withdrawn and had a bad time in social situations.

"I didn't relate my own lifestyle to that of women in general because I was not concerned about my role as a woman or what other people expected women to be. There was never much talk about the women's movement on the tour, where the whole world is reduced to what's happening on a particular green at that moment. It's so narrow, playing golf, because of the people and the nature of the game. The whole world could be collapsing around you, but if you make a 20-foot putt, everything is great as though it's the most important thing in the whole world.

"Golfers in general become pretty isolated; it is a very small arena, and they don't relate well to the outside world. I didn't think of it as normal or abnormal, and although I was intellectually aware it was an abnormal existence, emotionally I accepted and enjoyed it. I was so absorbed in golf, which is all-consuming and takes so much energy and effort that there was nothing left for anything else.

"Although I always read a lot and was interested in other things, all I wanted to do was play golf, think about it, and practice. It's not necessarily a good thing to be so totally absorbed because it's very narrow and limited, but winning makes it all worth it. Nothing can make you feel quite as good as winning a golf tournament. You've done the entire thing yourself. No one can help you. It's totally you. You get great satisfaction when you win, and you're rewarded directly according to your performance.

"As a golfer on tour, you become dependent on a protective environment, where you always have other people you know around you. Golfers feel pretty close to each other in an environment where they're always cared for and a lot of things are done for them; so that some people are very uncomfortable when they have to perform alone. You may be flying round the world, doing many things other women don't; so that you feel very confident in a lot of areas where you always have the protection of the group. You have to retain a strong independence from the golf course when you are on your own.

"I am very proud of being part of the LPGA, which is such a young organization and the most successful in the world of women's sport. A lot of people have given a lot of time and work to establish good policies and make good decisions, and so much has been accomplished to make the LPGA survive and grow. Sport is selfish, but off the golf course you can completely change your way of thinking so that it is for the good of the organization. Everyone should be proud to be part of the LPGA."

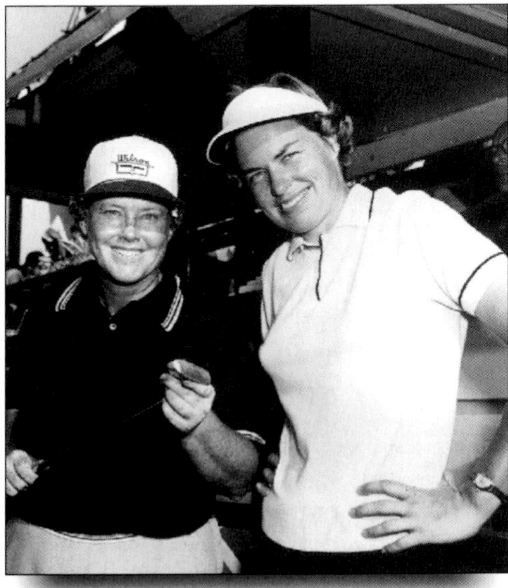

Patty Berg trained Betsy for the many clinics they did for Wilson.

Member LPGA Hall of Fame 1960

LPGA Victories: 1951 U.S. Women's Open, Sacramento Open, Hollywood Four-Ball. **1952** Houston Weathervane, Cross-Country Weathervane, Eastern Open, Western Open, Carrollton Open, Thomasville Open. **1953** U.S. Women's Open, Sacramento Open, Eastern, Texas Open. **1954** Tampa Open, St. Louis Open, Texas Open, Inverness Four-Ball. **1955** Carrollton Open. **1956** Tampa Open, Peach Blossom Open, Sarasota Open. **1957** U.S. Women's Open, Tampa Open, Lake Worth Open, Peach Blossom Open, Reno Open. **1958** Tampa Open, St. Petersburg Open. **1959** LPGA Championship, Lake Worth Open, Royal Crown Open, Babe Zaharias Open, Land of Sky Open, Mt. Prospect Open, Western Open, Waterloo Open, Opie Turner Open, Triangle Round Robin. **1960** U.S. Women's Open, Babe Zaharias Open, Cosmopolitan Open, Asheville Open. **1961** Cosmopolitan Open, Bill Brannin's Swing Parade. **1962** J.E. McAuliffe Memorial. **1963** Sunshine Open. **1964** Dallas Civitan, Vahalla Open. **1965** Pensacola Invitational, Waterloo Open. **1968** Mickey Wright Invitational. **1969** LPGA Championship. **1970** Dallas Civitan Open, Cincinnati Open. **1972** GAC Classic.

Betsy Rawls' LPGA Record

Year	No.of Events	Best Finish	Money	Rank	Scoring Average
1951	10	1	$1,520	NA	76.76
1952	12	1	11,802	NA	75.87
1953	19	1	9,790	NA	75.53
1954	16	1	6,805	NA	76.85
1955	18	1	5,292	NA	77.48
1956	20	1	5,924	NA	78.10
1957	19	1	9,812	6	75.36
1958	17	1	7,600	14	75.81
1959	26	1	26,744	1	74.02
1960	23	1	14,928	3	74.24
1961	16	1	15,672	5	74.38
1962	31	1	11,714	7	75.83
1963	34	1	6,645	4	74.70
1964	32	1	20,645	4	74.10
1965	30	1	12,148	10	74.97
1966	20	3	11,625	16	75.20
1967	25	T2	10,144	14	75.05
1968	26	1	14,530	12	74.54
1969	25	1	18,074	11	73.89
1970	18	T2	19,267	9	73.90
1971	18	T2	7,325	33	76.65
1972	20	1	12,880	28	75.80
1973	27	T3	19,646	26	75.86
1974	27	T6	7,595	49	76.81
1975	14	T25	1,622	78	76.43

Wiffi Smith

Wiffi Smith is not only a lovable character, she is one of the finest natural golfers to have joined the professional ranks. After a career of just under four seasons and nine professional victories, she was forced to leave the tour at 24 because of injury to her hands.

Her daredevil antics and pranks are still the talk of those who were her fellow professionals. At some of her golf clinics, she would arrive on her liver chestnut parade horse Flashy Mike, dismount, hit her shots, and ride away into the sunset. Her adventurous spirit accounted for some of her injuries, yet her resilience carried her through. When she left the tour, she went on to a new career of training and raising a pack of foxhounds in North Carolina, which became the focus of her life for many years.

Years ago a perceptive British golf writer called John Stobbs described Wiffi thus: "She stands on a fairway as if she had grown there." He conveyed the pure natural element of Wiffi in a golfing environment, where she is molded to the clubs through her hands and the golf course through her body. Says Wiffi: "You become the shot you are going to play, and in your mind you feel its totality: the hitting, the landing, the stopping. You get totally involved emotionally so that you lose yourself in the game; you become the game, the ball, the club. It is all part of your body from the ground upwards. When I had those feelings, I played my best golf."

Wiffi likens the epitome of the game of golf to the visual and sensual picture experienced by the great cook, the great pianist, the great gardener, the great tennis player, and all experts in their own field.

Wiffi's short golfing career was illustrious, with an amateur record that included 28 titles around the world. From winning all the Mexican garlands, she achieved victory in the 1954 USGA National Junior Championships. Reaching a peak in 1956, she won the Trans-Mississippi, the British Women's Amateur, the French Women's Amateur, was top amateur in the Jacksonville Open and the Titleholders, and was a member of the U.S. Curtis Cup team, all at 20 years of age.

I met Wiffi in the early 1980s when I was staying with Peggy Kirk Bell at Pine Needles, the delightful golf course nurtured and developed by Peggy and her late husband, Bullet. Peggy and Wiffi have a long-standing friendship over many years, and Wiffi says: "Peggy is one of the mainstreams of my life."

I was lucky enough to play golf at Pine Needles with Peggy and Wiffi as my companions, and it is

Wiffi had a fabulous amateur career and a brief one as a professional golfer due to injury to her hands. Here she is shown at the Curtis Cup, 1950.

one of my most congenial and outstanding golfing memories. Both were way past their heyday, but there was still the element of competition, the enjoyment and frustration of the game, the pleasant banter, the wonderful hands and swing that still belonged to Wiffi. Peggy continuously removed any little weed that might be showing through on a green. The overall enjoyment of being on a golf course in lovely weather with good companionship flowed through us all.

My relationship with Wiffi developed into one of much warmth; we met again at Marilynn Smith's Founders' Classic in 1987, and as friends we picked up where we last left off.

Wiffi is a private person in spite of her ability to amuse the crowd. As an interviewee she is not easy because her recall of happenings in any ordered sequence is hazy, and she looks to the present and the future rather than remembering what happened yesterday. An impish smile, a sense of humor, and a good use of imagery are all part of her communicative skills.

Wiffi was born in Redlands, California, where her father was an orange grower. She has a brother six years younger. "My nickname of Wiffi came about when my mother was pregnant and visiting Southern Mexico. The Zapotee Indians call an unborn child 'huiji.' When I was born, the name was adapted to Wiffi."

When she was 11, her parents divorced, and she and her mother, brother, and a cousin moved to Mexico, where she attended a French school and grew up speaking both French and Spanish. In 1956 her father died at 46: "He went to bed one night and never woke up." Wiffi lived with her mother until she began playing the professional golf tour. Then she based herself with Bob and Margaret Holden in Michigan. She had met the Holdens through Peggy and Bullet Bell, and they soon became like family.

"My father was a two-handicap golfer, my uncle a leading U.S. Army golfer, and I started playing at 13 in Guadalajara, where I was taught by a professional called Tom Garcia. I became good quickly, rapidly shooting in the 80s, and I started winning local and national tournaments from the age of 14. At that time my mother, brother, and I

Wiffi Smith was the winner of the British Amateur in 1956, in Berkshire, England. That year, she won the Trans-Mississippi and the French Open, and she turned pro at year end.

spent some months in England in Somerset where I had a cousin, and I played golf there on a nine hole course mown by sheep. Later I returned to play the U.S. amateur events and did pretty well.

"When I played in the Curtis Cup matches in 1956, in England, we were beaten as a team, but I won my matches. We went from there to play the French amateur, which I won, and following that I won the British Amateur at Sunningdale, which was one of the highlights of my life. In 1956, shortly before my father died, he saw me win the Trans-Mississippi, which pleased me because he enjoyed that, and it was the last time I saw him.

"By the end of 1956 I made the decision to turn professional, and my ambition was to become the best in the world. I was offered a contract with Spalding worth $3,000, which meant that I played their clubs, used their golf balls, and gave clinics. I budgeted to spend $500.00 a month and usually kept to that. I bought a 1928 Model A Ford for $1,000 bucks and, my God, I had some fun in it. It was green and called 'Susie,' and I went along at 45

Wiffi, with her foxhounds, transferred her pursuit of excellence to raising the best pack in America.

mph as the others were whizzing past me in their Cadillacs. Peggy [Bell] still has the car at Pine Needles.

"I did pretty well in my first tournament and later that season I won the Dallas Open. I was never out of the money, and when I won $15,000 one year, it was a fortune. When I was leading the 1959 Titleholders tournament in Augusta, I decided to try out a caddie's bike in the parking lot. I ran the bike into the back of a stationary car and jammed the bones in my hand. I still finished runner-up to Louise Suggs, but it was a dumb thing to do, and I permanently damaged my hand.

"That same year driving at night in the fog near Baton Rouge, I saw a white mule on the side of the road, but I didn't see the dark one in the middle, and I hit it. I got glass in my eyes, and I jammed my other hand. I was a real mess, and I couldn't find the mule anywhere.

"After I busted my hand the first time, I bought a piano and traveled with it in a Volkswagen bus. I thought playing it would be good for strengthening my hands. I loved horses, cars, and music, but I lived for my golf game. My whole purpose was to win, and when you're in that concentrated frame of mind, you're in a different space. It is easy to slip out of it and hard to return. I played by feel, whereas people like Mickey Wright and Betsy Rawls were intellectual players. Betty Jameson had the most beautiful hands, a great touch, and I would finish my round, go and watch her, and learn. I liked to make shots go through, around, or over the branches of trees, and I found it a marvelous thing to picture a shot and pull it off.

"By 1961 my hands were so bad that I couldn't pick up a piece of paper, and I had to leave the tour. I think that was when emotionally I came through the fallopian tube, and it was very tough because playing the tour had been my art, my mind, and my soul.

"I went to college for a while in New Mexico, studying biology and music. Then one semester before obtaining my degree, I quit over an emotional upheaval with a young man. I went back to Peggy and Bullet at Pine Needles, and while I was there, I was offered a job on a local farm with a pack of foxhounds. I loved it, and I wanted to raise the best pack in America. I bred them, trained them, rode to hounds, showed them, watched, read, and listened. I thought I would do that for the rest of my life."

Wiffi devoted most of nearly 20 years to her foxhounds. She also taught golf at Pine Needles and in Florida. She harbored thoughts of returning to the tour she had loved, and in 1975 she attended the qualifying school for the tour, where after such a long gap in competitive golf she missed qualifying by just one shot.

In 1987 she packed her bags and moved on to a property she found in northern California, an area she had enjoyed visiting as a youngster and where she always wanted to return. She learned the art of self-sufficiency, of living off the land. Just down the road there is a little golf course to which she probably sneaks when she has time between her home life and teaching at golf schools.

Playing the inaugural 1987 Marilynn Smith Founders' Classic in Dallas, Wiffi demonstrated her continuing rhythmic swing and natural talent: "I hadn't picked up my sticks for six months; nor had many of the others. There are very few women in the world who could play so well with as little time as we had to put into it. I'll probably spend the rest of my life assessing the emotional impact of that week."

Professional Victories: 1957 Dallas Open, UNSW Open. **1958** Peach Blossom Open, Rockford Open. **1959** Peach Blossom Open, Miami Triangle Open. **1960** Columbus Women's Open–Royal Crown, Peach Blossom Open, Waterloo, Iowa.

Wiffi, dog in tow, plays the piano out of her Volkswagen in 1960. After injuring her hands in several accidents, she thought playing the piano would strengthen them, but she left the tour in 1961 due to the injury.

Louise Suggs

I telephoned Louise Suggs when I was in Florida in the early 1980s to tell her about my project with a book on the LPGA and to ask her for an interview. Previously, we had been going to get together at the Dinah Shore, in which she was playing, but it did not come about.

Speaking to her later, she told me she wanted nothing to do with my book, and that if I wrote about our conversation on the telephone she would sue me. It seemed less than litigious, but I do remember telling her that if she had anything she wanted to say about the LPGA, surely now was her opportunity to do so. Sadly, she did not agree, and she is my one omission of a personal interview of all the women I approached.

Since that time I have seen Louise on several occasions and we chatted at the 1990 Women's Open at Atlanta. Talking about British professional, Laura Davies, and her potential in golf, Louise told me she would be happy to talk to Laura about golf course management, if it would help her. I thought it was a very nice gesture and passed it on to Laura.

Louise, in the 1990's, had a rapproachment with the LPGA, which resulted in her handing over to them, much valuable material for their projected Hall of Fame. Louise and I also came together, as we shared a breakfast table with Betsy Rawls, at the 1995 US Women's Open at the Broadmoor, when I enjoyed Louise's wit and her storytelling.

Both as an amateur and a professional, Louise was a very great golfer, often compared to Ben Hogan. In the book that she wrote, *Par Golf For Women*, published in 1953, Ben Hogan wrote in the foreword:

"The first time I ever saw Louise Suggs hit a golf-ball was in 1945, when we were partners in a 'pro-lady' event preceding the Chicago Victory Open. It was on the tough No. 2 course at Medinah, where the National Open was played four years later.

"Louise and I won that pro-lady competition, and after I'd watched her fine shot-making at Medinah. To me her later victories in the U.S. Women's and Women's Western Championships, and her triumph in every other major championship in the United States, and in the British Ladies' Championship as well, seemed the logical result. The swing she showed in 1945 was a beautiful thing—so smooth and rhythmic, so soundly joined together—she was bound to be a winner.

"If I were to single out one woman in the world today as a model for any other woman aspiring to ideal golf form it would be Miss Suggs. Her swing combines all the desirable elements of efficiency, timing, and co-ordination. It appears to be completely effortless. Yet, despite her slight build, she is consistently as long off the tee and through the fairway as any of her feminine contemporaries in competitive golf. And no one is 'right down the middle' any more than this sweet-swinging Georgia miss.

"Her game shows the benefits of a great deal of intelligent experimenting, study, and practice. Her timing and her consistently high standard of play, stay with her for the reason that she has got the fundamentals and the refinements down to where they reduce the margin of error to about its minimum.

"I know Louise to be a particularly keen student of golf, and have always been impressed with her sound concepts of the game. Her thinking in regard to good golf form is simple and basic. It is completely practical and free of the frills and theories that tend only to make a complex action of the golf swing.

"Because of this clear thinking and strictly fundamental approach to the process of stroking a golf-ball with maximum efficiency Louise is able to

Ben Hogan said "she was bound to be a winner, and she was." Louise won 47 tournaments as a professional and 20 as an amateur in one of golf's truly great careers.

impart to others these proven principles in thoroughly understandable terms.

"Anyone sincerely interested in playing golf well cannot help benefitting from the wealth of advice and instruction presented so ably by Miss Suggs."

Louise was an integral part of the LPGA from its inception. She was a founder. She attended the 1987 inaugural Marilynn Smith Founders' Classic, where she said at a celebratory dinner: "I can go back as far as anybody. The first time I ever saw Patty Berg I was 15 years old and playing her. I was three up on her, everyone came out to watch, and she beat me four and three.

"I made my reputation as an amateur golfer, as we all did. Only it was easier for me than for some because my family had a golf course. I was extremely fortunate to be blessed with a good temperament, good timing, and a kind of phlegmatic personality.

"When we began the LPGA, we were just an amateur group who started something. It's been fun. I appreciate being at this tournament, I am glad to play, and I hope we have some more."

A member of the Hall of Fame in 1951, Louise recorded 47 LPGA victories from 1949 to 1962, a remarkable achievement. In the 1949 U.S. Women's Open which Louise won at Prince George's Country Club, Landover, Maryland, she was 14 shots better than Babe Zaharias in second place, a record which still stands for the championship. Yet in the early days of the association, it was Babe whose personality overshadowed her and who attracted all the publicity.

In the October 1946 edition of *The Woman Golfer* magazine, the publication of the WPGA, reporter Jack Clowser records Louise winning the Western Amateur, defeating Patty Berg in the final:

"Louise Suggs played competitive golf for six consecutive days in Cleveland, and for six days was under par every round, on a 6500 yard course that is one of the most heavily trapped and wooded in that district.

"A simple statement, yes, and it furnishes the simple reason why the Georgia brunette towered over the field as she won the 46th Western Amateur Championship. For the week, Louise was eight strokes under par. The last two days of play were over a course so rain soaked that balls became buried on the greens. That signified that on the course nearly everything was a carry, and a big bounce was as rare as a house to rent.

"Small wonder that galleries at Cleveland Country Club departed swearing that here was the greatest woman golfer since Joyce Wethered. In 18 years of watching and covering golf, this reporter never has witnessed a more magnificent exhibition of consistent perfection."

Another extract from *The Woman Golfer* of 1946 praises Louise's performance in the Titleholders at Augusta Country Club: "Golf followers, who have never seen each other before, come up and begin a conversation on the fairways by noting the remarkable resemblance in style of Louise Suggs, the Georgia peach, and Ben Hogan.

"The first two days of play in the tournament, Eileen Stulb, whose home is in Augusta, had led with her 156 against Miss Suggs' 157. On the third round Louise passed her, and this is Louise's story from there on in: 'I had a stroke lead going into the final round ahead of Eileen Stulb, who certainly ought to know the course where she plays all the time. I finished with 314, and then I had to sit there in the clubhouse and hear about Eileen as she came in.

"'On the 14th, all she needed to tie me was to get straight pars. She parred the 14th, birdied the 15th, which put her one ahead. She got her four on the 16th but took a bogey on the 17th, which made her even with me, needing only a par on the 18th to tie for the tournament lead. Eileen has not played regular tournament golf and I guess that was what did it. She had a good tee shot, but got into trap trouble on her second. When she finished, she was two over par for the hole and I had won.

"'Did I see it? No, ma'am, not me. I heard all about it afterward, because I don't want to stand around and watch somebody beat me when I can't do anything about it.'"

The following extract comes from the 1957 Publicity Brochure of the LPGA:

FULL NAME: Mae Louise Suggs
NICKNAME: "Little Sister," "Sis," or "Miss Sluggs" (coined by personal friend, Bob Hope)
HOME CLUB: Sea Island Golf Club, Sea Island, Georgia
HEIGHT: 5', 5-1/2"
WEIGHT: 115
EDUCATION: Austell, Georgia High School
PARENTS: John Suggs (golf course manager and former pitcher with New York Yankees and Atlanta Crackers) and Marguerite Suggs
STARTED GOLF: 1933
PROFESSIONAL INSTRUCTOR: John Suggs
TURNED PROFESSIONAL: July, 1948
PROFESSIONAL AFFILIATION: MacGregor Golf Company and Sea Island Company
PREVIOUS EMPLOYMENT: Gulf Oil Company Service Representative
HOBBIES: Photography, swimming, dancing, music
PUBLICATIONS: *Par Golf for Women,* published by Prentice-Hall
LPGA OFFICES:1955–56–57 LPGA President
OTHER HONORS: Member, United Airlines 100,000 Mile Club

One name that has become synonymous with women's golf down through the years is the always popular "Georgia Peach," veteran Louise Suggs.

And it's only natural that the highly intelligent and talented member of golf's "Hall of Fame" should assume a double role as star performer and president of the Ladies' Professional Golf Association.

This combination seems to click with the Sea Island sweet swinger, as she completed her ninth tremendously successful year as a lady professional in 1956.

Louise, always one of the top five performers on tour since turning pro in 1948, again was one of the top standouts, winning three tournaments, finishing as the third leading money winner with $12,246, a stroke average of 75.96, and the third best rating of .840 in the race for the Babe Zaharias Trophy.

Undoubtedly Louise's biggest victory of the year came in the talent-heavy Titleholders Championship where she sank a pressure-packed 18-foot putt on the final hole to win her third Titleholders by a single stroke. Louise's other victories came in the first annual Havana Open and the big All-America Championship at Tam O'Shanter.

Besides these great victories, the rest of Louise's record that year was amazing with only four finishes out of the top six places. In fact, she had

Louise Suggs, a founder of the LPGA, quit the tour over a $25 fine. She is shown here at the 1946 Women's Western Open.

one string going where she finished no lower than fifth in 11 straight tournaments, tremendous considering the much improved competition in the LPGA in recent years.

Louise has always been a standout performer on the links ever since taking up golf when she was only 10 years old. Her father, John Suggs, a former member of the New York Yankees, owned a golf course in Lithia Springs, Georgia, and actually started Louise on her way to golfing gold and glory.

As she remarked about her early career, "By the time I was 15 years old I had gone slightly nutty about golf and was spending every minute on the golf course. Dad had shown me how to grip the club, and then he told me to just keep slamming the ball."

And slam it Louise did to reach the pinnacle in women's golf. At the age of only 14 she had already won the Georgia State Championship and went on to add further amateur laurels, including every major amateur tournament title available before turning to the pro ranks in 1948.

Her decision to turn pro was prompted by the fact that she had no more worlds to conquer as an amateur, and this decision brought about one of golf's truly tremendous careers. Louise won a total of 32 tournament titles in her first ten years as a professional, plus another 18 in her final five years on tour and at least 20 as an amateur.

The year 1953 was undoubtedly the most impressive for "Miss Sluggs" when she won a record 10 tournaments and set a record of $19,568. In fact, she is one of the very few women pros who has been able to win $12,000 or more in each of the past four years, proof of Louise's greatness.

Louise is a phlegmatic competitor on the course, but she acknowledges, despite her outward appearances, all is not serene inside. "I'm always seething," she says, "but when I quit getting butterflies in my stomach I'll quit golf, the thrill will be gone."

Always one of the leading performers in women's golf, Louise Suggs is destined to remain one of the LPGA's true luminaries for many years to come.

Betsy Rawls talked to me about Louise and said: "Louise was a very talented golfer, without question one of the best players we ever had. She had one of the best swings; she was one of the best putters and a great competitor.

"She had tremendous drive and was almost neurotic like most of our great players who seemed to have a lot to prove. Louise was definitely one of the greats. Winning was everything to her, and like Mickey Wright and Patty Berg, she couldn't tolerate losing.

"Louise was somewhat withdrawn. She never emoted much on the course or empathized with the gallery. She was very sensitive and took offense easily. She took offense at things I thought were ridiculous, reading into peoples' actions attacks on her that were not true at all. She overreacted in every direction—sponsors, players, press, and gallery.

"Louise respected the game, but she didn't like or respect Babe [Zaharias] because Babe disregarded the rules. Louise also resented the tremendous publicity given to Babe. She couldn't laugh at it.

"When Louise was president of the LPGA from 1955 to 1957, she was at her best, at her most well adjusted, because she felt she had the respect of the players. She did an excellent job, which gave her a little more self-esteem. Louise harbored everything. It was in her personality to do so, which was too bad because it helped cut short her career. It happened in 1962, when I was president of the LPGA and on the executive board of five elected officers who ran the association.

"At that time we had a rule that anyone entering a tournament and then failing to show up was automatically fined $25. Louise signed up for an event in Milwaukee, failed to show, and was fined the routine amount. She thought we had wronged her because, she said, she had set out in her car to come to the tournament and then decided her emotional state was not up to it.

"We considered it, decided it was not a legitimate reason and that fine stood. Louise was so upset that she quit the tour, virtually ending her career. She never played full-time again.

"Can you imagine doing that over a dumb $25 fine? She was at the height of her career and in her prime, when she quit. It was hard for me to understand that kind of thinking. I would have paid it for her myself, although the money was nothing to Louise. I forever regretted it for her, and I thought it was one of the saddest things in the LPGA history.

"She felt she was wronged, and she stuck to it because that's the kind of person she was. You can imagine how much a person like that needs to win. Sometimes weaknesses are strengths. Sometimes the things that made her that way also made her a great player.

"Louise's father, Johnny, who was the nicest man, was a professional baseball player, and her mother was the daughter of the owner of an Atlanta baseball team. The Depression came, the family lost the team and their money, and Johnny took a job as a golf course manager in Lithia Springs, where Louise and her brother grew up playing at his golf course. Her father taught her, and as a child she played barefooted. She was accepted and appreciated by her father, but she had to prove to her mother that she could do it.

"Louise became a fine player, winning lots of tournaments, including the U.S. Amateur and British Amateur Championships. She wanted to go to college, but her family couldn't afford it; so she went to work for Gulf Oil and played amateur golf when she could. Later she signed with MacGregor and earned good money on royalties from her own line of clubs.

"Louise is an interesting person. I've always liked her and enjoyed her. She is very intelligent, and if she feels comfortable and appreciated, she is fun to be around. In other instances she is completely irrational. People like that think emotionally, and that's it."

Member Hall of Fame 1951

LPGA Victories: 1949 U.S. Women's Open, Western Open, All-American Open. **1951** Carrollton Open. **1952** Jacksonville Open, Tampa Open, Stockfort Open, U.S. Women's Open, All-American Open, Betty Jameson Open. **1953** Western Open, Tampa Open, Betsy Rawls Open, San Diego Open, San Francisco Weathervane, Bakersfield Open, Philadelphia Weathervane Open, Cross-Country Weathervane. **1954** Titleholders Championship, Sea Island Open, Betsy Rawls Open, Carrollton Open, Babe Zaharias Open. **1955** Los Angeles Open, Oklahoma City Open, Eastern Open, Triangle Round Robin, St. Louis Open. **1956** Titleholder's Championship, Havana Open, All-American Open. **1957** LPGA Championship, Heart of America Invitational. **1958** Babe Zaharias Open, Gatlinburg Open, French Lick Open, Triangle Round Robin. **1959** Titleholder's Championship, St. Petersburg Open, Dallas Civitan Open. **1960** Dallas Civitan Open, Triangle Round Robin, Youngstown Kitchen Open, San Antonio Civitan Open. **1961** Royal Poinciana Invitational, Golden Circle of Golf, Dallas Civitan Open, Kansas City Open, San Antonio Civitan Open. **1962** St. Petersburg Open.

Louise Suggs' LPGA Record

Year	No.of Events	Best Finish	Money	Rank	Scoring Average
1950	9	1	$3,000	NA	76.30
1951	12	1	3,404	NA	75.53
1952	11	1	6,338	NA	75.24
1953	19	1	19,568	1	75.18
1954	16	1	12,061	NA	75.94
1955	15	1	11,003	NA	75.94
1956	23	1	12,246	NA	75.96
1957	16	1	9,207	7	74.64
1958	21	1	11,862	2	75.10
1959	20	1	16,936	3	73.58
1960	21	1	16,891	2	73.69
1961	17	1	15,339	4	73.87
1962	9	1	3,402	23	75.10
1963	7	2	4,418	20	75.30
1964	10	5	4,574	25	74.80
1965	5	7	2,122	31	74.82
1966	6	6	2,235	33	75.21
1967	7	4	5,579	27	73.92
1968	9	T9	2,581	41	75.34
1969	9	T21	5,200	33	75.90
1970	3	19	520	71	76.11
1971	5	15	1,120	62	75.86
1972	8	11	4,637	31	76.68
1973	1	42	750	88	77.78
1974	4	35	1,123	85	79.92
1975	3	53	507	101	78.11
1976	8	56	525	107	79.44
1977	1	67	505	112	83.50
1978	3	66	NA	NA	81.00
1979	2	67	NA	NA	80.25
1980	2	66	NA	NA	80.33
1981	1	NA	NA	NA	82.00
1982	2	NA	NA	NA	83.75
1983	2	NA	NA	NA	82.00
1984	3	NA	NA	NA	82.75

Kathy Whitworth

For a woman who says: "I have never had a great golf swing," Kathy Whitworth has had an inspiring career after an inauspicious beginning. She joined the tour at age 19 in 1959, played 26 events, and finished with a scoring average of 80.30, winning only $1,217.00. "You have dreams when you start and sometimes they are your only motivation. Then you get slapped in the face and learn that you have to be realistic. Before I could become great, I had to learn to break 80."

A legendary golfing figure, Kathy is a remarkable woman with an intensely competitive spirit. Her great playing career spanned the decades from the end of the 1950s and her phenomenal 88 career victories was an all-time record in men's and women's golf.

In 1982, she equaled and then overtook Mickey Wright, whose 82 career victories mark was the former LPGA target. In 1983, Kathy drew level with Sam Snead with her 84th victory; then she cruised ahead on her own with her first victory of 1984. She earned two more wins that season and another in 1985, giving her the unprecedented total of 88 victories spanning three separate decades.

In 1981, Kathy reached another milestone. She became the first LPGA player to reach $1 million in career earnings. The one gap, which she shares with Sam Snead, is the U.S. Open title, and ironically, it was her third placing in that event in 1981 that took her past the magic million. She would dearly love to have taken the title instead of the money, but was gracious in defeat: "I would have swapped being the first to make a million for winning the Open, but it was a consolation which took some of the sting out of not winning.

Although she has reveled in the game she chose as a career, Kathy has not come through unscathed. From 1965 to 1973, she achieved the leading money winner position eight times in nine years; she was second in 1963 and 1969, and third in 1964. The strain left her totally exhausted, and she suffered a breakdown, which changed her future attitude toward winning.

An intensely loyal LPGA woman, although one who has not always agreed with its decisions, Kathy was president of the LPGA in 1966, 1967, 1969, and again twenty years later in 1989. After she won the first Marilynn Smith Founders' Classic in Dallas in 1987, she spoke of her innate appreciation for those pioneer women who started it all: "I'm really grateful to the 13 charter members for having the courage to get the Association off the ground. They had almost nothing in 1950, but they had the guts to say 'We'll give it a whirl,' for which they deserve a lot of credit."

Kathy Whitworth's scoring average in 1959, her first year on tour, was a disappointing 80.30, but she quickly lowered it and went on to be the winningest pro ever (man or woman). When she left the tour in 1991, she had accumulated 88 career victories. Photo courtesy: LPGA.

Kathy Whitworth was the first LPGA pro to reach $1 million in career earnings. She did so at the 1981 U.S. Open when she finished third. Photo courtesy: LPGA.

A tall, strikingly handsome woman, always in fine physical shape, Kathy hardly appears to have changed through the years after she lost 60 pounds in the early 1960s. An admirably determined woman, Kathy veers toward the self-effacement typical of her generation, and deals with adversity by thinking there is always someone worse off.

With never a hair out of place, she has a certain aura of aloofness, maybe due to shyness, but it was most intimidating to me when I first saw her at the LPGA Colgate tournaments at Sunningdale, England, in the 1970s. My feelings were in no way reassured, when she made it perfectly obvious that she did not wish to talk to me for the purpose of my book. Wary of each other, it was some years before we sat down together at a tournament in Florida, and only after I told Kathy she could always refuse to answer any question. Quite to my surprise, she warmed to the interview, enjoying it more as it proceeded, and as the years went on, our association developed into a rapport and trust. She talked very frankly about her emotions as she responded to my questions.

Kathy was born in Monahans, Texas, the youngest of three girls, with sisters two and four years older. The family moved to Jal, New Mexico, where her father owned a hardware store, in which he and her mother worked. Her late grandfather had played golf, and Kathy got his clubs from her grandmother. She started playing at 15.

"I was athletic, loved tennis, and played sports of all kinds. School friends' families belonged to the golf club and urged me to play. I tried it and found golf to be a great challenge. I played nearly every day. I could play alone—myself against the golf course.

"I had an aunt who was a golfer, and after a year I played with her. I took lessons from the professional at Jal, who after two years sent me to Harvey Penick in Austin, where I would write everything down before returning home to work on it.

"I thought I was pretty good stuff right away, and I twice won the New Mexico State Amateur Championship. I played a couple of exhibitions at home with Mickey Wright and Betsy Rawls, where I was the big duck because it was my territory. I saw two professional tournaments and then was petrified out of my mind when I accepted an invitation to play the Titleholders in Augusta, Georgia. I did incredibly badly and took the Greyhound bus home.

"I graduated at 18 and got a scholarship to junior college in Odessa, to become a physical education teacher and to play on the golf team. I knew after half a semester I didn't want to stay and that there was a way to make a living in golf. My father and two other businessmen said they would sponsor me on the LPGA tour for three years, and the Wilson Sporting Goods Company took me on, starting me at $1,500 a year, plus expenses and $25 to $50 a clinic. That could keep you on tour a long time. I did 60 to 70 clinics a year for 10 years, and I wouldn't want to trade that experience, which was a big boost for me. I learned to handle crowds, and I gained self-confidence. I spent six to nine weeks being trained by Patty Berg in Florida and learned an awful lot from her, not only about clinics, but she helped me with my own game. I owe a lot to her and to Wilson.

"When I turned professional, women playing sport were not looked on as ladylike. My family backed me because they thought I should express my talent, and they felt it was possible to be a lady and still play golf. The stigma was there, but we were a strong group; so we survived.

"I joined the tour in 1959 when the fields were around 30 or 35 in a good week, the annual purse was about $200,000, and the players ran everything. The LPGA president was the tournament director, the executive board was the ruling body, we had tournament pairing committees, and everyone worked. It was nice, and you took a personal interest in the organization. Eventually I held every office, but I was a hopeless treasurer, and it was a godsend for me and the organization that I only served a short time. We all waited for our checks every Sunday night.

"Crowds varied according to parts of the country; the coverage was good from sportswriters in spite of having no press rooms and, of course, no television. Courses were never closed down. We played our practice rounds between the members; they teed off behind us during a tournament, and we shared their locker room.

"The sport was the thing. We enjoyed the competition and money was a necessary evil. We never thought of making a lot of money, neither in golf nor in other jobs. The opportunities for women were very limited in all fields; so why not do something you enjoyed?

"I always had aspirations of doing well at golf, of playing well and winning, but I got that knocked out of me right away. I played so badly, I almost quit after six months. I talked it over with my parents and Harvey [Penick]. Since no one was upset that I wasn't paying them back, the pressure disappeared, and I decided to give myself three years.

"I worked very hard and received a lot of help from Mickey Wright, Betsy Rawls, Gloria Armstrong, and Jackie Pung. I was so self-conscious about my golf; I thought everyone was looking at me. But they had enough troubles of their own and were more concerned with their games. The players were friendly. There was a great feeling of camaraderie, our goals were the same, and our motives were good, I made lasting friendships, and I wouldn't trade that time for the world. Later on, when the group became so much bigger, it was difficult to get to know people, and we lost the sense of family.

"My first goal on tour was to make money, but it was six months before I scraped in for $30. I was so delighted that it was like winning. I put a lot of pressure on myself, which I couldn't handle. I didn't win until 1962, when I was able to control myself and hit my best shots without thinking of winning or losing. After that, I never looked back, just forward, and I kept going. The competition was tremendous. It was great to be in contention every week. When you are young, you have the world by the tail, and everything looks great.

"When I won eight tournaments in 1963, I was living on a high. I got in a winning syndrome. I played really well, and it came easily. You don't think you're that great, but you're in the groove with good concentration. Nothing bothers you, and it is fun. Soon the spell breaks, and you struggle back up again. I don't know if winning is the best thing in the world, but it's a thrill. It is what you set out to do, so why limit yourself? It is great when your peers and great players congratulate you. I always got a real charge out of hitting a good shot or pulling off a trouble shot, whether or not I was the only one who knew about it.

"I look on the LPGA as a second family. I have made some close relationships, and when we are all retired, we will still be close wherever we are. Because I feel that closeness, one of the great thrills of my life was being inducted into the Hall of Fame in 1975, alongside other players of my era. It is the highest honor the LPGA gives to a player, and not many are going to make it. In my short speech, I tried to convey how much it meant to me and that maybe it meant more than winning.

"I always got excited about playing. I couldn't wait to get to the first tee. I am glad I was able to play head to head with Mickey [Wright] on several occasions. There was no one greater, and all the young players would gravitate over to watch her practice. She was a great motivator for me."

Kathy continued on her upward path until the end of 1973, when the emotional and physical strain took its toll and forced her to re-evaluate her goals. That year she had seven victories and topped the money list with $82,864.

"I won the last tournament of 1973, and my nerves were so bad I could hardly sign the score card. I was so exhausted and nervous I just scribbled my name. I remember it so well, and after the presentation I barely crawled back to my room, where I just died on the couch from exhaustion.

"After that winter, for the first time I didn't want to go back on tour. The seasons of 1974 and 1975 were traumatic. Previously I had always geared myself to go for number one all the time, and now I was forced to pull back, or I would not have been able to continue playing. I would find myself in contention and then shoot 80 the next day, which disturbed me. I didn't realize I was rebelling against being there. I thought about it and decided I was shooting a horrendous round to take off the pressure. Then I accepted the fact that it is nice to win but that you don't have to do it every week. You can be thrilled to bits by coming second because second is better than third. That attitude helped me, and I played better.

"In 1977, I again felt the strain. I remember winning the Colgate, which put me in number one position and the following week I promptly missed the cut. I will never forget missing the cut on Friday, waking up the next morning, disappointed and upset, and finding I couldn't move out of bed because my arms and legs felt like lead. I decided the Lord was telling me I couldn't take any more, so I lay in bed all day. You learn about yourself as you go along, and that year I didn't finish number one because I didn't want it. I probably never wanted it again. My mind and body rejected it as the pressure all returned—the demands on my time, the press, and the responsibility. When you are younger, you can handle it, but later I rebelled, and I made sure I didn't put myself through that again.

"During the latter part of 1978 and 1979 my golf deteriorated, although it turned around a bit in 1980. I had been in slumps before but not to that degree, and had it continued, I would have quit because it was too painful. When I won in a playoff in 1981, it was one of the big moments in my life, since it was important to know I still had the ability."

In 1981, when Kathy became the first woman professional to make a career $1 million, just ahead of JoAnne Carner in a much publicized race, she said: "I didn't want the build-up to get so out of hand with the media, I thought we would all have a heart attack, but it was great for the association." Her next milestones were passing Mickey Wright's 82 victories and receiving a telegram of congratulation from Mickey, and then the same accolade from Sam Snead on equaling his 84 victories. Kathy's three victories in 1984 and another in 1985 were remarkable achievements. Winning the inaugural 1987 Marilynn Smith Founders' Classic rounded off an emotional week of warm reunions and reminiscences, recreating the feelings that Kathy had earlier predicted would always be there among that close group of women.

As the 1980s progressed, Kathy's playing career was winding down: "I would love to play well so that I could feel I was leaving the tour on a high," she admitted at the time, "but I don't know if I can turn around my game. I would prefer to say I don't want to play any more rather than saying I won't play because I can't hit it. I'm sure it's an ego thing. I'm always going to want to play better; even when I'm 90, I hope I'll be able to play and not play badly.

"I enjoyed what I did on tour, and when I look at the alternative, what else would I have done? I can't think of anything I would have preferred. It didn't scare me to leave, because I felt I could get a job, which I would need, since I was not financially independent without one.

"I would not have had a different life, nor will I ever regret it. It's a sweet life. I was not on tour for the money, and I got more than my share of enjoyment out of my career. The life of a professional athlete is not hard, and I enjoyed every second—the traveling, the competition—and I never thought I was sacrificing anything. I would recommend it highly to any young girl who has the ability and who expresses the desire to do it. I am glad there is more opportunity for them now."

"By 1988, when Kathy was struggling with her game, she became vice president of the LPGA, a position leading to its presidency the following year. It was a time of turmoil in the administration, which led to the resignation of commissioner, John

Laupheimer, of whom Kathy was a staunch supporter, not having cared for the style of his more flamboyant predecessor, Ray Volpe. Ensuring that she had the support and confidence of the membership, Kathy continued in office. In 1989, thirty years after she joined the tour, Kathy became president of the LPGA for the fourth time. Her term of office coincided with the hiring of a new commissioner, Bill Blue.

Kathy said, "Being president is not an ego trip for me. I want to make it work and help the association, which in turn helps me. It is going to be tough and time consuming, but my career is pretty much over, and I'm willing to give the time. The job can detract from a younger player's game, but it's to the stage for me where my putter is older than most of the girls out here."

Kathy's year of presidency with Bill Blue was a troubled time for the association, since it became apparent he was not the right man for the job. Kathy describes it as "the most depressing and frustrating year I ever had as part of the LPGA. I have never been more scared of damage control running rampant."

Happily, the future of the LPGA turned around after Charles Mechem arrived at the end of 1990, but for Kathy Whitworth another battle was just beginning. Announcing her retirement in 1990, her financial worth was at an all time low. In 1981 Kathy entrusted her savings to a financial management company in California, only to see the company sink, filing for reorganization under Chapter 11 in 1986, with its lawyer-president going to jail for fraud two years later.

"It was very depressing, a sickening feeling that is hard to describe. You read about things like that and then cannot believe it has happened to you. After the initial shock, I realized I was young enough to get a job and make some money. I couldn't really cry because compared to many older people who lost everything, it was not nearly so brutal for me. You can wallow in it and not accomplish anything, or you can go on."

Kathy went on to sell her retirement home and to become involved with a Japanese consortium sending young women from Japan to America to train them as professional golfers. With appropriate advice from her own elderly and eminent teaching professional, Harvey Penick, and armed with his bible, The Little Red Book, she responded to the situation: "It has been terrific. The girls are great, very receptive, and they want to learn," she said.

Kathy Whitworth wins number 83 in 1982 at the Lady Michelob to surpass Mickey Wright in the number of tournament victories. Later, in 1985, she won her 88th tournament, more than any other man or woman golf pro.

Kathy threw herself with even more enthusiasm into the captaincy of the first U.S. Solheim Cup team, which met the Europeans at Lake Nona, Florida, in November 1990, trouncing the Europeans by $11\frac{1}{2}$ to $4\frac{1}{2}$. For Kathy, it was a week of delight to be back in the fray of competition, even if she was only at the helm. Chosen again in 1992 for the same job, this time with the matches in Scotland, Kathy made the journey, only to remain for one day. Her mother, who had been suffering from cancer for four years, suddenly died. "It is very hard to lose a parent," Kathy said later, "and in difficult times you do the best you can. The last four years my mother handled really well, and now I must not dwell on her death."

Kathy's fortitude has seen her through the tough times in her golf and in her personal grieving. She leaves a trail of outstanding memories for herself and those who follow her. "I treasure having been able to do something I really enjoyed. I was lucky to know at an early age what I wanted and to have the opportunity to do it. As I get older, I am more and more grateful.

"The highlights were not necessarily the victories but were more the experiences of being involved in the association, and knowing and meeting terrific people such as Patty Berg, Louise Suggs, Betsy Rawls, and Mickey Wright. It is wonderful just to have crossed their paths. I have a lot of memories: I saw the country by car, met all kinds of people, appreciated it at the time, enjoyed it so much, and played well enough to stay there.

"I don't think about the legacy of 88 tournaments —I did it because I wanted to win, not to set a record or a goal that no one else could surpass. I'm not some great oddity. I was just fortunate to be so successful. What I did in being a better player does not make me a better person. I'm not smarter or more intelligent than someone who digs a good ditch. I am proud for myself and what I did and that I gave my best shot. When I'm asked how I would like to be remembered, I feel that if people remember me at all it will be good enough."

Member LPGA Hall of Fame 1975

LPGA Victories: 1962 Kelly Girl Open, Phoenix Thunderbird Open. **1963** Carvel Open, Wolverine Open, Milwaukee Jaycee Open, Ogden Open, Spokane Open, Hillside Open, San Antonio Civitan Open, Gulf Coast Invitational. **1964** San Antonio Civitan Open. **1965** St. Petersburg Invitational, Shreveport Kiwanis Club Invitational, Bluegrass Invitational, Midwest Open, Yankee Open, Buckeye Savings Invitational, Mickey Wright Invitational, Titleholders Championship. **1966** Tall City Open, Clayton Federal Invitational, Milwaukee Open, Superfest Invitational, Lady Carling (Sutton), Lady Carling (Baltimore), Las Cruces Open, Amarillo Open, Titleholders Championship. **1967** Venice Open, Raleigh Invitational, St. Louis Invitational, LPGA Championship, Lady Carling (Columbus), Western Open, Los Angeles Open, Alamo Open. **1968** Orange Blossom Classic, Dallas Civitan, Baltimore Lady Carling, Gino Paoli Open, Holiday Inn Classic, Kings River Classic, River Plantation Classic, Canyon Classic, Pensacola Invitational, Louise Suggs Invitational. **1969** Orange Blossom Classic, Port Charlotte Invitational, Port Malabar Invitational, Lady Carling (Atlanta), Patty Berg Classic, Wendell West Open, River Plantation Open. **1970** Orange Blossom Classic, Quality Chek'd Classic. **1971** Raleigh Classic, Suzuki Internationale, Lady Carling, LPGA Championship. **1972** Alamo Open, Raleigh Classic, Knoxville Open, Southgate Open, Portland Open. **1973** Naples-Lely Classic, S&H Green Stamp Classic, Dallas Civitan, Southgate Open, Portland Open, Waco Tribune Herald Classic, Lady Errol Classic. **1974** Orange Blossom Classic. **1975** Baltimore Championship, Southgate Open, LPGA Championship. **1976** Bent Tree Classic, Patty Berg Classic. **1977** Colgate–Dinah Shore Winner's Circle, American Defender Classic, Coca-Cola Classic. **1978** National Jewish Hospital Open. **1981** Kemper Open. **1982** The Lady Michelob. **1983** Women's Kemper Open. **1984** Rochester Invitational, SAFECO Classic, Smirnoff Ladies Irish Open. **1985** United Virginia Bank Classic.

Unofficial Victories: 1971 LPGA Four-Ball Championship (with Judy Kimball Simon). **1975** Colgate Triple Crown. **1978** Ping Classic (with Donna Caponi). **1980** Portland Ping Team Championship (with Donna Caponi). **1981** Portland Ping Team Championship (with Donna Caponi).

Kathy Whitworth's LPGA Record

Year	No.of Events	Best Finish	Money	Rank	Scoring Average
1959	26	9	$1,217	NA	80.30
1960	22	2	4,901	NA	77.11
1961	15	2	6,853	NA	76.05
1962	28	1	17,044	NA	74.32
1963	32	1	26,858	2	73.90
1964	31	1	20,434	3	73.60
1965	30	1	28,658	1	72.61
1966	31	1	33,517	1	72.60
1967	28	1	32,937	1	72.74
1968	30	1	48,379	1	72.16
1969	28	1	48,171	2	72.38
1970	21	1	30,235	1	72.26
1971	20	1	41,181	1	72.88
1972	29	1	65,063	1	72.38
1973	31	1	82,864	1	73.12
1974	25	1	52,064	6	73.50
1975	21	1	34,422	9	72.96
1976	25	1	62,013	9	73.60
1977	25	1	108,540	3	72.16
1978	26	1	67,855	12	73.60
1979	26	T2	36,246	30	74.15
1980	29	T3	48,392	24	73.91
1981	27	1	134,937	10	72.40
1982	25	1	136,698	9	72.28
1983	26	1	191,492	5	72.33
1984	28	1	146,401	8	72.82
1985	22	1	95,606	21	72.82
1986	26	T5	54,774	46	73.80
1987	25	T11	18,653	101	74.76
1988	22	T12	16,683	107	74.63
1989	24	T30	11,054	134	74.79
1990	21	T31	6,652	153	75.22
1991	12	T28	2,636	178	76.04

Mickey Wright

Mickey Wright is a living legend and arguably the greatest woman golfer ever. I am thankful that I got to see that legend play golf. I first met Mickey when she was competing in the 1979 Coca Cola Classic in New Jersey. She played in tennis shoes, which she has done ever since she had two operations in 1974 and 1975 on her left foot for a growth known as Morton's neuroma.

After the final hole of the 54 hole tournament, Mickey was involved in a five way sudden death playoff with Nancy Lopez, Hollis Stacy, Jo Ann Washam, and Bonnie Bryant. At the opening short hole, Mickey, playing first, hit a superb five iron two feet from the flag, and the crowd went wild. The remaining players all made the green at varying ranges from the hole.

Lopez, then on the crest of her wave, holed her 25 footer for a birdie, the others dropped out with pars, and then Mickey sank her birdie putt from two feet. The legend, who joined the tour in 1954, and the young star, half her age, went to the next hole where Lopez won the title with another birdie. There is little doubt that everyone would love to have seen Mickey Wright achieve that win because of her greatness, her outstanding ability, and all that she meant to the game of golf. It would have been one more, to add to the 82 victories she amassed in the most outstanding golf career of all time.

Nancy Lopez said some years later: "Mickey Wright is the greatest golfer I've ever known. She wouldn't intimidate me now because finally I've acquired a confidence in myself, but in the playoff at the Coca Cola in 1979, I was intimidated. I remember her playing in tennis shoes, and she out-hit me, and I was pretty long then. I thought if I could beat her, what a great accomplishment it would be. I would be able to tell myself I had beaten Mickey Wright, the greatest of all time, and it would be a wonderful achievement. I also felt she might never win another tournament, and I would be the one who took that victory away from her. And she never did."

A tall, strongly built woman, Mickey has a marvelous, classical, rhythmic swing that makes the game look simple and effortless. It is a joy to

Many have described her golf swing as perfect. She was also perhaps the greatest player in LPGA history. Mickey Wright joined the LPGA in 1955 and won 82 victories in her amazing 26-year career.

watch her play golf. Professional Elmer Prieskorn, who often saw her play, says: "Mickey Wright hit more good shots accidentally than most girls did on purpose."

Betsy Rawls says: "Mickey was able to move the clubhead so fast and hit the ball a very long way because her mechanics were so good. She was strong, but she had no wasted movement in her swing so that everything contributed to moving the clubhead.

"As a personality, she didn't appear outwardly competitive or aggressive, although certainly she was. As a golfer, she stayed within herself, she gave everyone credit, and was the dominant star carrying the tour. To the public, she came across as very gracious and charming, and people liked her, although she was not outgoing. She was pleasant, even though she didn't like being sociable or care for the adulation. She didn't want people to bother her, but she didn't show it. She was a very controlled, unemotional person, who would never display any temper.

"Mickey was the best golfer we've ever had, and that I've ever seen. She had the right combination of a mechanically sound swing and enormous personal drive. It is hard to get that combination. At one time, the mechanics were too important to her, but then she realized that winning was more than hitting the ball well."

In fact, it was Betsy Rawls, who pointed out to Mickey Wright that she was becoming too intense about the mechanics of the game and that she should concentrate more on the ingredients of winning. Mickey says: "Betsy taught me the most important thing of all: to take responsibility for everything that happens to you on the golf course, not to blame the greens for bad putting, the caddy for bad club selection, or the fates for a bad day. She also taught me how important it is to maintain control of your emotions on the course, not to get excited about a birdie or get down about a bogey, but to save your emotional energy for the work at hand."

Mickey's career is remarkable, not only for the number of tournaments she won but for the number of major championships it included: four U.S. Open titles, four LPGA Championships, and

Mickey won the U.S. Open four-times — 1958, 1959, 1961, and 1964.

one Dinah Shore. She also achieved a record 13 victories in one year (1963), was leading money winner for four years, won the Vare trophy for five consecutive years, and, in fact, dominated the tour right through the 1960s.

Mickey admits to having become obsessed with winning, until it took over her entire life. Finally she had to retreat from her fixation to get her life into some sort of perspective.

She is a charming, soft spoken woman, intensely shy, which obviously has been an enormous strain in a life that has always put her in the limelight. She was the focal point of the tour in the 1960s, and every sponsor demanded her presence at each event. At one point, she also played 139 exhibitions a year for two years.

Meeting Mickey and seeing her play was a highlight in my life. When I first told her about the book I wanted to write and asked whether I could see her for an interview at a later date, I was surprised and highly encouraged at the alacrity with which she agreed. After my initial contact, I wrote to her and then did not hear from her for some time. When she did reply, it was with much warmth, encouragement, and an agreement to meet. It took some time for us to get together, and at one stage I felt maybe Mickey was going through some of those former pangs of apprehension in talking to someone who represented the press.

When finally the interview took place, it was during the penultimate tournament of her career, the Whirlpool Championship at Deer Creek, in February 1980, when Mickey talked with depth and honesty about herself and her emotions. A fascinating picture emerged.

Later, we corresponded again, with Mickey replying instantly to my further queries, one of which concerned her retirement. In July 1980, she wrote, "I think I'm retired, but I like to leave my options open."

In my letter to her I pointed out that our birthdays are within three days of each other, and she wrote back, "Remember, Aquarians are successful at what they put their minds to." When I told tour astrologer Joyce Kazmierski that both Mickey Wright and I were Aquarians, she looked at me for a moment and then pronounced: "So much for Astrology."

Mickey Wright was born on February 14, 1935, in San Diego. Her father was a lawyer, and her parents were divorced when she was three. Her mother remarried a man in the insurance business, and Mickey lived with them, acquiring two step-brothers, who were 14 and 16 years older. She continued to see a great deal of her father, who lived only six blocks away, and financially, her life was a comfortable one. Her father died in 1970, and her mother in 1990.

"My father was a tremendous motivation for me. Primarily, I wanted to gain financial independence from him, and then to prove to him what I could do. It is no coincidence that he died in 1970 and only one time in the following ten years did I play more than ten tournaments in a year. My father was a huge influence on my golfing life, and he never told me he thought I'd done well until it was all over.

"When I was ten years old, about the time my mother remarried, my father, who was a 15-handicap weekend golfer, introduced me to the game and had me taught by Johnny Bellante, who started Gene Littler. I took to it like a duck to water and a little later there was a picture of me in the local paper with a caption, 'The Next Babe?' You can imagine what that does for an 11-year old, and from that time on I was determined to become a professional golfer.

"When I was growing up, there was not any junior golf in San Diego. It is now the hotbed of junior golf, but that came a few years later. I gauged my progress by my scores. When I was 11, I broke 100. A year later I broke 90, and I broke 70 at 14. I had my own goals, which is what golf is all about. It is a very individual game of always playing the course without any competition between people, and that is probably why I like it. I played very little matchplay, and when I did, I couldn't play at all because I'm not a gut-level, gritty competitor in any way. Perfection motivated me, doing it better than anyone had ever done it, just as simply as that. To that end, I would practice for hours and hours. I beat balls and beat balls and beat balls.

"When I played golf, it was either alone, with my father, or with a few ladies at La Jolla. Juniors were not very welcome at clubs, which I think was a good idea. They had their place and were allowed on the course on certain days and hours, always accompanied by an adult. Nowadays, some juniors I see act as though they own the course. They think they are the members, which does not impress me because I've got an old fashioned view of golf. I hate to see the traditions disappear.

"My first tournament was the La Jolla club championship at 14, and I won it. Then I played in Los Angeles in the Southern California Junior Girls', and I won that, which took me to the club's professional, Harry Pressler. He was my coach and teacher from there on. He taught me to swing the club, and I spent about four years working on what he taught me. He had definite ideas on the golf swing, and four California state champions were his pupils. They and I swung the club the same way, and they were good golf swings.

"I had very little amateur experience, but when I did compete, my mother would drive me to tournaments. She was always greatly supportive of my playing. I was runner-up in the National Junior Championship in 1950, and then I was beaten by Betty Dodd in the final of the Western Amateur.

"My father, who was quite a bit older than my mother—he was 52 when I was born—twisted my arm and made me go to Stanford University for a year. He was of the old school who thought that women should go to college and get their teaching certificates; so they would have something to fall back on in life. He couldn't be budged from that idea until many years later when I had done well as a professional, and then he was 100 percent behind me.

"In 1954, I persuaded him that college was a waste of time; so he said he would give me $1,000, and I could go to Florida and play the tournaments until my money ran out. Then, I should get myself back home, forget golf, and go back to school. He didn't think I would achieve anything, and he was opposed to my playing professional golf.

"I went down to Florida and played two professional tournaments as an amateur. I led the first day at St. Pete with a 68, and had I been a professional, I would have won $345 in my first event. In the second tournament I would have won $450, which was quite a bit of money, as expenses were about $100 a week. That convinced my father. He said I could try professional golf, and I never had to take a penny from him after that.

"As I was always a professional in my heart and thought of myself as a professional, I did not have a transition to make in that sense. Most of the girls before, during, and after my time learned how to play golf when they got on tour, and the transition occurred in being a youngster who was getting out into the world. I was scared to death of driving a car across the country alone, of not knowing how to register at a motel—I was really green; and the hard part was learning how to travel. But, it was marvelous being part of a group where everyone was helpful because it was so small, and it was a matter of survival. We had to keep people out there, or there would not have been any tour.

"There never had been any statistics kept on the LPGA, and I was their first statistician. I'm a nut with figures and decided that I would start keeping records. We did everything ourselves; I was the secretary and kept the minutes. Then I was treasurer and wrote out checks. I was on the tournament committee, and later I was president for a couple of years.

"Everyone had something to do in our close-knit group; so sharing the work gave us a feeling of camaraderie, of pride in the growth of the tour and in the fact that we held it together. We were more of a family, which is still the way I feel about those people even if I don't see them for six months, a year, or more. You don't have to see people to feel close, but when you do meet, it's just like old home week.

Mickey visited the White Sands Missile Range in New Mexico on October 27, 1964, while playing in the Las Cruces Open. Photo: Warren C. Weaver, Civ., U.S. Army Photograph.

Mickey Wright wins her first major, the LPGA Championship, in June 1958. In all, she won this title four times.

"Unfortunately, at that time it was not acceptable for a woman to be an athlete. We all felt that when we were in public, we had to be 'on' like being on stage, and we had to watch our speech, our mannerisms, and everything we did. Not that anyone needed to, but when you are told that any woman who plays sports is nothing but an Amazon; then you have to try to counteract it.

"Of course, Babe was crude, and she couldn't have cared less. I was an amateur when I first played with her in 1954—in her last U.S. Open, which she won. We were paired together for the last two rounds and in one of them, her husband, George, stood in front of her on the course as she took off her slip, because it was such a hot day. I was totally appalled. She used awful language. I had never seen a woman like her, and I was embarrassed for her, but I needn't have worried, for it certainly didn't bother her.

"When I got to know Babe, I realized that she was having her fun in public and that really she was very sensitive and quite a nice person. I had respect for her, and she really made the women's tour. But, she was the complete opposite of me. She loved being in a crowd, which brought out her exhibitionist tendencies. A year after I joined the tour, she died.

"Babe was a marvelous athlete, but she couldn't carry Patty Berg's golf clubs. She wasn't the golfer that Patty or Louise Suggs were. Patty is the consummate perfect golfer for a woman, which shows in the fact that in her sixties she could still swing the club beautifully.

"It was some time after Babe died that the attention began to focus on me. I was winning tournaments in the 1950s, with 13 victories from 1955 to 1960, but it was not until the 1960s—1961, 1962, 1963, 1964—that I went from being good to being great, winning 44 tournaments in four years.

"The difference came in 1960, when I went to professional Earl Stewart in Dallas. He never touched my swing, as I knew very well how to swing a golf club, but he taught me to play and how to think. I moved to Dallas, and for a while he played golf with me every day. He was a slave driver, much more of a perfectionist than I, so far as winning goes, and he didn't care how I hit or swung the club. The object was to win.

"He would set goals for me every year—six tournaments this year, ten the next. When I won

13 tournaments in 1963, he just about broke my back by telling me it was a fair year, but that he would like to see me win 20 the following year. I nearly left the tour after that, even though I won 11 times in 1964.

"Although I had to prove to my father that I could make it on my own, money was secondary. I wanted to be the best golfer, and all I thought about was winning and doing it better than it had ever been done. During the time I was winning so much, there was a lot of pressure on me because I was also president of the LPGA for two years, and sponsors would threaten to cancel tournaments if I didn't show up. Consequently, I played very much more than I could physically and emotionally handle.

"Being president entailed going to every presentation, going to some type of Rotary Club luncheon and addressing them, attending cocktail parties every week, and introducing all the girls to the people at the party, plus running meetings and doing chores of a social nature that I didn't enjoy. It was a big responsibility. In addition, the pressure of the press can be very brutal. If you don't win, if you come in second or third, there are comments such as, 'What happened to you?', 'Is your game falling apart?', 'Are you over the hill?' This bothered me very much and for a time made me very cynical, which was a trait I did not like in myself.

"I never overcame my dislike of making a speech. I remember when I was inducted into the World Golf Hall of Fame in 1976 and I knew that I would have to make a speech, I sweated at home over it for months beforehand. I would practice, practice, practice because I found it so very difficult to get up and talk in front of people. I was always shy, never having been thrown into groups as a child; almost exclusively I was with older people. Either I was hitting balls alone, or I was playing golf with older people. My mother was a very modest woman who preached modesty, and my father was a very reticent man, a loner; it has always been more natural for me to back off from people.

"I got winning and golf and myself very closely tied up. Golf was me, and I was nothing without golf. Really I took it to an extreme for a while, which was very uncomfortable and certainly wasn't living life, but it is an easy trap into which to fall, especially when you have as much drive as I had to win. When you do win, it is total relief. Coming up to that last hole, you are scared to death, so afraid you will lose. If you are one shot ahead coming to the last hole, the only thing you can do is lose. It's very frightening always having your ego on the line.

Mickey found very little joy in winning, it was the fear of losing that drove her to become one of golf's greatest. Photo Courtesy: Golf Magazine.

"There is very little joy for me in winning. It is more, 'Thank God I didn't lose.' I've heard Billie Jean King say that what kept her going was total abhorrence of losing. For me, it was as if you didn't exist if you lost, and then I couldn't wait until the next week to win again. When you're shy and have inadequate feelings in other areas as I did socially, then everything gets tied up too closely with what you do in golf. It becomes too important to you as a person, shows how narrow you are and that you had better shake loose and find a little more dimension to yourself, which is what I did.

"I had hurt my wrist, or, who knows, did I hurt my wrist because I needed to get away? I don't know. But I left the tour in 1965, and I grieved. That was the first thing I did, a lot of grieving. My wrist was in a cast for about eight weeks, and while it was healing, I enrolled at SMU in Dallas for one semester and just hated it. I took two mathematics courses, philosophy, and psychology for six weeks and then dropped it because I thought it was a bunch of garbage. I did some volunteer work at an unwed mothers' home and branched out a little, trying other directions.

"Later in 1965 I returned to play 11 tournaments, and I won two, and then I was back full-time in 1966, with the pressure starting to build up again as I won seven tournaments. I decided to back off slowly, to gradually reduce the number of tournaments I played over a period of years, which I did, and it was a slow process.

"I have a theory that the adrenalin supply runs out when your body has pumped so much adrenalin over the years, and it frays the nerves; so that emotionally it wears you down. I think you have just so much of that to give. I was very fortunate to have the physical ability I had, the financial opportunity, and the good fortune to be born to whom I was so that I could play golf.

"The victory that meant most to me in my career was winning my fourth U.S. Open in 1964 in San Diego in front of my mother and father. My father was about 79 and not in really good health. He came to the tournament on the last day, and I needed a six-foot putt on the last hole to tie Ruth Jessen and go into a playoff the next day. I made that putt, I won the playoff, and it was the most thrilling tournament I have ever won.

"I have enjoyed the experience of doing something very well, and although I feel I made it happen, I could not have done it without Harry Pressler, Earl Stewart, or Stan Kertes, who helped me hit the ball longer. You have to want to do it enough, and you must feel that nothing else is as important.

"I have always said that people who win have 'it,' whatever 'it' means. Certainly it includes the ability to shoot 80 and look like a champion, to double bogey and never frown, to make a birdie and not get excited. You have to be able to control your emotions under tough situations."

Now, Mickey Wright is living in Florida: "I spend most of my time at the full-time job of living. You know, three meals a day, cleaning, repairing, yard work and the myriad of responsibilities of being an adult. I must say the real world is a lot busier than the unreal world of tour life, where you never fix a meal, wash a dish, make a bed, mow a lawn, repair

Mickey Wright was inducted into the World Golf Hall of Fame in Pinehurst, North Carolina, in 1976. A living legend in the golf world, she is considered by many to be the greatest woman golfer to ever have played the game. Today, she occasionally plays in LPGA events, but as she says, "I spend most of my time at the full-time job of living"

a faucet, or do much of anything other than hit golf balls and make it to a tee time.

"For fun I fish, I hit golf balls from my back yard out onto the 14th and 15th fairways behind the house, I read, and I watch and study the stock market. By most people's dreams, I don't suppose I am successful in the market, but I am accomplishing what I have set out to do. I have a decent income, keep up with inflation, and I don't lose money. Rather dull, but in its own way, quite rewarding."

Member LPGA Hall of Fame 1964

LPGA Victories: 1956 Jacksonville Open. **1957** Sea Island Open, Jacksonville Open, Wolverine Open. **1958** Sea Island Open, Opie Turner Open, Dallas Civitan Open, LPGA Championship, U.S. Women's Open. **1959** Jacksonville Open, Cavalier Open, Alliance Machine International Open, U.S. Women's Open. **1960** Sea Island Open, Tampa Open, Grossinger Open, Eastern Open, Memphis Open, LPGA Championship. **1961** St. Petersburg Open, Miami Open, Columbus Open, Waterloo Open, Spokane Open, Sacramento Valley Open, U.S. Women's Open, LPGA Championship, Titleholders Championship, Mickey Wright Invitational. **1962** Sea Island Invitational, Titleholders Championship, Western Open, Milwaukee Open, Heart of America Invitational, Albuquerque Swing Parade, Salt Lake City Open, Spokane Open, San Diego Open, Carlsbad Caver City Open. **1963** Sea Island Invitational, St. Petersburg Open, Alpine Civitan Open, Muskogee Civitan Open, Dallas Civitan, Babe Zaharias Open, Western Open, Waterloo Open, Albuquerque Swing Parade, Idaho Centennial Open, Visalia Open, Mickey Wright Invitational, LPGA Championship. **1964** Peach Blossom Invitational, Alexandria Open, Squirt Open, U.S. Women's Open, Milwaukee JayCee Open, Visalia Open, Tall City Open, Gulf Coast Invitational. **1965** Baton Rouge Invitational, Dallas Civitan. **1966** Venice Open, Shreveport Kiwanis Invitational, Bluegrass Invitational, Western Open, Pacific Classic, Shirley Englehorn Invitational, Mickey Wright Invitational. **1967** Shreveport Invitational, Bluegrass Invitational, Lady Carling (Baltimore), Pensacola Invitational. **1968** Port Malabar Invitational, Palm Beach Country Open, Tall City Open, "500" Classic. **1969** Bluegrass Invitational. **1973** Colgate Dinah Shore Winner's Circle.

Mickey Wright's LPGA Record

Year	No.of Events	Best Finish	Money	Rank	Scoring Average
1955	19	T3	$6,325	NA	78.04
1956	1	1	8,253	7	76.06
1957	24	1	11,131	3	75.38
1958	18	1	11,775	3	75.03
1959	26	1	18,182	5	74.51
1960	23	1	16,380	2	73.25
1961	17	1	22,236	1	73.31
1962	33	1	21,641	1	73.67
1963	30	1	31,269	1	72.81
1964	27	1	29,800	1	72.46
1965	11	1	8,888	13	73.10
1968	12	1	26,672	3	72.40
1967	21	1	20,613	4	72.65
1968	12	1	17,147	7	72.31
1969	21	1	17,851	10	73.92
1970	5	T2	4,436	45	74.08
1971	9	T3	6,575	36	73.35
1972	9	2	14,379	26	74.00
1973	8	1	36,262	11	74.27
1974	4	T21	1,929	74	75.66
1975	2	T22	610	99	74.17
1976	5	8	3,049	83	74.81
1977	11	T3	16,685	46	73.46
1978	6	3	9,175	70	73.60
1979	7	T2	8,892	79	74.14
1980	2	T33	554	146	76.00

The 1960s

The 1960s was the decade when Mickey Wright transcended to another level of golf to become a legend and the greatest professional the LPGA tour has ever seen. She added two U.S. Open victories in the 1960s to add to her two in the 1950s. She recorded 13 major titles—the most of any LPGA player; she had achieved 81 of her 82 victories by the end of the decade; her thirteen tournament wins in 1963 remain a record. It was not only the record books that made her so exceptional. It was the excitement of the rhythm, grace, power, and flow of her extraordinary talent, her constant search for perfection and her ability to achieve it, together with the combination of intelligence and physical talent, that produced Mickey Wright, the consummate golfer.

All the other women professionals speak of her with awe, and their greatest achievement is in going head to head with Mickey and beating her. Even Nancy Lopez felt this when Mickey was well past her prime in 1979, and Nancy found herself in a five way sudden death playoff, which included Mickey Wright. With just the two of them going down the second hole, Nancy birdied to take the title. Several years later, she admitted she was intimidated by Mickey at the time of the playoff, that Mickey out-hit her, and that she regards her as the greatest golfer she has ever known. Nancy said, "I thought if I could beat her, I would be able to tell myself I had beaten Mickey Wright, who is the greatest of all time, and it would be a wonderful achievement."

Betsy Rawls said of Mickey: "She totally dominated the sport in the way that had not previously occurred. The public flocked to see her because she was so spectacular. Even though Kathy Whitworth was winning a lot in the 1960s (56 victories compared to Mickey's 68), Mickey was considered so good, so impressive, that the other players would stand and watch her. They were in awe of the way she hit the ball and some of the things she achieved."

In 1960, Betsy Rawls entered the LPGA Hall of Fame, having been leading money winner the previous season with $26,744 and ten victories. She had won a total of 38 tournaments, including three of her four U.S. Open titles, but at that time, there were not any criteria for inclusion in the Hall of Fame: "You just received a telegram saying you had been elected," said Betsy.

It wasn't until 1967, at the association's annual meeting, in Corpus Christi, Texas, that it was decided to establish a Hall of Fame with definite criteria, exclusively for members of the LPGA, but automatically inducting those previously elected, who were Patty Berg, Betty Jameson, Louise Suggs, Babe Zaharias, Betsy Rawls, and Mickey Wright.

Mickey Wright was named Athlete of the Year by the Associated Press in 1963.

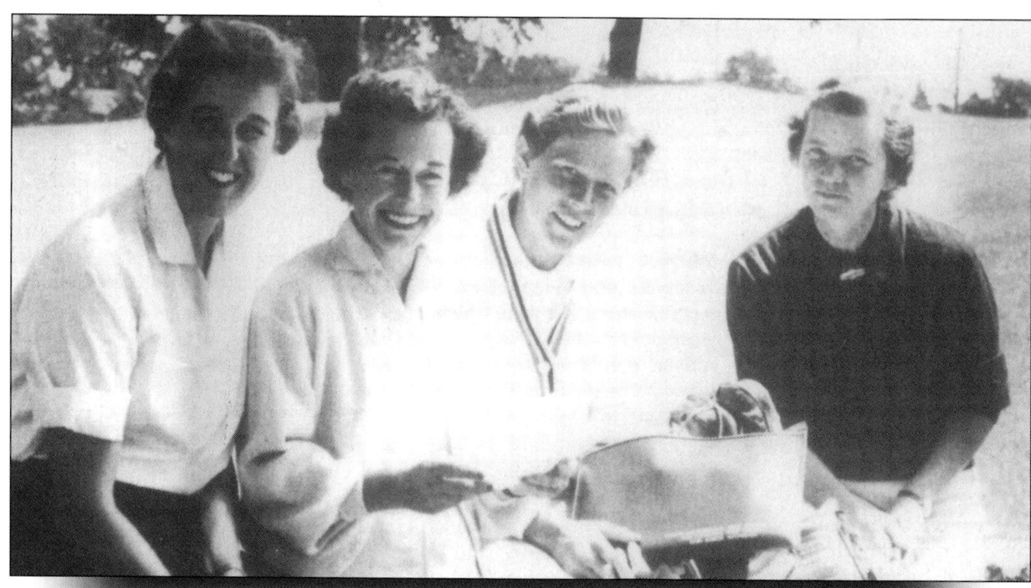

In 1967, LPGA President Marilynn Smith and Shirley Spork led the move to form an LPGA teaching division which held its first five-day LPGA National Golf School at the University of Michigan. Barbara Rotvig, Betty Hicks, Shirley Spork, and Ellen Griffin joined Marilynn as instructors at the school.

Qualifications for entry included being a member in good standing for 10 consecutive years and winning either 30 official events, including two different major championships or 35 official events with one major or 40 official events. Also included at that time was the provision that prospective inductees should have been retired from the tour for two years before entering the Hall of Fame.

In 1960, the daily events of the association were handled by the women professionals, who played their golf in addition to attending to every aspect of the tournaments, including setting up the courses, making the pairings, collating the statistics, paying the checks, and having a social chairman.

Fred Corcoran was in charge from an office in New York, and when his contract was up in mid-1960, the association retained him, but, in addition, hired Joe McDonald, who was out in the field as tournament co-ordinator and liaison officer, while Eileen Stulb continued to promote the organization from her office in Augusta.

LPGA President Marilynn Smith called a group of 23 players to order in a meeting and told them they had $12,000 in the bank, that there was a possibility of getting on television, and that a group insurance scheme was not recommended. At a tournament committee meeting, chaired by Mickey Wright, it was agreed a $25 fine would be imposed for "unaccidental breaking of the club and for late arrival or early leaving from a clinic".

Shirley Spork and Marilynn Smith led a group of women professionals who brought the teaching division into existence. Its first five-day LPGA National Golf School to help teachers of golf improve their teaching technique was held at the University of Michigan. It was so successful that it became an annual event, receiving its first LPGA subsidy of $750 in 1965. Ellen Griffin, Betty Hicks, Shirley Spork, Barbara Rotvig, and Marilynn Smith were all instructors at the first school.

In 1961 the most significant event of the decade occurred for the further promotion, organization, and expansion of the LPGA. When Fred Corcoran's contract expired, the women decided they wanted one person to devote more time to them, and they hired Leonard Wirtz to be in charge of tournaments and obtaining sponsors.

Lenny, known on tour as "The General," was formerly the assistant sales manager of MacGregor, in charge of the advisory staff. He was also a basketball official, a job he continued during the winters, and he promoted some of the women golfers. Both these latter involvements brought criticism from players, but he was the dynamic personality that the tour needed. Kathy Whitworth said: "Lenny gave us policies we live with today in our constitution and by-laws. He did a lot of good things for us. He fought for us, and he was concerned with our dress and our appearance."

Carol Mann said, "Lenny was a good friend of mine, and I thought he was so good for the tour and for the competitors."

I met Lenny Wirtz in the 1980s at the LPGA Championship. I found him short in stature and strong on humor and energy, with a likeable and forceful personality. He said: "I miss a lot of those women; they're greater than people credit them. I got closer to them than any tournament director because it was a small group, but I always tried to be fair. I was tougher on Mickey Wright than anyone out there, since she was the star. I always called her Mary Kathryn because that was her name.

"I was aware of their physiological problems, and I would take into account that some girls had periods that were so much more painful than others. On occasions I would bend the rules. I remember one player getting her period unexpectedly out on the golf course. When she asked me what to do, I let her ride in the cart back to the clubhouse. The others always looked to see how you were treating everyone, and when one of the women complained about the player riding in a cart, I said, 'Her monthly visitor came early.' She trotted off without a word.

"Being with the LPGA constituted eight great years of my life, and it was all because of the girls, who to this day are my friends. It's that friendship that I regard as more important than anything else. Every once in a while I see a quote that makes me feel good. At the time of my hiring I knew more than anyone because I had been exposed to golf all my life. I was born and bred in Cincinnati; I went to the University of Miami, where I was on the golf team, and I worked for MacGregor. I was hired by the LPGA for about 22 players, who had under $200,000 a year for 24 events, and I told them I wanted complete control of the tour.

"I tried to upgrade the quality of the sponsors; I cut the tournaments from four rounds to three, and shortened the courses, so that the women would be less tired and could produce lower scores to encourage greater publicity. I got them free cars from Oldsmobile and some sportswear. I arranged

Three legends of the LPGA are pictured at the 1961 Titleholders Championship which Mickey Wright won. Shown with Mickey are Louise Suggs, who won three Titleholders, and Patty Berg, who won four Titleholders events.

Mickey Wright and Betsy Rawls were both LPGA presidents during the time Lenny Wirtz served as Tournament Director. Both credit him for creating the growth needed to propel the tour into the decades ahead.

an insurance program, I considered hospitalization and retirement programs, and I worked so that a greater percentage of players were breaking even and making money. When I left at the end of 1969, we had 28 tournaments, 50 women, and $700,000 in prize money, having cut back from 34 events the previous season because the women found it too punishing a schedule.

"I paid for my own office and made that my responsibility. The women paid me a percentage of what I raised for them; so that if I didn't produce, I wasn't paid. It was a period of tremendous growth, of getting ourselves organized and knowing where we were going and how we were going to get there.

"It was an era when the girls really enjoyed the tour. I remember we played a tournament in California, where after one day it was so hot that I called the tournament, and we all went to the beach. The next day, when it was 112° the sponsor agreed to cancel it. Another time, at a tournament in Louisiana, the girls were sending me notes about the rain and the quagmire in which they were playing. I knew about it because I was out there, and I had to call the tournament after two rounds.

"Those were formative years for all of us. I was 30, married, with four children, all of whom came on tour during the holidays. We were all young enough that we grew up together. I am, and I was, a basketball official, and I was always criticized for it, but I wouldn't give it up. I agreed to get 35 weeks of tournaments, and I had 17 free weeks for basketball, starting at Thanksgiving.

"In the early sixties, if we had 1,000–2,000 people to watch 30 women, it was a good crowd. Later it grew to 10,000–20,000, but early on we had to play small towns to get any attention. It was difficult to get courses. We couldn't afford to rent them, so we had the members playing on the same course after the women had teed off.

"Our players shaped up really well as I introduced fines for everything: for throwing clubs, for language, for withdrawing from tournaments. I was judge, jury, and executioner, and they loved me or hated me. They called me the No. 1 money winner, since I took their fines, and I told them I was worth it. I used the money for a tour party at the end of the season. I'm proud of the ones who are still around, like Marlene Hagge, who once said to me: 'You're not always right, but you're never wrong.'

"One time at a tournament in Albuquerque, the local television company sent two people who had never before covered a tournament. On the first tee, Mickey [Wright] was getting ready to hit the ball, and the guy said, 'Wait a minute, I'm not ready with the camera.' On the third hole, where she was in the rough, the same thing happened, and again at the ninth. Mickey, who was very edgy at the time because she was trying to quit smoking, told him to stay away or she would bury a nine iron in his head.

"When she reached the par three 12th, she got ready to putt, and saw the guy lying on the green behind the hole. Mickey missed her putt. 'Mister', she said, 'come here.' Then she back-handed the next one, the next, and so on, until she six putted the green for a seven, and missed the cut.

"I flew into town that night, and Mickey and I had breakfast the next morning. She told me the whole comical story, after which, I said to her, 'If I'm Mickey Wright and you're Lenny Wirtz, what would you do?' She said, 'Mr. Wirtz, just tell me how much.' I fined her $100, and she paid up immediately.

"Mickey and I sometimes used to go fishing together, early in the morning, and I told her to put her money in stocks and how to do it, and the stock market became her second passion to golf. She was a woman who was driven by perfection, and it eventually drove her off the tour. I've never seen a woman play golf like Mickey."

In 1961, it was noted at a players' meeting: "The prototype image in the public's mind of a female athlete is not a pretty one, which holds true for any women's sport. Way back yonder there were too many Samsons and not enough Delilahs, and many people still believe this to be true, until they see differently. This element is being shattered by our dressing better and appearing as feminine as possible at all times".

Femininity in the 1960s was a key factor to acceptance by the public. A few of the women were regarded as tomboys, unacceptable in appearance and behavior, and this image, unfairly, would often be accorded to the women collectively. It was one that was hard to shake.

"Some women are never going to look feminine, and they look better in trousers. You could have put everyone in frilly clothes and had them all dolled up, but it wouldn't have brought crowds in greater numbers," Betsy Rawls recalled.

"The issue didn't keep the public away. They gradually learned that the women could play golf, and they liked their personalities. They liked Marilynn Smith because she emoted a lot; Patty Berg was well liked and never happier than when she was on stage; JoAnne Carner's personality and style of golf has always attracted people. The Bauers were popular and got a lot of publicity, partly because they were so young. They were on the cover of Life magazine when Marlene was about eight years old."

In the 1960s, the gradual exposure through television, combined with the aggressive marketing strategy of Lenny Wirtz, helped gain the public's interest. Lenny, who did a lot to change the image of women golfers, said: "I didn't sell the women solely on sex, more as feminine athletes, which is how they are attractive. They are also the best women golfers in the world, and I always tried to sell that. I was proud of their progress, and each one was like a daughter."

Mickey Wright wins again at the 1963 Dallas Civitan Open. She won 12 of 30 events she played in that year and a total of $31,269, the most she won in a year from 1955 to 1972.

Lenny Wirtz may have been proud of them, but in the swinging sixties the women's independent lifestyle was not considered feminine nor was their competitive aggression. However, they understood how to mask their true feelings, realizing that life as a professional golfer can mean outwardly denying the natural expression of your personality.

As the season of 1961 drew to a close, it was noted: "We have had four marriages, no divorces, one birth, a forthcoming engagement, and as yet, no scandals." Peggy Kirk Bell was teacher of the year, and Mickey Wright, at the beginning of her four-year run, was leading money winner for the first time, with $22,236 and ten victories. LPGA President Betsy Rawls, said: "This year has been marked by a distinct lack of dissension and conflict among the members and by an atmosphere of co-operation. Please accept my appreciation for making it a most pleasant year."

That same lack of conflict did not continue through 1962, when Louise Suggs was fined $25 for not turning up at a tournament in Milwaukee, an automatic penalty for not having given 48-hours' notice of pulling out. Louise thought she was wronged and ended her full time golf career in an episode which Betsy Rawls describes as: "One of the saddest in the history of the LPGA."

Although Renee Powell, following in Althea Gibson's footsteps, had her share of discrimination problems, to its credit, the LPGA would not tolerate anything less than equal rights for all of its members.

In 1962, the first LPGA Rookie of the Year award was given to Mary Mills, who went on to achieve her first victory as a professional by winning the Women's Open the following season. The year 1963 was delightful, in that the LPGA basked in the reflected glory of Mickey Wright, who as president of the association achieved a record 13 victories, which was something to astonish and to savor. Not quite so desirable was a comment recorded in the minutes of one meeting: "Complaints were received about a player cussing her caddie in front of the public and using other profane language on the course." Also recorded that year, with disapproval, was the notation: "Girls were moving balls out of holes on the greens, around their coin, sometimes a little ahead."

On a happier note, when NBC televised the LPGA Championship in Las Vegas, won by Mickey Wright, it was reported: "The girls looked well dressed and definitely like ladies." Possibly, the orientation rules were taking effect, as they read under the heading of *Proper Dress*: *"Cleanliness, including golf shoes; neat hair, wear lipstick, do not wear too short shorts nor too tight; do not wear sweat socks, wear only ladies' clothing, clothes must be pressed and neat."*

In 1963, Althea Gibson, famous as a tennis star for twice winning Wimbledon and once the U.S. Open, joined the LPGA tour as a professional golfer. Although Althea was not in the least militant and was in the parlance of the day termed "Negro," she was the first black woman to compete on the golf tour. Although Hawaiian, Jackie Pung, had not always had a smooth run in the 1950s, Lenny Wirtz fought for Althea's acceptance in the hostile atmosphere of the time, particularly in the South; he did the same for Renee Powell when she joined the tour in 1967.

Althea offered not to play in events which the LPGA might lose on her account, but if the black women professionals were not allowed into a clubhouse or faced discrimination, Lenny would refuse to hold the tournament. One such event was the Babe Zaharias Open in Beaumont, Texas, which Althea entered in 1964. Her entry was accepted on condition she did not enter the clubhouse. Althea played because she was trying to achieve her LPGA scoring average to qualify for the tour, but the following year, when Lenny Wirtz told the Rotary Club that Althea had to receive equal treatment, the sponsorship was withdrawn. Although Althea and Renee had their share of problems because of their color, the LPGA policy was always supportive of its members and their equal right to earn a living.

Mickey Wright entered the Hall of Fame in 1963, when she brought her total victories to 63, and won 11 out of 27 tournaments she entered. Her two years of LPGA presidency in 1963 and 1964, combined with extraordinarily high achievement, took their toll on Mickey, who said: "The job of president was very hard because it required so much time speaking at luncheons and civic groups. It involved extra appearances for local radio and television, and it meant introducing all the girls at each cocktail party after every Pro-Am. My terms of presidency came during two of my four best years on tour. I was in contention in the majority of the 57 tournaments I played, and I won 22 of them."

From the middle of the decade, Kathy Whitworth proclaimed her winning ability. She was ranked No. 1 for four years from 1965, the year that Mickey Wright's nervous system forced her away from full-time competition, and she played in just 11 tournaments. Mickey played the tour full-time for only three more years: 1966, 1967, and 1969.

The most extensive television exposure received by the association arrived in the mid-1960s, when the women became involved in a series entitled "Shell's Wonderful World of Golf." Separate men's and women's golf matches were played in countries around the world, and the program captured the imagination of viewers. The first television coverage for the Women's Open came in 1965, when Carol Mann took the title. The USGA forced ABC to take it by including it in a deal that went with the rights to televise the Men's Open. For ABC, the Women's Open was a token gesture that the broadcast company tried to avoid. They offered the USGA an extra $50,000 not to televise it, but to its credit, the USGA refused.

In 1967, a major stir was caused by the arrival of ten-year old Beverly Klass competing on the tour. The constitution of the LPGA did not allow Beverly to become a member until she was 18, but there was not an age requirement for competing amateurs, who were included in tournaments to make up the field. Jack Klass wanted his daughter to be a professional, and amid enormous publicity, the charade was played out. The child was banned after three tournaments—after beating a couple of women professionals when she broke 90 in an event. The LPGA passed a new by-law to exclude her, and Jack Klass promptly brought a lawsuit against Lenny Wirtz and women members of the board, for the tidy sum of $1.25 million for stopping his daughter from making a living. The protracted case was settled out of court more than two years later.

As the decade drew to a close, it was Carol Mann who reached her peak, winning ten tournaments in 1968. She was ranked at the top in the following year with eight tournament victories and $49,152. Carol reacted to her considerable achievements in the 1960s by saying: "I made a tremendous effort, and it still wasn't satisfying," but in the next decade she would discover great satisfaction in becoming the instrument for change that was crucial to the eventual well-being of the LPGA.

Debbie Austin

As an amateur golfer, Debbie Austin was told by a woman in junior golf that she would be labeled "the nice girl who would never make it." Almost living out that prophecy, Debbie entered professional golf in 1968 and progressed through nine seasons without a single victory. She showed steadily improving results, a reasonable income, and some high finishes, but there was never a victory for the young woman who considered winning to be of the utmost importance. Those nine seasons became an increasingly frustrating and depressing experience.

"My crisis point came when I finished 51st in the 1977 Dinah Shore. I was totally depressed, almost ready to give up. I am very emotional. I can cry at the drop of a hat. I'd be great in a soap opera."

Debbie Austin was always known for her outgoing personality, chatting and interacting with the galleries. It took nine years for her to achieve her first tour victory, but in 1977 and 1978, she fashioned seven LPGA wins and won the Australian Open by seven shots.

The year 1977 completely changed her status in the golfing world. She achieved five LPGA victories in one season and also won the Australian Open by nine shots. It was heady stuff. She was bubbling and riding high: the nice girl had made it.

Fairly short at 5 feet, 3 inches, Debbie is a bundle of highly strung energy. On tour, she was known for her interaction and chatter with the galleries, which she used to release surface tension. Underneath, she is a self-contained woman. She has always been encouraging and friendly to me and invited me to talk to her at her house in Florida, where her enjoyment as a homemaker was obvious.

During the 1980s Debbie was involved in the organization of the LPGA, serving on the player council and on the board of directors. Physical problems overtook her and restricted her playing schedule, during which time her main involvement was in the travel business.

Her background is interesting. She is a descendant of the highly unusual Oneida community from upstate New York, which was founded in 1948 by John Humphrey Noyes as an experiment in Christian communal living. Its philosophy for a group of some 300 people included eugenically selected children, in a process called Stirpiculture, where men and women offered themselves for mating, having first been chosen by a committee. Then, in every case, conception was planned by a committee and agreed by both parents, who did not become man and wife, but who were part of a system called "complex marriage."

The community lived together in a building called The Mansion, which still exists today in Oneida. The community looked after each other, established businesses, and the children were cared for collectively in a separate children's house.

A determined Debbie Austin collected five LPGA victories in 1977. Photo courtesy: Katherine Murphy.

The Oneida community came to an end as an organization in 1980, but the Oneida Silversmith Company is still thriving, and Debbie's father was a director. Debbie grew up in Oneida in an Episcopalian family of middle income, with a brothers Jim, 14½ years older, and Peter, 7½ years older.

"The Oneida community was very close, and everyone looked out for everyone else, which was perhaps not the best philosophy for making a career on the professional golf tour," Debbie admitted.

"When I got on tour, I was sometimes intimidated and put down, and I found there were some girls who did not acknowledge good shots or encourage other people, but I could never be like that. Being with women all the time in a competitive situation is difficult. They're very jealous of one another, and the tour is no exception. Many people come across as kind, but it's superficial, and if they could throw a dagger at you, they would. I didn't like that part of it.

"You have your clique of friends on tour, but how many friends do you really have? You could count them on one hand. You may think you have friends, but there are not many who care or who want to know about you when you need them. It's not all fun and games out there.

"You have great experiences, and I wouldn't have changed my life, but I was a wound-up ball on tour, and it would take me four weeks to unwind and relax. I am glad I chose golf as a career because I got over my shyness, I met tremendous people, and I traveled to places I could never have gone.

"I always felt I could win, but there comes a point when you wonder whether you have the capability to win. The tour is a lonely life and it's more lonely when you're not playing well. The days drag on. You keep working, and sometimes you improve, but the belief in yourself is what's missing.

"After the 1977 Dinah Shore, when I finished 51st, a professional golfer friend of mine in Palm Springs, Sherry Wilder, offered to work with me on my game. She gave me confidence and belief in myself and a more positive attitude. After working with her, I went to a tournament in Hilton Head where I saw a hypnotist. I needed all the help

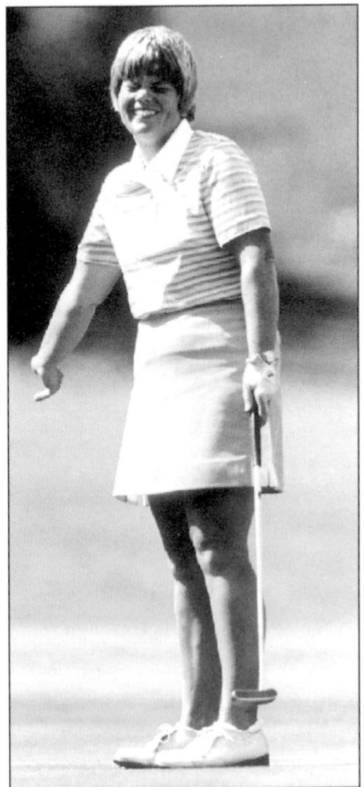

Debbie Austin didn't always enjoy her 20 years on the LPGA, but she persevered to make it pay off for her. Photo ©Phil Sheldon.

I could get. The hypnotist told me to believe in myself, and she taught me how to relax by squeezing my fists and by taking deep breaths.

"I played well that week at Hilton Head, and two weeks later I won the Birmingham Classic. I was ready for anything, and I was in some sort of a trance. When I won I was taken out of a cage. A terrible weight came off my shoulders, and I had the confidence and belief that I could win. Sherry was very positive and inspired me to do it again by telling me to go and win six tournaments in the season. I made it to five on the LPGA tour, and then I won the Australian Open by nine shots.

"After winning again in 1978 and 1981, I retained the impetus through 1983 and 1984 when I really wanted to play well. But, I didn't win. Joyce Kazmierski told me it was all in my head. She said that I willed whatever was happening."

LPGA Victories: 1977 Birmingham Classic, Hoosier Classic, Pocono Classic, Long Island Charity Classic, Wheeling Classic. **1978** American Cancer Society Classic. **1981** Mayflower Classic.

Debbie Austin's LPGA Record

Year	No.of Events	Best Finish	Money	Rank	Scoring Average
1968	23	15	$2,854	39	77.23
1969	26	T5	6,719	29	76.83
1970	18	6	3,996	35	76.24
1971	18	T4	6,455	23	75.20
1972	25	T3	12,502	25	75.37
1973	30	7	30,903	13	74.29
1974	26	3	24,439	20	74.91
1975	24	T3	20,559	19	74.11
1976	28	T2	31,999	17	74.24
1977	20	1	86,392	6	73.19
1978	24	1	44,768	18	73.60
1979	30	T7	33,597	33	74.39
1980	29	4	41,302	35	73.90
1981	26	1	72,881	14	73.34
1982	28	T7	33,105	46	74.07
1983	21	T5	26,685	68	74.13
1984	26	T4	33,074	61	74.39
1985	18	T19	3,873	153	76.28
1986	20	T38	2,589	164	76.45
1987	10	NA	NA	NA	79.16

Jane Blalock

Of all the LPGA members throughout its history, Jane Blalock was involved in the association's greatest and most explosive controversy, one which marred the LPGA and Jane's quality of life as a professional golfer. "It was a terrible time," says Betsy Rawls. "Everyone turned out to be a victim."

In 1972 Jane's alleged infringement of the rules came to light when she was the tour's leading money winner, which may have been relevant. In the early 1960s it had been noted in the minutes that "women had been moving their ball out of holes on the greens, around their coin, sometimes a little ahead." No action was taken against anyone until the Board took its decision to investigate Jane, on the basis of the number of complaints it received, although not one playing partner had ever refused to sign her card. It proved an episode in the history of the tour that was painful, costly, and which changed the entire structure of the organization.

Jane, an intelligent, articulate, high-strung and ultra-competitive woman, somehow learned to live with the tension that her situation produced, and she admits now that maybe she needs adversity to bring out the best in her: "When I was 16 years old and my mother and I went to the New Haven Country Club, I didn't like the attitude of the stuffy people. I said, 'They're going to hear from me,' and I shot the low score of the day, after which they paid a lot of attention to me and were nice to my mother. It's amazing how people change and how they are so success oriented. When I came on tour, the sponsors didn't have time for me, and it was a challenge to get some attention. I love challenges."

Jane showed her tough resilience as she responded to the challenge of the alleged infringement which resulted in an attempt to suspend her from the tour for a year. She slapped a $5 million anti-trust lawsuit against the LPGA and fought it all the way. She was awarded damages and costs, following which she wrote a book with Dwayne Netland, published in 1977 and called *The Guts to Win*.

The introduction was written by Billie Jean King, who said: "Few people I know are better qualified to discuss the alluring appeal of competition, because Janie is first and foremost a competitor, one of the toughest and most determined I have ever met. Considering what she has had to endure, the quality has been a priceless asset in her struggle to the top. Janie was accused by her peers without a trial. I cannot think of a more lonely place to be. At the time Janie's problems began, I had known her for only a short while. I was impressed with her skill and her drive. A lesser person might have crumbled under that type of pressure. Janie improved her game and came into her own as both a golfer and a person."

Later in her career, in 1981, Jane penned an article for the February 8th *Miami Herald* which

Always the competitor, Jane Blalock began her LPGA career as "Rookie of the Year" in 1969. She didn't miss a cut until the last event of the 1980 season. Photo courtesy: LPGA.

was entitled: *Isn't it time to promote talent not sex?* The content was an attack on the provocative pose of Jan Stephenson lying seductively on a bed, in the LPGA's Fairway Magazine, a method of selling of which Jane said: "Tour officials became so desperate for appeal that quasi pornography got the nod. Is our organization so unaware of the real glamour and attraction staring it in the face, that it must resort to such trash? With such an abundance of real beauty, must we really prostitute ourselves for the same type of lower form of exposure that we once had to?"

There was an ensuing furor for the whole year, and no one could have dreamed up a better PR exercise, as the LPGA and Jan Stephenson received local and national coverage throughout the season. Those for and against went on record and were quoted ad infinitum in every town they visited.

Jane's golf career has been distinctive, as she was "Rookie of the Year" in 1969, achieved 29 victories spanning a period of 15 years from 1970, and earned more than a million dollars in prize money. She was in the top ten money winners for an amazing ten years from 1971, and recorded her best season financially in 1985 when she won two tournaments. $192,426 placed her seventh on the money list. Her trademark as a player in earlier years was that she put her hair in pony tails and wore very short shorts.

My own relationship with Jane has been friendly without being close, and the longest time we spent together was over dinner one night when she was playing a tournament in England. I found her likeable, forthright and a good companion. As an interviewee she is excellent and helpful. She had a speech impediment when young and talks very rapidly. On one occasion I was interviewing her in a locker room in Dallas during a raging storm, and the lights went out. We were left in the dark, and I heard a voice ask, "Should we continue?" which we did for five minutes before the lights came back on.

"I was born in Concord, New Hampshire, having two brothers, seven and nine years younger. We were a close family. My father was in the Army, and a year after I was born, we moved to Portsmouth, a military town with a naval base that was home. We were upper class in that town, although we were middle income with Dad being a newspaper editor for the Stars and Stripes and then managing editor of The Portsmouth Herald.

"There was one golf course where my mother started playing with her friends. Dad played, and I would play with him. First, I used his clubs, but he was 6 feet, 2 inches; so I started caddying and baby-sitting to buy myself some clubs. My first tournament win was at 13, the Hampshire Junior in Concord. Winning a trophy at such a young age was a very motivating factor. It was good being recognized for doing something well, and my whole life I have had to prove something. I had an idea I could win, and I did.

"I have a competitive instinct, I just love competition. After my Dad retired and opened a small restaurant, I sat down with him one evening, and over dinner and wine we talked. He told me how he hated to lose, or not to succeed when he had some control over the matter. It was the first time we had talked about it, and he told me he didn't want to flaunt his competitiveness, nor could he tell anyone else how to be competitive, but he admitted he had almost willed the restaurant to be a success because he wanted it so much.

"I thought I was looking in a mirror, and at that moment realized how much we were alike. My mother is strong in a low key manner, but I picked up a lot of strength from my father. That sort of competitiveness has to be in the genes.

"Growing up I was never forced into competition, I did it by choice. I always won everything at school, where I felt it was my responsibility to live up to my talent, not to goof off. I was not upset if I lost, I would just work harder. Losing was all right and sportsmanship was stressed. My idol as a teenager was Wilma Rudolph, the black athlete who was an Olympic track star, and I wanted to be an Olympic athlete. When I met her in 1984 at a Women's Sports Foundation dinner, I told her I was so thrilled because she had been my idol.

"I spent a lot of time alone playing golf and developed a sense of a relationship between myself, the golf ball and the golf club: we were a team. I had always had very good powers of concentration and a consummate desire to overcome distractions. I never had a fear of losing, of thinking 'What if I choke?' I think of the moment, the shot, of being capable of being there, and capable of winning. Winning is never quite what you imagined. It is a satisfying feeling of inner strength when you conquer many obstacles—such as a good golf course, which is the enemy, together with JoAnne Carner, Nancy Lopez, Judy Rankin, or whomever you have to beat. It is a neat feeling to overcome the odds, but is never as exhilarating as you had imagined.

"In golf you don't share your win with anyone, which is one thing I've always missed so much—to be able to share victory with teammates, to hug and congratulate them. The loneliest feeling of all is winning in golf. You're everyone's enemy, you've defeated all your friends, and you're alone. People congratulate you, but there's no real sharing.

"When I'm playing well the round begins the night before in mental preparation. The build up is the excitement of winning. I don't want small talk and a lot of people. I want good conversation, to talk and move more slowly, as naturally I'm quick and my motions are brisk and rapid. I toss and turn in the night, and it's a good feeling. I know I'm going to be facing pressure. I look forward to it, and I dread it. I love the challenge of having to pull out a six-foot putt and succeeding. I used to play more from the heart; then I acquired extra ability and a better golf swing.

Jane was a rising star in 1972, winning the Colgate Dinah Shore, the Suzuki International, and three other events that year.

"I always get sick after I've won. I hide my stomach churning and feeling physically ill when I'm in contention, but I'm too drained to celebrate if I win. It takes so much more to win than to finish second: all that mental energy, concentration, and going a mile a minute—I feel great when I'm pumped up and playing for my goals.

"My most satisfying victory was in the 1972 Dallas Civitan Open, when I was in the middle of all the controversy and a lawsuit. I beat Kathy Whitworth in a playoff, where people were rooting against me overtly. I made a birdie and won, and it was like proving something. Adversity is a great challenge which brings out my total will.

"I was never interested in a golf career when I was growing up; I thought I would like the Foreign Service or politics. I was fortunate that my parents didn't put me into a compartment of marriage and a family. They allowed me to be who I wanted. My mother would say, 'Are you going to get married?' But more in the sense of, 'Are you happy?' I feel had I had children, I would not have been a professional golfer, because I believe in making a total commitment to whatever I do. You can manage, but I want to do something 100%. You can't have a family and professional golf and expect to do well without compromising. It takes an unusual husband. It can be done, but it is the exception.

"After I left high school, I majored in history at Rollins College, and I travelled with friends to play some golf tournaments. I worked as a waitress to earn money, and I did substitute teaching and a lot of skiing. Bob Toski helped me with my golf, and I won the North East amateur. He said I had a good touch and got the ball in the hole, and LPGA golfer Jan Ferraris urged me to turn professional, which I did in 1969 at 23, although I was scared.

"I won a tournament in my first calendar year and two events in 1971. In 1972, I was a rising star, I won the Colgate Dinah Shore, the Suzuki International, and was leading money winner with just over $32,000. My momentum was suddenly cut on May 20, 1972, after the second round of the Bluegrass Invitational at the Hunting Creek Country Club, Louisville."

That evening, Jane was called to an Executive Board meeting at her hotel, comprised of Cynthia Sullivan, President of the LPGA; Board members: Judy Rankin, Linda Craft, Penny Zavichas, and Sharon Miller. Marlene Hagge, a representative of the tournament committee, and tournament director Gene McAuliff were also present.

She was told that four spotters on the golf course (including one on a television tower who claimed that through binoculars she had seen Jane move the ball one inch) had observed her marking the ball incorrectly. They claimed she moved it 1–5 inches ahead, instead of replacing it correctly. She was informed by Gene McAuliff that she was being disqualified from the tournament. The reason given publicly would be on the technicality of signing an incorrect scorecard, for having played the ball from the wrong position. Further action would be taken, he said, by the Board. McAuliff also told her she might have to take a lesson on how to place the ball on the green, adding: "You are the first of this movement and your penalty may be severe".

Jane protested that 1–5 inches was ridiculous, but "maybe it was excitement or carelessness". Cynthia Sullivan told Jane: "We all know you have meant much to the LPGA, we're not trying to hurt you because we think the world of you, but we are in a position where now that we are aware of this situation, we must do something about it."

After Jane had left the room, the Board voted to disqualify her from the Louisville tournament, and to place her on probation for the remainder of 1972, when any infraction would mean suspension. They fined her $500.

It was the following week at the Titleholders at Pine Needles on May 26 that Jane was informed of the Board's decision. Jane says in her book that at this meeting her behavior was based on advice she took from professional Ernie Vossler whom she had consulted about her golf on the way to the Titleholders. She had also talked to him about the alleged infringement the previous week. As a result of her conversation with Vossler, she apologized at that meeting at Pine Needles for anything she had unintentionally done wrong, adding: "If all these things you say are true, I guess I've dug my own grave, and I'll just have to live with it."

However, the LPGA representatives heard it a bit differently. They maintained that when Jane was told she was fined $500, placed on probation for the remainder of 1972, and asked if she had anything further to discuss, she said: "No, I'm guilty of moving my ball from spike marks, out of heel prints and ball marks on several occasions. I've dug my own grave, so I'll have to live with it."

Although the matter might have ended there, it did not, as Jane's alleged remark was reported back to the rest of the players. Other alleged incidents were brought forward, implying that Jane's infringements had taken place over a period of three years. The Board then altered its original penalty, deciding instead to suspend Jane from playing on the LPGA tour for one year.
This decision brought them into line with a petition from 29 of the players who wished her to be suspended for the remainder of 1972, based on her alleged remark to the Board at the Pine Needles meeting. The Board said it had made its own decision before receiving this petition.

On May 30, the Board informed her of its decision at a most uncomfortable meeting in which both sides struggled. Reading the record of that meeting now, you can feel the tension. The women of the Board were trying hard to make their point, as was Jane Blalock, who said: "What I believe I said to you was that I have probably marked my ball incorrectly, that I cannot deny ever having replaced the ball in something like the spot I originally marked it. I can't say I've put back the ball in the same place every time. I'm not saying it was . . . I also said it was not an intentional act . . . I don't remember the words, but I wasn't trying to take advantage of the elements.

"I'm trying to be an honest person with you all. I think it's a hard thing to put it back in the exact same spot, but I'm not saying I know I have moved it intentionally. You don't do something like that intentionally.

"It's hard for me to be here, it's hard for me to talk to you. I didn't admit that I moved the ball intentionally, and I can't deny not putting the ball back in the same place. I made an informal statement and I said, 'probably.' I've always played by the rules, I've gone out of my way in many instances as I love the organization and the game of golf.

"I have never endured or been through a time as I have since our last meeting, and I don't think that any further punishment would make more of a mark or scar on me. I've lost my pride, I've been humiliated and embarrassed myself, and in front of my friends. I know a lot of people know about it.

"I'm trying to tell you what is coming from my heart. I don't think I'll ever do anything wrong ever again in my life. I won't speed or go through a yellow light; I've learned the hard way. It's going to take a lot of years and time heals some things, but I don't think anyone will ever forget this incident. There are some things where the scars are not taken away.

"I'm almost pleading with you. No one can benefit from what has happened or possibly could happen. Unfortunately I am in the limelight, having won a big tournament and being leading money winner. My future is almost in your hands. This is going to be very scandalous. It's not going to help; it's going to hurt me. It's not going to help the LPGA either.

"This isn't anyone's fault but my own, I'm well aware of that. I want to tell you the way I feel. I'm almost asking you for mercy. In a sense it's all a bit late, what's done is done and nothing can be rectified. I've got to live with it. I just want to be able to play golf, and I guess I'm asking you as human beings. I know I don't deserve any respect but just some compassion, somewhere. And, I'm just looking at the whole organization, the sponsors, the press and the publicity."

Many words were bandied back and forth in sometimes confused fashion, with both sides obviously feeling tense, passionate, unforgiving, unforgiven, in a sad episode that highlighted the difficulties for Jane and the tour.

Cynthia Sullivan told Jane: "We think you're a fine player, and you can win without doing any of this. The fact is that you have done it and been observed doing it. The faults have happened, and we have to deal with them on an impersonal basis. We feel for you. We may feel one thing, but our job and our position is to protect the whole organization and the field you're playing against.

"If we condone this and say that you're sorry and you're a good girl, it does not erase what has happened in the past. It is unfortunate that this is the way it has to be. Every one of us feels you're sorry, and you surely will never do it again.

"You say you've been through it, well we've been through it for the past two weeks. I don't think I or the other girls have slept because it's been a terrible decision, something that is weighing on our minds because we think so much of you. We're not being fair to the other girls, to our ethics, and to what we believe. And, we're not being fair to the game of golf where people honor the rules, and if they don't, they are penalized for it.

"We have no choice but to suspend you for a year from June 1, 1972. I know this is hard, a hundred fold on you, because of your position and your ability, but we've tried to come up with the fairest thing we could. We can handle it with or without publicity; it is up to you. I don't think the LPGA as a whole will be mortally hurt by this, and if you choose, you can say that you are not playing because of your back, or any other way you want to handle it.

"I know it's a shock. It's a shock to us, a shock to have to do it. It's the hardest thing I've had to do in my life. I don't think it was jealousy, but possibly you have not been playing fair with the rest of the field.

"Maybe I heard you wrong, maybe Judy (Rankin) heard it wrong, but we both heard what you said the same way—that you have moved the ball at the tournaments. We didn't want to hear you say that. The thing is very simple: if you're falsely accused, then we will be the first to want to see you play. If not, our hands are tied."

Jane's final remark before leaving the meeting, was: "Then you're judging me on just your word against mine."

What followed the board's decision was a legal suit, where Jane sued the LPGA for $5 million on the basis of the Sherman Anti-Trust Act, which covered the right of a person to earn a living and not be deprived of it by a group boycott. The final outcome was not reached until August 26, 1974 when Jane was awarded $13,500 under the anti-trust law. The LPGA had to pay its own legal fees of more than $200,000, while Jane's lawyers settled for $98,000 from the LPGA, although their bill was around $220,000. Her own out of pocket expenses amounted to about $40,000.

The reverberating effects of the case were in alerting professional sport to the restraint of trade act, and the whole structure of the LPGA, which came under Ray Volpe in 1975, was changed. A board of players could no longer discipline fellow competitors, and an advisory board of corporate executives was set up to work with two player representatives.

To this day there are members of the LPGA who feel thwarted that the issue of alleged rule infringement never entered the case and that affidavits were signed and never brought forth. There was a sense of frustration over the whole issue.

Of the way she marked the ball, Jane says: "Many players put a coin or marker right up against the ball so that it touches it, and sometimes the ball can move from that position. The rule says you have to mark it directly behind the ball. I put my marker a bit further back than most players, maybe up to half an inch; so that when I put back the ball and took up the marker, my knuckles would not inadvertently nudge the ball."

Reading through the mountain of data produced at the time, you feel the indignation of the group and you pick up a snowballing vindictiveness, as collective spying was followed by collective condemnation, punishment, and ostracism.

There was a weakness in the fact that no one ever refused to sign Jane's scorecard. Although the initial alleged infringement was handled properly and accepted, the further "evidence" prompting a change in penalty, was gathered quite improperly on "hearsay from other girls", without any specific charges by particular people, or of particular incidents, and without the opportunity to answer them.

Betsy Rawls says: "The problem was that we had no officials who ran the tour. If there is an alleged infringement a fellow competitor should say, 'You marked that ball improperly and that's a two-stroke penalty.' If there's a dispute you call an official to the scoring tent, settle it right there and that's the end of it. It should never go beyond that round of golf. Once a player signs a card, and a fellow competitor signs a card, that's it. You can't go back and say, 'You cheated two months ago.'

"The confusion was the result of the way we had always operated. The players handled everything to do with the business and running of the LPGA, including the rules and setting up the golf course. They shouldn't have been handling it, and they didn't cope with it properly, but they were in the position that it was their responsibility. With hired officials it would have been handled differently."

Carol Mann says: "We felt angry as a group with Jane because of the integrity of the game, and we felt guilt by association. We were wrong, not on merit but in the way we handled it, and it was a lesson we needed to learn. The tour was a hideous place, terribly difficult. It was the only topic of conversation with people sitting in little groups. At one point I left the tour, saying, 'This is ridiculous that there's such a cloud hanging over this place.' There was so much antagonism between those who were for and against, that it was an unhealthy place to be trying to compete. Also it gained so much media attention."

Executive Director, Bud Erickson, said at the time: "It was a traumatic decision that the executive committee made for the best interest of the organization and for the best interest of golf." While Jane issued a statement, saying: "Never in my life have I knowingly taken advantage of the rules of golf."

The media, sensing a feeling of victimization, was sympathetic to Jane, which further incensed the members of the LPGA. Three weeks after Louisville, when Jane had to post a $10,000 bond and obtain a temporary court injunction to compete in the LPGA Championship in her home town of Portsmouth, Joe Concannon wrote in *Golf World*: "Janie showed up on Tuesday at Pleasant Valley, and the atmosphere was as cool as the brisk New England weather. A cold front that settled later in the week was nothing compared to the way some of the girls felt toward Janie. It might have been justly called the Tension Open. The largest percentage of the gallery followed Janie, urged her on and in effect helped ease the tremendous pressure she was under. She stepped on the first tee to tremendous applause and an LPGA record number of newsmen and photographers."

"If I'd stepped on the first tee and been booed," said Jane, "I think I'd have gone back to the motel." By the end of the week, which was packed with tension, rumor, statements and denials, Jane, after finishing second to Kathy Ahern in the tournament, said: "The enthusiasm of the fans this week was tremendous. They stayed with me. I guess if I deserved it I would have been booed. I was very determined, my concentration was good, and I've seen friends I haven't seen in years. It's nice to be responsible for a record crowd (18,300 on Sunday), and maybe if it happens all the time, the LPGA will thank me.

Jane, whose hair fell out at the time, developed a nervous tremor. One time she was sent out on the course with the National Guard in attendance and says: "Had I killed someone I would have been treated better, it was like a kangaroo court. Disregarding the issue, the fact that a group could become so vindictive was almost equal to the Civil Rights movement. The way things transpired went far beyond anything to do with what happened."

Although as Jane admits, "it was a lonely vigil," she had a staunch supporter in friend, and fellow professional Sandra Palmer, who, in speaking out in support of Jane, was involved with the threat of lawsuits, which in fact did not materialize.

Jane says now: "Sandra felt an injustice was being done, and what comes back to me is such respect for her. I couldn't believe she had the courage to jeopardize her own performance and her relationships with other players. It was the only good thing that happened at the time. Even if I had been wrong, it was such an admirable quality that she had the guts to speak out for me. It was phenomenal and said a lot about her as a person. It is a very unusual character trait for people to go out on a limb and jeopardize their own well being for a principle. Too many people are into self-gain, and we don't often talk about principles any more, or stand on our own two feet for what we believe in."

In spite of Jane's regard for Sandra Palmer, when she wrote her book *The Guts to Win*, she inferred that Sandra had won a tournament from her with the use of gamesmanship as a weapon. Jane says: "It was not meant to be a cruel thing, it was bringing out different traits of different people on the tour. If you're telling the real story, you can't say someone does everything right. The publishers wanted a bit of nitty gritty to make the book sell, and it gave the public a better sense of what could happen."

Jane's own confrontations with authority led her more strongly towards her religion of Catholicism: "I've always been very much a believer, but on a scale of one to ten, I would say I was about a six. During my lawsuit, I went to bed every night with rosary beads as I thought some positive belief might go into my bloodstream."

When she met a Monsignor Kelley in Florida while playing an exhibition, she struck up a friendship, later unburdening herself to him. Then she obtained an audience with the Pope in Rome in 1974, arranged by the Monsignor. "I needed to get rid of the hatred in me that grew and grew as people continued to harass me. My audience in Rome was brief, the Pope did not speak good English, but he told me if I believed, everything would be all right."

Jane had sufficient energy not only for her golf and related problems, but also for the current issues of the day. "I was labeled a controversial person who speaks up for her rights, and I became involved in the Title IX Bill, which was designed to allow women to benefit at Federally funded educational establishments in equal proportion to men. Various women athletes including Olympic swimmer Donna DeVarona, Billie Jean King, and I, appeared on talk shows and did press conferences to publicize women's sports."

Jane also helped Donna Lopiano, Women's Athletic Director at the University of Texas, by carrying out an emotionally supportive role in urging athletes to contact Congressmen and Senators, to lobby them for equal funding. When the Women's Sports Foundation was started in 1974, as the result of a $5,000 award won by Billie Jean King, Jane was its golf representative.

With Billie Jean and others, she agitated for the Women Superstars event, which like that of the men brought together the whole spectrum of women athletes, competing against each other in sports which were not their own. Through that they met the greatest woman softball player, Joan Joyce, who later became a professional golfer. Prior to that, Jane and Billie Jean helped fund a professional softball league in 1975, which failed to become permanently established.

When the feminist movement arrived, Jane was not actively involved. "I identified with it to the extent that we were doing what feminists wanted others to do. As professional women we were ahead of our time and fighting for our place, but we led a sheltered life. We made money and had opportunities. Only now, unfortunately, do I feel a sympathy with them, which I wish I had felt at the time."

Throughout the period of her tribulations with the LPGA—other than in 1973, when she won a fourball championship with Sandra Palmer—Jane achieved victory or multiple victories each year. She consistently increased her earnings and remained at the top, until 1982, when she slipped down the rankings and was without a victory for three seasons: "I found my self-esteem severely injured. Part of the problem was mental, part injury, and part probably trying too hard. I didn't want to feel I had quit, but I wanted to feel free to go on to other pursuits without injuring my pride. For my pride, I wanted to win once more. Inside, I knew I could; so it was a challenge I set for myself.

"I wanted to do something outside golf, but I felt I hadn't earned it, and then I won the Kemper Open in March 1985. It was the most important day in my life, a turning point. I had a great year; maybe the best I ever played. With my victory in the Mazda Classic in Japan at the end of the season, in my own mind my career was over. I wanted to get up at the presentation and say, 'I've had 17 years, and that's it.'

"There were many other challenges and aspects of life that I wanted to pursue, while I was still healthy and energetic. You put everything you have toward one goal, and then you need somewhere to channel that drive and energy. Sometimes when athletes retire, they have a chance to make a lot of money by being put on a pedestal. People worship them as they attend award dinners and cocktail parties. Athletes are very driven; we work hard, have tremendous concentration, and whatever we do is from the inside. Therefore, suddenly, to take us and put us in token company jobs, without any purpose or function, is merely using us.

"To be a successful athlete is more than co-ordination and skill; there is some special inner quality that's required. Once you take that away, it is like stripping the soul and spirit from a person so that he or she no longer feels self-worth or significance. People are not successful by accident, it's something they possess. An athlete may always be recognized and can be used to tell stories and live in the past, but each needs to use whatever ability has made him or her successful, or something very special is taken away."

In 1984, Jane met the chief financial officer for Merrill Lynch, and because of her interest in the stock market and the financial world, she became friendly and kept in touch. Leaving the tour, she turned to stockbrokering and Merrill Lynch. She wanted to start from the bottom, and learn the business, taking all the appropriate courses: "When I took my exams with 150 others, I felt pressure as never before, and it was the most satisfying moment when I passed my exams and became a licensed stockbroker.

"What a contrast in my lifestyle to be working and living in Boston where my wardrobe was entirely different. I got to the office early because it was exciting, and I felt more full as a person. I went to the symphony, art galleries, the theater, baseball and basketball. I no longer talked golf or about what I did on the 17th. I didn't idly gossip; I talked business.

"It was important for my ego because I didn't want to depend on the tour for my sustenance or become a club professional or teach golf. I knew I was capable of doing other things. We all have brains, but people do not perceive professional golfers as intellectuals. Many women at that time were intimidated by the business world, but all the controversy in my life gave me strength to meet its challenges. I suppose something good comes out of everything, although I couldn't find it then.

"Changing lives is hard. It was very secure on tour, quite an irresponsible life with free time which is not well used. When I left, I missed the excitement and nerves, the applause, the recognition, the ego part. I missed walking up to the 18th green with the satisfaction of playing well, making that three or four footer at the last to win, and knowing only I did it. Nothing replaces the competition, but someday you have to leave it behind.

"Sometimes, sitting in the office, I would allow myself the luxury of thinking about the tournaments I had won, and it gave me a really warm feeling. My life was new and exciting, but everything changes, and you move on."

In 1989, Jane left Merrill Lynch to form her own Jane Blalock Company which consults with corporations on their golf and tennis marketing strategies. The company also stages and promotes tournaments. Joined by Silvia Bertolaccini, who retired from the LPGA tour, and four more employees, including a tennis professional, the company organizes executive women's golf clinics, company days, golf schools, and all aspects of golf as a business tool—in a market where 90% of the customers are male.

"It has grown by word of mouth, faster than I expected, and it has exceeded my expectations, as we hit on a need and successfully carved out a niche in a service industry. I apply the same self-discipline as I did in competitive golf.

Jane and Silvia continued in tandem until December 1994, when Silvia departed to take up the post of Tournament Director of LPGA Friendly's Classic. Jane became involved in running two Volvo Legends Tournaments for LPGA players over 45, which it was hoped would become an expanded circuit.

Sadly, in 1995, both of Jane's parents died within six months of each other. Jane, is, however, thriving in her life after the LPGA tour, in which her inspiration remains undimmed: "I am very lucky to be among interesting people in a field I enjoy and that is competitive. I have to be challenged; otherwise I get bored."

LPGA Victories: 1970 Lady Carling. **1971** George Washington Classic, Lady Pepsi. **1972** Colgate Dinah Shore Winner's Circle, Suzuki International, Angelo's 4-Ball Championship, Dallas Civitan Open, Lady Errol Classic. **1973** Angelo's 4-Ball Championship. **1974** Bing Crosby International, Birmingham Classic, Southgate Classic, Lady Errol Classic. **1975** Karsten-Ping Open. **1976** Wheeling Classic, Dallas Civitan Open. **1977** Greater Baltimore Classic, The Serra Coventry. **1978** Orange Blossom Classic, Wheeling Classic, Mayflower Classic, Golden Lights Championship. **1980** Elizabeth Arden Classic. **1985** Women's Kemper Open, Mazda Japan Classic.

Unofficial Victories: 1975 Colgate Triple Crown. **1977** Colgate Triple Crown.

Jane Blalock's LPGA Record

Year	No.of Events	Best Finish	Money	Rank	Scoring Average
1969	20	T7	3,825	37	76.84
1970	20	1	12,060	13	73.76
1971	20	1	34,492	3	73.22
1972	28	1	57,323	2	73.41
1973	32	1	40,710	9	73.11
1974	28	1	86,422	2	73.11
1975	21	1	45,478	6	73.00
1976	24	1	93.616	4	75.52
1977	24	1	102,012	4	72.48
1978	26	1	117,768	37	71.98
1979	25	1	115,226	7	72.15
1980	28	1	127,873	8	72.66
1981	29	2	96,962	12	73.05
1982	24	T5	45,295	25	73.47
1983	20	T5	40,145	40	73.75
1984	25	T3	45,893	50	73.72
1985	26	1	192,426	7	72.46
1986	20	T9	33,768	66	73.74
1987	8	T32	2,643	163	75.55
1988	3	NA	NA	NA	76.50
1989	2	T78	NA	NA	75.00
1990	DNP				
1991	1	NA	NA	NA	78.50

Althea Gibson

In the years 1957 and 1958 when Althea Gibson completed the double, winning Wimbledon and the U.S. Open at Forest Hills, she was the best woman tennis player in the world. In her book, which was published in 1959 and entitled *I Always Wanted to Be Somebody*, the last line reads, "I'm Althea Gibson, tennis champion. I hope it makes me happy."

Althea made it to the top as the first black woman athlete to achieve dominance in tennis. In her book, she says: "I refuse to turn my tennis achievements into a rousing crusade for racial equality. I won't do it. I feel strongly that I can do more good my way than I could by militant crusading. I want my success to speak for itself as an advertisement for my race. I feel our best chance to advance is to prove ourselves as individuals."

When Althea won her first Wimbledon title at age 30, in 1957, defeating Darlene Hard, the temperature on court was in the 90s. She was presented with the Wimbledon trophy by the Queen and describes it thus: "I walked up to the Queen, made a deep curtsy, and shook the hand that she held out to me. 'My congratulations,' she said. 'It must have been terribly hot out there.' I said, 'Yes, Your Majesty, but I hope it wasn't as hot in your box. At least I was able to stir up a breeze.'" In her speech at the traditional Wimbledon Ball that evening, Althea began: "In the words of your distinguished Mr. Churchill, this is my finest hour.'"

At the end of 1958, Althea became a professional tennis player, which in those days meant that she could no longer compete in the major tennis championships of the world. Together with tennis professional Karol Fageros, she joined the touring team of the famous Harlem Globetrotters, and they put on exhibition matches as a warm-up act to the basketballers. Althea won 98 out of 100 matches, and said at the time that she was making $100,000 a year, which was indeed riches.

Two years later, Althea was taken by a friend to Inglewood Country Club in New Jersey to play golf, and she became hooked on the game. She was offered the facilities of the club, and she took lessons from the professional. She was rooted to the practice ground hour after hour, day in, day out. She had found a new challenge.

Born in Silver, South Carolina, Althea moved with her family to Harlem where she grew up as a tough youngster who roamed the streets, ran away from home, and spent a lot of time at the movies. In a family of three sisters and a brother, she was the one always in trouble, and at 12, her father had ambitions for her to be a prize fighter.

Always a natural athlete, Althea excelled in physical co-ordination and recounts in her book that on a U.S. State Department tennis tour of Asia in 1957, she went to play some golf in Singapore, where her male playing partners, who admired her prowess, told her she was a natural-born golfer. "I didn't bother to tell them that I'm also a natural-born basketball player, baseball player, footballer, bowler, boxer, and that I shoot a pretty fair game of pool."

After rising to the highest level in tennis, she wanted to try another sport: "The challenge of being accurate, hitting a still ball and making it do what you want, opened another avenue of athletics for me. I was not ready to hang up my sports equipment; I still felt strong, agile, and my mind was clear on what I wanted to do. I had never seen a women's professional golf tournament. I don't think I knew any of the players, but there was a tour in existence for women, there was an organization, and I wanted to be a professional golfer. I spent every day practicing, as well as playing 18 or 36 holes. I turned professional in 1963, when I was 36 years old."

My own memories of Althea are of a superbly athletic Wimbledon tennis champion. I did not meet her until 1987, at the inaugural Marilynn Smith Founders' Classic in Dallas. When I asked her for an interview, she was not enthusiastic: "I don't consent to giving many interviews. I'm not a talker, and I don't remember a lot. I've had problems, but I've forgotten the details. I've forgotten a lot of things that I've gone through over the years. After they've happened, they're over. I don't need to hem and haw about them. I remember one club where they didn't want me to change my shoes in the clubhouse, but I've forgotten the name of the club. I know when I tried to have lessons with Betty Hicks in 1957 at Los Coyotes, California, I couldn't because the club wouldn't allow it. But there's a lot I don't remember. I don't know whether I'm lazy or I don't want to remember."

Althea offered me ten minutes of her time, which turned into more than an hour, during which she was interesting, helpful, and obviously obsessed with her golf. I went out to watch her play. Even at 60, she retained her athleticism, which combined with nearly six feet of height gave her considerable power. However, it was an obvious drawback that she lacked golfing muscle memory or the intuitive feel for the game, which comes from it being your dominant sport.

Lennie Wirtz, the LPGA tournament director in the 1960s, remembers Althea Gibson's arrival on the tour. "She was the first black. I came from the North and was stupid and ignorant about the segregation rules down South. There were sponsors who didn't want her, and I talked to her and promised to replace those sponsors as soon as I could.

"I remember going into a restaurant with her, and the waiter wouldn't come to our table and serve us. I told her not to make a scene, and we walked out. There was also a golf club where they said Althea could play the course, but they didn't want her to use the john or the locker room. We got a new sponsor and venue for that date.

"Althea is a great athlete, but when she joined the tour, she was past her prime. She tried to be mechanical rather than natural; she used her athletic talent, but she had no consistency and was a very slow player. One time, when she was leading after the first round, I had to impose a two-stroke penalty for slow play. I really took some abuse from everyone for doing that."

Althea Gibson won her first Wimbledon Women's Singles title in 1957 at age 30. In 1963, she joined the LPGA, and golf was her new and consuming challenge. Photo credit: Popperfoto.

Fellow professional Marlene Hagge, who became a friend and sometimes a roommate of Althea's, comments: "She probably doesn't want to remember the prejudice. There have been some black militants in sport. but Althea was smart and never militant. We had trouble, especially in the South, and we said we wouldn't play unless Althea could be treated like everyone else. I'm proud of the LPGA and what we did. I complain and gripe at times to the LPGA, but when it comes down to basic values, it does the right things.

"I started rooming with Althea by chance. I'm always for the underdog, and when I had driven from some place to Columbus, Ohio, I walked into the hotel around midnight to find them telling Althea that she didn't have a reservation. I guess when they took it, they didn't realize she was black; so I said, 'Come on in with me,' and that's how we started rooming together.

"When Althea came on tour, she represented a threat in that if she had wanted to make waves, her voice would have been listened to because she had been a star and a well-known name in tennis. But Althea always had the wisdom to know what she could change and what she had to accept.

"She was welcomed on tour, since most sports people respect champions. She had a tremendous amount of talent, but she came into golf too late. Although she was used to competing, performing, and winning, she couldn't learn the finesse, the finer points of the game. It takes a long time to acquire muscle memory. Had she started younger, she would have been a star.

"I was her friend. She was a very nice person. I felt good about being able to help someone, and we were equal friends. If she was your friend and knew you were on her side, she would do anything for you. She helped me; I felt very safe with her, since she was a very strong person. She achieved a lot just by being out there."

When Althea joined the tour in 1963, she competed in six events, but did not reach the required scoring average, so she put in some more practice, returning in 1964. She qualified for her player's card after four events. The tour guide of that era records that 1967 was her best year, with $5,567.50 in official money, from playing 25 events, in which her scoring average was 75.82 in 78 official rounds.

Although some say that Althea thought she was going to join the LPGA tour and shoot "lights out," she says: "It was very frustrating. I didn't like it at all, having been a winner in one sport and good at all other sports. My expectations were to be a good golfer and to shoot the best scores my talent would allow. I can remember a 68; otherwise I was in the high 70s and low 80s. It was not only frustrating; it was embarrassing. I always worked on my game to find out what I was doing wrong. I had the physical and mental ability. I felt strong, I learned from the good professionals, but I did not lower my scores.

"I was often too upset, frustrated, and depressed to sort it out. I would shoot a bad round, and I couldn't sleep at night. My body would be tired, I needed to relax, but I would start thinking about my swing. I would visualize myself, try to figure out the answers, but I couldn't translate from tennis to golf, even though the tennis swing is very similar to golf. In tennis it was automatic, while in golf, I would think about the swing plane and repeat the same mistakes. I didn't win Wimbledon until I was 30, but I had been playing tennis almost all of my life. I had won all over the world, and it was second nature to me.

"I am a Virgo, and they say Virgos are perfectionists. Maybe I am too much of one, especially when I cannot sleep because I am thinking what I can do to

New York paid tribute to Althea on July 12, 1957, after her first Wimbledon tennis victory. It was important to her that she set a good example for others to follow. She did just that in tennis and golf. Photo credit: Popperfoto.

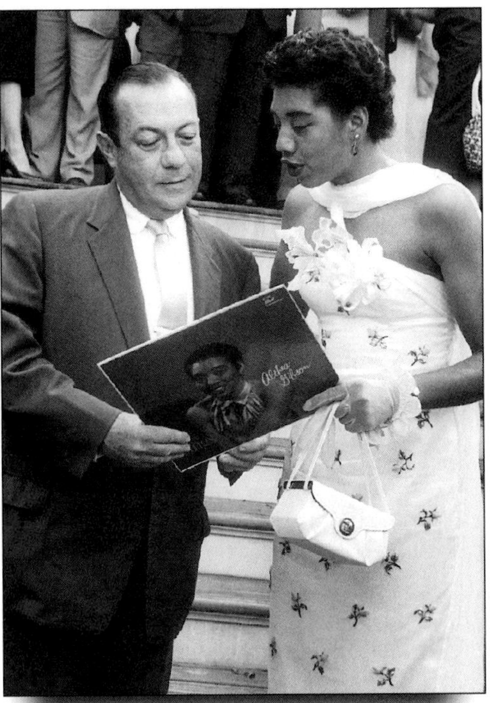

Althea is seen here with Mayor Robert Wagner, at the Althea Gibson Day celebration at Gracie Mansion. Althea presents the mayor with her first album of her own songs. Photo credit: Popperfoto.

improve. I still do it at 60. I don't think anyone expected me to win this tournament [1987 Marilynn Smith Founders' Classic], but I expected to win it. There's pride in performance. You want to do well for fans and supporters, and not get out there and make a fool of yourself.

"When I was on tour in the 1960s, I enjoyed it because I liked traveling from city to city. I've always been a loner, but gradually I got a little friendly with some of the girls. Marlene Hagge and I liked each other. She's a nice person, who appreciated my talent as the first black woman on tour.

"I tried to set an example for future young Negro women. I did the same thing in tennis. I set an example of courtesy, obeying the rules and not going against officialdom. That's the way I lived, the way I wanted to live for those others coming one day in the future. I like to say, 'Althea Gibson set a good example for others to follow.'

"When I found I wasn't making money or getting into the winner's circle and I was putting out more than I was bringing in, golf became a waste of time, even though it gave me enormous pleasure. I left the tour at the end of the 1960s, and I made a movie called The Horse Soldiers with John Wayne, William Holden, and Constance Towers.

"I don't remember how I got the part. Maybe it was just being Althea Gibson. It was a Civil War epic, and I was the lady's girl, complete with bandanna and long skirt. Once I'd learned the words, I got on and did it. It wasn't difficult. It was a way of making money to pay the rent and be self-supporting. That's the way things were during those years.

"Through the 1970s I was working with various companies doing PR, and I started teaching tennis in New Jersey. I was appointed manager of recreation for the city of East Orange, and then I became the first Female State Athletic Commissioner. Now I am doing a second term as a board member for the state Athletic Control Board, which governs and sets rules and safety regulations for boxing.

"I have enjoyed the pleasure of being blessed with a body to be used in the physical endeavor of athletics, but the most enjoyable thing is that when you accomplish things, the public becomes aware and appreciates you. Through my athletic endeavors, I received many awards. I was selected as the Babe Zaharias athlete of the years 1957 and 1958. I was given numerous other awards, including two doctorate degrees that entitle me to call myself 'Dr. Gibson.' I've got awards crowding me out of my apartment.

"God gave me many talents. Being competitive is a natural instinct, but you want to do it in a subtle way. Sometimes people with so much ability flaunt themselves, but instinct taught me not to do that. I remember the first time I played Wimbledon; it was 1952, and I found that my opening match was on the center court. I felt sick to my stomach, uneasy, but I talked to myself in the locker room to get over my nervousness. 'All you want to do on center court is just watch the ball, not look around. Don't flaunt being the first Negro woman on these hallowed grounds,' I told myself.

"I received instructions on bowing to the Royal box, but I didn't look up, I looked at nothing. I went

Tennis star Althea Gibson, like Babe Zaharias, brought her many athletic skills and competitive drive to the LPGA in 1963, but she didn't earned her players card until 1964. Though she failed to win a tournament, she brought celebrity to the tour. She is shown here during a golf match in Kingston, Jamaica. Photo credit: Popperfoto.

to the umpire's section, sat down, got my racquet out, and never looked at the packed stadium. The match began. I watched the ball and won the first set 6–0. Then I looked around as if to say, 'How do you like that,' and lost the second set 0–6. I eked out the match, winning the third set.

"Winning the U.S. Open gave me the most pleasure; my first was in 1957. I was in my own country, in front of my own people, and I loved coming back the following year to defend successfully. At that stage of my career, I could have intimidated others, but I knew as a champion that I was better than others, and I never flaunted it. If I can intimidate someone with my achievements, that makes me happy.

"I still feel I've got some golf left in me. I've got to practice, to make my hands, legs, body, and my mind work in unison. I want to prove I can be a winner as a woman golfer. I'm an athlete, and I will always be an athlete as long as I live."

Althea Gibson's LPGA Record

Year	No.of Events	Best Finish	Money	Rank	Scoring Average
1964	17	T19	$561	38	77.73
1965	19	T15	1,215	33	77.97
1966	23	T6	2,737	27	77.53
1967	25	T3	5,567	23	75.82
1968	19	6	2,339	42	77.69
1969	24	T21	1,925	44	78.28
1970	7	T2	3,654	37	75.39
1971	8	T13	1,730	50	77.00
1972	4	T27	1,670	63	78.40
1973	3	T46	588	95	80.77
1974	7	T17	1,240	84	76.88
1975	5	T30	1,025	89	76.66
1976	3	NA	NA	NA	82.67
1977	4	T52	186	119	78.82

Sandra Haynie

Sandra Haynie is one of the greats of golf. She has the distinction of having managed two separate and highly successful golf careers. Her additional role was in guiding and inspiring tennis professional, Martina Navratilova, to her first Wimbledon singles victory in 1978 and to the top of her sport.

It was during her break from golf in 1976, when she was injured, that she became mentor to Martina Navratilova. Although Sandra knew nothing about tennis, she learned very quickly and used her theories on applying yourself to winning at sport with remarkable success. "I felt she was super talented but could be a lazy person. Her father had driven her, but she could not do it on her own and wanted me to take on that role."

Sandra's first golf career lasted from 1961 through 1976, and the second burst came with a remarkable return in 1981, when in four consecutive seasons she recorded three victories, including a major, and she won nearly half a million dollars. In comparison, her early career earned her just under $400,000, and she achieved 35 victories in 14 seasons.

Of medium height and compact build, she is a highly cerebral golfer, who has such a wonderfully fluid and trained golf swing that she could play the tour and do most of her practicing in an armchair. Her finest achievement came in 1974, when she won the LPGA Championship and U.S. Women's Open within a few weeks of each other.

I met Sandra at a tournament in Dallas, and she was friendly, helpful, and an excellent interviewee. Her mental approach to the game fascinated me, and her concentration was obviously phenomenal. But above all, she made the game appear simple and uncluttered. Having honed the mechanics, she has superb visualization with which she creates her shots.

Her background is that of an only child in a middle income family where there was not a lot of money. "I was born in Fort Worth, and my father was in insurance. He then built a country club in Austin, Texas, and I lived there from the age of 12. I started playing golf at 11, through my father, who was a scratch golfer, and my mother, who did some secretarial work and was also a golfer. We played together.

"When I was 14, and my handicap was five, I won the state Publinx tournament, which I won again the following year together with the Texas State Championship. In 1960 I won the Trans-Mississippi, although I didn't enjoy matchplay and was not very good at it.

For Sandra Haynie, the highlight of her career was winning the LPGA Championship and the U.S. Open in 1974, making her the only person since Mickey Wright to win the two titles in a single season. Photo courtesy: LPGA.

"At the age of 12, I was invited to play in a practice round with Babe Zaharias and Betty Dodd, who were playing in the Texas Open at Rivercrest Country Club. Babe hit it so far and was such an impressive athlete that I went home and said, 'That's what I want to be, a professional golfer.'

"I was raised to be independent, and as an individual in sport, you learn discipline at a young age. I have always kept everything inside and never talked about what was bothering me, especially when I was younger. I guess it came from growing up on a golf course, where if I had a problem, I was the one who had to solve it. I spent many years accounting only to myself. I loved all sports, and I missed a lot of school to play golf. I left school at 17, turning professional in December 1960, and my parents were supportive.

"I wanted to play the tour, and I was convinced I would make it, but I had no expectation of winning a tournament. Although I was not intimidated by the women on tour, I had great respect for players like Mickey Wright and Betsy Rawls because they were so good.

"I had always led my own life, and I knew you had to be selfish to be successful. I put everything into golf that might have gone into a family because my golf career meant everything to me. I never understood the people who asked me when I was going to quit golf and get married. A woman doctor doesn't give up her career because she gets married.

"In the 1960s, you played golf because you loved it, and in the hope that someday the tour would improve. The money only meant that I could support myself, that I could take a trip or do what I wanted. I had a contract giving me a yearly salary with Spalding, but I never gave clinics or exhibitions because I didn't enjoy them.

"I found out I had talent, but I didn't win my first year. I made enough money to get by and then won back-to-back the second year, with the excitement of beating Mickey Wright by one shot for my first victory.

"From then on I won every year, once or more, and winning made me appreciate my talent and what I could do with it. You measure yourself against the best, and it is a good feeling to play your best against the best. You don't get that feeling many times in your life, and there is nothing else comparable.

"Winning is 50 percent talent, although it always requires 100% concentration, and you need a lot of discipline and confidence in yourself. The golf course is the loneliest place in the world. You are responsible for every shot, good and bad. You need to have hit enough golf balls, to know whether you can dig far enough down, to come up with the right shot at the right time.

"Almost the most important facet of any athlete is to know yourself, to know whether you have the calmness, thought pattern, and ability to use your imagination in order to win. There are so many things you go through mentally that by the time you get over the ball, the golf swing should be automatic.

"When I learned how to play golf, I learned from a Scotsman called A. G. Mitchell. I learned how to use my mind, as much as I learned to use my muscles. I always picture what I am going to do, and I always like to step behind the ball and look at that picture. I used to get teased on tour because I didn't practice a lot, but I didn't have to, since a lot of my preparation was mental.

"Some people think they have the proper picture, and then they get over the ball and start fiddling with their golf swing and wonder what their hands are going to do. If you have the right picture, your hands will follow it. We have great players who use visualization and others who are good strikers and rely on sheer ability.

"Desire to win goes without saying. If you don't have desire and nerves, you won't accomplish anything. When I quit playing the tour, I joked that it was nice to wake up in the morning and not feel sick to my stomach. When I was on tour, I could never eat breakfast, which was just something I went through. People asked why I endured it, but it was just part of it, and if I wasn't nervous I wouldn't play well. Nervousness is part of dealing with the sport, of being excited about what you're going to do and finding enthusiasm from it.

"If you don't feel nervous, you haven't the will to win. I am a firm believer that not everyone has the ability to be number one, or wants to be, but that doesn't mean you can't find your own level and get all the enjoyment and fulfillment that you can. It's important to recognize your limitations.

"The highlight of my career was not in winning the 1974 Open. It was the combination of having won the LPGA a few weeks before and being the only other person since Mickey Wright in 1961 to win the two titles in a season. That was the top. Also, the manner in which I won the Open at La Grange, Illinois, was very satisfying. Most Opens are lost, not won, but I made a 70 foot birdie at the 71st hole, and then birdied the 72nd hole for victory.

"Soon after, I took a club job at Fort Worth because it sounded like a heck of an opportunity. I had just set myself up for the future with two victories, but it beats me now why I took the job. It was a bad business decision, which didn't work out, and I returned to the tour.

"I had been part of the organization and seen it grow, and I was involved in the running of the tour, working on the board for six to seven years. In the 1973–74 period I was vice president to Carol Mann, which was a great experience. She was one of the best things that happened to the LPGA, and I respect the things she did. She was an excellent president, who had a lot of class and made many changes. I was hard to get along with on the board. If you had something constructive to say, I'd listen forever, but if you wanted to bitch, I didn't want to hear it, and they would say, 'Don't go to Haynie.'

"By 1976, I had circulation problems in my left hand, which was a build-up of scar tissue, and I lost the feeling in the last two fingers. I couldn't hang on to the golf club, and the doctor said I could learn to live with it or have an operation. I had the operation. I didn't play golf for a year and started a sports business.

"In April 1976, when I was still playing golf, I met Martina Navratilova, who was then 19. She was competing in the Superstars' competition in Florida. We began to talk about what you have to give to your sport, and in spite of having won the previous week, Martina said she was not happy. She knew she could do more. She asked me for advice,

Sandra Haynie won the 1974 U.S. Women's Open, one of 42 victories she carded while on the LPGA tour. She entered the LPGA Hall of Fame in 1977.

and I gave her things she could understand and use on court. She did them and liked them. I had always wanted to give something back to sport, and I love working with young people because they are delightfully enthusiastic and flexible. You can mold them a little, give them suggestions, and let them fly. I like to work on the head, on concentration, and not on the game.

"Martina moved from California and bought a house in my hometown, Dallas, which we shared and used as an office. I became her agent, did her schedule, her finances, and was with her lawyer when he handled contracts. I worked with her until 1980. I took a crash course in tennis because I didn't know anything about it. For weeks I watched every tournament I could, scouting to learn peoples' strengths and weaknesses. Players would come and sit with me, and I learned by listening to them.

"I worked on Martina's weight with a training course, and her weight dropped rapidly. I found out what she was experiencing on court and would suggest ways to make her more positive. I showed her that it was her perfectionism that made her question line calls or lose her temper.

People who expect a lot from themselves also expect it from others. Martina did not tolerate mistakes from other people well, and we talked about it a lot. People are going to make mistakes, and you have to learn to be tolerant of mistakes so they are not destructive to you. You have to take the energy you would have used to get mad to play better on the next point or game. You must concentrate on one point at a time, go for it, close it out right away, and not look ahead. You can apply the same principles to learning how to conduct yourself on the golf course, tennis court, or football field.

"Martina was going through a really rebellious period in her life, and 1976 was a horrible year. She had defected from Czechoslovakia in September 1975, giving up her family and her country for tennis, which was a huge decision. She was discovering she was alone, unhappy with herself and her weight, questioning why she had done it, and she was struggling with her emotions.

"Soon, things started to change, and it was a time of building and understanding what this complex person was all about, what she was going through, and how to help solve some of her problems.

"The public relations side of it was hard for a while. Martina was a tough interview, who would tell someone they had asked a dumb question. She was guarded and felt the press was abusive because of her defection and because she drove a Mercedes, made a lot of money, and liked expensive jewelry. She felt she was being picked on, and maybe it was partly true.

"I worked with her to turn it around; so she could tell other people who had been born in the U.S. that they had had the opportunities to enjoy all these things that she had never known, and was finding out about now.

"I hired a PR company to help with good exposure and to make people see her in a different light. I put her into a position to give something back, with her becoming a spokesperson for Big Brothers and Big Sisters.

"In 1977, Martina was a different person, and in the opening tournament of the season she beat Chris Evert in straight sets in the final. It was wonderful to see her starting to reach her potential.

"By 1978, she was blowing everyone off the court, winning 37 straight tournament matches. In July, she achieved her first singles victory at Wimbledon, defeating Chris Evert. Four days later was she ranked number one in the world. It was as satisfying to me as winning a golf tournament. To be able to have whatever it takes to bring that out of someone else, was really exciting."

In her book, *Being Myself,* Martina says this of Sandra Haynie:

"I went out to watch her play a golf tournament. I was fascinated by her play. As nerve wracking as golf can be, she was so calm, so cool. When she putted she used the same routine every time. She was so organized, so orderly, with her beautiful swing.

"She struck me as different from a lot of tennis players I knew. She was quiet, self contained—maybe the result of years spent standing over a ten foot putt with no opponent, no moving ball, no way to burn off her energy.

"After a day of talking with Haynie I knew she was the friend I needed. She was older, wiser, and a champion in her own right. She didn't need my money or my fame to feel good about herself.

"Haynie was so easy going it was easy to take advice from her. She never tried to pretend she knew anything about tennis, but she did understand what it was like to compete. Tennis is a different game from golf, but Haynie understood the inner strength you need for either sport.

"She was a good calming influence on me for a few years, but I was trying to find the world outside, and Haynie was happy sitting around watching TV. She was very quiet, and she didn't go out—not that I was much for night life either, but I wanted to get around a little more. She was like a guru to me for three years, and she helped me as much as she could, but I was young, and I had to find out about the rest of the world."

By 1981, Sandra was once again playing a full schedule on the LPGA tour. Her tremendous comeback started with a victory in the Henredon Classic that year, followed by two victories in 1982, including a designated major, the Peter Jackson Classic.

"My wins after my return, and in particular my first victory, gave me giant satisfaction. I felt very confident and got myself into a position where I could dig down inside and bring to the surface what I needed to make my game work for me and victory. I am a conservative player, and I try not to reach extreme peaks and valleys in a round; so I never felt extremely nervous. I maintained a level where I just felt I could make it happen. I had a nice reception to my comeback, which I enjoyed. I had worked hard for it mentally and practiced harder because you need to play yourself back into shape. There is nothing the same as playing tournament golf."

Sandra continued her success on tour until the end of 1984, when injury to her knee resulted in three operations. Her health has been a problem from the age of 33, when she developed progressive arthritis, and physical problems have affected her back, hand, and knee. Since her retirement from golf, she has suffered from hepatitis and other health problems.

Business interests through her golf career have included being involved in a T-shirt company, restaurant design and management, and golf club repair with her father.

Being off the golf tour and looking for a new lifestyle has required some adjustment: "I found it hard to be forced into making the decision to leave golf. I did feel deprived for a while, and it is hard to go through the times when you miss the competition. I don't miss the travel, but after doing something you love for a long period, you realize there is no feeling to replace the competitive adrenalin and excitement.

"I don't see myself as a selfish person, except with my golf. When I tried playing a few tournaments in 1986, my knee didn't hold up, but I also realized that I had become a bit more giving after being away from golf, and I didn't want to return to that type of selfishness.

"I have done some teaching locally, also with a few of the players on tour, and I find it gratifying that they ask my advice. I have a continuing involvement in a local arthritis foundation where I work not only with children, but also with their parents who need a lot of support. We have been pretty successful raising funds and continuing the educational process on arthritis. I'm on the board of directors, and I enjoy it."

Member LPGA Hall of Fame 1977

LPGA Victories: 1962 Austin Civitan Open, Cosmopolitan Open. **1963** Phoenix Thunderbird Open. 1964 Baton Rouge Open, Las Cruces Open. **1965** Cosmopolitan Open, LPGA Championship. **1966** Buckeye Savings Invitational, Glass City Classic, Alamo Open, Pensacola Invitational. **1967** Amarillo Open, Mickey Wright Invitational. **1968** Pacific Open. **1969** St. Louis Invitational, Supertest Open, Shreveport Kiwanis Invitational. **1970** Raleigh Invitational, Shreveport Kiwanis Invitational. **1971** Burdine's Invitational, Dallas Civitan Open, San Antonio, Alamo Open, Len Immke Buick Open. **1972** National Jewish Hospital Open, Quality First Classic, Lincoln-Mercury Open. **1973** Orange Blossom Classic, Lincoln-Mercury Open, Charity Golf Classic. **1974** Lawson's Open, LPGA Championship, U.S. Women's Open, George Washington Classic, National Jewish Hospital Open, Charity Golf Classic. **1975** Naples-Lely Classic, Charity Golf Classic, Jacksonville Classic, Ft. Myers Classic. **1981** Henredon Classic. **1982** Rochester International, Peter Jackson Classic.

Unofficial Victory: 1982 Portland Ping Team Championship (with Kathy McMullen).

Sandra Haynie's LPGA Record

Year	No.of Events	Best Finish	Money	Rank	Scoring Average
1961	12	10	$3,709	21	77.32
1962	17	1	6,608	16	75.66
1963	29	1	13,683	9	75.14
1964	29	1	17,061	7	73.80
1965	30	1	17,722	5	73.94
1966	31	1	30,157	2	73.09
1967	27	1	26,543	2	72.81
1968	26	1	25,992	3	77.36
1969	20	1	24,276	5	73.15
1970	19	1	26,626	2	72.95
1971	20	1	36,219	2	73.03
1972	25	1	39,701	5	72.93
1973	25	1	47,353	7	73.43
1974	24	1	74,559	3	72.75
1975	19	1	61,614	4	72.00
1976	18	T2	38,510	14	72.82
1977	1	NA	NA	NA	78.00
1978	3	T11	2,221	104	73.50
1979	6	T13	5,829	93	74.36
1980	7	T9	9,712	84	74.27
1981	25	1	94,124	13	72.89
1982	29	1	245,432	2	71.86
1983	23	2	108,136	13	72.82
1984	17	4	26,165	75	74.24
1985	DNP				
1986	5	T11	9,012	124	73.06
1987	DNP				
1988	12	T10	14,217	119	73.97
1989	23	T12	50,687	57	73.07

Joyce Kazmierski

Joyce Kazmierski's playing career spanned from 1968 to 1986 and included her taking an active part in the running of the LPGA organization. Although her consistency put her in the top 40 in career money earnings, she never won an event in all her years on tour: "I have always had an image of myself coming close, not winning."

Two years after she became president of the LPGA in 1984, she found her playing ability was waning. In order to remain on tour, she resigned as a member and became a tour caddie, which status excluded her from clubhouses and locker rooms: "I missed the food and the camaraderie, but I could choose my own Portajohn."

Born a Catholic, her religion had a large influence on her personality, in that she found it hard to shake off feelings of unworthiness with which she was indoctrinated as a child. "I've been working on getting rid of them, but it's evident in my behavior and feelings that there's an element of 'O Lord, I am not worthy,' which was a prayer I said. For me, those words have had a continuous subconscious power. I have rebelled against all Christian religions because they teach self-negating, instead of life-enhancing, attitudes."

Joyce Kazmierski is one of the people with whom you sit down to have a chat, and four hours later you're still going at it hammer and tongs and having a great time. I look forward to seeing her because she's warm, humorous, introspective, analytical, forever probing, honest, and open. She has probably analyzed herself and her emotions from before her birth, right through her life, to death and beyond. With a fascination for astrology and numerology, she became the tour's favorite chart reader, and it was always good for some publicity. She is of medium height and build, and when she wears her contact lenses her light blue eyes darken to china blue.

"I was born in Pontiac, Michigan, and grew up in Detroit. I was the first baby to be born in Pontiac on the day the Second World War ended—VJ Day—and although many babies were called Vee Jay, my parents, being good Catholics, chose Virginia Joyce and always called me Joyce. To this day my uncle has always called me VJ.

"I was the third of four girls. Eighteen month intervals separated the first three girls, then seven years later came the last one, Susan. Having been the baby of the family for so long, I carried some resentment about Susan, but she was very cute, and we all played mother with her.

"My father, a practical and frugal man, was a toolmaker at Cadillac Motors, a skilled laborer who became a master craftsman on machine maintenance. As the children grew older, my mother did a little part-time work, and although there was not a lot of money, I never had the feeling we went through any hard times.

"The Catholic religion was a large part of our lives, going to church and mostly parochial schools. Right through high school we would leave home at 7 a.m., go to 8 a.m. mass every morning at school, and go to catechism once a week. I didn't enjoy religion, but I liked learning Latin. There was a constant dosage of discipline, and you never really questioned it. It was based on faith, and if you didn't have it, there was something wrong with you.

"At my first confession at seven, I said that I had lied seventeen times and disobeyed my parents twenty-five times in those seven years. There's a series of prayers before confession leading up to communion that are symbolic, traditional, and ceremonial, and a seven year old doesn't understand them. It petrifies a little kid, gives you a feeling of sinfulness and unworthiness, which usually the child carries throughout life.

"At college in an intellectually inquisitive atmosphere, I started to question my religion. If the Catholic Church loses anyone, often it is in college, and at about 21, I rejected Catholicism. I was away from home sufficiently that my parents were not monitoring my attendance at mass. It was very painful for me being my own judge and critical parent. The priest in whom I was confiding had no compassion. His attitude was that I had to be a good Catholic.

"Once I made the decision to break away, I felt good about it, but you have to work through the guilt. All four daughters are not practicing Catholics in spite of being raised as such, but we are as aware of our spirituality as any human can be. Our parents were not encouraging, but they prayed for us and said, 'Whatever makes you happy,' which is a positive acceptance.

"I had a fairly normal, harmonious childhood, and we spent quite a bit of time with four male cousins down the street. I had strong feelings about helping my mother, but I felt a bit servile. I was not domestic and didn't want to cook or sew. I did have a doll, but I preferred being the tomboy, climbing trees and playing baseball with the boys.

"I strongly identified with my father, who was very athletic. I wanted to go bowling and play golf with him. He gave me a lot of support, unspoken love, and I wanted to identify with him. He started golf when I was eight, and then two years later found me a junior golf school in Detroit, where you got six free lessons and could play the local nine hole public course for 25¢. Dad thought it was a good opportunity, and I loved it. I was in it for six years, learning the basics. My dad and I would practice together and sneak onto a private golf course to play a few holes in the summer evenings.

"The first year I shot 67 for 9 holes, and then with a 54 the following year I won a competition. I won the Detroit Junior Girls title in 1958, 1959, and 1960, and I was Detroit district champion in 1964, 1966 and 1968, but it wasn't until I was 17 that I played my first national competition.

"Growing up, I always felt a bit awkward about my self-image, and my identification with sports. Every so often my mother would insist I wear a skirt, but as time went on I got more reinforcement from people in high school and at college, where it was all right to be in sports, and come hell or high water that's where I wanted to be.

Joyce Kazmierski played her first national competition at 17; she joined the LPGA in 1978 after playing amateur golf for six years. Photo credit: Lester Nehamkin.

"The mainstream of thought was that academic learning was acceptable for a woman but ultimately she should get married, have children, and be domestic. In my junior year in college, I thought seriously about marrying a guy I was dating, who said 'One of these days you'll find out golf isn't everything.' In one sense he was right; in another he indicated he did not understand. He was putting me in a wifely, female role, and I decided against marriage. I had kept myself in the feminine role in the relationship because I thought that was how to act around men, and although I felt the pressure at college to find a husband, social life was a minor part of my life.

"A bit later when women's lib started, everyone was re-evaluating. I didn't identify with it strongly, more with my sisters. My oldest sister, Mary Lou was unmarried and a secretary in San Francisco, and the next sister Jo Ann, who was born to be married, did just that and started a family immediately. There was no pressure on me from my parents.

"When I got on tour, my Pro-Am partners who were always men, would say, 'When are you going to stop this and get married?' I used to answer I'd

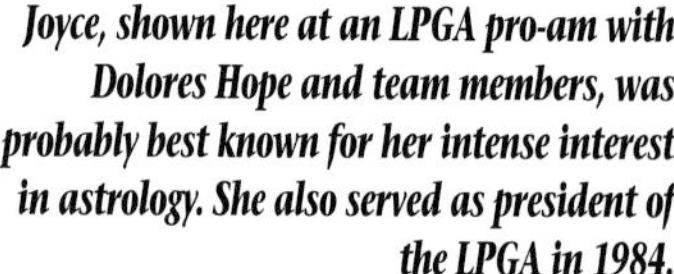

Joyce, shown here at an LPGA pro-am with Dolores Hope and team members, was probably best known for her intense interest in astrology. She also served as president of the LPGA in 1984.

probably do it for a couple of years, quit the tour and settle down. I always maintained that if I chose marriage, I would leave the tour. I could not do both. I would not want that split loyalty.

"Maybe I've chosen not to get married because I wanted to play golf, and getting married would interfere. People say what a sacrifice, but it's not because I've done exactly what I wanted to do. It's like telling someone who's married with children that they've sacrificed their freedom.

"I went to Michigan State University, which had an outstanding golf course. There was not a girl's team or club, and no intermural golf competitions, but I could practice and play golf. I started with a major in journalism and then I switched to English, hated it, and switched to history. When I left college with a degree in social sciences, I taught school for a year in a Detroit suburb and lived at home.

"In 1968 I went to Pinehurst to play in the North-South and stopped in Atlanta to see an LPGA tournament. I had won the Women's Intercollegiate and State championships twice, was runner-up in the 1965 Trans-Mississippi, and a semi-finalist in the 1968 U.S. Amateur. I was going to make the big decision on whether to turn professional or not. Eventually I said, 'It's now or never,' and at 23, I joined the LPGA tour in August and I played nine tournaments that season.

"The tour averaged 40–45 players, the average purse was $17,000, and three-day tournaments were the norm. Lennie Wirtz was the executive director based in Cincinnati, and we were really struggling. He was an aggressive little individual, who would stand up for the rights of the players. When certain clubs refused to let us wear slacks even in 40° weather, Lennie would say, 'We'll take our show elsewhere.' If black professional Renee Powell had trouble getting into a clubhouse, he'd threaten to leave.

"Although the players were pretty well in command of the organization, they eventually felt Lennie was too dictatorial, and some of them resented his conflicting loyalties as he managed some of the players. He left in 1970 and was followed by Bud Ericson, who was there until Ray Volpe arrived in 1975. It was Carol Mann's insistence and drive that made the new era of the LPGA happen in the 1970s, and I'm glad we had a Carol Mann who said, 'We're going to change things.'

"I was on the executive board from 1974 until 1976 and then on the player council, which was set up with five groups according to playing experience. Each group had a representative member on the council. The president and vice-president of the organization were elected by the total membership and those slated for the board of directors. The tour was a small sorority, which is something you lose as the organization grows. There was genuine concern from every member as to where the association was going. We had our share of jealousies and envy, but the positive element was much stronger.

"The image of the tour was not very good, since the women could not find clothes that were specifically made for golf. That didn't occur until the 1970s. In the early 1950s all sport was considered masculine, and if a group of women wanted to do a masculine thing like play golf, everyone asked what was wrong with them and why weren't they at home having babies?

"Sex is a viable selling point for the tour. Though I never liked the idea of stooping to that level, it was evident we needed to. It was hard to convince people they should respect a woman athlete for her ability. Many people are turned off by women athletes and see them as masculine sportswomen. As women, we know there are masculine characteristics within us and that people are not pure feminine or pure masculine. There are men who love to cook, love to cry, and women who are extremely aggressive. The point is to find out where you best fit in, function, and grow. There are only so many super machos and so many Miss America pageant types. Some men and women need to bounce their male and female characteristics off the opposite sex; for others it's not such a big issue. Women have shown their feelings and emotions from the time they were little girls, and you just need the courage within your head to live your life as you wish and know that we do not all think alike.

"When I turned professional, my ambitions were vague. I could see myself earning money, but obviously I did not perceive myself as a tournament winner because I never won a tournament. I now know that all the times I said I wanted to win, I really didn't. It was a daydream rather than a deeply felt desire, and from a religious past I had a repressive false humility where you don't appreciate yourself for what you are.

"The reasons I didn't want to win are foolish: I didn't like feeling nervous, I didn't want my knees to shake, my hands to sweat, or to feel physically uncomfortable. The motivation was to become comfortable by getting myself out of that situation. I told myself that it was all right to be physically uncomfortable, that it's fear creating the physical manifestations, and I asked myself what I was afraid of. There were times I was afraid of winning, times I was afraid of losing.

"I played professional golf from 1968, and I had an image of myself coming close, but not winning. That's where I'm comfortable. You build your security around it and decide it's all right not to want to win. I'm a perfect example of it being all right.

"You need to respect, love, and feel good about yourself. You want respect from your peer group and always from your mom and dad. You say, 'I'll win and prove to Mom and Dad that I'm OK.' I have limited myself, denied myself the experience of winning a tournament for reasons which I feel are all right. The power is in your own mind, and you choose where you put it.

"Money is important, but I've tried not to use it as a measuring stick. I never worried that much about it, since I felt I could support myself, or I fantasized about living with my family. I always wanted to be a professional, and I let my imagination run, about whether I could handle money or whether it would have been a powerful aspect in my life. The point is that Nancy Lopez knows what she wants in life and gets it. Her success has given the whole tour an identity and has pulled in the galleries who help to pay our salaries.

"I'm not miserable. I'm very happy, and winning a tournament would not make me a winner in life. There are many sports people who feel that way. I never lacked motivation, I could be happy and successful without winning. To me, winning a golf tournament has been finishing second, so I've won eight tournaments. For someone else it's a bit different.

"My interest in learning about myself from a different perspective came from my curiosity in 1968 about paranormal psychology and astrology, which was then in the realms of the occult and hocus pocus. A friend of mine in Michigan was studying to be an astrologer. Through talking with her and doing my chart, the more I learned, the more my understanding helped me to be patient with myself. I studied by reading and talking about astrology for two or three years, and I began to do charts for some of the women on tour.

"I'm only super-conscious of lunar cycles and Mars, which is the force of energy. I could say I want to know my energy level and need to consult the planets, but I know the answer if I ask myself. Since I'm as gullible as anyone else, I consult the planets and then make them say whatever I want, good or bad. There are not good or bad signs or aspects, it depends on your interpretation. Astrology reinforces your ideas and so does numerology, phrenology, reading the palm or the foot. Astrology can give an indication of what might happen, but what actually happens is up to you.

"My sun is in Leo, rising sun Aquarius, moon in Scorpio, which shows not the greatest harmony in the world. I'm suited to outdoor activity and I don't need astrology to tell me that. I love variety and travel.

"You always have the power to change whatever is there. You have a propensity to do certain things, but you can change it. I believe we choose when we're going to be born and when we die. It is always you who allows something to happen or not."

In 1984, Joyce served as president of the LPGA. By 1986 her playing status had become non-exempt, which meant she only would be able to play about seven tournaments a year without prequalifying. Trying to prequalify in Florida for the first three tournaments of the 1986 season, she missed all three and decided it was time for a change.

"The previous three years I was beginning to hate the game; I was 90 percent negative and felt that playing was in my past. Maybe it was time to lay it aside and establish a travel business or teach clinics. Sandra Spuzich knew that I was not happy playing, and said, 'If ever you want to caddie, let me know.' Although it meant giving up my membership of the LPGA, I liked the idea, and as a Class A member I could be taken back into the fold in the future. Most of my friends were on tour, I would be able to continue to travel, which I love. It would be fun to be still involved in the game and a nice farewell to the tour. Until then, I had always known what I would be doing throughout the years. It had been like going to college forever.

"I went home and asked my folks what they would do in my situation. My father said play the tournaments where I could get in. My mother said she never wanted me to turn pro in the first place, but that she was behind me because I wanted to do it. My mother astonished me, since I never knew that.

"My first year as a caddie for Sandra was a wonderful experience. Observing such a great player and such a high skill level, I learned a lot about the technical aspects, and she had the best caddie out there. I really spoiled her.

"I was a bit worried about how it would look to all the sponsors who I had known as a competitor and as LPGA president. I didn't care about the players because I knew that they understood on some level. I always seemed to bump into the main sponsor, and I found most would say, 'What fun. Isn't it great?'

"The transition phase was a bit scary because I like my life ordered. I was not Joyce the golfer. Who was I? I had to find out."

Joyce later joined Colorado teaching professional Pat Lange, a women's golf club manufacturer, in the golf travel business. Together they design and host golf vacation trips in the U.S. and United Kingdom. Joyce also became hooked on teaching golf, which she does locally in Indianapolis at the Brownsburg Golf Club, a daily fee course of which she says: "I could not have it any better if I owned it. I love teaching. I wish I had realized it 20 years ago. It would have been a whole lot easier. I'm a holistic teacher. I teach the whole person, and I go back to basics. If your fundamentals are not right, your structure will be like the leaning Tower of Pisa. The more I teach, the more I love it. I've found myself: I'm Joyce the teacher."

Joyce Kazmierski's LPGA Record

Year	No.of Events	Best Finish	Money	Rank	Scoring Average
1968	9	T22	$377	53	78.26
1969	28	7	2,895	41	77.94
1970	19	T8	1,245	49	78.40
1971	20	T10	2,548	44	77.51
1972	30	T8	6,727	38	76.59
1973	32	2	38,973	10	75.06
1974	28	2	19,634	23	75.15
1975	29	4	20,098	20	74.08
1976	27	T3	26,417	22	74.73
1977	26	2	29,180	22	74.44
1978	29	2	37,323	26	74.65
1979	29	2	47,395	22	74.28
1980	30	T8	24,489	22	74.28
1981	25	T3	18,924	65	75.56
1983	24	T13	10,741	58	75.39
1984	26	T10	11,157	115	75.37
1985	26	T29	6,184	143	75.77

Carol Mann

When I first met Carol Mann, I dropped all my pencils, I was so intimidated. She is 6 feet, 3 inches tall, has a deep, strong voice, and a confident presence that is deceptive, since she has been at times the most insecure of people. She is warm, vital, intensely emotional and has a rich form of expressing herself:

"As I'm getting older, I'm not now willing to put myself in the kind of physical shape I was in previously, just waking up. I miss the physical side; I will miss it more than any other thing. I've had it with dieting, I hate it. I hate cellulite too, but you just have to put up with it. If you get it, you get it.

"The beautiful things that happen on the inside, in the heart, the mind and the soul—I cherish those. I hope that getting older for me isn't too painful, like death. I don't know much about death. I don't think I'm going to like it a whole lot—my own, or that of anyone I love very much. I think it will make me mad, like one of those freaky accidents."

Carol is a larger than life person in every sense of the word. She is very giving, and much of it has been for the benefit of the LPGA and for women. She pinpoints an interesting feature about women athletes and those women who achieve: "If anyone were to judge us by our walk, they would not think we were too feminine. We are committed people who walk with a purpose. Look at anyone walking to a commitment, and they walk with drama and purpose. I defend that, it's a very logical thing. I agree with Gloria Steinem who said, 'If a woman is doing it, it's feminine.'"

Joyce Kazmierski says of Carol: "She was a very good role model, who was not the masculine type. As a woman with great leadership qualities, she could survive the confusion, and she was not afraid to ask questions. You could say the girl had balls."

Carol's impact on the LPGA was enormous. She achieved 38 career victories in the 1960s and

Carol Mann was a larger than life person in every sense of the word, and her impact on the LPGA was enormous. Photo courtesy: Wilson Sporting Goods Co.

1970s. She got into the Hall of Fame, and in the mid-1970s took the LPGA into the modern era, with the hiring of Ray Volpe during her office as president of the organization. Her drive and energy were responsible for that period of change, and like many people in office, she suffered when it was over. "When I stopped being president of the LPGA, I was depressed for eight months. I couldn't let go."

I first met Carol in the late 1970s, when she was married to golf professional Jim Hardy (they divorced in 1988). She has always been willing to help and communicate, and she is someone I look forward to seeing, both because I like her as a person and because I enjoy her depth and immediate intensity of conversation. She has become a woman of style, but she has a vulnerability just below the surface.

"I was born in Buffalo, New York, which is not the greatest place in the world, except to leave. My father and mother both worked for Chevrolet. They met there, and I was raised in a middle income family in Baltimore, with four younger brothers—16 months younger, twins five years younger, and another 10 years younger. I wouldn't speak to my mother for a month when the fourth child was a boy because I wanted a sister, but I was allowed to name him. I called him Bunky, since I had a crush on a boy with that name. Bunky in Baltimore means 'friend.'

"I was an anemic child, skinny and very tall at nine, when I started playing golf. Both my parents played, and my father bought me some right-handed clubs although I was naturally left handed. They were awkward, but all right. I took lessons and got deeper and deeper into it.

"My mother, who encouraged me, walked the fairways with me to count my strokes. My drive came from wanting to be with my father, who was away working all week. I thought I would be able to play with him on weekends, but he didn't want to pay any attention to me. We weren't close, but I wanted to be, and that's the way it was, by his choice.

"I went to a private girls' school, which was the only one that would take me at five. At first, I was so nervous I went to the bathroom the whole time. It was a Catholic school, and by third grade I had decided to become a nun. I had rosaries and all the works. At age eight, a year later, it was decided I should leave.

"I missed the place so much that I was sick all the time at public school, where I had nose bleeds. I was so unhappy that I went back to the nuns half way through the year. It was a good place to learn, where I felt happy and special. When I was 13 and the family moved to Chicago, I stayed in Baltimore for an extra six months.

"In the summer I played golf with my brothers, the shortest of whom was six-feet two-inches. I was athletic and captain of gym, which I hoped would

In 1960, Carol joined the LPGA. Patty Berg helped her become a member of the Wilson Sporting Goods Professional Staff, and Patty taught her how to do clinics; something Carol and Patty are both remembered for today. Photo courtesy: Wilson Sporting Goods Co.

Carol Mann won the 1965 USGA Women's Open, her third tournament victory. When her career ended, she had won 38 tournaments and earned a place in the LPGA Hall of Fame.

get my father's attention, but it was my mother who was still watching me.

"In Chicago I joined Olympia Fields, a famous old golf club, and I stayed out a lot playing golf rather than looking after my brothers, who were only to be tolerated. My mother criticized me and said, 'Who do you think you are?' It bothered me that I wasn't fitting in, and I thought, 'One day I'll show you.'

"I went to tournaments on trains and loved it: the challenge, the circumstances, and my changing golf ability. I idolized Babe Zaharias, Patty Berg, and Mickey Wright. At 16, with a seven handicap, I went to play the club championship. I was walking to the first tee when the mother of a friend told me the ladies didn't want me to play because they knew I would beat them. It wasn't fair. She wasn't very happy telling me, and I felt banished.

"At 16, you don't have the poise to cope with it, and I ran crying to the club professional. He was really mad. I was really unhappy. Finally, the ladies agreed to let me play the first nine holes the next day, as well as round two, and another nine holes and the third round the day after that, so I played 27 holes a day. I won. I beat them all by 10 or 12 shots. It was sad for adults to behave that way, especially as they always wanted me for the club team.

"At 17, when I won the Junior Women's Western Open, I was awkward, shy, without any poise, and I giggled. I had a pony tail, wore shorts, and was gawky and ugly, but it changed my perspective to have played so well.

"A few weeks later I won a tournament in Chicago, and then I went with Patty Berg to the Western Open in Seattle. We went by plane, and Patty was so nervous she was saying the rosary the whole time. I was paired with Mickey Wright in the tournament. I was scared to death and didn't do well. The women were terrific, fun, smart, and very nice to me. I knew I wanted to be a professional, but I wasn't good enough.

"The following year I went to the University of North Carolina in Greensboro, where Ellen Griffin was teaching and I was a phys ed major. After two years I told her I didn't want to be a teacher. I wanted to do a degree in kinesiology, anatomy, and physiology and relate them to golf. It wasn't an available course; so I quit.

"I played the 1960 Women's U.S. Amateur, and in the third round I played a woman on her birthday; when she won at the 17th hole, I said, 'Happy Birthday,' and I felt she should win. I had played a pregnant woman in the second round—it was a wonder I didn't lose to her—as I had felt badly about winning. Competing and beating people are not easy for me. I want to do well, but I can't stand matchplay.

"In October 1960, I turned professional, and Patty Berg helped me join Wilson Sporting Goods. In my first tournament I had the flu, and a 102° temperature. It was freezing cold and raining, and I shot 89. I five-putted one green because I didn't know how to take relief from the water. In my second tournament I came in sixth. I won just over $300 and was off and running. My first year I won $2,600, which was not very good, but I learned some poise, and Patty taught me to do clinics with her and Judy Kimball.

"I loved being on my own, traveling and working at the sport. I asked Mickey [Wright] and

Betsy [Rawls] for advice. I admired them. I was lonely, flitted from group to group, and enjoyed the fun, warmth, and closeness of the tour. Marlene and Bob Hagge sort of adopted me.

"In 1962, I was at a tournament where I met Manuel de la Torre, the professional at Milwaukee Country Club, and I went to him for lessons. He transformed my game, the heavens parted intellectually on the golf swing, and I worked with him over the next 16 years. I won my first tournament in 1964, the Western Open, where there was no information or communications about how the others were doing. After I chopped along the last hole I said, 'Who's doing well?' I was told I had won by two shots, so I threw a champagne party for the press to be like Tony Lema. I won $1,200, the champagne cost me $120, and I had blisters from popping every cork myself.

"In 1965, after I won the Open, I felt let down, and I said to Marlene Hagge, 'Is this all there is?' She was soothing, but I'd worked so hard that I couldn't imagine why I didn't feel more overwhelmed. Later I realized it is the doing that is the achievement, not the winning. The fun of doing spurs you on.

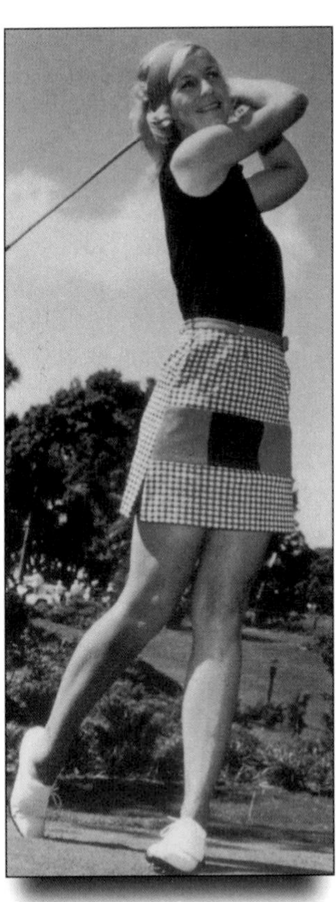

Carol Mann won ten tournaments in 1968. In 1969, she was also the leading money winner, but she never believed she accomplished enough in those days. It drove her greatness. Photo courtesy: Wilson Sporting Goods Co.

"In 1968, I won ten tournaments, and in 1969, I was leading money winner, having won eight tournaments. I had made a tremendous effort, and it still wasn't satisfying. I said to my father: 'Daddy, is this all there is to life? Is this all the accomplishment I can expect? Is this the only kick I'm going to have? Do I have to keep doing this?'

"He replied, 'No, baby, this isn't all there is.' It was the most profound conversation I'd had with my father, who died in 1993; yet it was not direct, not to the point, and I couldn't say what I was feeling. I knew something was wrong, but I didn't know how to resolve it.

"I was a bit depressed for a lot of reasons. I was not terribly satisfied with my career in golf. What would I be like at 50, at 60? I became very critical of the lifestyle. I wanted to set records, to be one of the best, in the Hall of Fame, but I never thought I was worthy compared to Patty Berg, Mickey Wright, Betsy Rawls, and Kathy Whitworth.

"I had a conversation with Mickey Wright. I asked her, 'How would I do head to head with you in a tournament?' I told her I thought I could beat her, and she agreed, letting me know that she had faith and confidence in me. It was a big accomplishment for me to feel more of an equal, but I don't feel I ever accomplished enough compared to others, and I never had the quality of Mickey Wright, all of which partly provided the motivation.

"I worked so hard on intellect and on psychology, reading Norman Vincent Peale's *The Power of Positive Thinking,* and Bob Hagge did self-hypnosis with me, but it didn't always work. I was proud of my inner achievements but not too proud of the external ones. My personal development grew; so that I became flamboyant in my dress and my actions, and I was comfortable being watched, which was a big achievement, since I had been embarrassed by how I looked. I had been an ugly duckling in school uniforms, and I never had much flair for dressing. My body was not bad. I had no boobs, good legs I was told, and not much else to go with them. I wore glasses that were too small for my body, but I never thought about them or how I looked.

"I got Marlene Hagge to help me with my dress and make-up. I told her I looked like a whore, so she helped me buy clothes, and I spent a fortune. I wore pastels, short skirts, and stockings to match. I got extra attention, won ten tournaments, but I was more on the fashion pages than the sports pages. A lot of the players laughed at me, but I could take it because I wanted to do it as a female.

"I was naive, but I knew there was Marlene Hagge and then everyone else. We wore baggy shorts and mannish shirts, and she was always glamorous. There was very little feminine about us. I knew Marlene was heterosexual and some of the rest of us were, but we didn't dress like heterosexuals.

"What was I? I had my sport, my idols whom I loved, and I wanted to be close to them. One told me she couldn't hang around me very much. When I asked why, she replied that she couldn't keep it platonic. I didn't understand, although intellectually I did inside.

"I flirted on the outskirts and in a way it gave me a kick that someone wanted me. It didn't happen, and maybe I didn't want it to. I thought about it, whether it was right, and I kept on thinking about it. I prayed to God to help me not think about her. It was very hard, since I loved her, but it was not necessarily sexual. I adored her ability, her achievements, and the very feel of her.

"Our tournament director, Lennie Wirtz, told all of us: 'Play really good golf, and do it like a female.' Although, at times, I've been outspoken in articles and criticized homosexuals on their masculine presentation, which hurts everyone, I believe that in society you have all sorts and that people have a right to be how they are, dress how they want, and it should be less of an issue.

"We need recognition for our ability, for our humanism, not for how we look or whom we sleep with. I understand people's curiosity, but the real issue is playing golf and doing the best we possibly can. So much is sold on sex and a lot of people only know about Nancy Lopez. It's all right to piggyback on that image, but we are alive first. Sex is second.

"Lopez is a genius at relating to others, a very controlled woman who only shows what she wants, and she is different in her softness. We were never encouraged to be soft. We had to be tough, strong, and impressive as golfers. They were writing, 'leggy Carol Mann,' but they didn't say anything about my performance or understand it from my point of view. We had fines for showing emotion, not happiness. In golf you don't get much happiness to show—there's frustration and anger, and happiness for one person a week.

"Women golfers want people to see more of them than their bodies. They are serious and like to be treated that way. They want people to see how they relate to a golf club, a golf ball, a flag, a hole. It is a very sexual thing we are doing. Golf is a sexual game; it is a beautiful thing, sensuous, with the grass and the sunshine.

"My one objection to the tour is that we don't afford ourselves the opportunity to embrace enough of life. The lack of awareness of what is going on outside is sometimes extraordinary. Women want to include more things in their lives. It's in our nature to do so—not to be boxed in. We are a bit warmer than men and more interested in people, but being a great performer creates insecurity.

"My own insecurity made me wonder when the pressure would get to me and when I would blow it. In the 1974 U.S. Open, when I was leading by a shot going into the third round, I was 10 feet from the hole at the first, with the chance for a birdie. I got up to the putt, I was standing over it, and I couldn't move a muscle. I had mild hysteria, but I wasn't shaking. I stepped away, my legs moved, and then I went back and hit a terrible putt, which went five inches right. Finally, I got it in with body movement.

"At the second, I wedged to a foot from the hole and left the putt short, paralyzed again. I missed the green at the third, chipped to 30 feet and made it: a big switch. I had a five shot lead going into the final 27 holes, and I blew it.

"I hated being so human, so vulnerable in my head. I thought it was in my head, when, in fact, it was a fault in my ball striking, but I'm so emotional that the outcome was more important than the method. Sometimes I was so frightened that I would shake visibly over putting."

From September 5, 1973, until May 31, 1976, Carol was president of the LPGA, during which time Ray Volpe came into office.

"My golf seemed so secondary while I was president. In 1975, I played 28 tournaments, won four, and was third money winner. I could barely get to the course in time to tee off; there was so much other activity. I burned myself out a bit, and by June 1976, I went down the tubes. I had launched a ship, and then I had to let it go, which was not easy. I was depressed thinking that no one on tour would say *thank you* to me for what I had done. Some would, others never would, and ten years later, players wouldn't give a damn.

"I chartered a 60-foot cruiser yacht in July 1976 and cruised for eight days. It cost me a fortune. I had a cook, a captain, and went with a crazy childhood friend, Pam Moore, from New York. It was very heady, and I could talk to her. It was glorious. We ate tuna fish, laughed, sunbathed topless, read Woody Allen novels, and I hit golf balls off the bow of the yacht. It was a totally refreshing experience.

"While I was on tour, I always felt I wouldn't get married, that I would continue to have a series of affairs. I was elusive. I couldn't settle down because I traveled so much, and I didn't know enough about close relationships. In a way it was an excuse for saying, I live this life so I can't be close to anyone. I wanted to get close, preferably to a man, although I love women and respect them a great deal, even if being close with them is not where I come from.

"I had a few provocative friends on tour, and one of them, Mary Mills, said to me: 'I'd like to see you run for president of the LPGA, do what you've got to do, and then get married and have some babies.' I thought about that, but by 1976 I was tired of relationships turning out badly, and I said, I'm going to be alone, count me out folks, I withdraw. I wouldn't date anyone, until six months later when I met Jim [Hardy] at a cocktail party. I was really scared because I knew he could undo me.

"It was at the Gene Autry Hotel in Palm Springs, and I was there to observe a John Jacobs golf school. I saw these eyes come round the corner and I said, 'Who is that?' I met Jim, and he complimented me on my clothes. Later we had a beer. He was so shy, but he asked wonderful, bright questions. I was supposed to be a golf star, he was a golf teacher, and I was less shy. We watched the golf school together, had a great simpatico, and we married two years later in April 1979. He was divorced and two years younger.

"In the winter of 1978 I had a hysterectomy because I had a fibroid tumor. I was upset that I wouldn't be able to have children with Jim.

Carol was president of the LPGA from 1973 to 1976, and her golf game often took a low priority to her management of the association. Shown here with Kathy Whitworth and Lenny Wirtz, tournament director, Carol ultimately changed the course of the LPGA when she urged the association to bring in Ray Volpe as the new commissioner of the LPGA.

Since leaving the LPGA tour, Carol was named an honorary member of its teaching division for her golf education commitments. She has also served as trustee of the Women's Sports Foundation since 1979 and was its president from 1985 to 1990. She remains active in the Foundation's work today.

I never thought of a traditional marriage, and although it would have been dangerous to have had a child so late in life, the choice had been taken away. I didn't like that. It was hard not to be in control, as I had controlled so much of my life. I had once been pregnant and had an abortion, and I felt I got paid back for having done that.

"I had never lived with anyone before; so I was a spoiled brat with regard to sharing a life. We lived in Palm Springs, and Jim helped me not to be so spoiled. My love increased, deepened, changed to a higher regard. We became better friends, argued and accepted it.

"He was kind when people said, 'Are you Jim Mann?' and he teased me, but I would never have married a man who couldn't handle it. I was always afraid of someone marrying me for that, or that I would do it in reverse.

"Our financial affairs were a 50/50 deal. I didn't have a lot of money, neither of us did, and we both needed to work. I had been wasteful. I had earned enough to have some, but I never managed it properly. I saw it as something to use rather than save. I was embarrassed about not managing better because I was supposed to be smart and terrific."

In January 1987, Jim and Carol separated, and a year later they were divorced: "I thought I got married forever, but it seems that I married someone who had been divorced once before, and it was easier for him to give up on the marriage than it was for me.

"Maybe my values were a little unrealistic. I thought we were very compatible people, and we could still be friends, but you could say that we had irreconcilable differences. Jim remarried, and I plunged myself into my work. It is a pattern I have followed before, and I understand it."

In 1980, Carol was faced with her declining golf ability and the eventual parting from the tour, of which she said: "The women represent so much more than a family. They are the only people who know what you really go through; there is a kinship that cannot be replaced.

"I also did not want the next generation to replace me. It is always difficult for an athlete. All of us want it to go on forever, to put things in a time warp. It is difficult to discover you can't perform.

"In 1980, in Dallas, in the Mary Kay Classic, I couldn't finish the round. My skills were not up to the quality of the golf course, which wasn't that tough. I reached the 12th green, had a putt for a bogey, and I didn't hole out. I whacked my ball right across the green into a hazard. My partners were stunned, and I said, 'Sorry ladies, I hope I didn't scare you. I just can't hack it any more.' And, I walked in.

"I went home to Palm Springs, into nothing. I went farther into nothing, when NBC, for whom I'd done some work, called to say they wouldn't need me any more, because they had cut the budget.

"I practiced through the winter of 1980–81, went back on tour, and made $960 in eight tournaments, To begin with, I was very nervous and excited, and I putted terribly. Then I fell back into feeling it was the same old stuff, and that I stood to lose more being out on tour than I had to gain. The real attraction of being on tour is nothing to do with money. It is not material; it is spiritual. I can't say enough about my love for golf, and how I love the pursuit of its mastery.

Carol enjoys conversation with golf greats Mary Lena Faulk and Ben Hogan at Marilynn Smith's 1987 Founders Classic.

"Now, my life is two things, profit-making and otherwise. My profit-making life is built around golf. I subcontract to companies to go to men's tour events to communicate to their customers about golf. I give golf lessons on table cloths, in notebooks, or programs. I talk about every aspect of the tournament with people who have never been before, or with those who have.

"My non-profit-making life is centered on the Women's Sports Foundation. When I was nominated president in 1985, I asked how many days a year it would involve? They said about seven to ten, but they did not know me well enough to realize that I couldn't be president and only give that little time.

"I feel sport needs to be grass roots, and it can help change society. Sport is a reflection of society, a developer of the mind and body. Supposedly, academics develop your mind and leave out the body, which is not right and that is the reason for the existence of sport.

"Women athletes are still not acceptable. I believe in freedom of physical self-expression, not only in the approved list of those sports considered feminine, such as dance, ice skating, and aerobics, but there is a whole other list, at present unacceptable. Little girls need the opportunity to use their bodies in movement, not just to please and attract, nor do I want women to be men, but they need a gamut of self-expression.

"At times, my own image has been a compensation for the wrong reasons. In the early 1970s, women in the women's movement were burning bras, and a lot of us on the golf tour, who did not want to be associated with them, paid lip service but did not want to be thought of that way, even though we were living it. If you live a sport that is white and male dominated, you have to play more by their rules to get what you want. I want equal appreciation for how good women are.

"Now I can cope with getting older. I'm more comfortable with myself, I have wonderful friends, I've had a fine life, I've walked on the moon. I enjoy being a person, and getting old and dying are fine. I never think how people will remember Carol Mann. The mark I made is an intimate satisfaction."

Member LPGA Hall of Fame 1977

LPGA Victories: 1964 Western Open. **1965** Lady Carling Open, U.S. Women's Open. **1966** Raleigh Invitational, Peach Blossom Invitational, Baton Rouge Invitational, Waterloo Invitational. **1967** Tall City Open, Buckeye Savings International, Supertest Open. **1968** Lady Carling Open, Raleigh Invitational, Shreveport Invitational, Bluegrass Invitational, Quality Chek'd Classic, Willow Park Invitational. **1969** Raleigh Invitational, Dallas Civitan Open, Lady Carling Open, Southgate Open, Tournament of Champions, Molson's Canadian Open, Mickey Wright Invitational, Corpus Christi Open. **1970** Burdine's Invitational. **1972** Orange Blossom Classic, Lady Carling Open. **1973** Sears Women's Classic. **1974** Naples-Lely Classic, S&H Green Stamp Classic. **1975** Borden Classic, George Washington Classic, Dallas Civitan Open, Lawson's Open.

Carol Mann's LPGA Record

Year	No.of Events	Best Finish	Money	Rank	Scoring Average
1961	24	11	$2,165	29	78.37
1962	26	T4	5,329	21	76.76
1963	30	5	6,789	16	77.43
1964	23	1	6,792	15	75.76
1965	30	1	20,875	3	73.95
1966	30	1	23,246	4	73.81
1967	26	1	24,666	3	73.12
1968	32	1	45,921	2	72.04
1969	29	1	49,152	1	72.88
1970	15	1	20,907	15	73.89
1971	14	T4	11,290	17	74.86
1972	21	1	36,452	8	74.13
1973	24	1	47,734	5	74.30
1974	22	1	47,720	7	73.70
1975	21	1	64,727	3	72.48
1976	19	4	26,665	21	74.02
1977	21	T2	41,533	17	73.85
1978	16	T4	6,125	74	75.90
1979	12	T9	10,438	75	74.58
1980	15	T13	3,541	114	76.37
1981	14	T14	4,592	115	76.22

Mary Mills

Mary Mills is a personable woman, a graduate in philosophy, who in the LPGA handbook of the 1960s listed the German Idealists and French and German Existentialists as her favorite authors. She is introspective, a high achiever, who has an obvious interest in the physical and mental aspects of life, and her penchant outside golf is toward the arts and literature.

She has had a great enjoyment of the game of golf, pain in leaving it as a way of life, and her forte was not in the aggressive head-on confrontation but in winning as the result of playing well enough to do so. She enjoyed the kudos, liked the satisfaction of earning a good living, but she never really relished winning at all costs or wanted to push herself to achievement like the greats, since she found the thrill of winning a short-lived emotion and the price too high to pay.

She has been concerned with the issues of her time, with the blacks in the U.S. and in South Africa, with feminism and the role of the woman, and with the Vietnam war. She insists that she was an onlooker rather than a crusader, as her life was taken up with being a professional golfer and she could not succeed if she drifted too much from golf. Yet, when she went to the Far East to entertain the troops at military bases during the Vietnam war, she was reading a book on the historical involvement of the French in Vietnam.

After achieving state and local titles as an amateur golfer, her impact on the LPGA tour was immediate. She won the first awarded "Rookie of the Year" title in 1962, achieved the U.S. Open title as her first victory in 1963, took the major title of the LPGA Championship the following year and again in 1973, in a total of nine career victories.

Mary has a languorous athletic flow, and she speaks quite slowly. We have been friendly over the years, with a conversational rapport that has not diminished, and she has entertained me in her distinctive home on the beach in Florida.

Mary has always encouraged me with the book and offered me any help she could give. She is tall at 5 feet, 8½ inches, has a serious look behind her glasses, an attractive smile and face, and lovely hair.

Mary was born in Laurel, Mississippi, the hometown of her maternal grandmother, and brought up in Gulf Port on the Mississippi Gulf Coast. She is the eldest of five children, having a sister one year younger, a brother five years younger, and twin sisters ten years her junior. It was a middle class family, her father worked in the retail lumber business and her mother was his secretary.

"We were all very different children. I was athletic and loved being outdoors. My father and I were not close, but he encouraged me to do things that were worthwhile because it improved his image. He was a perfectionist, whose children were an extension of his ego, and he instilled in me a necessity to achieve that would be hard to shake. As a family of English/German origin, we did not show much emotion, but my deep affection was for my mother. I would like to have felt the same for my father, but he did not seem to have time for his children. I was in my late teens, when my father died in his mid-30s of a kidney disease. It was before the days of dialysis. When I was 25, my mother died, at 51, of a heart attack, and I was devastated.

"We were a close family on my mother's side, with my financially secure grandmother being head of the family, and we all depended on her. With both my parents working, we were raised by household help.

"As a child I wanted to do something important, and my first ambition was to be a great artist. I was also very good at swimming, diving, and tennis, and I started playing golf at 11. I took to it immediately, and when I was 12 and saw the movie about Ben Hogan, *Follow the Sun*, I decided I wanted to be a professional golfer.

"When I was 13, I shot a 67 and won the state Amateur Championship; a tournament I won eight years in a row. I played national competitions, and I was better at medal play than matchplay. I enjoy doing something well, and I like relating to the physical and mental aspects of golf, which put me on such a high level. I enjoy the notoriety and attention that come from success; I use other people as a yardstick, but I don't like head-to-head competition, I prefer to beat the course and a group of people.

"Academically, philosophy and English motivated me, and I obtained a B.A. in philosophy at Millsaps College. I combined that with playing in first place on the men's golf team, but I was not on a golf scholarship, since there wasn't one.

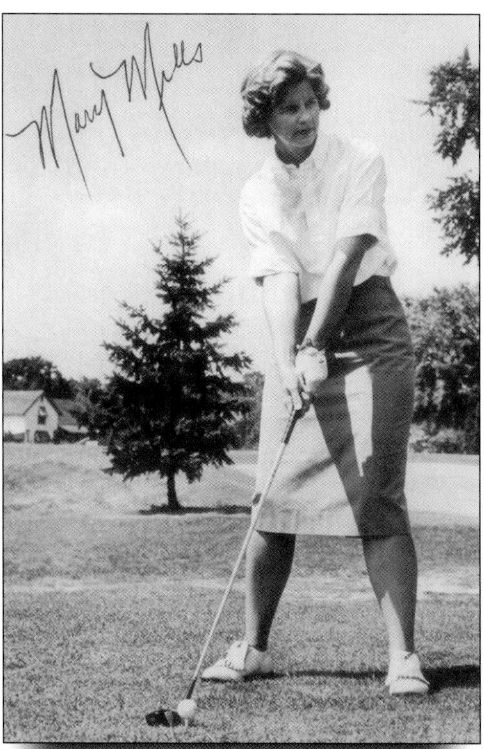

Mary Mills won the first LPGA "Rookie of the Year" title in 1962 and followed that with her first victory, the U.S. Open, in 1963. In 1964, she won the LPGA Championship.

I retained my interest in the arts and visited black colleges on an exchange program in Jackson, as I felt that I was a nonconformist. I thought there was discrimination against blacks and women, and I tried to demonstrate my feelings about it.

"In the South, women were supposed to support the male and be creative in the home. Sports for women were not that acceptable. I saw my own female role as being a person rather than identifying with my sex and becoming a crusader. I preferred positive action and left others to expend negative energy in reacting. I could identify with Amelia Earhart, who moved against the grain in a very positive way. My hero in golf was Ben Hogan, and I thought professional golf offered me a positive way to establish my equality.

"I couldn't see any difference between being a professional golfer or an artist. To me, golf is like a performing art, like ballet. You are given a certain circumstance, you take the objective reality and conform it to an idea in your head, and that is creative. Golf is little different from deciding what you want to do with a lump of clay, except that at the end you do not have an object to show; you have a few press clippings and a lot of memories.

"When I graduated, I turned professional, joined the tour, and was proud of my status. I wanted the attention, and I thought it looked like a lot of fun. The upper middle class circles of the country club looked up to people who could play, even if they didn't understand the discipline and dedication needed for the lifestyle. I believed that I would play until I was 30 and then do something else.

"I soon found out that although women professionals were acceptable in golfing circles, we received some very cruel treatment from the press. They would see a chunky young kid in Bermuda shorts, with untidy hair and a masculine, athletic walk, and the public was not ready for it. They wanted very feminine heroes, and we are not very feminine people in the way the world looks at us. We are very real in that we enjoy what we do, and we are healthy female athletes who exercise our bodies every day. But why should we crush our own personalities and be pushed into presenting a false image of dainty femininity just because society creates that role for us? My work is to play golf, to be aware of what I feel inside, and I do not have the time or energy to absorb all those outside feelings of society.

"My first week on the LPGA tour I won $100, then the next weeks $200, and $800, and as it was only costing $250 a week, I felt I had all the money in the world. After that, I had no money worries, I was paying my way and performing at a high level. Being independent probably kept me in golf. I really enjoyed the sport. Money was the icing on the cake, but the freedom gives you so much self-respect.

"Winning the U.S. Open as my first victory in my second season of 1963, was a highlight at 23 years old. I was wet behind the ears, but that week I was in a dream world, above the pressure, and I felt it was my destiny to win. My golf swing and putting were so good, and I was so in tune with what I was doing.

"Although I won my next major, the LPGA Championship in 1964, I didn't feel I dominated the sport or presented a real challenge. Mickey Wright and Kathy Whitworth were dominating, and Mickey tried to challenge me to do more, but winning didn't really mean that much to me. It was fantastic for a few weeks, then I was disillusioned and said, 'Is that all there is? Why go through all that, when it is so short lived?' I loved the sport, the self-respect, and being successful, but the people who win all the time are the leaders in our field of endeavor. I don't envy them living in turmoil, but they are driven to do it and to make things happen. When I play my best golf, I am in total inner turmoil, almost sick to my stomach. You get so keyed up, your body is not at a normal level.

"For such short-lived satisfaction, I was not driven like Mickey Wright or Sandra Palmer. Those people end up performing at very high levels, but I was not willing to expend the extra energy and pay the price. I don't need to keep on winning or shooting 68 to feel adequate. I prefer to accept my inadequacies. I'm not a driven person; so I probably won't get ulcers or have a nervous breakdown.

"My father had brought me up to achieve because males motivate children that way. In early childhood I felt my mother loved me no matter what, but I had to prove myself to my father. He wanted to bask in the reflection of my achievements, and I wish I could sit down and talk to him about it.

"Later, when I won my majors with everyone watching, I learned about the intense moments of winning. We all sacrifice a lot for that intensity of feeling. You put your reputation, your sense of self-worth, on the line. It takes only a few seconds to win or lose, and it can be devastating. You have to hypnotize yourself into thinking only of the activity of the moment; and it becomes all very momentary."

Mary became an established winner and, through golf, pursued life in other directions. In the winter of 1969–70, she visited major American bases in the Far East during the Vietnam War. She gave golf exhibitions and clinics, talked to the troops, and formed her own opinions. "Although I was reading the history of the French and their association with Vietnam, I was not a crusader. I wanted to travel, to see for myself, but I was not thinking in political terms. I did the golf side, and afterwards I visited the hospitals, where many of the guys were mentally disturbed, had malaria, or were hooked on drugs. It was a disturbing sight, and so was the sensation of looking over a B-36, which was built totally to destroy."

The following winter, Mary went to South Africa in a group of ten people, asked by South African professional Sally Little, to introduce women's professional golf to her country; "We played golf in the major cities and saw the country, undeveloped according to its potential, because of its political troubles. It appeared to be in a situation parallel to the U.S. at about 1900, except that the blacks outnumbered the whites. Obviously, it was going to be a matter of time before they stood up, but they were not going to be suppressed forever.

"I remember when I had my success in the 1960s, they put on a Mary Mills Invitational event in my home town in Mississippi. Some tournaments called their event an invitational, so they didn't have to invite the black professionals, like Althea Gibson and Renee Powell. I thought that it was very antiquated, but in the middle of trying to play golf, I couldn't fight politically. I couldn't handle it."

Mary found that physical injury played a large part in the life of a touring professional: "I had a great many injuries, and sometimes I never gave myself a chance to heal, since I would not pace myself properly. If you don't play, you feel the whole tour is passing you, so you push your body past its limits. Golf is a driving force and important to me, and when I played Ben Hogan clubs and worked for his company, I talked to him about it. He said that he thought his putting yips came because his nerve endings got worn, and that if you changed your style drastically, you could possibly work with different nerve endings.

"I know that when I was in my 20s, my body functioned as smoothly as silk, but 20 years later, my connective tissue was stiff. Although my golf muscles functioned pretty well, I hadn't the same endurance. It is very hard for athletes to accept body change, and it is the sad thing about staying in a sport for so many years. I started seriously thinking about leaving the tour in 1979 because although I was financially in reasonable shape, I wasn't playing well enough to continue, something that was painful to realize. I played 15 years of professional golf and enjoyed every minute of it. Golf was my life from the age of 11. It is very scary to think of doing something else when you are not trained for it.

"For a while I combined some photography, which I had always done, with playing golf. Then I played my last full season in 1980. After that, I taught golf for two and one-half years. I enjoyed some of it but found it very painful because mentally I would like to have played for another five years.

"A few years after I quit the tour, I decided I was becoming an alcoholic like my parents, and in 1985 I quit drinking. My parents were both heavy drinkers and both died young. They were never abusive to us children in any way, but because I felt I had a chemical predisposition to follow in the family footsteps, I went to a psychologist and sorted out that problem."

Mary joined a food company, working as a sales consultant for its catering division at golf and tennis tournaments. She then took her real estate exams "in order to earn some money." By 1991, she decided her career path should change. Wanting to become a golf course architect, she embarked on a four year masters degree in Landscape Architecture and Design—probably the only philosophy graduate to do so—at the Florida International University in Miami.

Writing her thesis in 1995, in order to pursue a second career, Mary reflected on the memories of her 20 years on tour: "What stands out are the trips I took, the winning, meeting so many different people who have brought out my personality. I would like to have had nine lives so that I could have been an artist, a philosophy professor, gotten married and had a family like my sisters. But it is a specialized world, and I had to cut out other things to do one thing fairly well. Some people can combine them, but I never found anyone with whom I could do that, or maybe I didn't look hard enough. I burned my bridges in my 20s, made a choice, and I think it paid off. I performed very consistently, at a high level, and even though I may be dissatisfied, I was adequate because I didn't divide myself. I have taken in other things in life by osmosis."

LPGA Victories: 1963 U.S. Open. **1964** Eugene Open, LPGA Championship. **1965** St. Louis Invitational, Pacific Classic. **1969** Quality Chek'd Classic **1970** Len Immke Buick Open. **1973** LPGA Championship, Lady Tara Classic.

Mary Mills' LPGA Record

Year	No.of Events	Best Finish	Money	Rank	Scoring Average
1962	20	2	$8,091	11	75.14
1963	22	1	9,252	11	75.44
1964	29	1	13,963	9	74.61
1965	25	1	13,007	7	74.09
1966	20	T2	12,823	10	74.69
1967	25	T3	10,012	12	74.71
1968	29	T2	10,792	17	74.99
1969	26	1	14,588	17	76.05
1970	20	1	15,054	10	74.17
1971	19	3	15,246	11	74.60
1972	22	T2	13,527	22	75.02
1973	29	1	47,638	6	73.63
1974	28	T2	30,914	16	74.04
1975	18	T4	11,653	38	74.35
1976	27	T5	19,874	29	75.33
1977	24	4	30,933	21	74.16
1978	27	5	31,460	34	74.26
1979	25	T13	12,087	68	75.73
1980	25	T22	9,726	83	75.56
1981	25	T12	10,545	90	75.63

Sandra Palmer

When you haven't seen Sandra Palmer for a while, you forget how small she is, both in height (at 5 feet, $1^1/_2$ inches) and in bone structure. Yet there is nothing frail about her; she has a fierce grip, a strong sense of determination, and she has dedicated herself to her chosen sport. "People made fun of my fast, flat swing, but I had an inner drive to get better. I never dreamed I would one year be leading money winner."

Perhaps, as a small person always wanting to prove she could make it against those who are bigger and stronger, Sandra propelled herself to impressive heights. She started on the LPGA tour in 1964, with her most lucrative season coming more than 20 years later in 1986, when she won $148,422 in a great year that included a tournament victory. She was still competing in the mid 1990s.

She was a U.S. Open winner in 1975, the same year she was leading money winner, finishing fifth and third the two previous years. Her first official victory did not come until her seventh season, but her dedication to the game has been complete. Only in the 1980s was she able to take off a day from hitting a golf ball and feel comfortable about it. Doubtless her small stature meant that she had to work harder, but her intensity of concentration made her enduringly successful.

Although Sandra began life on the "wrong side of the tracks," she attained an attractive lifestyle, through hard work, she is always most generous to those who are close to her.

The relationship between Sandra and myself started on a tenuous footing, for she was suspicious of me and my intentions in writing a book. She read the synopsis of my idea and was singularly unimpressed. Later, I was taken to her home in Florida by a mutual friend, and as the evening wore on, she became more accepting, until eventually we struck up a friendship that has been lasting, rewarding, supportive, and mutually caring. We keep in touch, have stayed in each other's homes, and although fundamentally we are disparate people, we enjoy the relationship.

When Sandra was born in Fort Worth, Texas, her mother was 16, and much of Sandra's early life was spent with her grandmother, since her young mother married and divorced twice. "I had a sister type of relationship with my mother," Sandra says.

Aged 11, she moved to Maine with her mother and father, and it was there she took up golf: "We lived in the country, and I saw the golf course from the school bus. I got off and watched. Later, I started caddying, and I made more money than my mother, who worked as a waitress or in a store.

1975 was a great year for Sandra Palmer. She won the U.S. Open, the Colgate Dinah Shore, and was leading money winner on the tour.

"The professional at the club took me into the shop in the summer, and I got my first set of clubs. I entered a tournament, shot 98, and wrote my grandmother, who was really excited at my score because she thought the higher the better. I enjoyed playing golf because I could do it without anyone else, and since I was very shy, I spent a lot of time alone. I was always a loner, and I still am.

"By the time I was 14, I was back in Fort Worth, living with my grandmother again. I played the West Texas State Championship at the Glen Garden Golf Club, and I won it. The president of the club, Ed Warren, and his wife Vita took a great interest in me. They were in their 40s and didn't have any children, and eventually they asked me to live with them. My grandmother encouraged me, for she thought I would have greater opportunities; so at 15, I moved in with them. Ed was an assistant postmaster and Vita a chief superintendent of government personnel.

"They were wonderful people; both had a great sense of humor, and they never argued, which was very different from being around people so often in conflict. I always introduced them as my parents, since it was easier, although I called them Vita and Ed.

"Living with them brought me so far out of my shell that at school I was voted homecoming queen, and I became a cheerleader. When I was 19, 20, and 21, I got engaged to the same person. I guess his ambitions did not coincide with mine. By that time I wanted to play golf, and he wanted me to be at home. I don't think it would have worked out.

"I went to North Texas State, where I majored in biology and physical education, and I spent all my spare time playing golf, winning local Texas championships. The year after I graduated I taught school in Arlington, and nearly every weekend I had golf lessons with Harvey Penick in Austin, (he died in 1995). He was like a father and more to me, all through my career. I leaned on him a lot, called him frequently, and talked emotions and technique with him. He always encouraged me, telling me to picture the perfect shot. That is the hardest thing to do, but it is possible when you play really well.

"By the summer of 1964, with Harvey's encouragement, I turned professional. I had met

Sandra Palmer was a small package with a small, flat swing, but Harvey Penick, her teacher, always encouraged her and realized her potential. Sandra is shown here at the Colgate LPGA tournament at Sunningdale, 1977. Photo ©Phil Sheldon.

the LPGA tournament director Lennie Wirtz, but I really had no idea what to expect. Many people thought it was too rough a life and frowned on it as a masculine thing to do. I didn't care because I just wanted to play golf.

"When I joined the tour, the emphasis was on golf; later the issue became appearance. There have been times when I have been very self-conscious about my appearance—about my hair, how I'm standing, if I've shaved my legs, just dumb things which surely are not the most important. Anyway it is hard to look your best when you play golf.

"My first tournament as a professional was in Dallas. I was not very confident, and I had no idea how I would perform. I was paired with Ruth Jessen, who had a 64; I shot 78. I was not intimidated by the other women, but I was by the golfing standards of those such as Mickey Wright,

Kathy Whitworth, Betsy Rawls, and Sandra Haynie, and the classic swings of Wright and Haynie were the ones I most admired.

"I kept practicing to get better, and I knew I didn't have a lot going for me because of my size, which also made it difficult to identify with other players. People made fun of my fast, flat swing, but I was good at concentrating, and I had an inner drive to get better.

"It took me five or six years to really improve. At first there were lots of adjustments. It was lonely, but you were out there and had to survive, which is just about what I did through the 1960s.
I was not liked a whole lot because I had been brought up always to introduce myself to people, which made the other women think I was cocky.

"I feel the ego of small people needs to be fed more, and although I have had a lot of people care about me, I know I've cared about me the most. Because of my size and people saying I couldn't do it, I found it important to prove that I could overcome my size. I was used to being out-driven, and if JoAnne Carner is on her game, you're not going to beat her or the long hitters on a wide open course. However, because I was great at matchplay as an amateur, toward the end of a tournament I could apply that ability in head-to-head confrontation. I don't know how I achieved what I did, but it must have been my way of becoming accepted. I got everything I could out of my game, even though I would upset myself a lot with emotions.

"In 1970, I won an unofficial tournament in Japan, which was nice, and then I had a pretty exciting victory in Las Vegas in the Sealy Classic, which was a Pro-Am tournament. I was paired on the last day with pro football player Joe Namath. Coming into the last hole I had a one-shot lead, and I hit my second into the bunker.
I blasted out, my ball ran into the hole for an eagle, a two-shot victory, and I won the largest check in golf at the time: $10,000.

"My biggest thrill came in 1975 when I won the U.S. Open, the Colgate Dinah Shore, and was leading money winner. Winning the Open was a dream come true, and I had to grit it out after an opening 78. You need a lot of heart, you must never quit, but physical strength is an asset, which I built up by hitting golf balls, running, and swinging a weighted club.

"The money has been very important to me because I never had any growing up, although I never wanted for anything when I lived with the Warrens. Now, even though I know I have money in the bank, there is that little remaining insecurity, so I still watch what I spend and have a habit of not throwing things away."

In 1972, Jane Blalock was accused of cheating by her fellow professionals after the second round of the Bluegrass Invitational, and she was disqualified on the decision of the tournament committee. The following week before the Titleholders at Pine Needles, Jane was fined $500 and put on probation. Sandra Palmer won the Titleholders by 10 shots. A week later in Baltimore, Jane was told that a petition had been signed by 29 of her fellow players, and she was suspended for one year. That action resulted in two years of tumult on the LPGA tour, where Jane Blalock's friends were few and far between.

Sandra, a loyal person and a good friend of Jane's, was one of the very few to stick by her and leap to her defense over the alleged cheating incident. Yet, when Jane later wrote her book, *The Guts to Win*, published in 1977, she first acknowledged Sandra's defense of her and then intimated that Sandra had won a tournament from her on one occasion, by practicing gamesmanship.

Sandra says: "Jane was my friend. When she said she had not done anything I believed her and went to bat for her. I am glad I did because the handling by the LPGA was wrong, and it was terrible the way people treated her family. Some good things came out of it, in that the constitution was altered so that a player could only be suspended by the commissioner, and fellow competitors could not act as judge and jury.

"I know taking the stance I did, hurt me a lot, but I am tough. The other players treated me as though I had done something wrong. No one would play a practice round with me; so Jane and I were thrown together. You could have committed murder and been more forgiven. The biggest sin in golf is to be accused of cheating, and I'm not sure whether Jane did or not, but certainly the way things were handled by the LPGA was not right.

"I sacrificed a lot, but once I was in it, I couldn't just walk away; so I followed it through. It hurt me as a person. I became withdrawn, unsociable, and I didn't trust people. I might have been like that anyway, but it was magnified by the situation. People would just stare silently, which dispensed with the idle chatter, and it enabled me to get out and concentrate.

"At one point I was put on probation for one of my comments about Marlene Hagge, after which I was going to sue the LPGA, Marlene was going to sue me, but the lawsuits were dropped and amazingly, Marlene and I became great friends again.

"I was hurt by Jane's book, and I lost a lot of respect for her. I never received a book or an explanation, and I never asked her about it, but I thought she fired a cheap shot. I never did anything to hurt her. I thought I was her best friend, but it was as though that was all forgotten. I felt really stupid after the book came out; I don't think I would treat a friend like that. You don't have too many. I was the only one who ever said anything good about her through the bad times, and if later she couldn't say anything good about me, she should have left it out.

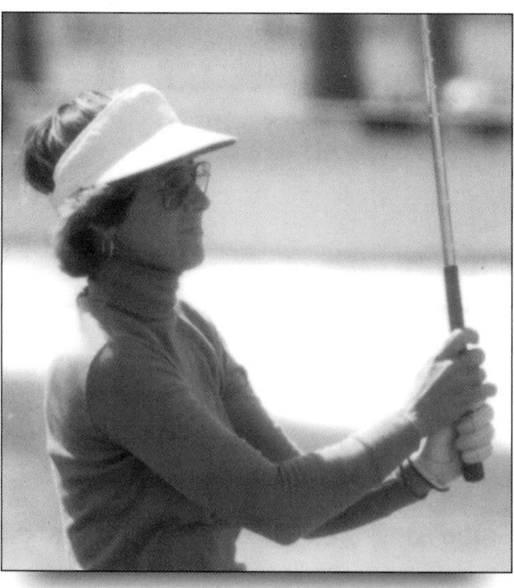

Although she had her doubts about continuing play after 1977 when she struggled to win, Sandra applied her usual hardwork and grit, coming up a winner again in 1981, 1982, and 1986, her biggest year ever. She still palys on tour today. Photo courtesy: Katherine Murphy.

"I know Jane has been marred by it all; it may be that she brought it on herself, and although she will always have a little cloud over her, Jane is not a bad person. She is kind and pretty understanding."

Sandra, whose career victories total 21, was a regular winner until 1977, when there was a gap of four years. Inevitable doubts crept in: "I thought I would give up. When you don't win, it is hard because people question you all the time. I was always too much of a perfectionist. I could only tolerate being in contention and playing well.

"There was a time when panic would set in if I thought about not being on tour. It was as though my whole being was built around it. It wasn't until 1982 that I took off a month at the end of the season and found I didn't miss playing golf, although I still wanted to play the tour. Throughout my career, I have always worked on something because you must believe in your mechanics or stay home.

"Over the years I have thought of becoming a coach at a university, doing television work, going back to school, qualifying as a physical therapist, or being a harness racing driver because I like the speed and the challenge. I have questioned my not getting married, but find it is nice not to have to answer to someone, to be my own boss, to come and go as I please.

"I don't like being alone, but I can cope with it. I have a lot of strength having had to fend for myself, and I have achieved much more than I thought possible. For someone my size it is quite an accomplishment to be leading money winner. It may not sound like much, but I pride myself that I have done better on tougher golf courses where my accuracy and consistency have counted, not length."

Sandra won in 1981, 1982, and 1986, when she had a tremendous season. She continued to win through 1986, and in 1987 played in the first Marilynn Smith Founders' Classic in Dallas, where she finished third. She won the second year. Always an LPGA woman, she was jumping up and down

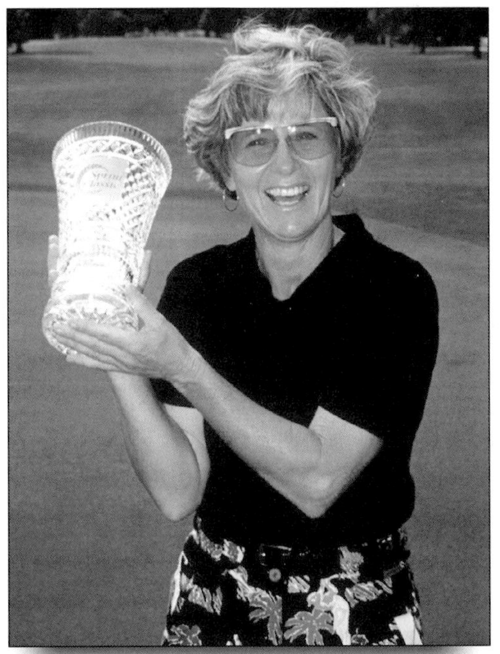

Sandra celebrates her victory at the Sprint Senior Challenge in 1993. She won the event again in 1994 and 1995.

with excitement at the inaugural tournament, seeing all the greats of the past, some of whom she had played alongside. "It was the most thrilling tournament I ever played. It was so wonderful to see people I'd only heard about for so long, such as Wiffi Smith, whom I loved, and Joyce Ziske, who just has the greatest golf swing.

"Ben Hogan presented the charter members with their jackets. It was a nice recognition for those women. But the real thrill was to see the closeness of everyone after all the years. To have that feeling of belonging was a very emotional experience. It was great that all those players paid their own way to come to the tournament and compete. They really laid themselves on the line years ago. How brave they were to do it for all of us."

LPGA Victories: 1971 Sealy Classic, Heritage Open. **1972** Titleholders Championship, Angelo's Four-Ball. **1973** Pompano Beach Classic, St. Paul Open, National Jewish Hospital Open, Cameron Park Open, Angelo's Four-Ball. **1974** Burdine's Invitational, Cubic Corporation Classic. **1975** U.S. Women's Open, Colgate Dinah Shore Winner's Circle. **1976** Bloomington Classic, National Jewish Hospital Open, Jerry Lewis Muscular Dystrophy Classic. **1977** Kathryn Crosby/Honda Classic, Women's International. **1981** Whirlpool Championship of Deer Creek. **1982** Boston Five Classic. **1986** Mayflower Classic.

Unofficial Victories: 1970 Japan Women's Open. **1991** Centel Senior Challenge. **1992** Centel Senior Challenge. **1993** Sprint Senior Challenge. **1994** Sprint Senior Challenge. **1995** Sprint Senior Challenge.

Sandra Palmer's LPGA Record

Year	No.of Events	Best Finish	Money	Rank	Scoring Average
1964	22	T8	$1,580	31	77.74
1965	28	T3	4,384	25	76.81
1966	29	T4	4,976	24	76.57
1967	27	T5	7,265	18	75.28
1968	31	T2	16,906	8	74.56
1969	29	T2	18,319	9	74.36
1970	20	T2	18,424	8	73.53
1971	21	1	34,035	4	73.92
1972	28	1	36,715	7	73.32
1973	34	1	55,439	3	73.24
1974	30	1	54,873	5	73.75
1975	25	1	76,374	1	72.72
1976	26	1	88,417	5	72.81
1977	27	1	82,919	7	73.20
1978	27	T3	44,498	19	73.58
1979	27	T2	50,892	21	73.48
1980	30	T3	73,598	12	72.92
1981	27	1	63,596	17	73.40
1982	25	1	73,993	19	73.35
1983	25	T7	33,523	51	73.98
1984	23	T4	46,655	48	73.44
1985	26	T4	39,013	57	73.73
1986	28	1	148,422	14	72.71
1987	28	3	73,373	32	73.45
1988	29	T2	79,656	36	73.25
1989	21	4	31,646	83	74.39
1990	24	T18	31,540	104	74.25
1991	23	T12	24,293	117	74.15
1992	15	T24	13,332	141	74.24
1993	7	72	1,773	176	75.67
1994	10	T61	1,563	177	75.32
1995	16	T11	20,035	134	74.50

Sandra Post

For Sandra Post, golf and the LPGA have been an obsession since she was six years old. In 1954, she was taken to a tournament by her father and met professional golfer Marilynn Smith. Her fascination was reinforced two years later when she shook hands with the great Babe Zaharias shortly before Babe's death. Sandra idolized the women professionals and corresponded regularly with Marilynn Smith. In 1968, at 18, she became a professional. "All my life I wanted to be a professional, and when I turned professional I cried because I was scared to death." Remarkably, she won a major event in her first season, the LPGA championship, by defeating Kathy Whitworth in an 18 hole playoff.

She married in 1970 and divorced three years later because she was so conflicted between trying to be a wife and wanting to be a successful golfer. "I was unhappy playing housewife, and I missed the tour. When I went to play, I was torn. I was always in the wrong place." She competed very little for those three years, and then returned to climb back up the ladder to success.

While recognizing the tough lifestyle on the LPGA tour, Sandra enthused about it in romantic, wide-eyed fashion: "It gave me the opportunity to travel the world, to go to places such as Bali, Kuala Lumpur, Hong Kong, Japan, and Europe. I met and played golf with sultans and presidents. What farmer's daughter from Canada could ever imagine doing that?" When she left the tour in 1983, she had achieved eight victories and won nearly $750,000. She gives the impression of a highly strung disposition, with an uneven temperament that can make her communicative or withdrawn. She talks rapidly and was keen to be interviewed. Her answers were frank, yet she has learned to contain her emotions and talk in a fluent verbal style rather than calling on emotional depths. She is attractive and always well dressed.

Sandra was born in Oakville, Ontario, with one sister, five years older. Her father was a fruit and vegetable farmer, and during her years of growing up, both her parents worked on the farm. They were a middle income family. When she was five, her father, who at one time was a scratch golfer and played in the Canadian Amateur Championship, gave her a cut-down wooden club and encouraged her to swing it.

"In his heart he always wanted a son and never had one. Being an athlete himself, he was determined to make one of his little girls into an athlete, and golf was more suitable than hockey or baseball.

"During the cold winter months, the family went down to Florida for some sunshine, and it was in 1954 that we first found the LPGA tour at St. Petersburg. My father saw some signs for the Orange Blossom Classic, and since I had shown an interest in golf, he told me that we were going to the tournament the next day.

"When we got there and started walking round, I picked up Marilynn Smith, who was awfully nice to me. She spoke to me, gave me a golf ball, tees, and a glove, and that was it—she was my idol, and I was her shadow for the whole week. I fell in love with the game and decided it was what I wanted to do.

"I went back from the tournament and all I did was mimic what I had seen the women doing with a golf club. Little kids have an easy time imitating, and I developed a natural swing.

"Every winter after that, we centered ourselves where the women professionals were playing in Florida. When I was seven, I told Marilynn Smith I was going to be a professional, and she was most encouraging. I wrote to her about once a month, telling her how I was playing, what tournaments I had played, and she would write back. I still have all of her letters. I copied everything she did. When Marilynn had a rabbit's foot on her skirt, I had one; she wore a tam, I wore a tam; she played Spalding clubs, so did I.

"When I went to a tournament in 1956, I met Babe Zaharias, who died in September that year. She was in a wheelchair, and I knew who she was, and I had heard people talking about her. I went up to her and shook her by the hand because I thought that someday it might stick in my mind, and it has. I was a real fan of all the women out there in the 1950s, and I had pictures and kept a scrapbook about them.

"Trying to play golf at home was difficult because as a child I was not allowed on a course until the age of 11; so I went to the range. When I was nine, my father spoke to the superintendent at the club, who said he knew how keen I was, and although I was small for my age, he said I should play and tell everyone I was 11, which is what I did. I entered a parent and child competition with my father, which we won, and I was given a white electric mixer as a prize. I wondered what it was.

"By the time I was 13, I was a good player, and over the next few years I won three Ontario Junior Championships, the Ontario Ladies' Amateur, and three Canadian junior titles. I went through high school and then decided to turn professional at the beginning of 1968 when I was 18.

"All my life I had wanted to become a professional, but I didn't know if I was good enough to make it on tour. We weren't playing for enough money to make money interesting, but I wanted to prove I could do well for my own satisfaction. I could have remained a big fish in a small pond in Canada, but I wanted to play against the best in the world.

"To get on tour, you needed two letters of introduction, and I got mine from Marilynn Smith and my golf instructor, Sybil Griffin. You earned your card out on tour if you finished in the top 80 percent of the field in two out of three consecutive tournaments.

"My parents were delighted at my decision. They gave me $400 and a car and told me they would send me more money. I told them not to, unless I called, and I never did.

Sandra is shown here when she won the 1974 Colgate Far East Open. She also captured the LPGA Championship in 1968 and back to back Dinah Shore tournaments in 1978 and 1979.

"When I turned professional, I cried because I was scared to death. For the first nine holes of my first tournament, I hardly stopped crying, and it was difficult to see the ball. It was a three-round event, and I played well enough to finish in the top 20, and I earned $155, which was great.

"In my third tournament, I had the first hole-in-one of my life. I got $1,000 for it and finished sixth. Then I started to get lonely and scared, and the money began to dwindle, but I did not call home.

"I went to the LPGA Championship at Pleasant Valley with $250 in my pocket. After four rounds, I was tied with Kathy Whitworth, whom I had met when I was younger, having played an exhibition with her. We had to play an 18-hole playoff the following day.

"All I was thinking was how great it would be to be second in the LPGA Championship. I thought of myself as runner-up and was overjoyed, since I never considered beating Kathy. The next day

I could do no wrong. I started birdie, birdie, eagle; I chipped in, holed a wedge shot, and kept it going to finish in six under par 68, beating Kathy by seven shots. I won $3,000, a bonus from Spalding of about $1,500, and I thought I had all the money in the world.

"After that I wanted to go home; so I told our tournament director, Lennie Wirtz, I was tired and going to take a rest. He said that as LPGA champion, I had to play the next week, which I did and finished third. I went on to be Rookie of the Year and to finish 12th on the money list with $13,509 at the end of my first season."

The following year, 1969, Sandra again did well, playing 22 tournaments, four fewer that the previous season, but ranking 20th with $11,269. In 1970, she was married, and her game and her income slumped. She played in 11, 13, and 15 events, over a period of three years and won little money. She found herself in a quandary, a woman torn between wanting a career and trying to combine it with the role of homemaker and wife. To play in tournaments you have to travel, and to build a relationship you need to be at home.

"My husband, John Elliot, was a golf professional from Fort Lauderdale. When I married and didn't play much golf, I became unhappy playing housewife, and I missed the tour. When I went out to play, I was torn; so I felt I was always in the wrong place. I couldn't get my head straight. We were both too young and decided to go our separate ways. It took me a long time to rebuild.

"It takes two special people for a woman to be married and to be on tour. We have some successful marriages, but it's difficult. It's difficult if you're single. It looks like all glamour, glitter, and gold, but it's not. It is very gruelling. If the right combination is there, it can work, but I wouldn't try marriage again until my career is finished.

"I learned a very hard lesson. I can't believe a divorce can be easy; and mine was really tough. I was so young that it was very hard on me. I pulled on all the resources I had, and I found out I was a hell of a lot stronger inside that I ever knew. The experience helped me become a stronger and better person.

"I had to open myself up and say, 'What are you made of? What is inside?' I really dissected Sandra Post, and so many times I thought I wasn't going to make it. What did I really want? I wanted to be a good player on the tour and to use the talent God gave me. If He would only give me one more chance, I wouldn't blow it—I made Him that promise. I'm not religious to the point where I go to church, but I'm a Christian, which gives me all the strength I need, and I do it my way.

When she left the tour in 1983, Sandra Post had traveled the world, won eight tournaments and nearly $750,000. "What farmers daughter from Canada could ever imagine doing that," she commented. Photo courtesy: Katherine Murphy.

"What I had going for me was that I didn't have any children and at the time of the divorce in 1973, I was only 24. I love children—I gravitate to them and they to me on the course. But, biologically, I would have to do something fairly quickly to have any of my own. I know that when I am about 50, if I don't have any children, I will regret it. I am well aware of that. I made the decision, which is a hard one, and I will cope with it. You have your career, and it's difficult to interrupt it, but some weeks when you only make $200, you wonder whether it is really worth it? I don't know. Unfortunately, that is a question you can only answer when it's too late.

"To some people the tour is a drug because it's so much of your life, your friends, and everything you know and have done has revolved around the tour and the game. But a future without the tour doesn't scare me at all. I know I can do other things because I like people, travel, and I have corporate associations and could get a job if I wanted one.

"I don't regret my life because it has been too wonderful. I've played the tour with annual purses going from $500,000 to $7 million. I've seen television arrive, and I have been part of almost everything that has been exciting on the LPGA tour.

"I always knew it would grow. For a few years, we would take two steps forward and one back. Finally, with an accumulation of variables, it began to take off: David Foster and the Colgate tournament; television and commercials; moving from Atlanta to New York; and Ray Volpe. The timing was right with the arrival of sex symbols Laura Baugh and Jan Stephenson; then with Nancy Lopez, we had a product to sell, and it went really well for us.

"I am thankful I was on tour with Mickey Wright. She is the nicest, sweetest lady to play golf with—quiet, unassuming, and what a great player. I also experienced the dominant eras of Kathy Whitworth, Sandra Haynie, who is one of the greatest players we ever had, Carol Mann, Judy Rankin, and Nancy Lopez.

"After my divorce, I pulled myself back up slowly, to win the Colgate Far East tournament in 1974. I also won two tournaments in 1978, including the Colgate Dinah Shore, which I won again the following year, when I finished second on the money list to Nancy Lopez.

"People built up stories about Nancy at that time, about the rivalry and hard feelings between the two of us, because her picture was on the 1979 Colgate program cover instead of mine, after I was the 1978 winner. We needed something new, something to grab the public attention, and Nancy was great for us all. She loved it, was new to it, and had so much more to give, and I'd been around a long time. She was great copy, and people loved her.

"Out on tour, we see each other every day, and we share an awful lot. We have all gone through it together. We've all sacrificed, we're all dedicated, we have a lot of common bonds, and we all want to succeed in our own way. Not everyone is going to succeed like Mickey Wright, Nancy Lopez, Sandra Post, or Judy Rankin. It's a crazy game, and when you've been on tour a long time, you have to know how to be rational or you can be awfully hard on yourself. I don't want to beat myself to a pulp thinking how someone else has more than I have or how I deserved more than she did—that would be a terrible way to live. You play as hard as you can, forget it, and go on to the next week.

"I was still young, when people looked at me and knew I was a veteran. They said, 'She's got to be 50; she's been on tour forever.' I heard them saying it, and it was all right because I didn't see myself out there when I was no longer a contender and out of the top twenty. There were too many strong young players coming up to have their turn, as I had once had mine.

"The game of golf has been so good to me, and I love it. When I think of it all from the very inception, it is almost like a fairy tale. Shaking Babe's hand, idolizing Marilynn Smith, playing in an exhibition with Kathy Whitworth, turning professional, winning the LPGA Championship so soon, going through a traumatic divorce, rebounding to make it back up, being exposed to so many wonderful people, and being financially rewarded for it. I couldn't have paid for what I have

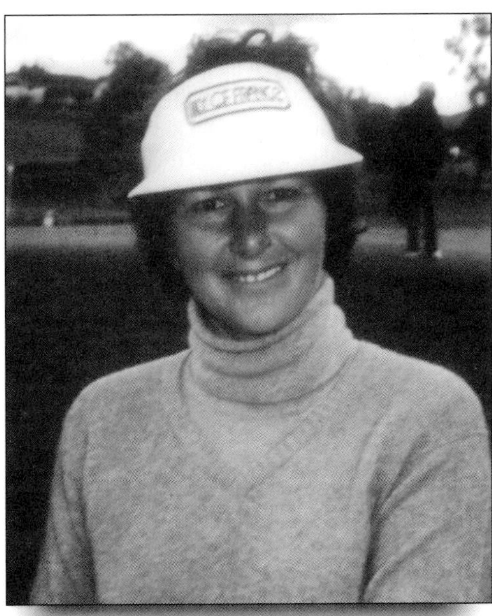

Sandra left the tour in 1983 due to injuries, but she found another career teaching and broadcasting—golf, of course. Photo courtesy: Katherine Murphy.

learned. What an education I've had. There isn't a college in the world that could teach you what I've learned. Life has been very very good to me, and I feel most people out here should appreciate it."

Sandra left the tour in May 1983, when she was nearly 35. Until her last two seasons, when she dropped out of the top twenty, she had enjoyed a successful career at the top, although one that was interrupted by marriage and divorce. With injuries worrying her, she decided to take a sabbatical to think about life and maybe do something else.

"Although I was relatively young, I had seen friends struggle with the decision of how to leave the tour, and you wonder how you will make the transition and handle it. I felt the time was right, but I never dreamed I would be able to do the things I did."

She branched out by going into sports programs on radio in the Toronto area and did television commentating for the LPGA Du Maurier Classic, which is an annual major tournament in Canada. She was also involved in public speaking at sports celebrity banquets.

After a year in the media, Sandra began teaching golf, which she enjoyed, especially teaching juniors. She became involved in raising money and being on committees of charities. "The charities are my children. I admire Judy Rankin and Nancy Lopez for combining family and golf so well, but not all of us could do that. I will not now have my own children—I have a niece and nephew—but I am sure one day I will get married, and I am currently engaged to someone.

On Christmas Eve, 1992, Sandra married the Hon. John McDermid, P.C., a former Federal Cabinet Minister in the Canadian government, who retired in 1993.

John, who says, " I am a better golfer since I married Sandra," helps her to run three golf schools a year. Sandra has a busy year-round teaching program, which takes in about 800 people. She has produced two instruction tapes and is a golf commentator for ABC sports, for ESPN, Prime Sports Network and CTV. John and Sandra built a new home in 1995, in a tiny community of 20 houses outside Toronto, where there are at the bottom of the garden.

"I have no regrets at leaving the tour and am in contact through television and the people I know out there. I still play golf for fun, and I hit the ball really well.

"I am proud of the LPGA and of each and every individual who is a member. I always respected my peers and all the girls I played with, whether they were number 1 or 100 on the money list. Some have more talent than others, but we have all paid a price, some a bigger price, to be where we are. Everyone counts, and we need every member we have who is a good player and ambassador for the LPGA."

LPGA Victories: 1968 LPGA Championship. **1978** Colgate Dinah Shore Winner's Circle, Lady Stroh's Open. **1979** Colgate Dinah Shore Winner's Circle, Lady Michelob, Real Estate Classic. **1980** West Virginia Classic. **1981** McDonald's Kids Classic.

Unofficial Victories: 1974 Colgate Far East Open.

Sandra Post's LPGA Record

Year	No.of Events	Best Finish	Money	Rank	Scoring Average
1968	26	1	$13,509	13	74.92
1969	22	T2	11,269	20	74.97
1970	11	T9	1,765	44	77.18
1971	13	T3	6,954	30	76.13
1972	15	T11	3,875	49	76.14
1973	29	5	20,409	23	74.96
1974	26	1	32,140	15	74.06
1975	22	2	34,852	10	72.98
1976	25	2	51,747	12	73.70
1977	26	2	77,727	9	72.55
1978	26	1	92,118	7	73.43
1979	27	1	178,750	2	72.43
1980	27	1	102,822	10	72.88
1981	27	1	71,191	15	73.61
1982	24	T14	22,363	63	74.11
1983	14	2	24,726	70	74.55

Renee Powell

Renee Powell is black and beautiful. Fellow professional Debbie Meisterlin Steinbach says, "She is so black, and she talks so white. Do you know what I mean? I used to room with her, and I would hear her talking, turn round to answer and be astonished because I never thought of her as black. She is a really nice person, who had a terrible time, and I am glad that things are now working out for her."

Debbie Meisterlin sums up Renee Powell, a woman who was caught uncomfortably in the middle of two worlds, never knowing where she belonged and often rejected by both sides. She grew up almost as a lone black in her neighborhood, during her schooldays in amateur golf, and then as a professional. She identified with the white world in which she lived and married, and was devastated by divorce from a white Englishman.

Her first real contact with the black community came after she quit playing the tour in 1980, when she became involved in promoting golf in black U.S. colleges and in black Africa. It was an instinctive antidote to all those years of trauma, as a child and as an adult in an often hostile environment.

In spite of facing a lifetime of color prejudice, Renee remains a charming, unaggressive woman, whose physical frame became positively frail when she was most stressed, but she has a resilient inner strength. She attracted much media attention as she trod paths that plunged her into territory sometimes elating, sometimes abusive, and always lonely.

Renee's father, in reaction to the prejudice he experienced, built his own Clearview golf course. This allowed Renee to participate in a sport she could play on her own. Her father, a professional golfer, lived through his daughter, nurturing all his hopes in her. Renee did not triumph on the LPGA tour, but her victory came in having the courage to survive it.

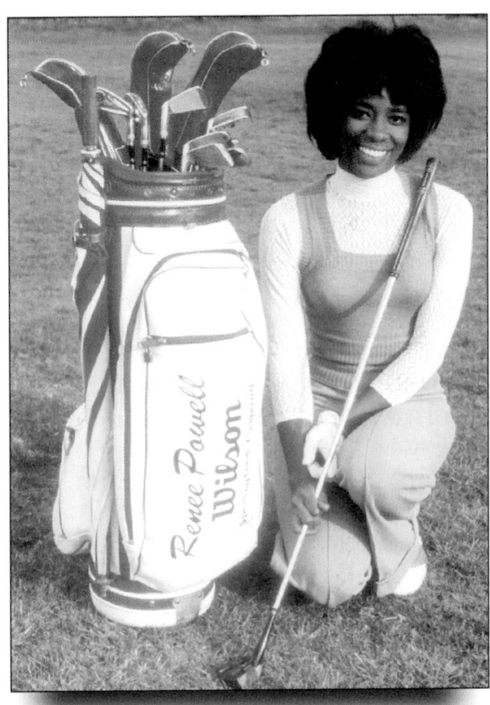

Renee overcame many prejudices growing up in an all white environment to become a popular LPGA player. While she had no triumphs on the tour, her victory came in having the courage to survive.

In 1992, the Powell family gained recognition of their collective endeavors when Renee received the Jack Nicklaus family golf award from the National Golf Foundation. It is given to families "who have made substantial contributions to the game and exemplify the ideals of golf and family." Some flowery language from a sport that has been in no way exemplary in its ideals concerning race and gender, and which still has a long way to go.

My relationship with Renee is warm and friendly, and she has stayed in my home. Although she blocks out periods in her life that are too painful,

Renee Powell's father, as a reaction to prejudice he had experienced, built his own golf course so that Renee would have the opportunity to play the sport he loved. Photo: Peter Dazeley.

she is a forthcoming interviewee, who provides a realistic picture of the problems she has faced, without wanting you to feel sorry for her.

"I grew up in East Canton, Ohio, about ten miles from where my father was raised in a very small town where we were the only black family and where my grandfather worked in an industrial plant. My father was very interested in all sports, playing football, basketball, and golf. They allowed him on the local golf course, but warned him not to bring any other blacks. He went to Wilberforce University, a black college, where he played in the first interracial golf matches. When he got out of school, he faced a lot of problems, since it was the time when the Ku Klux Klan were burning their crosses.

"He and my mother made their home in the predominantly white East Canton. My father had a job as a security officer. I had a brother five years older who was killed, and another brother six years younger.

"My father went into the Army during World War II, into the black division, and he was stationed in England for three years, where he managed to play some golf. That was when he made plans to build a golf course after the war, because of the prejudice he had faced. He returned to East Canton, designed the course himself, and built it with some partners who later dropped out. When it was finished, he turned professional. He was a scratch golfer, but because of racial barriers, he was not allowed to join the men's PGA, nor could he participate in any PGA tournaments because until 1961 there was a Caucasian-only clause.

"Right through school I was the only black pupil the entire time, although there was a Portuguese girl at high school. At my first public school, a little boy chased me in the playground with a knife, and when I ran inside, the teacher sent me out again. In third grade I had two good friends who one day came to school and said, 'We're not allowed to play with you any more because you are colored.' I was eight years old, and I went home and cried, but how do you explain that sort of prejudice? My parents tried, telling me I had to get used to these things and it would change when I was older, but to me it was a shocking thing that one day you were friends and the next day you weren't.

"School was very difficult. There was a song, 'My Old Kentucky Home,' which was going to be sung at a PTA affair, and instead of the line 'The darkies are gay,' there was the alternative 'The old folks are gay,' but this teacher decided to use the word 'darkies.' I wouldn't sing it, and she told me I couldn't take part. Again, I went home crying. There were so many incidents of this nature that I was taken out of public school and sent to a Catholic school, my mother being a Catholic and my father a Baptist.

"Socially I was a loner, and because we lived in the middle of a golf course, I started playing golf when I was three. I spent all my spare time there. Taught by my father, I progressed well, entered tournaments when I was 12, and played off scratch at 10. I won plenty of tournaments, but I found a lot of prejudice, particularly from girls from the South who would ignore me. I had trouble getting into some tournaments, and I never played the Ohio State Amateur Tournament because of racial prejudice, nor could I play the Trans-Mississippi, the Western Amateur, or the North and South. The North and South finally sent me an invitation to play its tournament the first year I was a professional, and therefore ineligible.

"When I was 12, I saw my first professional tournament in Ohio, where I met Marilynn Smith, who was then president of the LPGA. She was its fashion plate. She made a big impression on me; she talked to me, gave me golf balls, and after that always sent me encouraging notes and golf balls at Christmas.

"When I went to Ohio University, which was 200 miles from home, I was one of two black girls, and I was isolated in a dorm of 250 girls. I was captain of the girls' golf team, and when I transferred two years later to Ohio State University, which was of a higher standard and had two good golf courses, I was captain of the women's team. I studied speech and hearing therapy, with a minor in psychology, and tried to combine it with golf.

"In 1967, at 21, I decided to turn professional with the financial help of my parents. I knew many of the women professionals from my amateur days, and it seemed a reasonable life where you could make money and enjoy what you were doing. I didn't visualize it as glamorous, and it isn't, but I underestimated how strenuous it was playing golf all the time. I started my first season in July, picked up some money, and was doing reasonably well.

On January 21, 1979, Renee Powell became the first black woman to become a golf professional at an English club when she took over at the Silvermere Golf Club in Surrey. Here she gives her first lesson to 16-year old Russell Wright, her assistant at the club. Photo credit: Popperfoto.

"Once in Florida when another girl and I decided to room together in private housing, the woman expecting us wrote to say how excited she was at having two of us stay with her. Until she found out about me, and then she told the other girl she could stay, but I couldn't because of my color. I was disappointed that the girl stayed and let me find somewhere else, since I thought that she was more than an acquaintance and that I could count on her as a friend.

"I felt that people needed to stop being so ignorant, and I talked to black baseball and football players about the prejudice they encountered. I also talked to golfers like Charlie Sifford, Pete Brown, and Lee Elder, who said they didn't know how I managed on my own. Althea Gibson had turned professional in 1963 and played the tour, but she had grown up in New York City where it was rough, and she could take care of herself.

"I felt even more alone because neither group wanted to accept me—neither the blacks nor the whites. When I grew up at a private school, playing golf, the blacks thought I considered myself better than they were, and the whites didn't like me because I was black. I was upset that people would exclude me, and I am sure very few of the people on the LPGA tour could have withstood all the things I went through. It would be interesting to see someone as the only white on a black tour.

I was pleased to be on the golf circuit because I loved the game, but I grew up quickly to find life isn't all a bed of roses. I knew I could play well, but my golf suffered for years from all the pressures, and I didn't want to be defeated because I knew other blacks wanted me to succeed. A lot of people run into prejudice and change their name, but it is difficult to change your color.

"There was a time when I was so terrified I thought of carrying a gun, and I know if I had shown the abusive letters to the FBI they would have allowed me to, but I decided against it. Generally, I kept myself mentally balanced by blocking out the prejudice because it affected me so badly. I felt I could work it out with the help of God. I believe in prayer and that God is a good God.

"My life was further complicated by my father looking at me and seeing the life he never had, due to racial barriers; if I had a bad score, it was as though my father had done it, and I was lucky to remain sane because I was totally influenced by him and trying to fulfill his ambitions.

"I did not have any really close friends on tour, but I did meet some families to whom I became close, though I would only see them once a year. I had been forced by circumstances to be alone growing up; so that I preferred it and became more independent.

"Until I went to college, I never dated. I put a shield around myself for protection. It can be difficult to be a lone female on tour because you often get approached by guys who, if you reject them, say, 'Are you gay or something?' I did try to figure out the gay element, and then I decided it was not my problem. Whatever goes on behind closed doors is someone's own business. There are a lot of families who know and don't accept it, saying, 'Where did I go wrong? What did I do? I have failed.' I do not condone it, but I think a person has a right to choose. After all, I have been in a minority my whole life.

"For the first couple of years on tour I lost money, but then I improved, and I represented the Wilson Sporting Goods Company at exhibitions and clinics, and I had speaking engagements. One of my most rewarding experiences came at the end of 1971, when Mary Lou Crocker and I went on a State Department trip all over South Vietnam for three weeks. It was a morale boosting exercise into the middle of the jungle, all of it a war zone, and we had a male escort, whom Mary Lou later married. We got up at 5:30 a.m., went to hospitals, shook hands, hit balls whenever possible, maybe into the sea from a hospital ship, and I felt like Miss World because the guys were all so grateful. I had my eyes opened to the drug and racial problems, and I was so against what we were doing over there. When I came home, I phoned wives and parents to pass on messages. Soldiers who returned would phone me and come to tournaments occasionally, and I visited veterans' hospitals. I met a lot of troops, particularly black troops, who were giving their lives in Vietnam, but the ones who came home were once again second-class citizens, who couldn't get housing or work or were given menial jobs because of their color."

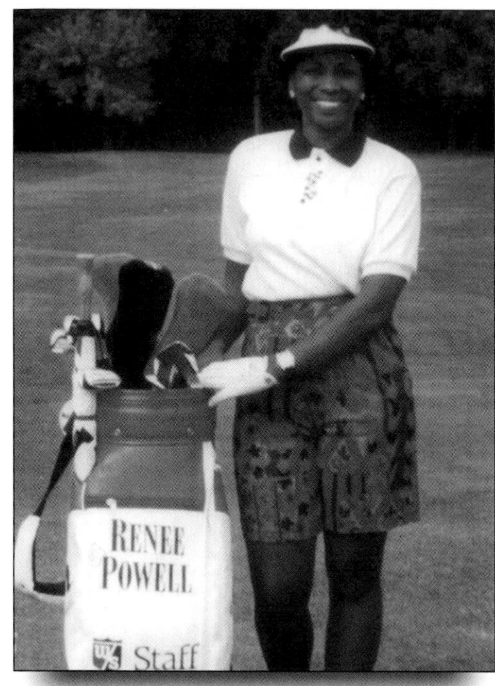

Renee Powell currently works with several African countries to develop golf programs for young people, and she continues to give clinics and to hold tournaments to benefit the United Negro College Fund.

In the 1970s, Renee went to England for the Colgate European Open, a tournament that was played at Sunningdale in Berkshire. There she met Chris Lawrence, a white, English accountant who was involved in making a film for television on women golfers, in which Renee took part. They struck up a friendship that later turned into marriage and finally ended in divorce.

Although Renee gained self-assurance while she was with Christopher, her marriage breakup was so devastating that she prefers to block it from her mind, along with the hysterectomy she went through in 1977, when she had a benign growth.

"At the time of my hysterectomy I was not shattered because I would be unable to have children, because Christopher had been married before and had two daughters whom I regarded as my adopted children.

"I let down my shield in marriage; I was shattered when it broke up. I was so embarrassed at getting divorced that I put a glass around myself so people wouldn't bother me. I wasn't well; I didn't have a marriage, a home, or golf which I had given up; my weight went down to 90 pounds. I couldn't sleep. I was a zombie who felt there was nothing in my life.

"I hated the game of golf, blamed it for my problems, and blamed my family for my growing up in a game that ruled my life. I think it is possible to be married and play golf, but it takes a husband who is a very secure individual, particularly when his wife is getting attention from everyone and travelling the world. It is as difficult for a man to accept the role reversal as it is for a woman to get to the top.

"I left the tour in 1980 because of personal problems. I found I had to come back into the world again, and I needed to build my own ego and mentally keep myself together. To avoid dwelling on my personal life, I became a workaholic, haunting the libraries, and throwing myself into research to find out about black colleges in the U.S. I had no idea there were as many as 168, but I put together a golf program for some of them in an area where I could drive from one to the other. Golf was being used so much for business purposes that I felt I could communicate the benefits of it. I wrote to them, outlining my ideas of a golf clinic and speaking program. The first year I visited 16 colleges, the next 28, all with the help of sponsorship from the Wilson Sporting Goods Company and Lily of France.

"I was fascinated to learn about the schools, and it was the first time I had ever mixed in a black group of people. I have never known where I fit into society. I have always been a citizen of the world, perhaps being most comfortable outside my own country. I found the work in the colleges challenging and interesting. Although I was something of a celebrity to the students, I was a real person to whom they could relate. They accepted me, and I accepted them. The media picked up on the project, which became very successful.

"At the same time, I went to Washington to research going to black countries in Africa, also to promote golf. I got Pan Am to sponsor me, and I went to Kenya on my first trip, which went well. My real break came when I went into the Embassy of Trinidad and Tobago in Washington, where the ambassador was the only person who played golf. I got to see him. He was so fascinated by the fact that my father, a black man, had built his own golf course that he came to visit us in East Canton, and then he introduced me to everyone I wanted to know in Washington.

"My African trips became so successful that after President Kaunda asked to play golf with me when he visited Washington, the U.S. Information Agency decided to use me as an ambassador to African countries, and they sent me on golf trips. In Africa, although I am a black American, they take pride in my talent."

"Looking back at my life, I think all things happen for a reason so that you end up stronger and wiser. Just to survive professional golf has been an achievement, that I have had to fight for the whole way. As everyone is aware, golf is not a popular sport among blacks, but somehow I have pulled myself through."

Renee remained a card-holding member of the LPGA and is a head professional at the City of Cleveland Golf Club in Ohio; she continues to give clinics and exhibitions, and holds a celebrity tournament at her father's course benefitting the United Negro College Fund. Her tours of black colleges and her trips to Africa are still part of her life.

Renee Powell's LPGA Record

Year	No.of Events	Best Finish	Money	Rank	Scoring Average
1967	14	20	$770	39	78.00
1968	23	T7	1,480	44	81.27
1969	20	T11	3,074	40	77.70
1970	16	T19	982	53	77.79
1971	16	T16	1,341	52	77.71
1972	24	T4	6,111	42	77.22
1973	29	T7	6,115	52	76.75
1974	21	T13	4,638	61	76.21
1975	12	T18	2,087	73	76.53
1976	18	T11	7,840	61	75.66
1977	18	T19	3,535	86	76.27
1978	NA	NA	NA	NA	79.45
1979	NA	NA	1,087	NA	77.89

Judy Rankin

Judy Rankin is a rare breed, admitting she played golf for money rather than titles or fame: "In spite of the fact there wasn't much money out there in 1962, it was the reason I turned professional. I care a great deal about the game, but I was not on tour for the love of it." For the first six years of her career, she never won a tournament, but fittingly she was the first player to break the $100,000 barrier in 1976, when she won $150,734. She is a direct, likeable woman, good to interview because she tells you her strengths and weaknesses, her emotions, and the facts and reality of a situation in a forthright manner.

She was a role model as the first woman professional golfer to combine being highly successful on the LPGA tour, together with having a husband Yippy, son Tuey, and a good, lasting family relationship.

What strikes you about Judy is her tiny frame, which might seem fragile, but at 5 feet, 3 inches. She generates power that has been built up from the age of six, when she first swung a golf club. From eight to eleven years old she was a Pee Wee Champion, and at fourteen became the youngest golfer ever to win the Missouri State Women's Amateur Championship, a title she won again two years later. At 15 she achieved the distinction of being low amateur in the U.S. Open.

Judy took an active part in the running of the LPGA tour, from carrying out every duty the women performed in the 1960s to being on the executive board in the early 1970s. She was president in 1976, when she was leading money winner, a feat she achieved again the following season. From 1970 to 1979 she was a dominant force, finishing only once out of the top 10 money winners.

"I was born and raised in St. Louis, and when I was six my mother developed a malignant brain tumor, which resulted in her never walking again. She lived three and a half years longer than the doctors predicted and died when I was 11. My father told me as soon as my mother became ill that she would die from the illness, and we were thrown very much together.

"My father, Paul Torluemke, was in the advertising business, and our middle income family was hit hard by thousands of dollars of medical bills. My mother's illness was hard on me, but it was 10 times harder on my father. Now I'm a mother, and I miss my mother almost more than I did as a child. I was very close to my father's mother, and later my father remarried. I have a half brother.

"My father took care of me, and our difficult times made us closer. He played golf for fun and

Judy Rankin competes at the Colgate tournament, Sunningdale, 1977. Just a year earlier, she was the first player to earn more than $100,000 in a single year. Photo ©Phil Sheldon.

would play with me when I started at six, for it was a way we spent time together.

"At first I bugged my father to hit golf balls, and when he saw how good I might be and had an inkling of what doors it might open for me, he was really encouraging and ambitious for me. He taught me and continued to do so right through my playing career. He persevered when it would have been easier to give up and go fishing. At times we would get very frustrated with each other, but it did make my life a lot nicer, and my success made him happy.

"I have always had a slight build, and at 14, I weighed only 80 pounds, but it wasn't a handicap. I was a long hitter because clubhead speed can be generated by a smaller person. Although when you are competing, it would be nice to be bigger. I never found anything more strengthening than beating golf balls. Go and hit 1,000 balls on a windy day, and you'll strengthen everything.

"I played golf about seven months a year. I won tournaments from the age of seven, and it all came rather easily. I never really wanted to be a professional because you couldn't make any money in golf in the 1960s. When I was 17, I had an offer from a sporting goods company to turn professional—they would finance me to travel on the tour—and I took it, joining the LPGA in 1962.

"Although there were lots of good times, the first couple of years I was fairly miserable and homesick, and I didn't play to my capability. I was supposed to be able to win, but I always finished second and didn't win until I was 23.

"Whereas some players think so forcefully they can achieve things, I was always a bit scared of everything, a realist without any false confidence. My emotions would get in the way, my heart would beat faster as I got excited, and I realized I couldn't afford to get too high or low. I eliminated the emotion, I quit trying to win, and after deciding to make as much money as possible and not caring whether I ever won, I won the following week and realized that previously my emotions had destroyed my golf game.

"In 1965, I won nearly $13,000 and started to make a profit, something that continued in my career. It didn't cost a lot to be on tour. I drove

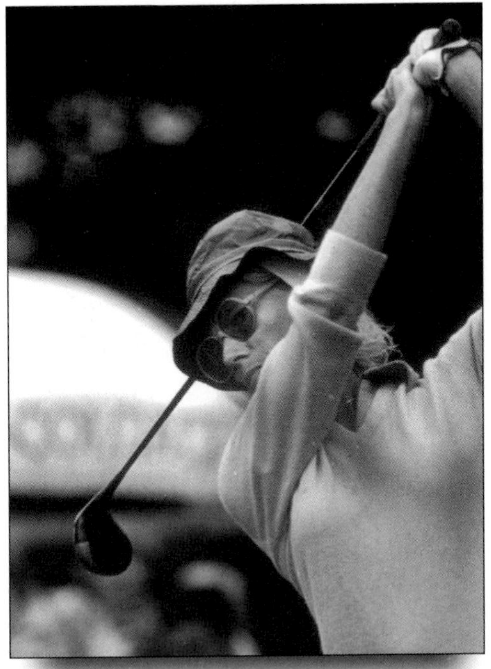

From 1970 to 1979, Judy Rankin was a dominant force on the tour, finishing in the top 10 money winner's list each year but one. She won seven times in 1976 and set an LPGA record of 25 top-ten finishes in 1977. Photo ©Phil Sheldon.

everywhere, and my first winner's check was $1,800. My father spent whatever he had on me, but it was never easy to come by money.

"It is a plus to be able to do something as nice as golf to earn your living, but I wouldn't compete if it weren't profitable. There would be no point. It is hard for me to believe professionals who say they are out there purely for the love of golf or for the trophies.

"My husband admits my working has provided some luxuries we would not otherwise have had. I did not play to support us, but I did play for the money and the independence it brings. I had a son at home, and if there had not been practical reasons for my playing golf, I would have been with him.

"It pleased me no end to set the record of being the first to win $100,000 in a single year. It's nice that it is permanently there, and that no one can take it away from me. I never believe things until they happen, and then I'd like to stop everything

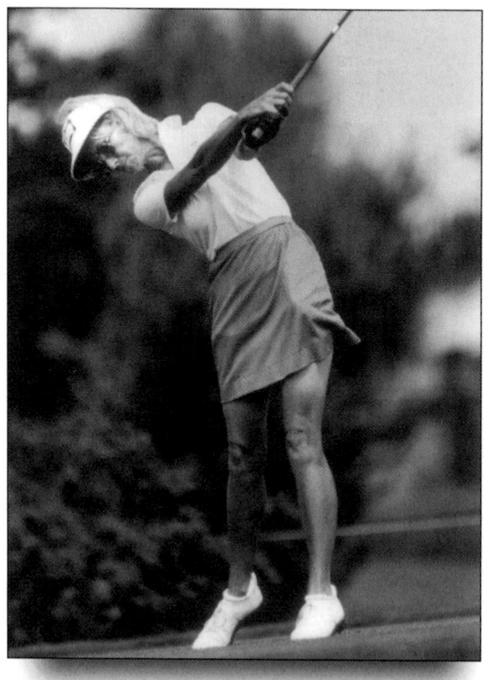

Judy Rankin, after leaving the tour, became a highly-respected golf commentator for ABC television. Her latest challenge is that of captain of the 1996 U.S. Solheim Cup team, which will demand her skills as a player and leader.

for five minutes to take it all in. It was a fantasy come true in 1976, and maybe I enjoyed it more than anyone else ever did.

"That year sticks in my mind as the epitome of playing a competitive sport with your friends and enjoying it. It was special. There was never another year like it, and I was president of the LPGA. When you are president, you have so much to do that you don't have time to dwell on yourself, and you play better. Normally you're so self-oriented that it's bad.

"It was nice that so many of the players were rooting for me to pass the $100,000 mark. I have never been super-confident, I'm not shy or backward, but I never thought of myself as number one. I was raised to remember that no one is better than anyone else, and sometimes I remember it so well that it's terrible. I'm just as happy to stay in the background. It's not very important to get in the papers.

"My husband Yippy has been very supportive, and he has such a competitive nature he could get me fired up when I lost enthusiasm. We met in a Pro-Am in 1967, when I was 22—he is four and a half years older—and we got married four weeks later. We couldn't afford the phone calls, and maybe that's the best way to do it. Yippy is in the insurance business and has interests in oil; so we set up home in West Texas." Their son Tuey was born in 1969.

Judy is realistic about the unusual lifestyle on tour. "Living with a bunch of women is at times a lot of fun. We can sit and have the best time laughing and enjoying ourselves without a drop to drink. There is a little jealousy or cattiness on tour, but you're accepted by everyone because you are a professional golfer. To some degree we're protected from the outside world, and as a result it can be hard, almost boring, to live in a town where your friends are housewives and you have nothing in common. As professional golfers we're a rather strange breed of women because our interests are so different."

Continuing to play through physical problems in the early 1980s, Judy was forced off the tour at the end of 1983 with a back problem that had caused her considerable pain for several years. After treatment by injection, which only worsened her condition, she had surgery in 1985. By the time she had recuperated sufficiently to continue playing, her desire had evaporated: "I was an intense player, who performed best when I gave my all. I lost that intensity and with it the desire.

"Having grown up on tour from 17, my closest friendships were there, in a life I knew, which was my comfort zone. I was lucky that when the public adoration was over I could fall back on my home and family, which I really enjoyed.

"All my life, every day of the week had been concerned with winning and losing, and it was a relief not to continue such an up and down affair. I was more emotionally wrung out than I knew. I'm not sure I have a great competitive nature, but with my back against the wall, I'm a fighter. I enjoy victory, dislike losing, and when I'm thrown into the arena, I'm tough, but I don't think I have to compete to be fulfilled. Truly competitive people always want to be in the fray. If I had not had some God-given ability, a father who persevered and taught me, and a very competitive husband who kept me up in my professional career, I don't know how much fight I would have shown.

"Players like Nancy Lopez and Jack Nicklaus are totally calm and in control, and their nervous systems do not take the same strain under the gun. My emotional turmoil amounted almost to fear, something I had to overcome to win. With Lopez and Nicklaus, part of their talent and the aura that people see is their great inner belief, whereas most of us see our failings."

In 1984, Judy became a golf commentator for ABC television and for both women's and men's golf. It is a working relationship that has lasted into the 1990s: "I have been encouraged, and I have enjoyed feeling part of the group of men with whom I work. The fact I'm still around attests to their openness. Sometimes women feel compelled to push too hard when it's more important to stay in the job than to make demands which may mean you lose it."

Judy's greatest pride is in the successful combination of her golfing and family role: "Juggling a home and family has been a big effort, but I made a statement in showing that you don't have to give up all other aspects of life to be good at playing golf. I didn't set out to blaze a trail. It just happened that way. The LPGA needed my image as a wife and mother in those early years when the picture was not pretty enough. Argue about the right or wrong: the truth is that the best way to help yourself is to have physical appeal and immense talent. Those are the people who get noticed.

"I received great enjoyment from my golf, from the LPGA tour, and financially the grass never looked greener elsewhere. I don't know where a woman could have earned the same money."

LPGA Victories: 1968 Corpus Christi Open. **1970** George Washington Classic, Springfield Jaycee Open, Lincoln-Mercury Open. **1971** Quality-First Classic. **1972** Lady Eve Open, Heritage Village Open. **1973** American Defender, Lady Carling Open, Pabst Classic, GAC Classic. **1974** Baltimore Classic. **1975** National Jewish Hospital Open. **1976** Burdine's Invitational, Colgate Dinah Shore Winner's Circle, Karsten Ping Open, Babe Zaharias Invitational, Borden Classic, Colgate Hong Kong Open. **1977** Orange Blossom Classic, Bent Tree Classic, Mayflower Classic, Peter Jackson Classic, Colgate European Open. **1978** WUI Classic. **1979** WUI Classic.

Unofficial Victories: 1974 Colgate European Open. **1977** LPGA National Team Championship (with JoAnne Carner).

Judy Rankin's LPGA Record

Year	No.of Events	Best Finish	Money	Rank	Scoring Average
1962	15	T10	$701	41	79.08
1963	23	5	2,539	33	78.44
1964	29	T3	8,630	13	74.99
1965	28	2	12,237	9	74.54
1966	30	2	15,180	7	74.52
1967	12	T2	4,600	29	74.59
1968	9	1	8,617	23	72.75
1969	16	2	16,310	14	73.79
1970	19	1	22,194	5	73.33
1971	21	1	17,924	9	74.18
1972	29	1	49,183	4	73.08
1973	33	1	72,989	2	73.08
1974	26	1	45,882	9	73.68
1975	21	1	50,174	5	72.32
1976	26	1	150,734	1	72.32
1977	28	1	122,890	1	72.25
1978	22	1	51,306	15	73.54
1979	25	1	108,511	8	72.68
1980	17	2	54,182	21	72.63
1981	22	T2	48,198	27	73.61
1982	20	T16	15,452	80	74.38
1983	16	T18	8,637	110	75.13

The 1970s & 1980s

The 1970s

Jane Blalock, Carol Mann, Ray Volpe, and Nancy Lopez were instrumental in the wave of change that swept through the 1970s. Jane Blalock and her alleged infringement of the rules in 1972 resulted in a $5 million anti-trust lawsuit, which dragged on and almost bankrupted the LPGA. But unhappy period as it was for everyone, it resulted in significant reorganization. For the first time, running the tour was taken out of the hands of the women who were playing on it.

Carol Mann was responsible for the vital change of direction in the LPGA's administration. In 1975, Ray Volpe was hired as the LPGA's commissioner. A dynamic man, he was the first to bring professional marketing expertise to the organization.

Nancy Lopez exploded into the limelight with her dark hair, shining eyes, and charming personality. She came as manna from heaven, achieving nine victories in 1978 and eight in 1979. With magnetic appeal, she took the LPGA to its highest profile, as Ray Volpe capitalized on her natural assets. A born communicator, she spent hours handling the insistent demands of the media, and when Nancy spoke to you it was as though you were the one important person in the room. Kathy Whitworth, who in her day had shunned the limelight, admitted: "Had someone else been winning besides myself who had more charisma, we might have grown faster in that earlier era."

Although the happy combination of Volpe and Lopez had a dramatic effect on the tour's public image, the LPGA's first commissioner was too flamboyant a personality for a few of the women, and some of the older members found it hard to come to terms with him taking the power out of the hands of the players. It was a wise move for the expansion of the LPGA to appoint a board of directors, which included members of the corporate world, but it was a jolt to those players, who for two and a half decades had run everything themselves.

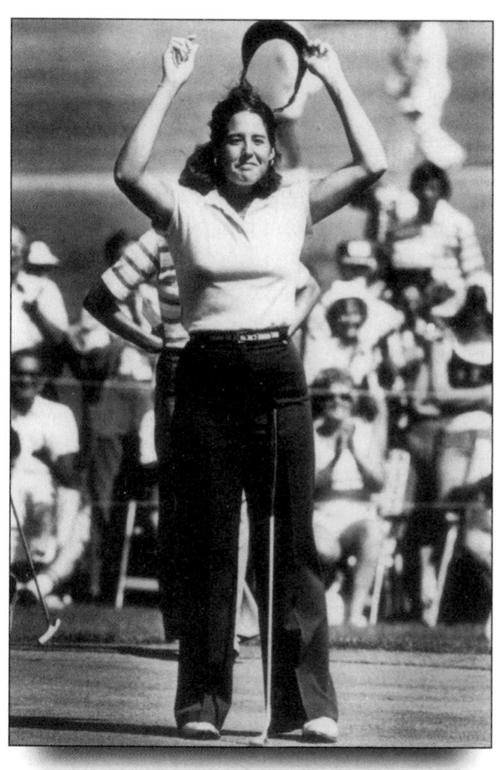

Glamour and prestige came to the LPGA in the 1970s, carried first on the shoulders of Laura Baugh and Jan Stephenson; then by the talented and charismatic Nancy Lopez, named "Rookie of the Year" in 1978.

In financial terms the tour grew from $435,000 and 21 events in 1970 to nearly $4.5 million and 38 tournaments nine years later, with the added perk of national television coverage scattered through the season. In spite of a promised $50,000 a year from the LPGA in 1975, Ray Volpe had to generate enough income to pay his initial salary, as the coffers were bare from the long-standing Blalock battle, which he finally brought to a conclusion.

The first qualifying schools for players to get on the tour began in 1973, with two each season in January and July. This lasted until the 1980s, when two pre-qualifying events were added before the final qualifying school, so great was the demand for places.

In the 1970s, attitudes about women shifted perceptibly as the feminist movement got into its stride. The law affecting sportswomen in colleges decreed through Title IX that Federal money allotted to education establishments had to provide equal funding for both sexes, which resulted in the beginning of golf scholarships for women.

Most of the women professional golfers did not identify with the struggles of the women away from the tour. They had their role model pioneer golfing predecessors and their own internal independence, and they were too caught up with their own survival as they fought to make a living and gain recognition for themselves in professional sport.

Carol Mann said: "The women's movement came along, where people were beating their chests and saying, 'Bravo, I'm a woman.' At first I didn't like some of the militancy. I was out there doing my thing; so I didn't feel I was being put down. People on tour spoke about it in a negative way, referring to it as 'militant,' 'bitchy,' and 'you must be kidding if you want to talk about it.' I read about it and heard Jane Blalock speak about it very well, but I was afraid to talk out because I felt I wasn't smart enough."

In corporate terms, the man responsible for providing big money in LPGA tournaments and thereby giving the women the most important asset of all—rising self esteem—was David Foster of Colgate. David loved golf and travelling with the women professionals, which he did worldwide. The company put up huge sums for a network of tournaments, and he pursued a dream, although it was his enviable manner of so doing that was partly responsible for his later downfall.

Says Joyce Kazmierski: "David did it in royal style, and all the players had their expenses paid travelling first class worldwide. I remember coming back from the Far East one time when Carol Mann had an eight foot spear, 27 pieces of checked baggage, and Colgate had an excess baggage charge which totalled $10,000. We didn't take advantage; we just enjoyed it."

In sexual terms, the more reticent players of earlier eras were astonished by the provocative antics of Laura Baugh—small, petite, and blonde. She capitalized hugely on her obvious assets, and she was later followed by the even more flamboyant Australian, Jan Stephenson. Whereas Laura was often almost a winner and attracted huge crowds, Jan entered the winner's circle and became the tour's sex symbol. With a theatrical penchant for excitement, Jan made male fans melt at the sight of her and lust after her, although often to little avail, since she had a tough protective layer. Laura and Jan carried the tour in their more calculated manner, until Nancy Lopez took it by storm with her girl-next-door appearance—no obvious promotion of sex, but the projection of a very womanly image. Some rumors of jealousy may have been justified, but on the whole, the women knew that they needed all these correctives to the less acceptable reflection of the athletic woman.

The hiring of Ray Volpe required all the tremendous energy of Carol Mann, who was more fulfilled being the catalyst for change than she had been winning the U.S. Open and becoming leading money winner. As president of the LPGA for three years from 1973, Carol fired former executive

David Foster, the driving force behind Colgate and the Colgate Dinah Shore Winner's Circle, pushed tournament purses higher with his showcase event. Kathy Whitworth was the winner in 1977. Photo courtesy: Katherine Murphy.

The winning U.S. Curtis Cup Team of 1976 included (left to right) Nancy Lopez, Carol Semple, Cindy Hill, Barbara McIntire (captain), Nancy Simmons, Barbara Barrow, Donna Horton-White, Beth Daniel, and Debbie Massey. All but McIntire, Semple, and Simmons eventually became LPGA professionals.

director Bud Erickson "in a taxi cab in New York in December 1974" and in a most business-like fashion set about finding his replacement. Ray Volpe came out on top of 600 applicants in a series of interviews devised to find the best man, even if he had no golf experience.

Ray said: "Not having tunnel vision about golf was an advantage. I knew about my product, and most people didn't. The more I met the women, the more I liked them, until my whole attitude toward women changed to a deep respect for the women's cause as a way of life.

I believed in them as people and athletes, and I admired their great belief in themselves. I said, 'These women are terrific. How come I don't know about them? If I believe they're terrific, it will be easy to get across their spirit, pride, and competitiveness to the public.' I realized the power of women being responsible for spending seven out of ten retail dollars, since women decide about houses, appliances, schools, and food, while men kick a car tire and pretend to choose the car."

The man from Brooklyn, former vice president of marketing for the National Hockey League, was given the news of his appointment by Carol Mann at Kennedy Airport: She said: "I had just lost a playoff to JoAnne Carner, and I met Ray in my golf clothes, with my current flame on my arm. I shook his hand and said, 'You've got a job if you want it. Do you want it?' He said, 'I sure do.'

Ray set up an office in New York, hired a public relations director and publicity co-ordinator to service the networks, magazines, and sponsors, and he formed a marketing arm for the LPGA. With his eye for publicity, he had Kathy Whitworth inducted into the Hall of Fame in 1975, getting the clause rescinded that stated you had to be retired for two years from the tour to qualify. For the first time the criterion dealing with the number of tournaments won was laid down for inductees into the Hall of Fame.

Ray Volpe was named LPGA Commissioner in 1975. His marketing savvy enabled the tour to grow rapidly. By 1979, the total purse was nearly $4.5 million.

In 1977, the LPGA Hall of Fame moved with great publicity from its original home of Augusta Country Club to reside at the World Golf Hall of Fame in Pinehurst, where Carol Mann and Sandra Haynie were its first inductees. In later years, as the LPGA moved its offices, the Hall of Fame went with it "in a cardboard box," as Betsy Rawls put it, until a new home was built in the 1990s in Daytona Beach.

Ray Volpe's admiration of the LPGA women was obvious, and although Nancy Lopez provided the vital impetus in the late 1970s, Ray was careful not to demonstrate any favoritism. He said: "The whole tour is not Nancy, nor is it marketed on her alone. Nancy is all heart—the golf swing is a tool—and heart makes the difference. Everyone loves sporting heroes, and the excitement of sport makes it easy to sell. My job is to promote the well being of 160 players, but I can capitalize on Nancy because when she smiles there's not a smile like that in the whole world."

On the cusp of the decade there was every reason to smile, for Nancy, for Ray, and for all the women of the LPGA who were benefiting from the most exceptional period of growth the tour had ever known.

The 1980s

In tune with the era, life on the LPGA tour in the 1980s had quickened its pace. A glossy sheen of glamour, money, and stars made it seem like progressing into a round of successful parties, where the top golfers moved with managers, endorsements, and sponsorship. The tour received the television exposure so essential to growth and reacted to the media's obsession with women, sex, religion, and sport. The LPGA had blood pumping through its veins as Ray Volpe established a lifeline to the corporate world, which appeared to create more wealth and a greater reward. When Judy Rankin pointed out that in real terms they weren't any better off than a few years previously, it was slightly deflating to Ray Volpe, but it highlighted the fact that for many people financial growth just manages to keep abreast of inflation. Nancy Lopez remained the star of the tour and its most consistently successful golfer, playing herself into the Hall of Fame. The LPGA reached its zenith, and then as the decade progressed, it had to confront encroaching competition for sponsors.

In 1981, a landmark was reached in sport, when Ray revealed that the Internal Revenue Service had approved the LPGA's proposed retirement program. It was the first deferred compensation program for athletes in a non-team professional sport. It was a fine plan for the current and future members of the association, but it was particularly heartwarming that those who had been involved over the past decades were also to benefit. The inspirational combination of Ray Volpe and Debbie Massey, the LPGA vice-president and subsequently president, worked on it tirelessly, and Debbie says: "I had a magical relationship with Ray, and we were two personalities who wanted to go somewhere with the organization. Ray was a visionary. He's a stimulating man, not a great administrator, but his ego is so intact that he never got bigger than himself."

Ray made a huge impact on the LPGA and on many of the women, who in turn affected him profoundly. Betsy Rawls, a loved and revered woman and a member of the Hall of Fame, resigned in 1981 after six years as tournament director of the LPGA and a lifetime's dedication of supporting its birth and growing pains after seeing it achieve fruition. Ray expressed the sentiments of the association, when he said: "I have learned to respect and admire Betsy Rawls greatly. Her dignity, knowledge, experience, and inspiring ways, are extraordinary talents given to few individuals. It would take volumes to represent her many attributes, but suffice it to say that the combination of qualities she brought to the LPGA are impossible to replace, and her contributions to the association are immortal."

Ray's decision to move in 1982 to the next area of excitement, cable television, left a void at the LPGA. At the time of his departure, he said: "Emotionally it is very hard to leave, and it was difficult to tell the players face to face. I felt I was losing my friends. I hope they know I'll be around for them if they need anything in the future.

"I could never function with the players in the way I would have liked. I couldn't tease them or take them out one at a time; I couldn't play golf with them in Pro-Ams, have them to my house for dinner, fearing that someone would say something. I would like to have been closer.

"I never thought I would feel for the players emotionally, or worry about their finances and how they were treated as women. It is good to see the players emerge and find their way, have pride and respect, and to know they are big time athletes. I feel good that I've made a contribution to their feeling of self-respect and independence.

"The biggest male chauvinist pig in the world has become a lover of women golfers. I don't know if I really believed in women's sports, if the cultural movement of women in this country made me believe it, if it was my closeness to the players where we were all fighting on the same team. I felt it was the players and me against the world, and I had to go out and get our share so that we could exist and build the tour. Because of that need, we were tied together very quickly, but I never thought the No. 1 player on the money list was more important that anyone else—it was one player, one vote. I thought they should regard themselves as a team of only a few hundred in the world. I feel very proud of the women. They can win more friends in a hurry than anyone. Everyone respects them because they play golf better than anyone else, but because people love them, it puts a momentum behind everything the tour is doing.

John Laupheimer left the USGA to become LPGA commissioner during the 1980s. He brought strong administrative experience to the tour. Photo courtesy: Katherine Murphy.

"I can never be part of the players. You go only so far and then you're locked out. All the men on the staff feel that. You're not a golfer, you're not a woman, but you have to have a professional relationship and a caring one."

Following the exuberance and inspirational qualities of Ray Volpe could not be an easy task for any new commissioner. John Laupheimer, formerly with the USGA, was chosen partly for his image as an establishment figure, and he also followed the pattern of alternating between quiet or more vociferous men at the helm, who were woven into the pattern of change right through the decades of LPGA history.

John was considered to be strong on the administrative side, where Ray had been lacking, and it was thought that consolidation rather than aggressive marketing would be of prime importance for the next few years. As it turned out, choosing Houston as a new headquarters in 1981 proved disappointing, since the boom town floundered when the bottom dropped out of the oil market. About that same time a men's Senior Tour appeared in Houston. It was an overnight success and had an adverse affect on the women's tour.

John Laupheimer had his admirers, one of whom was Kathy Whitworth, a strong critic of the volatile Ray Volpe: "I liked John very much," says Kathy, who was LPGA vice-president when John resigned at the end of 1988.

"He worked very hard and brought a lot of respect and stability to the LPGA. I was sorry he went. He was such a low-key personality that he didn't generate a lot of enthusiasm—it was not his style. He was a quiet plodder, not an outgoing man, but he did a lot of good things.

"He reorganized the office, got good personnel, and generated loyalty. The sponsors were not overly impressed, but in some ways they held him in high regard. The tour grew every year, and maybe there was not a lot of excitement, but it was stable. John did more good things for the LPGA than Ray Volpe, who brought publicity and hype and did not manage it very well."

Paula Marafino, who arrived with Ray Volpe and rose to become the administrative director, was a stable lifeline for the players, who all knew they could contact her if they needed something. As Joyce Kazmierski remarked: "Paula was an unsung hero, the cement that held the organization together." Paula had an attractive personality of warmth, perception, and intelligence, and you knew that she cared. She had her finger on the pulse of the organization, and she agonized for some time before moving from her close family and the city of New York to Houston, where she provided some essential continuity in the affairs of the LPGA.

"It was dynamic in 1975 in New York," said Paula. "We had a small staff working in an electric atmosphere of a daily snap, crackle, and pop. The staff was young, creative, and innovative, and it was hard to keep up with all the sponsors who wanted to be involved. We were best at building relationships, at creating and bonding loyalties. We were honest and fair, gave straight answers, and good service. We built up a presence and a relationship with the media so that the LPGA had appeal. Obviously you expect a see-saw with each administration, but the move to Houston was dynamic at the time, and the opportunity was there. It was only when the former dynamism receded that it became a morbid place to be."

Sadly, a disillusioned Paula left the LPGA in 1986, after giving so much to the organization. Two years later, the LPGA teaching division recognized her exceptional contribution by making her an honorary member.

As the 1980s produced the normal insecurities resulting from change in administration and headquarters, the presentation of the women golfers fluctuated between the wholesome Nancy Lopez to sex symbol Jan Stephenson, posing controversially on a bed with her dress hitched up toward her navel in the LPGA's *Fairway* magazine. The athletic woman of the 1980s, the career-minded and assertive woman, had little sway with the general public, who still preferred the woman as wife, mother,and sex symbol.

The sometimes perceived unfeminine image with which the LPGA has struggled for so many decades dates at least as far back as Babe Didrikson Zaharias, who as a boyish-looking athlete in the 1932 Olympics was termed "hirsute" at the most polite. Later, Babe made a conscious effort to change her appearance, which superficially altered dramatically, but she remained essentially an athletic woman. In the 1940s, Ellen Griffin discovered the hostility toward women in physical education, while Betty Hicks, of the same era, said succinctly: "If there weren't any men around, you were a lesbian, and if there were too many, you were a whore."

Athleticism is rarely considered feminine, yet emphasizing athletic qualities can be an adaptation to pursuing a career in sport. Many women may grow up as tomboys, identify with fathers or brothers, or have looked to a male golfer as role model for lack of a female. The wearing of trousers or shorts, the striding out on a golf course, playing competitive sport all year, can create an athletic woman who appears intimidating. Women in sport can find it difficult to get validation from men, who do not see them as homemakers and the physical support of the family. Some men think that women playing sport want to be men.

Innuendoes, whispers, and accusations of lesbianism follow the tour, which sometimes results in fear, hostility, and ignorance. Some obvious reasons for the women sticking together include sheer comfort in friendship, not having to make an effort at the end of a tiring day, not having to play the sexual game with a man, or simply choosing to be with women. There is also an element of it being easier to opt for a relationship with another woman.

When I arrived on the LPGA tour in the late 1970s, I was as curious as anyone about the women's sexual proclivities. As time wore on, I realized that some prefer men, some women, and others are bisexual. There are those who are single, married, divorced, and some with children. Sexuality assumes more importance for some of the women than others, but the amount of energy devoted to it is secondary to the effort put into golf and competing.

I am questioned constantly about lesbianism on the tour. On one occasion when I was covering a tournament in Boston, I saw Hollis Stacy and greeted her in my normal way with a big hug, only to be asked the next day by an American journalist whom I did not know, how "my friend" was doing

Kathy Whitworth set the record for men and women golf professionals winning her 88th tournament in 1985. Photo courtesy: United States Golf Association.

in the tournament. The implication was obvious though misguided, and I began to realize that gestures I had never before considered, were taken by some people as proof of your chosen sexual preference.

It was at first unusual to me to be in a predominantly female environment, but then I found it very relaxing, a nice change to be relating to independent women, to my own sex, and it gave me a greater understanding and more empathy with women in general. No one grabbed me in the shower, made my life a misery, or tried to "convert" me. I have chosen my friends, and we remain as we are.

Although the public may be titillated by gossip about an LPGA lifestyle, sometimes creating an apprehension for those who consider joining the tour, the reality is of natural intimidation in joining a group rather than any sexual harassment. Nancy Lopez said: "The biggest personal pressure comes from wanting to be accepted, not from gays. If some younger players feel pressured, they had better stop and look at themselves because the problem is theirs. You have to be grown up on tour."

The trend to be more forthcoming about sexual preference is only rarely acceptable. In general, anyone straying from the path of marriage and children has been swimming against the tide. Opting for the mainstream of society has to be the easier avenue, and certainly one that most parents would prefer their child to choose, because of the hostility that homosexuality can generate and the difficulty as a parent of parrying the inevitable question about your offspring getting married.

Some women discuss lesbianism with their parents; others do not. No woman on tour would risk disclosing her lesbianism publicly, partly to avoid reflecting an unacceptable image for the LPGA and the tour but also because, in personal terms, it could cost her a sponsor or any potential future sponsorship.

One woman golfer is prepared to talk about being a lesbian but remains anonymous. Her experience is purely individual rather than typical of other women on tour.

"If you come from the South, having an affair with another woman is probably equated to sleeping with a big black during the Civil War.

"I remember when I was in college, a gay woman used to come and visit one of the people in the house where I lived, and I thought, 'Is this woman going to make a pass at me? What am I going to do?' I felt uncomfortable being around her. I didn't know how to react, and it was a big thing. It may be more open now, but it was, and is, regarded as aberrant and weird.

"Some players who are not gay jump on it, are scared of it, or are scared that they may be thought to be gay. Gay people have low credibility; they are thought to be irresponsible and promiscuous. No one wants to come out in print as queer or gay. They used to tar and feather people and run them out of town. It may be better now, but it is still socially unacceptable. The only way for me to be socially acceptable is to get married. I could marry a gay man, have my 'Mrs.,' and people would not think I was gay. It gives you a way to get by.

"It is a huge issue in the sports world. Athletes generally, are more sexual than other people because they are more in tune with their bodies, more aware of them. It becomes a matter of, which stigma do you want? Do you want the stigma of going out and finding a different guy each week and sleeping with him, or the stigma of developing a meaningful relationship with another woman? I don't know a man who would put up with my being away so much of the year, with my lifestyle, or would come and see me every weekend. And I'm not prepared to drop my career and go running home because he's lonely.

"You can't be non-sexual. We were not put on earth to be singular individuals, without sharing ourselves and our experiences with another person, male or female. So you have to find a balance between your career and your relationships, and you can only put so much time and energy into both. I'm sure there's some man out there for me who would put up with everything, but it's been easier for me to find a woman. Almost all of the women go through a relationship with a man.

"I have never closed myself off. There were many men I was dating over a period of about three years where the whole game was bed-oriented: 'Let's jump in the sack.' It's exciting to begin with, when you feel wanted, wonderful, and beautiful. It's a great thing for someone to desire you, but I want to be desired for myself, my personality, my intellect, and my own being; not because my legs open up. I got tired of that.

"I met a woman who was interested in me as a person. It was the most refreshing, exciting thing that had ever happened to me. From being a loose woman and feeling guilty about that, I added a little more guilt because it was a woman.

"I haven't a right to judge anyone's sexuality. What's the difference between what they do when they close the door at night? How does it affect the product they endorse or the golf they play?

"A couple of years ago another woman warned me that you never admit to being gay, and I thought: 'How depressing to have this huge part of your life that you can never discuss in an honest way.' It's a denial, and you have to make up stories. I feel sorry for people whose parents don't know and can't relate to it, or who have to have it hidden from them. My mother has an excellent attitude: she says it doesn't matter whom you love, but that you love, that you find love and share it.

"There are times when all I want to do is just shock someone. Supposing we all came out. Would that shock people, open their eyes, and make them look? Of course it wouldn't work, it's not worth it, and you would blow your career.

"On the tour there have been some who feel they need to be self-proclaimed crusaders against gays and warn everyone who comes on tour about them. But, gays don't make it unpleasant for you if you're not gay, and no one gets hold of you. If you have an experimental nature, you may try it; if you haven't or you have made firm decisions before you come out here, you won't. The youngest person to come on tour is 19 or 20, and by that stage having someone approach you isn't going to change your life unless you want it to.

"Some people think it's a phase you go through out here. 'It's easier to be involved with a woman than a man. It will pass. There's a man out there for you, for sure.' I've never put away the possibility that I'll get married and have kids, although I'm not 'gung ho' on children because the whole experience scares me. I love children, and maybe I'd like to adopt one and have the experience of raising a child. That could be just another cover to let me think that I'm all right, making it acceptable to be gay right now. Most people want to be normal and do the accepted thing.

"Getting involved with another player on tour is very hard. There's so much involvement in working on my game that I don't want a relationship with someone who plays golf. I don't want to compete in a relationship, but it might be less lonely."

Attracting its share of the lonely as well as the religious is the tour's Bible study group, the "God Squad." One member was quoted as saying: "We do what we can to neutralize lesbian notions." However, unlike lesbianism, Christianity is a self-professed proselytizing religion, and a percentage of the women are fundamentalists, whose born-again Christian missionary zeal has at times irritated those on tour who are outside it.

Jan Ferraris, not a member of the Bible study group and on the tour through 1984, said: "As self-sufficient, rational people with a strong faith in God, we are sometimes scared by this religious minority group, which makes a lot of members uncomfortable.

When we see people being almost manipulated, who are a little weak at the time, it's frightening.

"Sometimes I played with one or two of them, and there was a crusade to get me involved. Jimmy Jones got started when people signed over everything to him, and any form of fanatical religion is frightening. People at a low ebb are susceptible; so they join in, instead of doing something on their own. Cults are made up of weak people who are grabbed at weak moments.

"I was approached to come to the group's first seminar in 1981, by receiving six telegrams every two weeks. I object to that and to being told that if I haven't played well it's all right, Jesus loves me, and I should take him into my life."

The Christian movement on tour peaked in the 1980s, coinciding with the fervor of television evangelists, one of whom affected Beverly Klass sufficiently to convert her. Margie Davis, a fundamentalist, was the first group leader. She came from an organization called Sportsworld Ministries, founded in the 1960s. Known as "Godwoman", she was the organizer of the tour's religious group: "I provide leadership, and I see my role as a friend, a listening ear, a guide on how to grow as a Christian. I'm supporting what the LPGA is for. I want this sport to be really credible. The women are paying a great price to be out here, and if I can help a girl become more successful, that's what I want to do."

Margie left the tour after she married and had two children, and was replaced in 1984 by a likeable, down-to-earth woman called Cris Stevens, a born-again Christian from Alternative Ministries. Cris came with a degree in human services, a master's in counseling, and had worked for ten years on a federal women's program in areas of sexual discrimination, harassment, and disability management. She not only became a group leader, but included in the program, organized trips to communities in the southern Appalachians to build low-budget homes.

Betsy King joined the tour in 1977 and the Christian Fellowship in 1980—"My worst golf year." Betsy, who didn't win for six and one-half years, told herself, "I'm going to be the best non-winner on tour." But from 1983 she became one of its most successful players, heading the money list in 1984 and coming in second in 1986 and 1987. In 1989 she won the U.S. Women's Open and five other tournaments, and was leading money winner with a record in excess of half a million dollars. The 1990 season saw her successfully defend her Open title and win two more events, including the Nabisco Dinah Shore, a major. By 1995, Betsy was a member of the Hall of Fame.

In 1988, at the U.S. Women's Open, I talked to Betsy in the clubhouse at Five Farms Golf Club, Baltimore, during which time there was a huge storm with thunder and lightning.The lights went out, and candles were lit. I asked her to explain the practice of talking in tongues and at one point as the storm thundered round, she launched forth, talking what sounded to me like gibberish. Later she sent me a book on spiritual gifts.

"Talking in tongues is a controversial subject among Christians," she told me. "I don't think it relates to salvation. It is associated with the charismatic movement, and it is evidence of being baptized with the Holy Spirit. It is a miraculous gift, whereby you can stand up in church, speak in a language no one understands, and someone else stands up and interprets it as a message. It's a prayer language, where you don't understand what you're saying, but your spirit is praying. I've done a lot of study on it.

"After being a Christian for three years, when I didn't know what speaking in tongues was, I went to a prayer meeting with Barb Thomas and Kathy Baker. They opened the Bible and said, 'All you need to do to speak in tongues is ask the Lord, and he'll give you the ability.' They put their hands on me and prayed I would receive it, and I started talking in tongues. I believe it was genuine. A lot of people say you don't have as much power as a Christian without it, and some believe it is of the devil.

"There is a danger of getting hung up on the experience and of seeking that alone rather than being obedient to God. I feel funny doing it here, but I could do it right now. I don't know what I'm going to say." Betsy then spoke in a sing song, rhythmical, unintelligible to me, tongue.

"I can do it if I want to. Some people feel it's emotional, psychological, or selfish. Some think that you build yourself up and can serve others better. Sometimes it's falsified, but it can be genuine. Witch doctors do it, and earlier religions have done it. You can feel closer to God. It's almost like a shiver down my body, but it's just an experience, and you can't worship experience."

As the 1980s progressed, it reflected further shifts in the golfing world. In 1987, Ayako Okamoto became the first foreign woman professional ever to lead the money list and be Player of the Year. The growing influence of European golf as a world force was highlighted by professional Laura Davies from England, winning her first event in America, taking the 1987 U.S. Open title, in which she defeated JoAnne Carner and Ayako Okamoto in an 18-hole, three-way playoff. Since Laura was not yet a member of the LPGA tour when she won, it led to an historic amendment of the association's by-laws to exempt its Open champion from attending the 1987 qualifying school to achieve LPGA membership.

The following year, as Laura added two further LPGA victories and won tournaments in America, Europe, and Japan, another European professional, Liselotte Neumann from Sweden, startled the Americans by emulating Laura. She won the U.S. Open and was named Rookie of the Year.

By 1989, the LPGA teaching division had blossomed to nearly 500 women, while the tour, worth $13 million for 36 tournaments, operated three qualifying schools in the competitive scramble for membership. The women of the LPGA tour were a pampered elite, recognized for their excellence. They acquired an image consultant, a traveling gymnasium, and a free child care center. They were given lists of local facilities, discounted hotel rates and courtesy cars, and hundreds of volunteers each week catered to their needs.

Marketing man William Blue succeeded John Laupheimer at the end of 1988. Kathy Whitworth, 30 years after joining the LPGA tour, became its president in 1989 for the fourth time, following a gap of 18 years. Bill Blue was an unhappy experience for the LPGA: "We hired a firm of recruitment consultants, thinking that this was the right way to find a new commissioner," Kathy Whitworth said. "I felt it was all right to hire a marketing man but not to put him in charge of the association. It proved a very bad mistake. It was the most depressing and frustrating year I ever had.

Jan Stephenson's sometimes suggestive poses on posters and in the LPGA's "Fairway" magazine added glamour and controversy to the tour.

"Judy Dickinson as vice-president, was restructuring the administration to include an executive committee with six players on the board, changing it from four players, five independent members, and players who had no power to fire or hire. In 1990, it was very difficult when the chairman of the board and some others on it appeared to be in Blue's corner and did not support the players. It was the 'good-old-boy' syndrome, implying 'These girls don't know anything about the business world.'

"I've been through a lot of changes, but I was never more scared of the rumors running rampant. The sponsors were ready to jump ship. We told them we understood and that we were going to make changes. Luckily they stayed with us."

From 1986, Kathy Whitworth had to deal with her own tough personal problems which lasted over the next few years. Yet, this remarkable woman at the helm at the end of the 1980s was a wonderful reminder that the women of the LPGA could and did survive, gloriously.

Amy Alcott

Amy Alcott takes herself seriously in an endearing way, and sometimes when she talks, she sounds like a romantic novelist: "When I was 18, my mother put me on a plane to Miami to the qualifying school, and with a tear in her eye said, 'I've taught you everything I can teach you. Off you go.'"

You warm to Amy, and there are times when she seems like a big kid, hamming it up for the audience, but underneath is a real professional. At a tournament she is a golf writer's dream, a natural communicator who partakes in excellent press conferences. She has a sense of drama, giving the emotional factor as well as delightful asides—such as the trials of being a short-order cook in the Hollywood Butterfly Bakery, where she invented the "Amy Alcott" sandwich. Since 1975, she has attracted her own fan club called "Amy Alcott's Allies," and fans appear wearing T-shirts which proclaim "The Kid Has Class."

At first acquaintance, Amy suggested I should talk to her agent before I interviewed her for a book. Later, she was keen to be a part of it, and we struck up a lasting friendship.

Amy speaks fairly slowly, in tune with her general rhythm and pace. On the golf course, you feel that although she has a quick swing, her walk is purposeful, and she plays at a measured pace that continues throughout the rest of her life.

Something of a prodigy at 19, when she turned professional in 1975, she promptly created a record by winning the third tournament she entered. She went on to achieve victory in 15 out of 17 seasons into the 1990s. Five major victories included a U.S. Open win by nine shots in 1980, which in the steamy conditions of Nashville, Tennessee, was astonishing. Her sixth season took her past the $1 million mark in career earnings, and she became one of the whiz kids of the tour as she continued to play winning golf.

After her major victory in the 1991 Nabisco Dinah Shore, Amy needed one more victory to enter the Hall of Fame, which has proved elusive through 1995. The incessant questioning by the media has been a tough burden to carry. Her mother died at the end of the 1980s, her father some years earlier, and Amy needed time to come to terms with her loss, and with the effort required for another victory after 17 years on tour.

"Losing both parents is very hard. You have to make adjustments in your life and face your own mortality. It is also a slight letdown when you

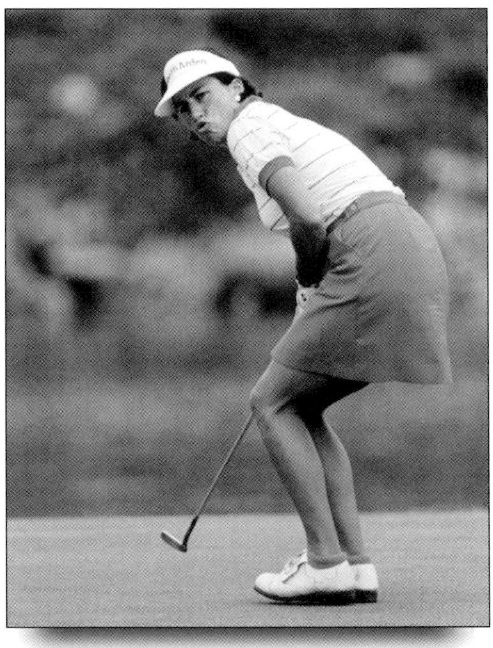

Amy Alcott, former U.S. Junior and U.S. Women's Amateur champion, won the third tournament she entered after joining the tour in 1975. Later, she won at least one event in 15 of her first 17 seasons. Photo ©Phil Sheldon.

realize that the emphasis in your career has shifted from being totally centered on golf, to one in which golf is merely an important part of your life. It may seem fractional, but it is a big difference when you no longer are eating it, breathing it, and sleeping it. Nor is it true to say I have the same fire and motivation I had at 20.

"I have to strive for this final accomplishment, one I know will happen, but one more tournament win will not prove anything to me. The pressure is always with me because I can't get up in the morning without someone asking me about it. I feel I deserve to be in the Hall of Fame, and it will be a real relief when it happens."

Involving herself in different projects, Amy has included her own annual tournament in aid of multiple sclerosis, serving on the board of directors of the LPGA, on the President's Council against Drug Abuse, the board of the Women's Sports Foundation, and as a playing editor of Golf Digest.

Amy was born on George Washington's birthday, February 22, and quips: "I've told a few lies in my life." She is of Jewish parentage and her father, who died in 1980, was a dentist. Her parents divorced when she was 16 years old, and her mother later became successful in the real estate business.

She grew up in Santa Monica, where the family moved when she was six months; she has a brother seven years older and a sister four years older. Her family lifestyle reflected a middle to upper income background: "Other people regarded us as the nouveau riche of Southern California, but my parents wanted to give us all the benefits for which they had worked. I didn't grow up like a rich kid, but we were comfortable and it was a great existence. I loved all sports and the athletic outdoor life. Although my parents were not golfers, my mother sent me off to play golf as a junior and told me she didn't care whether I shot 68 or 108. She would still love me. She was very much a Jewish mother in her own way.

"I was not very religious, but I went to Sunday School for a year with my sister. I have tremendous respect for my religion, and my parents taught me to be proud of it. I have my own idea of being a good Jew. I've read a lot about the culture and what it means. Being brought up in a Jewish home, you

The highlight of Amy's career was winning the 1980 U.S. Open by nine shots, but her greatest achievement would be entering the LPGA Hall of Fame. Photo courtesy: Katherine Murphy.

are instilled with the drive to succeed, to excel, to be one step better. As role models, there are not many Jewish athletes, but there are plenty of stereotypes of the Jewish woman who is busy trying to find a doctor and get married.

"I stayed with my mother when my parents split up, and although I'd sensed that it was coming and felt it was right for both parents, it did affect me. I was always family-oriented, and often I would go somewhere and wish I had my dad with me. I continued to see him, and we were close until he died.

"Growing up, I never had a lot of friends. I felt like an outcast and not like all the girls at school, who made fun of me. I was a loner, very much misunderstood. I had a seriousness about me that people considered strange.

"I was a tomboy, athletic, and the best girl in school at sports. I had tremendous desire from within to do well. I was born to be a fighter and to be competitive, which I don't think you learn—it is born in people who are successful.

"I read books on golf and idolized Jim Thorpe and Burt Lancaster. I started playing golf in the backyard at seven and took lessons at Walter

Keller's indoor school in West Los Angeles two years later. The family didn't belong to the country club, and it was difficult for juniors to play, so I used Walter's net and his electric putting machine. He taught me the basics and has been my pro ever since. He became a second father to me.

"When I was 10, I lied and said I was 14 so that I could get on the golf course. From that time I played junior tournaments and accumulated 150 trophies. My competitive desire increased, and I was playing against girls such as Hollis Stacy, Debbie Massey, and Nancy Lopez.

"I never thought I wanted to be a professional, but I dedicated myself to the sport, and it happened. I was always a very organized person, a perfectionist, who became frustrated when I couldn't do something right. In recent years I've found that it can drill a hole in your stomach, since things are never going to be perfect. Even if I let myself go, I like to be in control.

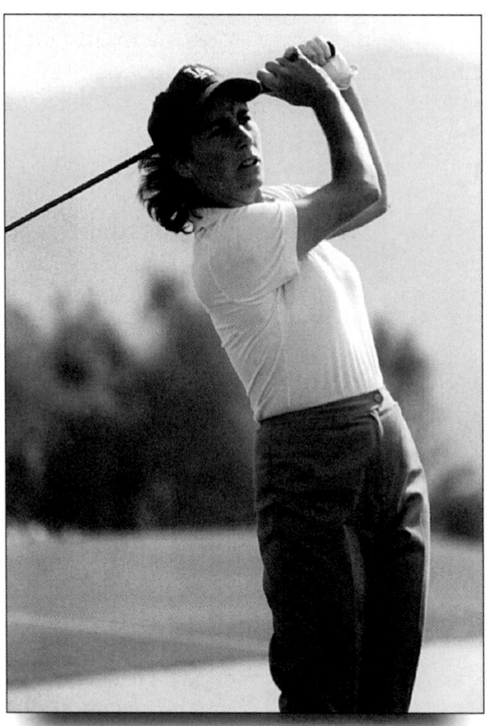

After her major victory in the 1991 Nabisco Dinah Shore, Amy needs just one more tournament win to enter the Hall of Fame, which has proved elusive through 1995. Photo credit: Katherine Murphy.

"At 17, I won the U.S. Junior Championship and did well in the U.S. Amateur Championship. I won three junior tournaments in Los Angeles and was considering whether I wanted to play college golf or become a professional and play against the big girls. I tested myself in 1974 by entering two professional tournaments as an amateur. At the second one in Sacramento, I led the field the first day, and in both of them I tied for low amateur, so I knew that I could play with the big girls, and I felt, 'Let's go get them.' I went to the qualifying school in Miami when I was 18, and I barely qualified, making it by one stroke.

"In 1975, three weeks after I was on tour, I won the Orange Blossom Classic. I had an outstanding rookie year, setting a record by winning $26,798. It bothered me that I never got the publicity I thought I deserved, but realistically women's golf was nothing at that time. Purses averaged $30,000–$40,000. The old guard dominated the tour, and I came along as a 19 year old kid, gave it all I had, made a 20-footer on the last green to win, edging out Sandra Post. They thought it was a fluke, but I continued to prove to them and to myself every week that I could play.

"I never thought about winning, I just knew I could. I feel I live to win, and there's nothing like the thrill of it. You go out and beat everyone, and you feel good inside. There's a real sense of accomplishment, a lot of happiness and reward for all the hard work, but you know you can always be better, and you can never conquer the game.

"The pressure is exciting, and I like it because I'm a masochist. Everyone who plays the game is part masochist. She wouldn't play unless she wanted to inflict a little pain on herself. I like challenges, I live for them, and I don't know if I'll ever be satisfied. The tournament is a stage, and the golf course an arena, where you bring the best athletes to compete. One person wants to make enough to pay the hotel bill, someone else wants to make the cut, another wants to reach the playoff, and Amy Alcott wants to win.

"The attention you get is important because everyone needs to be appreciated. I used to play the game to be recognized, but I don't care so much about it now. Not many people really know about the women's pro golf tour, and in the overall realm of life, it's not that important. Sometimes I think I'm more important than I really am, but I know I'm a great player because I've proved it, and I don't need someone to keep telling me all the time.

"When I came on tour, a lot of people thought I was cocky. I would sometimes say something to the press to make a good story, without realizing I had to live with my peers. I felt I was different and lived on another planet, and even now I don't have a lot of friends on tour. I'm wrapped up in being me, and I find it hard to open up and make friends; so people give up on me before I feel comfortable with them.

"I feel a part of the tour only in the sense that everyone plays golf, but I don't feel a sense of belonging. The other people are my competitors, and I've never lost sight of that. I am friendly, but I can't maintain close relationships because on the first tee, I go to work. I need to be cocky and to be a loner to be a winner, and the successful people are the ones who handle that.

"I always wanted to become a great golfer, and I wasn't interested in settling down and having a family. Golf has been so much of my life that sometimes I feel I'm in a cage, and I have sat in so many hotel rooms and wondered about what I am doing.

"Money is important because it brings privacy and the freedom to do things for myself and for other people. It gave me a nice house, nice car, investments, and the lifestyle of a top player. When I came on tour, I had a two-year deal with 15 local sponsors who put up $1,000 each. I hated owing anyone anything, and I paid them back each year with a percentage. I have been on my own ever since. I believe in strong, independent women who know themselves and their own minds. I believe in equal pay, equal opportunities, and I don't like discrimination. My freedom to do what I want means everything to me.

"The highlight of my golfing career was winning the 1980 U.S. Open at Richland Country Club, Nashville, by nine shots. Ever since I was little, I wanted that title, and it became a fixation. The heat and humidity that week in Nashville was intense and obviously was going to be a factor. Everyone was moaning about it, but I took it in my stride. I was in a trance. I played hole by hole, counted them down, forgot the heat, and the golf flowed. I wanted it that much more than anyone else, and I'm hard to beat when I'm in a trance.

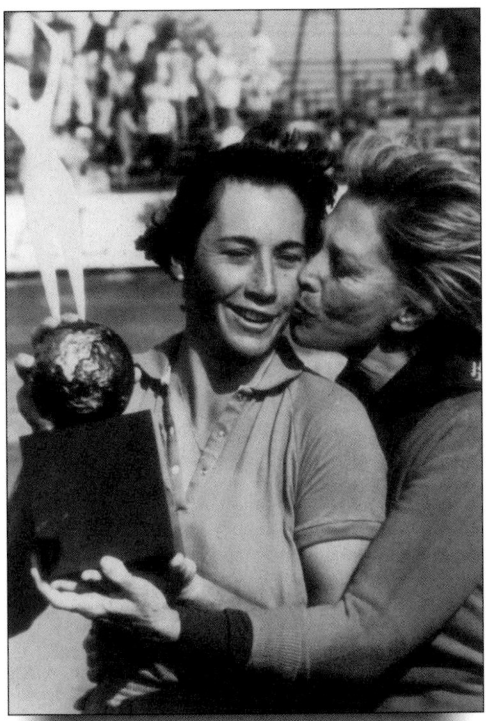

Amy Alcott is congratulated by Dinah Shore after becoming the 1983 Nabisco Dinah Shore Champion. She won the event two more times, in 1988 and 1991.

"Normally in a tournament you jockey for position until the last day, when you are psyched up and you realize that everyone is going to make mistakes and whoever makes the fewest mistakes is going to win. In that Open, everyone said it looked as though my name was on the trophy after the opening round.

"Everything was under control, and I maintained it by not eating heavy meals, by closing the curtains and lying down in my room, and by sleeping a lot. I got incredibly tired from the effort of playing and from the heat, but the momentum was with me. The course was tight and needed left-to-right shots, positive, aggressive shots, which suited my game. The greens were fast and undulating, but I had a good touch and didn't three putt all week.

Every once in a while I thought, 'Oh my God, this is the U.S. Open,' but I never really felt the pressure, and I feel I have what it takes to win more Opens. At the end, I knew finally it was over and I'd won, but I was so spaced out I hardly realized it was by nine shots.

"After that, when people announced me as U.S. Open Champion on the first tee, my drive would automatically go 10 yards further. No one can ever take it away, and what I did in winning was greatness. That gives me pride because it is one thing to want it and another to do it. That one achievement is worth a lifetime of working for it."

LPGA Victories: 1975 Orange Blossom Classic. **1976** LPGA Classic, Colgate Far East Open. **1977** Houston Exchange Clubs Classic. **1978** American Defender Classic. **1979** Elizabeth Arden Classic, Peter Jackson Classic, United Virginia Bank Classic, Mizuno Japan Classic. **1980** American Defender/WRAL Classic, Mayflower Classic, U.S. Women's Open, Inamori Classic. **1981** Bent Tree Ladies Classic, Lady Michelob. **1982** Women's Kemper Open. **1983** Nabisco Dinah Shore Invitational. **1984** United Virginia Bank Classic, Lady Keystone Open, Portland Ping Championship, San Jose Classic. **1985** Circle K Tucson Open, Moss Creek Women's Invitational, Nestle World Championship of Women's Golf. **1986** Mazda Hall of Fame Championship, LPGA National Pro-Am. **1988** Nabisco Dinah Shore. **1989** Boston Five Classic. **1991** Nabisco Dinah Shore.

Unofficial Victories: 1986 Mazda Champions (with Bob Charles).

Amy Alcott's LPGA Record

Year	No. of Events	Best Finish	Money	Rank	Scoring Average
1975	21	1	$26,798	15	73.52
1976	28	1	71,122	7	73.54
1977	28	1	47,637	14	73.57
1978	29	1	75,516	9	73.06
1979	26	1	144,838	3	72.43
1980	28	1	219,887	3	71.51
1981	26	1	149,096	7	72.33
1982	26	1	169,581	6	72.27
1983	25	1	153,721	8	73.05
1984	24	1	220,412	5	72.34
1985	26	1	283,111	4	71.78
1986	23	1	244,410	4	71.99
1987	26	2	125,831	17	72.57
1988	26	1	292,349	7	71.71
1989	25	1	168,089	18	72.16
1990	23	2	99,208	42	73.12
1991	23	1	258,270	13	72.43
1992	22	T8	100,064	55	72.70
1993	22	T6	60,518	76	72.91
1994	22	4	154,183	35	72.13
1995	19	T5	70,883	71	72.86

Laura Baugh

When Laura arrived on the LPGA tour in the 1970s, she was the first real glamour girl since the Bauer sisters back in the 1950s. Although the earlier women made good money, the tiny, blonde, blue-eyed Laura was able to capitalize on her looks with far higher financial reward. It was at a time when glamour could be exploited since the women were starting to be seen on television, and Laura's dainty image was a real bonus. Mark McCormack's IMG marketed her from the age of 17½, even though she was not eligible to join the professional tour until her 18th birthday. She took professional status and was sent on a tour to Japan. Later followed lucrative commercial endorsements that included calendars, modeling and one-day appearances for company days.

Laura Baugh's glamorous personality belies the protected, moral woman underneath. Following a disastrous three week marriage and divorce, she wed her original sweetheart, South African golfer Bobby Cole, and they had a daughter, Chelsea, born in 1982. Four years later they were divorced, but Laura still spoke warmly of her former husband, whom she continued to see. After two years apart, they remarried and Laura gave birth to three more children in four years: Eric was born in June 1988, Haley in April 1990, and Robert in March, 1992. In 1993 her fifth child, Michael, was born, and in April 1995, Evita Beau completed the half dozen. Five weeks later, Laura was back on tour and finished 44th—her urge for children and golf apparently insatiable. Her golfing ability undiminished, she said: "I am hitting the ball farther and playing better than ever."

The strain, however, of competing on such a tough tour in conjunction with the steady production of children and caring for all of them, meant that by 1992 Laura dropped out of the top 90. Entry to tournaments could be uncertain, or she would need to rely on sponsors' invitations, which was not to Laura's liking. She returned to the tour's qualifying school after 19 years to try to regain her exempt status.

"It is a hard thing to do at 18, but it is a lot harder at 37, especially when there are only 18 exempt places and 125 players. It was an ugly,

At 18, Laura Baugh joined the LPGA in 1973, bringing her glamorous personality to the tour. She also brought a strong golf game with her and was named "Rookie of the Year." Photo Courtesy: Wilson Sporting Goods Co.

nerve-wracking experience." Laura gained her exemption, finishing in seventh place. Although the LPGA allows players a medical extension for keeping their tour card, there is no specific maternity clause, and as a result many young mothers drop off the tour. It is a glaring gap in the 1990s, of particular concern to Laura.

"It is embarrassing that a women's tour does not have a maternity clause. If you stay home and play in ten tournaments or fewer, you can claim a medical extension, treating pregnancy as an illness when it is something natural. The LPGA should study the maternity clauses of top companies and work out a fair policy. Child day care at our tournaments every week is really good, but we need to straighten out maternity leave to keep the moms on tour."

As a child, Laura was pushed by an ambitious, strong father, who urged her to play golf at two. She achieved an excellent amateur record, including five Pee Wee titles, a 1970 Junior world title, the 1971 U.S. Amateur Championship, and membership on the 1972 Curtis Cup team. Laura has carried an irksome tag of the glamour girl who has not won a tournament; yet she is a fine player who works hard at her game with particular emphasis on chipping and putting. In the back of her mind she feels her petite frame may mean she tends to be more tired over the closing holes, resulting in loss of concentration.

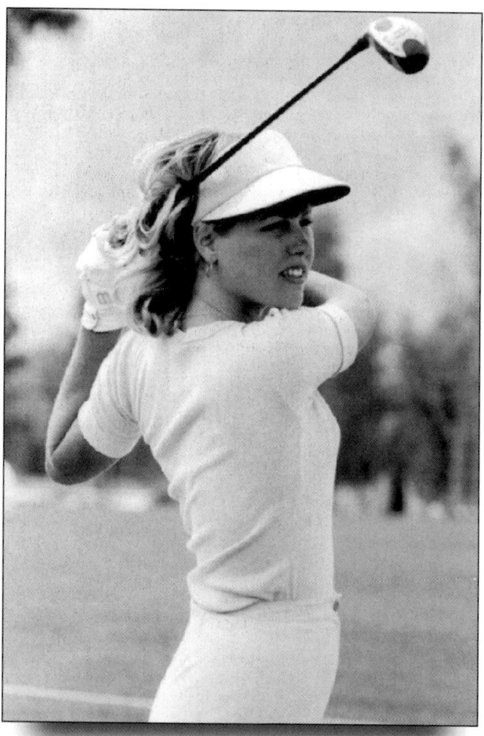

Laura's popularity and talent helped boost the LPGA's purses during the 70s and 80s. Photo Courtesy: Katherine Murphy.

She tied for second in her first tournament on the LPGA tour, repeated that placing, and was Rookie of the Year 1973. Since then, she has frustratingly achieved eight more second place finishes. Having joined the tour in the early 1970s, Laura has absorbed its culture and history and revels in the fact that she knew and played with some of the greats from the past: "I played with Mickey Wright when she won the Colgate Dinah Shore in 1973, and I just wish some of the young players now could have seen her swing—she was so far ahead of her time. She had a very controlled game and only used her power when she needed it. Betsy Rawls, Patty Berg, and Carol Mann were all playing when I turned professional, and Judy Rankin was one of the best ball strikers of all time. I'm just happy to have played through those years."

Laura is an appealing woman who appears fragile but is obviously strong. There is a feeling of insecurity about her, coupled with a confidence of manner from so many years of being in the limelight. We met over the years, more in passing than in any sense of being friends, and I know and like her husband. Because there were so many demands on her, it could be difficult to set up appointments, but whenever we talked she was warm, frank, and forthright and was happy to give me the time.

Laura was born in Florida and has brothers three and seven years older. Her father, a lawyer, was a pentathlete in the 1948 Olympics, and the family was together in Florida until Laura was ten, when her parents divorced, and she and her mother went to live in California.

"I didn't realize how drastic it was to get divorced. Looking back, it has resulted in my being warped in a few ways so that I had to be taught to trust and taught to love. I was always a bit skeptical, too.

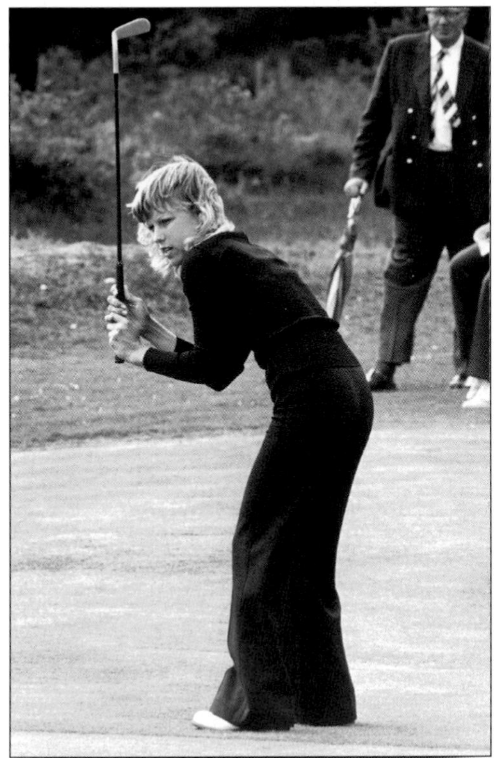

Laura Baugh placed in the top 90 until 1987, successfully combining family and career. She was mother to six children born from 1982 to 1995. Photo: Peter Dazeley.

"I was always close to my dad, but we drifted apart, and then I became close to my mom. Later, my dad told me how much the separation affected him, as we had been so close. He remarried, but it didn't last long, while my mother never dated or remarried.

"My dad was very competitive and played golf, and he started me playing at two. I won a tournament when I was three, but I was pushed and pushed by him, and I got sick of it. There were times when I had a lot of fun, but when I was so young, I would rather have been a bit more of a kid and gone to the movies.

"In California, my mom and I didn't have much money. I tried playing golf on public courses, got kicked off, but I liked the challenge. I really enjoyed golf when I started to play with high school and college boys. I loved the competition. I excelled at golf and won the majority of tournaments I played.

"Money was so short that I lived off of child support, but those years were probably the happiest time in my life. Money is very nice, and I love the things it can buy. It gives you security, and it's fun. I like nice restaurants and clothes, but I had a lot of fun eating hamburgers and living off a couple of dollars.

"I saved some money at 14 and went to the U.S. Open, where I missed the cut by one shot. I have always played in it ever since. When I was 16 in 1971, I became the youngest ever to win the U.S. Women's Amateur Championship. That same year I went to Britain to play its Amateur Championship. What a humbling experience it was! I thought I was hot stuff, but Mickey Walker killed me in the quarter finals, beating me 6 and 5. She was tremendous.

"Having won the U.S. Amateur Championship, the next step was to turn professional. I took the opportunity to do so at 17 1/2 when IMG offered me exhibitions in Japan. The money was attractive, and it was professional golf. Six months later at 18, I went to qualifying school and was runner-up.

"I wasn't intimidated when I came out on tour. I was supposed to be good, and I led the first two rounds of my first tournament, finishing tied for second. I got an enormous amount of publicity because I was the image the tour wanted to project. It worried me when people said: 'She makes money because she's attractive, and she's not a good player, not one of the top ten.' The top women golfers are on the LPGA tour, and if that's where you are, you are good.

"I probably haven't achieved what I could have, and it's frustrating not to win. I wish I had won some tournaments; I do expect to win, but I don't live and die on winning, which doesn't mean I try any less.

"Being a woman golfer is a weird life, rough, crazy, and like a drug. It is rougher on women than men. I love to cook, and I don't like eating out all the time. I like to travel but not being in a different town each week. I don't mind the girls out here. I don't have any enemies,and some are friends. I have had more men friends than women, but if I met a man on the golf course I wouldn't go out with him. My social life usually consisted of room service and watching TV.

"I have been very lucky and got a lot of benefit from all the publicity I have had. I don't know if the tour got as many benefits as I did. The publicity came at the right time for promoting the tour, and since I didn't have any money, it was wonderful for me. I felt fortunate to have the chance to do it, and I worked really hard. You can get someone at 17 to do a lot of work because she has the energy, no responsibility, and it is exciting."

Laura's life and responsibilities changed in 1980. Not until she was 20 did she go on her first date, and the young man was Bobby Cole, a South African golfer who had a brilliant amateur career. He turned professional in 1967, playing the U.S. PGA tour, where his most successful years were 1974, when he won almost $60,000, and 1986, when he made $88,472.

Laura met Bobby in 1975, dated him, and expected that they would marry. When this did not happen, she rushed off at the beginning of 1980 and married club professional Wayne Dent, the second man she had ever dated. The marriage lasted a disastrous three weeks, and they divorced by the end of that year. A day after the divorce came through, Laura and Bobby Cole married in South Africa, just a week after Bobby won the South African Open. They had a quiet, spontaneous wedding in a Methodist Church in Cape Town.

They seemed the ideal couple and were locked into golf and an outwardly demonstrative, loving relationship. After Laura had a miscarriage, their daughter Chelsea was born in 1982, and the little nuclear family appeared devoted. They traveled on both tours, often all together, and doted on Chelsea.

Some cracks began to appear, and in 1985 they were divorced, Laura receiving custody of their daughter. Having traveled with Laura on tour before her daughter married, Laura's mother now came to help care for Chelsea. Laura continued to be fond of Bobby: "I'm very proud of Bobby, of his golf game, and I think he's a very nice man. Chelsea and I see as much of him as possible. I feel that both of us playing professional golf was a problem. For a couple of years Bobby lost his card, which was important to him, and it is possible that he felt because of me and my golf, he hadn't succeeded in his golf. That was a big responsibility on my mind. I have some wonderful memories, but I cried a lot when we split up. I know it can be tough without a father, but I also know you can manage, even without great financial assets.

"I miss Chelsea all the time when I'm not with her, and she cries when I leave to play golf, but it's probably good for her to have a break from me during the day. Children are fascinating at any age; everything is new, exciting, and fun. My mother helps me, and I have back-up systems, and financially I provide all the support. I wish I had more energy and time for my golf, for Chelsea, and everything, but definitely Chelsea.

Laura's good looks and winning ways translated into lucrative endorsement contracts. She often earned $10,000 a day for modeling clothes or appearing in calendars. Photo Courtesy: Katherine Murphy.

"I don't date, and I don't have boyfriends. I think men are wonderful, and it's not that I wouldn't like to have relationships, marry, and have a whole bunch of kids. But, I have Chelsea and her father to consider. I have the time I spend with her, plus playing golf and working out. That's my life, and I love it.

"After I had Chelsea I lost about ten pounds, and I went down to 105. I'm 5 feet, 5 inches, and people kept asking me what was wrong and why I was so skinny. I may be thin, but I like it. Oddly enough, in spite of my size, I play long courses really well. I have a good short game, I chip well, and I'm a streak putter. I practice hard, so that in 30 minutes I do what most people do in one or two hours.

"I've been out here a long time, and I'm still relatively young. I still do calendars, and I'm proud of them. One of the assets of being thin is that you look good in a bikini and in clothes. I don't have that much time; so I have to be expensive. I can earn $10,000 a day, according to the time I spend, and I always make up to half a million dollars a year, off the golf course.

"I love quality and expensive things, and it costs me a lot to live in a very nice lifestyle. When you've driven a Jaguar and a Porsche, it's hard to go back to ordinary cars. Property is the greatest buy in the world. I love buying homes and decorating them. I have four homes. My brother lives in one in Florida, I lease one in Palm Springs, I want to sell the one at La Quinta, where Bobby and I lived, although I tried to give it to him.

"Winning and being in the hunt have always been important to me. I do wonder whether people feel I should have won. I don't know why I haven't, but I know it's been hard for me so many times. Maybe I'm just supposed to finish second a lot. The most important things to me now are my family and our health, so I don't really worry any more about not winning.

"I would love to be a married woman. I would like a man to really love me, and I'd love to take care of a man. I don't mean financially; I've done all that. I would like to cook for a man, have romantic candlelit dinners, have his children, and I would also like to play golf if the family could do without me for a while."

Laura and Bobby's remarriage took place on April 11, 1987: "Bobby is still a nice man, and things that previously had seemed important were not any longer. I'm a perfectionist, and I expect a lot, but with maturity I realize I'm very lucky to be Bobby's wife, and he's a wonderful man. It's important to have someone you like and love, and it is important for children that you keep together. I dislike some of the immoral things I see around me, and I feel like shaking people and telling them that kids are important.

"Bobby and I set up a new home together in Florida, and for the first time in 20 years my whole family was near me. I need to be a mom; I do it better than I play golf. I have to be the best mom, even if that means playing mediocre golf. I played when I was seven months pregnant and missed the cut. I love being pregnant, and I would like six children, but I don't know if that will work out.

"There are so many things I would like to do in golf with teaching, clothing, and television commentating. I would love to teach women to play golf because I'm a small person and could really help the average woman. It frustrates me so much when we are compared to men, who are always stronger. Women should stand up for each other. We don't want male hormones. We are the best women golfers in the world and should be very proud of that. Hitting it like a woman is great, so is capitalizing on the sexy young players and the moms on tour.

"My dedication to golf is not complete because I have my family. I would love to have won a lot of tournaments, but I would much rather have grandkids coming through the door."

Laura Baugh's LPGA Record

Year	No. of Events	Best Finish	Money	Rank	Scoring Average
1973	16	T2	$14,657	35	74.02
1974	29	2	35,563	12	74.03
1975	24	T4	16,902	25	74.44
1976	24	T2	26,654	19	74.13
1977	27	2	46,373	16	73.03
1978	27	4	37,469	25	73.76
1979	24	T2	44,361	23	73.73
1980	24	T8	21,379	59	74.51
1981	15	T3	21,034	62	74.12
1982	DNP				
1983	13	2	34,029	49	74.21
1984	19	T2	47,232	47	73.06
1985	22	T3	49,301	46	73.56
1986	16	2	50,412	51	73.81
1987	15	T33	8,158	112	75.26
1988	1	NA	NA	NA	77.50
1989	14	4	29,413	88	73.80
1990	15	T6	50,644	77	72.60
1991	16	3	70,920	67	73.29
1992	17	T5	33,790	107	73.84
1993	9	T38	3,482	165	75.17
1994	17	T9	17,796	132	74.90
1995	5	T18	6,037	174	74.15

Silvia Bertolaccini

Silvia Bertolaccini is a delightful, statuesque woman from Argentina, who came to the LPGA tour almost unable to speak English. "A lot of the time I cried because it was so difficult. There were times when I thought if something happened to me and I died, no one would ever find me." With courage and determination, she overcame the problem of being so far away from home without the security she had known in her close, affluent family. She made her mark in a foreign country which, after 12 years, she adopted by becoming an American citizen.

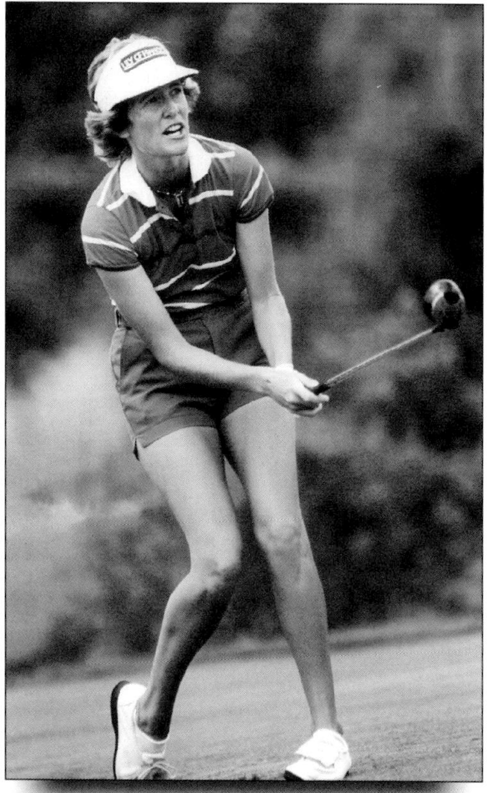

Coming to America to play golf was not easy for Silvia Bertolaccini, she spoke no English and had to fend for herself. Today, she is an American citizen. Photo ©Phil Sheldon.

She is charming and intelligent, outspoken but thoughtful, and I enjoy seeing Silvia although I am not a close friend. She can be humorous in the English language, and I am sure has an excellent sense of humor in her native tongue. In Florida, I saw her achieve her fourth LPGA victory, which gave her not only a great deal of pleasure but the impetus to continue a career—a goal not always easy to sustain. She succeeded in becoming financially independent in the United States. Worried about life after golf, she made a relatively smooth transition into business alongside fellow professional, Jane Blalock, who set up her own company to provide golf and tennis marketing strategies for the corporate world. She then branched out on her own.

Silvia was born in the small town of Rafaela, northwest of Buenos Aires. Her father is a doctor, and she has a brother two years older and a sister one year older. Both her parents play golf, and her father, a seven-handicap golfer, taught her the game and took her to local tournaments.

She won her first tournament at 12 and progressed by winning the amateur championships of Argentina and Colombia and performing well in the World Cup and international team championships. At 19, she went to college in Buenos Aires for a year, studying economics, but she quit because in Argentina "women didn't need to go to college."

"I belonged to a course where Roberto de Vicenzo was a member, and I played a few rounds with him. He told me not to get mad when I missed a shot, and I learned a lot from watching him.

"My dream was to play in the United States, having read the magazines and seen pictures of the courses. When I was 24 and staying with friends in

Colombia, I met a man from Houston called Charlie Smith. He offered to sponsor me on the LPGA tour. It sounded crazy, but I said, 'Why not?' He said, 'Do you speak English?' And I said, 'No.' He then asked, 'Do you drive a car?' And I answered, 'Yes.' He told me I could learn English. My parents supported the idea of my turning professional, but some people thought I was crazy. There were one or two women in tennis, but otherwise not any professional sportswomen from Argentina.

"I went to the LPGA qualifying school in July 1974 and missed by two shots. I returned to Colombia to practice golf and learn some English, but I couldn't say much. In January 1975, I finished second at the qualifying school and found myself on the tour. I didn't really identify with the other women since my heroes had been Jack Nicklaus, and Roberto de Vicenzo, but I was happy to be out there.

"It was very hard not speaking the language, and for about six months I felt awful. Everyone helped me with plane reservations and getting around, but I had to get up in the morning, have breakfast alone, and I had to eat alone in the evenings. Sometimes I would go with other people, but I couldn't join in the conversations; it was hard. After a while I started to stay in private housing, which meant I had company, and it helped me learn English. I watched TV, read magazines, and after about two years I began to feel that I belonged.

"I could play a Pro-Am and actually talk to my partners. Before that, I just had to smile and smile. After I finished my round, I would always go out and watch the best players to learn from them, and as my English improved, I relaxed and my golf game got better.

"My first victory in the 1977 Colgate Far East Open was very exciting. Winning kept me going, although I have always known my limitations and wouldn't have said I could be number one. Making money also keeps you going, and it is important. After two years in the U.S., I was supporting myself. It means a lot to me to have my own house and car, but the feeling of doing well and being at peace with myself is even more important.

Silvia's first victory in 1977 was at the Colgate Far East Open. She recorded three more wins before retiring in early 1990. Photo courtesy: LPGA.

"My motivation was there from always competing, but in my role as an independent woman it has been hard to go home. It is incredible how sport and sportswomen are so accepted in the United States, whereas at home, my sister and a lot of my friends are married with children. I feel rather apart from them. Golf has made very little impact in South America, and not many people have understood my life on tour. They think it's just fun, not work, hitting balls 10 hours a day, and calling it a job. They feel you hardly deserve what you get, but that doesn't matter to me. I have lived in another world, so different that it makes it hard to communicate with my old friends, but I have been happy and proud of being a member of the LPGA. I'm interested in its future, and I would not want to have done anything else."

By 1984, Silvia had not won for five years and was feeling despondent until her victory at the first tournament of the season: "I had a good year, and I thought things would be better after that victory. Instead, I fell back into a slump." By 1987, she was working with teacher Gardner Dickinson and more hopeful, but still wary.

"I was curious to see how much the damage of playing poorly for such a length of time would affect me. You go through all the different stages of gaining confidence, but still having doubts—of saying I'm not going to be a leading money winner, but I can make a living. You ask yourself whether you can be in the top 20, and if not, why are you out here? I am happy to have won four tournaments, although I wish it had been more, but at least I got to know what it's about, and I am pleased to have made a good living.

"When you grow older, you are not as patient with yourself; you tend to think you are too old and should look for something else. You want to hang on, play a few tournaments, and try to find a job that will fit in with your knowledge. I knew that I liked finance, numbers, and business, but was not sure what to do.

"Deep inside I wanted to remain on tour since I still had the desire to play well. You create a way of life, and after 15 years, my support group was the tour and my friends. I left in 1989 and for about a year I wondered what I would do if I started hitting the ball better. It took me that time to realize I wasn't going back, that there was a new breed of younger players, and that golf was something I did in the past. Now my mind is so far away; I don't even dream of competing.

"Joining Jane [Blalock] in a business which allowed me to use my knowledge acquired in golf was a perfect combination. I always enjoyed the corporate aspect, and it was good to realize I could do something other than play golf."

In December 1994, Silvia moved on to become Tournament Director with responsibility for staging, marketing and selling the LPGA's first Friendly's Classic in Agawam, Mass. "I am pleased to be out again involved with the tour, " she said. "There are a lot of new faces, but I am impressed by a very nice group of women, who are extremely good golfers and who communicate well with the public. They are down to earth, friendly, and corporate America should be there chipping in to support such marketable women."

In 1987 on Friday, 13th March, Silvia became an American citizen, and was proud of it: "I was brand new like a baby, a new-born American. I never thought I would do it. My father encouraged me because of the situation in Argentina and the length of time I had been living in America where I have made my home. I didn't feel too much until the ceremony, when all of a sudden it was quite emotional. You go before a judge, have to be sworn in, raise your right hand and pledge allegiance to your new country. It was nice. I enjoy American politics, and I voted in 1988 and 1992, which was exciting. With a military government I never had that opportunity in my own country."

LPGA Victories: 1977 Colgate Far East Open. **1978** Civitan Open. **1979** Colgate Far East Open. **1984** Mazda Classic.

Silvia Bertolaccini's LPGA Record

Year	No.of Events	Best Finish	Money	Rank	Scoring Average
1975	24	3	$8,408	45	75.60
1976	28	2	31,344	18	74.36
1977	28	1	56,520	12	73.72
1978	27	1	53,935	14	73.97
1979	29	1	76,244	13	73.58
1980	31	T6	37,674	39	74.14
1981	29	T6	30,181	50	74.14
1982	28	T6	42,628	34	73.85
1983	27	T5	33,930	50	74.27
1984	25	1	62,259	30	74.03
1985	26	T5	38,347	58	73.86
1986	23	14	17,805	97	73.71
1987	21	T33	9,466	126	75.15
1988	22	T21	10,557	134	74.57
1989	18	T48	2,093	169	76.18
1990	4	NA	NA	NA	NA

Pat Bradley

Pat Bradley, known as the most consistent woman professional golfer, took her place as the 12th great player to enter the LPGA Hall of Fame. In 1991, at 40, she realized a dream 17 years after joining the tour: "I completed my mission," says the woman whose 30 victories include the 1981 Women's Open. In that same period she recorded an astonishing 55 second place finishes.

Her achievements were reflected in the statistic of her being the first player to exceed cumulative earnings of $2, $3, and $4 million in 1986, 1990, and 1991 respectively. Each time she won a tournament, her mother would ring a Swiss cow bell on the back porch of her home, a tradition which began after Pat's first victory in the 1975 Colgate Far East Open, then an unofficial event.

In 1986, Pat pushed herself to the limit and achieved five victories, including three of the four majors; she won a record $492,021, had a scoring average of 71.10, winning the Vare Trophy and the Player of the Year. She considered herself one of the greats, suitable for the Hall of Fame.

By 1988, she was fighting Graves disease and finished 109th on the money list. But only three seasons later she responded by reaching the ultimate peak in her career.

An interesting, driven woman who loves a challenge, Pat is a strong, powerful player who appears emotionally controlled in a world of her own on the golf course. In spite of a brusque manner, which probably stems from growing up as the only girl among five brothers, she is a woman who talks very honestly about her emotions and was surprisingly revealing of herself.

During the week of the inaugural 1987 Marilynn Smith Founders Classic in Dallas, Pat—far too young to compete—took the time to attend, and played a role as a starter. Brimming with excitement at mixing with the LPGA Charter Members and players of past eras, she told them emotionally at a celebratory dinner: "I never before had an idol. Tonight, I have all of you as my idols." At the 1995 US Women's Open, Pat was one of the few women professionals to attend Patty Berg's golf clinic as an excited and captivated spectator.

Intimidated by Pat in earlier years, I have come to enjoy the honesty and emotional depth she has shared with me, and she has always been helpful in setting up meetings with me.

"I was born in Westford, Massachusetts, into a middle income family, with five brothers, two older and three younger. My folks sold ski equipment, and as they both worked, we fended for ourselves. We were survivors.

Pat Bradley was the 12th player to enter the LPGA Hall of Fame, 17 years after she joined the tour. Her achievements include being the first player to exceed cumulative earnings of $2, $3, and $4 million. Photo credit: Katherine Murphy.

"At times it was tough being the only girl; with five boys you can get set apart. I didn't have a sister as a chum, so my mom was my sister and my best friend, and we stuck together. Looking back, I wouldn't have wanted it any other way: I have great brothers, and I have enjoyed them very much.

"They were extremely competitive, so I learned about competition very young in life, which was a big help. I started to ski at six, and in my junior year of high school, I trained with Olympic skiers. I dreamed of the Olympics but didn't give it enough effort.

"I took up golf at 11, through my dad, who was the big influence. He was an average player, a caddie in his younger days, and he believed in golf as a game of ladies and gentlemen, of honesty and etiquette. He wanted all of his children to experience its greatness, which we did. I was the only one to do it at the highest level, as a professional.

"Dad took me to Nashua Country Club, where we became members, and I began taking group lessons. He made sure I had the best equipment, all the opportunities for learning and working on my game. Although I had natural ability and talent, I did not become good very quickly. In national amateur tournaments or the U.S. Amateur, I was easily beaten by girls who played the game year round instead of seasonally, as I did. I won regional tournaments; so that locally I was a star, although nationally I was no one. There was not a major improvement until I went to school in Florida, and I considered turning professional as my ability and maturity improved. I played a lot of college golf, and in my last year, 1973, I went to the LPGA qualifying school in Miami. I won it and was really excited by my victory.

"I didn't know what to expect on tour; I had no idea how to travel or play for money. I was green. My dad, two of my brothers, and a group of men at Nashua gave me a three-year sponsorship contract worth $12,000. The first year I made $10,000 and paid back $5,000; the second year I made $28,000, paid back another $5,000 plus a bonus; the third year I made $84,000 and was off and running. Money is wonderful in that it gives you freedom of choice, and it will come if you shoot the right numbers. I've fared well in that department.

"I felt very comfortable on tour. I gravitated to the older players, learning from Judy Rankin, Sandra Haynie, Donna Caponi, Marlene Hagge, and Sandra Post. It didn't come easily, but I strived mentally and physically, learning course management, patience, and realizing that working on my game around the greens was the most important part. "I remember Susie Berning coming up to me as I was chipping 50 balls all over the place. She told me that I should work on quality, not quantity, that I should take 10 balls and put them within three feet of the hole, and I've always remembered that.

"I believe that over the years of a career, consistency is the winner. Winning is extremely important, since we're only out here to win, but you can't be a winner every week. It is important to get the best out of a week when you can't win. A lot of my seconds came from being down the field, not giving up, and shooting 66 to finish second.

"I have to work on my emotions because I'm very sensitive, and it's a never-ending battle for me to control myself. I can be easily hurt, and at times the tour gets pretty tough. If you're not strong, you get swallowed up. I'm still searching for strength; I give myself pep talks: 'Relax, be patient, things will turn around. You're being tested; they're trying to make you strong by giving you little challenges. It's up to you to meet them and succeed.'

"I felt that being known as the most consistent player was a compliment. I never wanted to be a fly-by-night player. The most important thing was to be in the hunt and know my day would come. By 1986, I had paid a lot of dues and put in my time. Finishing first is easy—there are no questions to be answered; finishing third is no problem, since there are two ahead of you. Finishing second leaves all the questions to be answered. Finishing second over the years helped me build character, and it also helped me have one of the most distinguished years of any golfer in the history of the game.

"I have been a very consistent and very good player, but I really believe that in 1986 I was tapped to be a little bit more distinguished than the other players. I think somewhere, someone up above picked me to have a year that will go down in golfing history and will make me just a little more special than other people. I feel that over the course of my career, playing as much as I have and doing what I have done, 1986 was truly a year for Pat Bradley.

"I got tremendous enjoyment from it. I honestly wish everyone could experience what I did in that dream-come-true year. I was invincible. I felt it every week. I was so strong mentally and physically. It was incredible. I could do no wrong; no matter where I was I could make something happen, and I did. I did it at the Nestle, the DuMaurier, the LPGA Championship, the Dinah Shore, and the S & H Classic. In every tournament I did something spectacular, and it was the most incredible feeling I've ever experienced.

"It makes all the blood, sweat, and tears worthwhile. I'll never forget it. I remember every emotion, every feeling. I was alive in 1986. I was at the height of concentration, the height of excellence from April until the first of September. For five months I was at the highest peak of my physical and mental ability, which is incredible when you consider being the ultimate for that long a period. Sometimes you have a week, and then you get it again a couple of months later.

In 1986, Pat achieved five victories, including three of four majors, and she won a record $492, 021. She had a scoring average of 71.10 to win the Vare trophy and become "Player of the Year." Photo courtesy: Katherine Murphy.

"I was completely exhausted in November when the tour was over. I had done what I always wanted and worked for. I had become Player of the Year. It took 13 years, and I would have loved it six or seven years earlier, but that was not Pat Bradley's time frame. My time frame happened the 13th year I was on tour, and I'm very thankful.

"The Hall of Fame is important," she told me some years before being selected, "but it is not the same stress and strain as Player of the Year. It was only in 1985 that I thought of the Hall of Fame, but for 12 years I had Player of the Year in my heart and mind. I honestly have to admit that if a year like 1986 can't put you in the Hall of Fame, maybe it's not worth being in it. I need nine more victories, which is not impossible, and I'd like to get in, but it could take a little time.

"I believe there could be justification for altering the criteria for the Hall of Fame. I don't want it to change and all of a sudden have an asterisk by my name because I got in under different rules, but it needs to be considered. There were only 45–50 women when the rules were made and now there are 144 every week. It's a controversial and sticky situation that may not be changed five years from now.

"I feel I am one of the greats—the statistics and the victories speak for themselves. I may not be up there attracting publicity or may not be a household name; I may be far behind in superstar quality, not as acceptable as some others, but in facts and figures I'm up with the greats.

"I enjoy communicating, doing my job, answering questions directly and to the point, but I'm not in for a popularity contest. I grew up with five brothers not showing their emotions—I'm sure if you got into the psychology of siblings and emotions, it would explain a lot. I didn't see a lot of emotion, so I hold mine in and don't let down my guard, which is not so appealing to people.

"I'm much better on a one-to-one encounter than in a group. I'm a lot shyer and less outgoing than people think. I veer away from the gallery on the golf course. My visor is down, and I keep my head straight toward where I've got to go. Nancy Lopez, JoAnne Carner, and Hollis Stacy can play to the galleries, and I accept and respect them for that, but please respect and understand me for what I do. It is the way I am."

Those were Pat's reactions to her great year of 1986, which drained her so much that her earnings dropped in 1987 by nearly $350,000, and she won only once. By 1988, the year her father died, she was tired, shaky, and still trying to compete, in spite of warning symptoms.

"I had never been ill, and I thought that I was over-reacting to 1986 and that all I needed was a good tournament. I lost so much strength I couldn't hit a wedge 80 yards when usually I hit it 105 yards. My hands were shaking so hard that one day I put my club down behind the ball on the fairway, moved the ball, and had to take a penalty stroke, I couldn't control the tremors.

"I looked healthy, but inside I was a mess. There was such denial; I thought I was having a nervous breakdown. In April I went to a hospital in Dallas, and tests revealed I had Graves disease, stemming

Pat Bradley, 1981 U.S. Open Champion, has collected 31 career wins thus far on the LPGA. Her most recent victory was the 1995 HEALTHSOUTH Palm Beach Classic.

from an over-active thyroid. I had treatment, started medication, and slowly began to feel better.

"In a way it was a blessing in disguise because I had been humiliated by going from No. 1 to 109th in a short time, from $492,000 to $16,000. After the diagnosis, I had a new challenge, a goal of coming back to where I knew I should be.

"My dad's goal was for me to reach the Hall of Fame, and I had a fear of failing him. For many years I felt in my heart I was Hall of Fame material but not in my mind. I was not completing the mission. You're so close, yet you're so far. When I said I thought I had done enough to get in the Hall of Fame, I was telling myself not to worry, everything would be all right. It was a defense mechanism to take off some pressure.

"My year began slowly in 1991, until April when I won the Centel Classic and vaulted to No. 1. Nothing much happened through the summer, no one bothered me, and then I had three victories in September, which happened so quickly—the last two, back to back—they caught me by surprise.

"I was still not the focus of attention at the MBS LPGA Classic, my final victory for the Hall of Fame. I played the Pro-Am at 7 a.m. and never saw the press. I shot 70 the first round and was not in the picture, either then or on Friday and Saturday, when I was four shots off the lead. On Sunday I didn't take the lead until I birdied the 13th, and picked up two more shots at the 14th and 17th, before bogeying the 18th to finish 11 under par. I thought the competition was behind me. I didn't realize that Michelle Estill had already finished 10 under, or that I had won from her by a shot.

"When I was told, I broke down and cried in the scorer's tent because I realized my mission was finally over and complete. It was a tremendous relief. Commitment was the key, and I had made it. Nothing came easily to me, and I'm a perfect example of it happening, of not having it handed to me. You can have success, failure, setback, and defeat, and rise above it."

Pat's ultimate goal that year was combined with the outstanding achievements of winning Player of the Year and the Vare Trophy for the second time, of being leading money winner with $763,118, and passing $4 million in career earnings.

Her induction into the Hall of Fame took place on 18th of January, 1992, at the Ritz-Carlton Hotel in Boston: "It was very emotional. My whole family was present, except the one person who was meant to see it, my dad. But, it was my opportunity to thank all five of my brothers, who sacrificed so much for me and allowed me to get the attention when we were growing up.

A scoreboard at the MBS LPGA Classic recorded Pat's march to the LPGA Hall of Fame. Her Mother always rang a bell on her back porch for each of Pat's victories. That bell will also reside in the Hall of Fame. Photo courtesy: Katherine Murphy.

"I was very, very proud of my speech, which started out in fairy tale land with my dad the king and my mom the queen. They had five princes and only one princess. I took a quality of each of my brothers and said how that quality was also within me and had helped me become who I am today.

"I talked about the legends of women's golf of whom I had always heard, and said I was so proud to walk beside them and no longer in their shadows. It was a memorable, perfect evening. It is most satisfying that when you are born into the world and hope someday to make a statement, that accomplishing this goal means my name will live on in the game of women's golf, especially LPGA golf. It is a legacy of which I am very proud, and I have been very fortunate to do well in my sport.

"I have reaped tremendous rewards and had a lot of heartbreaks and setbacks. It has been hell at times, which made me strong enough to deal with the ups and downs. I'm very blessed and extremely thankful.

"My mom has retired the bell, which has rung 30 times, and when the Hall of Fame is built in Daytona, the bell will rest there."

Member LPGA Hall of Fame 1991

LPGA Victories: 1976 Girl Talk Classic. **1977** Bankers Trust Classic. **1978** Lady Keystone, Hoosier Classic, Rail Charity Classic. **1980** Greater Baltimore Classic, Peter Jackson Classic. **1981** Women's Kemper Open, U.S. Women's Open. **1983** Mazda Classic of Deer Creek, Chrysler-Plymouth Charity Classic, Columbia Savings Classic, Mazda Japan Classic. **1985** Rochester International, du Maurier Classic, Nestle World Championship. **1986** Nabisco Dinah Shore, S&H Golf Classic, LPGA Championship, duMaurier Classic, Nestle World Championship. **1987** Standard Register Turquoise Classic. **1989** Al Star/Centinela Hospital Classic. **1990** Oldsmobile LPGA Classic, Standard Register Turquoise Classic, LPGA Corning Classic. **1991** Centel Classic, Rail Charity Golf Classic, SAFECO Classic, MBS LPGA Classic. **1995** HEALTHSOUTH Inaugural.

Unofficial Victories: 1975 Colgate Far East Open. **1978** JC Penney Classic (with Lon Hinkle). **1989** JC Penney Classic (with Bill Glasson). **1992** JC Penney/LPGA Skins Game.

Pat Bradley's LPGA Record

Year	No.of Events	Best Finish	Money	Rank	Scoring Average
1974	26	5	$10,839	39	75.38
1975	24	2	28,293	14	73.40
1976	29	1	84,288	6	73.28
1977	26	1	78,709	8	72.62
1978	29	1	118,057	2	72.31
1979	28	2	132,428	4	72.31
1980	31	1	183,377	6	71.95
1981	31	1	197,050	3	72.15
1982	29	4	113,089	11	72.29
1983	29	1	240,207	3	72.06
1984	28	2	220,478	4	72.05
1985	28	1	387,378	2	71.30
1986	27	1	492,021	1	71.10
1987	23	1	140,132	15	72.71
1988	17	T11	15,965	109	75.19
1989	26	1	423,714	4	71.00
1990	28	1	480,018	5	71.13
1991	26	1	763,118	1	70.66
1992	24	T2	238,541	19	71.60
1993	25	T3	188,135	27	71.96
1994	23	T2	236,274	20	72.03
1995	25	1	386,904	11	71.70

JoAnne Carner

JoAnne Carner, née Gunderson ("I was known as The Great Gundy and I loved it"), is one of the all-time greats in golf, in both amateur and professional ranks. This is a woman who has gloried in competition, in head-to-head battle, and who has thrived on making golf a lifetime involvement, for the sheer enjoyment she has derived from the game.

Her marriage to a considerably older man, Don Carner, when she was 24 gave her financial stability. Theirs has been a close and interdependent relationship—of traveling the tour for many years in a luxurious trailer, owning a boat, fishing together, and enjoying JoAnne's golf. Don has been her most valuable critic, guiding and criticizing JoAnne's golfing game with her eager consent. When I asked JoAnne about the age gap between her and her husband, she told me to ask him, and Don Carner informed me: "There are two things we do not discuss: JoAnne's weight and my age."

JoAnne Carner won the 1971 U.S. Open and to date is the only woman to have won the USGA Junior, Women's Amateur and Women's Open titles.

Although JoAnne came relatively late to the LPGA, at 30 in 1970, no one arrived with a more illustrious amateur career: five U.S. Amateur titles, the 1956 U.S. Girls' Junior title, and membership on four Curtis Cup teams. So high did she rank as a golfer that in 1969, as an amateur, she won what was then the biggest money tournament of the LPGA circuit, the $40,000 Burdine's Invitational in Miami.

As a professional, this Hall-of-Famer has 42 career victories and was the second woman, after Pat Bradley, to achieve $2 million in career earnings. Twice a winner of the U.S. Women's Open, she is the only woman to have won the USGA Junior, U.S. Amateur, and U.S. Women's Open titles.

JoAnne, who has always given the ball a tremendous whack and been happy to play attacking, adventurous golf, has attracted huge crowds. Her pressure-easing habit of cracking humorous one-liners has been part of the fun of following this legend of golf. Never a health fanatic, JoAnne enjoyed smoking, drinking, and eating, until in 1987 her health was suffering and doctors diagnosed a systemic yeast infection. She went on a drastic diet, which produced a dramatic weight loss.

After twelve consecutive years with at least one victory, the spell was broken in 1986, but JoAnne showed little sign of wanting to hang up her clubs and go fishing.

In a press room environment she responds well with some good repartee, but on a one-to-one basis, she is more defensive. Although I found her quite difficult to interview, I feel I often did not ask the right questions. In spite of this, some very good material emerged, showing a woman who reveled in the game of golf and the excitement it had brought her.

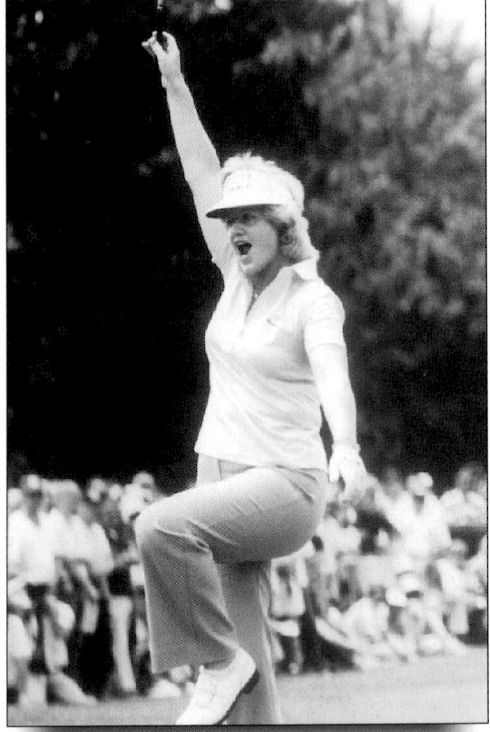

A triumphant JoAnne Carner has always had the ability to play to the crowds. Photo Courtesy: LPGA.

JoAnne was born in Kirkland, Washington, just outside Seattle. She grew up in that area, the youngest of five children, with three older sisters, and a brother, Bill, only 13 months older. Her father was a carpenter, and after JoAnne graduated from college, her mother worked in a department store.

"Bill and I were like twins growing up. Whatever he did, I did. We hunted together for golf balls and sold them on weekends; he worked at the local nine-hole public course, and I tagged long. When I found some old hickory-shafted clubs, I hit balls in a field, aiming at the cows. Because I wasn't allowed on the course when I was younger, I went there at night and played moonlight golf. I had terrible trouble trying to find my ball among the weeping willows.

"Neither of my parents played golf, but they were very encouraging. I had lessons from a man called Gordon Jenkins, who was a good golfer. He entered me, at 14, in my first tournament. Playing with a 24 handicap, I sent two balls out of bounds, three-putted three times, and won with a 79. They screamed blue murder, and the following week when I did the same, they cut my handicap to 12.

"Later, when I became the State Public Links amateur champion, I was given an honorary membership to a private club in Seattle, where my father did carpentry work. I was runner-up the first time I entered the National Junior at 16, and the following year when I won it, I was also runner-up in the U.S. Women's Amateur. When I won the National Junior, they gave me a ticker tape parade from Seattle to my hometown. It was really exciting. They did it again when I won the 1974 Women's Amateur, and they put on a huge banquet as well.

"That first U.S. Amateur victory was a huge thrill. I really loved playing head to head, and I enjoyed all my battles in the Curtis Cup matches. I was the youngest member of the team in 1958, undefeated in my career as an individual member of four Curtis Cup teams, and I just loved everything about amateur golf—to this day I still do. My parents supported me through my amateur career, and the fact that they raised us as individuals developed my competitive instincts. My mother was a horoscope nut, and having read all the characteristics of the signs, she told me I was a typical Aries; stubborn, big-headed, adventuresome, and I loved to win.

"As an amateur I would analyze my opponents. With some, you win the first hole, and you know you have them beaten. Others could be off and running and shoot 33 for the front nine, and then I would tell myself that a player is only hot for nine holes and that it would be my turn soon on the back side. I was a cat-and-mouse player, going ahead and falling behind, and winning 80 percent of my matches from behind. My theory was to get my opponents trying to make birdies, and then I knew I had them. They would go for the pin and end up in the bunker with a bogey. I was uninhibited as an amateur, I always thought I

At age 30, JoAnne turned professional, and no one arrived on the LPGA with a more illustrious amateur career: five U.S. Women Amateur titles, the 1956 U.S. Girls' Junior title, and membership on four Curtis Cup teams.

could play and never thought there was anyone better. I was a natural at golf, and although I always wanted to win, I would want other people to play well rather than win with a runaway victory. Some people are afraid to win, others are afraid to lose. I think winning is a lot more fun.

"In 1957, I think I was the first U.S. woman golfer to have a golf scholarship. I went to Arizona State University, but the problem was that there were only two intercollegiate tournaments a year, and I couldn't play on the boys' team, which upset me.

"While I was at college, I played the 1958 Western Open, a professional tournament in Seattle that no longer exists. I shot 72 the first day, and the next day when I went to practice, the women professionals tried to make me gas it. Fay Crocker stood and analyzed my swing; so I asked if I could watch her hit balls and then needled her so much she couldn't get it airborne. I was paired to play with Marilynn Smith, and when I hit a shot three feet from the hole, she said, 'Why didn't you hit a seven or eight iron instead of a punched nine?' I replied, 'I got it three feet from the hole. What do you want?'

"I was really harassed, and they tried to put me off my game; so before my round I practiced at a local nine hole course. I arrived at the tournament, putted a little, and then went straight off the first tee, all of which made the women madder. Betsy Rawls was running away with the tournament, I was playing well, and although I nearly choked over the last couple of holes, I got two pars to tie for second with Patty Berg."

After JoAnne graduated from college with a physical education degree, she stayed in Phoenix and went to business school. She worked in insurance, then in an electronics company, where she met her future husband, Don, who had been previously married. They were married in 1964, when JoAnne was 24. Don was president of the electronics company and also had a jewelry business. "He was the rhinestone king of costume jewelry." At first they lived in Seconk, Massachusetts, and built a par-three executive golf course in Providence. They later sold the course and their house, living for a long time in a trailer. In 1979, they bought a home in Palm Beach.

Don Carner says: "I was successful before I met JoAnne. Financially, I have accomplished just about everything I wanted to do in my life, and I have been happy to play the supporting role. We never spend much money except to live on the golf tour, since our needs are not that great. The age gap has never worried us—I just wonder how she will spend all the money when I kick the bucket. She doesn't need to work another day for the rest of her life. I have taught her to be independent and to think well; we both go to the lawyer and the accountant, and I keep her informed on investments; so she can do it herself one day.

"We never have arguments because there is no point in being mean to someone. We depend on each other in our relationship and do everything together. I get stirred up watching her play golf, and JoAnne is like a stake horse in a fine race, who sometimes gets tired from playing too much."

JoAnne says of her husband: "Don has been a big influence. He has handled all the business side of my life. I regard money as the end result of all my winning, but I have seen women golfers and athletes who end up with nothing. Don has invested my money, which represents security for the future. He has observed my golf, analyzed it, motivated me, and kept me sharp. Everyone thinks we're crazy to be together so much, but we thoroughly enjoy doing everything together. When I once went alone to England for a tournament, I didn't enjoy it because Don wasn't there. We have only been separated for a few days of our marriage.

"Golf is a funny sport in that you have to eat, sleep, and drink it. We have lived in a trailer apart from the tour crowd for much of the time because as a group, the women can be very picky and negative, talking a lot about the bad things, while I like to talk about the good. We don't socialize that much, and the trailer provides a salvation for looking at green grass, a river, a lake, going fishing and being relaxed. We eat well, and Don is the better cook; we have a telephone, a television, and it is all very comfortable. I play better golf living in our trailer.

"At one time in the early 1970s I was voted in as secretary or treasurer of the Association, I forget which. I did it for two months and quit. The president and vice president controlled and organized everything, and I said, 'You don't need me. You have already made all your decisions.'

"Don and I sometimes talked about having children. Every once in a while we would get loaded and wonder what kind of pup we might have produced, but to me you have to do one thing or the other. Some people have raised kids and stayed on tour, but I don't think I could have done that."

When they first married, Don traveled the amateur circuit with JoAnne, where she remained because she loved it so much. Then, after years of dominance, she ran out of amateur challenges. Her foray into the 1969 Burdine's Invitational, and her victory against the top women professionals, was followed by needling them as she declared that a team of amateurs could defeat the professionals in matchplay or strokeplay. She added: "Right now I can think of only three pro golfers I would rate top notch—Mickey Wright, Carol Mann, and Kathy Whitworth . . . and Mickey is past her peak." Her impudent challenge was studiously ignored.

In 1970 JoAnne joined the professional tour, and she says: "When I first played as an amateur with the professionals in 1958, the women's image was horsey-looking, suspected lesbian, tough and swearing. I think I had a lot to do with the change when I turned professional. Because I had such a good reputation, a lot of mothers and fathers said, 'It must be all right. I needn't worry about my daughter.'

"Really, I consider, it is all a bit overplayed because it depends on your background how you turn out. You only have to see a Judy Rankin out there with a husband and a child to know that you can marry, raise a family, and travel a lot. I see a woman athlete's life as nothing but good. It is hard working, and I consider my life to be about as normal as you can get. I do everything with my husband, and it is a business from nine to five, seven days a week."

Although she won a tournament in her first season and won the Women's U.S. Open and another tournament the following year, JoAnne did not consider herself a dominant figure until

JoAnne, shown here in 1990, was admitted to the LPGA Hall of Fame in 1982. She won 42 tournaments by 1985 and is still a popular player today. Photo ©Phil Sheldon.

JoAnne is a fierce competitor, a great winner, and, above all, always a favorite with the galleries. She received the LPGA's 1995 William and Mousie Powell Award, voted by her peers, as the person who best exemplifies the spirit, ideals, and values of the LPGA.

she won six events in 1974: "I expected to take over the tour immediately. Sandra Haynie told me it would take four years, and I said baloney, but it did. I was used to matchplay and winning, not staying there and grinding it out for $500. I was a very good driver and fantastic with a wedge because in those days I practiced so much. Then, when I turned professional, I started steering the ball to try to get more accuracy. I practiced too much and thought beating balls was the only thing to do because Mickey Wright and Kathy Whitworth, two great all-time winners, were forever working on their games. Mickey had the best swing of any professional who has ever played the game. Everyone could watch her and figure out something, but basically, many of the women don't have great swings.

"In 1974 when I needed to straighten out my mental attitude, it was New York Yankees' manager Billy Martin who helped me. He told me not to analyze what I was doing with every club in the bag on the practice tee before I played. He said I should use the time strictly as a warm up session to loosen the muscles, and maybe use not more than a seven iron. His advice made me stop over-analyzing and work out my problems after my round, and I went on to be leading money that year."

JoAnne had to learn how to make the most of her tremendous talent in the professional ranks. In spite of her great record, she still feels she has not played to her potential, but the other women and the competition have helped to fire her:
"I have never had any trouble controlling my emotions. My problem has been to gear up—I have to drink five cups of coffee in the morning. However, being paired with good players like Jane Blalock, Sandra Palmer, Judy Rankin, Hollis Stacy, and Sally Little is motivating, since they play well and force you to do the same.

"Concentration and getting involved with the shot are important, but if I get too serious I can't play. I relieve the pressure by light chatter with the gallery, although I never get into conversation. I enjoy being able to show more emotion as a professional. I get so enthused with the golf that if the ball is going for the pin or in the cup, I am the first one to yell. Every day I tee it up in a tournament, I try to win. Unless you want to win every week, you're playing for third, fourth, or whatever.

"I get excited with pressure, not nervous, and I love to feel I can win and that I can pull it off. You have to learn how to compensate for being pumped up, and only you can do it. I used to spend a lot of time working on trouble shots; so that I could be wild and still recover. I'm a shotmaker, and the greatest fun to me is pulling off a particular shot because I love the challenge. Mickey Wright, in her time, and Hollis Stacy, are the only other players who thoroughly enjoy a real shot. Winning the U.S. Women's Open twice has provided the peaks for me because it is always a true test which requires lots of shot making."

JoAnne's career continued in an upward spiral of victory and reward, but in May 1979 she had a motorcycle accident in Tennessee. She hit a rock in the road and went over the handlebars. She injured her wrists and tendons, and sat on the sidelines until almost the end of the season: "I got depressed, and drank and ate everything in sight. I gained 45 pounds, and it was murder to get them off. It was the most frustrating time I've ever had. It was nice that people would phone and write and tell me they missed me. I had a good welcome back."

JoAnne continued to win, until in 1982 her winning the World Championship of Women's Golf gave her 35 victories and a place in the Hall of Fame. Before she attained it, she stated: "I would like to make the Hall of Fame before I retire or die." She passed the million dollar mark in 1981, and her highest earnings, $310,399, were in 1982. She continued winning until 1985 when she suffered with back trouble and played fewer tournaments. In 1992, at 54, JoAnne played herself magnificently into a playoff with Tammie Green, and, sadly, history has to record that the great veteran lost on the first extra hole. In 1994, JoAnne was the winning Solheim Cup captain, at the Greenbrier, West Virginia, an honor and an achievement she relished, as one of the greatest matchplayers of all time.

JoAnne does not see anything beyond golf and will stay on tour as long as it is enjoyable. "I know I am a legend in my lifetime, and I love taking on the rookies. When they said I was getting too old some years ago, I worked very hard on my game, and I felt I was getting better and better. I get pleasure from playing well, and I believe you can intimidate the majority of the field. I enjoy my golf more than anyone. I could go and play all by myself, without any gallery, and be in seventh heaven."

Member LPGA Hall of Fame 1982

LPGA Victories: 1970 Wendell West Open. **1971** U.S. Women's Open, Bluegrass Invitational. **1974** Bluegrass Invitational, Hoosier Classic, Desert Inn Classic, St. Paul Open, Dallas Civitan, Portland Classic. **1975** American Defender Classic, All-American Classic, Peter Jackson Classic. **1976** Orange Blossom Classic, Lady Tara Classic, Hoosier Classic, U.S. Women's Open. **1977** Talk Tournament, Borden Classic, National Jewish Hospital Open. **1978** Peter Jackson Classic, Borden Classic. **1979** Honda Civic Classic, Women's Kemper Open. **1980** Whirlpool Championship of Deer Creek, Bent Tree Ladies Classic, Sunstar '80, Honda Civic Classic, Lady Keystone Open. **1981** S&H Golf Classic, Lady Keystone Open, Columbia Savings LPGA Classic, Rail Charity Golf Classic. **1982** Elizabeth Arden Classic, McDonald's LPGA Kids' Classic, Chevrolet World Championship of Women's Golf, Henredon Classic, Rail Charity Golf Classic. **1983** Chevrolet World Championship of Women's Golf, Portland Ping Championship. **1984** Corning Classic. **1985** Elizabeth Arden Classic, SAFECO Classic.

Unofficial Victories: 1977 LPGA Team Championship (with Judy Rankin). **1978** Colgate Triple Crown. **1979** Colgate Triple Crown. **1982** JC Penney Classic (with John Mahaffey).

JoAnne Carner's LPGA Record

Year	No.of Events	Best Finish	Money	Rank	Scoring Average
1970	18	1	$14,551	11	74.52
1971	18	1	21,604	6	74.24
1972	26	4	18,902	15	74.62
1973	26	2	19,688	25	75.60
1974	26	1	87,094	1	72.87
1975	23	1	64,843	2	72.40
1976	27	1	103,275	3	72.38
1977	25	1	113,712	2	72.51
1978	23	1	108,093	4	72.01
1979	15	1	98,219	9	72.40
1980	26	1	185,916	5	71.89
1981	28	1	206,648	2	71.75
1982	26	1	310,399	1	71.49
1983	22	1	291,404	1	71.41
1984	18	1	144,900	9	71.79
1985	19	1	141,941	11	72.04
1986	18	2	82,802	26	72.65
1987	17	T2	66,601	41	72.50
1988	17	T2	121,218	21	71.77
1989	16	T2	97,888	38	72.69
1990	17	T2	87,218	48	73.07
1991	20	8	86,874	56	73.00
1992	19	T2	175,880	29	72.08
1993	18	2	134,956	41	72.46
1994	17	T15	55,474	86	73.02
1995	11	T9	38,033	98	73.68

Beth Daniel

When 5 foot, 10 inch, Beth Daniel arrived on the LPGA tour at 22, she would swish the club through the air and the ball went a country mile. Equally, she might bang her club on the ground and be fined by an LPGA official.

"My temper is frustration with myself," Beth said at the time. "When I hit a bad shot, I know I can do better, and maybe I've put a bad swing on it or I should have changed my club. So, I'm frustrated. I need to feel like that to push myself and work harder at the game.

"I was fined about four times in two years for throwing clubs and felt I was labeled for life, which upset me. I'm a dedicated athlete who wants to do the best I possibly can, and out of all the fines I deserved only one—when I threw a club at a tree, and Betsy Rawls was sitting there. I deserved that. I don't feel I disturb other people—maybe I do—but others have disrupted me. On one occasion, a player in contention missed her putt and slammed her putter into her bag as I was over my putt. I backed off, and then missed to lose the tournament.

"I don't necessarily call mine a temper. I'm an ultimate perfectionist, who can throw a club or a little fit after a shot and then come back to the next shot without being affected. If it was true temper, it would affect the next shot and the next hole."

Beth's golf was not affected by her misdemeanors, nor was she labeled for life. She made her mark as an amateur and early on the LPGA tour. She was resoundingly heralded as the next superstar, the woman to challenge Nancy Lopez. She is slim and athletic, attractive in her own style. When she was younger, she seemed to lack confidence in her appearance.

Beth was Rookie of the Year in 1979, during which she won her first tournament. She followed by reaching the No. 1 spot in 1980, with record earnings of $231,000, four victories, and she was Player of the Year. Her next three seasons were equally illustrious, as she continued to win five events in 1982, and tie for second place in the U.S. Open. She set a financial record of more than $200,000 for three seasons from 1980, and it appeared that the superstar was on her way.

By 1984, Beth was troubled with back problems, and she did not continue to scale heights. However, she had a good year in 1985, when she

Beth Daniel won the 1975 U.S. Women's Amateur and won it again in 1977. Since joining the LPGA in 1979, she has won 32 events.

had one victory and was eighth on the money list. But, the woman who had been so exciting, with such a glossy future, settled for being one of the better players on tour, earning good money as stardom receded, and as victory eluded her completely for three seasons. It was a painful time for Beth.

In 1988 she made strides forward, climbing up the money list with some good performances, and in the Atlantic City LPGA Classic, she held a comfortable lead in the last round, at one time 10 shots ahead of Juli Inkster. But, Inkster's final round 65 to Beth's 72 forced a play-off, which Inkster won with a par at the first hole. That year, Beth's health suffered, and mononucleosis was diagnosed.

I have known Beth since she joined the tour. I like her style and over the years have enjoyed talking with her. She has always been frank about herself developing from an impetuous and successful young woman of immense talent, to become increasingly torn between weighing her privacy against the demands of success, later, she developed a second career of stunning achievement.

Refreshingly outspoken, she became confused about her goals, which affected her confidence and ability on the golf course, although there were always sparks of her real talent. As she matured and learned how to handle her lifestyle and how to make her talent work for her, she seemed happy. This was reflected in her rewarding resurgence. From 1989, she stormed forth with multiple victories and a glorious year in 1990, when she won seven times, was Player of the Year, and won the Vare Trophy.

Beth's amateur background was one of great success. She twice won the U.S. Amateur championship in 1975 and 1977, twice played Curtis Cup golf. She collected many other amateur and college titles. She graduated from Furman University with a degree in physical education.

Beth was born and brought up in Charleston, South Carolina, with a brother six years older and a sister three years older. She comes from an upper middle income family. Her father worked for Coca Cola, and both her parents played golf.

"I liked all sports, and at 14 I was only five feet tall, but I grew very quickly, so that I was 5 feet, 8 inches, at 16. I started playing golf at eight, when we played as a family. Sometimes I would play with my father and his friends. My parents tried to emphasize the enjoyment of competing, but winning was always very important to me. I had to win to achieve; otherwise it was not worth it.

"I was always a perfectionist, although later it was just as fulfilling to know I'd done my best. I showed my frustration by throwing a club, but I didn't think I had the worst temper on the tour. The first year I got mad and didn't know how to cope, but gradually I calmed down. I will never be a person who doesn't show emotion, because I care too much.

"When I joined the tour, I said I would stay only three years. I hated the tough lifestyle. It helped that I had played amateur and college golf. From about 14, I wanted to be a professional, and I joined the tour to see how good I could be. Majors are the most important ones to win, and I want to set records in the number of tournaments and major championships I win. I hope one day to be considered the best. I visualized achieving all I wanted in under ten years and saying goodbye to the tour to settle down and get married.

"I didn't expect to do so well so quickly. In 1980, I felt I could intimidate the whole field, that I could win every time I teed it up, which is a feeling that everyone would like and only a few achieve. It is a feeling of power, of others backing off, which makes you feel superior to everyone else on the golf course. No one charged. They knew I was going to win, and they played for second place, and I felt I would beat them all.

"It is exhausting mentally, but you're high, it's so much fun, and it's the ultimate to win. You work so hard at such a difficult game and finally winning makes it all worthwhile. Winning and losing are a state of mind, and you have to want to win, not just say you do. Early experiences of winning force your mind into the right track, but a lot of people lose because they don't know how to win, or how to psyche themselves up, and they don't want it enough.

"Any time you have a chance to win, your mouth gets dry, your throat gets tight, your breathing becomes shallow, your heart beats faster, and you feel pressure. You can fall apart as though

Beth was "Rookie of the Year" in 1979, winning her first LPGA tournament and nearly $100,000. Photo ©Phil Sheldon.

you have no control over yourself; you can hit a shot into trouble, get uptight, nervous, and play yourself out of the tournament; or you can calm down and deal with it. If you're in contention regularly, it becomes easier, but it's equally easy to back off and to think of any number of excuses as to why you don't want to win: 'I don't know what to say in my speech,' you tell yourself, or 'I don't want to win because the press will be after me next week.'

"I guess I would like to be No. 1 every year, but it takes a lot of time, and it is very tough to handle success. I want to win, but do I want to devote that much of my life to being a winner? There are a lot of demands off the course, and I'm not sure if I want to give up that much of my time.

"People pry so much; they're so intrusive; I respect my privacy. Nancy enjoys the attention, but I don't particularly thrive on it; I like to turn down appearances, which doesn't make me popular, but I don't enjoy doing them. I'm very shy, and I dislike people latching on to me because I'm Beth Daniel the golfer.

"I find it hard that there is such an emphasis on good-looking athletes. Although we play golf for a living, we are judged by our appearance, and I think it is fine for Jan Stephenson to project herself as she does—everyone wishes she looked like Jan Stephenson—but some people are born better looking than others. What can you do if you're big-boned, stocky, or a big person? You're born that way. Losing weight isn't going to give you an attractive face. You dress and look as good as you can, but it would be a joke if I tried to look like Jan."

By 1987 Beth had struggled through a degenerative disk and experienced serious putting problems. She became disillusioned. "My disk improved, but my golf hasn't been good, and the missing ingredient is the mental part," she said at the time. "I've been out here a while, and it's harder to motivate myself to be a good putter, especially a short putter. Now it's really mental. I can stand on the practice putting green, and it's fine, but it's not the same once I get on the course.

"I want to be out here. I still enjoy the game, and although I don't enjoy playing poorly, I like the challenge. I don't feel I'll ever reach my prime. I never got as good as I could have been. It doesn't matter when you reach it as long as you do reach it. The last three years have been so bad according to the goals I set that I got very depressed. It is stupid that everything is based on what you shoot, and it's tough going through the despair, but I think I am going to come out of it, and I'll be all the better for it.

"Finishing 13th on the money list in 1984 was terrible for me. I thought it would be my worst year ever. I was 8th in 1985, and then I played awful golf to be 21st in 1986. There's a fine line between even par golf and four- or five-under, and when you play badly you seem to get all the bad breaks.

"It takes a lot out of you to be at the top. I didn't enjoy the extra demands, with everyone tugging at me in every direction. I don't miss that part of it. I know the attention is all part of it. When you're not playing well, no one cares. Maybe I'm not ready to put up with the attention. When I am, maybe I'll start playing better. My pride tells me I want to play better.

"Sometimes my golf embarrasses me—when I miss a short putt or come to the 18th where there's a big crowd and I'm plus four for the day. I don't want to hide because people still enjoy watching me play, and if I didn't feel that, I'd retire. It's amazing how many people don't know what you're shooting, and they come and say, 'I love the way you swing, the way you hit the ball.'

"I used to let my feelings hang out, but now I keep them in. I still fling a club here and there, but nothing like before, when I used it as a motivator to kick myself. Now I just mope along, which is far worse. When I was 22, I thought, 'It's a party. You just go out and play golf.' I didn't care if I hit it out of bounds because I could make a couple of birdies, and I had the ability to let myself win. I know I'm still capable of winning if I'll allow myself to do it, but whereas it was once so easy, now it's so hard.

"It is stupid, but I get to the point where I want to cry, where I do insane things on the golf course, and think, 'Why is it this way?' I'm a pretty tough cookie, and I tell myself it's a cycle and eventually a cycle has to end, but it's hard to ride it out, and that's what I've got to do. A lot of people reach their peak in their thirties."

By the end of 1994, Beth had 31 victories, including one major, the LPGA Championship, and she had become a contender for the Hall of Fame, needing either one major or four more victories.

It was a remarkable turnaround for the woman who took three months away from the tour in March 1988, suffering from exhaustion and mononucleosis. She returned a new woman, who not only achieved some of her goals, but also was involved from 1989 to 1992 on the Player Council and executive board, at a time when more power was given back to the players to control their own destiny.

"When I thought about what I would do for a living if I didn't play golf, I decided I didn't want to end my career on a down note. I came back with a lot of motivation to prove myself again; I almost felt like a rookie. The illness was a blessing in disguise. To win again and have a good year in 1989 was encouraging, and although 1990 will go down in my career history as the best, it was a real watershed. It meant a lot, because I had gone through such a low period when most people thought I was possibly washed up.

"To be consistent enough to win the Vare Trophy in 1989 and again the following year meant a lot to me, and it was very satisfying to win the 1990 LPGA Championship playing against the best. To have, in 1990, one of the greatest years of anyone in LPGA history, also gave me real satisfaction knowing I had won the week before and three weeks previously and that I could do it again. I had reached a maturity where I knew that the feeling didn't happen often, and I cherished it rather than taking it for granted, as I did when I was younger.

Beth Daniel won seven times in 1990 and was named "Player of the Year." She also won the Vare Trophy for the lowest scoring average. That year she was selected to play in the Solheim Cup competition at Lake Nona, Florida. Photo ©Phil Sheldon.

"I came on tour and said I would quit when I was 30, but now I look forward to the next year. As a professional athlete I have certain motivations that keep me in the game. I have tournaments I want to win, private goals to achieve.

"I am now comfortable with my image, and I think maybe I have been misunderstood. My great love for the game motivates me to work as hard as I can to win. I speak my mind, and my words have often been misinterpreted by the media. The only time people had sympathy for me was after I was ill, and they saw how hard I worked to come back.

"People thought I had tremendous talent and didn't do anything with it. I was always a hard worker, but my air on the golf course is a little aloof, I get into a shell, which looks like I'm over-confident and I don't care about people. I'm intense and totally different on the golf course. Sometimes my mother doesn't recognize me. I'm very competitive, and that part takes over sometimes, causing me to slam a club to get the adrenalin flowing. Off the course, it takes an awful lot to make me angry. On it, it doesn't take much at all.

"Suffering makes you tougher and more appreciative. I would never want to live through it again, but those hard times made me a better person and a better golfer. You can't be on top all the time. I arrived cocky, wanting to prove myself as one of the great players, and ultimately I humbled myself.

"You have to have a little luck on your side in this game. It helps more than anyone will ever know. It's so true that when you're playing well, your ball hits a tree in the middle of the woods and kicks out on the fairway, and when you're playing badly, it never fails to go in deeper. That's the game which drives us all crazy and makes us keep playing."

LPGA Victories: 1979 Patty Berg Classic. **1980** Golden Lights Championship, Patty Berg Classic, Columbia Savings Classic, Chevrolet World Championship of Women's Golf. **1981** Florida Lady Citrus, Chevrolet World Championship of Women's Golf. **1982** Bent Tree Ladies Classic, American Express Sun City Classic, Birmingham Classic, Columbia Savings Classic, WUI Classic. **1983** McDonald's LPGA Kids Classic. **1985** Kyocera Inamori Classic. **1989** Greater Washington Open, Rail Charity Golf Classic, SAFECO Classic, Konica San Jose Classic. **1990** Orix Hawaiian Ladies Open, Women's Kemper Open, Phar-Mor in Youngstown, Mazda LPGA Championship, Northgate Classic, Rail Charity Golf Classic, Centel Classic. **1991** Phar-Mor at Inverrary, McDonald's Championship. **1994** Corning Classic, Oldsmobile Classic, JAL Big Apple Classic, World Championship of Women's Golf. **1995** PING Welch's Championship (Boston).

Unofficial Victories: 1979 World Ladies. **1981** JC Penney Classic (with Tom Kite). **1988** Nichierei Ladies Cup U.S.-Japan Team Championship. **1990** JC Penney Classic (with Davis Love III). **1991** Konica World Ladies. **1995** JC Penney Classic (with Davis Love III).

Beth Daniel's LPGA Record

Year	No.of Events	Best Finish	Money	Rank	Scoring Average
1979	25	1	$97,027	10	72.65
1980	27	1	231,000	1	71.59
1981	27	1	206,977	1	71.87
1982	27	1	223,634	5	71.66
1983	23	1	167,403	6	72.29
1984	23	T2	94,284	16	72.68
1985	27	1	177,235	8	72.19
1986	24	T2	103,547	21	72.71
1987	26	T2	83,308	29	73.12
1988	18	2	140,635	17	71.80
1989	25	1	504,851	2	70.38
1990	23	1	863,578	1	70.54
1991	18	1	469,501	4	70.94
1992	23	2	329,681	11	71.64
1993	23	T2	140,001	40	72.25
1994	25	1	659,426	2	70.90
1995	25	1	480,124	6	71.33

Laura Davies

In 1994, Laura Davies at 30 acquired the mantle of the best golfer in the world—male or female—as she devoured tournament victories the way she once swallowed Coca Colas. She won the Thailand Open at the beginning of the year, the LPGA Standard Register Ping in March, then back-to-back in May she was victorious in the Sara Lee Classic followed by the LPGA Championship, sponsored for the first time by MacDonald's at the DuPont Country Club. She had won MacDonald's tournament the previous year. Four birdies in five holes from the 11th in the final round, en route to a three-shot victory, gave the television audience and huge galleries of more than 40,000 the full magnificence of this outstanding woman golfer's game. It was her second U.S. major and her ninth triumph on the LPGA tour.

Betsy Rawls, a member of the LPGA Hall of Fame with 55 victories, in charge of the LPGA Championship, said: "The first time I ever saw Laura, I thought it was inevitable she would win a lot. At first she took off the pressure by trying to convince herself that winning didn't matter; then, emotionally, she accepted it as the most important thing in the world.

"She is a great champion, who admits weaknesses, who is modest and unassuming. There is no hint of bragging. People like her a lot and enjoy watching her play. Very unusually for a golfer, she does not take herself too seriously. She can laugh at herself, which is a very likeable quality. If she is on tour another ten years, her entry into the Hall of Fame is inevitable."

Laura is a woman who loves setting records, and in 1994, she hurtled round the world to become the first professional golfer ever to win on five tours. She dominated world rankings, achieving eight tournament victories. She also was the first Briton ever to top the LPGA money list, which she did with $687,201.

For so many years, Laura had been hearing that she should win every tournament she entered, yet she knew, that like everyone else, she needed to serve her apprenticeship before she could fulfill her great promise, before she could reach any level of consistency.

When Laura won the 1987 U.S. Open at 23 before she joined the LPGA tour, defeating JoAnne Carner and Ayako Okamoto in a three-way playoff, it was as startling a victory as when the French amateur golfer Catherine Lacoste, took the title twenty years previously.

Laura hits the golf ball farther than any woman in the history of the game, regularly driving it 250 yards, and on occasions sending it well in excess of 300 yards. An inveterate gambler, she always has taken chances, and this penchant for taking risks, combined with her power, which allows her to attempt shots no other player would dare, creates an awesome sight on a golf course. Laura will smash a ball over trees and all obstacles in sight, pulling off miracle shots to land on some far distant green. A swashbuckler of the long game, she has a most delicate touch around the greens, but consistency used to elude her, and many are the putters that have been thrown in waste bins or discarded in disgust at her own performance.

In the early days of Laura's career, if she was putting poorly, she would appear to lose interest and turn in high scores, which reflected her intense frustration and an inability to cope with her imperfections on the greens. A self-taught, instinctive golfer, who plays by feel, Laura would change her grip, watch the method of Seve Ballesteros, or talk to Nancy Lopez, Patty Sheehan, or others she admired, but never has she acquired a teaching guru or become bogged down by technique.

"Vicariously, Laura learns by osmosis," says fellow professional Mickey Walker. "She assimilates knowledge in her own time and in her own way. It is not that suddenly she sees the light in a big public display, but the results are profound over a period of time. Her golfing brain is phenomenal."

Often criticized for her lack of dedication to the practice ground, Laura has followed her instincts through some outstanding years, during which people unfairly have expected more of her because her natural talent made them think she should win every week. Had Laura settled in America and played only one tour, undoubtedly she would have improved more quickly and won more consistently at an earlier date, but her continued loyalty to a European women's tour has been its greatest blessing. Winning the U.S. Open so early in her career was something she did with tremendous flair and inspiration, yet it set her up to be knocked down in a world where she had precious little experience. Taking the U.S. and British Open titles, leading the European money list for her first two years as a professional, winning on both sides of the Atlantic, in Japan, and on other world tours, has been all the more remarkable for her ability to adapt to the constant change in environment.

Her inspirational quality was first demonstrated as the force behind the upsurge of a women's tour in Europe. Swedish professional Lotta Neumann followed Laura's 1987 U.S. Open success with a victory in 1988. Laura's four LPGA tour victories in four years set the pattern from 1988 onwards. Then, the driving force of Laura's determination took the whole European 1992 Solheim Cup team to a glorious 11-½-6-½ victory, the one that she so craved against the Americans: "This must lend credibility to a women's European tour," she said, in the year that it meant more to her than winning the U.S. or British Open titles.

As a young girl she was painfully shy; she still picks nervously at her clothing, a gesture retained from childhood. Her mother says, "She always wore two layers of sweaters." Intensely sensitive to criticism, she used to march round furiously as a young professional, to "sort out" any journalist she felt had criticized her unfairly.

Laura first came to prominence as a talented, wild-hitting, 20-year old amateur on the British and Irish Curtis Cup side at Muirfield against the Americans. There she defeated the experienced campaigner Anne Sander on the last green in her singles, one of two matches she played. The Americans won by the narrow margin of 9-½-8-½, and it was the beginning of the rise of women's golf in Europe.

She turned professional in 1985, and in only her second tournament was runner-up to Jan Stephenson in the Hennessy Cup in Paris. Laura went on to become a star and the leading money winner in Europe her first two seasons.

Laura's achievements have been remarkable, and so is her manner of controlling her nervous system. Like everyone else, Laura has nerves, but constant activity diffuses them. Her boundless energy and her way of embracing life with open arms keeps her highly active brain occupied. Laura is the same on the golf course as off of it, which is a great strength.

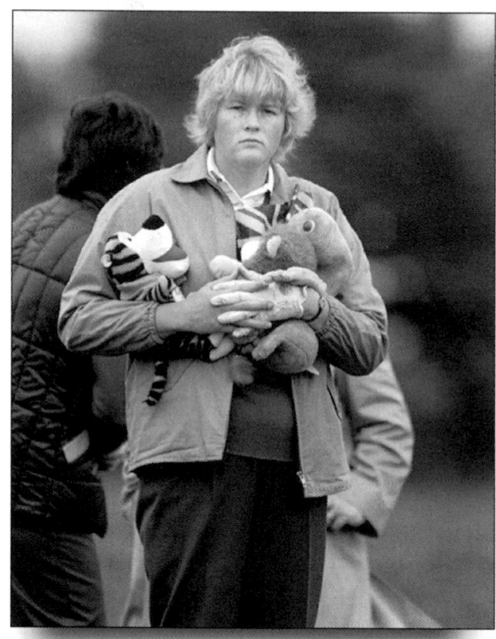

Laura and friends gallery the 1984 Curtis Cup matches at Muirfield. She won twice, defeating the experienced Anne Sander on the last green in one match. Her performance signaled the rise of women's golf in Europe. Photo ©Phil Sheldon.

Although Laura in now much more self-assured in public speaking, she used to be shy to the point of fear. It did not stop her winning, but she likened her horror to that of "a trapeze artist with vertigo." A warm hearted, generous woman, Laura has an instantly appealing quality. Others would like to enjoy life as much as she does.

Laura loves fast cars, gambling, and sports, and her chosen career of professional golf feeds her competitive desires. She indulges herself as she does her family and friends, looking after all those who are close to her.

Laura is a powerful figure who wears her mantle lightly. Inspirational to others, she has matured with success. She has absorbed and processed it, in a way that has been enriching rather than detrimental. As a youngster, she had a temper, and she would moan about her golf. However, she has always handled the demands of success with equanimity.

Like many others, I feel a great affection for Laura, and I love her generosity of spirit. She and I have had a friendly relationship over the years, and she has always been forthcoming, honest, humorous, and helpful. Having covered women's golf on both sides of the Atlantic, I have an appreciation for just how much she has achieved, given the circumstances.

Laura was born in Coventry, England, and she has a brother, Tony, three years older. When she was three, Laura's family moved to Marietta, Georgia, where her father David took a job as a design engineer for Lockheed. Three years later when her parents divorced, Laura and Tony moved back to Surrey, England, with their mother, Rita. Both parents remarried; her mother to Mike Allen in 1974, and her father later in the United States. She has a close bond with her family on both sides of the ocean.

"I come from a good family base. Uncle Mike is not my dad, but I've known him so long that he and my Mum have had pretty equal influences on me. When I began competing in America, I saw more of my dad. We disagree, but we get on very well. My family and friends have been the greatest incentives in my golf.

"I started playing golf at 14 with my brother Tony. I have always been sport mad and played hockey, rounders, netball, and ran cross country at school. I've been 5 feet, 10 inches, as long as I can remember. Tony and I were always competitive with each other. We had bets on everything we did. I wouldn't have a putt without a bet on it. Even at Trivial Pursuit we would play for a fiver (£5.00) or there was no point. I'll always want to win because I'm so competitive. That will never change. The day I don't care, I'll give up.

"I left school at 16 and brought down my handicap from 26 to scratch in two and one-half years. Tony also became a good golfer, and sometimes I outdrove him. My Mum and Uncle Mike helped support me as I played golf all summer, and then I took jobs in the winter at a supermarket, a garage, and working for a bookmaker. As a family, we were a champion ten pin bowling team, and I had the lowest handicap and the highest average (158) of all the women in our league.

"I won some local golf events, became an International in 1981, won the English Intermediate and Welsh Strokeplay titles, and I was lucky enough to be selected for the 1984 Curtis Cup team, in which I played really well.

"At 21 I turned professional, deciding to give it a go and stick to it if I was any good. I couldn't have stayed out there missing cuts every week, I would have given up. I had ambitions, which I kept to myself. I borrowed £1000 from my mum, who was working part-time for a builder, and in 1985, I joined the European tour, which had only been in existence since 1979."

Finishing second to Jan Stephenson in her second tournament was a tremendous achievement for Laura. She was insensitively fined £50 by the then executive director for wearing allegedly "scruffy trousers." At the time Laura had no money and was not an easy size to fit, and Jan Stephenson leapt to her defense. "Laura's got so much talent; it would have been irrelevant if she had played in her bra and pants. You should encourage players of her ability. She could be the Seve Ballesteros of the women's tour," said the prophetic Jan.

Laura went on to win the Belgian Open with a dramatic eagle-birdie-birdie finish and led the money list in her first season, rushing home to shower gifts on her family.

As leading European money winner, she was invited to the Dinah Shore in March 1986, and playing after a winter break of five months, she reveled in just being there. "It was out of this world in Palm Springs, not only as an amazing place, but I had a huge condominium with three bedrooms and three bathrooms, and it was like a palace. I loved the Mission Hills golf course; the greens were unbelievably good, and the practice facilities wonderful. It was my first experience with American tournaments, which are run for the professionals, and they really look after you. Even though I got a bit nervous and missed the cut by a shot, it was a great experience.

"My next American tournament was the 1986 U.S. Open at Dayton, Ohio, where in the last round I was paired with Pat Bradley, who was dominating the season on the way to winning five tournaments, including three majors. I don't think Pat noticed me. She had tunnel vision and was totally concentrated on her own game. I had never seen anything like it. She hardly spoke four words, but she told me at the end of the round that I played well, it was nice to see me, and she hoped to see me again. She shot 69 and finished tied for 5th. I had a 72 and tied for 11th place.

"I realized that America was a very different kettle of fish. The women were very, very good, although not unbeatable. You had to play your best golf to win tournaments."

In her second European season, Laura won two tournaments before taking the British Women's Open title at Royal Birkdale in Lancashire: "When I hit my six iron to the final green I knew it was perfect, and walking up, I remembered that once in Sweden when I had six putts for a playoff, I putted from the front of the green right off the back. This time I two putted for a birdie.

"Coming into the final tournament of the European season, the Spanish Open, I knew I had to win to go ahead of Lotta Neumann, who was the leading money winner at the time, and I was determined to do it. I was amazed when I made it happen, and although it's not in my nature I did jump up and down with excitement.

"I had won four tournaments, the British Open, and £37,500 for the season, which was a fortune (an average annual wage for a woman was £6,000). I knew it could take forever to make a million, but I realized my ambition was to go right to the top. I was greedy for money because that was what it was all about. It might have sounded mercenary, but I wanted to make as much money as I could, as quickly as possible, not to get out of golf, but because I wanted to win for my family and for the money. My Mum, Uncle Mike, and my brother all got great pleasure from my success, and I was pleased. They had struggled to support me as an amateur. I felt it was as much their success as mine, and I wanted to be able to do something for them."

In 1987 Laura, top European for the second time and the British Open champion, was again at the Dinah Shore, where she was not accorded any status and was sent off at 7:30 AM. She came in and led the field with a six-under-par 66. John Cherwa of the Los Angeles Times, who had not seen Laura hit a shot, wrote: "The leader is Laura Davies, a 23-year old lass from England, who despite her six under par 66 is not expected to be

Laura beat out Ayako Okamoto and JoAnne Carner in a play off to win the 1987 U.S. Open. She was also winner of the British Open that year. Photo ©Phil Sheldon.

leading after Sunday's final round. Leading a golf tournament after the first round is akin to leading the 10,000 meter walk after the first lap. Who really cares? Davies won slightly more than 37,000 British pounds in 1987, which equates to about $50,000 here in the Colonies. The winner of the Dinah Shore gets $80,000. Better tell Maggie Thatcher there's no need to hang by the phone."

Cherwa may have thought he was funny, but Laura did not. Her veteran playing partner, Marilynn Smith, was more perceptive: "I'm really impressed with your girl," she told me. "She knows how to manufacture shots, has tremendous power, a lovely touch, and her composure is wonderful. It's rather refreshing she is so shy."

After Laura was paired with Nancy Lopez and finished tied with her for 33rd, the American star commented: "I think if she gets it all together, she could dominate over here." Laura sent her father to get Nancy's autograph on her visor because she was too shy to ask.

Back home in England, Laura became the part owner of a greyhound called Dominique, which was awarded the title "Bitch of the Month" in March 1987 for its excellent performance on the track. After fellow professional Dale Reid backed the greyhound on an off night, she quipped: "I reckon Laura's the faster of the two, and more talented too."

In July 1987, Laura was at the U.S. Open, at Plainfield Country Club in New Jersey, and for the first season she was employing her brother Tony as her caddie, a happy relationship that lasted five years. In a frustrating week of rain delays, Laura played some magnificent and consistent golf, never exceeding par with rounds of 72, 70, 72, 71, to get into a three-way playoff for the title with the legendary JoAnne Carner and Japan's Ayako Okamoto, who became the 1987 LPGA leading money winner and Player of the Year. Astonishingly, victory that Tuesday in the longest Open on record, went to Laura as she birdied the 14th and 15th on the way to a 71, two ahead of Okamoto and three in front of Carner.

"It was fun. The other 141 competitors would love to have been in that situation, but there were only three of us. We had the bonus that we still all had a chance; so I thought 'Why feel sick or nervous about it?' Mentally I had written myself off, thinking it was too early to win something so big, and I thought, 'Get out there, enjoy it, don't make a fool of yourself, congratulate the winner, and be a good loser.'

"All the way round I kept my cool and the only time I felt pressure was on the 18th tee. I looked at Tony and said, 'If I make a four here, we could win this.' That put on the pressure, but I made the four anyway. Afterwards it was all unbelievable. I was downing champagne, doing interviews, I was at 35,000 feet and could hardly realize I was U.S. Open champion and at the same time British Open champion."

Ayako Okamoto, overawed by the English woman's power, commented: "Laura's golf is on another planet." While JoAnne Carner summed it up: "When Laura hit the ball, the earth shook."

Later that season, at a specially called meeting, the LPGA passed an amendment to its by-laws allowing non-tour members who win a major championship or domestic LPGA event, to be exempt from the LPGA qualifying tournament as a condition of LPGA membership. Quite rightly, the 1987 U.S. Open champion would not be going to qualifying school.

By the end of 1987, Laura had the U.S. Open title, was second money winner in Europe, and had finished as runner-up in the British Open, after rushing back with the huge U.S. trophy to compete the next day without a practice round.

All the pressure was on Laura in 1988 to prove she was not a fluke winner in America, and after missing the cut in her first two LPGA tournaments, she won at her fifth outing, the Tucson Open, where she led the field with an opening record-breaking 63. She was two ahead after three rounds and went on to win by one shot with a ten-under par total when she birdied the final hole from a bunker, pushing Robin Walton, Patty Sheehan, and Jan Stephenson into 2nd, 3rd, and 4th placings.

Sandwiching European, American, and Japanese tournaments, she missed three consecutive cuts on the U.S. tour before bursting into form again to win the Jamie Farr Toledo Classic. There, she overtook her hero Nancy Lopez on the last nine holes with a birdie-eagle-birdie flourish. Her final 69 gave her a tournament record 11- under, 277 total and victory by three shots.

"There's no messing about," commented Laura. "I either miss the cut, or I win." JoAnne Carner said: "We don't think of Laura as a rookie. We're just petrified when she makes the cut." Laura had played 12 tour events, missed the cut in five, won two, and earned enough to keep her card for the following season. In July, Laura was defeated by one shot in the major Du Maurier Golf Classic, where Sally Little took the title on a birdied final hole. Laura's hectic schedule was tiring, but she added to her credit with five victories in Europe and one in Japan, where she defeated Jane Geddes in a playoff.

"It was an incredible year. It all happened so quickly, and everything kept going right even though I missed so many cuts. I consider I was very lucky, but I would not think of myself as exceptional, unless I won 35 tournaments and got in the Hall of Fame in a shorter time than Nancy Lopez."

In Britain, Laura was an exceptional enough talent to be awarded the MBE (Member of the Order of the British Empire) which she received from the Queen in October 1988: "Getting my MBE was the most exciting moment of my life. After walking through the corridors of Buckingham Palace, I ended up in front of the Queen in the State Ballroom. She talked to me about winning the U.S. Open and what a great achievement it was, and she asked me what other tournaments I was playing. She pinned the silver medal on me, which was on a red ribbon. I was really impressed with the whole ceremony."

In the 1989 season Laura finished second in the Women's Classic in New Jersey, won the Lady Keystone Open (her third LPGA title in two seasons), and was 13th on the money list, playing in 18 events. In Europe she won one tournament.

"I decided to spend more time on the practice ground," Laura says, "as I wanted to become more consistent, but I knew I didn't have the temperament of a Betsy King, and that if I did it her way I would give up the game. Betsy is totally dedicated to golf and practices every minute of the day. She probably even practices putting on the carpet in her hotel room. I'm terribly competitive, but I would soon burn out and get fed up if I practiced as much as she does."

Part of Laura's enjoyment in life has been her gambling. "Once you start gambling because you think you can make money at it, you're in trouble," she says. "The week of the tournament in Las Vegas is one of non-stop gambling for me, but other than that it's maybe once a week at the dogs or playing pool. Over a week in Vegas, you cannot physically win money. It's almost impossible.

"It's part of my personality to gamble. I enjoy the adrenalin pumping so hard that it's like being up there with a chance of winning a tournament. Sometimes I stop when I'm ahead, and I've walked out of a casino in London and run to the car because I won so much money I was afraid of being mugged.

"Lots of people gamble to try to win money. I gamble for fun, and I know I will lose. Gambling and golf go hand in hand. Nine out of ten golfers gamble, even it it's only a $10 Nassau. I'm sure some people think I'm mad, but I think they're

Laura is in an obviously thankful mood at the 1991 British Women's Open in Woburn. That year she won the Inamori Classic in California and placed fifth on the European Women's Tour. She also began dieting and lost 50 pounds during the fall and winter. Photo ©Phil Sheldon.

mad—some of the stuff they go for, like drink, drugs, or smoking.

"Losing at gambling doesn't bother me, but playing badly on the golf course upsets me. I'm not a compulsive gambler who plays golf; I'm a compulsive golfer who plays at gambling. I love it when I win, and that's the thrill, but gambling is well down my list of priorities. Golf is No. 1."

For Laura, a struggling 1990 season resulted in a second placing at the Kemper Open, a win in the Biarritz Open, and representing Europe in the inaugural Solheim Cup team against the Americans at Lake Nona, where a predominantly inexperienced European team was trounced $11^1/_2$ to $4^1/_2$. The highlight of Laura's week was when Nancy Lopez asked for her autograph on her souvenir program and when, together with Alison Nicholas in the foursomes, they defeated Lopez and Pat Bradley by 2 and 1: "It ranks very high in my career to beat Nancy, right up with winning the U.S. Open," she said.

Nancy Lopez was enthusiastic: "Laura has the charisma to be a superstar, and she has the game. She's a great asset to our tour, and I keep asking her if she is going to play full time in the U.S. Maybe she will next year. We need her on our tour. She's a drawing card, and people want to see her hit the ball. Laura is one of a kind."

The Englishwoman was still determined to support her home tour and continue her demanding worldwide schedule. Remarkably, in March 1991 she won the Inamori Classic at Stoneridge Country Club in California without once using her driver, her confidence having been dented by increasingly erratic tee shots. Judy Dickinson, who tied for runner-up, said, "There aren't many who could do that." JoAnne Carner stated, "The amazing thing is that Laura won while she was in a slump."

In 1991, Laura achieved a career low round 62, in the LPGA Rail Charity Classic, and she won the Inamori Classic, her fourth LPGA title. In Europe, she achieved victory in the Valextra Classic. Of prime importance for Laura that season was the beginning of a diet which resulted in the shedding of more than 50 pounds over several months. "In September that year I was watching American television and saw the L.A. Dodgers' coach Tommy Lasorda. He was advertising a slimming aid which seemed effective and simple. He had become really slim with a vitamin and mineral enriched powder that you mix with cold milk or hot water as a flavored drink.

"I bought a couple of cartons on the way to the course each day, had one for breakfast, a couple of bananas as I played, and then another carton after my round. It wasn't the easiest thing I've ever done because I felt very hungry and got terrible cravings. I'm a chocoholic, and I gave up chocolate and ate a peach or bunch of grapes instead. When I craved ice cream, I had frozen yogurt, and I ate more vegetables and sensible food.

"It's like jet lag; you get over it quickly if that's what you decide to do. It's all in the mind. The mind sorts out the good from the mediocre on the golf course, and the champions can make things happen. Losing weight was a challenge, and I love to test myself because it is very satisfying. I enjoy saying, 'I've done it, stuck to it, and won.' It was one of the greatest achievements of my life."

In 1992, the year that Laura led the European money list for a record third time, she also reached the height of her inspirational powers by making her teammates in the 1992 Solheim Cup at Dalmahoy believe in a European victory. All season she worked at it. "It is the most important week of the year, since a win will reflect so well on our tour," she said. "Winning in front of British crowds is what I want. Our captain, Mickey Walker, is the best person, and she will choose a perfect team. She's top class and can be my captain for the next ten years. She's been there and done it; you can respect someone like that."

With the inspiration of Laura out front leading the charge and Mickey quietly putting together the pairings and smoothing the way, the European women professionals enjoyed their greatest moment in golf as they swept onwards to a $11^1/_2$ to $6^1/_2$ victory against the Americans, who had been made 6 to 1 favorites, by the bookmakers. It was a stunning achievement.

By 1995, Laura was again dominating world golf, leading the US money list and dancing in and out of top position in Europe as she juggled her commitments on both tours. She was aiming to top

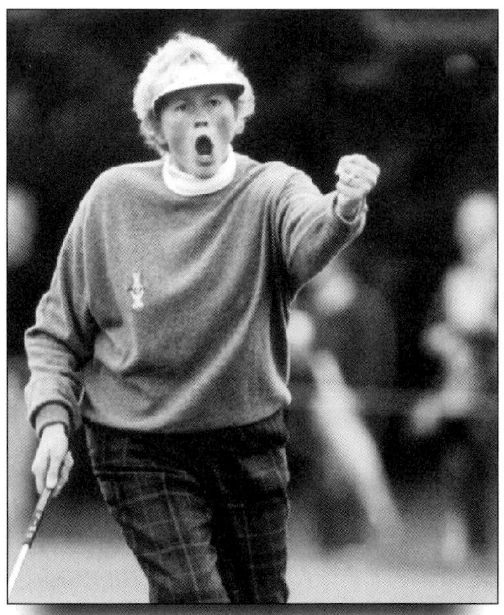

Laura reacts to her birdie on the second hole at the 1992 Solheim Cup in Dalmahoy, Scotland. With Laura's inspiration and Captain Mickey Walker's adept pairings, Europe's women professionals won 11½ to 6½ against the Americans who had been 6-1 favorites. Photo: Richard Saker/Allsport.

both money lists at the end of the season, an ambition she described as "massive pie-in-the-sky," but she wanted something to aim at. When she won for the fourth time in 1995, the Irish Open in July, it was by a record 16 shots and a record 25-under par.

As Laura continued to rocket 'round the golf tours of the world, she increased her victories to seven (four European, two LPGA, one Japanese), but it was not enough to eclipse the astounding year of Annika Sorenstam, to whom she kept taking second place. The Swedish professional dominated in unprecedented style by becoming leading money winner in Europe and America, as well as LPGA Player of the Year and Vare Trophy winner in 1995, records Laura would dearly loved to have set.

When Laura won in Japan at the end of the season (her 40th worldwide title), she received the hefty $108,000 prize, a diamond necklace and a large Mazda car. Afterwards, she said that possibly in the next five years, she might like to play a full season on their tour, provided she made it through the qualifying school. Another challenge for Laura, who remarked: "I feel thoroughly at home in Japan, and they give very generous prizes."

Mickey Walker acknowledges the extraordinary role that Laura has played throughout her golfing career: "Laura was simply willing the Solheim Cup victory. No one could have imagined we would have won by such a huge margin, but Laura has an incredible influence and power over the players, it's as though she is God. She doesn't realize it, and they don't either.

"Laura is Laura, unique in every sense, as a talent, a person, in whatever she has done. Her individual feat as a non-cardholder of the LPGA winning the U.S. Open will never happen again. Whatever she achieves in the future, she will be the dominant personality in European golf. There will never be another Laura."

LPGA Victories: 1988 Circle K LPGA Tucson Open, Jamie Farr Toledo Classic. **1989** Lady Keystone Open. **1991** Inamori Classic. **1993** McDonald's Championship. **1994** Standard Register PING, Sara Lee Classic, McDonald's LPGA Championship. **1995** Standard Register PING, Chick-fil-A Charity Championship.

Highlights of European Tour: 1986 McEwans Wirral Classic, British Open, Greater Manchester Tournament, Spanish Open, Belgian Open. **1987** Italian Open. **1988** Biarritz Open, Italian Open, Ford Classic. **1989** Laing Charity Classic. **1990** AGF Biarritz Open. **1991** Valextra Classic. **1992** European Open, English Open, BMW Italian Open. **1993** Waterford Dairies English Open. **1994** Irish Holidays Open, New Skoda Scottish Open, Itoki Japanese Classic, Alpine Australian Masters, Thailand Open. **1995** Evian Masters, Guardian Irish Holidays Open, Woodpecker Women's Welsh Open, Wilkinson Sword Ladies English Open, Itoki Japanese Classic.

Laura Davies' LPGA Record

Year	No.of Events	Best Finish	Money	Rank	Scoring Average
1988	21	1	$160,220	15	72.98
1989	18	1	181,574	13	71.87
1990	18	T2	64,863	64	73.72
1991	23	1	200,831	20	73.16
1992	21	2	150,163	39	72.94
1993	16	1	240,643	20	72.00
1994	22	1	687,201	1	70.91
1995	17	1	530,349	2	71.37

Chako Higuchi

Born in 1945, Chako Higuchi became such a Japanese superstar of women's golf in the 1970s that she was recognized in the streets of Tokyo. People would stop and clap their hands together excitedly as she passed by.

Although Chako won the JLPGA Championship for eight consecutive years beginning in 1969, it was her victories overseas that established her stardom. She won the Australian Open, the 1976 Colgate European Open, and finally a major title, when she took the 1977 LPGA Championship in America.

Chako has a distinctive, if unorthodox, swing, which has worked beautifully over the years. "I just remember her swaying off the ball and how accurate she was with her woods," says British professional Mickey Walker. "She never showed any emotion. You wouldn't have known if she was shooting 68 or 88, which is a great asset in playing golf. That sort of control is one of the reasons the Japanese have made such incredible strides in world golf."

A charming woman, Chako was as responsible for the rise of women's golf in Japan as Nancy Lopez was in the United States. A pioneer in every sense of the word, she and Marbo Sasaki played in America on the LPGA tour. At the same time, in Japan, they were involved in the beginnings of the JLPGA with professional golfer Ayako Nihei and the Dunlop-employed Sho Tobari, who organized and promoted the early men's and women's golf tournaments.

Ayako's purpose was to establish a strong JLPGA; she became its first elected president: "I never thought of what people might say when I turned professional. I played because I liked the sport, and I wanted to establish women in it. Women professional golfers have acquired better status than women in other jobs, so that it is an attractive life to them, perhaps an ideal. The JLPGA was lucky to have Chako, who appealed to the public and to sponsors with her personality and her ability."

Sho Tobari says even more adamantly, "Chako was the focus for the Japanese women's tour." Sho, a university graduate and golf team member, did not turn professional when he left the university in 1967, as the social status of a professional golfer

Chako Higuchi won the LPGA Championship in 1977, her first major U.S. title, although she had won the JLPGA Championship eight consecutive years beginning in 1969. Photo ©Phil Sheldon.

was then very low. He became a golf ball salesman for Dunlop, and because the company wanted to sell more golf balls, he persuaded them to sponsor the first Dunlop tournament for men in 1968: "Television executives thought old movies would get a better audience rating than golf, but they ran it to very successful viewing figures," he says.

Sho's involvement in men's and then women's tournaments deepened with the formation of Dunlop Sports Enterprise. "Women's golf was minor because women were not admitted as golf club members, but with the beginning of the women's movement in the early 1970s, I thought it had a future. As men's golf became more popular, we began using Chako as a vehicle, and women's golf started to move.

"By the mid-1970s Chako was an idol, playing tournaments, doing exhibitions and clinics. I told her to go to the U.S. in 1970, when there were hardly any women's tournaments in Japan, and she played from January to May in the U.S., and then I built the tour around her in Japan. She was sponsored by Mizuno, with Masato Mizuno who was then a student, acting as her interpreter. Masato is now president of the company.

"Chako was strong and patient, and she practiced a lot. Immediately after she landed, she would be off to the course for practice. If she thought of something she wanted to try out on the journey, she had to rush to the practice ground. She is an athlete, a good fighter who had to strive for it all: prize money, tournaments, and sponsors. She is a born competitor who learned a lot from the Americans. When she saw how different she was with the sway on her backswing, it really embarrassed her. She was shocked, but she didn't change it. In Britain, Henry Cotton saw her when she won the European Open in 1976 and said it was an effective swing for a woman to use.

"Chako, who has a strong personality and is an independent woman, was the first stage in the development of Japanese women's golf. Ayako Okamoto was the second stage. I had faith in their ability and eventually got the women on television. For Ayako Nihei, doing the organization and administration of the JLPGA in the early days, it was very hard, particularly when the women broke away from the men's PGA in 1967. It was a real struggle."

In the Japan of the 1960s, there were 580 golf courses and 1.5 million golfers. This increased to 1700 courses and 12 million golfers by the 1990s.

Sho Tobari formed his own company to run 25 men's and women's tournaments; he remained on the Dunlop Board as a non-executive director; he became a television commentator with his own show, and started to design and manage golf courses. Twenty-five years after he began, he said: "I still love the game of golf."

In 1976, I saw Chako win the Colgate European Open at Sunningdale, and I also watched her play on the LPGA tour. I did not know her well, but when I interviewed her in Japan she was charming, helpful, and too shy to speak to me without an interpreter.

Born and brought up in Tokyo, Chako was motivated by being sixth in a large family of two boys and six girls. Her father, who is no longer alive, was in the food business, and he struggled to support them.

"I was a track and field athlete at school, and I started golf at 16, when I went to live with my older sister, who was working as a locker room attendant at a local golf course. She lent me her clubs and told me that I could hit balls at the range for nothing. I was there from 9 a.m. to 5 p.m. every weekend.

"I began caddying for Torakichi Nakamura, a famous teaching professional, who won the individual and team event when the Canada Cup was in Tokyo in 1957. He taught me the game physically and mentally; he made me run every morning and hit 1,000 balls a day until I cried.

"There was no proper women's tour, but I turned professional in 1967 and worked at the Kalagwe Golf and Country Club. When there were two or three tournaments a year, I won them all, and people considered me very competitive. There were few women professional golfers, since most girls worked in banks and department stores and married at 22 and 23. You became a professional to raise your status and get away from this image. To a lot of women I became an idol, and the attitudes toward women professionals changed as the tour grew.

"I practiced hard to win tournaments; I was expected to win all the time, and I tried to meet those expectations. The younger professionals aspired to do the same and to become better professionals. Money and independence were important, and I was happy to earn as much as possible. When I had won 50 tournaments, I still wanted to win more because I enjoyed winning.

"In 1969, Marilynn Smith, from the LPGA tour, was in Japan to do a clinic, and I was supposed to play with her. Marilynn caught a cold and couldn't play, and I was really disappointed because I wanted to compare myself to the Americans. When Mizuno offered to sponsor me to go to the U.S., I jumped at it. There was no qualifying school in 1969. You had to finish in the top 80 percent for the first few tournaments. I went for three months with Marbo Sasaki, and I was so homesick, I wanted to return as soon as I arrived. We played ten tournaments, and I was crossing off each one. I couldn't wait to get home. [Chako was laughing at these memories.] My best finish toward the end of that first visit was ninth.

"My first round, I shot 42–38 for 80. I was so nervous; I was in all the lakes and the rough. I didn't know what I was doing. I had a really bad time. I was surprised there were so many good U.S. professionals.

"I went back every year for 10 years, and I improved and made money. I liked studying golf by watching the other golfers, and I had ambitions to finish well and to win in America, which I did. I wanted to win a major, and in the 1977 LPGA Championship I led for three days. Then I got nervous, since I was ahead of Judy Rankin and Sandra Post, and I thought I would not win. By then, I was very consistent, and I hardly ever missed a fairway. On the final day I played my best golf, and it turned out to be the best of all. It was the most exciting moment of my career, and I was so happy to win a major that I thought I could quit golf. But of course that was not what I wanted to do."

At 26, in 1972, Chako married Japanese professional golfer, Isao Matsui. He played the men's tour and had his own television program. Four years older than Chako, he helped her with her golf game, and she ignored the people who said she was a success on tour and he wasn't.

Chako juggled golf on both sides of the Pacific and was an idol to women in her own country. Photo courtesy: LPGA.

"At that time, a Japanese woman was meant to walk behind her husband, never stand before him," she recalled. "I cooked for my husband when I was home, and I accepted most of his decisions but not all of them. In some ways I was a typical Japanese wife doing everything at home and waiting for him. Then I would go out on tour, where I was completely free, and forget it all.

"I thought that I could get married, have children, and still be a successful top golfer because I had seen Judy Rankin do it in America. You only need to see one person as a role model. After I married, so did many other Japanese women professionals, and I was pleased."

In 1980, Chako miscarried and afterwards still went on winning tournaments. Her first marriage ended in divorce in the early 1980s, and she married her present husband, Otsuka Yoshihumi, and they have one daughter Lisa, born in 1986. Otsuka is in real estate and a six-handicap golfer.

Chako, as a wife and mother, continued to win golf tournaments in Japan: "I became an emancipated woman through patience, with practice, and by wanting everything so hard. It all developed through my golf and my personality. I have done things for my own pride because others think I can't and because I want to show people that others can follow."

U.S. professional Sandra Palmer, a good friend of Chako's for many years, says, "Her concentration and ability to stay focused is exceptional. With her big turn and unusual backswing, the concept of keeping her eye on the ball is the last thing she would do. But she always knows where the ball is, and she has a very pretty tempo.

"One of the top golfers for many years, she was one of our first International competitors and very good about learning English. She was good for our tour and has a great sense of humor. When she won our LPGA Championship, they gave her a ticker tape parade in Tokyo.

"When I went to Japan in the early 1970s, I took Chako an Elvis Presley album—you would have thought I had given her a diamond bracelet. I have never seen her so excited. The next day she gave me a pearl brooch larger than a 50¢ piece. She is such a generous woman that if you like her sweater, she goes and buys one for you.

"She was the first top female professional golfer in Japan, where everyone knew her the way they knew the Emperor. She handled herself so well and had a perfect image for a role model. You couldn't have had a better pioneer than Chako. She was a wonderful good-will ambassador."

LPGA Victories: 1976 Colgate European Championship. **1977** LPGA Championship.

Career Highlights: 9 times JLPGA champion, winner of 71 career victories worldwide, including the Japanese Women's Open 4 times, winning approximately $3.784 million from all sources through **1992**.

Chako Higuchi's LPGA Record

Year	No.of Events	Best Finish	Money	Rank	Scoring Average
1970	10	T9	$2,810	41	74.86
1971	10	2	9,714	19	74.33
1972	3	T14	1,702	73	77.49
1973	8	2	10,180	41	73.84
1974	6	6	9,602	44	74.00
1975	9	T3	15,678	28	73.13
1976	15	1	57,389	10	73.82
1977	14	1	30,897	18	73.62
1978	9	T5	19,320	NA	73.55
1979	6	T2	26,675	NA	72.17
1980	1	3	12,250	73	72.33
1981	DNP				
1982	2	T12	2,790	129	73.00
1983	1	T21	2,606	146	73.67

Joan Joyce

When I first met Joan Joyce in the latter part of the 1970s, I was struck by her extraordinary athletic quality and the purely physical enjoyment of sport that flowed through her. "I cannot imagine being a housewife in a kitchen, which has to be the most boring thing in the world." A tall, big-boned, powerful woman, she radiates physical presence, although the only sport I have seen her play, golf, is not her natural milieu.

Joan was the greatest woman softball pitcher in the world, with all sorts of records that unfortunately I do not comprehend, but it is obvious that as a softball player she is held in awe.

At the age of 37, while a softball professional, she joined the ranks of the LPGA, having qualified in 1977, only 18 months after starting to play golf seriously. She tried to combine her two sports until 1981, when she decided to focus solely on golf. Winning $31,000 on the golf tour in 1984 was a tribute to her guts and determination.

To change your muscle memory at such a relatively late stage in life in order to compete successfully in another sport is an almost unrealistic task, yet Joan has never seen it in that light. Like the highly athletic Althea Gibson, who switched from tennis to golf, Joan had high expectations and to this day has not altered them. She is a woman who makes no concessions, who resists any physical ailment, and who revels in competition. Winning has always been important; yet as a golfer she has had to settle for a lesser level of achievement. It would be a masochistic endeavor, had she not enjoyed it so much.

My relationship with Joan has never been close, but she has always been helpful, forthright, and willing to be interviewed. She talks frankly about the prejudice of society against the athletic woman.

By the late 1980s Joan reduced her tournament appearances to work for a custom golf club manufacturer, and she was enjoying teaching golf in Florida.

Joan was born in Waterbury, Connecticut, the eldest of three children, having a brother one year younger and a sister ten years younger. Her father worked as a factory foreman doing the 7 AM–3 PM shift, her mother in a lipstick factory on the 3PM–11 PM shift, and it was her father who influenced her most. He was a softball and basketball player and coach and would take Joan and her brother with him.

"We didn't have a choice; we just learned sports. I was naturally competitive with my brother, or anybody I could find to catch with me. At 10, I was a pitcher for the Park and Recreation Softball team; I could throw underhand, run, get balls from everywhere and get people out.

"Three years later I tried out for the Raybestos Brakettes, an amateur softball team playing at the highest level, and I was a second baseman and outfielder. They didn't know for a year that I could pitch underhand, and if we were 10–0 ahead they would let me pitch a little.

"At that stage I didn't know or care what other people thought about my softball—I enjoyed it, and I was out there playing the same sport as my father.

"I finished high school and started a degree in Physical education at South Connecticut College but dropped out after six months. I worked for eight months in public relations for the Raybestos Company, which makes brake linings, but I couldn't stand the 9–5 job. I left and worked for a bowling alley for a while and became good enough at bowling to represent them in tournaments. After that, I became a basketball coach in a Catholic school.

"I was a basketball official going to a game, when I saw a nun coaching her team, trying to get the girls to do a weave. The kids couldn't understand it; so I offered to help her. I got them doing it immediately, and she offered me the coaching job. I thought it would be fun, and I was the physical education teacher for three years at Waterbury Catholic High School. Catholicism is not a big influence on my life, but I'm a pretty good Catholic, and nuns have been some of my best friends.

"The job at Waterbury led to my returning to get my physical education degree, which I did in three years at Chapman College in Orange County, California. When I was 20, I was engaged to be married for a year, but in those days you were expected to be engaged for about five years, and I felt I was much too young. The fellow made it clear that I could go ahead and achieve whatever I wanted, but there were so many things I wanted to do, and I felt I couldn't inflict that lifestyle on another person. I needed to be free. My parents never put any pressure on me to get married or to have children.

"I don't know whether I would like to have had my own children, although it would probably be fun bringing up kids. My brother has a couple whom I love, that I take out and spoil to death, but I'm not sure I would like to have been tied down and to have had to be there all the time to take care of them, which is tough and confining. I like doing too many other things. I have no regrets at anything I have done. I have totally enjoyed everything, met a whole lot of neat people, and had a good time."

By the time she was 18, Joan had been a softball pitcher at the national level and had found out there was prejudice against women athletes: "In 1956 when I was just entering high school and playing sports, people thought that a woman playing any type of sport was awful. Women weren't supposed to sweat or feel the same as a man competing. Although I knew a man could be stronger, I also knew I could think as well. I could do what I wanted as well, and why were people giving me a hard time?

"There were so many frustrated women who would like to have been athletes but were not because society said you shouldn't do it. I have met plenty who have said, 'I wanted to do that, but I couldn't.' I felt sorry for them and told them they should not accept society's attitudes. I never bought the fact that I couldn't be competitive. I was fortunate growing up as a woman athlete in Connecticut, where we had outstanding opportunities in sports, and I could play 40 games of major league caliber softball and basketball in a season.

"Everyone knew Joan Joyce in basketball, in softball, and as a volleyball official. When the

Softball great Joan Joyce honed her golfing skills on the mini-tour before she qualified for the LPGA. Here, she is shown with Suzanne Jackson, Group Fore's tournament director, who later became the LPGA's tournament director, and San Francisco journalist Nelson Cullenward.

Joan came to golf from softball where she was one of the leading pitchers in the world. She recorded 725 wins and 42 losses in her 25-year softball career. Among her records are 150 no-hitters and 50 perfect games. She also pitched a 157 scoreless inning streak, and once she struck out Ted Williams in an exhibition. Here, she is shown with Kathy Neal, a star softball player who joined Joyce on the Group Fore mini-tour in the 1970s.

feminists came along, I didn't identify with them, since I was so busy enjoying what I was doing, I didn't need to. I have lived my own life from the time I was 13.

"Billie Jean King has done more for women athletes than anyone else, with her ability to speak out, to get attention, and have people take notice. By the 1980s the woman athlete was acceptable.

"Sport is fun. It takes a lot of work to became a winner, and most people don't want to put in that much work, but I'm a competitor, and I will do the best job I can at whatever I'm doing. I may not win, which doesn't bother me, but I don't enjoy losing either.

I didn't want to be the greatest softball pitcher in the world; I wanted to be the best at what I was doing. I could throw a softball. I worked very hard, and all I knew was that I had a softball in my hand, that someone was coming to bat against me, and that I was not going to let that person beat me. I just work at what I do to become the best. I think I know why I have pitched better than other people. I would get a lot more hyperextension of my shoulder taking the ball back. That gave me a much better arc to control the ball, and I have used my legs very well.

"I pitched for 25 years and recorded 725 wins and 42 losses. I'm toughest when it is tough, and I liked it best when I was in trouble. There is an inner drive which makes you competitive so that by nature you cannot let anyone beat you. I felt the pressure in softball from 1958, when I became known as the best softball pitcher in the world. Everybody who came out to face me wanted to beat me—not my team, but Joan Joyce. They would get their charge out of beating me because not too many people could do that."

Joan, who was a star, first in amateur, then professional softball, formed a professional league with backing from Billie Jean King and professional golfer Jane Blalock. Joan was the driving force of the Connecticut Falcons. "I was interested in establishing a professional softball league, not so much for myself but for all the high school and college players who would one day like to play professional softball. It came close to being successful, and since a lot of it depended on me, I didn't want to leave it." In 1981 the softball league failed for lack of funds, and Joan played full time golf.

In October 1975, she decided she wanted to try to qualify and to play as a professional golfer, while continuing to support the softball league. Joan made it through the LPGA qualifying school 18 months after she took up the game, which was astonishing. Trying to combine the sports, she did not earn sufficient money to keep her card in 1979 and had to qualify again in 1980.

"Golf was a new challenge, and I was starting at the bottom of another sport. I had always been able to hit the ball, since I swung at it a few times in 1960, and it had traveled a good distance. When I became a professional, I would see people hit the ball well on the practice range and then leave it. If I was hitting it well, I'd stay out there for hours. It was so much fun, I didn't want to leave. I figured if I did it enough times, my swing would start repeating itself on the golf course, and I had to keep doing it until I knew what it felt like. When you get into trouble, you must let your body respond to what it automatically knows. I was always in good physical shape. I did a lot of running, but I don't see golfers as real athletes, although they are improving.

"When I arrived on tour, I had to worry just about hitting the ball, and no other professional can know what that is like. I played with a lot of fear, since I had no idea where the ball was going, and often I couldn't hit a green with a pitching or sand wedge. The first ball I hit in a tournament went miles, but to the right and out of bounds, and I was incredibly embarrassed. At the beginning, all I did was hit the ball hard and far, but I never knew where it was going.

"I had to make an emotional adjustment from team sports, where basically people care about each other, to golf, where no one cares. At first, I had a terrible time, because I would get so excited, and no one wanted to hear about it."

After her finest season in 1984, Joan was not well, and in the middle of the following year she had a hysterectomy. She was so anemic that she was close to needing a blood transfusion. Although she had a vaginal hysterectomy, rather than being surgically cut, her recovery rate was phenomenal.

"I wanted to go home two days after the operation, but the doctor persuaded me to stay one day longer. I couldn't wait to get out of the hospital, and I was marching round the corridors. Within ten days, I played 36 holes of golf in one day, and although I was a little tired, I was fine. Three weeks after the operation I was playing a four- round tournament in Canada.

"After my operation I didn't play as well, which was very frustrating, since there are times when I can play this game. The whole problem as I see it is a physical skill breakdown, not related to my operation or to my age. I don't make any concession to age. How could it have anything to do with it? I can walk the golf course as well as anyone, I'm as strong as anyone, I can think as well. How could it be age?

"When I began playing, I went out and hit it, hit it again, and somehow got it in the hole. Now that I play a whole lot better, I can't handle the bad shots as easily, so I put too much pressure on myself. What is frustrating is that I have not played golf with the ability I would wish, so that I could have combined it with my knowledge of competing in everything else."

Joan Joyce's LPGA Record

Year	No.of Events	Best Finish	Money	Rank	Scoring Average
1977	8	T57	NA	NA	81.73
1978	21	T18	$3,148	95	77.84
1979	17	T45	1,703	116	77.72
1980	11	T15	3,029	118	76.69
1981	30	T6	14,146	77	75.52
1982	30	T6	17,743	74	75.52
1983	28	T14	9,060	108	75.68
1984	30	T6	31,483	65	74.67
1985	27	T28	4,160	150	76.54
1986	28	T28	7,484	132	76.27
1987	20	T21	5,314	148	76.04
1988	14	T20	5,100	156	75.19
1989	14	T43	2,505	167	76.41
1990	12	NA	NA	NA	NA
1991	12	NA	NA	NA	NA
1992	13	NA	NA	NA	NA
1993	8	NA	NA	NA	NA
1994	6	NA	NA	NA	79.17
1995	DNP				

Karolyn Kertzman

Karolyn Kertzman was on the LPGA tour from 1971 through 1982. Never a tournament winner, her best year was 1974, when she was 34th on the money list with $13,774. She projected the beauty queen image: tall, with long, curling auburn hair, and she used her glamour as an antidote to being in the world of sport, since she didn't like the look of the tough woman athlete. "There is a bit of a stigma that if you play golf you must be queer. I fought it by keeping my hair long, by looking feminine, and making my statement louder."

With a strong, assertive personality, she was sometimes outspoken in her criticism of her fellow professionals, although she appreciated them and accepted the quirks of the lifestyle. Unlike most of the women, Karolyn would enter a bar on her own and eat and drink alone, rather than be with a group or order room service.

When Karolyn married Richard Hansard in 1977, he took her name. After she left the tour and they worked together, their stormy relationship resulted in eventual divorce: "I made him take back his own name," she says with some satisfaction. An unhappy Karolyn started drinking: "It's not good to work with your spouse. You're together 24 hours a day." Worse was to follow, when it was discovered she had brain cancer. A large tumor was removed, which later grew back, and a second operation was performed. Karolyn's indomitable spirit and her humor survived, and in 1992 she married Robert Lahonde, this time taking her husband's name.

An attractive woman, with warmth and humor, Karolyn would always go out of her way to come and chat when she saw me on tour. She gave me her opinions without any reservation, on tour and again 10 years later.

"I was born in Rapid City, South Dakota, and was brought up with two brothers—huge men—seven and eight years older. The family moved to San Diego when I was two, and my father had jobs as a farmer, a plumber, working in a bar, and building airplanes, while my mother was a waitress in an exclusive restaurant. We were a middle class family, with a housekeeper, and we never did without anything. We were all indulged children, allowed to do our own thing.

"My dolls went in the closet, and I got my extreme competitiveness from my brothers, who would wrestle with me on their knees. I started playing golf with them at seven, because it wasn't physically painful like football. I won a junior trophy and joined the famous junior golf program in San Diego. I was a scratch golfer at 16, before my teenage revolt against my parents occurred, and I did not want to dedicate myself to golf. At 18 all my friends were running off and getting married, and that's what I wanted to do.

Karolyn Kertzman spent 12 years on the LPGA. Although she never won a tournament, she continues to win the biggest battle of her life, relying on the inner strength, determination and grit she developed while on tour. Photo courtesy: Katherine Murphy.

"Then I changed my mind. I had worked at a golf course and didn't like working for other people. When my mother took me to play in a Pro-Am in Palm Springs, I decided that professional sports were glamorous and that I was going to join the LPGA tour, although I had no idea what I was going to do as a professional golfer.

"I worked to get enough money to join the tour, and I went to Florida to a tournament in 1971, when I was 20. It was terrible. I forgot to make a hotel reservation and was nearly in tears until someone fixed me up with a local family. The wind blew, I played a practice round with Sandra Haynie, Carol Mann, and Gloria Ehret, and I was in awe of the high caliber of play. I shot 80, 80, and I was terrified. The players were taking yardages, and I'd never heard of that, but at the same time I was fascinated by it all. I played five events that year and full time in 1972.

"There was a small, close-knit group of about 60–70 players, a great group of women who took me under their wing. I couldn't believe how nice they were. I was a greenhorn; yet I could learn to play golf from the greats on tour, who willingly gave me advice.

"Although I had a few friends, I never felt I got along personally with the women as a group. I was interested in the group and would defend it to the hilt, but I felt like an outsider and a loner. I always tried to be nice to younger players and welcome them aboard. The tour had its image problems, and you have to accept the gay element because there are gays in everything. But I can't condone it, and it bothers me, partly on religious grounds—I was raised a Catholic—and partly because I don't understand it, and I'm not part of it. I feel the same about homosexual men. I don't think it's right. God created man and God created woman, and that's how it should be.

"Far too many girls get caught up in things they would never have done in different circumstances. At some point in your life, you are vulnerable, and I dislike anyone who preys on vulnerability. I don't like lecherous men, who grab hold of me. I made a pretty strong stand with my views and sometimes I was too strong for some people, but that was their problem, not mine.

"My golf made slow, steady progress. I learned as I went, with 1974 and 1976 being my best seasons. When I was single, I was having too much fun and found it was awfully difficult to play golf with a hangover. Later, my golf became important to me, and I paid my penance by working really hard.

"In 1974, I met my first husband, Richard Hansard, who was running a tournament. We were together for three years before we married. I wasn't going to quit golf to get married, nor would I have asked him to quit his job, as head of promotions for the Sacramento Union newspaper, to marry me. It is very difficult for a man to step back if it is the woman who is in the limelight, although most women do it in reverse. I'm a strong-willed, domineering, independent woman, which comes from traveling so much. I never thought I would find a man with whom I could spend the rest of my life, until I met my husband, who I felt was the most liberated man I had known. I didn't need a man to take care of me; I needed someone to share my life. Our marriage didn't make any difference—it was just a piece of paper.

"Richard was ten years my senior, which could have been a hindrance. I felt a younger man might adapt more easily; so I was shocked when he went to my father and asked him if it would be all right for him to take our family name. It was totally his idea. I would never ask that of anyone. He told my dad it was the only gift he could give me, and he felt I'd worked hard to be known out on tour, so I should not give up my identity. I wouldn't have cared, but he did, and said it was easier for him to give up his name. My dad said he was certainly gaining a son and not losing a daughter. I felt Richard wasn't getting such a great name, and it took a very strong and stable man to take a woman's name.

"In spite of telling people that he got married and changed his name, and that's all there was to it, he had a lot of problems—with his passport, with affidavits, and with discrimination. Women's groups were delighted and wanted to involve him, but he declined.

"I believe in equal pay for equal work and that we've all benefitted from the women's movement, but I can't take the whole package; I just support certain parts of it. I am a liberated woman and have never minded sitting at a bar on my own if I wanted a drink. I could afford to buy my own, and I feel I have every right as a human being to do what I damned well please. I'm not there to pick up anyone, and if someone tries to buy me a drink, I say, 'No thank you, I'm not interested.' I've been in a bar, been sent a drink and refused it, and then sent one back, paid for it and left the bar. You can always ask a bartender to tell someone to go and jump. It's very easy for me because I used to play golf with bartenders back home; so I would go and talk to bartenders when I was on tour and never thought anything of it. I also used to work as a cocktail waitress at one time; so I had no inhibitions about going into a bar.

"If I am hungry and there's no one with whom I can eat, I'll eat alone in a hotel restaurant. I don't enjoy eating alone, but it doesn't bother me, because I regard it as a relaxing function and I get sick and tired of hotel rooms.

"I liked playing golf and making a living at something I enjoyed, but it was not always easy to survive financially. And sometimes I found it necessary to find a sponsor. I would get depressed at not winning, and the lifestyle can be very hard. At times the human psyche is so negative that it is difficult to be 'up' every day. You can't get excited at a good round or depressed at a bad one because you need to maintain an equilibrium to play consistently. I find this difficult, since I'm a very emotional person. I flare up, explode, I'm very verbal, and then it's all over."

Karolyn left the tour at the end of 1982, with an injured shoulder that had aggravated her for some time: "I had 12 years out there and met some wonderful people." She returned home to study marketing and business statistics and take classes to find out where her talent lay. She worked in media sales at two radio stations in the Sacramento area before setting up a marketing company with her husband in 1985. Spending 24 hours together, everyday, did not help their relationship. They parted, and some years later, divorced.

When Karolyn had to face her illness and the first operation in December 1987, she did so alone, with tremendous courage and a will to live: "Can you believe they told me I had a tumor the size of a golf ball? Amazing, but that was how they described it. When I was in hospital, I talked to God, asking for his guidance, which He gave me. He put a warm cloak around me, and I knew that everything would be all right."

After surgery, she was boosted by support groups and a good friend, Johanna Johnson, in Sacramento. "Johanna is five years older, and I have known her for a long time. She laughs, has a good time, and helped me find out that no matter what happens, you can laugh. I used to be quick-witted; now I'm quick-hearted. With the first operation I had a 50–50 chance of not making it off the table; the second time in 1989, I was given two years to live. It was hell, but I always tried to find the funny parts, and I still get letters from people with whom I went through radiation. They remember I always came in laughing and smiling. I got involved in cancer and brain tumor support groups and learned how to help people. I have seen so many people so sick, and we've lost a lot, but we can still laugh and have a good time."

Karolyn lost her beautiful auburn hair, some of it permanently, from radiation burns. "I wear wigs. I'm a blonde, it's great. It's not that important, and it's interesting that I met someone who accepts it and who has really cared for me. We met after my second operation, in one of the programs I attended, and we married in July 1992. I never liked myself before, but now I think I'm a nice person. One thing I know, is that I'm alive, really alive, from the inside out instead of from the outside in."

Karolyn Kertzman's LPGA Record

Year	No.of Events	Best Finish	Money	Rank	Scoring Average
1971	5	T22	$448	NA	NA
1972	18	T17	2,706	52	76.73
1973	28	T6	7,610	50	77.47
1974	28	T4	13,774	34	75.43
1975	14	3	7,818	46	74.58
1976	19	T6	13,914	47	76.48
1977	19	T5	8,605	62	75.51
1978	15	T10	10,849	64	74.96
1979	NA	NA	6,042	92	74.98
1980	NA	NA	11,593	78	75.10
1981	NA	NA	8,581	101	75.35
1982	NA	NA	2,282	131	75.57

Betsy King

Ask Betsy King to describe herself and she replies instantly: "I am very analytical and very religious. No, I hate saying it that way. I just say I'm a Christian. I work pretty hard, I'm self motivated, and would be the same in any job I did, since I'm very competitive. I always wanted to win at Monopoly, to beat my brother at everything; at basketball I would make him play 20 times until I beat him.

"As a golfer, I felt I should tone down my competitive nature because it's not beneficial to take things too personally. You can get jealous of other people. Early in my career I was jealous of other peoples' achievements, which is not right, not a correct emotion. Yes, it is human, but as a Christian trying to work at being more Christ-like, it is not good. Jesus wasn't jealous, and my goal is to be more like Christ. I realize, though, that it is an impossible goal to achieve, since Christ had to come down from the Cross because no one can reach perfection. When you become a Christian, you have amazing grace, and for the rest of your life you are supposed to try to become better, which is where forgiveness comes in. I don't know how many times I have prayed for patience. And the fact is, I'm almost more impatient with autographs and all that stuff than with golf itself."

Betsy King, an intensely competitive woman. She tries to come to terms with her nature through her born-again Christianity, from which she derives great sustenance. In the 1980s history section of this book, Betsy explains the practice of talking in tongues, an ability she possesses.

Though Betsy is not easy to know, I've grown to enjoy her, and following one discussion, she sent me a nice note ending with a quote from 2 Corinthians: "Aim for perfection, listen to my appeal, be of one mind, live in peace. And the God of love and peace will be with you."

Betsy has always striven hard to prove herself in golf. In July 1977 when she joined the LPGA tour, she told herself: "If I don't win in my first year, I don't belong here." By 1983, her tune had changed to reflect her disappointment: "I'm going to be the best non-winner I can." Finally, in 1984, Betsy exploded into action on her way to a remarkable career, including back to back U.S. Open victories in 1989 and 1990, the 1992 LPGA Championship, and twice winning the major title of the Nabisco Dinah Shore. On June 25, 1995, having plodded through 41 tournaments without a victory, Betsy played her way into the Hall of Fame. It was her 30th win. She birdied the final two holes of the ShopRite LPGA Classic for a two-shot victory and inclusion in the Hall of Fame as the 14th member of an august group of women.

Betsy King won the 1985 British Women's Open in Moor Park, Herts. It took her nearly eight years to win her first LPGA tournament; but in 1995 she won her 30th to enter the Hall of Fame. Photo ©Phil Sheldon.

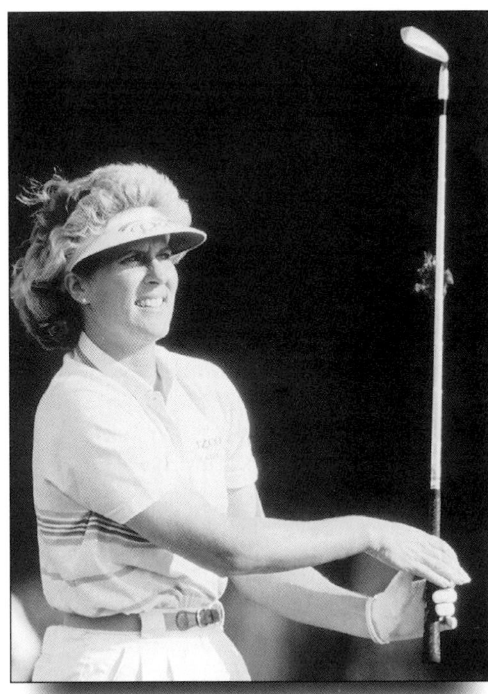

Betsy says, "My faith gives me perspective." It has also given her the ability to become one of the LPGA's top golfers, having won the U.S. Open back to back in 1989 and 1990, the Nabisco Dinah Shore in 1990 and the LPGA Championship in 1992. Photo by Jan Traylen: ©Phil Sheldon.

"I always felt I would do it," Betsy says. "Although the longer time goes by, the harder it gets, and the mounting pressure was only equivalent to that I experienced in the Solheim Cup. My faith helped, and I am a grinder, a perfectionist, who battles for my own satisfaction."

"It was gratifying to have my peers come out and support me and congratulate me. Towards the end of your career you appreciate it more, knowing that you must have been a good player. It all adds to the concept that we're a family from generation to generation. It must have been God's timing, because my parents were there and the next day I had a Pro-Am in my home town nearby. There were 30 people waiting in the lane to my parents' house to meet me. It was very touching."

After an outstanding season in 1989, Betsy admitted: "There's such a fine line between having a good year and a great year." In 1989 she won her first U.S. Open, she included five other titles, won a record $654,132, and was Player of the Year for the second time. The first was in 1984, the year she finally joined the winner's circle with three victories. In 1987, when she won four tournaments, she also captured the Vare Trophy. Betsy's reticent nature ("you should meet my dad if you think I'm an introvert") and lack of interaction prompted headlines: "The Invisible Woman." Journalists failed to come to grips with her personality or, as they saw, the lack of it. Betsy is, in fact, outspoken in an honest manner and stands up for herself when she needs to.

As defending champion at the 1991 U.S. Open at Colonial Country Club, Fort Worth, Betsy quite rightly felt it was a disadvantage to be paired with two amateurs in the first two rounds. She accepted one of them, the U.S. Amateur champion, but remarked of the second: "It is weird, I am surprised."

When a journalist posed the question: "This part of the country used to have two LPGA events in the 1970s; have you any thoughts on why an area like this doesn't have one LPGA tournament now?" Betsy replied by talking about the failing economy, the extreme heat in summer, and playing opposite men's football. Was she disappointed, she was asked? "To be honest, I'm not," replied Betsy. "We're doing very well where we are right now, and in my mind it is a loss for Texas, not for us. The LPGA doesn't need to come to Texas to be successful, and although everyone may not love me for saying that, it's true. I enjoyed it when we played at Bent Tree in Dallas, which is a nice course, but Texas is a hard place for us to play. There is a lot of "good old boy" mentality, and that's always hard to deal with."

Betsy's comments were right on the nail, but when it was splashed all over the newspapers the next day. That the U.S. Open defending champion had criticized the "good old boy" mentality in Texas, brought out the knives. Unfairly, Betsy had to defend her position. She had been justified in speaking out, although little of her reasoning appeared in print. "The press is supposed to report the truth, not make up stories," Betsy complained.

Betsy comes from a middle class family—a physician father, a brother one year older, and golfing parents. She began to play golf at 10, although she preferred basketball, softball, and field hockey.

"I didn't play much amateur golf except for the U.S. Juniors twice, and we had no girls' team at high school. In my junior year at Furman University, where I was a P.E. major, I injured my knee playing basketball; afterward I concentrated on golf. Since I didn't want to teach P.E., I turned professional at 22 in 1977, sponsored by my dad, and within a year I supported myself.

"I started going to the tour's Christian Fellowship in 1980, my worst year in golf. It helped me keep things in perspective. Sometimes the tour is lonely; so when you are with people who care for one another, the social aspect helps. People say joining the fellowship is a crutch, but I believe the Bible is the inspired word of God and He can do things through me. I believe everything in the Bible, but it is open to interpretation. You could spend your whole life on it.

"I believe that God created Adam and Eve and that evolution is wrong; we did not evolve the way evolutionists say we did. I accept that Christ died and rose from the dead. If you are imperfect, you need to accept Christ dying for your sins. I know I'm imperfect, that I may be better than many and my good may outweigh my bad, but this is a fallen world. We are imperfect, and that is why there's a heaven. Heaven is going to be better than this.

"As a Christian you should lead a better life, but it doesn't mean you're going to be better than everyone else. Other players see the human side of you and how you get angry on the course. To my great disappointment, the hardest group to reach is my peers because there is an element of judgment—that it is all right for them to make mistakes but not for me as a Christian.

"A fellowship meeting is not the threatening environment people imagine. I would invite someone if I thought the time were right, that they were struggling and looking for something. The Bible commands us to go into the world and preach the Good News to all creation. I understand that people feel it's an imposition, but we are called to be witnesses like the disciples, and we don't need to ram it down someone's throat.

"My faith is most important to me and carries into my golf. Your relationship with the Lord is first, unless you are married, when your marriage comes first and then your ministry. I haven't married, and I didn't date a lot, coming from a background where a lot of guys didn't go out with girls playing sports. I never went to the prom, and I didn't miss it that much because I was doing sports and studying. As time goes on, you wonder about getting married, but it would be very tough to combine it with being at the top. I haven't been around kids that much, and without obligations you have more time to devote to golf.

"I probably don't come across that well to the public, but I don't want to change. I want to be honest, and the only emotion I sometimes show is anger, which I know is wrong. Golf is a way to make a living; it can't be more than that, because you can't base your self-worth on something which is just another day at the office. It is impossible to get psyched up every day and live and die by what you do, but I do care about it."

In 1980, when her golf game was floundering, Betsy met respected teacher Ed Oldfield in Chicago, who became her instructor and golf mentor in a long-lasting relationship. She would hit up to 800 golf balls a day to attain the improvement she wanted and the breakthrough she so obviously craved.

"In my first victory, I had a three-shot lead in the Kemper Open going into the last day, and it was on national television. I was worried, since I thought it was easier to come from behind, but until you win, you don't realize that you don't have to play perfect golf to achieve victory."

Passing that first hurdle, Betsy became an increasingly impressive and confident golfer and a consistent winner. After she won her first U.S. Open on the magnificent Five Farms golf course in Baltimore, she was on a winning roll in 1989, her most outstanding season. That championship was the highlight of her career, since it was her first Open title, and the terrain was such a tough challenge. The night before her victory, she called Ed Oldfield, who told her to continue with what she was doing.

"I hit a lot of good shots, had confidence in my swing, and putted well. Sometimes as a kid you think, I've got this putt to win the Open, and I did that as an adult on a practice green the week before I won. It was my 15th Open, and playing so many, you feel you should win at some point.

"My faith gives me perspective. Scripture tells you to forget what is behind and press toward what is ahead, toward the goal to win the prize. The hardest thing is to forget what is behind. I use my faith as my sports psychologist. Why not get it from the guy who knows everything? I've learned that all I need to do is try the best I can, to play to the best of my ability. Whatever happens, even if I shoot 85, my parents are still around, and I still have my friends. That is the most important thing.

"Did I feel much emotion when I won at Five Farms? Yes, the fans were hollering like a baseball game, and I thought for a second I was going to cry when I reached the last green. I was slightly scared, but enjoying it, and trying to respond the best way I could. When I go to a play or a concert, I get choked up when someone receives a standing ovation, and I cry. It's funny to get a standing ovation yourself."

Successfully defending her title the following year did not give Betsy similar satisfaction because it was at the expense of Patty Sheehan's devastating collapse. "Patty had a couple of bad rounds, with the weather working against her, and she had only 35 minutes to tee off again before the final round, instead of going home and returning the next day."

As Betsy advanced toward the Hall of Fame, she left Ed Oldfield for the first time in her career in late 1991. Then three weeks before the LPGA Championship in May 1992, at Bethesda Country Club, Maryland, she resumed the relationship. The tournament was the first of three victories that season.

"I played my best four rounds ever in the LPGA Championship, on a good golf course, not too long but without much roll due to rain. I putted well, played well, and after I made two bogeys on the front nine the second day, I never made another bogey the rest of the tournament." For Betsy, it was her fifth major. She won with rounds of 68, 66, 67, 66, and a record 17-under-par 267 total, by the huge margin of 11 strokes from JoAnne Carner, Lotta Neumann, and Karen Noble.

Having Hall of Fame status, Betsy will contemplate her future commitment to golf and to her religion. It is something she regards with an honest assessment of her own strengths and weaknesses.

"I do a lot with the Fellowship of Christian Athletes," she says, "and they have indicated they would give me a job as a lay preacher or help me get into it, but I am not sure I could possibly do it. I am not naturally a people person, and you need a lot of compassion in that position. I get up and speak fairly well in front of audiences, sharing my faith, but on a one-to-one basis, I am a little judgmental. I'm such a perfectionist, I don't know if I could handle it."

Member LPGA Hall of Fame 1995

LPGA Victories: 1984 Women's Kemper Open, Freedom Orlando Classic, Columbia Savings Classic. **1985** Samaritan Turquoise Classic, Rail Charity Classic,. **1986** Henredon Classic, Rail Charity Classic. **1987** Circle K LPGA Tucson Open, Nabisco Dinah Shore, McDonald's Championship, Atlantic City Classic. **1988** Women's Kemper Open, Rail Charity Golf Classic, Cellular One–Ping Golf Championship. **1989** Jamaica Classic, Women's Kemper Open, USX Golf Classic, McDonald's Championship, U.S. Women's Open, Nestle World Championship. **1990** Nabisco Dinah Shore, U.S. Women's Open, JAL Big Apple Classic. **1991** LPGA Corning Classic, JAL Big Apple Classic. **1992** Mazda LPGA Championship, The Phar-Mor in Youngstown, Mazda Japan Classic. **1993** Toray Japan Queens Cup. **1995** Shop Rite Classic.

Unofficial Victories: 1981 Itsuki Charity Classic (Japan). **1985** British Open. **1990** Itoman World Match Play Championship. **1993** JC Penney/LPGA Skins Game.

Betsy King's LPGA Record

Year	No.of Events	Best Finish	Money	Rank	Scoring Average
1977	8	T15	$4,008	83	74.46
1978	29	T2	44,092	20	73.90
1979	31	2	53,900	19	74.15
1980	32	T5	28,480	50	74.54
1981	31	2	51,029	22	73.96
1982	30	T5	50,562	28	73.71
1983	28	T2	94,767	14	72.88
1984	30	1	266,771	1	71.77
1985	28	1	214,411	6	71.89
1986	28	1	290,195	2	71.75
1987	28	1	460,385	2	71.14
1988	28	1	256,957	8	71.81
1989	25	1	654,132	1	70.58
1990	28	1	543,844	3	71.32
1991	26	1	341,784	9	71.50
1992	28	1	551,320	2	71.50
1993	28	1	595,992	1	70.85
1994	27	2	390,239	9	71.52
1995	26	1	481,149	5	71.24

Beverly Klass

When Beverly Klass was 10, her father, Jack, tried to put his daughter on the tour as an LPGA professional. After three tournaments, she was banned by a new ruling, and her father constantly threatened the LPGA with litigation over the next two years. "He was a man with visions of grandeur, who thought he could make money out of his daughter, with endorsements and golf exhibitions," says then-tour director Lenny Wirtz.

Beverly was a precocious talent, who suffered a bizarre lifestyle of insecurity and stormy, inadequate relationships. As a result, she became a conflicted personality, a child who was a compulsive liar and expert manipulator. Talking to her now, you sense the turmoil of her life, the vulnerability, the defense mechanisms, and an understandable craving for love, attention, and success.

In 1976, at 18, Beverly returned to the LPGA tour. Her background had made it hard for her to relate to people; yet the environment of the tour provided security, continuity, and a place in life. That Beverly functions so well is remarkable, and her 1984 season, when she twice finished second and won $51,572, was an admirable achievement. She has plenty of golfing talent; she is a long hitter and a fine putter. As an amateur, she won more than 25 state and city tournaments, including the 1974 Los Angeles Junior Open. "I knew in amateur golf I was the best, and I watched others trying to beat me."

Talking to me on several occasions, Beverly has always been warm and friendly, though guarded to a degree. She admitted that it would take days to relate her life's happenings. There is a fascination in listening to her tales and her fanciful style of expression. I admire her resilience and instinct for survival. She is a likeable, high-strung woman, who, when I first met her, had nails bitten right down and would nervously chain smoke through an interview. Later she seemed calmer and happier.

Her background of family turmoil, drug problems, psychiatric institutions, and custodial care led to her becoming a born-again Christian in the 1980s, embracing it with tremendous fervor. Her father died in 1982, and she says: "I was in Japan at a golf tournament when he died, and previously we had been in contact, but we were not close. It is hard to say what I feel about the

Beverly shows the style that made her a phenomenon at such a young age. After three tournaments on the LPGA as a professional at age 10, she was banned by the LPGA. She returned at 18 and played for 13 years.

relationship, since I have no comparison. It just happened that way."

Beverly was born and grew up in Encino, California. She has one older and one younger sister. The family is Jewish, but there was little in the way of religion. Her father was a building contractor, and her mother looked after the home and later worked in the jewelry business.

"My father started me playing golf at three, although his sport was baseball. I had a baseball grip, swung the club like a bat, and hit the ball a ton. I played my first tournament at seven and won it, following which I entered the National Pee Wee tournament in Orlando at eight. When I won it by 65 shots, they said it wasn't fair to the other kids and asked me not to return.

"My father pushed me to hit more than 300 balls a day at a range. He wanted to take the credit for my golf, and I used the situation by asking him for an hourly wage to practice. I didn't have time for friends, homework, or anything else. There was constant pressure and a situation of fear. When my dad got home, he'd say, 'Did you practice?' I'd tell him, 'Mom didn't take me,' and she'd tell him I hadn't asked her. She didn't want to take me, and I didn't want to go. Everything in the family revolved around me and my golf, and if my mom wanted to go out for dinner, she'd get me to ask my dad for her.

"In 1967, when I was 10, my dad went to the LPGA and said, 'My daughter would like to play in your events. What do we do?' The LPGA had an age rule of 18 for joining the Association but not for playing in their events, so I was able to pay $50 more than the other players to enter a tournament as a non-member of the association, and I beat a couple of professionals; so I couldn't have been all that bad. I played in three tournaments, until the women decided it was bad for me to be out on tour. But meanwhile, the galleries had tripled.

"It was great, I wish I could have stayed out there. I don't think I was too young. Just because you're a kid doesn't mean you can't work at it and improve. After I left, I quit playing golf for three years, until I got back my amateur status in 1970."

In Beverly's first tournament, the Civitan Open in Dallas, she earned her only money, when she

Beverly poses with Jack Nicklaus. As a very young player on tour, she created quite a controversy, but her play also brought galleries to the tour.

won $31.25 in the Pro-Am. She came in last with scores of 88, 88, 90, 99, for a 365 total. In her next tournament, at St Louis, she shot 85, 82, 92, which did not put her quite at the end of the field, and in the Eastern Lady Carling, her rounds of 86, 92, 92, and 270 total, put her just 63 shots behind Mickey Wright's winning score of nine-under-par 207.

The week of the Lady Carling, the LPGA passed a new by-law into its constitution, saying that no one under the age of 18 could play on the tour. A furious Jack Klass flung a $1.25 million lawsuit at the association in retaliation, suing tournament director Lenny Wirtz and the LPGA officers individually, each for $250,000.

"I remember it well," recalls Lenny Wirtz. "A week after the new by-law, Jack Klass made a grandstand entrance at the tournament, complete with Beverly and photographers. They marched to the registration desk; so they could photograph her being refused entry. He said we were depriving her of making a living. We said she should be at school. We tried saying it was a violation of child labor laws for her to be out there, but because the women are self-employed, that law did not apply.

"He was very aggressive and domineering, and Beverly and her mother, who was a very nice woman, appeared to be scared to death of him. We all felt sorry for Beverly, who didn't know what was going on. I don't think she wanted it. She didn't know the rules, couldn't understand the rule book, and when there was a problem on the course, she would burst into tears.

"Jack tried to slap an injunction or lawsuit on us every week, and after the first one was thrown out of court in Worcester, Massachusetts, we finally made a deal to pay him off with about $7,000, to get rid of him and defray his lawyers' fees."

Beverly entered the 1967 U.S. Women's Open, which was won by French amateur Catherine Lacoste. Beverly shot 96, 96, which was better than one professional and one amateur, and which earned her an automatic $100 for competing as a professional.

The result of all this chaos in Beverly's life was that she broke down under the strain. Continually pushed by her father, she drifted into the drug scene of "pills, barbiturates, and what have you." Continual stormy scenes at home resulted in her leaving and returning on nearly 200 occasions in the next few years. She stayed with anyone who would take her into their home.

"I was given psychiatric help, which was a type of escape. I was in psychiatric hospitals for months at a time, sometimes as a voluntary patient, sometimes involuntary. I suppose it helped, in that I'm here now. Eventually, though, I had to help myself. I had a lot of fights at home, when my parents would kick me out or I ran away. The police would find me and send me to Juvenile Hall, which is a junior prison where you go to school; it is very strict, you eat starchy food, and it has high walls.

"I was sent to the state mental institution, which is a gory experience, and some of it is very frightening. One time when I laughed, they had a man hold me down, give me a shot in the ass, and tell me not to laugh; they don't want you to laugh or cry. They like you to be a zombie. They gave me a drug which knocks you out, and I was laying in bed all drugged up, when some girl came over and started kissing me. I threw her against the wall. I tried to sit in the background, to play it cool and be normal, which I was.

Beverly gets a few tips from Arnold Palmer. He must have been impressed with her win at the National Pee Wee tournament in Orlando. At 8, she won by 65 shots, a record Arnold, or any pro, has never achieved.

"Looking back, I see how dumb and funny some of it was; often those treating you need the help. Counselors could be on a power ego trip and want to keep you there. Because of my dad, I was confused, and felt I was being manipulated all the time. I never got credit for anything I did because my dad took it all. It was an ego thing with him.

"I became very smart at manipulating everyone into taking me into their home. When I got kicked out of a variety of schools, I would stay with teachers and do some dope with them. It was a wild life, a weird experience, but I guess I have a strong survival instinct. I enjoy being with people, and I observe a lot, but sometimes I feel insecure and inferior. For a year, I went to Pierce College in California, where I played on the men's golf team. The guys hated me. No one liked me except the coach, but it was kind of fun.

"At 18, I turned professional, went to the LPGA qualifying school, and came in fourth. When I arrived on tour, some of the women said, 'Welcome back,' and some sensed I was saying, 'Fuck you' because I was still mad at them. They had killed me off when I was 10, because they didn't want me to play with them when I had the potential to beat them, and they didn't like all the attention I got. I was glad to be back in 1976; I was older, hitting it past the other women, and I wanted to make them play for second. I wanted to win, to be comfortable with my life.

"When you win, there are a lot of things that go with it. Winning means being No. 1. It means money and people around you. When you win, all of a sudden people say 'hello' to you. When you shoot 89, they don't know you exist. They think you're an oak tree just standing there, and they never talk to you.

"If I'm on the golf course hitting a golf ball, I'm very aggressive. I don't feel particularly female or male in that role, more of a human being where I am just the best. I feel I can beat a guy on the golf course, and I'm not supposed to; so what does that make me? I knew I could beat the guys on the men's team at college, and sometimes I did. I didn't grow up as a female; I was born a woman (I was never a lady). I was a person born to play golf. It's better than sitting in an office at a typewriter.

"I have thought about having my own family, but I couldn't do that and play golf. If I had kids, I would have to adopt them, since I don't have nine months to spare to be pregnant. Time is very precious to me. It takes a lot of it to be a good golfer, and I've been doing this for all but three years of my life. I could do things other than golf, anything I want, but I did golf best, and I want to do golf; so in my case, the man would have to be the wife in the family.

"I get a high playing golf. I almost like getting in trouble on the course; so I can get out of it. Maybe that applies to me generally. As a professional I like playing golf, but most of all I enjoy the attention. The tour provides somewhere to prove to myself what I can do, and I would like to have proved it to my father. I don't know why I haven't achieved more, but I find discipline the hardest thing.

"I have come to realize just how dominant my father was and what effect my family has had on me. My mom put a restraint order out on me; she doesn't like me very much. My dad neglected her for years because of my golf; so she felt left out. She was placed in a mental hospital and tried to kill herself. There was always fighting and anger. My older sister has also been on drugs and hospitalized, and there is not any relationship between me and my sisters. The whole family fought, and I worried about it and my golf.

"I lied a lot as a child, and I didn't have any friends, girls or boys. There were a few short-time boy friends, but I thought boys were naive and dumb because I had been around and was mentally older. I had some inner strength at an early age, and instinctively knew I was going to become a professional golfer. It was like destiny, and the destiny is not yet over."

In 1986, Beverly became a born-again Christian, and a year later she described the experience and told me about the impact it made on her: "I fired my caddie during the tournament at Tucson and went back to my hotel because I had a really bad stomach pain. I was doubled over. The TV happened to be on in my room, and it was the Oral Roberts Prayer Line. They said, 'If you want to get a healing, call this number.' I was desperate; so I called, and the lady said to me, 'What can I do for you?' I told her I had this terrible pain in my stomach. 'Do you know Jesus?' she said. 'I'm Jewish,' I replied. 'Would you like to know him?' she asked, and I replied, 'Sure.' 'We'll pray to get Jesus into your life, and then we'll pray to take away the pain,' she told me.

"I confessed to Jesus. You say what's called the sinner's prayer, and then through faith, Jesus comes into your life. After the first prayer, God's presence filled my hotel room. It came down and lifted the pain from my stomach. Before we got to the healing prayer, I was so ecstatic, I was on the floor yelling at the woman, 'He just did it. He took out the pain.' And she said, 'I know He did.'

"Ever since then, I have been having incredible experiences with God. It's completely changed my life, and I've been leading other people to the Lord. I go to Bible study group on tour and a Christian Love Fellowship church at home in Florida.

"I've had a lot of rotten things happen in my past, and I've received prophecies from God through other people, about things that went on, which only God could know and not some stranger in a church; so I know it's God who has told me. He knows I have been hurt. The first prophecy came eight months after I accepted Jesus and was born again. Being born again is not a religion; you are born again and given his spirit.

"Five months after I was born again, I was with Betsy King at a tournament in Ireland, and we went to a Full Gospel Fellowship meeting where there were about 30 people, and someone said, 'Anyone who wants to receive the baptism of the Holy Spirit, raise your hand,' which I did, even though I didn't know what it was.

"I found out it is a confession that you want the Holy Spirit to enter your body with evidence of speaking in other tongues. I was standing there,

Beverly enjoys a light moment on the tour. In 1986, she became a born-again Christian, and for the first time, her life found meaning and purpose, outside of golf.

and a guy was explaining the Holy Spirit, and I didn't hear a word, but I was prompted to look up over his head, and as I looked at the ceiling above him, the air was peach colored, and it descended on me. I fell backwards, which they call going out in the power, being slain in the spirit. The power of God is so strong you can't stand in His presence. This peace came over me as I was going back. Since then I've seen this charismatic movement happen in churches, but at that point I'd never seen or heard about it, and it happened to me. It happened to Paul in the Bible, when the power of God knocked him from his horse to the ground. When it happened to me, two people caught me who had seen it before.

"I was on the ground, and I couldn't move, talk, or open my eyes. I was conscious, and I knew it was God. The peace of God was all over me. He was trying to fill me with the Holy Spirit. He stimulated my vocal chords so that I said, 'Thank you, Jesus' about 20 times, although no one heard me except God. It was funny because my knees raised up about a quarter of an inch and God pressed them back down. This happened again and again. I'll never know what it was, except the Bible says, 'We wrestle not against flesh and blood but against the principalities and powers of darkness.'

"Before all this happened, I had been having problems with a couple of girls on tour who were good friends of mine and Christians. I wasn't in the church, but I had been praying to God, saying, 'You're sending me these people as friends to be joined up in a bond of peace. What should I do?' After I had joined the church, I woke up one morning, having prayed the night before, and as I got out of bed, an audible voice, which was God, said to me: 'I'll take care of them. You go and play golf.' God said that. I heard his voice, which was so powerfully sweet, pure, peaceable, and lovable that the walls were listening. Everything stopped. I got a whole vision behind the voice, and He said: 'They've hurt you, and that's OK because I'll send new people to you.'

"I've received about six different prophecies from the Lord. He gave me a vision for 1987 and 1988 on tour, which I prefer to keep to myself, and another telling me what tournament would be

Beverly, as an adult, competed at the 1984 Dinah Shore at Mission Hills. It was her best year, but she left the tour in 1988 after playing just 10 tournaments. Photo ©Phil Sheldon.

mine on the LPGA tour. I had set my goals too low, and He gave me a higher one out of thin air. He told an elder of my Church a certain way for me to practice and for how long. When I draw nigh to God, He draws nigh to me.

"When I was in Hawaii, I went to an inter-denominational Assembly of God Church, where they have praise and worship. I was standing there singing songs to the Lord, when the music finished, and some guy started speaking in tongues. It got dead quiet, and I thought someone would interpret. He stopped, and all of a sudden this thing rolls up inside me, up my stomach to my neck. My mouth is shut, and I'm supposed to interpret the tongues, but I didn't want to say it.

"Then God spoke to my heart and said: 'You'd better say it.' I had no idea what was happening, but I opened my mouth and the words came out: 'Notice I haven't forsaken you. I know my sheep. I dwell among my brothers. I am the Lord who gives to the blessed abundantly. Jesus is the Lord.' Then it faded out, and they all went crazy and loved it.

"That church needed to hear that, and He used me to do it. They'd had prophecies in the church before, but at this time there was tension in the church, and they needed to know God had not left them. I was an outsider without any idea of all this, but it was a confirmation to them, and it is how God works.

"Nothing happened in my life until I opened my mouth and said, 'Jesus, I need you.' As soon as I did, I had my first experience of God within seconds. It was nothing to do with Judaism, although Jesus was a Jew. Jesus is the ultimate sacrifice, and whoever asks him into his life will have eternal life. That's what the Bible says, and the Bible is God's word.

"God is moving in this day and age like I've never seen: on television, in new churches, and I'm seeing people get born again, everyday. People ask what's so different about me, and it is God's glory which just shines through me.

"God is even helping me with my finances. Two people gave me checks for $500 and $5,000, which were offered to me when I needed them. God drops into someone's heart and says, 'That girl needs money.' He supplies all my needs, and He's moving on my behalf. He does that for all his believers. If you put God's name in this book, he'll help you write it and make it a success.

"My inner strength was leading me in my early years; it could have been God's spirit. Your will, desire, love, peace, joy, and happiness come from God, who gives us the free will to choose whether to have life or death.

"If we go back to Adam and Eve, if Eve hadn't eaten from that tree, there would be no death. He gave them free will, and He said, 'Don't eat from that tree.' The serpent said, 'Go ahead,' and Eve disobeyed God. They weren't physically supposed to die. They lived 1,000 years, and others lived 200–300 years. Eve disobeyed, and all that sin came into the world, as Satan came down to earth with two-thirds of the angels that he had taken.

"God now is leading me along. I call my mom occasionally, and she is doing all right. God has removed from my life a lot of unforgiving feelings I had toward my father and mother."

In March 1988, Beverly left the tour and went to live in Florida, where she started teaching golf and continued her involvement with the church into the 1990s.

"I was a bit burnt out and haven't decided whether or not to go back to the tour. Realistically, I would need a sponsor. I still have an ambition to win, and it wouldn't be a very big struggle for me to return. I have always golfed, since I was three, and I miss it a little, especially the competition. I don't miss the companionship, because you make acquaintances on tour, and everyone is friendly, but they are not friends.

"I am enjoying teaching golf, and my students are doing very well. I'm getting good results and more and more students. I find it takes a lot of discipline to have a 9-to-5 job. I have been helping in the church, doing bruised heart ministering with battered women and those suffering from drug and alcohol abuse. I help with children and do missionary projects, which I find more satisfying than hitting golf balls week after week.

"God has some kind of calling for me, which is not yet clear. It might be short missionary trips like one I made to Honduras, where they are years behind, there is all kinds of disease and poverty, and they are still practicing voodoo. We went with preachers who preached the gospel. We told the local people that they were on the wrong track and that sacrificing and worshipping animals doesn't give you eternal life. It was a pretty awesome experience and makes you thankful for your own life. I may go into the ministry or back onto the golf course. Time and God will decide."

Beverly Klass' LPGA Record

Year	No.of Events	Best Finish	Money	Rank	Scoring Average
1976	25	T11	$3,436	79	77.92
1977	25	T5	11,805	52	76.00
1978	25	T7	5,817	75	76.97
1979	31	T7	21,544	54	75.36
1980	32	T13	9,047	88	75.89
1981	28	T3	16,168	72	75.60
1982	30	T5	37,534	39	74.29
1983	25	T18	8,672	109	75.62
1984	31	T2	51,572	41	74.32
1985	29	T21	19,546	91	74.85
1986	29	T11	19,624	95	75.05
1987	27	T13	24,010	86	74.47
1988	10	T13	5,553	154	75.12

Kathy Linney

Kathy Linney was an inspirational and courageous woman, who did not become a professional golfer until she was 29. She struggled for many years with cancer, and at the age of thirty six, she died. "She was a woman of intelligence, and she always used it wisely," said her mother Doris.

Academically bright, with a degree in mathematics and a professional background of systems analysis, Kathy decided to follow her heart and try to become a professional golfer. She joined the tour in 1976 and was diagnosed with breast cancer only two years later. Amazingly, she stayed out on tour, playing as much as she could between operations and while she was undergoing chemotherapy.

I first met Kathy just after her best career performance. The whole tour was rejoicing when she finished tied for fourth in the 1980 Birmingham Classic, only a month before her third operation. She was a warm, friendly woman who often had a deceptively healthy glow. She talked with candor about her illness, confronting it, wanting to hang on to life, and at the same time realizing that it could slip from her grasp. Only once she admitted: "I'm tired of being tired."

After battling cancer and its debilitating treatment, Kathy Linney finished fourth in the 1980 Birmingham Classic. In 1981, she received the Ben Hogan award, given to the person who has overcome a serious illness to play golf again. Photo credit: Katherine Murphy.

She would tell me about her operations and unpleasant treatment, never asking for sympathy, only appreciating the depth of support she received from those around her. She was an inspiration in her fortitude as she faced illness and death. Fellow professional Cathy Duggan, her closest friend on tour, who gave so much in practical and emotional support, says: "Kathy always wanted to be independent, however ill she might be. She did not want to burden her family, to whom she was very close, or her friends.

"She was such a great person that it was a real blessing to have a friend like her. She was never a liability, and she would say to me, 'Duggy, this cannot be a Florence Nightingale relationship.' There were times when she got angry about what was happening, but she managed those times. Even when she was really sick, she would do something like running, to vent her emotions. She had an unbelievable faith in God, which gave her great strength, and her relationship with Him was a very personal one.

"She was immensely interested in everyone on tour, in what they were doing, and she always empathized with others and their problems as though she had none. She gave me hope on the level of friendships she attained, on how people care. I have tremendous memories of what a fun person she was; the enjoyable things we did overshadowed the sad things. She was truly a courageous person and a master at handling adversity."

In 1981, Kathy Linney was the overwhelming choice of golf writers to receive the Ben Hogan award, given to the person who has overcome a serious illness or injury to play golf again.

Kathy Linney was born at Camp Shelby, Mississippi, where her father was in the Service until she was five years old. Then the family moved to New Jersey, and he became part owner in a women's sleepwear business. Her father died of cancer at the age of 51, and later her mother remarried. Kathy had two brothers, two and five years younger, and the family was upper middle class.

She told me in 1980, "We all played golf, but my father was not as interested, and we only joined the Plainfield Country Club after we moved to New Jersey. My mother was the real influence. She took me and my brothers out when I was 13 to see who could break 100 first.

"I played local amateur tournaments and won a few things, including the New York Metropolitan Championship. I didn't play golf when I went to Marymount College, where I majored in mathematics. I never considered professional golf as a career option. In 1964, when I was 18, the tour did not look viable in terms of making a living.

"I wanted to be independent, and I worked as a computer programmer for AT&T; then I got my Master's in mathematics at the University of Wisconsin and took a job with Mountain Bell in Denver as a systems analyst.

"I was cruising along in the job, and thinking and reading about golf. I had taken only two formal golf lessons up to the age of 27, when I saw the Colgate Dinah Shore on television and thought the tour looked pretty healthy. I thought it would be nice to do something I really liked. I missed playing golf, and my brother, two years younger, had become a professional. I wondered if I was having a pipe dream, and only one friend thought it was a good idea.

My father had died in 1969, and my mother didn't approve of my becoming a pro golfer. She didn't say, 'Don't do it.' She just said, 'Aren't you tired of it yet?' Later she realized it was a fine decision, but initially she thought I would be happier getting married and settling down. I never thought I was making a choice not to do that, but golf is fairly consuming, and it would be hard for me to be married and play golf. I still hope that sometime I'll get married."

"In 1974, I quit my job, took lessons for three months, worked hard, and went to the North and South at Pinehurst to prove I could make it. In the qualifying round I made an 11 on the second hole, because I hit three consecutive trap shots over the green out of bounds. I missed qualifying by one stroke, and I was crushed. I thought, 'Perhaps it's not for me. It's too devastating when you fail.'

"I went on and played the summer amateur tournaments and won everything. I vacillated a lot, but I thought maybe it was possible. I went to the January 1975 LPGA qualifying school and didn't come close. I was so uptight because I had to prove to the world that my decision was right.

"Rumson Golf Club in New Jersey offered me a teaching job for the summer, which allowed me to learn more about the game and practice. I went to the July qualifying school, not feeling prepared, and I finished fifth, won a check, and got my LPGA player's card. I went back to the club until the end of the season.

"Starting on tour in January 1976, my ambition was to stay out there, and I barely sneaked through my rookie year. I was financed by some family money. When my mother remarried in 1973, she sold the family home and divided the proceeds between the children.

"My golfing age on tour was that of a youngster, but since I was chronologically older, it meant that I was more patient and realistic in my goals. It helped me to be tenacious, to hang in through all that's happened, and to cope with the crises in my career, which may end sooner than I would like. In my second year on tour, I operated at a deficit but learned as much as most people know when they start the tour. I was doing okay in 1978, my third year, when I got sick.

"I had gone through an operation previously, when I was 23, for a melanoma tumor related to a mole, which meant a radical groin dissection in the left leg and groin; and that cancer did not recur.

"In 1978, I had a lump in my breast which had been there a year. I had been to a doctor because I had a fibrocystic disease and a biopsy in the early

1970s, but it was diagnosed as a common benign condition. The lump changed dramatically, and in June, when I was stretching to get into bed, I felt pain. The lump was huge. The doctor thought it was mastitis. I looked healthy, the mammogram showed nothing, but a biopsy in August proved it was highly malignant and had traveled into 17 of 27 lymph nodes. I had a radical mastectomy, losing pectoral muscles on my right side, followed by radiation and chemotherapy because of the high probability of recurrence.

"My first reaction to the operation was that I would come back and play golf, if possible. Having that desire was a big help. I met Liz Boyer, who taught yoga, mastectomy rehabilitation classes, and dance at a New Jersey YWCA. She took a personal interest in me as an athlete and worked to increase my body awareness, which was zero. She educated me on muscle groups and where to find my strength.

"I had chemotherapy for two years from November 1978—two weeks on and two weeks off. I had to see whether I could incorporate it into a career. At the age of 32, I didn't have time to wait two years and start again. Statistically, the cure rate is much higher with chemotherapy. Without it, 50 percent live five years with the type of cancer that I had; with it the figure goes up to 70 percent. The chances are good, but it's a real drag, with the nausea and drinking lots of water during treatments.

"In 1978, I played the Group Fore mini-tour and made enough money, but I didn't do anything terrific because I had lost a lot of distance from losing the muscles on my right side. By spring 1979, I thought maybe it wasn't worth it, and I wondered what I was trying to prove. In the summer I went to an LPGA tournament in New Jersey, saw my friends, and that's all it took. I knew I wanted to be there. I joined the LPGA tour again in January 1980 and stood on the practice tee with all those strong females and felt like a real weakling. I had to tune out that feeling and realize I could make pars and birdies my own way.

"I had to become comfortable about the days when I was so bad I didn't look like I belonged in professional golf. My ego was on the line because I don't like to look ridiculous, and I have professional pride. Whatever I did was great with the girls, and that gave me a lot of psychological energy. I give them a lot of credit for the success I've had in overcoming my problems. If they hadn't cared about me, I wouldn't have had the motivation to get back. They were terrific.

"I limped along, made the cut, missed the money six times, and was getting frustrated. Something would always go wrong in four rounds, and it became like a wall I couldn't get through. In Raleigh in the spring, I made the cut and missed the money for the umpteenth time. I got on a plane, felt really fatigued, and thought maybe I couldn't do it. 'You can't admit defeat. You're an intelligent person,' I told myself. 'Try something constructive, a new approach.' I got films of my swing, saw an age-old error, and went to play in Orlando, where I hit the ball really well and missed the cut. It was mental.

"The following week in Birmingham, I was determined to give it my best effort, not to think back or ahead. In my entire life I never concentrated so well, and I finished fourth. It was the highlight of my career. Maybe all that struggle had to happen to get me to maximize my talents. It was great, a real thrill.

"Two weeks later I pulled a muscle in my back and was very tired. Another lump appeared under my other arm in March, but there was nothing in my breast. I waited until May when there was granularity in the breast, and I had an immediate biopsy. It was malignant, and I needed a modified radical mastectomy, leaving the muscle there. The arm would recover, but it sidelined me. It also meant another two years of chemotherapy—not my favorite thing.

"Following the operation, I played five tournaments, knowing I was not really competitive, but physically and psychologically it helped rehabilitate me. I'm pretty tired now [this was said in San Jose in 1980], and I don't feel equal to starting a tournament tomorrow, but it's the last tournament of the season and maybe a miracle might happen." (It did not. Kathy had to withdraw after one round.)

"Through all this, I feel the influence of my parents has been significant. My father's parents were poor Irish immigrants, and he had to fight for anything he got in life. He was successful, and he encouraged us never to give up. My mother's family was German—tenacious and stubborn, and she encouraged us to try new things.

"The person I am has been made better by the things that have happened to me. I wish it would all go away because who likes chemotherapy and surgery, but I can't do anything about it. If I said, 'Gee, I got a bum rap in life,' that would interfere with my ability to enjoy the time I have left in each day.

"I made a decision when I had my first surgery that it would not interfere with my life, and luckily after the operation, I needed only a surgical support stocking for four years. This latest illness had interfered with my career, but it has brought things into my life that would never have happened. It's not been all bad.

"I confronted death at 23 with the terror of having cancer. I knew I could die. I still realize that, but it hasn't bothered me that much. Everyone's going to die sometime, and I feel I'm not going to die before my time. I've had a really interesting life, in which I may not have done everything there is to do, but everyone misses something.

"It's hard to think about dying when you're out here playing golf on a sunny day, and I choose not to. But I know it's a possibility, and I must face my

Kathy Linney Boulevard at Sweetwater Country Club, Houston, official home of the LPGA in the 1980s, was a tribute to her indomitable courage and spirit.

limitations. An awareness of death is good in that it motivates you to get on with your life. It has improved that quality of my life.

"I've had a lot of attention since a story was written about me in Newsweek, when I was in the hospital in June 1980. It acted as a catalyst; so newspapers and television have followed me ever since. It has been a brand new experience for me, since no one ever wanted to write about my golf before I got sick. It was never worth it, except at Birmingham. You normally earn the attention I've had by merit.

"I feel the attention I'm getting is important because if people know a person can play professional golf after having two mastectomies, another cancer operation, radiation, and chemotherapy, they should be able to go on with their own lives and do what makes them happy. That motivates me more than anything.

I don't care if people know the Kathy Linney story—which is invading my privacy a little, but what I represent is important and can make a lot of people happier, and that makes me feel happier. Cancer is not the end; there is a lot of living you can do along with the problem. I could lie awake at night thinking, 'What if I'm dead this time next year,' or that I might get something else horrible and need to have a limb cut off. Those things do cross my mind, but right now I don't have to worry about them.

"I never was planning to be No. 1 on the money list. Starting at 30, I looked on it as another experience in my life, and I've had a good time in spite of all the things that have happened. The LPGA administration and players have been incredibly supportive; so that I want to make it, for all the people believing in me and pulling for me. It's a great motivator, and sharing the experience makes it meaningful.

"It's interesting that it probably took getting sick for me to feel a part of the tour. I never was that good a player and didn't know people that well. I was scared of not feeling equal to Carner or Whitworth. When they took the time to send me cards, call me on the phone, I thought, 'They're human beings, not just unapproachable stars.' Since then, I've had a much better time out here."

Kathy received the Ben Hogan award, which was presented to her at the U.S. Men's Open at Merion in June: "I knew I had won it just before Christmas 1980, after a sportswriter called my brother. When my brother told me, I thought he was kidding, even though I'd been nominated. I felt good to have won it.

"There was a big dinner, and everyone was staring at me for an evening. I got up to make my speech and said that my family had provided me solid support in such an insecure profession, and they were always there for me when the money ran out and so forth. I said that my close friends kept me sane, reminded me who I was and what I was trying to do, and that the LPGA gave me moral and financial support. I thanked the golf writers who voted me in for telling my story with sensitivity and dignity and not making it a soap opera. Then I lost all my train of thought for a few seconds. You're up there, and all you can see is lights. I looked for my family, and my mind went blank. Then I remembered my message to these people, that the Ben Hogan award belonged to others as much as to me, that you don't do these things alone, that everyone had helped and supported me, and I wanted them to know. It was a lot of fanfare for little old me—the USGA, the LPGA, the press, everyone at the Men's Open focusing on me for that moment. I went home and was sick for the next three weeks."

Kathy began the 1981 season after a tough winter: "I'm still taking chemotherapy, and I battled with flu through the winter. I don't know that I'm up to playing right now, but it's good to be out here. People probably often feel this rough and play professional golf, but I have to be a little careful because I lack the force to fight off things, due to my suppressed immune system. I'm being pulled in two directions. I should be careful, but I don't want to coddle myself. Hopefully, I'll have the wisdom to pull out if necessary, but the important thing is to be here, even if the ground's a little shaky.

"It lifts my spirits immeasurably to see everyone, and considering the transient types that we are, the group support is wonderful. If you're married, there's a family unit, but our bigger family is out here. You feel something that gets in your blood, and it makes you do all these crazy things to play golf. If I can keep my head above water physically and get to the end of the year, I'll be almost through the treatment, and then I'll be too old to play golf."

Kathy was fit enough in 1981 to play only one tournament and one more round in the final event of the season. After that, she moved to Houston, where she worked at the new home of the LPGA at Sweetwater as a liaison between the architect and builder and the LPGA tour. She died in 1982, and in Sweetwater there is a street called Kathy Linney Street in her memory.

Kathy Linney's LPGA Record

Year	No.of Events	Best Finish	Money	Rank	Scoring Average
1975	2	T43	$110	117	79.66
1976	23	T33	1,226	99	78.11
1977	22	T13	4,181	80	76.02
1978	NA	NA	4,466	89	75.78
1979	NA	NA	NA	NA	79.75
1980	NA	T4	4,279	110	77.14
1981	NA	NA	NA	NA	77.50

Sally Little

Sally Little, South African born, became a naturalized American in 1982 because it was the country where she lived, but she remained close to her roots and her family, particularly her father. Until his death in 1986, he was the overriding influence in her life. "When he was dying in South Africa, I spent 10 days with him, and it was the greatest experience to have been there. I had a wonderful time with him in spite of the circumstance."

She avoids political discussion and controversy by not talking about it. As a youngster of 19 joining the LPGA tour, she performed extremely well but was overwhelmingly homesick. Much of her playing career has been dominated by poor health—she had a hysterectomy in her mid-twenties, with some devastating results, but since 1976, she won 14 tournaments, including two majors, and she made an excellent living out of the sport she loves.

She is a woman who is immensely aware of physical attributes and well being; yet when she arrived in the U.S., she became overweight from feelings of insecurity. Soon, she slimmed down to become a glamorous, trim, athletic, attractive woman.

Sally has always gone out of her way to be friendly to me, coming over to shake me firmly by the hand when I arrived on tour in America. We had met previously in England, and when I first interviewed her, it was at her lovely home in Florida. She is surprisingly revealing in an unemotional way on somewhat emotional and personal subjects, which makes her a good interviewee.

Sally was born and brought up in Cape Town, where her father worked in insurance. She has a sister four years older and a brother four years younger. The family was affluent, with servants and a luxurious lifestyle. This was normal for many whites in South Africa, but it contrasted greatly to her life in the United States, when she first arrived.

"I grew up having everything I wanted. I was very fortunate. My dad worked awfully hard to give it to me, which left me with a strong feeling for him. He was an excellent natural athlete, an all-around sportsman, who acquired a two handicap in three years. If it weren't for him, I would never have taken it up. I didn't like golf as a child of 11, but my father told me to come and watch, and said he would pay me to pull his

Sally Little thought she would take the LPGA tour by storm when she joined it in 1971 as the first South African to turn pro. Instead, she found it rough, but she did win $1,670 and was named "Rookie of the Year."

cart, so I started playing at 12 with my father as my sole teacher.

"I played with my dad and other men at the club, since the women didn't want to play with a child. The men made me play off their tees, and I mimicked them and became more aggressive. At 15, I had a seven handicap, but because golf was unpopular for youngsters, I was embarrassed, and I would go and play secretively.

"When I was 15, I had an accident on the back of a boyfriend's motorbike, badly breaking a femur, which put me in hospital for three months. When I came out with my leg in a caliper, I would go and chip and putt to pass the time. I learned to love it, and I decided to dedicate myself to it. I started winning a year later. I won the Western Province two years running, the Transvaal Strokeplay and Matchplay, the 1971 South African Amateur Championship, and I finished low individual in the World Team Championship in Madrid even though countries were threatening to boycott the tournament because of the South African competitors. Mixing politics with sport is really sad because the athletes are the only ones who get hurt in the long run.

"At 18, I was engaged to a guy seven years older. My father fought it because he didn't want me to get married so young. He didn't say, 'You can't get married,' but when my fiancé and I had trouble, my father said, 'You're very young, you have a tremendous career ahead of you, and you could blow it all. Why don't you have your career and then get married?' I was engaged for a year, but I broke it off because my fiancé didn't want me to play golf. You can't do that to someone—it totally destroys a healthy relationship.

"In 1971, I was the first South African woman to turn professional, and I joined the LPGA tour. I was very immature at 19. I thought I was going to kill them, to take America by storm. I had been built up in South Africa, and although I'm not exactly a cocky type, I thought I was hot stuff. I played so much golf in America; I burned out in a month. Although I competed in only seven events, I won $1,670 and was Rookie of the Year. I didn't play well for quite a few years, but I was lucky that in those days there were only about 60 players, there

Sally became a U.S. citizen in 1982. Since joining the LPGA in 1971, she's earned more than $1.7 million in prize money. Photo courtesy: Katherine Murphy.

was no school, no halfway cut, and the pressure was very different.

"It was an awful adjustment, and it was tough being so far from home without my support system. I found it hard to get settled. I couldn't iron a shirt or balance a checkbook. They thought I was dumb, but I learned quickly.

"My ambition was to be No. 1 in America. You need a tremendous ego. The more ego you have, the more constantly motivated and successful you are. A lot of people don't like the word ego, but there's nothing wrong with it. It is probably instilled in you from your upbringing. My father was a super athlete so that being around him I wanted to be a good athlete.

"Most people don't think of golfers as athletes. I think you have to be an athlete to hit the ball, but you can be out of shape. The definition of an athlete is someone who is totally co-ordinated, has timing, grace, and rhythm. If I'm in good shape, I know I'll do better. I can't stand being fat, and I perform better being thin. We're on stage, and it's important to look good. I'm very self-conscious.

"I'm an athlete who likes looking good, but I don't consider myself a sex symbol, nor should I be sold that way. It is nice to look good, but it sometimes annoys me when people go overboard on looks. People have tried to sell me for my face, and I don't like that because I consider my ability a lot better than my face.

"Physically, women are fantastic. If your body can be active all the time, you are going to have a better and longer life. If you look at an athlete's body, it is beautiful. I don't like the muscular look, but I like the firmness in place of flab that comes from activity. It is beautiful to watch men and women athletes perform. There is nothing prettier than seeing what a woman athlete can do with her body and how much discipline she has. You need self-discipline to succeed.

"I have always set myself high goals on tour, but at first I could not reach them; so I changed them. Instead of trying to win, I tried to finish in the top 20. I didn't know how to win, and when I had the opportunity, I would choke like a dog. I didn't like the word choke, but I learned to accept it. I got so nervous, I couldn't handle it, and being self-conscious, I didn't want to make a mistake. Then, of course, I wanted to satisfy my ego. I took the club back so quickly that I ruined my timing, my arms got tired, my legs started to wobble,and I choked. No one in this world who is a winner hasn't choked, but you learn how to handle it and accept your failures.

"I remember one time in the early 1970s in Orlando, I led the first day, did well the next day, and was leading after three rounds. I was playing with Kathy Whitworth, who was dominating the tour, and I was so nervous and uptight that I couldn't get the club back or feel the swing. I shanked three or four shots into the gallery. I've never been so humiliated. Talk about destroyed. Everything you have worked for disappears.

"It was amazing, but after that experience everything changed. I thought about it a lot, and got rid of those feelings. However, my first win in the Women's International at Moss Creek in 1976 was a miracle, since I tried to choke. I won with a sand shot out of a bunker. You fantasize about how you would like to win, and that week I led all the way, playing really well. I got very nervous in the last round, with Jan Stephenson chasing me. On the 16th, I heard she was leading by one shot. It blew my mind, and I birdied to tie; she bogeyed and I was one ahead, then I bogeyed the 17th. At the 18th I thought I'd blown another tournament. After a terrible drive, I was shaking like a leaf. With a five iron in my hand, I stood over my second shot telling myself 'You can make a birdie,' and I hit a good shot out of the rough, but it catches the bunker. I can't believe it. 'What are you doing to yourself?' I asked. 'You really love to persecute yourself. At least you could get it on the damned green.' People said I looked so cool as I went shaking into the bunker, but I don't remember a thing. All I know is that it went in the hole from 80 feet, and I went bananas. I still shake whenever I'm keyed up, but it's a different kind of nervousness that I enjoy more."

Sally's golf improved steadily from her beginnings in 1971, reaching a peak in 1982, when she won three tournaments including the Dinah Shore which had become a major, and she had her highest earnings of $228,941. From 1974, she was continually dogged by poor health. She had two operations for ovarian cysts and a hysterectomy when she was 26, in 1977.

"I never had menstrual problems growing up, but by my third year on tour I was doubled over on

From 1974, Sally was plagued by poor health, but by 1982, she was on top of her game again, winning nearly $229,000. By the end of 1982, abdominal and knee surgery sidelined her again. Photo courtesy: Katherine Murphy.

the course with pain. From then on, I always fought my health. I was very young to have a hysterectomy, but I had really bad endometriosis. It was endangering my health, and there was nothing I could do. It could be hereditary; my grandmother had died of cancer at 42. Needless to say, I was very upset. It was a very emotional thing for me, something lots of people have mental anxiety about.

"My family might have liked me to have children, and I love children; so it really hurt when I knew I couldn't have any. But with my career, I'm not sure I would have had children. Maybe I'm too selfish for a family.

"After my hysterectomy, I had to take hormone pills which messed me up for some years. With any stress, I could get a hot flash, and I was always experimenting with dosages. It was a nasty experience, trying various drugs which caused huge mood swings. Sometimes I tortured myself trying to play golf. I didn't know what was going on with my body.

"By the end of 1982 I needed further abdominal surgery, and then I had knee surgery, which meant that I played only nine tournaments in 1983. It was then that I decided to try a metabolic diet with vitamins to control the weakness in my immune system, and I built myself up to become my strongest since my early years. Now, I don't have highs and lows, and I work out in the LPGA fitness trailer.

"When I was so low, I thought of giving up, but someone told me that I had a great gift in golf, and with it, I could give so much enjoyment to other people. I realized I wasn't ready to close the door.

"I used to be afraid of not having golf as my career, and then I realized it didn't matter. I knew that I could give up golf and do something else, but I don't think too many of my peers can say that. It is horrible and sad to judge yourself by your golf scores, live by a number, but unfortunately we do not know anything else. It is hard to let go of something that is an extension of your whole being.

"My best year was 1982, and I got a great deal of attention, but those people evaporated when I was sick. It hurt me when people said, 'Why don't you give up?' It made me think that you have to be more selfish with your time when you are at the top."

Sally had lots to celebrate at the 1988 British Women's Open, but her big win at the DuMaurier Classic that year in Vancouver vindicated her lengthy struggles against illnesses that had plagued her since 1974. Photo by Jan Traylen: ©Phil Sheldon.

In 1979, Sally's parents went to live in America but found it a hard transition and returned to South Africa when her father was not well in 1986. In March that year, he was dying, and Sally returned home.

"I spent 10 days with him when he was dying. The worst would have been not to be there. It was hard; yet it was good. I don't have bad feelings about his death. Mostly, he was coherent, and I had a wonderful time with him. People say, 'How can you say it was so nice?' It just was.

"One day when he was in bad shape, not talking any more, I told him about the problems I was having with my golf grip. I got the Tommy Armour book from which he had taught me and told him that I'd finally read about my problem and how to solve it. He was squeezing my hand, and it was a very special time for me. I have had some very special moments with him.

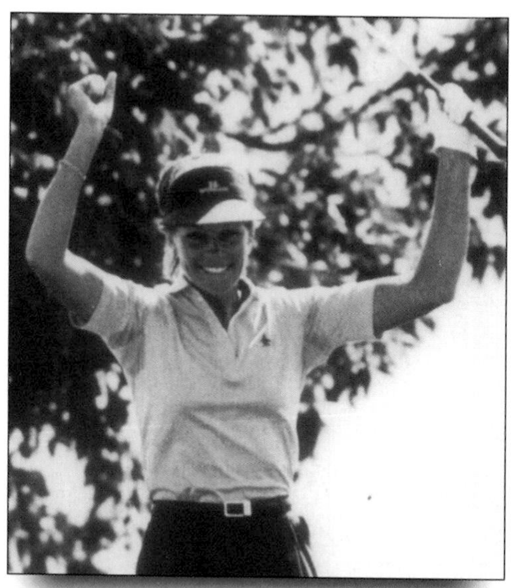

All is well that ends well, and for Sally Little, winning the Nabisco Dinah Shore in 1982 was one of her greatest moments.

"Since my father died, my mother moved back to America to live in California with my sister and her family. I live in California now, and in recent years I have become close to my brother who lives in Florida—we have created a wonderful friendship—and sometimes he carries my bag.

"He worked for me in the 1986 Open, which we almost won. It has always been my biggest dream to win it, and even though I lost the 18-hole playoff to Jane Geddes, I felt I had won because I won a huge battle with myself. When you are not well, it is difficult to concentrate, and I had lost a lot of confidence. Playing so well in the Open made me realize I had a tremendous future, and the desire which had been taken away from me was stronger than ever."

It was two years later that Sally received the Ben Hogan award, given for overcoming serious illness or injury, when she reached the fruition of her battle against ill health, winning the 1988 DuMaurier Classic in Vancouver in a dramatic climax. With Laura Davies pounding at her heels, Sally saved her par from a bunker at the 17th, and then, having seen Laura come out of a bunker at the 18th to within six inches from the hole, Sally sank a 35-foot birdie putt for victory.

"I felt those last six years of struggling drop away. They left me. I was nervous, my concentration had wobbled slightly, but when I saw the winning putt drop, I realized the struggle had been worthwhile ten times over. I had battled my health with so much patience that I had felt alienated from competition and being in contention. My pride made me carry on and turn it around."

In an emotional telephone call to her mother, Sally told her: "This one was for dad. I want you to know that he was with me on the 17th and 18th holes."

LPGA Victories: 1976 Women's International. **1978** Honda Civic Classic. **1979** Bent Tree Classic, Barth Classic, Columbia Savings Classic. **1980** LPGA Championship, WUI Classic. **1981** Elizabeth Arden Classic, Olympia Gold Classic, CPC Women's International. **1982** Olympia Gold Classic, Nabisco Dinah Shore, United Virginia Bank Classic, Mayflower Classic. **1988** DuMaurier Ltd. Classic.

Sally Little's LPGA Record

Year	No.of Events	Best Finish	Money	Rank	Scoring Average
1971	7	T20	$1,670	51	76.38
1972	23	T5	8,260	33	76.11
1973	30	3	9,335	45	75.99
1974	23	T7	13,353	35	75.18
1975	14	T11	7,107	50	74.62
1976	25	1	44,764	13	73.77
1977	21	T2	67,433	10	73.01
1978	24	1	84,895	8	73.15
1979	27	1	119,501	6	72.66
1980	28	1	139,127	7	72.49
1981	26	1	142,251	8	72.37
1982	27	1	228,941	3	72.05
1983	9	T15	3,792	139	75.48
1984	25	2	75,561	21	73.16
1985	23	T4	54,310	42	73.79
1986	21	2	55,802	44	73.83
1987	27	T14	38,495	62	73.78
1988	26	1	139,781	18	73.20
1989	22	T18	15,854	118	75.68
1990	14	T11	26,541	108	74.03
1991	28	T2	134,859	34	73.26
1992	28	T8	88,400	60	73.04
1993	26	T12	49,658	89	73.12
1994	25	T5	98,115	56	72.90
1995	24	T10	56,186	82	73.24

Nancy Lopez

Nancy Lopez is one of the greatest women in sports. Her outstanding success in golf is not just contained in the amount of records she has set, or the achievements she has managed, or the charm with which she has done it. She combined becoming one of the greats in golf with the role of wife and a mother to three daughters. She passed the $1 million mark in winnings the year her first daughter was born, and she gained entry into the Hall of Fame just eight months after the birth of her second daughter.

Nancy has made everything appear easy, but she admits the toll: "You kind of hold your breath when you play golf, and it has aged me. The reason I've won is my desire to win combined with the ability to be able to do it."

When she was 26, with the same amount of career victories as her years and with nearly $1 million in winnings, she said: "I feel a lot older than I am, especially on the golf course. It seems like I've been out here a long, long time. The first few years went by really quickly, but I was so busy that I never had time for myself. I was always playing golf, doing interviews, or signing autographs. I was never able to relax and celebrate my victories. I didn't have fun or enjoy the time because I had to grow up too quickly and had to make so many important decisions.

Nancy was not moaning about her lifestyle or anything it brought her, including a first marriage and divorce. She was being realistic about the result of the pressures that were put on her by the LPGA and by the demands of the media.

She is a physically appealing woman, with dark hair, brown eyes, and a warm dazzling smile. Her fluctuating weight has never detracted from her appeal. She was God's gift to the LPGA, and carried the banner for the tour from her first full season in 1978, through the next decade, and into the 1990s. Nancy Lopez has been the only modern household name in women's golf. Although other players have had their share of the limelight, Nancy has been the LPGA's most continuously saleable commodity and the perfect vehicle for a women's golf tour. Her attraction is universal, her patience remarkable, and she is a natural at public relations. She looks at you straight in the eye and makes you feel you are the most important person in the room, when she addresses you. The great Mickey Wright, recognized the potential of Nancy Lopez in 1978, when she said: "Never in my life have I seen such control from someone so young." In 1979, Nancy defeated Mickey Wright at the second hole of sudden death at the Coca Cola Classic, and the older champion, near the end of her career, never had the chance to win again.

Nancy, who came from a lower income family in New Mexico, said: "Before I was what I am now I wasn't anything. I wish people wouldn't put

Nancy's first win during her rookie year came at the Bent Tree Classic, the first of 47 victories that would enable her to enter the LPGA Hall of Fame in 1987. Photo courtesy: Katherine Murphy.

celebrities on such a high pedestal, because we get spoiled."

Debbie Massey said: "By and large, because of her upbringing, Nancy has a fairly aggressive attitude in business. She didn't have an easy life. Golfing circles were not very happy to have her initially, but when she started playing good golf, she won her first amateur state championship at 12, and things changed tremendously for her and for her whole family. She loves her family. Her mother was an especially wonderful woman; her father is wonderful too. When you look at Nancy, you see a big family, and what she meant to them. I know how she feels about her father and felt about her mother.

"Financial and social reward meant that her motivation started to climb, and that's where her aggression comes from. She doesn't have a killer instinct. She wants to win from within and has been highly motivated for years. You can't play to that level of excellence without it."

Nancy had an outstanding amateur career. She won the New Mexico Women's Amateur at 12 and two USGA Junior Girls Championships in 1972 and 1974, as well as three Western Junior titles. She was a member of the Curtis Cup and World Cup teams in 1976. As an amateur, she tied for second in the 1975 U.S. Women's Open. A professional in 1977, before the LPGA qualifying school, she finished second to Hollis Stacy; in 1989, she was four shots behind winner Betsy King, for another second, and the U.S. Open title still eludes her.

Nancy enjoys setting records and made a dynamic entrance onto the tour. In her opening season of 1978, she became the first player in LPGA history to win five consecutive tournaments on her way to nine victories. She was the first professional golfer, man or woman, ever to be Rookie and Player of the Year in the same season, when she won a record $161,235 and the Vare Trophy for the lowest scoring average of 71.76. Throughout 1978, she never finished lower than 25th in any event.

Following that startling debut she won eight tournaments in 1979, prize money of $197,488, and again achieved the lowest scoring average of 71.20. Nancy Lopez had set the world of women's golf on fire.

1987 was a great year for Nancy. She won the LPGA Championship after sinking this final putt.

Nancy's private life, which inevitably became very public, had to fit in with her golf career. Her marriage to Tim Melton on her 22nd birthday in 1979, when she became Nancy Lopez-Melton, broke up and was in the divorce courts by 1982. Later, the same year, she married baseball star Ray Knight and kept her maiden name playing professional golf, perhaps an indication of a more mature and stable relationship.

Nancy was born in Torrance, California, and brought up in Roswell, New Mexico. Her sister, Delma, is ten years older, and Nancy grew up almost as an only child, since her sister married and left home at 17. Her father, Domingo, had a car body shop, and her mother, Marina, who looked after the family, died unexpectedly at 54 in 1977, following an appendectomy shortly before Nancy went on tour. A devastated Nancy said that her mother's death helped to strengthen her own mental power: "I felt my mom was there in spirit, and I wanted to show her I could do well." Determinedly, she won her first professional tournament, the Bent Tree Classic at Sarasota, and dedicated it to the memory of her mother, tears streaming down her face as she achieved victory.

Nancy's early years were nurtured by her father, who refused to let her wash the dishes at home, for fear that she might spoil the hands that were going to help her become a golf champion. He was grooming her for stardom and working hard to finance her. His own natural sporting ability resulted in his playing golf to a three handicap.

"I started playing golf with my dad at seven, and I competed in my first Pee Wee tournament at nine, which I won by 110 shots. My dad never pushed me, but he set goals and rewarded me if I achieved them by giving me presents. Golf was always fun, because I was trying to beat him and win for what he would give me. Later, he gave me a car for winning a tournament.

"He encouraged me to practice, told me that I needed to practice to win, and sometimes he would come with me. I would play and practice for hours everyday. I would like to have done things with my friends, but because I wanted to win at golf even more, I practiced harder and harder.

"Winning is not just that; a lot of people practice hard, want to win, and can't do it. Your mind controls what happens, and mentally I was able to make myself win. You feel high when you win, which is enough justification.

"However, I wanted to win for my parents because they sacrificed a lot for me to play golf. They were always there when I needed them, and I wanted them to be proud of me. I couldn't do anything except play golf to repay them.

"The incentive was even bigger when my mother died. Before she died, I was playing well and thought maybe I could win my first tournament. I thought about the money I would win and the things she never had that I could buy her. I didn't become successful until after she died, and her death really motivated me, although I couldn't buy my father the things I had wanted to buy my mother.

"It was my dad I wanted to make proudest of me, to repay him for what he did, but when I was young I never realized I could be that good. I never said, 'Boy, I'm really good, I'm going on tour.' I played a lot of amateur golf and enjoyed it very much, but when I finished as runner-up in the 1975 U.S. Open as an amateur, I was surprised. I never thought I could come that close to winning or playing well with the professionals, but that result changed my mind.

"With the help of Dale McNamara, the golf coach at the University of Tulsa, I got the first women's golf scholarship and stayed there for two years. It gave me the confidence to think I could do well on the LPGA tour, which I joined in 1977 after qualifying in the July school. A week earlier, I had a boost of confidence, when I placed second in the U.S. Open.

"My dad wanted to sponsor me, but I wouldn't let him; so there was tremendous incentive to make enough money to play the following week. I enjoyed having my parents with me and felt they helped me to play well. Some players, particularly when they're young, don't like their parents at tournaments because they feel more pressure. I like to be with my friends and family, and I like to be alone. I don't get bored; I'm not dependent on having someone there.

"When all of a sudden I started to play well and to win, I made a lot of money on and off the tour. In one year, I went from earning $500 to $12,500 for a company day. It was a new experience. I was shocked at such a big jump—$500 had seemed like a million to me. I laughed and said, 'Why would anyone pay you that much to play golf?'

"At first I didn't feel part of the LPGA; I felt nervous and scared, and I didn't want to step on anyone's toes. You need to go to meetings to know what's going on, but I was doing so much away from golf that I was too tired to sit and listen to everyone gripe. It wasn't really in me to get up and tell people what I thought.

"Everyone has her own little group on tour, but I don't. I tried the Bible study and enjoyed it, but I didn't feel I belonged or could go out with them and have a good time. I don't like groups. I prefer to be with one or two people or on my own. You have to be a loner to be successful. Anyone you hang around with can change your attitude and make you negative.

"Success can make things difficult. After my first two years, the press would write about me even when someone else was winning a tournament and I was losing. I won five in a row in 1978, which caught peoples' attention. The galleries grew, and it was pretty exciting. It's hard to win five in a row but that type of achievement excites me so.

"When you become very good at what you do, other people think you are changing, but I think they change. For some reason, they don't know how to react to you; they feel that because you are doing really well, you're not going to talk to them any more. It was difficult to get close to people, although I felt they respected rather than resented me. Finally I became friendly with people more like I am and who think as I do.

"After my first year I thought, 'I could be a flash in the pan,' and I was also determined to prove I was not. I was determined not to fall on my face, though it is easy enough to choke yourself to death trying to win. I proved myself in the second year, winning eight times, but because I didn't win until the end of March 1980, I was constantly being questioned on why I wasn't winning.

"It bothered me. I felt like yelling at them that I was human. They spoke as though I would never play well again, and I nearly went crazy. I was depressed, crying; I felt close to a nervous breakdown, and I thought about quitting. Supportive fans wrote and said they loved me, win or lose, and that took off a lot of pressure.

"I told myself that if I was sweet when I was winning, I shouldn't be nasty when I was not. It was really important to keep myself together, not to show it was a big deal; so I talked to the press when I wasn't playing well. It's easy to snub them when things go wrong, but I kept my cool because I wanted the admiration of people more than anything. I wanted them to say, 'She's playing badly, but she's still smiling.' Nothing else mattered."

Nancy won five tournaments in a row in 1978, and nine for the year, including the LPGA Championship. She was off to a fast start and was named "Rookie of the Year" and "Player of the Year" — the only pro, man or woman, to achieve both honors in a single year. Photo courtesy: LPGA.

When Nancy was 20, she was engaged to a college boy friend for a few months: "We broke up after I left school, but he came and spent time with me when my mother died. As someone else in my life was gone, I clung to him. Then I broke it off, because my career was important to me. I wanted to date other people, but I felt I was in prison."

A few months later, Nancy met Tim Melton, a sports broadcaster: "He was the guy. When I met him, I knew he was the person. I once told my mother: 'If I ever marry, he's going to be tall, dark and handsome, a good Christian, who doesn't smoke or drink.' My mom said, 'You'll be looking for a long time.'

"Tim fit the mental picture I'd given my mother. There was an outline in my mind, and he belonged in that empty space. He was such a gentleman. He was 30; I was 22, and I felt my mom would have been pleased with him. Dad met him when I told him we were engaged. He was quiet for a little while, started to cry, then said, 'Are you sure? If you're happy and that's what you want.'"

Tim and Nancy married at the beginning of 1979 and were divorced in early 1982. Before Nancy married, she said: "It is sad to see people get divorced. I hope Tim and I never get divorced or have those kind of problems. I feel I could tell people what to do to make everything all right."

Nancy's celebrity status created problems for them both: "It was hard on Tim. I had to make him feel sure I loved him to make him feel secure. He had no identity, and people would talk to me as though he wasn't there, which hurt him and bothered me. It was hard on him that when I appeared, I took over. I always grabbed him by the arm and said, 'Don't let it bother you.' He put up with it.

"The problem was that I was too young to realize who or what I needed in my marriage. As I grew up, things between Tim and me changed. We didn't have fun any more. It was really tough, because I had never seen myself in that situation. It was hard to settle for a divorce, when it had upset me so much to see other people get divorced.

"When I was separated from Tim, I met Ray, who was already a friend. It all happened in a very short time that we got together; Ray is more like I am."

Ray Knight also had been married before, and when Nancy and Ray married in September 1982, Nancy began a new life with a very different husband, five years her senior, who was already a National League baseball star in his own right.

"I had 60 offers to play college baseball and football on a scholarship, but I chose to play pro baseball. I signed out of high school with Cincinnati," said Ray. "I felt I was good enough to be a professional athlete and earn lots of money. I had three different fan clubs in the U.S., but I was not nearly as well known as Nancy, because in team sports the national recognition is for the team. I have had a lot of adulation, but Nancy has had much more national and worldwide acclaim.

"I have had no problem with my ego because I've never been the kind of person who wanted adulation. I want people to respect me, but I'm much better in the background. I'm strong willed, and I'm not a follower. I'm backing Nancy when I'm out with her, not following.

"I come from a very close family, that has given me a tremendous amount of love and security, and I love people as a result of that. Nancy is the same, and I don't mind talking to people about my wife and her career, which are important to me.

"I have my own identity. I've been blessed with talent, and I make a tremendous amount of money, so I'm very secure. I love people to adore Nancy,

Nancy triumphed on tour in 1985. She won five times, including the LPGA Championship. Photo ©Phil Sheldon.

and it makes me feel good to know she's respected by a lot of people. As her husband, I love and admire that. You can judge someone on how other people take to them, and Nancy has a reputation as a sound and solid person, who is very sweet.

"I stay in the background when I'm watching Nancy, but she knows I'm there. She smiles, winks, or throws me a kiss. She never takes me for granted and always lets me know she is aware of my presence.

"Nancy and I are very much alike. She's the most honest person I've ever met, the first I've met who is as honest as I am. I say what I feel; so does she. Our goals basically are similar. When two people are in love, their professions come second, and their love and their relationship come first. That's the way it is with us.

Nancy has successfully combined family and career, setting records in tandem with raising three daughters. This photo was taken during the 1990 Solheim Cup competition. Photo ©Phil Sheldon.

"I have put Nancy's career before mine, and the reason I have been able to do that is because she gives me security as a husband. I know she respects me, never puts golf or people before me; so it's easy to say, 'Go and play golf,' because I know she likes to be with me. She makes me feel so at ease that I don't mind if she plays golf for another 20 years.

"The big thing is understanding a professional athlete. I know what motivates Nancy and what she needs because I need the same things. It's easy to know when to back off or when to apply pressure. I'm so competitive that sometimes I'm very demanding, but Nancy understands."

Nancy said: "I've never felt a career is more important than a family, and life in general. I play golf because I enjoy it, and the money is great, but you have to be happy outside your golf to succeed. I need to be happy first and then play golf. Although golf has been part of my life for so long I'd probably be lost without it.

"It think it's good to be away from each other a little, but I don't like being away from Ray. I want to play well, and if I need to be away from him to do that, I will, but I'll miss him a lot. I know what it takes to win, and I have to push myself to do that. I have to decide whether I want to win or be an average player. I want to win for Ray and my dad because they give me so much support.

"I like to compete in anything I do and I'm aggressive on the golf course. It is not in me to curse or swear, but I love to cry, and that's the way I show my anger.

"It is hard always to put on a public face, and sometimes I want to freak out, but it is important to me to keep a good image. My image reflects on me, my husband, my family, my life. Everyone should be good in public.

"I know that, because of who I am, I get treated differently. Normal people don't get such friendly treatment. If you're in a store and you hear them whispering, 'That's Nancy Lopez,' they come up and give you the royal treatment. I hate it. I think everyone should be treated the same. It's nice to be treated well, but not differently, because I'm not any better than anyone else, and I don't think God would want me to feel that way.

"This world would be a better place if people didn't think that if you have money, you're everything, or if you have none, you're nothing. It would be better if everyone were treated like a celebrity. I don't like phoniness.

"Sometimes it's nice to have a little bit of power, which money and success give you, but it's wrong to think you're better than anyone else. It's good to have people say, 'Hi Nancy,' even though they don't know you.

"I've enjoyed the recognition I've had over the years. The way for it to continue and to have people remember me, is to go out and win. I've been spoiled a bit by the recognition, but I like it and wish it could be like that forever. To keep winning and be known is the greatest experience you can have, especially at a young age. I wish everyone could have it. It motivates me to accomplish things no one else has ever done."

Nancy continued to set records in tandem with producing three daughters, and traveling with them and a nanny on tour. Ashley Marie was born on November 7, 1983, and Erinn Shea on May 26, 1986, Torri Heather on October 30, 1991.

In 1985 Nancy won the Player of the Year Award and the low scoring average with 70.73, both for the third time. In 1987 she became the youngest ever entrant into the Hall of Fame, gaining her 35th career victory at the beginning of the season, when she won the Sarasota Classic. It was a poignant moment, since that same tournament had been her first professional career win and one she had wanted so badly in memory of her mother.

When Nancy won in 1987, she was just six months short of ten years on tour, and according to LPGA rules could not be inducted into the Hall of Fame until July that year. When it took place, it was a glittering and emotional occasion. Nancy was gracious and charming among the sparkling diamonds of Tiffany's in New York where the ceremony was held.

Following her January victory, she said: "Getting in the Hall of Fame is what I always wanted to do. I don't feel I'm in yet, because they haven't inducted me. They should induct you before ten years when you meet all the criteria. Ten years shouldn't have anything to do with it. It would make me the youngest to get in, in that time, which is a record in itself, and I like to set records. It would have been nice if they had inducted me right after I made it.

"I feel honored to be with the other women in the Hall of Fame. I have always respected them and what they have done for women's golf. I look at each player, and some are already legends while others will become legends as time goes by. I feel I'm a great now, being in the Hall of Fame, having accomplished what I've done and being with the greatest golfers. I feel great that I can say I'm one of them.

"Trying to win more than Kathy Whitworth's 88 victories would be impossible, juggling my home and tour life. I'll play as long as I can win, as long as it's right for my family.

"Sometimes I have felt guilty about what I have been doing. I'm starting to get over it, but I think Ray gets a little cheated. He's so good because he doesn't put pressure on me, either to play or to stay at home. He's very understanding and sacrifices a lot. He's not selfish about it, but I still feel pretty bad. You don't get over feeling guilty, but you feel better about it, especially if the person you're married to makes it easy for you.

"I've become more organized; so that when I'm home, I cook, wash, and grocery shop. I have very good help with the children, both at home and when they come on tour; so that I don't really need to worry.

"My mom raised me in an old-fashioned way, where the woman did everything for the man, and the man was the one who went out, made all the money, and gave her the luxuries. Sometimes I think I would like a daughter of mine to marry someone really rich, stay home, and be a mommy. I wouldn't mind her having a career, but not one

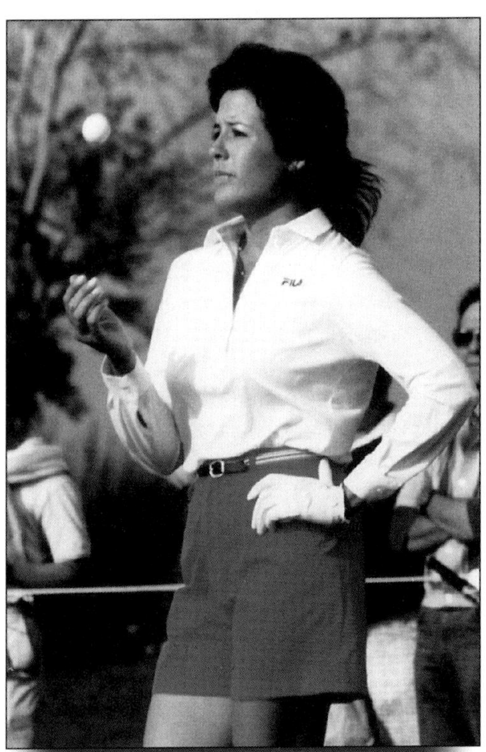

A confident Nancy Lopez was on her way to becoming the youngest qualifier for the LPGA Hall of Fame. She had to wait six months to be inducted as the rules for admission required that a player be on tour for 10 years. Photo courtesy: Katherine Murphy.

of traveling, and not separately, as Ray and I do. I wouldn't want her to go through that.

"I still do a lot of public appearances and other work, and since I enjoy communicating, it is easier for me than some. I used to agree to everything, until I realized I couldn't keep doing that. I was either going to drive myself crazy or burn out. When I'm not playing, I don't want to be doing an appearance somewhere. Although I hate to refuse, because it may be for a good charity, but I just can't take that time away from my family anymore.

"I'm still excited about playing. I want to relax and play the best golf I can; even if I haven't the pressure of getting in the Hall of Fame. I don't really worry about winning the U.S. Open; I may never win it. As an amateur I never won the U.S. Amateur. If it's going to happen, it will. I've tried to make it happen, and it hasn't; so I'm just going to lay back and let it happen if it's going to.

"I know that when I retire from golf I will miss the excitement of competing, a lot of my friends, the crowds, the feeling of making a five or ten footer on the last hole, and winning. That's a great feeling, something no one can feel unless he or she has been in that situation. It's wonderful to have that power of being able to compete and win.

"I would like Nancy Lopez to be remembered as a great competitor—a good winner and a good loser. I hope people will remember me as a friendly person. Some professional athletes are so tied up with themselves they forget what got them there. I want to be remembered as a person who appreciated what was done for me."

Member LPGA Hall of Fame 1987

LPGA Victories: 1978 Bent Tree Ladies Classic, Sunstar Classic, Greater Baltimore Classic, Coca-Cola Classic, Golden Lights Championship, LPGA Championship, Bankers Trust Classic, Colgate European Open, Colgate Far East Open. **1979** Sunstar Classic, Sahara National Pro-Am, Women's International, Coca-Cola Classic, Golden Lights Championship, Lady Keystone Open, Colgate European Open, Mary Kay Classic. **1980** Women's Kemper Open, Sarah Coventry, Rail Charity Classic. **1981** Arizona Copper Classic, Colgate Dinah Shore, Sarah Coventry. **1982** J&B Scotch Pro-Am, Mazda Japan Classic. **1983** Elizabeth Arden Classic, J&B Scotch Pro-Am. **1984** Uniden LPGA Invitational, Chevrolet World Championship of Women's Golf. **1985** Chrysler-Plymouth Charity Classic, LPGA Championship, Mazda Hall of Fame Championship, Henredon Classic, Portland Ping Championship. **1987** Sarasota Classic, Cellular One–Ping Golf Championship. **1988** Mazda Classic, Al Star/Centinela Hospital Classic, Chrysler-Plymouth Classic. **1989** Mazda LPGA Championship, Atlantic City Classic, Nippon Travel–MBS Classic. **1990** MBS LPGA Classic. **1991** Sara Lee Classic. **1992** Rail Charity Golf Classic, Ping–Cellular One LPGA Golf Championship. **1993** Youngstown-Warren LPGA Classic.

Unofficial Victories: 1980 JC Penney Classic (with Curtis Strange). **1987** Mazda Champions (with Miller Barber). **1992** Wendy's Three-Tour Challenge (with Dottie Mochrie and Patty Sheehan).

Nancy Lopez's LPGA Record

Year	No.of Events	Best Finish	Money	Rank	Scoring Average
1977	6	2	$23,138	31	73.24
1978	25	1	189,813	1	71.76
1979	19	1	197,488	1	71.20
1980	24	1	209,078	4	71.81
1981	24	1	165,679	6	72.10
1982	22	1	166,474	6	72.10
1983	12	1	91,477	15	72.59
1984	16	1	183,756	7	72.00
1985	25	1	416,472	1	70.73
1986	4	2	67,700	35	70.29
1987	18	1	204,823	7	71.91
1988	22	1	322,154	4	71.40
1989	21	1	487,153	3	70.73
1990	18	1	301,262	8	71.33
1991	12	1	153,772	26	71.69
1992	21	1	382,128	8	71.05
1993	19	1	304,480	14	70.83
1994	193	T2	197,952	25	71.98
1995	18	3	210,882	28	71.83

Debbie Massey

Debbie Massey is an emotional, humorous, resourceful, and physically strong woman, with innate drive and a forceful, direct personality. Her capacity to be interested and involved in other people and projects is unusual for someone in such an egocentric job. She has been involved with her family, with her father's death and that of friend and teacher Ellen Griffin. She was an officer for three years in the LPGA, after only three seasons on tour. Her adventurous urges have been satisfied by taking time off to go skiing, scuba diving, and mountain climbing in the Himalayas.

She pushes herself to the limit, liking to experience everything with the greatest possible intensity: "Maybe two or three times a year I know I am a fantastic machine, a perfectly tuned instrument, performing to the top of my capability." She drains herself emotionally, enjoys being a leader and in control: "I like to feel in control all the time, in my personal life and on the golf course. In order to perform to my maximum capacity, I need to maintain a level of calm, no matter what is going on around me."

Taking matters decisively into her own hands, Debbie left the tour later in the 1995 season and then announced her retirement with a press release. She knew it was an emotional moment and did not want any fond farewells, from the women she had enjoyed as a competitor since 1977. She departed without a clear vision of her future and then launched into some player management projects.

Debbie had an impressive amateur golf record and represented her country in Curtis Cup and World Cup teams. She finished seventh as an amateur in the 1974 U.S. Open after leading three rounds. When, as a professional, she led going into the last round of the 1979 U.S. Open and failed to win, it was the heartbreak of her golfing life. She won the following week on the rebound and did not win again until 1990.

From 1980, she flung herself into the vice presidency and presidency of the LPGA for a unique three years when the LPGA structure was reorganized. Her involvement was at a pivotal point, where decisions had to be made on establishing a new home for the LPGA, which came to rest in Sweetwater, outside of Houston, Texas. An innovative pension plan was being set up for the women professionals, and it was also the end of an era with Ray Volpe's departure at the end of 1981 and John Laupheimer's arrival.

Debbie was my first interview in 1980, and has encouraged me all the way with this book. After

Debbie Massey, two-time winner of the British Open (1980 and 1981), is shown here winning her first one.

reading my initial synopsis, her enthusiastic reaction was: "It's great. It made me tingle right down my spine."

Our friendship has been close over the years. We have stayed in each other's homes, met each other's respective families, traveled together, and knew that it was a friendship for life, where each could call on the other at any time.

Debbie was born in Grosse Pointe, Michigan, the eldest of three children, with two younger brothers, in an upper middle class family. They lived in Chicago for six years and then moved to Bethlehem, Pennsylvania.

"My father was a graduate of Michigan State University at 20, when he went into a trainee course for Bethlehem Steel. He worked his way up to become the vice president of sales. He was probably the last person to have been a lifetime career employee. My mother's father, who died young, and her uncle were members of the Grace family, which was a dynasty of the American steel business, and my great uncle operated Bethlehem Steel for over 40 years.

"My father worked very hard, and my mother did volunteer work, but mostly she was concerned with learning to play sports that she wanted us to play as we grew up. She learned to ski, and so did each of us as soon as we walked. She was a good horsewoman, and I loved watching her exercise polo ponies. I had a strong desire to follow in her footsteps, but I had an allergy to horses. She was very instrumental in my upbringing, and I loved it. We all played baseball and football. We were an athletic, outdoor family, which was wonderful.

"As a child I was scared of my father; having talks with him was scary. We were never put into specific roles. We did things as a family unit, but I remember that on one of my brothers' birthdays, when I was about 14, my father was taking a group of boys to a baseball game, and I asked to go. Teasingly, he told me to stay home and do the dishes with my mother, and I socked him right in the stomach, hurting my hand. I burst into tears as I ran into the kitchen. As it turned out, mom and I had a great time, but my initial reaction was, 'Don't exclude me. I've proved myself to be one of the guys in the way I can compete and understand sports. I'm as good as any of the people you're taking.'

"We are a close family, and I have very happy childhood memories. I could not have acquired the confidence or desire to do what I want, without the encouragement I received. Whatever I was good at was nurtured. The moment I lashed out at my father was the one moment he tried to put me in a role of which I knew nothing. Normally, we all did the dishes, and all of a sudden I was with mother, helping, and that was not comfortable.

"I was competitive within myself as far back as I can remember. I was not achieving to get praise at home. My parents took great pride in what I did, and I cared about pleasing them, but I cared about pleasing myself much more. My parents were both good golfers, and I went with them to the Shore Acres Golf Club outside Chicago to learn golf course etiquette before I was allowed to pick up a club. I loved the adventure of tending pins and raking bunkers. I pitched balls into a bucket in the back yard, and I started playing golf at 14. I was down to single figures in three years.

"I went to Westover girls' boarding school in Connecticut, which was an adventure, and I enjoyed the discipline, even though I fought it. At the University of Denver, which had no women's golf team, I minored in sociology, which was fairly elementary, but which stimulated me to consider things carefully. I often have conversations with myself over important issues.

"Playing golf mostly on vacations, my amateur golf continued, and after leading the 1974 U.S. Open for three rounds and finishing seventh, people asked why I didn't turn professional. I'm pretty much goal oriented, and I wanted to win the U.S. Amateur. I never did, but I played Curtis Cup and World Team golf twice.

"When I played my second Curtis Cup in England in 1976, the teams had an audience with the Queen at Buckingham Palace. We were instructed on how to curtsy, and we had to wear white gloves. If you were spoken to, you spoke, saying, 'Your Majesty,' the first time, then 'Ma'am.' You could shake her hand if she offered it.

"She met the teams as we filed past; then we had coffee, and it was very awkward when she came

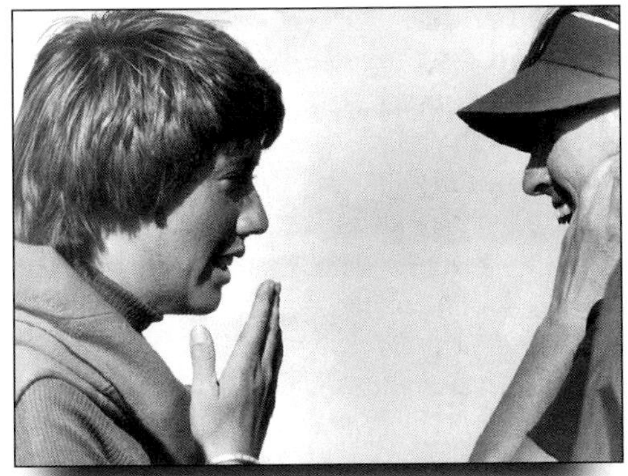

Two best friends and tough competitors, Debbie Massey and Carol Semple, confer during the 1976 Curtis Cup.

over and initiated some conversation. We were petrified. Of course, I was the first to open my mouth, and I squeaked something. I had seen the yacht, Britannia, in Bermuda, and I asked her whether she liked traveling by boat, since I knew she was due to visit America in it. She said she loved it because it is like taking your home with you. Immediately, I felt easier. I knew she was going to see her daughter in Canada; so I asked her whether she was nervous watching her ride. I told her my mother got so nervous watching me on the golf course that she hid behind trees. The Queen said she got nervous, too. She was such a gracious woman and appeared to enjoy the conversation which came so easily to her. She even apologized for not knowing anything about golf. She was very regal, and I was in awe.

"After my second Curtis Cup, I turned professional at the end of the season, when I was 26. I always knew I wanted to be a professional, and that I wasn't going to be satisfied unless I had the intensity of LPGA competition to find out whether I was good or not. I knew that I could become an artist at what I was doing, as I had a sound understanding of the form of the sport.

"The artistry comes with feel and sensitivity. These are not innate; you can learn them. You feel something once and then learn how to bring it back, again and again. You feel it in your fingers, in the calmness of your body motion in competition. To play golf well, I don't need to be psyched up every time, because I'm psyched up enough by wanting to be good. But, I had to develop sensitivity and feel in order to perform to the point where I could win, where I was relaxed enough to make touch shots and sink putts.

"I really like to challenge myself, to see what I can do. I'm a good competitor, with a good mental attitude, and I'm objective. I laugh at myself; I look at myself and say, 'You jerk,' when I've done something stupid, or I say, 'You're really great; you did more than I expected of you.' Being in tune with myself is my strength.

"I know that being a professional golfer sounds like a very ego-involved trip, but really it isn't, because if you're confident and happy with what you're doing, you take people along with you.

"I was excited about my possibilities as a person, and I wanted to develop them. Going into professional golf, I set out to be satisfied with what I planned to do for ten years. That way, I thought I'd probably end up as one of the best. I saw myself becoming a good golfer, with high hopes of contributing something to golf.

"I have never found that being a woman is a minus. Certain characteristics taken on by the female athlete are termed masculine by some people, but I've always been more accepted than rejected, revered rather than repelled, because of my athletic ability.

"The first time I was ever conscious that some women considered a woman's role an inferior one, was when the women's movement got going in 1974–75. I objected violently to it and had great discussions with people who were for it. I watched women on television or read about them, and thought, 'They're having problems I've never had,' but the women's movement accomplished what it should for a certain number of women. I don't identify with too many movements since I feel liberation comes from within, not from without.

"I feel I'm living in the real world except when I'm in competition. I read the papers, listen to the news, keep good track of what is happening. A lot of people playing professional golf do that, but usually you talk golf because that's what people want to talk about. Consequently, those outside golf feel you are more interested in the sport than in world affairs.

"When I'm in competition, I hope I'm not leading a normal life. Usually, I don't get out of bed until I've thought about the golf course I'm playing, especially if I like it. Then I can't stop thinking about it—it's almost like being in love. I'll go to bed, and my last thought will be: 'God, it's so hard, so good; it's asking so much from me.' I wake up thinking, 'Now we have to handle it,' but you have to court it as you would a beau in whom you were really interested. You don't want to turn him off by being too obnoxious. You handle him just the right way. He might respond appropriately, and you might be rewarded. You have to be ready to face the course, get on the first tee, and feel comfortable with the place.

"Sometimes when I arrive at the club, I'll sit in the car and think for 15 minutes. On the practice ground I'll think about the golf course, practice the shots I'll need, and deal with how well or poorly I'm doing. Even if you're swinging badly, you should be able to shoot 72 if you are a good player. You may know some part of your game is wrong, but you put tremendous faith in the part that is right. You have to deal with what you are doing, or you are dead.

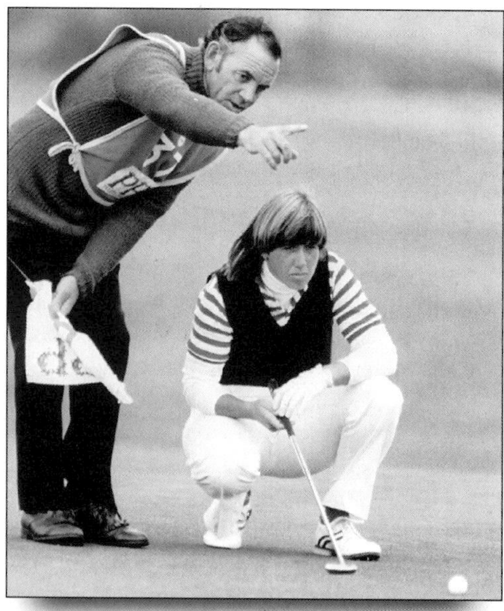

Debbie Massey, defending champion at the 1982 British Women's Open in Royal Birkdale, came to the LPGA with an impressive amateur record. Photo ©Phil Sheldon.

"After I've played, I have a beer with my pals. I'm a lot of fun. I laugh and joke, and getting together in the locker room is a real source of camaraderie. My competitive round is very important. I enjoy what I do, and I'm tired afterwards; I'm tense, I chat, listen to funny stories, release a bit, but I don't think or talk about my round. I wait until the next day to concentrate again.

"Professional golfers often don't mix with outsiders because of their desire to be alone. I relish my times alone, in an airplane or a car; even the silence of nature courts me—I love it. When your business is on the golf course, it is public, and anyone can read in a newspaper what you've made at the end of the week. 'Sorry that last putt cost you $1,500,' someone will say, and you have to sit and discuss it. It is all very open, what you have done on the battlefield. I give 100 percent of myself to the public, from the minute I arrive at the golf course to the minute I leave six or seven hours later. That's what I'm paid to do. When I leave, it's my own time.

"Sometimes at meals, you are tired; people come over, and you're hospitable when someone asks why you missed that last putt to lose a tournament. You would like to pick up your chicken tetrazzini and put it on top of the person's head. Instead you say, 'Excuse me I'm having my dinner. I'd love to talk with you another time.' Sometimes it is difficult to have the fortitude to answer that way.

"You need to be a loner at times to be successful. You have to sit back, criticize yourself, and if you're really going to make an impact, you have to separate yourself and say, 'I am special. I recognize this.'

"There is a fear of winning and a fear of losing. I'm scared to death to lose. That surge of adrenalin when you are charging is the most fantastic drug. If anyone ever bottles it, we're in big trouble because I'd pay through the nose for it. Physically, you've never been as strong—mentally, never as sharp—as when the adrenalin flows. Adrenalin will flow when you're close to death. I will cope with death, and sometimes I look forward to it because I've been excited in situations close to it.

"One time skiing in Utah, it was snowing very hard; I had a white-out where I lost all perception of the horizon, and I skied over a cliff. I landed and went sliding down the hill. I couldn't stop. I put my fist in the snow, rolled over and over, and stopped. I looked up and there was a boulder five feet in front of me. If I'd struck it, that would have been cookies. What a great feeling it was to stand up, look at that thing, know you beat it, and to have been so aware the whole time. I wouldn't trade that for the world. To many athletes, death is the ultimate challenge, your ultimate match.

"For me, winning the U.S. Open is the ultimate, life and death. All my life I grew up sinking three foot putts to win the U.S. Open, the most important tournament in the world. To have a three-shot lead going into the final round in 1979 and then to blow it, was really hard to take. I blew it all on the front nine, came back to tie going down the 18th, and then lost to Jerilyn Britz. I had made a surge forward; then I realized it was gone, out of my grasp. It was really tough. I felt terrible. The face you saw was honest, absolute heartbreak, complete momentary loss.

"You say, 'Get me out of here, bring me a big helicopter, hook it onto my bra strap, and carry me off to New Jersey. I'm making a fool of myself in front of all these people.' I walked off the green, watched Jerilyn sink her putt and knew I must go and shake hands. It was a tough thing to do because I felt so low. But, you get yourself back to the level where you can congratulate your opponent for having beaten you. It takes energy, but I did it. I'll never forget losing. It was too big a test to have lost; it will help if one day I win it.

"In Wheeling the following week, I won because I lost the Open. The last round at Wheeling was really cold. I was wearing a ski jacket, hat, and gloves, and I thought, 'At least give me some good weather.' I kept asking myself, 'How much do you want to win?' I really wanted to win. I played well and sank some good putts.

I talked with Debbie again in 1987 after she had been on tour ten years: "In the last two years I lost my greatest teachers; my father and my golf teacher, Ellen Griffin, died. Going through my father's death was beautiful, and I am happy I was able to do that.

"Ellen was my teacher for two and one-half years, although I'd known her much longer than that. She was a real teaching professional, and every person Ellen worked with felt she was special. She never lost the line between professionalism and intimacy. I'm not good at taking criticism, yet I never felt Ellen criticized me, and as close as we were, she was always my teacher. Since her death, I've tried to develop a relationship with other teachers, but I walk away because the professionalism isn't there. I miss her so much.

"I haven't changed my sights with my own game, I'm coming to grips with the way I am. I can't play golf really well, incessantly; I need to do other things. I need to pursue other interests as hotly as golf. I was never possessed by golf, like many great players or those not so great, but I thought maybe I should be and that it was appropriate behavior for a pro golfer. I gave it a try; I didn't like the person I became, and I decided I preferred to enjoy the rest of the world, rather than just one little world.

"I love golf more now. After 10 years on tour, you have to decide what is going to make the remaining years meaningful, part of a growing experience, and to get ready for what's next. I'm winding down on tour, although I still want to win. Having a winning attitude is feeling you can win every time you tee up. Whether or not you do, is in the cards—I still feel I can. I fight to get into contention; I am uncomfortable out of contention. I don't have to win every week, but I need to feel I can win, or I can't enjoy it. I haven't changed much at all; I expect to win a tournament—two, three, or four this year. Certainly I expect to be in that position every time I play.

"My running for office in the LPGA after I had been on tour only three years was because Carol Mann chose me. She was president of the association, involved with its future, and at different times she told me the association needed me, that I was 'the gal for the job.' When I was vice-president in 1980, it was decided that the term should be limited to two years. A little later it was changed so that the vice president automatically becoming president after a year. I was vice-president to Shelley Hamlin in 1980 and 1981, then president for a year.

"At first I was terrified. I didn't know where the tour was coming from, even if I knew where it was going. I didn't want it to lose its continuity because those founding mothers of the tour had such wonderful dedication, motivation, and ideals. I wanted to preserve it all. The tour had grown so much that some of the older players weren't comfortable with what was happening.

"When Shelley and I were in office, she said to me, 'You do what you have to do,' which was great. She did her part, and I did mine. I stopped the player council from having to defer to the membership all the time, and I used parliamentary procedure at meetings to get things more organized.

"New York was not working as the headquarters for the LPGA, because it had become too expensive and was not a golf-related site. The LPGA was not a megapower with a lot of money. We had to choose between Phoenix, Florida, Palm Springs, and Houston. The player council, which made the decision, opted for Houston. There, we developed Sweetwater, with the golf course and all other leisure facilities as the showcase for the whole property.

"When the idea of a pension plan came up, I loved it and jumped on it. It had never been done before—the men's PGA had been turned down by the Internal Revenue Service. It was the first time an organization of individually contracted players could get deferred compensation. We wanted to reward people who had been on tour in earlier years, so we allocated $100,000 to founding and charter members, $400,000 to current players, incorporating criteria for the different categories of players and compensation.

"It was a very creative period of my life; it was like learning the fundamentals of the golf swing and knowing you could go out and do something with them. Ray [Volpe] and I knew the principles, and we put them into action. Shelley did too.

"I had a magic relationship with Ray. We were two personalities who wanted to go somewhere with the organization. I had two years with him and my third with John Laupheimer. Ray was a visionary, and we went out on a limb and could see the same things. He's a stimulating man, not a great administrator, and he knew instinctively when it was time to leave. He had the mind and grace to leave his job at the propitious time, and I hope I have the same instinct for leaving competitive golf. He came in, zoomed to the top, said, 'I've done the best I can; now find the next person.' Ray's ego is so intact, he never got bigger than himself.

"I was so involved with what I was doing with the LPGA, I was a physical wreck. The hours I spent were hours I could have spent on golf, or sleeping and resting. I gave so much time and effort, and I loved it.

"By the time I left the tour, the whole image of women's golf had changed. Women became accepted by other women athletes, whether they were single, married, or pregnant. You could have your husband and babies, you could date, fall in love, go out dancing, and you could play on tour. The whole peer attitude shifted; it was so healthy. It became the real world, where there are people who are married, pregnant, single and having babies, and where there are people who are gay. All of that is found in the world of women's professional golf; it is very nice."

LPGA Victories: 1977 Mizuno Japan Classic. **1979** Wheeling Classic. **1990** Mazda Japan Classic.

Debbie Massey's LPGA Record

Year	No.of Events	Best Finish	Money	Rank	Scoring Average
1977	26	1	$45,962	15	73.60
1978	19	2	70,211	11	73.29
1979	19	1	57,778	17	73.61
1980	19	2	65,239	15	73.49
1981	23	2	48,777	25	73.78
1982	16	T14	15,310	81	74.70
1983	23	T2	67,920	25	73.69
1984	23	T5	41,914	52	73.59
1985	24	T3	58,162	35	73.85
1986	24	T2	122,495	15	72.99
1987	22	T6	52,502	51	73.39
1988	23	T2	115,426	25	72.38
1989	19	T4	74,919	42	72.70
1990	23	1	166,661	19	73.01
1991	21	2	127,308	39	72.85
1992	20	T3	94,301	57	72.72
1993	10	T12	20,985	125	73.41
1994	9	T5	24,638	123	74.71
1995	11	T11	29,465	116	73.60

Ayako Okamoto

The anxiety was evident when Ayako told me: "Sometimes I want to run away from golf, from the golf course, and from the media. I have no privacy, and it is tempting occasionally to run away from everything. Really, I enjoy the game and the lifestyle, and learning how to hit and control the ball has always been a fascination. Fortunately, I have had money to help protect me from people."

A strong, compactly built woman, Ayako Okamoto has an enviable golf swing and a consistency that has kept her in the forefront for many years, in spite of some back problems in the mid-1980s. As a woman who makes shyness an issue, she has not enjoyed the intensity of the spotlight, particularly from a hungry Japanese media. They have followed her every move, not only on home shores but also in droves on the U.S. tour, where her personal Japanese press corps have, on occasion, almost outnumbered the press for the rest of the players.

Ayako is a remarkable woman of great achievement. She came to golf late, at nearly 23, and rose to dominate golf in Japan, where the sport is revered. She achieved the superstardom usually reserved for pop cult figures like Madonna. She then went to America, where, combining the playing of two tours, she rose to the top. She became the first foreign professional in 1987 to take the LPGA Player of the Year title, and she led the money list. She won four tournaments in one season, and her winnings exceeded $1 million.

To be pulled between two tours is hard enough, but to have to adapt to a different language, customs, and food was not easy. Ayako achieved it with grace and distinction, acquiring friends and admirers of her personality and her golf game, wherever she traveled. She now has homes in Tokyo and California.

Ayako Okamoto won the 1984 British Women's Open in Woburn by 11 strokes, a prelude to her outstanding career on the LPGA tour. Photo: Jan Traylen/©Phil Sheldon.

In 1984, the Japanese media followed her to England, where she took the British Open title at Woburn in Bedfordshire. In appalling weather conditions that made shot making impossible for the rest of the field, Ayako produced immaculate golf to take the title, pulling away to a phenomenal 11 shot victory. "I remember the clouds," Ayako said. "If you reached up with your arms, it seemed you could grab them." It was a season of rare excellence, one that included two U.S. victories, and of which she said: "With every single shot I felt I knew which way the ball would go. If there was one blade of grass between the ball and the club I knew how it would react. The entire year was like that; I felt I reached the height of my technical ability, and I was hitting the ball the best ever; my moment of impact was so precise, it was a joy. It was what I had been searching for all my career."

When in 1993, I telephoned Ayako's office in California to set up an interview at a U.S. tournament, I was informed that a "courtesy fee" would be required, but after I explained that I had never paid anyone in golf for an interview, it was not mentioned again, and I received most helpful assistance and courtesy from everyone concerned with the Japanese players and their tour.

Knowing that Ayako speaks English, our interview began in that language, but once an interpreter arrived after 10 minutes, Ayako understood the questions but replied entirely in Japanese: "I am not happy if I don't speak perfectly," she told me. We covered a wide range of subjects, and she was helpful, patient and answered every question after thoughtful attention. Although at times, I found speaking through an interpreter to be frustrating, her strength of character and her intelligence shone through.

Ayako is the sixth of seven children, with five older brothers and a sister. Her parents are farmers, "not rich, not poor," she says. Now a wealthy woman, she does not reveal much about her assets: "I don't like an elaborate home, and as a single woman, I live in a condominium. We have a rule in our family that what we make we keep to ourselves. I don't support my parents, but when they come to see me in Tokyo I give them a little allowance."

Ayako was born in Hiroshima in 1951: "I went to junior school there before going to high school in Osaka. My father remembers World War II, when he did not get a good impression of American people. My parents survived the atom bomb, although some distant relatives in my town were killed. The day the bomb was dropped, my parents were in the fields, and they saw the mushroom cloud some distance away.

"When I am in America, I try to turn my attention away from the war, and if I do hear something against the Japanese, I pray and wish that it is not from the close people I know. I introduce my American friends to my father and my family. Whoever I like, they have to learn to like and accept. My father has no ill feelings toward my friends."

Ayako grew up with a great love of sport and an outstanding talent for softball. She excelled enough to become the No. 1 woman in Japan: "I left school at 18 and wanted to go to college, but my softball coach told me I had to work for a company and play softball. Although I didn't think he should decide my life, I contracted to do office work,and I continued playing softball until I was 22 years and 10 months. Then my manager advised me to take up golf, where I could play tournaments and earn money teaching. A year later, I turned professional.

"After working on my game for three to four months at a golf range and a private club in Osaka, I shot 47 for nine holes. I had worked as a caddie and learned the rules and the etiquette, but I was surprised I became good so quickly. I played from sunrise to sunset, even turning the lights on to the putting green when it got dark; so that I could practice. I got up at 5 a.m. and didn't finish until 9 p.m. in the summer.

"Although I didn't think of it at the time, being a woman professional golfer, creating records and history for Japanese women, means that your status goes up. To me, women and men are different whether we like it or not. Mentally, we are equal, but not physically. In Japan, women have been taught to think that men control the world, and women assist them. Now we are more Westernized; we realize what an important role women play in the world. Even in the days of the Samurais, the intelligent women kept crying out that women were equal to men, but society would not allow it. Slowly it is changing, and women professional golfers are playing a very important part.

"Having gone to America and seen the raised status of women through their eyes, I grew tremendously. If it were not for that and my golf, I would have had a very different life. I would have looked at successful women and been very envious of what they had done. I might have regretted that I had not tried it. With my personality I would have pursued a goal or a dream which could have been living happily as a married woman with two children. But, playing golf is very selfish, and I do not think it is fair to have a family.

"I do everything to the best of my ability always. I give 100 percent. My motivation is wanting to be the best at whatever I do. The money is important in securing some privacy, but it does not make happiness.

"Feelings of invincibility have come easily. At 30 I had a premonition that I would became one of the top three golfers in the world. At times, I have looked at a golf course and had a feeling or a premonition that I would win a tournament. Wanting to win and achieving it are difficult to explain, but winning gives me a chance to further my ambitions and goals.

"There have been times when winning has been easy, when I'm prepared mentally and no matter how well the others are playing, I'm on such a mental high and my ability is so far above everyone else that I can focus my attention so well on each shot. I know I can win.

"Being an athlete, I express myself on the golf course. If I had had the ability to express myself in another form, I would have been a great writer; you need your soul to write. I read everything: love stories, mysteries, books about philosophers, and people in history, and I compare myself to them.

"I have always been very emotional. Your emotional state can alter a golf shot, or your emotions can change after you hit a shot. In golf it is all about how you control your emotions. The Japanese nature not to show your emotions has been very helpful. I am proud of being Japanese and of our long history, although I find it boring and difficult to read."

Ayako first met Chako Higuchi when she was 24, on the day that she got through her second attempt at the qualifying school for the Japanese tour, just a year after taking up the game. Chako was then the superstar of Japanese women's golf, playing in both the U.S. and Japan, but the younger woman, perhaps being too shy, did not ask the more experienced golfer for any advice. After emulating Chako and becoming the No. 1 golfer in Japan, Ayako decided she should test herself in America. "A lot of sponsors felt I was being selfish leaving Japan, because I was a big

Ayako Okamoto points with pride to another long one-putt. In 1987, she was the first foreign professional to become LPGA "Player of the Year," and to lead the money list. She won four tournaments, and her total career earnings surpassed $1 million that year. Photo courtesy: LPGA.

name over there. But, being No. 1 in Japan was not like being No. 1 in America. I had a feeling I would get to the top of the LPGA tour and when it became reality, I was able to go anywhere in the world and walk with my head up high. I was very proud.

"I only knew school English; so the language barrier made it hard, but at 30 I was determined this time to do what I wanted. I qualified at the January 1981 school and played eight LPGA tournaments that year; my best finish was fourth place. Everyone helped make it go smoothly, and I felt very comfortable. I learned English for day-to-day living and to speak with friends, but I am not an outgoing person. Instinctively, though, I can understand people and what they are like from their body language and their manners. Because I am very shy, I don't enjoy the attention you receive when you are successful. I keep my mouth shut ["Oh, she does Liz," said the interpreter with a smile. "You should hear some of the interviews."] Even among friends I sit and observe. I am interested in human beings, and I analyze them and why they are successful. One person may have no brain and be physically very talented or vice versa, but if you have no brains, you do not last very long.

"For me, talking is a tedious duty. I went into sport to play, not to talk. I know if you have better scores, you have to talk; but, I think you need to enjoy sipping a cocktail before the revolutions in your brain become faster, that way your speech is smoother."

"Ayako's American career spiraled upward until she reached the zenith of technical perfection in 1984. The following year she suffered from a herniated spinal disc, which affected her performance, but she climbed back up, reaching the top position in 1987. "I felt that if I didn't do well in America, everyone at home would say, 'I told you not to go;' so it was a great incentive to reach the No. 1 ranking.

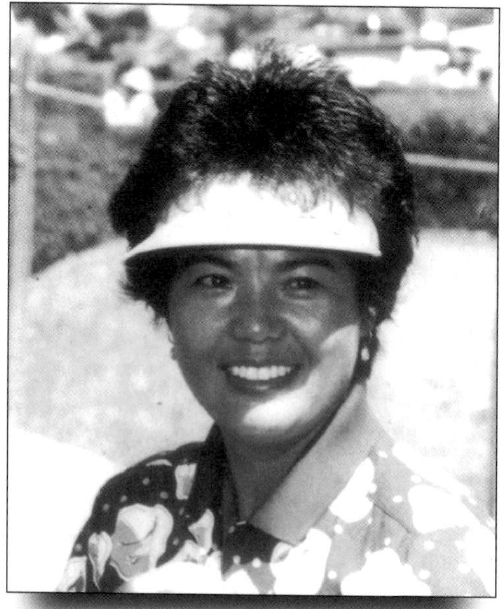

Ayako was victorious on several continents, winning the British Open in 1984, and competing in both JLPGA and LPGA events through 1995. Photo courtesy: Katherine Murphy.

"My strengths have been that I think positively, I am patient, and I delete trivia. I am a mixture of my parents, although neither one is quiet or reserved, and I have inherited a certain clumsiness from my father. If I cook, I cut myself; if I iron, I burn myself. Eating crab I cut my finger, or I trip on the carpet in a hotel. I embarrass myself constantly, even though I have an image of being cool and debonair.

"What has made me most proud in my career, is the growth of my personality. You may think that is funny. But I have a lot of friends, people who care, and that means more to me than anything."

LPGA Victories: 1982 Arizona Copper Classic. **1983** Rochester International. **1984** J&B Scotch Pro-Am, Mayflower Classic, Hitachi Ladies British Open. **1986** Elizabeth Arden Classic, Cellular One–Golf Championship. **1987** Kyocera Inamori Classic, Chrysler-Plymouth Classic, Lady Keystone Open, Nestle World Championship. **1988** Orient Leasing Hawaiian Ladies Open, San Diego Inamori Classic, Greater Washington Open. **1989** LPGA Corning Classic. **1990** Sara Lee Classic. **1992** McDonald's Championship.

Career Highlights: 3 times JLPGA champion and won the Japanese Women's Open in **1993** en route toward 37 JLPGA tour titles through **1993,** winning approximately $3.06 million from the Japan tour alone through **1993.**

Ayako Okamoto's LPGA Record

Year	No. of Events	Best Finish	Money	Rank	Scoring Average
1981	8	4	$14,147	76	73.67
1982	14	1	85,267	14	72.60
1983	25	1	131,214	10	73.01
1984	27	1	251,108	3	71.92
1985	18	2	87,497	23	72.53
1986	24	1	198,362	9	72.07
1987	24	1	466,034	1	71.36
1988	20	1	300,206	6	70.94
1989	19	1	205,745	6	71.66
1990	21	1	302,885	7	71.57
1991	17	2	349,437	7	71.54
1992	15	1	229,953	20	71.48
1993	15	T7	61,504	76	72.78
1994	8	T19	32,318	116	72.88
1995	5	T21	19,951	135	73.20

Patty Sheehan

When Patty Sheehan let a 11-shot lead fade in the final round of the 1990 U.S. Open in Atlanta, losing the title to Betsy King, Judy Rankin in her capacity of television reporter, pushed forward a microphone to allow the watching audience to hear Patty's immediate reaction. What riveted viewers saw, after such a public demise, were tears streaming down the cheeks of a suffering, almost-incoherent woman.

"It was very difficult," Patty recalled. "I was crying, I felt rotten about myself, and I thought, 'Here I am having just lost the Open, and it would look like sour grapes if I didn't talk to Judy.' It would make me look bad, and I would feel that I had let down the public, who wanted to know what had happened. So I talked to her, I did the right thing in dealing with the situation honestly, and everyone knew how I felt, because they felt as bad as I did. Afterwards, I had hundreds of letters from people telling me they cried right along with me, and I gained more friends from losing the Open than from winning it. That was an experience in itself."

Patty Sheehan knows the loss will always haunt her, in spite of winning the U.S. Open twice, first in 1992 and again in 1994. A lesser woman might have sunk, but Patty not only has outstanding talent, she has great heart and courage. She suffered, she was humiliated, and she rose above it. With her three victories in 1992, and finally with a five shot win in the 1993 Standard Register Ping, she entered the Hall of Fame as its 13th member.

"I feel inside I should be there because I stepped up and achieved that level, and there's a place for me beside those greats. I'm not bragging; I just feel that way. The level of competition on tour now is so keen; it is quite a satisfying achievement."

Patty's amateur golf career included winning Nevada and California state titles, the AIAW National Championship, and being runner-up in the Women's Amateur Championship in 1979. She was a member of the 1980 Curtis Cup team, winning all her matches.

When she arrived on the LPGA tour in 1981, at the relatively mature age of 25, Patty won a tournament in her first full season and was Rookie of the Year. Her 1983 Player of the Year award was followed in 1984 by winning the Vare Trophy.

Patty Sheehan, in triumph at the 1980 Curtis Cup in St. Pierre, brought an outstanding amateur record to the LPGA when she joined it in 1978. Photo ©Phil Sheldon.

She has been a consistent winner, including two U.S. Open victories and two LPGA Championship titles. She won the 1992 British Open Championship and played in the Solheim Cups of 1990 and 1992.

Patty is 5 feet, 3 inches, a compact woman with an enviable golf swing. The suffering she experienced on the Atlanta golf course in 1990 had been preceded by the trauma in 1989 of losing her home in the California earthquake, and then finding it was uninsured. To combat that loss financially, her earnings in 1990 were a remarkable $732,618, reflecting five victories: "I had an incentive. I had to pay the bills."

When I first knew Patty, I found her reserved, but as the years progressed, our relationship became more relaxed and friendly, until finally she surprised me with the depth of feeling she revealed.

Born in Middlebury, Vermont, into a middle class family, Patty has three older brothers, all high athletic achievers. Her father was a college sports coach in Vermont, and an Olympic ski coach; her mother taught nursing and did seamstress work.

Patty has the victory cheer down pat. This time she won the 1984 LPGA Championship, her second in a row as she won the title in 1983 as well.

Patty started skiing as soon as she could walk and competed in downhill racing, being cited as the best 13-year old in the country in 1967: "As the only girl in the family, I became an over-achiever." When she was 10, the family moved to Lake Tahoe when her father changed his job from coaching to become a ski resort manager.

"I started golf at five because the whole family played, but I took it up seriously at 14. I was down to scratch at 18, when I went to the University of Nevada, and then I transferred to San Jose State, where I was No. 1 on the golf team and won the 1980 National Intercollegate.

"I was always very competitive. I saw myself as a winner from a very young age. I played with boys all my life, and I seemed to be their equal, if not better. I never thought of myself as anything less than a winner. To be successful, you need drive, determination, and a belief in yourself, and some kind of peacefulness about what you are doing.

"When I arrived on the LPGA tour in 1980, I was intimidated, but it didn't last. My family sponsored me, and I needed their support only for a month, because I was lucky and played well. Money is a bonus. When I came out on tour, I concentrated on playing well and letting the money come as a result of my play.

"I feel a little misplaced and out of my era, because I have great empathy with the women who started the tour and where they are today. The majority of players have forgotten where we came from. I appreciate the history, the grand old women of golf who played their hearts out and sometimes hardly got paid for what they did. They caravanned in cars and picnicked at the side of the road, and I would have loved to play in that era. I am very appreciative, though, of all we have now, of my talent, and of the money I can make.

"I see myself as a multidimensional person, who likes to ski, play tennis, go to the theater and art galleries. I love the mountains and the beach. Sometimes, I think sport is undesirable because people get so involved in it. They let it ruin any home life or personal life, and it affects the way

Patty enjoys her Women's Open Championship Trophy. The tournament has been the source of her greatest joy and disappointment. Photo: RLG ProImage, Inc.

they feel about themselves. I enjoy making really good golf shots, hearing the crowds, and being in the limelight. I'm very comfortable out there; so sometimes I feel molded into the golf course. Inevitably, that is combined with periods of unrest and uneasiness. I try to be slow and easy on the course, which is hard because the lifestyle is always on the move at a fast pace. I sometimes feel I'm on a treadmill. I walk the same golf courses and keep coming back to the same clubhouses, and it all becomes repetitive.

"I became involved in charity work because I care about people and particularly about children. I chose a Group Home Society, at first giving them clothes and a pool table, and then I supported a house which was named Tigh Sheehan. Some of the children were very disturbed, and it was difficult to break through to them." Sadly, the charity later disintegrated when funds disappeared.

On October 17, 1989, Patty attended baseball's World Series in Candlestick Park in San Francisco as a guest of Willie McCovey, a former player for the San Francisco Giants. "I was in Willie's suite at the stadium when the earthquake struck at 5:07 p.m. I had been in several earthquakes before, but none as big as 7.1, which really jolts you. Everything shook and jiggled for several seconds. In the stadium, we lost all communications, and although everything looked fine, we realized there was not going to be a game, and it was probably worse than we thought.

"I left the stadium with a friend, and as we drove we heard on the car radio about the collapse of the freeway and bridge, and we were told people had been crushed. The traffic was horrendous, and we took a detour off the freeway to Juli Inkster's house. It was pitch black, and we couldn't find the way up the drive. The devastation was pretty bad at her house. Everything had gone flying, and all the glass and china was smashed. We were in shock that a big one had finally hit. We helped her clean up the house. There were smaller tremors every 15 minutes, and we would all grab each other for safety.

"The next morning it took two and one-half hours to go 30 miles to my home in Scotts Valley near Santa Cruz. When I reached home, I found a piece of beveled glass 8′ x 8′ broken in half, and it had been thrown into the kitchen. Everything breakable was broken, my crystal trophies were all shattered, the television and stereo were on the floor, the structure of the house had collapsed, and the antique furniture was tipped over. Later, my then manager told me there had been confusion over the house insurance and that I had none. After renting a place in Reno, I had $2,000 left in my pocket at the end of 1989. In January 1990, I spent more than that to get to Jamaica, and I went out and won the tournament because I had to. Nearly all of the $732,000 I earned that year went to pay the bills."

Patty's intense desire to win an Open title had been frustrated over the years, when she finished tied for second behind Jan Stephenson in 1983 and second to Lotta Neumann from Sweden in 1988. Her most devastating experience on the golf course came during the 1990 U.S. Open at the Atlanta Athletic Club, where, in a storm-lashed week, the frustrating delays were interminable.

"It was difficult to cope at Atlanta with the USGA's handling of the event. I got my round in the first day, but the second was a nightmare. It seemed to last forever. My second round on Friday started at 7 p.m., when I played 4 or 5 holes and then was told to come back at seven the next morning. I was hitting balls at 6 a.m. on Saturday in the pouring rain, and the round was called again. We were told to check back at 10:30 a.m. I ate breakfast and dallied around before returning to the course at 1 p.m. Half the field had finished the second round on Friday and had Saturday off, but I got through my second round at 6 p.m. on Saturday, having started out at 6 a.m. I was nine shots in the lead at the halfway stage, and we were to play two rounds on Sunday.

"I was up early the next morning, but I was so tired that I didn't eat any breakfast. By the fifth hole of my third round, I was hot, I felt a bit weak, and I was losing strokes. When I went in the water and double-bogeyed the 18th, I had dropped back to three ahead of the field. I was finding it difficult to function, and I later found out that I was hypoglycemic. With only 35 minutes before my final round, I went to the locker room to get a turkey sandwich and some Gatorade. Going back out, I didn't feel any better, and I continued to lose strokes. After nine holes, I was one behind the field. Beginning the last nine, I felt a bit better, and I birdied the 14th and 15th.

"Just as I was about to hit on the short 17th, a marshall yelled, 'Stand, please,' which rattled me. I tried to regain my composure, but I hit my four iron into the right bunker and had no shot. I bogeyed the hole to go one behind Betsy King; so I needed a birdie at the 18th to tie. When I reached the green, I couldn't get my 30-foot downhill putt up to the hole. I made a weak effort leaving it short. It had been a gruelling two days and a painful emotional experience. I had owned the Open. It was in my hands. I could break a leg and still shoot well enough to win, but I hadn't been able to do it. I cried for about an hour and then with my chin up, I walked outside to face people.

"The following week I went to the tournament, and the players left me alone because they didn't know what to say. They would see me coming and walk the other way, which was an interesting learning experience. What do you say to someone who has lost the Open like that, except, 'God, I'm sorry.' It was as if someone had died. Although there was nothing to say that could ease the pain, 'Hi' might have been nice.

"I double-bogeyed the first hole of the tournament, and thought, 'Why did I come here?' Then I picked myself up and played really well until the 17th hole on the final day, which I bogeyed to tie Beth Daniel. I lost to her in a playoff, but I was proud of myself for getting on with it, for not letting the Open destroy me, which could have happened. I also realized that I shouldn't put such intense pressure on myself to win an Open, that it was not worth the pain or ruining my career. I don't know how long I will be emotionally vulnerable. Maybe I am still. It keeps coming back when people mention it or something happens to bring back that memory. There's a little scar inside.

"I did not watch the 1990 Open tape, although maybe I could have gotten it out of my system so that I didn't have to think about it any more." Patty eventually dealt with the aftermath of losing that Open and regained her fighting spirit to win back-to-back tournaments later in the season. In 1991, she had one victory, and with her equilibrium restored in 1992, Patty came into the U.S. Open at Oakmont Country Club with back-to-back victories.

"My attitude for the week was to work on two swing thoughts: a good turn and a slow tempo. I was not going to worry about anything else. I figured I couldn't be any more devastated and disappointed than I had been in 1990; so everything was going to be better. I had a wonderful sense of humor about everything. I felt

Patty hoists the championship trophy for the 1992 British Women's Open. In her 16 years on tour, she has won at least one tournament every year but two. Photo: Jan Traylen/ ©Phil Sheldon.

fine, nothing bothered me, and everything was rolling off my back. I wish I could have such a wonderful attitude every week. I played my usual practice round with Juli [Inkster] on Wednesday, and she was hitting the ball so well, I thought, 'She's the one to beat.' At the end of the round, she said, 'See you Sunday' and I replied, 'That would be great.'

"The tournament started, and there were a few rain delays, but I maintained the same tempo all the time, which was wonderful and strange. About three months before the Open, something unusual occurred which could have significantly affected me; I had my normal period, and then I got it again 10 days later, and then 20 days after that, following which it reverted to my normal 28-day cycle. The difference was that the timing of my cycle had changed, which had never before occurred. Every previous Open I had played, I had either been premenstrual or right on my period. This time, I had my period before the Open, and going into it, I felt fine. I thought it was significant. Your emotions can be a little schizoid before and around your period, and I thought, 'This is it. There's either something wrong with me or it's happening for a reason.' It was definitely a contributing factor to my level emotional state that week at Oakmont. I hit each shot, chased the ball, hit it again, and didn't worry about any bogeys. I kept having enough birdies to bring me back.

"Just as we had predicted, I played with Juli in the final round. She was leading the tournament as rain and lightning appeared before we struck our second shots to the 17th green, and play was halted. I saw her reaction, which was shock. I had just three-putted the 16th to go back to two behind her, and I was a bit annoyed about it.

"I went to the locker room and knew I had time to regroup, to forget the three-putts, and to concentrate on getting birdies on the last two holes to get into a playoff. I cussed myself for 15 minutes; then I was serene and alone, after which I chatted with friends for one and a half hours. The pressure was off, and more than likely I was not going to win, since I didn't figure Juli would make any mistakes. After a 1 hour, 45 minute, delay, I hit a few balls and felt relaxed as we resumed play.

"My tee shot at the 17th landed on a replaced divot, and when I returned to hit it, I thought, 'That's a stroke of luck to have a perfect lie and not be in the divot.' I hit my sand wedge, and my ball finished inside Juli's ball. She putted and lipped out. I lined up my 15-foot putt and told myself to get the ball up to the hole, and I sent it right in.

"At the 18th, I missed the fairway, and when I saw my ball in casual water, I asked for relief. I was able to drop in the fairway, which was another stroke of luck. Juli hit a good one to the green first, and I had a shot of 160 yards. I took a five iron and said, 'Make this the best swing of your life.' I hit the ball very well; it stopped a little inside Juli. Being the smart competitor she is, Juli lagged hers up for a tap in. I knew the line of my putt was a little outside the hole, and I struck it dead solid perfect. It was right in the heart, the whole way.

"I had tied Juli to get into an 18-hole playoff the next day. It was so exhilarating, with the crowd right on top of the green, and I was getting another chance to win the Open. I was so excited, and it was probably as much emotion as I've ever shown.

Patty has continued to win every year since the 1992 Open—five more tournaments, including the 1993 Mazda LPGA Championship and the 1994 U.S. Women's Open She was inducted into the LPGA Hall of Fame in 1995. Photo courtesy: Jean Kalich.

I milked it with my fist in the air. I saw the faces of disbelief and amazement, and it was the most exciting moment I have ever spent on a golf course. Juli had a look of disbelief as she thought, 'God, I had it in my hand, and then it was gone.'

"That night, as the tournament had ended for everyone else, I took my clubs back to where I was staying with friends. The next morning, I left my clubs behind, and after I reached the course in 40 minutes, I had to turn round and drive back to the house like Mario Andretti, praying there were no cops. I was lucky, and after I had warmed up on the practice tee, I was ready to go, the adrenalin was pumping, and I was thinking, 'This is a good omen.'

"Getting a birdie at the first where Juli barely made par was a boost, and when she missed a four-footer for birdie at the second, it was a key point for me. The thought ran through my mind that she might not have a good putting day because she hadn't started well, and it came true. She missed a lot of short putts. She played better than I did tee to green, but I got it up and down for par six times, and I was five shots ahead when she three-putted the 16th. I felt I had it in my hands. I relaxed and made two bogeys, but I didn't care.

"It was such a great comeback from 1990, and emotionally it healed so many wounds. It was the most significant win of my career, because I overcame so much doubt. It would have been very hard to live the rest of my life without winning an Open. Now, I feel I'm on vacation from adversity, and that 1992 Open victory made me a different person—much happier and more content. If I never win another tournament, I'm still complete because that was the one I wanted."

Member LPGA Hall of Fame 1995

LPGA Victories: 1981 Mazda Japan Classic. **1982** Orlando Lady Classic, SAFECO Classic, Inamori Classic. **1983** Corning Classic, LPGA Championship, Henredon Classic, Inamori Classic. **1984** Elizabeth Arden Classic, LPGA Championship, McDonald's Kids Classic, Henredon Classic. **1985** Sarasota Classic, J&B Scotch Pro-Am. **1986** Sarasota Classic, Kyocera Inamori Classic, Konica San Jose Classic. **1988** Sarasota Classic, Mazda Japan Classic. **1989** Rochester International. **1990** The Jamaica Classic, McDonald's Championship, Rochester International, Ping–Cellular One Golf Championship, SAFECO Classic. **1991** Orix Hawaiian Ladies Open. **1992** Rochester International, Jamie Farr Toledo Classic, U.S. Women's Open. **1993** Standard Register Ping, Mazda LPGA Championship. **1994** U.S. Open Women's Championships. **1995** Rochester International, SAFECO Classic.

Unofficial Victories: 1992 Weetabix Women's British Open, Wendy's Three-Tour Challenge (with Dottie Mochrie and Nancy Lopez. **1994** JC Penney/LPGA Skins Game.

Patty Sheehan's LPGA Record

Year	No.of Events	Best Finish	Money	Rank	Scoring Average
1980	6	5	$17,139	63	72.86
1981	25	1	118,463	11	72.52
1982	25	1	225,022	4	71.72
1983	26	1	250,399	2	71.72
1984	22	1	255,185	2	71.40
1985	24	1	227,908	5	71.59
1986	24	1	214,281	7	72.17
1987	23	2	208,107	6	71.83
1988	23	1	326,171	2	71.56
1989	20	1	253,605	5	71.24
1990	25	1	732,618	2	70.62
1991	22	1	342,204	8	71.49
1992	22	1	418,622	5	71.30
1993	21	1	540,547	2	71.04
1994	18	1	323,562	13	71.65
1995	17	1	333,147	14	71.69

Muffin Spencer-Devlin

Muffin Spencer-Devlin, a woman of fertile imagination, is one of those characters of the LPGA tour, who, because of her wonderful storytelling abilities, is a boon to journalists. It is positively enticing to lap up her tales of reincarnation: of former lives as King Arthur, a black Matabele king, and a Samurai Warrior. As a woman who has marketed herself admirably, she nurtured at one time the habit of walking backwards uphill on golf courses to keep fit. Her ambitions outside golf have run to being an acupuncturist, a sports or news broadcaster, or an astronaut. She hosted a television show in Japan after learning the language when she played on the Japan LPGA tour in the early 1980s.

Muffin is tall, glamorous, and outspoken, with modeling being included in her list of achievements. She posed for the LPGA's Fairway magazine on several occasions—in 1982 becoming the reincarnated picture of a famous Betty Grable pinup pose: all swimsuit, long legs, and piled-up hair. "I expect I was chosen because I have long legs. The make-up artist was magnificent. I have had fun selling sex and women's sport, and I believe it is all part and parcel of it."

Her tempestuous past includes going into extreme highs and lows full speed ahead. Given the name Helene Harrington after her maternal grandmother, she acquired the nickname Muffin at birth when after a forceps delivery, her grandmother remarked that she looked like a muffin. Her hyphenated surname includes that of her father and also her stepfather, to whom she was very close.

When I first met Muffin, she was a wild, but attractive personality, playing the mini tour without a great deal of success but with plenty of gusto, trying to get through the qualifying schools and failing. Over the years, we have visited each other's homes and have had wide-ranging discussions. Muffin has an exaggerated style—her eyes opening wide as she spins her tales. She has progressed, from the woman who looked as though she would never amount to more than a tearaway character, to a golfer in the winner's circle. In 1985, her best season, she earned $133,372.

Muffin was born in Piqua, Ohio, and grew up with a brother two years younger. The family was wealthy on both sides. Her father, who was partial to alcohol and some wild living, was a traveling salesman for a company that made blankets. After divorce and re-marriage, he retired in the early 1960s to enjoy his pastimes. He died in 1975 at the age of 54 by choking on a piece of steak.

Both her parents played golf and were low handicap club champions; her mother, formerly Pat Harrington, was a fine amateur, who often found herself competing against and losing to Babe Zaharias in the first round of matchplay

A gleeful Muffin, at the 1985 British Women's Open in Moor Park, celebrated her best year on tour that year, winning $133,372 and finishing 12th on the money list. Photo ©Phil Sheldon.

events, and consequently was nicknamed *The Consolation Kid.*

"I started playing golf at five with my parents on weekends. I had a five iron and a putter. When I was six, my parents were divorced, and my brother and I went to live with my grandmother in Shaker Heights, Ohio, until my mother married Bill Devlin, a senior vice-president with a stocks and bonds company, in December 1964. The family, which now included three stepsisters and a stepbrother, went to live in Long Island, New York.

"At college I met a guy in the theater department, went gung ho into that, and left to become an actress in New York City. The nearest I came to acting was doing some modeling, being a costume mistress, and a fashion show co-ordinator. It was the beginning of my depression, of manic highs and melancholic lows. These mood swings later were diagnosed as resulting from low blood sugar, but at the time I thought I had a whirlwind inside me.

"I saw several psychiatrists and went into three different mental homes. I was drinking and taking drugs; I would sometimes take lithium to stabilize my condition, then I would chuck it. I muddled through, I couldn't cope, and one time I flew off to London for a month, saw a show every night, and then went home even more depressed.

"I was incapacitated and supported by my family, which in 1976 took me down to Florida, where they lived after my stepfather retired. Driving back to New York through Pinehurst, I entered the North-South tournament, in spite of not having played golf for two years, and I won the last flight. From there, I went to watch the Women's International at Moss Creek and met up with Hollis Stacy and a bunch of women I knew, who were professionals. They were having a great time on the LPGA tour; so I decided to work on my game and try to qualify for the tour.

"I missed the first qualifying school in January 1977 by a bunch of shots; so I went out to California and played the Group Fore mini-tour. Eventually, I plunged into a manic phase. I spent all my money and got into a load of trouble. To try to recoup, I painted houses, until later that year I quit drinking and went back on lithium.

"At one time, I got the shakes on the golf course—I had muscle tremors. A lot of that phase was frightening, particularly when I got arrested for a driving offense or when I went into mental highs and lows. A manic high gives you a wonderful feeling of grandeur, of powerful control; while a low leads you to hide in bed all day. Who can say whether it is body chemistry or outside influence?

"The mini-tour gave me a lot of experience in traveling, in week-to-week competition, and in handling myself and other people. They accepted me out there, which was for me a much needed thing; so I could come out of being crazy. The film *One Flew Over The Cuckoo's Nest* was so very close to what it had been like for me.

"I tried the January 1978 qualifying school after a hernia operation, and missed; then I played well on Group Fore, but missed by six shots at the July school. Following that, I was introduced to Arthur Kaslow in California, a nutrition expert, who said I had a classic case of low blood sugar, and he gave me vitamins and a special diet, and my manic state receded, although I was apprehensive for at least six months.

Muffin got her game together after playing the mini-tour to qualify for the LPGA, and then she went on to win three tournaments. Photo ©Phil Sheldon.

"When I became involved in nutrition, in health foods and physical fitness, I also delved into EST and Scientology. I became an active conservationist, getting onto the board of the Pacific Whale Foundation. My interest in Scientology led to a fascination for reincarnation, in auditing sessions where you explore past lives, and I was finding real things that had happened to me. I discovered in one session that I had been an 18th century stevedore on the Liverpool docks in England. I didn't understand the connection, but I was fascinated. I explored reincarnation further, and when I was visiting England, I was convinced that I had been King Arthur in a previous life. As a child and later, I read all there was about King Arthur, and I was so comfortable in England that I felt I must have known it previously. In South Africa, my connection was with a very big, black, Matabele king, who ruled with a rod or iron; while in Japan, I was sure that I had been a Samurai warrior.

"Toward the end of 1978, I began to feel great. I started to play golf well, and in January 1979, I was fifth in the qualifying school. The two previous years had been a real struggle, but suddenly I discovered I had inner resources and I had heart. I didn't go off the wall any more, nor was I on the roller coaster of peaks and valleys, I was hanging out in the middle zone.

"I got out on tour, and I could be wacky and zany, but I had to improve my golf because I really wanted to be a good player. My first victory did not come until 1985, when I won the Master Card Invitational in Virginia, coming from nowhere on the last day to shoot a 64. That tournament was a satellite event the same week as the World Championship of Women's Golf, so the top 12 players were not there. When I won my second tournament, the 1986 United Virginia Bank Classic, coming from behind with a 69 on the last day, it was a vindication of my first victory. All the normal complement of top players was there, and I had beaten the best.

"I see myself as a person who struggles back, not as one who gets in front and runs. I thrive on coming from behind. I feel I play well enough to be consistently in the top ten, and I have it in me to win majors. It is my goal to be the best putter and bunker player the world has ever seen, to take the weaker points in my game and work on them. I don't know that I particularly want to be in the No. 1 spot, or that I want to give it the required dedication, focus, and single-mindedness. I would like to win one, two, or three tournaments a year, and I would be quite happy playing in the top ten for the rest of my career. I just want to feel comfortable and realize my potential. Instead of putting on the blinders, I want to hang in and enjoy a life that isn't just golf."

Muffin, with Harpo the clown, could be wacky and zany, and when she wasn't struggling with the demons inside, she could play golf well enough to win. Photo courtesy: Katherine Murphy.

In 1987, Muffin was troubled with a persistent back problem that carried over into the following year and caused her to withdraw from several tournaments. She tried to work on the mental aspect of her problem, using meditation: "I feel I have a potential in golf; so far I have fallen short of it. I want to realize it, since I am knocking on the door. It is depressing to be faced with the possibility of giving up. I don't want to stay out on tour past my time, nor do I want to quit early; so I feel a certain need to push myself, and hopefully it will work. By God, you have to be an optimist to get along in this life."

By 1989, Muffin's career appeared to be blossoming as she won a tournament at the end of the season, in which she took home a much-needed $86,380. A commitment to a newly acquired home in California was proving costly, and her victory was timely. In spite of a financial breathing space, her mental state started to become unstable as a personal relationship fell apart and her stepfather,

Bill, to whom she had been close to as a child, was dying at 85.

"I had a niggling feeling of depression, and by Christmas when my mother and brother came to California, it was a real chore to put one foot in front of the other. I didn't realize it, but I was heading for one of my worst-ever depressions, since a combination of factors prevented me from rising out of the morass.

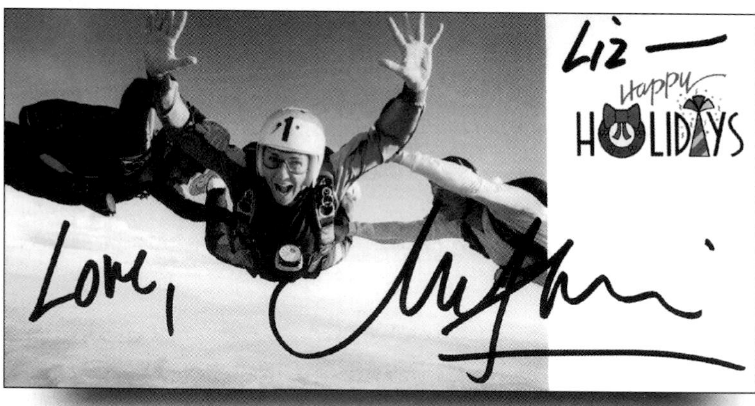

An irrepressible Muffin sends her holiday greetings to the author, who like many friends, coaxed her to seek treatment for her manic depression.

"The 1990 tour started in Jamaica, and I was lying on a couch with the blinds drawn staring at the ceiling, trying to gather some energy to make my reservations. Somehow I reached Jamaica. I told my caddie I was a basket case and that he should lead me round. I don't know how it happened, but I finished fifth and felt no euphoria at all.

"The following week I was in Florida with my mother, and I never got out of bed. I contemplated suicide, but the impact of my death on those who would find me kept me from doing it.

"Bill died in February. By then, I was on Prozac and feeling a little better, but it was short-lived. In March, I went into a manic high. At the Dinah Shore, I threw a water bottle at my caddie and was warned about my behavior. After that, I went to make a video in Portugal, and no one there knew me."

"On my arrival in England, where I went to play in the Ford Classic, a European tour event at Woburn, Bedfordshire, I booked into a hotel in London. The next day I went to get a rental car, and no one could give me directions to the course. As a result I got lost, got stuck in traffic, and telephoned the course. When I arrived, I was told I could have the Pro-Am day off since I had missed my starting time. A little later I was asked to play in an added group to which I agreed, although I had sent my caddie away on an errand.

The tension began when I was told to take a pull cart, which I thought was an insulting suggestion to a professional golfer. It mounted further when only one of my three partners could play, and the others were eternally hacking for five hours in the trees. At a dinner in the evening in Woburn Abbey, the home of the Marquess and Marchioness of Tavistock, I arrived late. When I found I was sitting with the same guys, I went to the top table, where I found the club director's wife, and I sat by her.

"When I went to inform my Pro-Am partners of my change of table, a tour official told me I had to sit with them or leave, at which point I pounded my fist on the table and said, 'I'm a fragging American and no one treats me like that,' and I stormed out. I made up the word 'fragging' instead of saying something worse."

The next day, Muffin went to the golf course and conducted several press conferences, wearing a German style officer's cap. She had been barred from the tournament and was headline news. I had not been at the dinner the previous evening, but I arrived at the course, recognized her depression and manic state, and confronted her. She readily agreed to go for treatment.

"I went back on lithium," she recalled, "and went into a rather zombie-like existence, never too excited or depressed. My self-esteem was low because I wasn't playing well, but my treatment did not change until March 1992, when I saw a holistic psychiatrist who put me on a vitamin and amino acid program. It had an unbelievably good effect on my brain chemistry. My constant, terrible anxiety receded and then disappeared.

"Looking back at my manic states and the incidents, they are funny and regrettable, but as a free spirit, I don't feel constrained by the mores of society; the rules don't necessarily apply to me. In a light way, I feel I can get away with just about anything. I would love to have skipped the depressions but not the manic highs, which were much too fun. They wreaked havoc, and I may wish I hadn't made an ass of myself, but I wouldn't trade those highs for the world. Very few people get to feel like that, and it is pretty amazing."

In 1996, Muffin became the first LPGA professional to come out publicly as a lesbian, when Sports Illustrated ran an article in which she revealed her sexual identity. Cathartic for Muffin, her action had the approval of her sponsors and many of her peers. Commissioner Jim Ritts offered a mature and commendable reaction: "When you label someone with a single word, a stereotype gets attached, and the individual's real qualities get clouded. Muffin is dramatic, she's warm, she's funny, and she's a truly gifted athlete, who has had to contend with great travails in life. If someone tags her gay and never experiences the rich colors of her life—well, it's a lost opportunity for them."

Although a few players said: "Well, that's Muffin blowing the lid off," Swedish professional Helen Alfredsson was more representative, declaring in Sports Illustrated: "If you dare to be happy, people should accept that."

All of Muffin's sponsors reacted positively and continued their backing. One said he and his staff knew Muffin was gay, but it was not an issue. She will continue to participate in board meetings and represent them at functions and corporate outings. This response firmly contradicted the finger pointing in 1995 by television commentator Ben Wright, who stated that lesbianism on the LPGA tour was losing them sponsors.

Muffin, the woman with a big heart and broad shoulders, reflected: "I am practiced at stigma busting after 15 years of talking about the problems of manic depression; so it was less scary for me to come out as a lesbian. I don't want to sensationalize it or make a circus of it, nor do I want to be regarded as the elected head-lesbian of the LPGA. I just don't want to live a secret life anymore.

"I am sure my action will follow me for the rest of my life, but as Anais Nin, wrote: 'There comes a time when the risk is greater to stay in a tight bud, than to allow the petals to blossom.'"

LPGA Victories: 1985 MasterCard International Pro-Am. **1986** United Virginia Bank Classic. **1989** Cellular One–Ping Golf Championship.

Muffin Spencer-Devlin's LPGA Record

Year	No.of Events	Best Finish	Money	Rank	Scoring Average
1979	22	43	$2,527	112	77.39
1980	27	T13	7,904	92	76.05
1981	25	T16	13,501	79	74.99
1982	21	T3	26,066	59	74.55
1983	22	T14	27,686	63	74.03
1984	26	2	73,324	23	73.62
1985	28	1	133,372	12	72.42
1986	23	1	104,034	20	73.55
1987	23	T2	85,176	28	73.08
1988	16	T12	21,877	96	73.85
1989	25	1	86,380	38	73.32
1990	12	T5	21,591	113	76.58
1991	21	T28	13,170	146	74.89
1992	27	T2	79,388	65	73.39
1993	21	T10	35,730	104	73.59
1994	21	T6	59,294	80	72.95
1995	22	T7	100,449	58	72.62

Hollis Stacy

Think of Hollis Stacy, and you picture one of the most fluid, beautiful golf swings in the game, one that other professionals love to watch: "Basically, I just swing the club. When I was young, I went to the Masters at Augusta, where I got autographs and watched Julius Boros. He was my idol. I would imitate his swing and copy his tempo, and he remained one of my favorites."

Hollis revered the Women's U.S. Open championship above all others and was able to harness her great talent to win the title on three occasions, one of only four women to do so: "After I won my first Open, no other tournament seemed important."

One of ten children, Hollis emerged from the pack: "It is tough on others in the family to be known as my sister or brother. It can be a little uncomfortable, but they are supportive and love it when I do well. We never sat down together as a family, except at Christmas and Thanksgiving, because there wasn't enough room."

When Hollis plays golf, she blends into the course as though it is her natural habitat. Pretty, with a lively personality, her trait of a wandering mind earned her the nickname of "Spacy Stacy." Hollis is a popular figure, to whom people like to relate. I have seen her walk through public places where people, knowing her or not, forcibly stop her to have a conversation.

"I hate people grabbing at you when you're successful. I don't like being loved for having won a tournament or a lot of money; it is a false security. I hope people like my style of play, which I use as a tool for communicating, but they should like me when I miss the cut. Don't tell me I'm wonderful just because I play good golf."

Hollis admits that playing through the best years of her golfing life alongside Nancy Lopez was difficult for her and for others: "Sometimes I feel I never really became a super player because even though I won three Open championships and all my other tournaments, it was always Nancy who mattered and was promoted. I understand that she was interesting because she was married, divorced, remarried, and had children, but when I was young and felt as good a player as Nancy—if not better. I sometimes felt a bit depressed about not being as much in the limelight.

Hollis Stacy is one of only two players to have won the USGA Junior Girls Championship for three consecutive years, 1969-1971. Remarkably, she also won three USGA Women's Open titles in 1977, 1978, and 1984. Photo courtesy: LPGA.

"Maybe a few dumb things didn't help—when I was uppity or acted like a star instead of a human being. I said a couple of obnoxious things to players, I was occasionally difficult about press days, or a pain to people as a result of being needed all the time. It makes you realize you're human and you have problems and frailties just like the guy next door.

"But I feel like I am the example of the professional woman athlete [much laughter here from Hollis]. I'm feminine, very independent, and I've made some good investments. I relate well to people, and I'm smart at public relations. I'm very positive about being a professional athlete, I have a good disposition, and there should be more of me on tour. Most of the time I'm very modest, but I feel I am an asset and good for women's golf."

Hollis, whose mother Tillie has been a staunch USGA woman committee member, came up through the traditional ranks of amateur golf. She was one of only two players to win the USGA Junior Girls' Championship three years consecutively, from 1969 to 1971. Her 1969 victory at the tender age of 15 years, 4 months, makes her the youngest ever to take the title. She was also the 1970 North-South champion and a member of the 1972 Curtis Cup team.

Immediately after she turned professional in 1974, Hollis did well. In her first full season of 1975, she won the then-considerable amount of $14,409 and continued to make a good living at the game, passing the $1 million mark in 1985.

Hollis was one of the bright young stars in women's professional golf. She started winning in 1977, with two titles and the U.S. Open. She then successfully defended her U.S. Open title the next year and won the Open for the third time in 1984. Reveling in head-to-head matchplay from her amateur days, Hollis has been involved in seven career playoffs and won six of them.

When Hollis came on tour at 20, she appeared to be interested in competing only when she was in contention. At other times, her attention wandered, her mind switched off, and she merely played 18 holes. The U.S. Open was her prime target, and those victories and that championship have stimulated her beyond all others. For a time she made a huge effort to concentrate whatever her situation, but her inclination has been to get excited only on the big occasions.

Hollis and I became close friends, even if we were out of touch. A generous woman, she showered me with hospitality and gave me a marvelous tour of her hometown, Savannah. I have stayed at her various homes, stayed with her friends, and often she arranged accommodation for me on tour.

She is a great companion but not terribly easy to interview, since she gives you either the unprintable or not too much at all. I was surprised to find that she is incredibly untidy, since most good golfers I have met are exceedingly neat and orderly.

"I was born and brought up in Savannah, Georgia, the fourth of ten children. There were seven girls and three boys with an age range of 16 years, and I was the second girl. My father is an architect, and besides making babies he was quite an athletic fellow—a college football player and, at his best, a two-handicap golfer. My mother married at 19, had her first baby at 20, and her lowest handicap was 10.

"I had a very healthy upbringing in a large family where I was always trying to please my parents or prove I was something special. I did it by playing golf and being good at it. I also went to church all the time, every day during Lent. I fasted on Friday, and I was a good little Catholic girl.

"After a regimen of Catholic schools through the 8th grade, except for my 6th grade year at public school, I realized that I'd been stifled as an individual. I didn't like the nuns beating me on the knuckles with rulers and intimidating me. I was shy, sat at the back of the class, and learned not to answer back. I always stood up and curtseyed when a teacher came into the room, which I continued on my first day at public school, and everyone stared at me. I caught on really quickly.

"I was a good, solid B student, who always made C in religion because I couldn't relate to the catechism and all that. I made an A if they scared the hell out of me. I rejected religion when it changed from Latin to English, and I then comprehended what I was saying, rather than just chanting ignorantly. My best friend and I started questioning what we were doing, and we rebelled together.

"Everyone in the family went the same way except my Mom, who still prays for all of her children. Dad went to church on special occasions. I was closer to my mother than my dad, with whom I fought because we're so much alike—we're

Hollis seen here on tour in 1981, during the LPGA Championship, claims she has the killer instinct, but she rarely loses her temper in a tournament. Photo: ©Phil Sheldon.

both bull-headed. He worked at home and was around all the time.

"I always played golf alone, not with my dad. He would give me lessons, and we both got irritated until I'd walk off the course. Tempers flew, and we could never play together and enjoy the round. Even now my father will try to give me a lesson because he wants me to do so well.

"I won three consecutive National Junior championships. I won the North-South at 16, played Curtis Cup golf, and thought I was going to be a die-hard amateur.

"I spent two years at Rollins College on a sports scholarship, where I was unhappy. I did not accomplish anything, but I did go on a trip to Russia, which was something I'll never forget. It made a big impact on my future. I thought about the people in Russia who couldn't do what they wanted and how I was blowing my opportunities. I decided I should do something I enjoyed, go and make some money playing golf, and see how far I could get.

"After two years at Rollins, I decided to quit, and I remember being very upset driving home, pulling off the road, and having a good cry. I was lucky when I met Jim Flick, who helped me more than anyone with my swing and mechanics, because my swing was a bit flippy as an amateur.

"Although I went out on dates and had good friends, the most important things in my life were my family and my golf. I began to feel guilty about the money I was spending on amateur golf, since we had some tough times at home financially. Money is important. I'd be lying if I said I have played for sheer pleasure. I enjoy my comfortable lifestyle, and I have had to play well enough to meet those standards. I play to win golf tournaments; if I played just for the money, it would detract from my ability and my concentration, but I like to be financially secure through my golf. When I needed money for paying taxes, I won a tournament.

"In temperament I've got the killer instinct, I'm aggressive to a degree, and I very rarely lose my temper in a tournament. I feel more aggressive when everything's going my way, so that if I'm involved competitively, I'll shoot the lights out, whereas if I'm not, I may as well not even tee it up.

"If I can't communicate with the golf course, I tend to do badly. I rise to a good course; I feel gypped on dinky ones, since I'm more of a purist. I play my best golf on Open tracks because they are generally the best and because it's the biggest title. I like to use my talents as a golfer. I feel I have more shots than most players, and I like to feel challenged by the golf course.

"I went to the July 1974 qualifying school, and although I was a nervous wreck, I managed to get through. I joined the tour, and I was completely lost, homesick, and lonely. It was a tough transition from amateur to professional, and I learned the hard way, since I am not the type to listen—I bang my head against the wall.

"By 1976, I was enjoying the tour. Winning my first tournament, the 1977 Lady Tara Classic, was the most exciting moment of my life. My father walked up to me on the 12th hole of the final round and said, 'Quit choking.' I went birdie, birdie, par, par, birdie, birdie, and beat JoAnne Carner by one shot. I was really excited, but I didn't cry. I've never cried for winning or losing, but I'm very calm after I win, very satisfied.

"I had won a tournament and my goal for 1977 was to win a major. I didn't play well for about two months before the Open, and I was so tired that I took off the week before and relaxed. I wrote down what I had to do to win the Open, and I played nine holes with Betty Jameson in Florida, who told me to work on tempo. Peter Kostis, who had been helping me, gave me some swing thoughts, and I went up to Hazeltine just hoping I wouldn't embarrass myself.

"The weather was 99 and humid, but I was hitting it fairly well, which was a good sign. It is a tough course, but I gave every shot 100 percent effort, which I can't say I've always done in other tournaments.

"I led the whole way after an opening round of 70. My concentration was good. I was not thinking about my swing, only of the next shot and what the ball was supposed to do. I didn't hear anything. I was nervous, but I was occupied with playing and with interviews. At night I had room service and got about two hours of sleep.

"There were interruptions from thunderstorms all week, including the last day, when Nancy Lopez was on my trail all the time. She had just turned professional and hadn't yet gone through the qualifying school. I pulled ahead of her at the 12th, where I parred and she double-bogeyed and by the 18th I had a three stroke lead, which gave me a pretty good feeling. I thought of my family and my friends in Savannah as I beat Nancy by two shots. I was choked up, but I didn't cry. I felt that once I made up my mind to do something, I could do anything I wanted.

"My Open victories all seem to have come after not playing very well, and the last, in 1984, was particularly satisfying because people had forgotten about me. I was interviewed only once that week, I wasn't ahead until the 72nd hole, I never gave up, and I beat Amy Alcott by one shot.

"All my life I have aimed for the Open, putting so much emphasis on it that I couldn't get up for anything else. I used to visualize Billie Jean King holding up the trophy at Wimbledon, Mickey Wright holding up the U.S. Open trophy, and I always had a vision of my emulating them.

"I love to play golf, and the more I realize how much I love it, the better I play. But, I can lose my enthusiasm and get bogged down with the difficulties I face earning my living as a professional golfer. The constant travel, the problem of forming a relationship, and the eternal focus on yourself and fulfilling your ego are the demands of the job."

By 1988, Hollis had not recorded a victory since 1985 and said: "I love the discipline and the competition, which is now even greater, but I don't like having to grind it out to pay the bills. You lose an edge after playing on tour for quite a long time, and the less you play, the better you feel, but the result is that you get less competitive.

"I have developed outside interests, becoming involved in working on golf course developments and with a research foundation for a degenerative medical condition. This makes it harder to focus completely on golf, but I wouldn't have it any other way. I feel more whole even if my golf game is hurting a little."

Hollis continued to play the tour and raised her game enough to win a tournament in 1991. "That victory gave me a lot of confidence; so I played very well the following season and was surprised

Hollis Stacy has carded 18 tour victories thus far, but she has always been driven to win the U.S. Open. She accomplished this three times and nearly won the prestigious title several other times. Photo courtesy: Katherine Murphy.

not to win, although I shot 62 in Seattle, a career low round. Now I would love to win an LPGA championship. I have never won one and would be thrilled to take that title playing among my peers."

In 1992, Hollis went as an LPGA representative to Augusta National, when it was being suggested that golf should be reintroduced into the Olympics in 1996. "It was as though I had gone full circle. I got up and said how my parents had brought me to Augusta as a child, and it was a dream come true as I sat on the practice tee watching my idol, Julius Boros.

"I hope the Olympic Committee brings golf to Augusta. It would be a gift to the golfing world, like a Jew going to the Wailing Wall or a Muslim to Mecca. Maybe they will break down the barriers in golf which have been far too exclusive. They have not got a woman member at Augusta, and I would love to be asked. I might feel a little nervous when they sent out their bills each year, and they might feel the same when they realize I would need at least three tee times for all my family."

LPGA Victories: 1977 Rail Charity Golf Classic, Lady Tara Classic, U.S. Women's Open. **1978** U.S. Women's Open, Birmingham Classic. **1979** Mayflower Classic. **1980** CPC International. **1981** West Virginia LPGA Classic, Inamori Classic. **1982** Whirlpool Championship of Deer Creek, S&H Golf Classic, West Virginia LPGA Classic. **1983** S&H Golf Classic, CPC International, Peter Jackson Classic. **1984** U.S. Women's Open. **1985** Mazda Classic of Deer Creek. **1991** Crestar-Farm Fresh Classic.

Hollis Stacy's LPGA Record

Year	No.of Events	Best Finish	Money	Rank	Scoring Average
1974	2	T2	$5,071	60	76.40
1975	24	T4	14,409	33	74.48
1976	27	2	34,842	16	74.45
1977	27	1	89,155	5	73.05
1978	28	1	95,800	6	72.53
1979	28	1	81,265	11	73.18
1980	26	1	89,913	11	73.21
1981	27	1	138,908	9	72.47
1982	28	1	161,379	8	72.50
1983	26	1	149,036	9	73.00
1984	24	1	87,106	17	73.10
1985	24	1	100,592	18	72.62
1986	23	2	104,286	19	72.29
1987	24	T3	86,261	24	72.89
1988	16	T10	34,091	72	73.17
1989	23	T2	134,460	24	72.73
1990	21	3	64,074	65	73.89
1991	20	1	114,731	45	73.03
1992	24	4	132,323	44	72.43
1993	21	2	191,257	26	71.87
1994	25	T9	96,124	58	72.38
1995	23	T9	76,840	67	72.92

Debbie Meisterlin Steinbach

Debbie Meisterlin's place on the golf tour from the mid-'70s to mid-'80s is that of a young woman who arrived with stars in her eyes and could never live up to her great expectations: "When I joined the tour, I saw myself on the front page of *Sports Illustrated*, setting course records and performing in front of thousands of people. I rehearsed all kinds of acceptance speeches. I rehearsed waving to the crowds in the mirror; I was so hyper, I was always smiling, and I could never shut up. I was really going for it. Nancy Lopez was nothing compared to what I was going to be."

Debbie is a small, pretty blonde, with a hyperactive personality that bursts out and bubbles over at the top as she expounds in rapid fashion on herself, on the tour, on her emotions, and on how she survives.

At one point Debbie asked me why I would want to include her in my book; at another she told me what a great interview she had given me, and she was right. We met several times over the years to chat, and she thanked me for taking an interest in her career.

Debbie had to learn to come to terms with her emotions getting the better of her. In spite of a considerable golfing talent, the emotional aspect of the sport finally drove her off the tour. Talking to Debbie, you get the impression that her brain is one step ahead of her, that she cannot produce the words quickly enough. She is honest, good fun, an excellent interviewee. Very quickly after she left the tour, she met her future husband, John Steinbach, and was married and settled into a life of marital harmony.

Debbie was born in Long Beach, California, growing up in Orange County, with two older sisters and two younger brothers, each of them one year apart. Her father sold real estate, and her parents were divorced when she was 12; her mother remarried soon after. Her stepfather and one brother played golf, but she escaped to the golf course from school, as although she loved all school sports, she found it was unpopular for a girl to excel in them.

Debbie Meisterlin knew she could be an asset to the tour, and she had her winner's speech well-rehearsed. Victory eluded her, but she did make her mark, winning many friends and supporters for the LPGA. Photo Courtesy of Golf Pro magazine (1993).

Her handicap came down dramatically in one year from 29 to 9, and she was hooked. "I lived for the game. I woke up thinking of it, went to sleep dreaming of it, played by flashlight, chipped into trash bags, and it became an addiction. I played junior golf with Laura Baugh and Amy Alcott and did quite well, winning some tournaments. But I was more into the social side of things.

"I quit golf when I got my first boyfriend in my senior year of high school. I went to junior college for a year doing physical education, and I waitressed to pay for it, living in my own little apartment.

"Then I read about my friends on the LPGA tour, and I realized I should have practiced harder and there was a real future in golf, a lot of money to be made. I got myself a scholarship to the University of California at Fullerton, where I stayed for a year, before going to Mission Hills for two years, working in the professional's shop and learning golf from Johnny Revolta at Tamarisk."

Debbie played in the first ever women's mini-tour event in Riverside, California. "There were only six of us in the Group Fore tournament. We played a pro-am, and each of us paid $300 which went into the purse. I knew I would win it, but I didn't. What makes me really mad is that the girl who did win never played golf again and went home to pump gas or something.

"When I went out on tour in July 1975, I needed money, which was a terrible pressure, and my first sponsor was a doctor who bet a lot on horses. He gave me $20,000, and we were to go 50/50 on my winnings. When I got sick the first year, he dumped me because he didn't think I was strong enough to be a professional golfer. My next sponsor owned race horses, and he gave me what money I needed, but I never made enough to pay him back, and although he was nice about it, he also dumped me. In my third year my sponsor was a retired professional basketball player, a nice guy who ran into financial problems of his own; so he backed out in mid-year. I had to leave the tour and teach golf, so I could pay back the money and pay my outstanding bills.

"Sponsorship is very hard because it is extremely difficult to sell yourself as an investment. You need to find someone who has so much money that you're a tax write-off. Usually you are going to men and appealing to their egos, but it would be better if they liked you as a person and wanted to give you a break.

"Mark McCormack signed me up after I had appeared in the LPGA's Fairway magazine as a model, looking pretty good. Also, I had played a friendly game with Arnold Palmer, and I shot 68. That was enough for McCormack, and it was exciting for me and made me feel good.

"McCormack is wonderful, if you are playing well and making a lot of money. But I was never doing well enough financially on the tour; so I had to keep doing exhibitions to earn the money to stay out there, and the exhibitions became more important than the tournaments. I lost my perspective, and my golf got worse. In retrospect, I would prefer to have become a great player and then signed with McCormack, but we all feed our own egos, and it was a good arrangement for us both.

"Six years after I joined the tour, I found it quite startling to realize that financially I had not moved. I had only gone in a circle. I had grown a lot, and it was a tremendous experience and education about life. Even though the golf was hard, I thought every minute was phenomenal, and I learned to toughen up.

"At first I was fearful, polite, and nice, but it's an extremely intimidating place, and after a few bad stares and unkind words, I learned to dish it back in order to survive. I've seen girls come and go who just couldn't handle it. I'm still intimidated by the women, and it makes my stomach curl to think of going back to play a couple of tournaments. On the other hand, they are an exciting, powerful, different, and aggressive group, with all the qualities that women really want in themselves. But for me, being that way every day, week after week, year in and year out, was emotionally exhausting. I didn't have the make-up for it. I was too caught up in the emotional side; so that I never really allowed myself to go and get on with my business."

Debbie survived on tour until 1986, when she realized she could no longer compete. One of her finest moments was at the 1983 Women's U.S. Open at Tulsa (won by Jan Stephenson). Debbie was in contention until the last nine holes, when she let her emotions push her down the field.

"You see the winners, and there is something different about them. It is almost psychic. You can feel it in their whole being. They've got it together, and you can sense it. You know when Jan Stephenson is going to win, you can tell from the way she's walking and carrying herself. The same applies to Nancy Lopez, when she's stalking a putt and you know it's going in. You can feel it with Amy Alcott. There is something they create, a belief in themselves, a confidence, which doesn't die. It is a feeling that everything is going to be all right, and if you miss a putt you go on to the next one and keep constantly working at it. Finally, I realized I was never going to be like that, but I am glad I joined the tour when I was young and single, and I see it as a positive thing, not a failure.

"Changing your life is not tough, but the decision to do so is a difficult one. It is like getting out of a relationship which you know is not working. For all those years I was married to golf, and for about the last two, I knew we were heading for a divorce, and I figured we should just be friends.

"When you make the decision, it is a tremendous relief; you sleep better, you feel better, particularly after having all those feelings of not wanting to quit, of fighting, hanging in, and draining yourself. When you say it's over, you have fresh energy to create new things.

"I didn't make it in golf, and maybe those dreams are still there. I feel that what held me back from being a great player were my putting nerves and wanting it all so badly that I defeated myself. You have to get to the point where your ego doesn't need to win tournaments to feel that you are worth something; then you will be all right. When you make golf your priority and that is all you have, your life is miserable if you play badly. If you play well, everyone loves you, and life's great.

"The superficiality out there is reflected in your relationships with men. They are not based on reality—they pick you up because it is glamorous to be associated with someone on the tour. The men don't know who you are; they don't care about you, only that you're a professional golfer. It is: 'How far do you hit your drive,' and 'Have you ever played with Nancy Lopez?' I felt extremely vulnerable, and I was often very lonely.

"When I came off tour, I went to see the Taylor Made company, whose clubs I had played, since I wanted to work for them. I met John [Steinbach], the national marketing manager, and we went out for lunch, and then we went out for dinner. Two meals made the match, and we've been together ever since. I moved in within two weeks, we were married within a month, and we are inseparable. We're crazy about each other.

"My type of marriage would not have worked on tour, since my husband likes me with him, and I like being with him. Maybe it will wear off, but at the moment we really love it.

"I still practice my golf and play a couple of tournaments. I feel I was on tour in the hottest years of the LPGA, the exciting times of Ray Volpe and Nancy Lopez. Ten years later, the tour didn't seem to be much hotter.

"Now golf is booming off the tour. I do a half hour program on cable television, which is shown nationally, and we get so much mail that we need an extra secretary to deal with it. It's a hot thing. Golf is now a yuppie sport, and I'm still part of it."

Debbie Meisterlin Steinbach's LPGA Record

Year	No.of Events	Best Finish	Money	Rank	Scoring Average
1975	28	143	$447	107	77.57
1976	20	21	2,544	84	76.94
1977	25	9	7,090	65	75.79
1978	29	T12	13,030	56	75.30
1979	24	T5	11,732	70	75.56
1980	28	T17	5,913	105	76.42
1981	21	T16	7,350	106	75.86
1982	2	T31	915	144	74.00
1983	21	T11	23,116	72	74.42
1984	24	T6	20,687	97	74.06
1985	27	T38	10,407	119	75.49
1986	19	44	6,003	142	75.87

Jan Stephenson

Every women's golf tour needs a Jan Stephenson. Jan has been the woman with the greatest sexual appeal the LPGA has known, and both they and she capitalized on it.

Deservedly, she attracted enormous publicity. Her private life often resembled a soap opera of the most fascinating order, but she also proved herself on the golf course by becoming a U.S. Open champion, the holder of three major titles and a multiple winner. Successfully, she combined glamour, money, sex appeal, and golfing achievement. Less successful have been her relationships with men. She has left a trail of three marriages, all ending in divorce.

A complex woman, Jan is a highly competitive, dedicated golfer, who for many years said she wanted to sacrifice having children to concentrate on her golf career: "I absolutely adore children, but I don't want a family, since I have a talent in golf, and I don't want golf and kids." This view was colored by her third husband, Eddie Vossler, who appeared to dominate Jan for many years. Later she tried unsuccessfully to have a child. Sadly she miscarried, and the biological clock had run down.

Her greatest bond, always was with her father, Frank. "He was a very gentle man; he was my motivator." He caddied for her in two of her three major victories. When he died from cancer at the end of 1988, Jan was devastated. The only man with whom she had had a stable, loving, and lasting relationship in her life had gone. It was not just the loss of a parent; it was the loss of a pillar of emotional support, of caring and devotion that could not be replaced.

"He was there every summer watching me play, and when I finished we would have a cup of coffee, discuss a three-putt, or just talk if I was upset. He was always there for me. After he died, I had to have psychiatric help to realize that my husband Eddie was not going to take over that role, since he had never been there in the first place. My father had helped me with my career, and once he died it was the beginning of the downfall in my marriage, which never really recovered."

Always dedicated to working on her golf, when Jan won the 1983 U.S. Open in Tulsa, she flew overnight to Chicago and back between rounds, to take a putting lesson from her professional, Ed Oldfield. That's how badly she wanted the Open title. She won it by one shot from JoAnne Carner and Patty Sheehan in the soaking 105° heat.

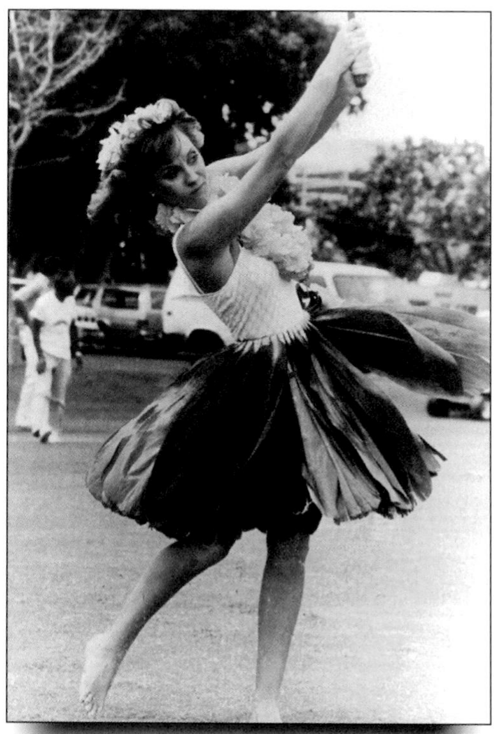

Jan Stephenson and the LPGA capitalized on publicity photo opportunities, this one during a tour stop in Hawaii. Photo courtesy: Katherine Murphy.

Jan has had her own airplane, boats, cars, and huge houses, and as much as she has enjoyed the fun, she has not had a great yearning for material wealth. Not conventionally beautiful, she is an attractive woman, who has always presented herself with drama and style. Her athletic body has projected eye-catching sex appeal, and she has been able to reap the reward, even though the workload has been demanding and time consuming. Her sexual poses may have been provocative, but there also has been an underlying humor in her approach.

Gracing the covers of countless magazines, she included a pose in a 1970s issue of Sport magazine in a tight-fitting bright pink top, obviously braless, which prompted a journalist to write: "She is a star and the crowds come to see her nipples as well as her niblick."

Annual pin-up calendars have had such titles as: "Come Play a Round With Me," and she was featured in Playboy magazine, not as a centerfold (which she was offered and turned down), but with a 20 questions article, where question number nine read: "Have you ever had sex on a golf course?" Jan replied: "No, I wonder why not; maybe because it's my office. I wouldn't want to have it in the bunker because of the sand. I'd kind of like to have it on the green. It would be nice and soft."

In answer to question 12: "Defend the proposition that golfers make better lovers," Jan said, "Maybe it's because they have such a good touch. In golf you have to be good in all areas; you have to be powerful, strong, have stamina and be able to control yourself. Plus, you have to have an unbelievable touch. All those things are important in making love, especially discipline and patience."

Surrounded by people wanting to grab her attention, it was not always easy to get Jan's time, but when she gave it to me, she was always an excellent interviewee. Over the years we established a good rapport. I enjoy Jan, her honesty, and ability to communicate. She is a woman of resilience, which she has needed in the many instances of drama she has attracted, and when she has allowed others to manipulate her life to her detriment.

Jan Stephenson parlayed her golfing career in Australia and Japan to become a leading LPGA player during the 1980s, winning the LPGA Championship and the U.S.G.A. Women's Open. Photo: Peter Dazeley.

As a youngster in Australia, Jan had an early marriage and divorce. Soon after she arrived in the United States in 1974, she met Texas businessman Eddie Vossler, who became her manager throughout a long and sometimes stormy relationship. After a particularly bumpy ride, she hastily married business associate Larry Kolb in March 1982. The disastrous liaison, which lasted only five weeks, resulted in several years of legal wrangling and drama.

After she left Kolb, he had her arrested during the practice round of a tournament in Birmingham, Alabama, saying she should be committed. For many hours, she was kept in a mental hospital, which included rough treatment and questioning, before Vossler obtained her release. Jan returned to play in the tournament, finishing 10th. Kolb also had her financial assets frozen and flew with a psychiatrist to Japan to confront her, stealing her passport from the tournament locker room. The psychiatrist was meant to remove Jan from the influence of Eddie Vossler, who said that Kolb had been cheating on her and stealing her money.

Jan returned to Vossler, and the battle of the two men and the woman golfer stormed on until October 1984, when finally a Texas court decided that Jan's marriage to Kolb should be annulled, since Eddie Vossler was already her common law husband. In spite of the wrangling, Jan won the 1982 LPGA championship and the Lady Keystone, and in 1983, the U.S. Open was one of four victories.

Her golf blossomed, her notoriety was sky high, and she could command as much as $10,000 a day for modeling, clinics, and exhibitions. Reactions from other women on tour have varied from a mixture of irritation, envy, and an acceptance that she pulls crowds through the gates.

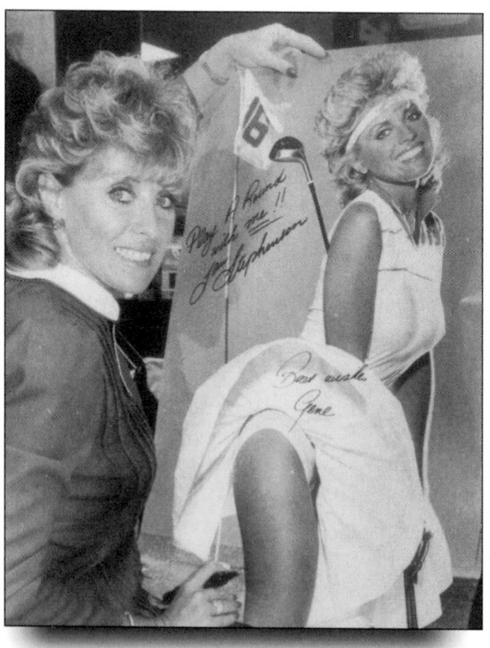

Jan Stephenson signed posters at the 1983 Nabisco Dinah Shore. The LPGA, in its own "Fairway" magazine, used Jan's sex appeal to promote the tour during the early 80s. It worked, but it was also very controversial, especially with some LPGA players.

Jan made a regular appearance in the annual LPGA Fairway magazine, and in 1982 posed as a look-alike of the Marilyn Monroe publicity picture for *Seven Year Itch*, with her skirt flying up as the wind blows from a grid at her feet. It was deliberately provocative but did not receive any adverse comment. The controversy came in the 1981 edition, in which Jan was photographed displaying her charms, lying on a bed with her skirt pulled thigh high. The implications were open to interpretation. "Stephenson Has It, So LPGA Flaunts It" ran one newspaper headline, in which a raunchy article began: "The Jezebel eyes beckon seductively, but it's the half-exposed body that really drives everyone wild—the men because it's so lusciously beautiful, the women because most of them are envious like alley cats."

By this time, controversy over Jan's magazine pose was at fever pitch among players and public. A February article in the Miami Herald by fellow professional Jane Blalock fanned the flames, when she wrote: "In the current issue of *Fairway* magazine, a publication produced by the LPGA, tour officials became so desperate for appeal, that quasi-pornography got the nod. The obvious question becomes: Is our organization so unaware of the real glamour and attraction staring it in the face that it must resort to such trash?" Jane Blalock felt there were plenty of players on tour with sex appeal, which was excellent for promotion, but the LPGA's own magazine had gone too far, and the pose was a type of prostitution.

With Stephenson's picture and Blalock's article, the LPGA couldn't have dreamed up a scheme guaranteed to get more publicity, as the arguments continued back and forth throughout the 1981 season, with blanket media coverage in every part of the country. Women and sex were selling the golf.

Jan Stephenson was born in Sydney, part of a middle class family, with a brother two years younger. Her father was a mechanic for the Sydney transport department, her mother an accountant, who did all of Jan's school homework.

"Our house was seven miles north of Sydney, and I was brought up on an ocean golf course, where it was inexpensive to play. My parents were both good tennis players, and my father was convinced I was going to be an athlete. When I was seven, he had me swimming and training every morning before school; I would do even more after school and on weekends. He started me at tennis when I was eight, and I showed promise, but I didn't like being pushed. At ten, I went with him to play golf, taking a canvas bag and some sawn off clubs, and I loved it. After that, I would play 54 holes a day.

"I was a loner as a child, and I still am. I spent a lot of time with my parents because as a girl who played good golf, I was a misfit. I gambled and played golf with the boys, but 99 percent of the time I was playing or practicing with my father. I didn't mix very much with other children, and I am still not very good with my fellow competitors. I like them, but I have trouble mixing with them, and when I go to my room and putt on the carpet, people think I'm a snob, but really I'm just not used to mixing.

"As a youngster, I became good at golf very quickly. At 12, I entered the New South Wales schoolgirl championship. I won it for the first time, out of six consecutive victories. At 15, I won the Australian Junior championship for the first of three times, and I was New South Wales junior champion for four consecutive years from 1969.

"It was all a dream come true, and I worked very hard for it. When I was chosen for the Australian team, I said I knew I would win my matches—which I did. It was then I decided I would one day like to be a professional in the United States and to be one of the best players in the world. From high school, I went for a year to college. I was a cadet journalist for a newspaper and magazine, but I didn't enjoy writing.

"I couldn't acquire a golf scholarship or a sponsor; so in 1972, at 21, I turned professional, entering my first tournament in Japan in 1973. I finished eighth. After that, I played in Australian LPGA tournaments and won five of the next ten tournaments. I was the top player in Australia, and I got a lot of publicity. Plenty of attention was focused on me. I was big time and expected to win.

"Coming to America was a slap in the face. When I joined the LPGA tour in 1974, no one cared; I had to do everything myself. It was really expensive, and like starting all over again from the bottom. Coming from another country, even though you speak English, it is totally alien. The food and customs were different. I had lived with my parents all my life, and suddenly I was shoved out alone; so I became very homesick, and I was always phoning home. I played every week, because I didn't have anywhere else to go. I was so overawed by idols like JoAnne Carner and Judy Rankin, that they didn't even seem human. Laura Baugh was the glamour girl, and no one paid any attention to me.

"I was pleased to be Rookie of the Year in 1974 with 14 finishes in the top 20, but it wasn't until I won a couple of tournaments in 1976 that I became noticed for my golf and as a glamour girl. It was a very hectic year, with exhibitions and promotions, which were making me a lot of money, but I had no private life, and I got too tired to practice. I know you only have to worry about hitting a little white ball into a hole, but I also worried about my appearance. The glamour image became exhausting, and I retreated from it by pulling my hair back and wearing trousers instead of shorts.

"I made a few friends who were close knit and not jealous, and I heard people say that the girls on tour would like me if they knew what I was like. I enjoy teasing and joking, but I'm a lot colder on tour than I am at home. I find it hard to make friends in my business life, and I have not made many men friends because men want romance. I could date all the time, but I have no desire to do that. I tell men I'm not interested; I don't want to go out with someone I don't know.

"Sometimes I think I should quit the tour for a few years to do something else, but then I decide I really love the game. What would I do if I quit? It would drive me crazy. After two or three weeks at home, I can't stand it and have to come back out on tour. The money is so good, I enjoy the crowds, and I love to play competitive golf. I hate playing for fun.

"The fun part is having a chance to win. I live, work, and dream of teeing off on Sunday morning in the last round, knowing I'm in contention with a chance to win. The momentum builds from feeling excited on Saturday and wondering what I'm going to wear the next day, to really getting into it when I see my name on the leader board on Sunday. I feel good when I'm in a winning position as I settle down, go into slow motion, and get increasingly stronger. People say I'm an aggressive person, but I don't feel that. I think I'm a quiet person but an aggressive player.

"The money from exhibitions and appearances used to mean more. It seemed so easy to make money on Mondays and Tuesdays at exhibitions, where I was paid $5,000–$10,000. I could make more there in one day than winning second or third prize. When the purses increased, I preferred just competing; winning meant more.

"I am very fortunate that money brought me three houses, lots of cars, my own airplane, and everything money can buy. It was really nice. Sometimes I feel insecure, doubt my own ability, and complain about my game, but I know this is the land of opportunity, and people here do love sports. It's a good feeling to do it all yourself, and I'm happy to have come here and made it. I loved it when my parents both came over and my dad caddied for me, and they saw people wanting my autograph. They knew that I was big time. They sacrificed a lot for me, and it was nice to know it was worthwhile. I spoiled them to death when they were here, and going home for Christmas always gave me the best feeling. I could be Santa Claus and take everyone what they wanted. I really got a kick out of it."

After Jan's famous bed pose in 1981, she said: "I knew there was going to be one on a bed, and the comments as it was taken, made me think it would be sexy. I first saw the picture in a professional's shop in Florida, and Eddie [Vossler] was with me. He said, 'You didn't tell me they took one like this,' and I replied that I didn't realize it would look that provocative. My first reaction was that it didn't look like me, especially in the face; I was shocked.

"I had no idea it was going to have such an effect on the players, and when I went into the locker room and heard the comments, I wondered what it was all about. I thought the picture was in good taste. The LPGA's marketing professionals had

Jan's swing, shown here in 1984, has held up throughout the years, but her talents have expanded to include golf course design and the production of an exercise video for people who have arthritis. Photo ©Phil Sheldon.

sanctioned it; so I was surprised by the reaction of the girls. I thought Janie [Blalock] was a good friend, and I was shocked by her article when I read it. A lot of girls were derogatory about me and the LPGA selling the tour with sex and the glamour girl image. Everyone is entitled to his or her opinion, but I was a little hurt.

"In 1976, when I first won, I knew they were exploiting me by taking advantage of my being a good-looking girl, and I felt it was all right, although my game eventually slumped. With the picture in *Fairway* magazine, I thought it was flattering to be asked to do it, and I'm certainly not ashamed of my body. Maybe I have always felt I'm average looking, and all the fuss surprises me, but I love to relate to the camera and play in front of it. I love having someone do my hair and make up. I love to wear pretty clothes. I would like to act and get into films. I always did dance and drama as a child, and I miss it. Acting is as competitive as golf, and I know I can compete in golf.

"I got a little anxious when they pulled up the dress for the magazine photograph, but everyone assured me it was fine; I wouldn't do a questionable picture for Playboy, but I thought the LPGA would handle it well. Everyone sells with sex; that's the way of life. The sexual angle may be over-emphasized, but anything that sells is good. In sport, you also have to perform and win, to get recognition and have the galleries.

"After all the publicity over the picture, I got a lot of good letters and a lot of bad ones. Some people said I was quite disgusting and told me I should be destroyed for being that kind of person, which upset me. They didn't know me or realize how much time and hard work I put into my golf. They didn't know that I stay in and eat room service 99% of the time, that I practice putting in my bedroom. I got so upset by the kooky letters, by people who said they would blow me up, that I wouldn't open letters any more. I sent them to my office. I'm serious when I'm on tour, dedicated to my career, and people take me the wrong way.

"When the publicity started, I thought it was fun and exciting doing so many TV shows, and then I got really tired. Everyone said it was great for my career and for the LPGA to get so much publicity, but I was getting so much attention, I forgot to devote myself to my golf, although I managed to win three tournaments that season."

Winning the 1983 Women's U.S. Open at Tulsa was Jan's greatest moment in her golf career: "I thought it was a compliment to be regarded as a sex image, but you have to win an Open before you can go in the record books as a top player. It's something I always wanted. I was thrilled when President Reagan telephoned. It gave me goose bumps when he said I had given him an enjoyable afternoon.

"I was even more delighted that my dad was there to see me do it; he wanted it so much. When I went in the water on the third hole in the final round, he left the course to be sick, and at the 18th he was crying. It was a highly emotional moment for us both.

"It was such a difficult tournament, on a golf course that was so damned hard, I didn't feel I had the edge or momentum. But I hung in there, and it was the best I've ever played. I wanted to win so desperately that when I bogeyed the last two holes, my lips were white with tension. I thought I was choking and going to lose, but I had done enough to earn the title. The six-over par 290 that I predicted at the beginning of the week, was my winning score."

Jan's career flourished, and the momentum continued through 1987, as she won three tournaments and was ranked fourth on the money list with $227,303. In 1988, she was flying back and forth to Australia when her father's condition worsened, and he died in December. The following year her caddie, Rick White, a former policeman from Fort Lauderdale who had been with her since 1982, also died of cancer: "He was my caddie, body guard, protector, and good friend. My life fell apart when I lost my team."

In January 1990, she was mugged in a parking lot going to a basketball game in Miami. As the man attacking her tried to twist the wedding ring off her finger, he fractured the bones in her hand: "The realization that everything could fall apart, that I would not have a career or anything, made me realize I would like to have a child. I had wanted a family for a few years, but Eddie as my manager was really against it because of it affecting my career. He didn't want children. When I became pregnant in 1991 and then miscarried after 12 weeks, I was a lot more upset than I realized. I had been having problems, and the doctors warned me, trying to prepare me, but when it happened, I was shocked and disappointed. I was surprised it took me so long to get over it. I'm not the crying type, but I was always crying after the miscarriage."

Divorce from Eddie Vossler followed, and with it went nearly $1 million to the man who had managed and controlled her: "Eddie was a major influence, and I cared so much about him I didn't want to admit failure, which is why I hung on so long trying to make it work. He wanted a divorce, and to keep control of me and my finances. I don't know whether he felt he needed to keep me

Jan loved it when her parents came from Australia to watch her play, and she was particularly pleased when her father caddied for her in two of her three major victories. Here, she is shown with her mother. Photo courtesy: Katherine Murphy.

around or keep me as part of his life. I had cared so much about him and about my game, that if it made him happy, he could take control. Eddie lived for my career. He made a lot of money out of it and from the divorce, which made me very bitter. It was hard for me to be the one doing all the work, sacrificing a family, and then he took so much from me. That's life, but the next time I will make sure my money is mine. I have been successful, earned a lot of money, and it's really been hard.

"You have to be compatible and secure to make a marriage work; you have only to look at the British Royal family to realize that. I don't know how many times Eddie was called Eddie Stephenson, and that is hard to handle. We had many large homes, cars, boats, and the jet plane, for which I had to do a lot of one-day exhibitions to afford it. Eddie liked the plane, and although I loved flying, I have never been ruled by wanting material things. I was so influenced by Eddie, that I had to be a different person around him. He was so controlled and unemotional."

By 1992, Jan's golf game had fallen apart after nearly 20 years on tour; she had miscarried, her marriage to Eddie was over, her father and her caddie had died, and she needed all her inner resources to gather herself together. A chance meeting with teaching professional David Leadbetter, the guru of many top golfers, led to an association, a renewed enthusiasm for the game she loves, and a new life. She set up home to be near Leadbetter in Florida.

"David and his team are so supportive and caring; it's a wonderful atmosphere. I was desperate because I had always hit the ball so straight, and then suddenly I would hit a shot way left and I never knew when it was coming. I decided I had to go down to see David and his team in Orlando, and I cried all the way down on the plane. Now, I am so fired up; I have the ambition of a rookie; it is wonderful to be with such nice people who all care. I have to have people who are prepared to put my golf game first. I'd like to finish my career on a good note. Nothing has ever come easily. I know you have to make sacrifices, and I have always been very disciplined.

"I have always had strong influences: my dad was strong and very sweet. I always said I wanted someone sweet and nice, and I have definitely not had that much success personally. I don't know why, but it is probably one of the down things in my life. A man would have to be so understanding to realize I have to give so much to my game, since I'm not a big strong woman with a lot of talent. I have never found anyone who understands that. My priority is still my golf, and people don't realize what I have been through personally and mentally, sometimes living on five hours sleep a night because I have had so much on my mind.

"I always felt I needed to have someone with me. Now I don't. I am finally secure enough to know I don't need an Eddie or anyone to take care of me. For the first time I feel I don't need a man to lean on, and it's very nice. It is nice to be myself, not to be judged by anyone. If someone doesn't like me, it's too bad. I'm learning about myself again and not worrying about what Eddie or anyone else says I can do. I've had the material things and the men who tried to control me. Now, I can enjoy family and friends and do whatever I want. I do a lot of charity work—I always have, since I have wanted to put something back.

"I hate getting old and wrinkled and not having a nice body, but the good thing about not being the glamour girl any more, is that I don't have to worry about that part of my life. I can find an excuse not to go to the gym. I can still do as many corporate outings for $15,000 a day as I want, and although they are tiring, it makes me feel very independent and secure. I have worked hard. I come from a small background in Australia, and I appreciate everything I have."

LPGA Victories: 1976 Sarah Coventry Naples Classic, Birmingham Classic. **1978** Women's International. **1980** Sun City Classic. **1981** Peter Jackson Classic, Mary Kay Classic, United Virginia Bank Classic. **1982** LPGA Championship, Lady Keystone Open. **1983** Tucson Conquistadores LPGA Open, Lady Keystone Open, U.S. Women's Open. **1985** GNA Classic. **1987** Santa Barbara Open, SAFECO Classic, Konica San Jose Classic.

Unofficial Victories: **1973** Australian Open. **1977** Australian Open. **1981** World Ladies. **1983** JC Penney Mixed Team (with Fred Couples). **1985** Nichirei Ladies Cup, Hennessy French Open. **1990** JC Penney/LPGA Skins Game.

Jan Stephenson's LPGA Record

Year	No.of Events	Best Finish	Money	Rank	Scoring Average
1974	28	T4	$16,270	28	75.24
1975	25	3	20,066	21	74.28
1976	25	1	64,827	8	73.38
1977	27	T2	65,820	11	72.52
1978	22	1	66,033	13	73.01
1979	28	T2	69,519	15	73.25
1980	21	1	41,318	34	73.82
1981	28	1	180,528	5	72.40
1982	21	1	133,212	10	72.30
1983	28	1	193,364	4	72.22
1984	29	T3	101,215	14	72.84
1985	29	1	148,030	10	72.95
1986	29	T2	165,238	12	72.06
1987	25	1	227,303	4	72.19
1988	25	2	236,739	9	71.29
1989	21	T3	71,550	45	72.57
1990	13	T10	31,070	105	73.63
1991	20	T3	49,467	88	73.39
1992	27	T3	132,634	42	73.20
1993	22	T4	161,123	36	72.19
1994	22	4	99,766	55	72.74
1995	20	2	72,822	70	74.04

Mickey Walker

Thirteen years after joining the professional ranks, when she took a club job as one of the first head professionals in Britain, Mickey Walker said, "The life of a tournament professional is a very selfish one. You are in an unreal world, where you are feted to an extraordinary degree. You are the center of attention and totally self-absorbed."

Mickey was one of the greats in European amateur golf, dominating in the early 1970s, when she won the British Women's Amateur title in 1971 and 1972 and was a Curtis Cup player in 1972. That same year she went to America and won the Trans-Mississippi, the first Englishwoman to do so since Pam Barton had been victorious 36 years previously. Mickey was the 1972 Woman Golfer of the Year in Britain.

"The Mark McCormack organization approached me, inquiring whether I was interested in turning professional. I said I was not. In my own mind, I decided that if I won the English championship in 1973, a title I was lacking, I would become a professional."

Mickey won that event, turning professional at 21 in 1974. She was the first British woman ever to do so specifically to play on the U.S. tour. She was also the first to be signed up with McCormack, which in those days gave you an added aura of success.

"McCormack arranged a five year club contract for me with Colgate for £5,000, rising to £7,500 and bonuses. I was to represent Pacific Harbour for three years, starting at £2,000 and rising, and I had a contract to make a television commercial for Colgate, which I did in 1975 with Carol Mann. I was incredibly nervous, not about making the commercial, but about spending the day with Carol, who was a superstar. Carol told me I looked great in the makeup, and I should always wear it."

Financially secure, Mickey went to the LPGA qualifying school, where she gained her card and then lost it by the end of 1974, having won only $838.75. She won the next qualifying school by seven shots, but struggled until 1976—her most successful year, when she lost in a four-way playoff in the Jerry Lewis Classic and won a total $12,150. Mickey, at her finest in matchplay golf, did not achieve her potential on tour in America. She developed an obsession with technique, falling into the trap of taking advice from everyone; so that she was totally demoralized by the time she lost her card in 1981.

When the women's tour (WPGA) began in Britain in 1979, she played some events on both tours. In 1981, she became chairman of the WPGA, carrying it through its most difficult years until in 1985, she helped it to settle under the umbrella of the men's PGA, where it experienced a period of stability and growth. Mickey won six WPGA

Mickey, here in the late 1960s, was one of the greats in European Amateur golf in the early 1970s. She won the British Women's Amateur in 1971 and 1972 and was on the 1972 Curtis Cup team.

tournaments from 1979 to 1984, and in 1982, with professional Christine Langford, became the first all-woman combination to win the Sunningdale Foursomes at Sunningdale, Berkshire.

In 1986, Mickey became the first full-time woman club professional to apply for a job and receive a formal appointment at the Warren Golf Club in Essex. "I regard it as my greatest achievement," she said. Warren Golf Club owner, John Durham, said: "Ten minutes after Mickey walked into the room, applying for the job, I thought, 'God, I hope she accepts. She's such a nice woman.'"

At 5 feet, 11 inches, Mickey has that slight stoop common to many tall people. An attractive woman of exceptional charm, she spent many years feeling awkward about her height and thinking she was not pretty enough to be marketable off the golf course. She lacked confidence in herself and her appearance, but as her achievements widened, her self-confidence grew, and she was able to become an inspirational leader.

As the European captain at all three Solheim Cup matches, in Florida, Scotland and West Virginia, held biannually from 1990, she earned the respect and affection of all her team. Playing the inaugural international competition between the professionals of the LPGA and European tours, the Americans whitewashed the Europeans at Lake Nona by $11\frac{1}{2}$ to $4\frac{1}{2}$. But, Europe then soundly beat the Americans two years later in Scotland $11\frac{1}{2}$ to $6\frac{1}{2}$. For Mickey, it was one of the most exhilarating moments of her career. It was a wonderful vindication of all she had worked toward, when the Europeans claimed victory against the American team that had started as the odds-on favorite by 6 to 1.

Mickey's exceptional amateur career established her name in British golf, and she has always been a much-admired figure in the game. Mickey and I met in the mid-1970s, when she took an instant dislike to my self-assured, opinionated, extroverted manner. "I thought you were all the things I wasn't, and I was overwhelmed," she told me later. In spite of that, we became close and lasting friends, often sustaining each other with long telephone conversations at all times of the day and night, in varied parts of the world.

Mickey Walker, always the tough competitor, captained the first two Solheim Cup matches. Photo ©Phil Sheldon.

Mickey, who has two half brothers—one two and one-half years older and another eight years younger, was born in Leeds and brought up in Kent, when her mother married a dentist, Julian Walker, whose name Mickey took and who has been a father to her.

"I started playing golf at 14 because my father, a Scot, played, and I copied him. Golf came easily, and at 15 I won the Kent Girls' Championship by 20 shots, after which I was selected for the Junior Home Internationals. Since I achieved what I wanted as an amateur, I decided to go to America after I talked to Vivien Saunders, who had played on the LPGA tour in the 1960s. She made it sound like a lot of fun to be in the best competition on the only tour there was at the time.

"I got through the LPGA qualifying school and went on tour, where I found everything very strange. It took me three months to make my first check. I traveled by Greyhound bus, and sometimes the people were so rough, I was afraid to get out of the bus when I reached my destination. I stayed in private housing, which was really nice, since the Americans are the most hospitable people in the world. I was impressed with the organization of the tour and the standard of play, but because I played badly and couldn't get any consistency, I was miserable for some time.

"I thought the women were aggressive, the top players uncompromising. I had imagined they would be more friendly as a group, but they had their own lives to lead, stayed in different places, kept to themselves and in cliques. As I was very shy, I didn't fit in, and I was scared of them. Karolyn Kertzman reduced me to tears one day on the golf course, over a rule I unknowingly infringed. Later, I realized it was their strong personalities that frightened me, but at the time, I felt inferior. They knew what it was about, while I had never before been responsible for myself. When I needed to survive emotionally, I would go on an eating binge because I was a compulsive overeater. It was destructive, but I could have done worse things.

"After my second year, I considered giving up. Growing up, I had been successful all the time fairly easily; so it was a big jolt to be unsuccessful for a long time as a professional. Instead of saying, 'I'm going to overcome it, prove I can be good,' I became full of self-pity and gave in. By nature I'm very competitive, but I'm not aggressive. After I gained some confidence and made some friends, I felt I was good enough to fulfill my potential. Luckily, I was able to support myself with my winnings, with my contracts, and with playing in golf days off the tour.

"My downfall came when I was playing badly and started to worry about my swing. I took advice from so many people, that I became confused, and I was prey to everyone who thought he or she knew the answer. I had a lot of natural ability, which I lost in a typically American way—by overanalyzing everything.

"My goals in golf have never been that clearly defined. They might have been by my parents when I was an amateur. But in America, I lost my direction, I wasn't single-minded enough, and I probably never had enough confidence in myself to realize how good I was. The result is that when you stop winning, you begin to doubt if you ever were good or will be again.

"I was working on my game, on wrong and on right things, feeling it was the only chance I had to compete, but my biggest problem was my mental game. I began thinking, 'It won't be too bad if I finish with 75,' which is an acceptance of mediocrity. I wasn't expecting, planning, or working to win. When everyone expects you to win, there's an element that's flattering, but it can be a negative factor, which makes you feel inadequate. People are telling you that you should be winning consistently, or you're one of the best, and if you don't win, then they say, 'What's happened? Why aren't you winning? You question yourself and can't come up with the answer. All of these things reinforces something you feel is lacking in yourself. People make remarks, without thinking or understanding, that you've tried your best, given 100 percent, and haven't won. It's not that simple to go out and win.

"Although I started to play better, to develop a sense of understanding, my performances in America were disappointing, and I became so miserable that when I lost my card in 1981, it was almost a relief. I was pleased to come home to a more comfortable environment, where I believed I was able to be a winner. Although I have never intentionally sought the limelight, I enjoy it. I like being recognized, interviewed, being thought of as a contender rather than making up the numbers. I don't believe there's anyone who can beat me when I play well."

Mickey returned to Britain, winning six tournaments in five seasons, and she served a four-year term as WPGA chairman from 1981.

"It was very satisfying, being involved in developing the WPGA tour and helping it through its crisis, when we had to decide on policies for the better future of the association. I remember Scottish professional Cathy Panton offering to contribute every penny of her savings to get the tour on a better footing, which represented the depth of our feelings. The association had been handled independently, but we needed a change and felt the men's PGA could stabilize the tour and give the organization added professionalism. The decisions were frightening at the time, but after the PGA took over in 1983, the tour improved dramatically.

"We sold the women professionals as being so much better than the men at providing excellent Pro-Ams. We developed a terrific reputation for looking after our Pro-Am partners, being entertaining, and having the added attraction of being women. The word spread, and many major companies wanted to sponsor women's tournaments because they wanted the women for Pro-Ams prior to their event.

"It was a learning process that I feel resulted in my greatest achievement, since I headed the most positive period in WPGA history in terms of regular tournaments and good prize money. I was dealing with areas totally foreign to me, such as legal and accounting problems, and I was really pleased to be involved. You face challenges and come out in your own eyes feeling good about having achieved something. It was a very positive time in my life, and now I feel proud of being able to handle almost any situation in a professional manner."

By 1986, in addition to not playing as well, Mickey felt she had experienced enough years of living out of a suitcase and decided to settle for the more stable existence of a club job: "A few years previously, I thought that I couldn't stand to be a club professional and put up with all the rubbish that people talk. But, I have found it to be an interesting and varied job. I enjoy teaching, which I did previously in North Carolina after I joined the LPGA teaching division and took its tests. I also qualified with the British PGA; so I'm fairly competent, although I'm sure I can learn a lot more. I've always enjoyed meeting and dealing with a variety of people, and I like selling. As a kid I sold lottery tickets for Gillingham, my local football club, and I loved it. If you can sell those, you can probably sell anything.

"I expected some initial resistance from the male golf club members, and while some of them took time to accept me, others were open-minded. Once word spread and I developed a good reputation as a teacher, men would come for lessons if they needed help. I've enjoyed being able to give through teaching, and the reward you get from helping people who appreciate it is tremendous.

"Teaching both men and women, you notice their different qualities. By and large men find the game easier because they are more co-ordinated and athletic; traditionally, men are more aggressive, which is reflected in their golf swings. In general, women are more willing to learn and listen, and want to work more on their game.

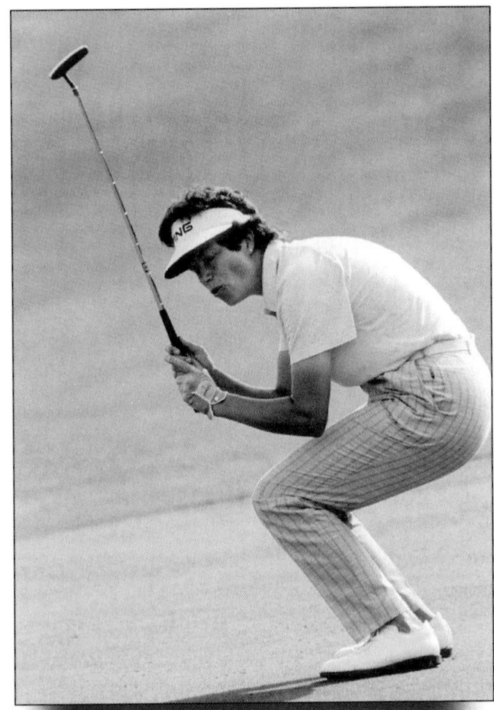

Mickey, at the B&H Mixed Team in 1989 in Spain, was instrumental in the development of the WPGA in Britain and for stabilizing it under the leadership of the PGA. Photo ©Phil Sheldon.

"As a club professional, I have had to adjust my ideas on the value of money, because playing tournaments you have the opportunity to be paid or to win a lot of money. In teaching, I have had to work jolly hard to earn £100, but the job has provided the security of knowing that I'm going to make enough to pay the mortgage, have a nice car and a reasonable standard of living. I really struggled in my last year of playing tournaments, and I was happy to have my best ever financial year when I started my new job. Sometimes as a club professional, you are the person serving behind the counter or telling someone they've gone off the wrong tee, which I found a big adjustment from my self-centered existence on tour. My golf improved without the pressure of tournaments, and I felt I could go on tour and win again, but I couldn't have tolerated the lifestyle.

"The tour changed after I left, in that professionals now have to work so much harder to survive the strength of the competition. I have tremendous admiration for the women, who need to understand their swing, the physical and the fitness aspects, and their own personalities. I was talented enough to perform well without working to any great extent on my game, and with relatively little application. The facilities were more restricted, and there was less emphasis on acquiring knowledge. Now, teachers as well as players need greater depth of technical expertise, since videos and computers have made teaching golf a science. You must have good sound knowledge for the best players to respect you."

In 1990, Mickey was appointed captain of the Solheim Cup team, which in its inaugural year had eight members, who traveled to Lake Nona, Florida, to face the Americans over three days of matches.

"It was an incredible honor for me, but it was tough for the team, since most of them felt inferior or were in awe of the Americans. It was almost impossible mentally to go out and beat them. They had that feeling of playing the greats, coupled with an element of hero worship, but it was a good and helpful learning experience."

The Americans defeated the Europeans 11½–4½, and no one was surprised. The European women realized that their American counterparts, while more confident and aggressive and better around the greens, were shot-for-shot no better than they. Two years later, Mickey Walker again was appointed captain of the European side when the matches, this time with 10 women on each team, took place at Dalmahoy in Scotland. "I'd have Mickey Walker as my captain for the next ten years if she would do it," declared Laura Davies, the inspirational star of the European side, and the British woman who took the U.S. Open title in 1987.

By 1992, the Europeans had improved in leaps and bounds. More of them had competed on the American LPGA tour and made their mark. It had provided an essential opportunity to raise their standard and test the water in the toughest competition in the world. As Mickey said before the confrontation in Scotland: "They now know the Americans are human and that they can beat them. Their LPGA experience was crucial to building up their confidence and obtaining a sense of self-worth, which is absolutely vital. The desire to win is greater as underdogs, and team spirit can carry you through. You can make things happen if you are committed, focused, and keyed up, but everyone will have to play great golf. As a captain, I have a feeling of total helplessness when the gun goes off. I can't do anything to make them play better shots."

Such was the reputation of the American side, with their massive total of tournaments and dollars won and their collective experience, that the British bookmakers made them odds-on favorites. When the matches began, the Europeans, inspired by the intense determination of Laura Davies, by Mickey their captain, and supported all the way by huge crowds in the sometimes sodden conditions

A delighted and excited 1992 European team hoists its hero Mickey Walker on their shoulders after defeating the Americans for the Solheim Cup at Dalmahoy, Scotland. It was one of the most exhilarating moments of her career.

of October in Scotland, produced superb golf in tough matches. The momentum was with them all the way to a famous victory of 11½ to 6½.

"To want to win is one thing; to make it happen is another," Laura Davies proclaimed. While Mickey Walker reflected her pride and joy when she said afterwards: "This is the sporting achievement of the century in European women's golf, and it should boost the morale of every woman. If the Americans are honest, they were not expecting it to be so tough. They thought they would win comfortably. Everyone copes with pressure at times, and everyone succumbs to it. No one can argue with the talent of our players; they are awesome. People know they have beaten the best in the world, which gives them such credibility. Winning meant so much to the European team. It gave them tremendous motivation and brought out their utmost talent. It is a trait encouraged far more in America: the ethic to work hard, and make the best of what you've got, test your ability and be successful.

"I feel more euphoria than satisfaction. I played a very small part, being responsible for the wildcard team selection, the pairings, and order of play. The first Solheim Cup was never going to be close. The second we seemed destined to win. I was astonished how well we played and by the whole team exceeding my wildest expectations. We won so convincingly. The result is great for golf, for our tour, and for the Americans.

Shocked by their defeat in Scotland, the Americans were out for revenge, and in 1994 at the Greenbrier, under the captaincy of JoAnne Carner, the matches were neck and neck until the final day, when the U.S. surged forward to defeat Europe by 13 to 7.

"It was a disappointing result after a close contest" says Mickey, who will take up the reins of captaincy again in 1996. "We have a real chance to win it back home in Wales. Europe is getting stronger all the time, with Laura Davies continuing to dominate as the world's best woman golfer. Annika Sorenstam won the 1995 US Women's Open and was player of the year. Alison Nicholas and Kathryn Marshall achieved their first LPGA victories; so we'll have a very strong team.

"I have enjoyed each Solheim Cup we have contested; I am fortunate to be part of the team, and it has been a highlight of my career."

European Tour Highlights: 1979 Carlsberg Tournament. **1980** Lambert and Butler Matchplay Championship. **1981** Carlsberg Tournament. ***1982*** Sunningdale Foursomes. **1983** Sands International. **1984** Baume-Mercier Classic, Lorne Stewart Matchplay Championship.

Mickey Walker's LPGA Record

Year	No. of Events	Best Finish	Money	Rank	Scoring Average
1974	25	T29	$839	94	79.03
1975	20	T42	467	105	78.62
1976	23	T2	15,011	42	76.28
1977	24	T9	12,150	53	75.64
1978	NA	NA	5,412	82	76.62
1979	NA	T12	5,121	99	76.78
1980	1	71	220	153	83.00

The 1990s

At the opening of the final decade of the 20th century, the LPGA watched the media herald the success of the men's Senior Tour. Though it took money away from the LPGA, it did not seriously threaten its continuing, loyal support.

The LPGA also endured an awkward management problem, when the hiring of Bill Blue, as Commissioner, undermined the women and their aims for the association. Judy Dickinson became LPGA President in 1990, and when Blue departed in September of that year, there was a collective sigh of relief.Jim Webb, a stalwart of the LPGA since 1982, was appointed Executive Director and was in charge during an interim period, backed by a good team which continued with him. In January 1991, Jim was promoted to Deputy Commissioner.

Elaine Scott, an Englishwoman who joined the staff in 1986 and rose to become Director of Communications in 1992, said, "Bill Blue was the wrong fit, a weak link, but we got by with a strong core of people. The players and sponsors pulled together, and it was uncomfortable in fits and spurts, but the experience was a positive one as we learned what we needed. It was a hiccup.

"The move to Daytona Beach from Houston, in October 1989, had an excellent effect on the organization, since the LPGA became a big fish in a smaller pond. If I go shopping and use my LPGA credit card in Daytona, people notice and are proud to have us in town. They are proud that the name goes all over the world, and that we're an integral part of the city and of the community. We have a presence in Daytona that we could never have had in Houston."

The association, together with local government became involved in a resort project that included a 36-hole public golf course, owned and operated by the city but known as the LPGA course. Tied in with it, is a five-star hotel, business offices, homes, the LPGA Hall of Fame, and the LPGA headquarters and teaching facility.

When Charles S. Mechem, Jr., became LPGA Commissioner on November 28, 1990, a huge smile broke out across the entire spectrum of the association. Charlie had retired as Chairman of Great American Broadcasting, formerly Taft, which had been involved for many years as a sponsor of PGA tournaments in the early 1970s and as a sponsor of the LPGA Championship from 1979-1989. Charlie had excellent contacts and relationships with everyone in the golf world. "It is quite scary," remarked Marlene Hagge. "I don't know anyone who doesn't like Charlie."

A close family man, he has two daughters and one son. His older, married daughter, is a

Charlie Mechem became LPGA Commissioner in 1990, offering to stay for five years. He was welcomed by players and sponsors, alike. During his tenure, purses grew, the tour became more settled, and the strength and depth of its players became greater.

JoAnne Carner was the 1994 Solheim Cup captain, and she led the team to its second victory over the Europeans. The Solheim Cup, sponsored by Karsten Manufacturing, is a biennial trans-Atlantic team match play competition between members of the Women's Professional Golfers European Tour (WPGET) and the LPGA. Photo courtesy: LPGA.

pediatrician, who completed her training three weeks before producing her first baby: "She is combining career and family with a vengeance," said Charlie. "I like young women who feel strongly about creating their own independent existence. I think it is healthy. I have never been threatened by women in business. In my former company, the treasurer was the first woman ever allowed on the floor of the New York Stock Exchange, and we had many women in important roles. I suppose any 60-year old man almost inevitably has chauvinistic threads, but I have not been conscious of them. I never thought gender had any bearing on a person's worth, and my wife and I encouraged our daughters to satisfy their own needs with a career, by raising children, or both. It was their choice.

"I have a great regard for women, for those who excel, and I especially admire people who play golf as I know how really difficult it is. I like the code of behavior in golf by which people live. I like the LPGA women, and my appointment at 60 possibly made it easier than if I had been 30 or 40. Some say, quite rightly, that there will be a woman LPGA Commissioner, but not quite yet is the feeling. I have been happy to be received so warmly and graciously."

Charlie offered stability and respect, and he was the right man for the moment as societal trends were on the move and he recognized them: "The falling of restrictions in society, however slowly it happens, will accelerate the growth of women's golf. Unless people take notice of changing patterns, they will find themselves increasingly isolated as pressures build up to do away with discrimination. The impact of Title IX is being felt now in sport and business, and the government is also affected. Having Hillary Clinton, a top lawyer, in the White House is symptomatic of a growing trend, highlighted by the first black woman in the Senate. This may seem remote from the LPGA's future, but it augers well."

The LPGA tour became a more settled place, where sponsors were delighted to support the women and the new commissioner. In 1993, the tournament calendar had 36 events, worth $21.43 million. As the strength and depth of players became greater, the tour was less dependent on Nancy Lopez, the star who had carried it for so long. However, Dottie Mochrie, Player of the Year and Vare Trophy winner for 1992, said, "Nancy is readily identifiable even from a helicopter; you can always tell where she is playing because of the crowds."

By 1993, players approaching qualification for the Hall of Fame were Amy Alcott, Patty Sheehan, Betsy King, and Beth Daniel. Discussion was volatile on whether or not to change the criteria for entry or even to accommodate a separate category retrospectively for those players who had contributed so much to the game and to the LPGA, with Judy Rankin, Marilynn Smith, Marlene Hagge, and Donna Caponi constantly mentioned.

Dottie Mochrie and Patty Sheehan were of the opinion that adjustments might be suitable, and they suggested a point system incorporating Player of the Year and Vare Trophy winners. They also thought that any major victory should be of equal value rather than requiring different major titles for qualification. Alternatively, change could be resisted, and inclusion would remain an outstanding achievement for the few. As Mickey Wright so appropriately remarked, "Not everyone was meant to be in the Hall of Fame."

The inaugural Solheim Cup, promoting competition between European and American women professional golfers, was launched in 1990, with competition every two years. Thus far, the Americans have won twice, in Florida (1990) and West Virginia (1994), and the Europeans once in Scotland (1992). The 1996 event is scheduled in Wales.

In tune with the 1990s, it was increasingly clear that women professional golfers were combining career and family. By 1992, the number of tour mothers reached 27 and the children 43. Child care facilities were available at each tour stop; yet as Laura Baugh, mother of four, pointed out: the LPGA had not formulated a maternity leave policy. The effect was that many women were finding it too tough to combine career and family. In 1993, the year that Laura Baugh gave birth to her fifth child, the LPGA announced that Smuckers had become the official child development sponsor, and that it would be operating child care centers at each tournament site from Tuesday through Sunday. Maternity leave remained to be solved.

In international terms, the LPGA was fairly insular, but the inaugural Solheim Cup between the American and European women professionals took place at Lake Nona in Florida in 1990. The Americans dominated with an 11½ to 4½ victory. The U.S. side was captained by Kathy Whitworth, the European by Mickey Walker, and the outcome was reasonably predictable as the European tour had been born only in 1979.

Two years later, with more Europeans having benefited from competition on the LPGA tour, the result was an astounding reversal at Dalmahoy in Scotland, in spite of the bookmakers quoting the Americans as overwhelming favorites. This time Mickey Walker and her team thrashed the opposition 11½ to 6½ in excellent matches. The result was superb for the Europeans, for women's golf, and for the prospect of the confrontation in 1994 at The Greenbrier in West Virginia.

As it turned out, the 1994 match, which received the event's greatest advance publicity and media coverage, was neck and neck until the final afternoon when the Europeans were unable to pull out their best and they slid to a 13-7 defeat. As each team has been victorious in the Solheim Cup, public interest has increased, just as it did with the men's Ryder Cup. Hopefully, the ground rules, which are constantly changing, will allow the women's Cup to flourish.

The 1990s saw an increasing number of European players on the LPGA. Britain's Laura Davies led the charge, and their impact expanded audiences and gave the tour worldwide marketing appeal. Photo © Phil Sheldon.

Internationally, the British Women's Open was incorporated into the LPGA tour in 1994, while in America, the women expanded their horizons and exposure to the public in 1992, competing and winning the inaugural Wendy's Three-Tour Classic, a competition with the men's PGA tour and the men's Senior PGA tour. "Televised at Christmas, it did wonders for women's golf," said Dottie Mochrie, who played alongside her idol Jack Nicklaus.

As the 1990s progressed, the biggest shift in player emphasis was toward a greater dominance by European professionals. Initially, this was set in motion by the 1987 and 1988 U.S. Open victories of Laura Davies and Lotta Neumann. Europeans consistently took the LPGA rookie titles: Swedish players Lotta Neumann in 1988, Helen Alfredsson in 1992, Annika Sorenstam in 1994; Scot Pam Wright in 1989, and Englishwoman Suzanne Strudwick in 1993. Belgium's Florence Descampe won an LPGA event in 1992, and the following year England's Trish Johnson created a record for the Europeans. She won back-to-back LPGA tournaments and led the money list for several weeks. In 1995, Alison Nicholas from England won twice, and Scotswoman Kathryn Marshall achieved her first LPGA victory.

Most of the Europeans juggle playing at least two tours, while Laura Davies set an all time record in 1994, by winning on five different circuits. At the end of 1995, she had acquired 10 LPGA titles, including two majors and 40 victories worldwide. In 1994, Laura became the world's top woman golfer and the LPGA's greatest asset, a role she had fulfilled for many years in Europe, as she won three LPGA tournaments and was leading money winner. Her delightful personality, her phenomenally long hitting, and the aura of success had everyone clamoring for her presence. Luckily, Laura has the knack of making it appear effortless to deal with such demands, as she smiles her way through and strives on to greater achievements.

In 1995, the extraordinary and meteoric rise of Sweden's Annika Sorenstam created a bevy of records, which included becoming the first golfer, male or female, to be the leading money winner in America and Europe (Laura was runner-up on both). Annika was also LPGA Player of the Year and Vare Trophy winner. Her first American victory was the 1995 US Open, after which she won two LPGA titles, two tournaments in Europe and two in Australia, achieving one of the most prodigious feats in golf at 24, in only her third year as a professional.

Annika Sorenstam won "Rookie of the Year" honors in 1994, and her performance in 1995 included capturing "Player of the Year" and Vare Trophy awards. Photo ©Phil Sheldon.

"I am not special. I come from a small town near Stockholm, and I talk to the leaves," smiled the winsome Swede, after her victory in the U.S. Open. Small in build, not a long hitter or an adventurous golfer, Annika relentlessly hits fairway after fairway, finds nearly every green and hopes to make a good putt. Her consistency is remarkable, her temperament always controlled. Although she can be visibly nervous, she uses her adrenalin to superb effect.

Annika admits that she grinds and grinds and never gives up: "As a person, I am a little shy. I am honest, I like to laugh, and I am always up for a

Three Swedish players took the LPGA by storm. Lotta Neumann won the 1988 U.S. Open, Helen Alfredsson won the 1993 Nabisco Dinah Shore and nearly won the U.S. Open that year. Annika Sorenstam became "Player of the Year" in 1995. All are a credit to Sweden's remarkable junior golf program headed by Pia Nilsson, former LPGA player. Photo ©Phil Sheldon.

challenge. I have achieved all I wanted in my career in one year, but there are a lot more tournaments to win, and I think I can play better. I know now that I can do it."

Annika may be the most extraordinary of Swedish golfers, but she is part of a tidal wave of talent to emerge from a small population that plays golf for only a short span of the year, due to climate and lack of light.

These women prodigies include Lotta Neumann, who serenely outplayed the field to win the 1988 U.S. Open in her rookie year at just 22. By the end of 1995, her considerable ability had taken her to a total of five victories on the LPGA tour. She added another win at the beginning of 1996.

A contrast in personality, Helen Alfredsson is an emotional, volatile, and talented player, whose highs and lows have enthralled the public. She made a run at the 1993 U.S. Open with a record 9-under par after three rounds and finished tied for second. The following year she shot the lowest round in Women's Open history, opening with an eight under par 63. That was followed by a 69, before she suffered a very public demise and dropped into a tie for ninth place. Helen won a major tournament, the Nabisco Dinah Shore in 1993, and another LPGA event the following season.

All three of these women, and many more Swedish golfers coming up through the ranks, are products of a remarkable junior golf development program in Sweden, headed by Pia Nilsson. In 1995, she became Director of Golf in Sweden, responsible for both men's and women's golf. She is a former Arizona State University, Suma cum Laude, graduate, and she competed on the LPGA tour for just over four years starting in January 1983. A wonderfully sane, thoughtful, and caring woman, Pia has orchestrated many of the innovative programs that have inspired emerging Swedish golfers. Having learned how tough, hard, and disappointing a life in golf can be, Pia became an independent person who understood discipline and trusted herself to take responsibility; she also studied the psychological combination likely to breed success in golf.

"As a golfer you have a mission, which has to be very clear in order to accomplish it. You need to know your strengths and take the consequences of your actions. It is how you interpret what happens, which is of prime importance. Some bad things will occur, and you have to look, act, and work on them for better future results. You must separate your performance from who you are as a person and not judge yourself on your results on the golf course, or your self-confidence can disappear down the drain. Whether you shoot 65 or 85, you must learn to value yourself."

Although Pia says she "didn't have the tools to do it" on the LPGA tour, she won eight Swedish tournaments and worked her way up the ladder in tournament administration. This included becoming a rules official, with Swedish and American certificates, and acting as a tour official for men's and women's golf in Sweden. She was captain and head coach of the National women's team, and she spread her wings to join the Board of the Swedish PGA in 1989, serving on the Committee responsible for Sweden's golf program.

"I always had a lot of ideas, different perspectives, and I listened to a lot of players. My appointment as Director of Golf caused some turmoil, but the aim is for Sweden to become a leading golf nation, and it is my job to make it happen. I am not afraid to do new things.

"There are programs for men and for women, but neither can afford to miss out on what the other is doing. I pop up at tournaments, watch players, and write cards for them on their swing, short game, body language, temper, pace of play, decisions made, and how they react to the crowd and acknowledge applause. I comment on practice methods, how to deal with a caddie, or other aspects of the tour. It is a form of tournament coaching which I wish had been available to me. I encourage the players to reach their potential as golfers and as human beings."

Dottie Mochrie, now Dottie Pepper after divorcing in 1995, began playing the LPGA in 1988. By 1992, she had topped the LPGA money list with $693,335. She also won the Rolex "Player of the Year" and Vare Trophy awards that year.

Sweden's program also includes "Vision 54" which attempts the seemingly impossible goal of encouraging players to make 18 consecutive birdies. "There is a mental block that you cannot birdie every hole," Annika Sorenstam says, "but in a way it should be possible. I don't think I can ever do it, but it is similar to a high jumper who sees the bar raised, thinks it's impossible but clears it, and then everyone else does it, too. It is in the head. I made six birdies in a row at the 1994 British Open, before I became so nervous that I was shaking and stopped the run."

By the end of 1995, Annika Sorenstam was the best golfer in the world, although world ranking showed Laura Davies in top place, Annika second, and Lotta Neumann fourth. Of the American tour players, Patty Sheehan entered the Hall of Fame in 1993, and Betsy King joined that elite group two seasons later. These two professionals, and Beth Daniel, Pat Bradley and Dottie Mochrie (who reverted to Dottie Pepper after divorcing in 1995) consistently took top honors during the 1990s; while Meg Mallon, an embryonic superstar, won four tournaments, including the U.S. Open and LPGA Championship in 1991, and she won two more in 1993. Also impressive were Kelly Robbins, Michelle McGann, Tammie Green, Kris Tschetter and Dawn Coe-Jones.

Ovations and awards handed out by the LPGA included one given to David Foster, who had done so much for the LPGA tour in the 1970s with his Colgate sponsored tournaments. He was recognized as the 1995 recipient of the LPGA Commissioner's award. The 1995 Heather Farr Player award, established in 1994, went to Shelley Hamlin. Heather, a promising young LPGA professional, died from breast cancer in her 20s, and Shelley, after a diagnosis of breast cancer which led to a modified radical mastectomy in 1991, had the courage and determination to fight back and return to the tour. She won the second and third events of her career, the 1992 Phar-Mor at Inverarry, and the 1993 ShopRite LPGA Classic, both inspirational triumphs.

In 1995, the McDonald's LPGA Championship was detrimentally affected by the ongoing subject of lesbianism, that has always enthralled some members of the press and the public, the nemesis

Kelly Robbins had her best year ever in 1995, winning $527,655 and capturing the McDonald's LPGA Championship amid the furor of unseemly comments about the LPGA by CBS broadcaster Ben Wright. She led the first two days, but the flap over lesbianism on the tour overshadowed her play and her one-shot victory over Laura Davies. Photo courtesy: LPGA.

that has dogged the women's tour throughout its history. "Flap over sexuality steals thunder from McDonald's LPGA," ran one local newspaper headline. And, indeed it did.

The "flap" concerned the alleged remarks of CBS golf commentator Ben Wright, an English resident of the United States. He was quoted by Valerie Helmbreck in the Wilmington News Journal as having pronounced: "Let's face facts, here. Lesbians in the sport hurt women's golf." He maintained that a homosexual image hindered corporate support. He also unpleasantly denigrated Laura Davies: "The woman's built like a tank. She's superwoman. She just beats the hell out of the ball."

This time the man with an over-inflated ego had gone too far, putting down women athletes with the same old suppositions. Although a few potential sponsors might be wary of the women's market, women's sponsorships in sport will never equal men's, merely because they are female—regardless of their sexual orientation. However, Ben Wright is not known for his tact and sensitivity; his alleged comments on the women's sexuality reverberated around the world.

Ben denied having made the remarks, and his CBS bosses closed ranks to support him, and he continued to cover the tournament. Unwisely, the LPGA advised Nancy Lopez to join him on air to cover the tournament, a move meant to lessen the impact of his statement, but one that clearly did little to make the problem go away. It was all highly detrimental to the Championship, which was won Kelly Robbins.

The issue dragged on through 1995, with a mass of articles in golf publications and two in Sports Illustrated, one of which reported that Ben Wright was reputed to have told a colleague over the dinner table that of course he made the remarks attributed to him. In 1996, CBS decided that Ben Wright would no longer cover golf, and he made an apologetic farewell.

The real answer is that no announcer should behave in such an unprofessional manner, where his comments and his presence impair the event being played. Ben Wright himself has said: "I have a grave fear that I'll never escape this. No matter what I do, I'll always be tied to this, and that makes me sad. Not exactly the kind of legacy one would wish for, is it?" If Ben Wright doesn't enjoy the legacy, maybe he should have thought more carefully about the consequences before he allegedly made his unenlightened utterances.

Later in the 1995 season at the U.S. Women's Open in Colorado Springs, journalist Bob Kravitz of the Rocky Mountain News took Johnny Miller to task for his comments on NBC. As professional Kris Tschetter played to The Broadmoor's 16th green, Miller's commentary included: "She has tremendous strength. She looks really feminine. She's a great looking woman, but she has strength too."

Kravitz welcomed Miller to "Ben Wright's world" and said the commentator implied: 'Hey, here's a lady who hits the ball a ton and she's a sweetie too!' Suppose Judy Rankin in her commentary told the world: 'Gosh, that Greg Norman just hits the ball a ton. And isn't he one hunk of a man wearing those butt-hugging pants? He not only plays golf beautifully, but in my humble opinion, he is the essence of masculinity.' "

At the end of 1995, a more positive and happy action resulted in the announcement of a new LPGA Commissioner. After an extensive search, Jim Ritts took over from Charlie Mechem at the beginning of 1996. Jim, 42, arrived with a background in journalism, communications, advertising, television sports, and educational programs. He attended five tournaments incognito during the interview process and was so impressed by the LPGA and its women, that he became "almost manic about getting the job."

Although in the mid-1990s, it would seem appropriate to find a suitable woman to lead the LPGA into the next century, and though I was certainly hoping it would happen, Jim appears to be an excellent choice. When I asked him whether he would have sought to appoint a female, had he been representing the LPGA, he replied equably: "Gender is not on my list. My contemporaries, male and female, are moving into key positions, but had there been two candidates of opposite sex in a tie-breaker, I would have chosen the woman."

His appointment was a unanimous decision, which is not difficult to understand. He has a personal warmth, an empathy, and a feeling for the LPGA women that reminds me of an earlier predecessor, Ray Volpe. Jim Ritts obviously cares; he has energy, enthusiasm, and the ability to listen in conversation. Taking over a thriving tour, which in 1996 has 39 events worth almost $26 million, Jim has delved into the history of the LPGA with a zest for discovering its women and their roots, which included reading the rough draft of this book.

As Jim researched the history of the LPGA, he was able to call on some of those early pioneers to help him gain a greater perspective. Betsy Rawls is one of those women.

Betsy has been part of LPGA history, never losing the link, since she joined as a player in 1951, and when she quit playing the tour, she became LPGA Tournament Director and then Executive Director of the McDonald's Championship, which in 1994 became the McDonald's LPGA Championship.

Out of those early LPGA years developed a glorious history, of which Betsy has been an integral part. She explains the common thread that kept her and all of the women on tour, a proud legacy for the women of the 1990s to carry forward: "The heart and soul of the LPGA, the whole reason it started and the reason it exists today, is that a group of women wanted a place to compete. They loved golf and golf competition, and this was a means for them to do that and hopefully to make a living at it. These women did not expect anything for nothing. They would do everything necessary to see to it that the LPGA survived. They were willing to work, to attend social occasions, to be nice to sponsors and spectators, and to make people like them.

"They ran the organization themselves. They constituted a totally unspoiled group and never expected anything to be given to them. They made sacrifices that are not necessary now; they were warm to sponsors and spectators, and they did not

Jim Ritts began his official tenure as Commissioner of the Ladies Professional Golf Association on January 1, 1996, succeeding Charles S. Mechem, Jr., who retired at the end of 1995 after a five-year tenure in that position. Jim brings to his leadership role, a wealth of experience gleamed from a 23-year career in communications and marketing/advertising.

1951 didn't seem that long ago when many of the charter members and past stars of the LPGA tour gathered at Marilynn Smith's Founders Classic in Dallas in 1987. Shown here are Bettye Mims Danoff, Alice Bauer, Marlene Hagge, Marilynn Smith, Shirley Spork, Louise Suggs, and Kathy Whitworth, still promoting women's golf well into the 1990s.

expect special treatment as men pros did. The women realized that they could not compete with men in the way they hit the golf ball; so they became more likeable as people.

"I feel proud of them all, and when I look back and see everything they did in the beginning, they were really unselfish, always doing the best things for the organization. It was remarkable. They always felt close to each other and were willing to work together, even in such an individual sport. Each one still feels part of the LPGA today, and each feels a responsibility for its success.

"After forty years, it is almost like a week ago when we meet each other. We feel very comfortable with each other; there is nothing to hide, no pretense, nothing to work through. Once you have shared something like those early years, it brings you close forever. It's a nice feeling. Whether or not we have anything else in common, we have a special feeling, having been through all that period of growth together and having competed with and against each other. I hope the women of today's LPGA retain that same closeness."

ACKNOWLEDGEMENTS

This book was a labor of love, which took almost 20 years from its very beginnings. Many people along the way offered their ideas, contributions, and encouragement; I am most grateful to all of them

Special thanks to the LPGA; to LPGA professionals Betty Hicks, Betsy Rawls, Debbie Massey, Joyce Kazmierski, and former LPGA Administrative Director Paula Marafino. They gave boundless assistance and support.

Thanks also to photographers Katherine Murphy, Phil Sheldon, and Peter Dazeley, the USGA photo library, and Bruce Matthews and Harold Roberts of *Gotta Have It Golf Collectibles* in Miami, who assisted in locating many wonderful, historic photos.

Bud Collins, of NBC and the Boston Globe, always knew the book would be completed, and without Sarah Beacham, who converted my entire handwritten manuscript to computer disks, it never would have happened.

Other vital links have been: Mark Lamirande and Bruce Fingerhut, in layout and design; publishers John Howard, Jill Langford, and Judy Horst, who brought the book to fruition.

Above all, I owe everything to my husband David, always my loyal supporter, to whom, with my family, Maxine, Richard, Elaine, Tabitha, Elijah, and India, I am devoted.

Liz Kahn

WPGA FOUNDERS

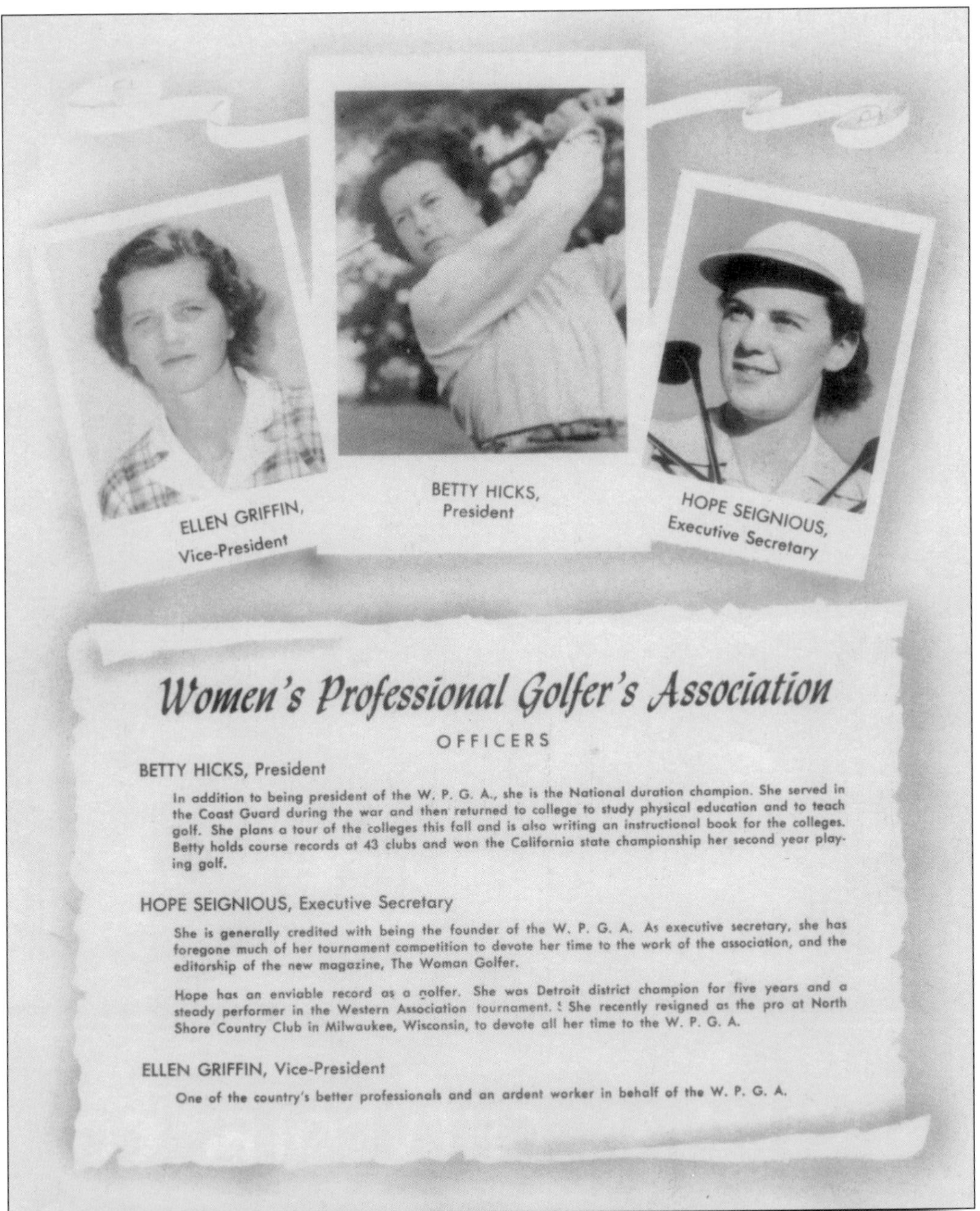

ELLEN GRIFFIN,
Vice-President

BETTY HICKS,
President

HOPE SEIGNIOUS,
Executive Secretary

Women's Professional Golfer's Association

OFFICERS

BETTY HICKS, President

In addition to being president of the W. P. G. A., she is the National duration champion. She served in the Coast Guard during the war and then returned to college to study physical education and to teach golf. She plans a tour of the colleges this fall and is also writing an instructional book for the colleges. Betty holds course records at 43 clubs and won the California state championship her second year playing golf.

HOPE SEIGNIOUS, Executive Secretary

She is generally credited with being the founder of the W. P. G. A. As executive secretary, she has foregone much of her tournament competition to devote her time to the work of the association, and the editorship of the new magazine, The Woman Golfer.

Hope has an enviable record as a golfer. She was Detroit district champion for five years and a steady performer in the Western Association tournament. She recently resigned as the pro at North Shore Country Club in Milwaukee, Wisconsin, to devote all her time to the W. P. G. A.

ELLEN GRIFFIN, Vice-President

One of the country's better professionals and an ardent worker in behalf of the W. P. G. A.

A page from the program of the first Women's National Golf Championship, Spokane, Washington, 1946. Courtesy: Betty Hicks.

LPGA CHARTER MEMBERS

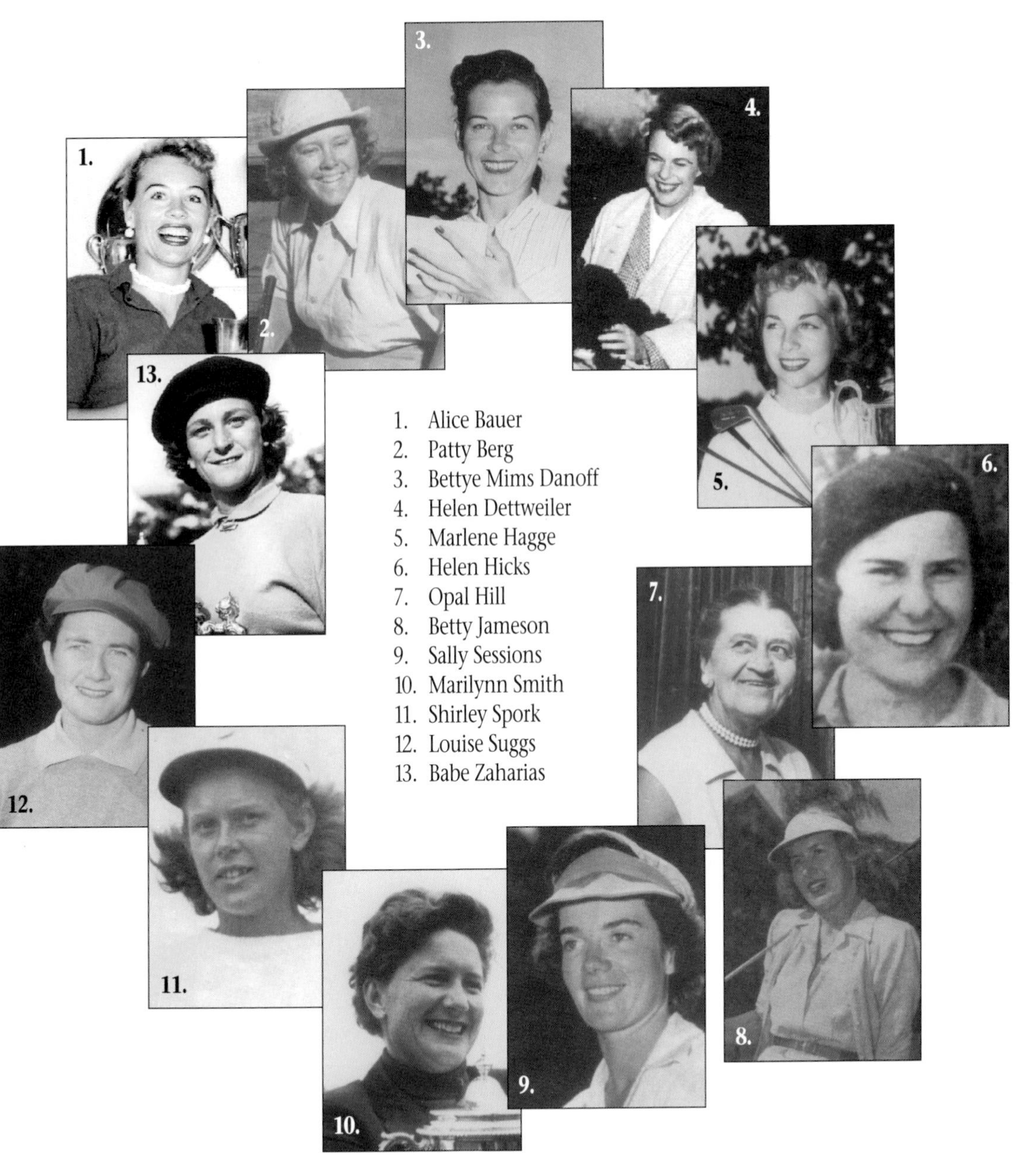

1. Alice Bauer
2. Patty Berg
3. Bettye Mims Danoff
4. Helen Dettweiler
5. Marlene Hagge
6. Helen Hicks
7. Opal Hill
8. Betty Jameson
9. Sally Sessions
10. Marilynn Smith
11. Shirley Spork
12. Louise Suggs
13. Babe Zaharias

Index